THE JUDAS WAR

THE
JUDAS
WAR

HOW AN ANCIENT BETRAYAL
GAVE RISE TO THE CHRIST MYTH

S.P. LAURIE

Published by Hypostasis Ltd.
71-75 Shelton Street, Covent Garden
London WC2H 9JQ

www.hypostasis.co
Email: info@hypostasis.co

Book cover design by BespokeBookCovers.com
Typeset by Euan Monaghan

ISBN: 978-1-912029-69-3

Also by S.P. Laurie

THE THOMAS CODE:
Solving the Mystery of the Gospel of Thomas

THE ROCK AND THE TOWER:
How Mary Created Christianity

For articles, information and news see:
JesusOrigins.com

Table of Contents

PART FIVE: THE CHILD OF SEVEN DAYS

Introduction

The Judas War is the longest conflict in history. It has lasted two thousand and seven hundred years, and may not yet be over. Starting with a betrayal by a king, it led to the destruction of a nation and the exile of her people. The Judas War gave rise to centuries of oppression, engendering a bitter hatred among its victims. Some of these victims, forced to live among their betrayers, separated themselves from their neighbours and followed their own religious direction. The bitterness of the Judas War was embedded in their writings and passed down from generation to generation. Long centuries went by, and this small, despised group appeared destined for extinction. Then just as the Judas War had all but died out, it flared up in a surprising way. The group gave rise to a new religion that spread across the Roman Empire. By a remarkable reversal, those who had been the original persecutors became the persecuted. They were now the exiles, living among a people whose very gospels cursed them with the ancient hatred of the Judas War.

This book is concerned with the origins of Christianity as it developed before the Jesus movement in the first century AD. The central thesis is that the Christ myth is very ancient. The original story of the crucifixion reflects events that started with the Judas War in the eighth century BC. As a result of these events, first Israel and then Judah were destroyed, the royal line of David was extinguished, and the temple was put to the torch. To the ancient mind, events on earth were a reflection of events in heaven. The cataclysmic destruction of Israel by the nations meant that something terrible had happened in heaven. The divine king of the Jews, the Christ, had been executed by the heavenly powers representing the nations. He had been crucified, suffering the cursed death of being hung from a tree. Although innocent, he had paid the sin price for his people.

The death of Christ in heaven was simultaneous to the destruction of the temple on earth and marked the start of exile. But it was all part of a greater cosmic plan that the God who existed beyond all things had prepared before time. The greater exile was not just that of the Jews but of all humanity who had been placed under the rule of evil angels. These

1

heavenly beings had crucified Christ, but they did not know the hidden secret. At the appointed time, Christ would be brought back to life, to end their rule and bring in a new kingdom of heaven for all those who loved God, both Jew and gentile.

And so the group of Christ believers waited for the resurrection through long centuries. The exile supposedly ended with the return of the elite Jews to Jerusalem following the Persian victory over the Babylonians in 539 BC. But the little group, the descendants of refugees, noticed no change. Evil ruled in the world; their neighbours oppressed them, the powers in Jerusalem viewed them with distaste, and the Jews were a subject people under foreign kings. The true exile had not ended at all. The rebuilt temple was false, a mere construction of stone, empty of the presence of God. There was no temple—God was dead and absent from the world. The group waited and waited. The question they constantly asked themselves was "When?" Everything happened according to God's plan. It was just necessary to elucidate that plan.

The Almanac was the group's solution. It organised time as seventy days from the beginning of the world and the creation of Adam to the end of the world, the apocalypse and the rule of Christ. Each of the seventy days in the Almanac was one generation and they were arranged in weeks of seven generations. At a higher level each of these weeks was thought of as a great day—the world would last for ten such great days. The group were sectarian but not isolated. They absorbed the writings produced by the powers of Jerusalem and by other sects. The details of the Almanac were filled in from these scriptures.

In the Almanac, the sabbath days were significant, and in particular the sabbath of sabbaths (the seventh day of the seventh great day). But beyond this common Jewish preoccupation with the sabbath, the group had a radical insight into the nature of time; the Almanac was symmetrical. The mathematical centre of the Almanac, the midpoint of all time, was the building of the temple. Time was reflected around this midpoint; events in the second half of history were the mirror image of events that had happened in the first half. In this mirror of time, things were reflected into their opposite. There was an ascent to the peak of the temple and then a descent. In the first Almanac day the world was created, and in the last Almanac day it would be destroyed.

There was a startling corollary to the symmetrical nature of time. In the mirror image the arrow of time would point backwards—time would flow in reverse. The Almanac could not only be read in the forward direction but also, more profoundly, from the end to the beginning. The sabbath was the seventh day. But if you counted time in reverse then the sabbath would be the first day of the week and not the last. The Almanac demonstrated that bad events happened on the forward sabbath and good events on this reverse sabbath. The true sabbath was not Saturday but Sunday.

The Almanac told the group exactly when Christ would return. The prophecy predicted that the exile would last two days, with the resurrection on the third day. These "days" could only be the great days of Almanac time. So the exile would take two great days or fourteen generations. The Christ would come after fourteen generations had elapsed starting from the destruction of the temple.

So they waited. The date was determined in Almanac time, but the translation to actual time allowed a great deal of latitude. It was a matter of opinion what counted as a generation and how many generations had already passed. Christ was expected to appear in the sky, leading an angelic army. But he did not come. The Almanac could be almost infinitely adjusted to cope with disappointment, but the waiting was wearing.

The situation of the Jews seemed to get ever worse, and by the first century, they lived under a brutal Roman occupation. At this time, apocalyptic expectation throughout Judea reached fever pitch. Then something happened that surely signalled the commencement of the end times. The Roman governor, Pontius Pilate, ordered the legionary ensigns, which the Jews regarded as idols, to be taken into the holy city. He was forced to withdraw the ensigns when a crowd of protestors offered their bare necks to the Roman swords, preferring death to living with the polluting presence of the ensigns. Were not these ensigns the "abomination of desolation" predicted in the Book of Daniel?

At around this time, a young demon-troubled woman in the group made an announcement. She was a virgin dedicated to God but possessed by seven demonic husbands. The woman said that Christ had come in spiritual form. He had been resurrected and reborn through her and had cast out her false demon-husbands. No one else could see him, and some wanted to have her put away as mad. Others wondered, for the woman was known to be a prophetess, and a few wished to learn more. The woman was a skilful shaman, and she took those curious few on a spiritual journey. She showed them the crucifixion of Christ, so they hung on the cross with him, they died, they went down into the darkness of the tomb, and they were reborn. And they too saw Jesus.

The woman started her movement with these first followers. Although other women would doubtless have been involved, the shaman selected twelve male disciples, representing the twelve tribes, as her core group. If the resurrection had happened, then the exile was over. But the end of exile also meant the return of the temple. God had not taken up residence in the corrupt temple of Herod. It remained as empty of God's presence as it had always been. The Lord had instead come into the humble form of the shaman. She was the new temple "not built by hands". So she was given a new name which indicated her divine nature. They called her by the word they used for the temple; "the tower", the Magdalene.

The shaman paradigm

None of this, of course, represents the standard paradigm of the origins of Christianity shared by almost all believing Christians and virtually all scholars. In this traditional view, Jesus of Nazareth was a wandering charismatic preacher who was crucified by the Romans at the instigation of the Jewish priests. His followers believed he was the Christ and that he had been resurrected after his death. They founded his church and spread his teachings throughout the Roman world. All of this comes from the gospels. Christians view these gospels through the lens of belief, whereas scholars are more sceptical but still accept the basic story.

The gospels originated with the Gospel of Mark, which was written in the 70s AD. This work was of embarrassingly poor literary quality, and it was quickly superseded by more polished productions; Matthew, Luke and eventually John. But all followed the same basic story established by Mark. The idea that Jesus had been crucified in the first century comes from a misunderstanding by the author of Mark. He knew that Jesus had been resurrected on "the third day", but he did not know about the Almanac and took the time quite literally. He also knew that the resurrection had occurred while Pontius Pilate had been governor of Judea and that it had happened on the first day of the week. From this, we get the gospel timing, with a crucifixion on a Friday, and the resurrection on Sunday. But the author of Mark had made a spectacular timing mistake. He had made Jesus dead for just two days rather than for six hundred years.

Once the idea that Jesus had lived and died in the first century became established, it was hard to dislodge. For most people, it is absurd even to suggest that Jesus had not existed in Roman-occupied Judea as a real man. So they might be surprised to find that there was controversy on just this point in the early centuries. The evidence for this is even in the New Testament. The letter 1 John comes from a group divided by a disagreement so severe that it ruptured their church into two. The author of the letter is writing to encourage his own side and denounce their opponents. As always, we only see the proto-orthodox side of the disagreement, but we can work out from the condemnations of 1 John 4:2-3 what the others believed. They maintained that Jesus Christ had not come "in the flesh", that he had not been a real, material man.

Reflection will show that it is the standard paradigm that is absurd. How could a crucified itinerant folk preacher be regarded within a few years of his death as the ruler of the universe? The idea would have been laughed out of court had people not had two thousand years to get used to it. The standard paradigm requires Christianity to have developed like no other religion on earth. A real "Jewish Jesus" could not have been a Christian because he could not have taught any of the things that Christians believed in the first century. So we have to imagine a complete U-turn with the real teachings of the founder discarded in favour of a completely different, and often diametrically opposed, set of beliefs. At the same time, the human founder is elevated to the status of God, which would surely be impossible in a Jewish context. My earlier book, *The Rock and the Tower*, goes into the scholars "it just so happened" explanations in detail to show why they must be abandoned. In their place, it develops the shaman paradigm.

The shaman paradigm is based on the simple observation that new religions typically start with an individual, a "shaman", who has revelations from a "visitor from heaven". The shaman passes down these revelations to his or her followers as the teachings of the new religion. People will not change their religious beliefs unless they think that some higher authority is commanding them to do so. No human would ever be accepted as such a higher authority. The authority has to be spiritual and heavenly, although channelled through some human agency. A shaman's first challenge, then, is to establish credibility with a group of followers, so that they accept the shaman as a genuine conduit for the visitor from heaven.

Christianity is unique in that Jesus is both the prophet and the subject of the religion. He never offers any authority for his teachings other than himself. Jesus is the Son of God who will rule the universe at the end of time, and as such, he is the ultimate authority. Jesus is able to annul the law of Moses because he is above Moses, and above the supposed divine authority that gave that law to Moses. This shows that Jesus cannot have been the shaman. A person holding the view of themselves that Jesus is supposed to have held would be insane, and insane people do not start powerful new movements. No, Jesus is the visitor from heaven. This alone can explain why he is both the source of the teachings and the subject of the religion.

If Jesus is the visitor from heaven, then he must have appeared through the medium of a shaman. The first shaman paradigm book, *The Rock and the Tower*, searches for the identity of the shaman. In that book, I show that there is only one possibility; the prophetess called Mary, who was known by both the titles of the Magdalene and the Virgin. The book explains why she must also be the mysterious person whom Paul calls by the name

Cephas, which, in Aramaic, means "rock". Cephas is typically translated using the Greek for "rock", as Peter. However, Paul uses both the names Cephas and Peter, which he would not do unless he needed to distinguish between two individuals. The first, Cephas, is the founder of the movement. The second, Peter, is the leading second-generation apostle, also called Simon. In the gospel stories, Cephas and Simon Peter have become hopelessly conflated into one person. So why would two individuals both be called by this strange name, "the rock"? Because it is not a name but a title. It is a direct parallel to Mary's other title, "the Magdalene" which means "the tower". Both the rock and the tower are found in a source which dates from hundreds of years before Christianity; the Animal Apocalypse from the Book of Enoch. The rock is the holy mountain, Mount Sinai, but standing beyond this for the "high places" at which the ancient Israelites worshipped. The tower is the temple. The rock and the tower represent the two places in which God was believed to come down to earth. The titles signify a shaman, a receptacle for God's spirit.

The Rock and the Tower is concerned with the story of the shaman and the religion she created. Mary cannot, however, have created Christianity in a vacuum. It is a necessary requirement that there was a pre-existing myth of the Christ. Mary cannot have invented this myth. Her shamanic role only makes sense if she lived among a people who were already fervent with expectation for the resurrection of the Christ. They had had a long, disappointing wait. So when Mary said that Christ had been reborn and had appeared spiritually through herself, they were already primed to believe.

The current book explores the myth of Christ primarily as it existed before Mary. Although it is a shaman paradigm book, it has the character of a prequel to *The Rock and the Tower* and can be read independently of that first volume. *The Rock and the Tower* was concerned with Mary and revolves around the story of the resurrection. This book is concerned with Christ and revolves around the crucifixion.

The crucifixion and Jewish guilt

In the gospel crucifixion accounts, there is an extraordinary hostility towards the "Jews". There are multiple stories that express Jewish guilt. Most obviously, it is the Jewish leaders who arrest Jesus, condemn him to death, and hand him over to the Romans for crucifixion. The Romans are presented as being almost innocent in contrast to the Jews. When Pilate, the Roman governor, wants to release Jesus, it is the Jewish crowd who demand that he be crucified. In Matthew, we have the chilling words shouted out by the crowd: *"His blood be on us and on our children!" (Matthew 27:25).*

These stories of the "Christ-killers" have led to numerous tragedies down the ages when Christian crowds would attack and murder the Jews who lived among them. The Jews were cast out from nation after nation by popular demand. They were forever looking for a new home, another place to lead a precarious existence. The strange thing about all this is that those who founded the Jesus movement were themselves Jews. We are left with a conundrum; how can a Jewish movement be so anti-Jewish? Scholars have attempted to explain this with their usual "just so" stories. It just so happened that the movement expanded among gentiles, and it just so happened that these gentiles blamed the Jews instead of the Romans for the death of Christ. This explanation makes no sense. It does not explain why every early document from the Jesus movement is anti-Jewish. It requires the hypothetical early pro-Jewish teachings of the Jesus movement to be abandoned within a generation, to be replaced by new anti-Jewish beliefs. And it is contradicted by the fact that the two most "Jewish" gospels, Matthew and John, are also the most anti-Jewish. Neither of these gospels was produced by a gentile.

This book will show how the real explanation for the anti-Jewish beliefs goes all the way back to the Judas War. The literal meaning of the word used for the "Jews" in the gospels is "Judean". Although it came to stand for anyone who was of Israelite or Hebrew descent, this was not the original meaning of Judean. A Judean was someone of the tribe or kingdom of Judah. The thesis of this book is that the first Christians were not anti-Jewish as we would understand the term. They were anti-Judean.

Two kingdoms

At one time, there was a people divided into two kingdoms—one to the north, one to the south. The northern kingdom was the stronger, richer and more splendid of the two. Their king lived in a magnificent palace, and their territory was secured by forts made mighty with earth and stone. They were breeders of horses and famed for their skill with the chariot. Their copper mines produced much wealth, and they exported olive oil and wine, trading with the Egyptians to the south, and the Phoenician sea people on the coast who took their wares across the Mediterranean world. They even had forts in the distant desert of Sinai to control the trade that ran from the east, through Arabia to the coast. The people of the southern kingdom came from the same hardy, hill-dwelling stock as their northern neighbours, but lived in the shadow of their greater twin. Their smaller territory was centred on their capital and its famous temple. The people of both the northern and southern kingdoms spoke the same language and worshipped the same gods in the same way, and prided themselves on being the chosen people of Yahweh. They both loved words and songs and the arts of literature. The scribes of the northern kingdom had even learnt to write, an innovation which trickled down to the south.

The two kingdoms were not allowed to live in peace. They existed on a political fault-line, between two of the world's great civilisations. To the south was Egypt and to the north-east Assyria. Egypt had long dominated them, but a period of relative Egyptian weakness had allowed them to flourish. This stability was upset by the growing strength of Assyria. The northern kingdom attempted to build an alliance of neighbouring powers against this looming Assyrian threat. But the southern kingdom would not join this alliance and did something extraordinary: it became a client state of the Assyrians to secure its independence from the northern kingdom. Then, when threatened by the alliance, the southern king paid a great sum of gold to the king of Assyria to persuade him to invade the northern kingdom.

As a result of this intervention, the northern kingdom was not just defeated but utterly destroyed. Its people were killed, or sold into slavery or exiled. Many were forced to flee as refugees to the only place they could—the southern kingdom. The northern kingdom simply ceased to exist. Its former land was incorporated into the Assyrian Empire, and people from other parts of that empire were settled into its now vacant farms and vineyards

The northern kingdom was Israel and the southern kingdom Judah. The Assyrian war started in 732 BC and ended with the destruction of the Israelite capital, Samaria in 722 BC. Judah remained an Assyrian ally throughout the war against Israel and thrived with the elimination of its northern competitor. When the Judean King Hezekiah eventually made the mistake of attempting to throw off the Assyrian yoke, his kingdom came within a hairbreadth of sharing the fate of Israel. But Jerusalem and Judah survived. They lived on for another century until the southern kingdom was destroyed by the Babylonians.

It is this destruction of Israel that I have called the Judas War. It caused a crisis which was to lead to the creation of both Judaism and Christianity. The Judean establishment was seen as having betrayed Israel. This was a particularly dangerous situation as Judah was now flooded by Israelite refugees. So it was necessary to put a spin on events. The Judean propaganda machine went into overdrive, and one result was the production of the Hebrew Bible (the Old Testament). The Bible was a Judean creation and had its origins in this period, although much of it was written or revised after the final Babylonian exile. The Judean scriptures often drew upon earlier Israelite materials, but these were reworked to give an appropriate anti-Israel slant.

The Judeans created a new pan-Israelite identity to unite the people, with the myth of the twelve tribes descended from both Jacob (the northern patriarch) and Abraham (the southern patriarch). The Judeans embraced the legendary Israelite kingdom of Saul. But in their account, it was superseded by the much greater kingdom of David and Solomon who supposedly ruled both Israel and Judah from Jerusalem. So it was the Judean kings, "the house of David", who had the divinely sanctioned right to rule over all Israelites. As for the fall of Israel, well, that was nothing to do with Judah. It was the Israelites' own fault. The Israelite kings had broken away from the united kingdom to establish their lessor state. The Israelites had then fallen into evil Canaanite ways, worshipping other gods than Yahweh. They had ignored the true Jerusalem temple and set up Canaanite style "high places". So God had summoned the Assyrians to destroy Israel.

This explanation required the development of a backstory. In this fictitious history, the Israelites were not Canaanites (as they really were) but had come into Canaan from outside. They had been given the land of Canaan in a sacred covenant with Yahweh. They only had to obey the law of Yahweh as received through Moses, and worship exclusively in the Jerusalem temple. But the kings and people of Israel had broken this covenant. So Yahweh had deprived them of their land.

The Israelites living in Judah were not convinced, of course. In opposition, they developed their own literature which told a very different story. They did not blame themselves for the disaster but the kings of Judah. One group expressed the betrayal by using a common literary technique of the time: the betrayers were represented as a significantly-named individual. This made-up person was presented as if he was real. The name of such a character was intended to reflect the party he represented. In this case the betrayers, "Judah and Jerusalem", were indicated through the name Judas Iscariot.

Although the Israelites did not control the official channels of transmission, much of their literature survived, ironically embedded in the Judean scriptures. Other texts went underground, to be passed down generation to generation in small sectarian groups. There was much diversity of belief and much confusion. Texts in this era were not static one-time-only creations—they lived, being repeatedly modified and even rewritten to meet the needs of each age. With the passage of centuries, people forgot the original context of the conflict. The Judean scribes were poets of extraordinary ability, and their creation was too good to ignore. So it began to penetrate the beliefs of the descendants of the Israelites. But the separation and hatred engendered by the Judas War persisted.

The Christ myth

The Christ myth was developed over the centuries by a group descended from Israelites living in Judah. They accepted the first temple and the right of the Davidic kings to rule, even as they condemned those same kings for their betrayal. They did not accept the second temple and had only a loose adherence to the law of Moses.

The word Christ is the equivalent of the Hebrew "Messiah" and means "the anointed one". The expectation of the Messiah was widespread throughout Judaism in both its official and dissident forms. In essence, the Messiah was an expected king who would redeem Israel and Judah to end the exile and establish the new temple. He would be a branch or shoot of David; the image is of a felled tree that re-sprouts and grows again.

You cannot separate Christ from the exile since the purpose of Christ is to undo the exile. So it is extraordinary that in the gospels there is a complete disconnect between Jesus and this concept of Christ. Jesus does not release the Jews from exile; he does not even try. He is not triumphant over the nations but is crucified by the Romans. He does not establish a new temple, but acknowledges the existing temple, even though that temple is destined to be destroyed in a few decades. Instead, Jesus has come to save the individual and conquer death. But how does this relate to the redemption of Israel and Judah? There seems to be not a single point of contact between the Jewish concept of Christ and the picture of Jesus that we find in the gospels. It is as if the Jesus movement has simply appropriated the title of Christ without any justification.

We will see how the original myth of Christ was all about the exile. His crucifixion is the beginning of the exile, his death is the exile, and his resurrection the return. But the meaning of the exile has been expanded. The term of exile has been increased sevenfold so that a day is like seven days. The scope has been increased to encompass all humanity and not just the Jews. And the oppressors are not human kings but the divine forces who control them.

The group believed that the world had been placed under the rule of seventy evil angels. These angels had been appointed by God to rule the nations, whereas Christ ruled Israel and Judah. With the death of Christ, the angels ruled the whole world. We can trace the seventy angels right back to the religious origins of the Israelites. However, as monotheism developed, the idea that God had appointed the angels caused a fundamental dilemma. How could a good, all-knowing God place humanity under these evil rulers? The answer to this problem was to split the deity into two. The true ultimate God was wholly good but remote and unknowable directly to humans. The God of the Jewish scriptures, who had manifested himself many times to the Jews, was an intermediary. This lower Yahweh was really an angel himself, although more ancient and powerful than any other angel. He was good but fallible and limited in knowledge. It was he who had appointed the angels and who had given the Jews their law. This lower Yahweh thought that Christ was his son; but in reality, Christ was the son of the higher God. At the time of his resurrection, Christ would destroy the seventy angels who had brought death to humanity. He would replace the lower Yahweh and rule a new heaven and a new earth.

I have called the expansion of the exile the principle of cosmic escalation. This phenomenon is found not just in Christianity, but also in the Hebrew Bible. It might be thought that cosmic escalation only happened after the fact of the exile, but this is not the case. Cosmic escalation draws upon a myth that was already ancient at the time of the exile. This myth is about the son of the benign father god, the creator of all things. This son-god dies and goes down into the underworld to dwell with death. After a period he is resurrected. He returns to destroy the seventy gods who ruled the world in his absence and defeat death, establishing his kingdom under the father. This pre-existing myth has combined with the political facts of the exile to give the Christ myth. The idea that the Christ, the Messiah, was a supernatural king was there from the beginning and evolved in tandem with the alternative interpretation that the Messiah would be a human king.

Such mythological explanations of Jesus have always encountered the problem that Christianity supposedly came from a Jewish monotheistic context that was deeply opposed to the polytheism of the pagan religions. This problem disappears if the Christ myth is far earlier than had been believed and first arose during the polytheistic phase before monotheism had become established. The mythology of the dying and rising god, which is the earliest and deepest layer of Christianity, did not come from outside. It was there all along, in the Canaanite foundations of Judaism.

Christianity has always been regarded as the daughter of Judaism, a relative latecomer which appropriated the older religion to its own purpose. This book will show that this view is incorrect. Christianity is not the daughter but the sister of Judaism. It can trace its origins back to the same era in which Judaism was formed, the tumultuous centuries of exile. Just as Judaism struggled towards monotheism, so also did those who believed in the Christ myth. It might be said that Judaism represents the perspective of Judah, and Christianity preserves that of Israel.

The child of seven days

Some seven centuries separated the Judas War from the Jesus movement in the first century. Proto-Christianity took shape during this long period. The Israelite group would have been among those who remained in Judah throughout the exile, and who opposed the returning elite Jews and their attempts at rebuilding the temple. But Jerusalem and the temple were reconstructed in the Persian period, and the power of the priestly class reinstated. The hugely impressive Judean scriptures, the Hebrew Bible, were taking something like their final form at this time. For the Jews, it was a creative age of great diversity of belief, of mutual hostility and loathing, and yet also of influence and interchange. Among those outside the temple circle, the mystical cult of Enoch became hugely popular in opposition to the priestly cult of Moses. The Judas War and the seventy angels provide the earliest strata of the Christ myth, but the development of the myth was heavily influenced by both the Judean priestly scriptures and the Enoch cult.

The interaction between the myth of Christ and the myth of Enoch gave rise to a new conception of the nature of Christ—he becomes the "Son of Man", a human. This provocative title contrasted Jesus to the seventy angels who were "sons of God". In the last section, we will look at two sayings from the Gospel of Thomas, which are evidence for a major development in the Christ myth. These sayings, interpreted correctly, tell us that Jesus was believed to have come to earth at three separate times in three different forms. Twice he has come as a human; first as the "child of seven days" and then, much later, as the "suffering servant". The third time he is resurrected in spiritual form through the shaman. We will see how the logic of the Almanac dictates these three appearances.

Great events were regarded as happening simultaneously at different levels of reality. There was a heavenly level, a national level and a human level. The crucifixion had taken place on all three levels. We will see how the gospel crucifixion account has been derived ultimately from the Almanac. In the gospels, the great days of Almanac time, each seven generations long, have become literal days of twenty-four hours. This is true of the resurrection which takes place on the third day. It is also true of Jesus' final day, which represents the seventh great day of Almanac time. The gospel account culminates with the crucifixion. This corresponds in the Almanac to the destruction of Jerusalem and the temple which took place on the "sabbath of sabbaths"—the seventh day of the seventh great day.

Applying this principle of correspondence, we will be able to place the crucifixion account in its original context for the first time. This will help us understand the many odd and bizarre features of the account. We will uncover the very considerable evidence that Judas Iscariot does indeed represent the betrayal by Judah that launched the Judas War. But before we can analyse the crucifixion account, we first ask a more fundamental question— "who killed Christ?" In our search for the answer, we will uncover a world ruled by angels. We will locate these beliefs in the real origins and religion of the Israelites as revealed by archaeology rather than the biblical account. We will then reconstruct the Almanac and explore its features and symmetries. It is the Almanac that gives us the key to unlocking the Christ myth.

Finally, in the Afterword, we will take another look at the Judas War in a remarkable contemporary account that has been hiding in plain sight. We will show how the story of David, Solomon and Bathsheba in the Bible started as a satire written by an Israelite scribe against the kings of Judah who had betrayed Israel. The satire gives us a first-hand taste of the bitterness felt by the Israelite refugees against the powers in Jerusalem.

This book researches the foundations of Christianity. The aim is to uncover the religious worldview which Mary inherited and in which she operated. This worldview will provide insights into many puzzling aspects of the early Jesus movement. But we should always remember that the shaman built a new spiritual religion upon these existing foundations. Christians today do not dwell among the ancient hostilities of the Judas War, but in the house that Mary built.

Part One

The Seventy Shepherds

1

Who Killed Christ?

The gospels tell us that the Romans crucified Christ at the instigation of the Jewish priests and authorities. In the post-holocaust era, scholars had problems with the Jewish part of this equation. The anti-Jewish polemic in the New Testament became unacceptable, so the idea of the "Jewish Jesus" became fashionable. Under this paradigm, the original Jesus movement was thoroughly Jewish and law observant. The anti-Jewish elements were a later development which emerged as the church expanded among gentiles. It was the Romans who were really guilty of the crucifixion. They executed Jesus because he was a dangerously popular figure and a potential rebel. The Jewish high priest acquiesced in this killing: better to sacrifice one man than risk revolt and mass retributions from the Romans.

Remarkably, this "Jewish Jesus" hypothesis is still widely accepted although contradicted by all the evidence. If the Jesus movement were good law-observant Jews, then why were they persecuted from the beginning by the Jewish establishment? We know the religious leaders wanted to destroy the movement because Paul was one of the persecutors. The antipathy was mutual—in virtually every early Christian text the anti-Jewish (anti-Judean) tone is prevalent. The gospels are unambiguous about the guilt for the death of Jesus. He was put on trial by the Jewish Sanhedrin who condemned him to death for blasphemy and passed him over to the Romans for execution. When Pilate wished to free Jesus, the Jewish crowd demanded his crucifixion. There is not a single early Christian source that assigns the chief blame for Jesus' death to the Romans. The Book of Revelation is anti-Roman to the core: it depicts Rome as a whore drunken with the blood of the saints.[1] Yet it never accuses the Romans of the death of Jesus. Why not?

➤ **Paul says that the "archons" (rulers) crucified Christ.**

The earliest texts in the New Testament are the genuine letters of the apostle Paul. These letters are a unique survival, an eyewitness account of the Jesus movement dating from decades before the gospels. And Paul, unlike the authors of the gospels, was in direct contact with the leaders of the movement. There is a famous passage in 1 Corinthians in which Paul talks about those who have killed Christ:

> *We speak wisdom among the mature, but not the wisdom of this age or of the rulers [archonton] of this age who are coming to nothing. No, we speak the hidden wisdom of God in a mystery which God foreordained before the ages. None of the rulers [archonton] of this age knew it, for had they known it they would not have crucified the Lord of glory. (1 Corinthians 2:6-8)*

This tells us that Christ has been crucified by the "archons" (rulers). These powers are "coming to nothing", a reference to the apocalypse which Paul believed was very close. The rule of the archons would then be replaced by the rule of Christ. What are we to make of this strange phrase "rulers of this age"? Does Paul mean the Romans? Then why does he not say so? The phrase gives a strong impression that the archons are divine beings.

Such was certainly the interpretation of the diverse Christian gnostic groups who flourished in the early centuries alongside the developing proto-orthodox church. In gnostic mythology, the archons were angels who ruled the world. They had been appointed by the Demiurge, the flawed creator who stood for Yahweh. The archons were evil and enslaved humanity. In the gnostic view, Christ came from the light that was far above the Demiurge and the archons. He descended with a mission to defeat the archons, to redeem humanity and to bring about a new kingdom of heaven.

> ➤ **The archons must be heavenly beings; otherwise, it makes no sense to say that they did not know the heavenly mystery.**

When placed in the context of Paul's argument, it is clear that the archons are heavenly beings. Paul is telling the Corinthians that a mystery was hidden before time: *"No eye has seen, no ear has heard, no heart has imagined, what God has prepared for those who love him"* (1 Corinthians 2:9). It is because the "rulers of this age" did not know this mystery that they crucified Christ. It is absurd to think of any human ruler, such as a Roman governor going about his daily tasks of administration, knowing of such a mystery. The mystery is heavenly, so the rulers must be heavenly also. They are angels.

➢ **In 1 Thessalonians, Paul appears to say that Christ has been put to death by the Jews. But this passage gives every sign of being forged.**

If we turn to another letter of Paul, 1 Thessalonians, then the mystery of Paul's words is apparently resolved. He meant the Jews of course:

> *For you, brothers, became imitators of the churches of God in Judea that are in Christ Jesus. For you suffered the same things from your own countrymen as they did from the Jews [Judeans], who killed both the Lord Jesus and their own prophets, and drove us out, and displease God and are against all men: forbidding us to talk to the gentiles who might be saved so as to fill up their own sins. But the wrath has come upon them to the end. (1 Thessalonians 2:14-16)*

However, this passage is suspected of being an interpolation or forgery even by many of these accepting the historical Jesus.[2] There are multiple things wrong with it:

- It adopts an external perspective on the Jews. Paul was himself a Jew and a former Pharisee and would never have written about "the Jews" in this way. While he had his differences with the Jewish law-abiding party of the circumcision, he never condemns the Jews in blanket terms like this anywhere else. Compare to Paul's genuine words in Romans: *"I ask, then, has God rejected his people? Never may it be! For I am an Israelite, a descendant of Abraham, from the tribe of Benjamin. God did not reject his people whom he foreknew"* (Romans 11:1-2).
- The idea that Paul was forbidden to talk to gentiles is inconsistent with his genuine letters. His arguments with the Jewish-Christians in Jerusalem were not about whether he could proselytise gentiles, but whether his new converts should be circumcised.
- According to the historical Jesus paradigm, the Romans crucified Jesus. In assigning guilt to the Jews, the author of 1 Thessalonians is reflecting the gospel version of events which is supposedly unhistorical.
- The real "smoking gun" for forgery is the final line: *"But the wrath has come upon them to the end."* The word here for "end", *telos*, can also be translated "to the utmost". It means that the Jews have received their ultimate punishment from God. This is a reference to either; (i) the Jewish War that led to the sack of Jerusalem and the destruction

of the temple in 70 AD; or (ii) the Bar Kokhba revolt in 132-35 AD, when the Jews were finally exiled from Jerusalem. Either way, these words were not written by Paul in the 50s AD.

> **The whole section of 1 Thessalonians 2 and perhaps the entire letter has been forged as a response to Paul's words in 1 Corinthians.**

Was this passage about the Jews interpolated into a genuine letter? It is more likely that the entire letter is a forgery or a such a heavy reworking of a short genuine Pauline letter that it amounts to the same thing. There are several features that are untypical for Paul. Unlike other letters, it seems to have been written for no immediate purpose. A large part of the letter is "paraenesis" meaning a statement of generally established teachings—it is boilerplate. Another warning sign is that this is the only letter in which Paul uses "we" rather than "I" throughout. It is true that the letter is supposedly from joint authors—in this case Paul, Silvanus and Timothy—but then so are other letters in which Paul uses "I".

Our primary concern here, though, is with 1 Thessalonians 2. We will show that this section, in its entirety, is suspiciously parallel to 1 Corinthians 2:1 to 3:3. In both cases, Paul starts by describing the manner he first adopted towards (i) the Corinthians and (ii) the Thessalonians. To the Corinthians, he says he did not come "with eloquence or wisdom" but "in weakness and fear, and with much trembling". This is vintage Paul. He assumes his usual false modesty and makes masterful use of paradox, giving an eloquent denial of eloquence. In 1 Thessalonians, Paul covers the same ground, but his prose is now plodding. He gives his audience a long list of all the bad things that he is not, before telling them all the good things that he is. He does not speak through "error" or "impurity" or "trickery". His words are "approved by God" and are not a "pretext for greed". He never uses "flattery" nor is he seeking "praise from men". This is not Paul. It is someone trying to be him but failing.

The smoking gun for forgery is the most problematic expression in this section:

> *"Instead, we were like infants among you, like a nursing mother caring*
> *for her children." (1 Thessalonians 2:7)*

What is the meaning of this odd idea that Paul and his colleagues are "infants" and also, jarringly, "nursing mothers"? These contradictory metaphors have caused consternation among commentators. In fact, the text has been changed by the copyists of some manuscripts to remove the difficulty. There is a variation in which *epioi* (gentle) appears instead of *nepioi* (infants). This variation is preferred in most modern translations because it makes more sense that Paul and his companions were gentle among the Thessalonians than that they were infants among them. However, the textual evidence for *nepioi* is very strong, which is why it is followed by the authoritative Nestle-Aland. Also substituting *epioi* for *nepioi* causes grammatical difficulties. The only reason for preferring *epioi* is that conventional commentators cannot understand why Paul and his companions should call themselves infants.[3]

We can find the real source of the infant metaphor in the document the forger is using as a template, 1 Corinthians:

> *"And I, brothers, was not able to speak to you as spiritual, but as fleshly, as infants in Christ. I gave you milk to drink, not solid food, for not yet were you able." (1 Corinthians 3:1-2)*

Paul undoubtedly intended "infants" here to mean the Corinthians. But the forger of 1 Thessalonians has made a mistake which gives him away. He has read this passage as a continuation of the theme of "weakness", "fear" and "trembling". So he thinks that Paul is describing himself and his co-author Sosthenes as "infants". Paul then goes on to say that he fed the Corinthians on milk. So the forger of 1 Thessalonians parallels this by having Paul call himself and his companions first "infants" and then "nursing mothers". Paul continues his self-praise for several more lines. Then comes the statement about the Jews killing "Lord Jesus" which is parallel to the archons crucifying "the Lord of glory" in 1 Corinthians.

The forgery of 1 Thessalonians 2 has been made by a member of the proto-orthodox church in the second century. Their purpose was to refute the gnostics who were using 1 Corinthians 2:6-8 to claim that heavenly archons crucified Christ. The forger based their passage on Paul's troublesome words in 1 Corinthians 2:1-3:3, and made their sock-puppet Paul state unambiguously that the Jews were guilty of the crucifixion. Read correctly, 1 Thessalonians is evidence for a heavenly interpretation of the archons. It shows that the proto-orthodox Christians were well aware of the embarrassing inconsistencies between Paul and the gospel version of events. They resorted to forgery to cover up these inconsistencies.

The parable of the tenants

There is one other early source which deals with the death of Jesus and which is independent of the crucifixion account in the gospels. I have discussed elsewhere the evidence that the Gospel of Thomas is earlier than any of the New Testament gospels.[4] Whether or not you accept such an early dating for Thomas, the parable of the tenants is certainly early, for it is also found in all three of the synoptic gospels. We will give the Thomas version first because it has certain features than indicate that it preserves the earliest form of the parable:

> *He said: "A good man had a vineyard. He gave it to some tenants that they might work it, and he receive the fruit from their hand. He sent his servant, that the tenants might give him the fruit of the vineyard. They seized his servant, they beat him, and almost killed him. The servant came and told his master. His master said: 'Perhaps they did not know him.' He sent another servant; the tenants beat the other one. Then the master sent his son. He said: 'Perhaps they will be ashamed before my son.' Those tenants, since they knew that he was the heir to the vineyard, they seized him and killed him. He that has ears, let him hear." (Thomas 65; TC 4:10)*

> *(Note: For the Gospel of Thomas, both the traditional and Thomas Code (TC) numberings are given throughout this book.[5])*

This is one of only two sayings in Thomas that could allude to the death of Jesus.[6] If the son is Jesus, then it is the tenants who killed Christ. But who were the tenants? There are other enigmas. Who are the two servants who go to the vineyard before the son? What is the meaning of the vineyard? And who is the "good man" who owns the vineyard? Is he God? If so, why is he so ineffectual? The ending of the parable is bleak—the son is dead. Have the tenants succeeded in their plot to kill the heir? Is there no resurrection? This deceptively simple parable leads us to some deep questions.

> ➤ **According to the Gospel of Mark, the "tenants" are the Jewish priests.**

To most Christians, though, there is no mystery about the parable of the tenants. The answer is set out quite plainly in the Gospel of Mark:

> *And he began to speak to them in parables. "A man planted a vineyard and placed a fence around it and dug a wine vat and built a tower, and rented it out to husbandmen and went into another country. When the time came, he sent a servant to the husbandmen so that from the husbandmen he might receive some of the fruit of the vineyard. And they took him and beat him and sent him away empty-handed. And*

*again he sent to them another servant, and they struck him on the head
and treated him shamefully. And he sent another, and him they killed,
also many others: some they beat, and some they killed. Finally, having
one beloved son, he sent him to them, saying, 'They will respect my
son.' But those husbandmen said to one another, 'This is the heir. Come,
let us kill him, and the inheritance will be ours.' And they took him
and killed him and threw him out of the vineyard. What then will the
master of the vineyard do? He will come and destroy the tenants and
give the vineyard to others. (Mark 12:1-9)*

To remove any doubt at whom this is aimed, the author of Mark adds
a comment: *"And they were seeking to lay hold of him but feared the people, for
they knew that he had told the parable against them"* (Mark 12:12). By "they"
is meant the *"chief priests and the scribes and the elders"* (Mark 11:27). So the
author of Mark interprets the parable as follows:

The tenants = the Jewish priestly establishment
The vineyard owner = God
The servants = the prophets
The son = Jesus

Both Matthew and Luke follow this explanation. It is consistent with
the gospel passion account in which the priestly establishment arrange for
Jesus to be killed. So is the author of Mark correct in his interpretation of
the parable? If we look in more detail at Mark's explanation, it falls apart.

➢ **The servants cannot be the prophets.**

In Mark, the servants represent the prophets, and some are beaten and
some killed. The first problem is that the priests did not actually kill the
prophets in scripture. It is true that two of the ancient kings of Israel supposedly killed priests or prophets. Saul killed the "priests of the Lord" for
siding with David. And Jezebel, Ahab's wife and devotee of Baal, killed
many "prophets" of the Lord.[7] It would be absurd to blame either episode
on the priests when it was the priestly caste who were the victims. In fact,
both episodes are examples of propaganda directed by the priests against
Israel. The only episode blamed on Judah was the killing of Zechariah at
the temple. But Zechariah was the son of the former High Priest, Jehoiada,
and it was Joash, the king, who ordered his killing.[8]

The second problem is that, according to the Thomas version, there were
only two servants. Taking the later understanding of who qualified as
a prophet, the traditional number was twenty-four. The original concept

of a prophet was much wider—in Jezebel's time, there were hundreds of prophets. But how could even twenty-four prophets be represented by just two servants? The author of Mark attempts to solve this problem by having many more than two servants. But scholars have long known that there is something wrong with the Gospel of Mark's description of the servants.

There are four versions of the parable of the tenants, and all four differ in this apparently minor detail of the number of servants. The authors of Matthew and Luke both changed the description of the servants:

Matthew has two groups of servants followed by the son.[9]
Luke has three servants followed by the son.[10]

The authors of these gospels would not have changed this detail unless they were aware of a problem with Mark. Note in particular the very odd change that Matthew makes in dividing the servants into two groups. The author of Matthew tends to be loyal to his sources, and this change indicates that he had an alternative source apart from Mark, which had a structure of two servants followed by the son. If we examine Mark, it is clear that extra servants have been added. The addition is clumsy: *"And he sent another, and him they killed, also many others: some they beat, and some they killed"*. Having some of the servants killed detracts from the climax of the death of the son. The reason for preferring the Thomas version as original is that it reflects the structure of three found in storytelling all over the world:

The first servant is sent, is beaten, and returns.
The second servant is sent, is beaten, and returns.
The son is sent and is killed.

The first two cases establish the pattern, and the third case partially breaks the pattern while bringing it to a climax. The human brain loves such patterns of three, and they predominate in traditional storytelling. Think of the story of the three little pigs:

The first little pig builds his house with straw. The big bad wolf comes and blows down the straw house and eats him.
The second little pig builds his house with sticks. The big bad wolf comes and blows down the house of sticks and eats him.
The third little pig is wiser than the other two. He builds his house with bricks. The big bad wolf comes and puffs and puffs but cannot blow down the house of bricks.

If the story followed Mark's approach, then the first two little pigs would be followed by something like; "then there were many more little pigs, some building houses with straw and some with bricks, and all were eaten by the wolf". If it followed Matthew, there would be a first group of little pigs building their houses with straw, a second group building their houses with sticks, and one little pig who builds his house with bricks. If it followed Luke, then we would have three little pigs building houses which are blown down before a fourth builds his house with bricks. Encountered as a nursery story, we would automatically reject each of these variations in favour of the structure of three.

The author of Mark has disrupted the original form of the saying to force it to match his interpretation that the servants are prophets. But they are not prophets—they are something else.

> ➤ **It would be impossible for human priests to have the motivation assigned to the tenants.**

The parable tells us why the tenants killed the son. They want to take the vineyard from the "good man". By killing the son, the vineyard would fall to them because the son was the heir. But how can this motivation apply to the priests and rulers of the Jews? They would have to know that Jesus was the Son of God and they would have to think that by killing Jesus they could steal Judah, the vineyard, from God so that they could rule it indefinitely. Put in these terms, we can see that the Mark explanation is absurd.

According to the crucifixion story in Mark, the priests kill Jesus because they do not know who he is. Had they known he was the Son of God, they would surely have feared God's wrath and the terrible vengeance that would ensue. Their crime depends on their ignorance. Yet the tenants are not ignorant. They know the son is the heir because that is why they kill him. This is not a minor detail, but the whole point of the parable. The tenants are guilty of insurrection against the "good man", and the murder of his son is a premeditated part of their rebellion. The human priests cannot have consciously rebelled against God, so they cannot have been the tenants.

> ➤ **The Gospel of Mark makes a connection between the tenants parable and the vineyard parable in Isaiah.**

Although we must reject the interpretation of the parable in the Gospel of Mark, it does give us one valuable clue. Unlike Thomas, the Mark version starts with the vineyard owner planting the vineyard, putting a fence around it, and building a winepress and tower. These details are significant because they lead us to the parable of the vineyard in Isaiah:

> *Let me sing for my beloved, my song concerning his vineyard. My beloved had a vineyard on a very fertile hill. He dug it and cleared it of stones, and planted it with the choicest vines. He built a tower in its midst, and hewed out a winepress in it; and he looked for it to yield grapes, but it yielded wild grapes. (Isaiah 5:1-2)*

In the interpretation of this parable:

The vineyard stands for the kingdoms of Israel and Judah.
The "beloved" who builds the vineyard is Yahweh.
The hill is Mount Moriah on which the city of David and the temple is built.
The watchtower is the temple.
The winepress or vat (for the vat would be used to press grapes) is the altar that stood in front of the temple.

The fruit of the vine which goes into the winepress is, symbolically, the sacrifices made on the altar. These sacrifices stand in the broader sense for the obedience of Yahweh's chosen people. However, the grapes turn out to be bad—they are "wild grapes" reflecting the uncultivated religion of the Canaanites:

> *And now, O inhabitants of Jerusalem and men of Judah, please judge between me and my vineyard. What more could have been done for my vineyard, that I have not done in it? When I looked for it to yield grapes, why did it yield wild grapes? (Isaiah 5:3-4)*

Because of this, Yahweh will destroy the vineyard:

> *And now I will tell you what I will do to my vineyard. I will take away its hedge, and it shall be consumed; I will break down its wall, and it shall be trampled down; I will lay it waste; it shall not be pruned or dug, and briers and thorns shall grow up. I will command the clouds that they rain no rain upon it. (Isaiah 5:5-6)*

This is a prophecy of the coming exile, the theme that runs through the whole of Isaiah. Although the "house of Israel" will be destroyed the main target of the parable is Jerusalem and Judah. The walls of Jerusalem will be broken down, and the city laid waste. The briers and thorns are an image of wilderness used consistently in Isaiah: the land of the Jews will be made desolate, and agriculture will cease.

> ➢ **An alternative explanation sees the parable of the tenants as being about social justice, with the vineyard owner as an exploiter. This explanation is inconsistent with the vineyard parable in Isaiah.**

There is one more interpretation of the parable of the tenants that should be mentioned. Others have also noted that the Gospel of Thomas version appears original and that the Gospel of Mark interpretation does not really fit. But they question whether the Thomas parable is really about Jesus at all. There is another, completely different, reading that sees the parable as concerned with social justice. In this view the man who owns the vineyard is an exploitative landlord. It has even been suggested that the word that describes the man who owns the vineyard, and which is usually restored as "good", is actually a much rarer word meaning "usurer". The word is doubtful because of a lacuna in the one surviving copy of the Thomas parable.

This reading would change everything. The man sends his servants to extract an exorbitant rent from the hard-working farmers, so it is not surprising that they are unwilling to pay and rough-up the servants instead. To resolve matters, he sends his own son, hoping that they will be awed by his status. But the tenants despise the rich heir to the vineyard and kill him.

This may give a more fashionable twenty-first century reading, but it leaves a bad taste in the mouth. For a start, what is the point of the story? Those listening to the parable in first-century Judea would be scratching their heads because they know how it would all end. The vineyard owner would go to the Roman authorities, pay the necessary bribe, and the Romans would then send soldiers to arrest and crucify the tenants for murder. How could Jesus be so naive to believe that they would get away with their crime and keep the vineyard?

Then there is the ambiguous moral status of the tenants. If the vineyard owner is exploiting the tenants, are the murderers not justified in their actions? Such ambiguity belongs to the modern university and post-modernism but is not found in ancient storytelling. The tenants are evil, and the storyteller would never excuse them.

Another reason for rejecting the reading of "usurer" is the correspondence between the tenant parable and the vineyard parable in Isaiah. They are too close to deny a link. Yet, in the Isaiah parable, the owner of the vineyard is Yahweh. No Jew would ever regard Yahweh as an exploiter. Nor could they accept that those who rebelled against Yahweh were anything other than evil. We must reject this modern idea that the parable is about social justice as unhistorical.

> **The surviving text of the Gospel of Thomas indicates that the servants were regarded as divine beings.**

The mystery of the two servants deepens with another clue. In the one surviving complete manuscript of Thomas, there are some small, apparently insignificant, lines over the first three letters of the Coptic word for "servant". These lines are present for both of the two servants. Such marks are called *"nomina sacra"* and occur very frequently in Thomas and other early Christian manuscripts. Most typically they appear over abbreviations used for certain sacred names, but sometimes, as here, they are used to indicate the special status of a name spelt out in full. The *nomina sacra* are marks of the divine. They are used for Jesus, God, the holy spirit, and a few other holy names. They are not used for prophets nor the purely human. We cannot tell at what stage the *nomina sacra* were placed over the two servants, whether they were original or a later addition. But it is certain that whoever first drew them regarded the two servants as being more than human.[11]

2

The Servants

The Book of Enoch

I long puzzled over the two servants, unable to make any progress. But
then, quite by chance, I stumbled across the two in an unexpected place—
the Animal Apocalypse in the Book of Enoch. Not only did I find the
two servants but also the answer to another mystery; the meaning of the
names Cephas (the rock) and the Magdalene (the tower). Finding these
links gave a sense of reaching far back into the past of the Jesus movement,
beyond the memory horizon of the gospels.

The Animal Apocalypse is the history of the world presented as an
animal fable. It is preserved in the Book of Enoch (also called the first
book of Enoch, or 1 Enoch, by scholars to distinguish it from the second
and third books of Enoch which were written later). The Book of Enoch is
a composite work, and its individual components would have originally
circulated independently. The church fathers talked about the Book of
Enoch, and it is quoted in the New Testament. Although it was thought
to have been lost, it had been preserved in the Ethiopian church where
it exercised considerable influence. It was rediscovered to western scholarship when the first copies were brought back by the Scottish travel-
ler J. Bruce in 1773. The only complete copies are in Ethiopic (Ge'ez), but
Aramaic fragments of all but one of the component works have been
found at Qumran among the Dead Sea Scrolls. Some of these fragments
relate to the Animal Apocalypse including one dated to 150-125 BC.[1] The
Animal Apocalypse must be at least as old as these fragments and the
original language was almost certainly Aramaic.[2]

According to Genesis, Enoch was the seventh generation from Adam.
There is actually another Enoch, the son of Cain who murdered his
brother Abel.[3] The two Enochs must have come from the same original
root which has split into a good and an evil branch. It is the good Enoch
that will concern us. Genesis says very little about him, but that little
includes a statement that fascinated the Jews:

> *So the days of Enoch were 365 years. Enoch walked with God, and he was not, for God took him. (Genesis 5:23-24)*

It was believed that Enoch had a special relationship to God having "walked with God" before "God took him". Enoch may have started out as a sun god. It is probably no coincidence that his life on earth was 365 years, equal to the days in the year. In Jewish belief, Enoch is one of just two humans who were taken up to heaven alive, the other being Elijah. The Book of Enoch is about Enoch's journey to heaven and about what he heard and saw there. It is a compendium of myths and stories that were not all originally connected to Enoch. But there is one meta-myth that runs through the Book of Enoch—the descent of the Watchers.

➤   **The Watchers are angels who disobey God and descend to the earth to take wives.**

The Book of the Watchers is the first part of the Book of Enoch. The Watchers are angels who have been appointed to keep guard over the earth. They look down upon the earth at the beauty of the "the daughters of man" and decide to descend and take wives. This has been forbidden by God and is a dangerous act of disobedience. The angels vow to go through with it together and descend to Mount Hermon under their leader Semyaz. Once on earth, the angels teach humanity knowledge of the arts and sciences. They take women as wives, and these wives give birth to giants who oppress the people. It is clear that multiple versions of the myth are combined in Enoch. In some places in the text, it is Azaz'el, rather than Semyaz, who is the leader of the angels.

The good angels, led by Michael and Gabriel, observe what has happened and inform God. He sends an angel to Noah to warn him that a flood is coming. Another angel, Raphael, is sent to bind Azaz'el and imprison him in a pit. Gabriel is told to take action against the offspring of the Watchers and make them fight against each other. Michael goes to Semyaz and the others to tell them that they will be imprisoned in a pit for seventy generations. At the time of final judgement, they will be condemned to eternal torment in the fire. After the angels and their children are destroyed, humans will live in peace and the earth will become super-abundant.

Up to this point, Enoch has not been involved with the Watchers, but now, oddly, they ask him to intervene on their behalf. This part of the book is confused, reflecting alternative traditions. In one of those traditions Enoch dwells in heaven:

… Enoch was hidden, and no one of the children of the people knew by what he was hidden and where he was. And his dwelling place as well as his activities were with the Watchers and the Holy Ones. (1 Enoch 12:1-2)[4]

However, in another tradition, Enoch is a man on earth who undertakes a shamanic journey to heaven. Azaz'el and the other Watchers come to Enoch to ask him to intercede with God on their behalf, to request mercy. Enoch writes down their prayer and sits by the waters of Dan, where he falls asleep. In his dream, he receives the judgement of God. They are not to be forgiven, nor will they be allowed to ascend to heaven again, but will be imprisoned in the earth for all eternity.

This is followed by Enoch's account of his ascent to heaven. It is unclear if this ascent is intended to be physical or a shamanic ascent that occurs in Enoch's dream. Enoch describes how he was taken up in the clouds of heaven and came to a wall of flame and white marble, inside of which was a great house of white marble. The house appeared to be empty, but then in a vision, Enoch saw a door which led to a second, infinitely greater house made of fire. These two houses represent the second and third heavens which lie above the first heaven, the sky. In this third heaven, Enoch comes to the throne room of God and the divine presence. He prostrates himself, and lowers his face, but is raised up by God.

God then repeats his decision about the fate of the Watchers. In this passage, it is said that the offspring of the Watchers will become evil spirits who will wander the earth. They share the heavenly nature of their fathers but are confined to earth because of the earthly nature of their mothers. These spirits are the demons whom the early Jesus movement believed haunted humanity. It is said that women will be particularly afflicted by them. The angels then give Enoch a tour of heaven and earth.

The story of the Watchers in Enoch is closely linked to a passage in Genesis:

And it came to pass when man began to multiply on the face of the earth and daughters were born to them, that the sons of God saw that the daughters of man were beautiful. And they took wives for themselves of any they chose. Then Yahweh said, "My Spirit shall not always strive with man, for he is flesh. Yet his days shall be 120 years." The Nephilim were on the earth in those days, and also afterwards, when the sons of God came in to the daughters of man and they bore children to them. These became mighty men of old, men of renown. (Genesis 6:1-4)

Here the Watchers are called the "sons of God" which is an expression used for the angels. As in Enoch, these angels see the beauty of the daughters of men and take them as wives. The meaning of the "Nephilim" is unclear, and they could be either giants or great warriors. The version of the myth in the Book of Enoch makes it clear that the Nephilim are the children of the "sons of God" and their human wives. The word itself comes from a root meaning "to fall" and may hint at the origins of the Nephilim as an alternative form of the fallen angels. The relationship between the Genesis passage and the Book of the Watchers is controversial. Does Enoch use the Genesis passage as a source, or does Genesis reflect Enoch, or do they both use another lost work? Most likely, Genesis is the earlier of the two. But the traditions about the angels must predate both.

> **The story of the angels in Genesis and Enoch is a combination of two formerly separate myths; the myth of the angels who descend to earth for seventy generations and the ancient myth of the flood.**

There is an awkward series of events around the judgement of the angels and the flood in Enoch. The fallen angels are judged and imprisoned in a pit at the time of the flood. Then, after seventy generations, they are judged and imprisoned in a pit. The repetition shows that there is something wrong here. The problem arises from combining the myth of the Watchers with the myth of the flood. It requires that the angels receive a preliminary judgement long before the final judgement. Another glaring problem is the persistence of evil after the flood. The Book of Enoch employs a messy solution—the children of the angels somehow survived the flood to become demons.

The problems arise because Genesis has conflated two formerly distinct myths; the descent of the angels to earth and the flood. The story of the flood is ancient, originating in Mesopotamia but found throughout the region. An Old Babylonian version exists on clay tablets dated to 1,700 BC, some thousand years before the Bible. In this version, the gods bring about the flood because they are annoyed by the over-population of humanity. The wise man Atrahasis builds an ark and saves humanity from destruction.[5] In Enoch and Genesis, we can see a hint of the original cause; it is the growth in the human population that sparks the angels' lust for women. The angels corrupt humanity and Yahweh brings the flood to cleanse the earth.

What was the form of the angel myth before it was combined with the flood story? The angels must have been on earth for seventy generations and are judged at the end of time. Evil is in the world due to the continued presence of the angels. Because the seventy generations did not fit in with the Genesis story, they were suppressed but remained in the Book of the Watchers.

The Animal Apocalypse

The Dream Visions constitute the fourth book of 1 Enoch. In these Visions, Enoch recounts to his son Methuselah two dreams he had as a youth. The first is a terrifying vision of the earth collapsing into the abyss. The second is the much longer Animal Apocalypse, an exquisitely worked out allegory of the whole history of the earth, from Adam to the final judgement. In the Animal Apocalypse, everything is reduced in scale; animals represent humans, and humans represent angels.

> ➢ **The Animal Apocalypse combines the myth of Adam and Eve in Genesis with the descent of the Watchers. In the Apocalypse, evil enters the world through the fallen angels and not through the snake and the apple.**

The Animal Apocalypse begins with a snow-white cow (Adam) emerging from the earth. He is followed by a female calf (Eve) with two other calves, one dark (Cain) and one red (Abel). The Apocalypse follows the storyline in Genesis; the dark calf, Cain, gores the red calf, Abel, who disappears. The dark calf then has many children by a female calf (we are not supposed to ask where she came from!).[6] In the meantime, the original female cow (Eve) and the bull (Adam) have two more snow-white cows, followed by other cows and dark heifers. One of these white cows becomes a great snow-white bull (Seth) from whom a tribe of snow-white cows will come.

In the Animal Apocalypse, the colour white represents purity. Humans start in a pure white state, and the Apocalypse ends with the restoration of whiteness. Unfortunately, "white" has come to mean a particular ethnic group, people of northern European descent. The myths emerged from middle eastern populations, and they did not regard lighter-skinned northern Europeans as being "white". Instead, they are thinking of white sheep or white cattle, or the way the light reflects from a pure white fabric or rock.

The Apocalypse now begins to follow the Book of the Watchers with the descent of the angels as fallen stars:

And as I looked, behold, a star fell down from heaven but (managed) to rise and eat and to be pastured among those cows. Then I saw these big and dark cows, and behold they all changed their cattle-sheds, their pastures, and their calves; and they began to lament with each other. Once again I saw a vision, and I observed the sky and behold, I saw many stars descending and casting themselves down from the sky upon that first star; and they became bovids [cattle] among those calves and were pastured together with them, in their midst. (1 Enoch 86:1-3)[7]

The stars are the fallen angels of the Book of the Watchers. They take the shape of cattle (men) and begin to corrupt humanity. They put out over-sized male organs to mate with the female cows (human women), who bring forth their offspring as "elephants, camels and donkeys", representing giants, monsters and demons. These children of the fallen stars bully and torment the cows and begin to kill and eat them.

The corruption of the fallen angels is ended by the appearance of four white persons (angels).[8] They take Enoch up from the earth to a high place and put him on a high tower from where he can see everything. The four then seize the first star, bind him, and throw him into an abyss. One produces a sword which he gives to the elephants, camels and donkeys who then fight and kill each other. Another binds the remainder of the fallen stars and casts them into a pit.

We should note the differences with Genesis. There is no garden of Eden, no snake and no story of Eve and the apple. Evil still enters the world through the female, but only because the fallen angels have impregnated the women. So there were two myths among the Jews for the origins of evil. But are these myths at heart one and the same? Does the snake, the purveyor of forbidden knowledge, stand for the Watchers? Is eating the apple a euphemism for sex?

> ➢ **In the Animal Apocalypse, there are two, and only two, humans who change into angels. These must be the two servants of the tenants parable.**

In the continuation of the story, we find the first clue as to the identity of the servants:

Then one of those four went to those snow-white bovids and taught (one of them) a secret: he was born a bovid but became a person: and he built for himself a big boat and dwelt upon it. (1 Enoch 89:1)[9]

Something very strange happens here. The white bull who builds the ark (Noah) becomes a person—so Noah has transformed from a man into an angel. He is one of only two animals in the whole of the apocalypse who become human. This means that only two people throughout history were believed to have become angels. These must be our two servants, and the first is Noah.

After the flood, the nations emerge from Noah's three sons. Each nation is represented by a distinct species of animal or bird. The Israelites come after the nations through a snow-white cow (Abraham) who gives rise to another snow-white cow (Isaac). This connects the Israelite patriarchs back to the line of snow-white cows to show that they were not descended from the nations. The representation of the Israelites then changes to a flock of sheep. From the bull-Isaac comes a white sheep (Jacob/Israel) who has twelve other sheep (the twelve brothers who give rise to the twelve tribes). The Apocalypse follows the Genesis story of Joseph and the sojourn in Egypt. The Egyptians are represented as wolves who oppress and eat the sheep. At this point, God enters the Apocalypse.

The "Lord of the sheep" (Yahweh) comes down and appears to a sheep (Moses). This sheep Moses will lead the flock to escape through a lake (the Red Sea) whose waters part to give them passage but close upon the pursuing wolves. The sheep now enter a desert where "they began to open their eyes and see". Moses goes up a rock (Mount Sinai) to meet the Lord of the sheep who appears on top of the rock to all the people:

> That sheep then ascended to the summit of that lofty rock; and the Lord
> of the sheep sent (him) to them. After that, I saw the Lord of the sheep,
> who stood before them; his appearance was majestic, marvellous and
> powerful; all those sheep beheld him and were afraid before his face. All
> of them feared and trembled because of him, and cried around to that
> sheep (who was) leading them and to the other sheep who was also in
> their midst, saying, "We are not able to stand before the presence of our
> Lord and to look at him." (1 Enoch 89:29-31)[10]

Moses returns to the rock, but when he comes down again, the other sheep have begun to go astray, and the majority have become blinded. Those that have gone astray he slays and the others he brings back into the fold. Although the description of the exodus is more detailed than the rest of the Animal Apocalypse, there is one thing missing. Moses does not come down with the tablets of the law, the Torah. The authors of the Apocalypse are following the Judean mainstream account of the Exodus, but they do not come from a tradition where the law was important.

After his descent from the rock, Moses is changed:

> *I continued to see in that vision until that sheep was transformed into*
> *a man and built a house for the Lord of the sheep and placed the sheep*
> *in it. (1 Enoch 89:36)*[11]

Moses is transformed from an animal into a human. This means that
Moses, like Noah, was believed to have become an angel. He is the second
servant. The two servants are intermediaries between heaven and earth
because they have both a human and an angelic nature. In the whole
of the Animal Apocalypse, only Noah and Moses transform into angels.
Even Elijah, who is taken up to heaven alive, remains a sheep.

The rock that the Moses sheep ascends is Mount Sinai. It gives us the
origins of the name Cephas (Peter in Greek) which means "rock". The
house that Moses builds is the tabernacle, the predecessor of the temple.
In the Animal Apocalypse, the temple is represented as a tower built
onto the house. From this comes the name Magdalene which means "the
tower". The Lord of the sheep appears to the sheep first on the rock and
then, later, on the tower. The names Cephas and Magdalene represent the
new mountain and new temple.

To find the two servants so close to the origins of the titles Cephas/
Peter and the Magdalene cannot be a coincidence. Those who wrote the
Animal Apocalypse drew on the same set of beliefs as those who founded
the Jesus movement. Most likely the authors of the Animal Apocalypse
were the ancestors of the group from whom the Jesus movement emerged.

The sign of an angel

> ➢ **It is clear from other traditions in the Book of Enoch that Noah**
> **was regarded as an angel.**

From the Bible we would not guess that Noah was an angel. The few
stories about him in Genesis show him as all too human. In one episode,
he gets drunk and falls asleep naked. His sons come in to cover up his
nakedness with a blanket while looking away. One of them, Ham, does
take a peek, and his son Canaan is cursed by Noah as a result.[12]

In contrast, the Book of Enoch gives clear evidence that Noah was an
angel. A section (1 Enoch 106-7) is believed to be related to a lost Book
of Noah.[13] In one of these passages, Noah's father, Lamech, describes his
birth:

> *"And his body was white as snow and red as a rose: the hair of his*
> *head as white as wool and his demdema* beautiful; and as for the eyes,*

when he opened them the whole house glowed like the sun—(rather) the whole house glowed even more exceedingly. And when he arose from the hands of the midwife, he opened his mouth and spoke to the Lord with righteousness." (1 Enoch 106:2-3)[14]

* *Ethiopic word for long and curly hair combed up straight.*

The baby Noah fills the house with light which recalls a saying in the Gospel of Thomas: *"There is light within a man of light, and he becomes light to the whole world" (Thomas 24; TC 2.5).* Lamech fears that the boy might be an angel:

> *"I have begotten a strange son. He is not like an ordinary human being, but he looks like the children of the angels of heaven to me; his form is different, and he is not like us. His eyes are like the rays of the sun, and his face glorious. It does not seem to me that he is of me, but of angels, and I fear that a wondrous phenomenon may take place upon the earth in his days." (1 Enoch 106:5-6)*[15]

Lamech appeals to his father Methuselah to ask his own father, Enoch, about the child. Enoch has disappeared to dwell with the angels of heaven, and Methuselah has to travel to the world's end to find him. There he calls out into space, and Enoch, hearing, comes down. Methuselah tells Enoch how Lamech believes that the child is not his son but *"in the image of the angels of heaven" (1 Enoch 106:12).* Enoch reassures his son about Noah. He tells him about the coming flood and how it will cleanse the earth of corruption, although he adds balefully that this will not be the end of evil. Even worse is to come, for he, Enoch, has read the secrets of the holy ones in the tablets of heaven.[16]

It is clear that there was an early tradition that Noah was an angel. If we look carefully, we can find a few hints of this in Genesis. The best-known story about Noah is, of course, the building of the ark and leading the animals and birds into the ark two by two. This is now seen as a child's story, but it was an attempt to explain the reasons behind natural catastrophes that killed large numbers of people. In Mesopotamian myth, the gods send the flood because the earth is overpopulated. In the Bible, it is sent to cleanse the earth of the corruption of the "sons of God", the fallen angels:

> *Yahweh saw that the wickedness of man was great in the earth and that every inclination of the thoughts of his heart was only evil continually. And Yahweh repented that he had made man on the earth, and it grieved him in his heart. So Yahweh said, "I will blot out man whom I*

*have created from the face of the earth, man and animals and creeping
things and birds of the heavens, for I repent that I have made them."
(Genesis 6:5-7)*

If Yahweh had carried out this resolution, there would be no life on
earth. Instead, he instructs Noah to build the ark and save both his own
family and the natural world. Genesis gives no reason for this change of
heart, other than that *"Noah found favour in the eyes of Yahweh" (Genesis 6:8).*
So Noah is not just someone who built a great boat, but the sole reason
why humanity was not wiped out. Genesis adds that Noah *"walked with
God [Elohim]"* a phrase that is also used of Enoch, but no one else. Clearly,
Noah was a very significant figure, perhaps originally on the same level
as Enoch. But among the apocalyptic movement, the myth of Enoch won
out. Enoch had been taken up to heaven to learn the secrets of the holy
ones, making him the perfect source for apocalyptic revelations.

> ➢ **There are similar indications of Moses' angelic nature.**

There are some Jewish traditions about the birth of Moses that are very
similar to those about Noah. In Exodus, the new-born Moses is described
as "fair" or "goodly" and in later commentary this became increasingly
exaggerated.[17] Josephus says that the beauty of the baby was so remarkable that passers-by would turn back in the street to stare at the child.[18]
In Jewish medieval commentaries, his birth is described in terms similar
to Noah:

> *"The parents of Moses saw the child, (for) his form was like that of an
> angel of God." (Pirke de Rabbi Eliezer Ch. 48)[19]*

> *"When Moses was born the whole house became flooded with light."
> (Midrash Rabbah, Exodus 1:20)*

These commentaries are comparatively late, but we can find in the Bible
an episode where Moses glows with light. In the Animal Apocalypse, the
change in Moses happens after he comes down from the rock (Mount
Sinai). In Exodus, Moses is on the mountain forty days and forty nights
communing with Yahweh, and neither eats nor drinks for this time.
When he comes down from the mountain with the tablets of the law, he
is changed, and his face shines. The Israelites are terrified of the transformed Moses:

> *And when Aaron and the people of Israel saw Moses, behold, the skin of*
> *his face shone [qaran], and they were afraid to come near him. (Exodus*
> *34:30)*

The word *qaran* means literally "horns". Most likely it is a figurative expression meaning horns of light. Sometimes it is taken literally, which is why Michelangelo's famous statue of Moses shows him with two horns coming out of his head. This gave rise to the superstition among some Christians that Jews had horns. Moses' companions cannot stand his glowing appearance, and he has to cover his face with a veil when talking to them. When he communes with Yahweh, he casts the veil aside.[20] If to shine with light is evidence of an angelic nature, then Moses has become an angel like Noah.

> ➤ **The fact that Noah and Moses were man-angels explains why the word for "servant" was written with the nomina sacra.**

We have seen how in the Gospel of Thomas, the word for servant was marked by the *nomina sacra*, which indicates a divine rather than human nature. The *nomina sacra* would not be given to two human prophets. It is only because the two servants are angels that they are marked with this line. This is no trivial point. It is difficult to think of any other credible explanation to the mystery of the *nomina sacra*.

The three laws

> ➤ **The two servants and the son each bring a law to humanity.**

The two servants and the son are Noah, Moses and Christ. One common factor between all three is that they each brought a separate system of law. Jews look to two sets of laws; the law of Noah and the law of Moses. Christians look to the spiritual law of Christ. The act of bringing a law to humanity sets the two servants on a higher level than the prophets. So it makes sense that the law-bringer must bridge the distance between God and humans by having both a divine and human nature.

> ➤ **The law of Noah applied to the nations.**

The Jews believed that Noah brought the law that applied to the nations, the gentiles. The law of Noah was given after the flood, at the time when the nations came into being from Noah's three sons. At this time, God blessed Noah and his sons. He told them to be fruitful, to multiply and to fill the earth. They were permitted to eat of all plants, beasts and birds. There was a basic requirement for animal welfare—they were not to eat the flesh of a living animal. Murder was forbidden on pain of death. And that is it! After giving this very basic law, God makes a new covenant between himself and all living things. He will send no more floods, and as a mark of his promise, he places the first rainbow in the sky.[21]

> **The law of Moses applied to the Jews.**

The law of Moses applied to the Israelites but not the nations. In the familiar story, Moses communed with God for forty days on Mount Sinai and came down with the tablets of the law. It is less well known that Moses descends the mountain with the tablets twice. The first time he smashes the tablets and has to go back up again.[22] (This is an example of multiple versions of a story being combined which is common in Genesis and Exodus.) In the Animal Apocalypse, God appears directly to the people. In Exodus, elaborate preparations are made for such an appearance, but God then changes his mind.[23] The final priestly editor of Exodus did not approve of the notion that God would appear to just anyone.

> **Jesus brought a new spiritual law for Christians.**

Christians do not follow the law of Moses because they believe that Christ's sacrifice ended the old law and that Jesus brought a new spiritual law. However, the question of whether the law of Moses continued to apply to the Jesus movement was controversial in the first century. Some Jewish Christians thought that it did, including the author of Matthew:

> *"Do not think that I have come to abolish the law or the Prophets; I have not come to abolish them but to fulfil them. For truly, I say unto you, until heaven and earth pass away, not one iota, nor one stroke, will pass from the law until all is accomplished." (Matthew 5:17-18)*

However, we will see that the logic of the Almanac requires the law to end with the destruction of the temple. The supposed law of Moses was actually a Judean invention from the period around the Babylonian exile. The Jesus movement came from an Israelite population and draws on traditions that are older than the book of Exodus and the law. In the Animal Apocalypse, when the sheep Moses descends from the rock, there is no mention of the law or tablets of stone. Instead, the focus is on the building of the tabernacle, which will become the temple. It was the temple and not the law that was important to the predecessors of the Jesus movement. They followed the biblical account and incorporated Moses into the Animal Apocalypse and the Almanac. But the law was never their tradition which is why the Jesus movement found it so easy to discard. The difficulty came as the movement expanded from the initial small group into the surrounding Judean population for whom the law was vitally important.

This difficulty is summed up in the intellectual struggles of the former Pharisee Paul. His attempt to reconcile his old and new beliefs has had a huge influence on Christian thought. It is ironic that many see Paul as the person who led Christianity in the direction of abandoning the Jewish law. We might almost say the opposite; that Paul gave the law far more prominence than it had for the founders of the movement. In the Gospel of Thomas, scriptural authority is almost causally dismissed:

> *His disciples said to him: "Twenty-four prophets spoke in Israel, and they all spoke of you." He said to them: "You have left out the living one in your presence and have spoken about the dead." (Thomas 52; TC 3.15)*

The living one is the spiritual resurrected Jesus who supersedes the authority of the prophets. Circumcision is dismissed in another saying;

> *His disciples said to him: "Is circumcision beneficial or not?" He said to them: "Were it beneficial, their father would beget them from their mother circumcised. But the true circumcision in spirit is entirely profitable." (Thomas 53; TC 3.16)*

In the new order, circumcision of the flesh is replaced by the circumcision of the spirit. Turning back to Paul, there is an explicit statement that the law of the Jews has been replaced by the law of Christ in 1 Corinthians:

> *To the Jews I became like a Jew, to win Jews. To those under the law I became like one under the law, (not being myself under the law) that I might win those under the law. To those outside the law, I became like one outside the law (not being outside the law of God but under the law of Christ) that I might win those outside the law. (1 Corinthians 9:20-21)*

Paul is no longer under the law of the Jews, but he is not lawless like the unconverted gentiles, because he is under the law of Christ. Nowhere does Paul agonise more about the apparent conflict between the Jewish law and Christian faith than in Romans:

> *Therefore, my brothers, you also died to the law through the body of*
> *Christ, that you should belong to another, to him who has been raised*
> *from the dead, so that we should bear fruit to God. [...] But now we*
> *have been released from the law, having died to what bound us, in order*
> *to serve in the new way of the spirit, and not in the old way of the letter.*
> *(Romans 7:4,6)*

The old law comes to an end at Christ's death; the new law comes through Christ's resurrection.

3

The Tenants

The quest for the servants has led us to the Animal Apocalypse, which is also the source of the names Cephas/Peter and the Magdalene. Can we find the tenants there? We will follow the Apocalypse from the point where the sheep Moses disappears.

➢ **The first temple is central to the Animal Apocalypse.**

Having mourned for Moses, the sheep cross over the stream (the Jordon) and come to a pleasant place in *"a land beautiful and glorious"* (Canaan, the Promised Land). The dogs, foxes and wild boars (the neighbouring nations) began to attack and devour them. So the Lord of the sheep raises a ram (King Saul) to fight the other animals. However, that ram (Saul) *"abandons his glory"* and begins to fight the other sheep, so the Lord of the sheep raises another sheep (David) as ram, and he becomes a *"judge and a leader of the people"*. The ram Saul is killed by the dogs (the Philistines) and David rules in his place. When David dies, his offspring (Solomon) becomes a ram and a judge and leader of the sheep (King Solomon). The wild beasts are all defeated and are not able to attack the sheep. We then have the building of the temple under Solomon:

> *Then that house became great and spacious; a lofty building was built upon it for the sheep, as well as a tall and great tower upon it for the Lord of the sheep; that house was low but the tower was really elevated and lofty. Then the Lord of the sheep stood upon that tower, and they offered a full table before him. (1 Enoch 89:50)*[1]

The house (the moveable tabernacle) has become enlarged and spacious, representing the temple complex where the people would gather for feasts and sacrifices. The tower is the actual temple building, housing the holy place and the holy of holies where Yahweh dwelt. The "full table" was the altar that stood in front of the main temple building on which animal sacrifices would be offered.

Afterwards, the sheep begin to stray away from the house. The Lord of the sheep calls a number of sheep to go to them (the prophets), but some are killed. One of these sheep (Elijah) is rescued by the Lord of the sheep and ascends to settle down next to Enoch. Eventually, the sheep abandon the house and the tower, and they become blind. The Lord of the sheep gives them over to the lions, leopards, wolves, hyenas, as well as the foxes and all the wild beasts (representing all the nations). The Lord of the sheep then leaves the house and tower (the presence of God leaves the temple), and the sheep are consumed by the lions (the Babylonians). Although Enoch tries to intervene on the sheep's behalf, the Lord of the sheep is content to let the slaughter proceed. The temple is then destroyed:

> "Then they burned that tower and ploughed that house. And I became exceedingly sorrowful on account of that tower, for that house of the sheep was being ploughed." (1 Enoch 89:66-7)[2]

We have already noted that there are no tablets of the law in the Animal Apocalypse, and in this account we see the central importance of the temple. The eyes of the sheep are open when they have the "house", the tabernacle, and then the "tower", the temple. The descent of the Lord of the sheep onto the tower is the high point of the Apocalypse. After this, there is a decline. The eyes of the sheep become closed as they stray away from the temple. When the temple is destroyed, the exile is complete. There is nothing in this about the sheep not obeying the law of Moses.

➢   **The authors of the Animal Apocalypse rejected the second temple.**

The Animal Apocalypse covers the rebuilding of the temple. After twelve hours, three sheep (Zerubbabel, Joshua, and perhaps Nehemiah) return to rebuild the house and the tower. However, the offerings they make on the table are impure and rejected. The attempted rebuilding only brings on yet more destruction. The sheep do not see properly, and their eyes are dim.

This detail tells us something fundamental about the authors of the Apocalypse—they did not accept the second temple and believed that the real temple had come to an end with the exile. It is not just a question of the rebuilders of the temple failing to meet some technical requirements relating to sacrifices. The sheep are exposed to their predators because they no longer have a house. The Lord of the sheep has left the original temple and does not descend onto the rebuilt tower. In the final apocalypse this false temple is ignominiously demolished and its contents abandoned in *"a certain place in the south of the land"* (1 Enoch 90:28). Just a few lines earlier the blind sheep judged as sinners are thrown into the burning abyss: *"and that abyss was to the south of that house"* (1 Enoch 90:26).

This place to the south of Jerusalem and Mount Moriah is the Valley of Hinnom, the site of child sacrifice, whose name Gehenna came to stand for hell. This shows the extent of the rejection of the second temple by those who wrote the Animal Apocalypse.

If they rejected the second temple, then the users of the Animal Apocalypse would also have rejected the authority of the temple priests. If they did not have a temple, then they could not follow the law of Moses. They were far from the mainstream and would have been regarded by their neighbours as heretics.

> ➤ **Those who used the Animal Apocalypse can be seen as the first Christians. They believed in a new kingdom and heavenly temple at the end of time to be ruled over by the Messiah.**

The authors of the Animal Apocalypse believed that the real new temple would come from the Lord of the sheep at the end of time and would not be built by humans. In place of the demolished second temple, the Lord of the sheep brings about a new and even greater house (the true second temple). Within this new temple both the sheep (the Jews) and the beasts and birds (the nations) are gathered together. Enoch is brought down to their midst together with the ram Elijah. The sword is laid down and sealed. The eyes of all are opened—there is not a single one who cannot see.

Then we have one of the strangest features of the Animal Apocalypse; a snow-white cow is born with huge horns. All the beasts and birds fear him and petition him. They are then all transformed into snow-white cows, and the first white cow becomes something else (the text is unclear here) with great black horns. The Lord of the sheep rejoices over all of the cows and Enoch is in their midst. He then wakes.

The great white bull is the most mysterious figure in the Animal Apocalypse. Although this bull is the supreme ruler at the end times, he is an animal, and hence human. Like Jesus, he is "a Son of Man". The white bull, as the last born, relates back to the first white bull, Adam. Similarly, Paul connects Adam to Jesus:

> So it is written: The first man Adam became a living being, the last Adam became a life-giving spirit. (1 Corinthians 15:45)

All the animals and sheep change into white cattle, taking the allegory full-circle back to the beginning. Mankind returns to its first unity; the distinctions between nations, and between the nations and the Jews, disappear. All are gathered in the new "house", the temple around the white bull. The word "Messiah" is not used but in the Animal Apocalypse, horns signify an anointed one, a king.

All of this is very similar to Christian belief. The final temple will not be built by hands. The Christ will come to establish his kingdom over both Jews and gentiles. There will be a new heaven and a new earth.

Under the traditional explanation, the Jews were expecting a military Messiah, a king who would free them from the Romans. But instead, Jesus brought a completely different and unexpected type of kingdom. The Animal Apocalypse shows that this is not true. Hundreds of years before the Jesus movement, some Jews were expecting a heavenly Messiah, just like Christ. The very earliest source for this heavenly Messiah is the Animal Apocalypse. This cannot be a coincidence. Once again, we have found a surprising link between the Apocalypse and early Christianity.

The Shepherds

> In the Animal Apocalypse, seventy shepherds (angelic rulers) are appointed over the sheep. They are destroyed after the final battle of the apocalypse.

The seventy shepherds are a striking feature of the Animal Apocalypse. After the sheep desert the house and tower, the shepherds are appointed by the Lord of the sheep:

> He then summoned seventy shepherds and surrendered those sheep to them so that they may pasture them. He spoke to the shepherds and their colleagues. "From now on, let each and every one of you graze the sheep; and do everything that I command you. I shall hand them over to you to be duly counted and tell you which among them are to be destroyed; and you shall destroy them!" So he handed over these sheep to them. (1 Enoch 89:59-61)[3]

In the allegory, the shepherds are men and so stand for angels. The Lord of the sheep asks other angels to watch over the shepherds and record their actions. The shepherds kill many more sheep than authorised and abandon the flock to the hands of the lions, leopards and wild boars. After the destruction of the house and tower, each shepherd takes a turn in pasturing the sheep before handing over to the next one.

The sheep wander into the woods and become mixed up with the beasts (the exile). The destruction continues until thirty-seven (an evident mistake for thirty-five) shepherds have had their turn. The sheep are then handed over to another twenty-three shepherds who each rule in turn and the persecution of the sheep by the other animals intensifies. The sheep are now attacked by the birds of the air, eagles, vultures, kites, and ravens who dig out their eyes and eat their flesh.

The reign of the last twelve shepherds is worse than all the rest. Yet in this period the eyes of some of the lambs begin to open. The birds viciously persecute these lambs, but they begin to grow horns. The lambs' struggles continue until a ram with a large horn emerges (a new king). There is a very confused account of a battle between the beasts, birds and the sheep. Some of the sheep remain blind and do not support the ram, or perhaps are actively on the side of the other animals. The shepherds join in, and they all attempt to break the horn of the ram, but he has help from the man (angel) keeping the record.

At this point, the action stops. The sealed books recording the shepherds' deeds are opened in the presence of the Lord of the sheep. He passes judgement on both the stars who descended at the beginning and the shepherds who ruled at the end. The blind sheep are cast into the abyss in the Valley of Hinnom where they meet a gruesome fate: *"I saw those sheep while they were burning—their bones also were burning"* (1 Enoch 90:27). The judgement is followed by the new temple and the white bull Messiah. It is all very similar to the Christian concept of the last judgement, hell, and the new kingdom of heaven. But who are the "shepherds"?

> ➤ The shepherds reflect a pre-existing myth that the world is under the control of seventy angels who rule for seventy periods. In the Animal Apocalypse, the rule of the angels corresponds to the exile.

The seventy shepherd angels have been inserted quite clumsily into the Apocalypse. The animal allegory would make good sense without them. Their appointment just before the destruction of the temple interferes with the flow of the action. In the Apocalypse, the rule of the angels is the exile. There is some evidence that they are organised into groups representing the nations who ruled over the Jews during the exile. There are certainly three groups, consisting of 35 (or 37), 23 and 12 shepherds. There is a hint that the first group is split into 12 plus 23, which would give a chiastic pattern of four groups; 12, 23, 23, and 12 shepherds.[4] There is also some evidence of a variant where the total number of shepherds has been made to equal 72.[5]

Four groups of shepherds could correspond to the four powers who ruled the Jews; the Babylonian, the Persian, the Ptolemaic and the Seleucid. If there were three periods, then the Ptolemaic and Seleucid periods could be combined as the Greek Macedonian rule which started with Alexander the Great. But however we organise the groups, neither the number of shepherds nor their actions make any historical sense. One fundamental problem is that the shepherds who rule after the three sheep attempt to rebuild the house can only correspond to the Persians. Yet this group of shepherds engage in excessive destruction, and the sheep are thoroughly dispersed during their oversight.[6] This is the exact opposite of the settled Persian period when the Jews returned to Jerusalem and rebuilt the temple. The Persians were regarded as benign rulers and received little criticism in Jewish writings. It would seem that the Apocalypse simply reflects a broad theme that the nations were all evil persecutors of the Jews and the closer to the end times, the worse the abuse.

The term "shepherd" indicates a ruler, a king. So are the seventy shepherds seventy human kings and emperors? The first problem is that there are too many shepherds to fit the period. Assuming an average reign of 20 years, then 70 rulers would cover 1,400 years, but the time between the beginning of the exile and the date of the Apocalypse is about 400 years. More fundamentally, the shepherds are angels and so cannot be human kings.

All of this is evidence that the shepherds have been inserted into the narrative from elsewhere. In the original source, seventy angels rule the world for seventy periods. The author of the apocalypse associates the shepherds with the exile and places them appropriately in the narrative.

> The fates of the fallen stars and the shepherds show that they are two versions of the same myth. Initially, the stars and shepherds were one and the same.

In the Book of the Watchers, the fallen angels are punished at the time of the flood:

> ... *bind them for seventy generations underneath the rocks of the ground until the day of judgement and of their consummation, until the eternal judgement is concluded. In those days they will lead them into the bottom of the fire—and in torment—in the prison (where) they will be locked up forever. And at that time when they will burn and die, those who collaborated with them will be bound together with them from henceforth unto the end of (all) generations. (1 Enoch 10:12-14)[7]*

The period from their imprisonment until the final judgement is "seventy generations". The coincidence between the seventy periods for which the shepherds rule and the seventy generations is striking. It suggests:

1. That each shepherd rules for a generation.
2. That the fallen angels and the shepherds were one and the same group, reflecting an original myth that the angels ruled the world for seventy generations.

The equivalence between the Watchers and the shepherds is indicated by their fates in the Animal Apocalypse. As in the Book of the Watchers, the fallen stars (the fallen angels) are bound in a pit at the time of the flood:

> *… and gathering and taking away all the mighty stars … bound all of them hand and foot, and cast them into the pits of the earth. (1 Enoch 88:3)*[8]

At the end times, shepherds and stars are judged together:

> *"Take these seven* [seventy] shepherds to whom I had handed over the sheep, but who decided to kill many more than they were ordered." Behold, I saw all of them bound; and they all stood before him. Then his judgement took place. First among the stars, they received their judgement and were found guilty, and they went to the place of condemnation; and they were thrown into an abyss, full of fire and flame and full of the pillar of fire. Then those seventy shepherds were judged and found guilty; and they were cast into that fiery abyss. (1 Enoch 90:22-25)*[9]

> ** The "seven shepherds" are a scribal mistake for "seventy shepherds" which appears in some copies as well as later in the passage.*

Both stars and shepherds meet the same fate, thrown into the same abyss of fire and eternal torment. The similarity between the stars and shepherds is obvious. The same myth is repeated in two slightly different forms.

Tenants and shepherds

➤ **The shepherds are the tenants of the parable. They are the same as Paul's archons.**

Everything leads to the conclusion that the Animal Apocalypse shepherds are the same as the tenants of the parable. If we look at both sources, we will see the close equivalence in the roles:

The Israelites:
The vine in the parable of the vineyard.
The flock in the Animal Apocalypse.

God:
The "good man" who appoints the tenants in charge of the vineyard.
The Lord of the sheep who appoints the shepherds in charge of the flock.

The evil angels:
The tenants in the vineyard parable.
The shepherds in the Animal Apocalypse.

In both sources, the shepherds/tenants are appointed legitimately but abuse their position. The shepherds/tenants must also be the same as Paul's "archons":

- Shepherd was a well-known metaphor for ruler or "archon".
- The seventy shepherds are angels who control the nations and who, after the exile, rule over the Jews; the archons are heavenly rulers over the world.
- The tenants kill the son; the archons kill Christ.

We are building a consistent picture in which archons, tenants and shepherds are three names for the same group of angels.

➢ **In Jeremiah, the metaphors of vineyard and flock are used inter-changeably and in conjunction with the shepherd metaphor. There is a close connection between these passages and the Animal Apocalypse.**

We have seen evidence for two metaphorical systems. In one the greater Israel (including Judah) is represented as a vine in a fertile vineyard. In the other, Israel is represented as a flock of sheep. We find both meta-phorical systems in the Book of Jeremiah, where they are even used inter-changeably in the same passage. The "shepherds" here are a metaphor for the King of Babylon, Nebuchadnezzar, and his allies and generals:

> O beautiful and delicate one, I have cut-off the daughter of Zion. The shepherds with their flocks shall come against her; they shall pitch their tents around her; they shall pasture, each in his place. (Jeremiah 6:2-3)

In this passage, the flocks are the Babylonian armies, and the daughter of Zion is Jerusalem. In Jeremiah 12, the sin of Judah is expressed using both metaphorical systems:

> *You have planted them, and they have taken root; they grow and bring forth fruit; you are near in their mouth and far from their hearts. But you know me, O Lord; you see me, and test my heart toward you. Pull them out like sheep for the slaughter, and set them apart for the day of slaughter. (Jeremiah 12:2-3)*

The Jews are (i) a plant that produces fruit, such as a vine and (ii) a flock of sheep "for the slaughter". In the continuation, the imagery is very close to the Animal Apocalypse:

> *"I have forsaken my house, I have abandoned my heritage; I have given the dearly beloved of my soul into the hands of her enemies. My heritage has become to me like a lion in the forest; she cries against me, therefore I hate her. My heritage is to me like a coloured bird of prey, the birds of prey all around are against her. Go, assemble all the beasts of the field, bring them to devour. Many shepherds have destroyed my vineyard; they have trampled down my portion. They have made my pleasant portion a desolate wilderness." (Jeremiah 12:7-10)*

The nations are compared to wild beasts and birds of prey who are assembled to devour Yahweh's "heritage", meaning Judah. This is very similar to how the animals and birds attack the sheep in the Animal Apocalypse. The passage explicitly combines shepherd and vineyard imagery: *"Many shepherds have destroyed my vineyard"*. Another passage addresses the judgement on the shepherds:

> *"Woe to the shepherds who destroy and scatter the sheep of my pasture!" said Yahweh. Therefore, thus says Yahweh, the God of Israel, concerning the shepherds who tend my people: "You have scattered my flock and have driven them away, and have not attended to them. Behold, I will attend to you for your evil deeds", declares Yahweh. (Jeremiah 23:1-2)*

The rule of the Messiah will replace the rule of the shepherds:

> *The days are coming," declares Yahweh, "when I will raise up for David a righteous branch, a king who will reign wisely and execute justice and righteousness in the earth. In his days Judah will be saved, and Israel will live in safety." (Jeremiah 23:5-6)*

The Messiah will be a branch of the house of David. It is the Christ who will end the exile and who will gather together Judah and Israel. Another prophecy concerns the length of the exile:

> "This whole land shall be a desolation and a horror; and these nations shall serve the king of Babylon seventy years. Then after seventy years are completed, I shall punish the king of Babylon and that nation, the land of the Chaldeans, for their iniquity," says Yahweh, "making the land an everlasting waste." (Jeremiah 25:11-12)

This prophecy, written after the event, is predicting the end of the Babylonian kingdom after seventy years. However, it is wrong in saying that Babylon would be an everlasting waste. Babylon remained a thriving, prosperous metropolis with a substantial Jewish population. Jeremiah continues by predicting that after the shepherds, the leaders of the nations who have enslaved Israel, will be punished:

> "Howl, you shepherds, and cry; and wallow yourselves in the ashes, you leaders of the flock: for the days of your slaughter and of your dispersions are accomplished; and you shall fall like a pleasant vessel. And the shepherds shall have no way to flee, nor the leaders of the flock to escape." (Jeremiah 25:34-35)

There is a close connection between these passages in Jeremiah and the Animal Apocalypse.

> ➤ In Jeremiah, the "shepherds" are the rulers of the nations that oppress Israel and Judah. However, the Animal Apocalypse reflects "cosmic escalation" of the shepherds and the exile.

In Jeremiah, there is nothing to suggest that the shepherds are anything other than human kings, with the chief shepherd being the king of Babylon. What is the nature of the connection between the Animal Apocalypse and Jeremiah? An obvious conclusion might be that the Animal Apocalypse has been influenced by the earlier Book of Jeremiah. But there is no straight read-across from the shepherds as represented in Jeremiah to the shepherds in the Apocalypse:

1. The shepherds in the Apocalypse are angels, not human kings.
2. The rule of the Apocalypse shepherds lasts far longer than the seventy years of physical exile in Jeremiah.
3. The seventy shepherds cannot be the gentile rulers of the Jews

during the exile because there are far too many of them. This is true even if we take the extended exile to include the Persian and Seleucid periods.

4. The best fit for the seventy periods for which the shepherds will rule is seventy generations.

These show that the shepherd myth in the Animal Apocalypse reflects "cosmic escalation". The exile becomes the servitude of all humanity under evil cosmic forces. We will see later that this cosmic exile reflects myths that were already ancient by the time of the Judean exile. It is likely that both Jeremiah and the Animal Apocalypse draw upon this earlier imagery. The duration for the exile in Jeremiah of seventy years is a suspiciously round number. It is not the correct figure for the length of the Babylonian exile, but it matches the seventy generations for which the angels will rule the earth. So aspects of the narrative of the exile may have been taken from the angel myth, and this exile narrative has then, in turn, influenced the development of the Christ myth. If so, cosmic escalation has not emerged after the exile; it has been there from the very beginning. Jewish perceptions of the physical exile have developed alongside the cosmic exile myth, and each has affected the other.

The ram and Judas Maccabaeus

➢ **The ram in the final battles is often identified with Judas Maccabaeus. This would mean that the Animal Apocalypse was written between 165 and 161 BC.**

Given the importance of the Animal Apocalypse to our reconstruction of the Christ myth, we must mention the theory that it was authored by a supporter of the Maccabees. This theory is the majority opinion among academics, although not quite a consensus. It rests mainly on the similarities between the ram in the final battle and Judas Maccabaeus.

The story of the Maccabees is one of the most remarkable and romantic, in the history of the Jews. In 167 BC, Judea was under the control of the Seleucid Empire and its Emperor, Antiochus IV Epiphanes. The Seleucids were Greeks, one of the successor kingdoms to the empire of Alexander the Great. Unlike his predecessors, Antiochus IV embarked on a project to convert the Jews to Greek religion and culture. The immediate cause of these actions was unrest caused by conflict between various factions in Jerusalem. The high priest Onias III had been deposed in favour of his brother Jason, who promised an increased tribute, and who led a party of

Hellenisers keen on introducing Greek customs into Jerusalem. It must have seemed that the old religion of the Jews was dead, and it was time to move on. Greek culture was impressive, with its sophisticated philosophy and mathematics, its literature and art. By contrast, the Jews were a failed people who had long since lost their independence. Although Jason started the Hellenising movement, he was also deposed when outbid by his successor, the corrupt Menelaus, who had no qualifications for the high priesthood and who proceeded even more aggressively with Hellenising policies. The old high priest Onias III objected, and Menelaus arranged his assassination. In 167 BC, Jason led a rebellion against Menelaus in Jerusalem which was put down by Antiochus IV. The king embarked on a brutal suppression of the Jewish religion and installed "the abomination of desolation" in the Jerusalem temple. It was probably a statue of Zeus and was intended to make the equivalence between Zeus and Yahweh. Antiochus sent his representatives around Judea to convert the population to the new worship and to quash any descent.

The Maccabean rebellion started with Judas' father; a village priest called Mattathias who was also called Hashmonay, from which we get the Hasmoneans. Watching in disgust in his home town of Modein as a neighbour accepted the new religion from the kings' representative, Mathias killed both men with his sword. He then fled to the hills with his five sons where he formed a band of guerrilla fighters. Surprisingly, they won a series of local victories over the government forces. After the death of Mattathias, his son Judas took over as leader. Judas Maccabaeus was a fearless and talented military commander who in his short career, won some amazing victories and secured a degree of independence of Judah from Seleucid rule. The struggle however continued. In 161 BC, Judas and his Hasmonean force came up against an enormous Seleucid army sent by the new King Demetrius I and led by Bacchides. Refusing to retreat, Judas died as he had lived; brave but reckless. His brothers succeeded him and from them came a dynasty of kings, the Hasmoneans. By an irony of history, they eventually became tyrants in their own right, opening the door for Roman occupation.[10]

In the Animal Apocalypse, the ram leads the flock in the final battles that precede the apocalypse and, unlike Judas, he does not die. So if the ram is Judas, then the Animal Apocalypse must have been written in the brief period in which Judas was triumphant but before he was killed— between 165 BC and 161 BC. There are several similarities between the description of the battle and the situation at this time:

- Some of the sheep oppose the ram and side with the animals. Similarly, many Jews supported the Seleucids.

- A lamb is killed by the ravens early in the conflict. This is seen as the former high priest Onias III.
- At one point, a man (an angel) assists the ram. This is taken as a reference to the legend that an angel intervened on Judas' side at the battle of Beth-Zur.[11]
- After a peace deal with the Seleucids, a series of ethnic wars between the Jews and the neighbouring peoples broke out. Judas and his brothers had to fight on many fronts. In the Apocalypse, all the animals and birds battle the ram.

➢ **The battle in the Animal Apocalypse is best explained as a generic end-of-times battle rather than relating to any particular historical event.**

Is the Animal Apocalypse a production of the Maccabees? Any similarity between Judas and the ram depends upon it being written in that narrow date range 165-61 BC. If we had independent evidence that the ram was Judas, then this dating argument would be valid. But in the absence of such evidence, the reasoning is circular and we can turn it on its head. If Judas is not the ram, then the Apocalypse could date from any time from within a few hundred years. The fact that we have to assume that it was written in such a short period of just four years for the ram to match Judas reduces the probability that the ram is really Judas.

Another obvious difficulty is that the ram's battle brings in the final apocalypse. Why would anyone writing in 165-161 BC think that the victories of Judas were signalling the imminent end of the world? The final battle is better understood as prophecy of the future—a generic "end of times" battle in which the ram represents the future military Messiah, the earthly counterpart to the bull, the heavenly Messiah. It is part of the myth that all the nations, the beasts and birds, will gang up on the Jews in this final climactic battle. The feature of the sheep with closed eyes could come from any sectarian group who were opposed to the "blind" mainstream. And the other points of supposed similarity to the Maccabean rebellion are not quite so impressive as they may at first appear:

- The death of the former high priest Onias III does not really match the lamb killed by the ravens. Onias was assassinated treacherously by the governor Andronikos at the instigation of Menelaus. According to 2 Maccabees, Andronikos was executed for the killing by the king.[12] The death of the lamb is quite different: a raven lifts it into the air and dashes it onto the ground before eating it. And the text has multiple sheep attacked at this point, and not just one.

- Although in the Apocalypse, the man (angel) intervenes on the side of the ram, the shepherds also take part in the battle (Enoch 90:13). So, unlike the Maccabean legend, there are angels on both sides of the conflict.

➢ **There are overwhelming religious differences between the Apocalypse and the Maccabees. And the key event of the Maccabean revolt is not reflected in the Animal Apocalypse.**

Not only is positive evidence equating the ram with Judas doubtful, but there is also strong contrary evidence that the Maccabees did not write the Animal Apocalypse. The religious viewpoint of the author of the Apocalypse is completely opposed to that of the Maccabees. And the most significant event that should have been included in the allegory if the ram were Judas is missing.

The Maccabean revolt was about the right of the Jewish people to live under the law of Moses and to worship Yahweh accordingly in the temple. The Maccabees and their supporters cared so passionately about the temple that they were ready to die for it. The high point of Judas Maccabaeus' career was the reconsecration of the temple as celebrated ever since by the festival of Hanukkah.

In contrast, the author of the Apocalypse did not mention the Jewish law and regarded the second temple as invalid. The second temple does not feature between its first rebuilding when the offerings are described as polluted until it is demolished and dumped in the Valley of Hinnom, Gehenna, at the end of times. Significantly, the Lord of the sheep does not come down onto the new tower, as he did on the first, but allows the sheep to be dispersed. Their eyes became dim-sighted. They wander and are attacked by the animals. There is no valid second temple.

Completely missing from the allegory is an allusion to the desecration of the temple by Antiochus IV which sparked the Maccabean revolt. If the author of the Apocalypse thought it fit to record the death of the former high priest, then why did he not include this much greater event, the "abomination of desolation"? This, after all, was the cause for which the Maccabees were fighting. And why was the rededication of the temple by Judas not included?

➢ **The Animal Apocalypse was not produced by the Maccabees but may have been edited to write in Judas Maccabeus as the ram.**

We must conclude that a Maccabean did not produce the Animal Apocalypse. However, the final battle may have been edited by an admirer of Judas Maccabaeus. It is suspicious that there are variations between manuscripts at the point where some of the sheep help the other animals against the ram. Such variations often indicate the hand of a redactor. There is also considerable repetition in the account of the battle; Nickelsburg shows how the account can be set out in two columns with parallel verses. This indicates our surviving copies of the Apocalypse have combined two different versions of the battle.[13] This leads Nickelsburg to conclude that the original Apocalypse was updated c. 163 BC.[14]

In one of the variations set out by Nickelsburg, there is no mention of the ram. So the ram may have been written into the second version which was based on the first. This would explain one of the most puzzling features of the Apocalypse—that there are two unconnected Messiahs. The ram leads the final battle, and his horn indicates that he is the kingly successor to David. Yet a completely different white bull rules after the end times.

If the ram is not Judas, then we must reject the narrow date range of 165-161 BC. The oldest extant fragment is dated 150-125 BC, but the Animal Apocalypse is probably much earlier than this. If the ram has been added by a Maccabean supporter then the original must be earlier than the Maccabees, perhaps from the third century BC.

4

The Vineyard Owner

The transformation of God

The vineyard owner in the parable of the tenants stands for Yahweh, and the tenants are the evil archons, the fallen angels. The idea of a multitude of gods/angels under a supreme father God is ancient. But as a new philosophical concept of God developed, it gave rise to a fundamental problem. How was it possible for an all-knowing God to make the mistake of appointing the tenant angels to rule the world? And why is the vineyard owner so ineffectual in dealing with their evil?

The myth of the Watchers was one solution—the angels were not appointed by Yahweh but had rebelled against him. Yahweh responds rapidly to their disobedience by imprisoning them and sending the flood to cleanse their evil. But this is not the form of the angel myth in the parable of the tenants.

The Jesus movement took a more radical approach of splitting Yahweh into two. The lower Yahweh ruled the world and appointed the angel-archons. But beyond this lower Yahweh, was an all-powerful, male-female, higher Yahweh who sent Christ to redeem the world. This higher Yahweh was so remote from humans that he could only communicate through intermediaries. One of those intermediaries was the lower Yahweh, and another the Christ. The lower Yahweh took on some of the attributes of the higher Yahweh, but his knowledge was incomplete. He believed that Christ was one of his sons. But Christ was really the one and only son of the higher Yahweh. At the apocalypse, the kingdom of Christ would supersede the rule of the lower Yahweh. The physical world and heaven that the lower Yahweh had created would dissolve and in their place would come a new heaven and a new earth.

The belief in a lower and higher Yahweh is no more than a logical extension of apocalyptic belief. This world must be destroyed because it is flawed and imperfect. But a perfect God would have created a perfect world. So the one who created the flawed world must be a lower imperfect God. The Christ will rule the new perfect earth and so must be perfect himself. From where did this Christ come? Not from the lower God, but from the higher ultimate God who is unseen but who lies behind the true nature of all things.

It might be thought that the belief in a lower and higher God is inconsistent with monotheism and could never have emerged in a Jewish context. In fact, the creation of two Yahwehs was first made by the Jewish priests as a result of the development of monotheism. The proto-Christians took it much further than the priests had intended. They equated the lower Yahweh with the God of the Jews, which meant that Christ was not just above Moses, but also above the one who gave Moses the commandments. This was why Christ was able to supersede the law of Moses. No wonder that the Jewish establishment regarded the early Jesus movement as heretics and set out to destroy them.

We can trace four stages in the evolution of the lower and higher Yahweh:

1. The creator God starts as an anthropomorphic father god. He has a wife and a large family of sons and daughters. He shows emotions, such as anger and lust. He feasts and gets disgracefully drunk.

2. The priests of Judah evolve a new concept of God; as unknowable and all-powerful. This God is not anthropomorphic—all images and idols are forbidden. This creates a dissonance with the God in stage 1 who is all too visible and human in the sacred literature. The priests solve the problem by separating the manifestations of God from the true form of the ultimate God. The visible manifestation of God to humans becomes an angel.

3. This angelic representation of God becomes viewed by some as a completely separate being. Ambiguity in scripture between the angel and Yahweh gave the notion that there were two Yahwehs— one higher and one lower. This is the stage of the proto-Christians; the lower Yahweh is the "good man" in the parable of the tenants. It is this lower God who has created the physical world. He has appointed the angels to rule, and it is from him that the Jewish law comes. In the original conception, this lower Yahweh was a legitimate extension of the higher Yahweh but limited in power and knowledge.

4. It is just a short step further to the Demiurge, the "half-maker", of gnostic myth. The lower Yahweh is no longer "good", but arrogant and ignorant. He is begotten from his mother Sophia, Wisdom, who descended from the higher God and became trapped in the material

world. The Demiurge thinks he is the one and only God and has created the archons to rule the world. Christ comes to redeem Sophia and the sparks of light, the human souls, that have come from her.

The angel of the Name

In scripture, we can track the evolution of the "angel of the Name" as a manifestation of Yahweh. When Yahweh appears directly to humans, this is often in the form of an "angel of Yahweh". This angel carries the divine name "Yahweh" which is represented in scripture as the tetragrammaton "YHWH". Because he carries the name of God, there is ambiguity between this angel and God. Originally the ambiguity did not matter because the angel was simply an aspect or manifestation of God. But it led eventually to the idea that there were two Gods.

> ➢ **The "angel of Yahweh" is used interchangeably with "Yahweh" in the accounts of God appearing to Moses, Hagar and Abraham.**

Moses' first experience of God was in the land of Midian at Mount Horeb, where he was shepherding his father-in-law's flock:

> *And the angel of Yahweh appeared to him in a flame of fire out of the midst of a bush. He looked, and behold, the bush was burning, yet it was not consumed. (Exodus 3:2)*

Moses turns aside to look at this burning bush and "Yahweh" calls to him from the fire:

> *He said, "I am the God of your father, the God of Abraham, the God of Isaac, and the God of Jacob." (Exodus 3:6)*

The apparition in the bush is called the "angel of Yahweh", then "Yahweh", then "Elohim" (God). When Moses pushes him for his name, he receives an enigmatic answer:

> *God said to Moses, "I Am who I Am." And he said, "Say this to the people of Israel: 'I Am has sent me to you.'" (Exodus 3:14)*

Another example concerns Hagar, the maidservant, who also sees God. She is the slave of Abraham's wife, Sarah, who is barren. Sarah solves this problem in the manner of the time, by sending Hagar into Abraham to have a child on her behalf. After becoming pregnant, Hagar slights Sarah who in return mistreats her until Hagar runs away. While fleeing in the wilderness, Hagar encounters God. She is told to return to her mistress, which she does and gives birth to Abraham's son Ishmael. By a miracle, the elderly Sarah becomes pregnant also and gives birth to Isaac. This toxic ménage-a-trois is resolved when Sarah pushes Abraham against his own better instinct to expel Hagar and her son into the wilderness. Without water or hope, Hagar abandons her child under a bush to die. But God appears to her again and directs her to a well.

The obvious purpose of the story is to explain why the Ishmaelites, like the Jews, are sons of Abraham. It casts them as children of the maid-servant/slave, whereas the Israelites are children of the wife. Given this Israelite viewpoint, the story is surprisingly positive about Hagar and Ismael. The two episodes of Hagar in the desert are two versions of the same story. In the first Hagar is visited by an "angel of Yahweh":

> *The angel of Yahweh found Hagar near a spring in the wilderness; it was the spring that is along the road to Shur. (Genesis 16:7)*

This "angel of Yahweh" is also called "Yahweh":

> *So Hagar gave this name to Yahweh who had spoken to her: "You are the God who sees me," for she said, "Here I have seen the One who sees me!" (Genesis 16:13)*

The episode is similar to Moses' encounter with the burning bush. In both cases, the apparition of God is called both "the angel of Yahweh" and "Yahweh". In both he is given another enigmatic name; "I am" and "the one who sees". The same ambiguity between God and the angel is also found in the second appearance to Hagar. This time the voice talking to Hagar is an "angel of God (Elohim)" and also "God (Elohim)".

The third example is Abraham's sacrifice of Isaac:

> *But the angel of Yahweh called to him from heaven and said, "Abraham, Abraham!" And he said, "Here I am." (Genesis 22:11)*

This "angel of Yahweh" tells Abraham to abort the sacrifice. The same "angel of Yahweh" (Genesis 22:15) calls out to Abraham a second time:

> *"By myself I have sworn, declares Yahweh, because you have done this and have not withheld your son, your only son, I will certainly bless you …" (Genesis 22:16-7)*

The angel is now called Yahweh. In all three examples the "angel of Yahweh" is used interchangeably with "Yahweh".

> **In Exodus, the Jews are led by an angel who carries the Name of Yahweh and who dwells in the tabernacle. This can be seen as an attempt to explain the tradition that the Name of Yahweh resides in the temple.**

In the previous examples, the angel is simply called an "angel of Yahweh". The idea that this angel carries the Name of Yahweh is found in Exodus. At one point, God comes to Moses to tell him his real name:

> *God said to Moses, "I am Yahweh. I appeared to Abraham, to Isaac, and to Jacob as El-Shaddai, but I did not reveal myself to them by my name, Yahweh. (Exodus 6:2-3)*

In the context of the Bible, this is very odd because Abraham, Isaac and Jacob already knew God by the name "Yahweh". The glaring inconsistency arises because Genesis and Exodus have been assembled from disparate and conflicting sources. The above passage must be very old because it does not take for granted the later identification between Yahweh and El. Yahweh was an imported God, associated here with Moses. The passage is revealing that Yahweh was the same God as El-Shaddai, a name for El. When the Israelites flee Egypt, Yahweh goes before them as a pillar of cloud and fire:

> *And Yahweh went before them by day in a pillar of cloud to lead them along the way, and by night in a pillar of fire to give them light, that they might go by day and by night. (Exodus 13:21)*

But then it appears that this Yahweh is really an angel:

> *Then the angel of God (El), who had gone before the camp of Israel, moved and went behind them. The pillar of cloud also moved from before them and stood behind them. (Exodus 14:19)*

Later Yahweh tells Moses explicitly that it is his angel who will lead them:

> *"Behold, I am sending an angel before you to guard you along the way and bring you to the place I have prepared. Pay attention to him and obey his voice; do not defy him, for he will not forgive rebellion, for my Name is in him." (Exodus 23:20-1)*

The angel is to be obeyed because be carries Yahweh's Name, and he will often be called Yahweh or El in what follows. We find the same personification of the "Name of Yahweh" in Isaiah:

> *Behold, the Name of Yahweh comes from afar, burning with his anger, and in thick rising smoke; his lips are full of fury, and his tongue is like a devouring fire. (Isaiah 30:27)*

In Exodus, when the tabernacle is completed, the angel descends into it:

> *Then the cloud covered the tent of meeting, and the glory of Yahweh filled the tabernacle. Moses could not enter the tent of meeting because the cloud had settled on it, and the glory of Yahweh filled the tabernacle. In all the journeys of the Israelites whenever the cloud lifted up from the tabernacle, they would set out. If the cloud was not lifted, they would not set out until the day it was taken up. (Exodus 40:34-37)*

The "glory of Yahweh" in the tabernacle must be the same as the angel in the cloud and fire. In the emerging narrative, the tabernacle would eventually be incorporated into the temple. The purpose of the narrative was to justify the Jerusalem temple as the unique dwelling place for Yahweh. The tradition that the Name of Yahweh dwelt in the temple would have predated the Exodus story. In 2 Samuel it is prophesied about Solomon:

> *He will build a house for my Name, and I will establish the throne of his kingdom forever. (2 Samuel 7:13)*

The house (temple) for Yahweh's Name is linked to the establishment of the house of David. After the glory of Yahweh has entered the new temple, Solomon gives a speech and reminds his audience of the words of Yahweh:

> *"'Since the day I brought my people Israel out of Egypt, I have not chosen a city from any tribe of Israel in which to build a house so that my Name would be there. But I have chosen David to be over my people Israel." (1 Kings 8:16)*

This is a transparent piece of Judean propaganda. The Jerusalem temple is the unique house for the Name of Yahweh, and the house of David alone has the right to rule all Israel. It renders invalid both the Israelite places of worship and the Israelite kings. Solomon continues:

Now it was in the heart of my father David to build a house for the Name of Yahweh, the God of Israel. But Yahweh said to my father David, 'Since it was in your heart to build a house for my Name, you have done well to have this in your heart. Nevertheless, you are not the one to build it; but your son, your own offspring, will build the house for my Name.'" (1 Kings 8:17-19)

According to this history, David conceived the temple, and his son Solomon built it. The idea that the temple was built for the Name of Yahweh would have meant no more originally than that it was dedicated to Yahweh. The Jerusalem priests, however, wanted to establish the temple as the unique dwelling place of God. So the Name became interpreted as a hypostasis of Yahweh, and the backstory of the tabernacle linked the temple to Moses. The priests are also struggling with a theological problem which is well expressed by Solomon:

But will God indeed dwell upon the earth? Even heaven, the highest heaven, cannot contain you, much less this temple I have built. [...] May your eyes be open toward this temple night and day, toward the place of which you said, 'My Name shall be there'.... (1 Kings 8:27;29)

Here we have the new conception of God who fills the whole universe. If so, then how can God be confined to a mere building of stone? The priests' solution was that the angelic Name of Yahweh dwelt in the temple. He functioned as an interface between Yahweh and humans. The priests could communicate with Yahweh by calling on the Name. This created a bridge between the primitive notion of a God who inhabits a house, a temple, and the new philosophical concept of a God who is everywhere and nowhere. But the idea acquired a momentum of its own in a direction which would have horrified its creators.

The gnostic Demiurge

We have traced the antecedents for the proto-Christian belief that there were two entities; Yahweh and the angel of Yahweh, also called the Name of Yahweh. We will now move forward several centuries to see how the idea developed after the initial phase of the Jesus movement. In the 60s AD, virtually all of its leaders of the Jesus movement were martyred. This brought in an age of chaos for the rapidly expanding church. The gospels were written in this era of chaos and quickly became immensely popular. The earlier traditions were preserved alongside the new gospel interpretations, and as Christians tried to make sense of the confusion, a vast diversity of belief emerged. Eventually, one strand, the proto-orthodox church won out. We can trace the origins of this proto-orthodox church back to the mid second-century with the early church father Irenaeus playing a key role.

The movements which flourished in the second and third centuries alongside the proto-orthodox church have become known under the broad label of the gnostics. Let us see how some gnostics regarded the God who created the physical world.

> **In the Gospel of Philip, the creator of the world is an imperfect angel and not the ultimate God.**

The second-century Gospel of Philip preserves many genuine early memories of the beliefs of the Jesus movement. So it is interesting that in this gospel the world is created by a lower "God" who is really an angel:

> *The world came into being through a mistake. For he who created it wanted to create it imperishable and immortal. He fell short of attaining his desire. For the world was never imperishable, nor, for that matter, was he who made the world. For things are not imperishable, but sons are. (The Gospel of Philip, NHC II (3) 75:3-11)*[1]

The world was created through a mistake, and the creator was "not imperishable" implying that he was not immortal. It may seem surprising that he is called a "thing" rather than a "son", but this tells us that he was regarded as an angel. The angels were created beings and hence "things" whereas the Christians were not created but were children of the ultimate God through Jesus ("sons" here should be read as including "daughters"). So we have the exact same belief as in the early Jesus movement: the creator of the world was a lower "God" who was really an angel, whereas Jesus is the "son" of the ultimate God.

> **The early Christian leader Marcion believed that there were two Gods; the God of the Jews and the God of Jesus.**

The proto-Orthodox church's most significant competitor was the movement founded by Marcion.[2] We only know about Marcion and his beliefs through the church fathers who opposed him, chiefly Tertullian who wrote a book "Against Marcion" which survives. Marcion was born about 100 AD at Sinope on the Black Sea coast and was said to be the son of a Christian "bishop", although such roles were not well defined at this time.

Marcion was probably from a wealthy family who were the patrons of a local house church. Certainly, when he came to Rome in 139 AD, he was very wealthy as an owner of ships. He offered to make a substantial donation to the church in Rome, but this was eventually rejected. The problem was that Marcion had a very different view of Christianity.

Marcion believed that there were two Gods; the God of the Hebrew Bible, the Old Testament, and the God of whom Jesus spoke. The first God was the creator of the world, the one we have called the lower Yahweh. The Jews were his chosen people, and he had given them the law. He was a just God, which made him also a harsh God. He had no mercy on law-breakers and had condemned his own people, the Jews, and all of humanity to death because they were unable to keep the law. Marcion pointed out the many passage in the Hebrew Bible where God acts violently. For example, when the Jews enter into Canaan under Joshua, Yahweh tells them to kill the local population, men, women and children. How can this genocidal God be the God of love and mercy that Jesus taught about?

According to Marcion, Jesus had come from a higher and previous unknown God. He was not a real flesh and blood man but only human in appearance—his true nature was spiritual and non-material. He made the supreme sacrifice and suffered crucifixion to redeem humanity from the rule of the lower Yahweh. In support of his beliefs, Marcion produced the first Christian bible. He included all of Paul's letters except for 1 and 2 Timothy and Titus, which modern scholarship considers to be later forgeries. To these, he added just one gospel, a modified version of the Gospel of Luke. Marcion's bible was the very first Christian canon, an idea that was later taken up by the proto-orthodox church giving rise to the New Testament.

The views of Marcion are very close to the picture we have uncovered of the early Jesus movement. He also believed in a lower and higher God. His lower God had also created the world, brought the law and was the God of the Jews. Marcion also had the correct belief that Jesus was not a physical man but had come in a spiritual form. He must have taken all these beliefs from traditions and texts in circulation in his home region of Pontius. But the knowledge that Marcion possessed of the early movement was limited and he was very much a speculative child of his times. His theories went in an extreme anti-Jewish direction, and he ended up rejecting the Hebrew Bible altogether, a point of view that would have been quite alien to the early Jesus movement. By the mid-second century, the gospels were widely known and accepted, so that Marcion's view of Jesus is heavily influenced by the gospel story. The result is that his non-material Jesus resembles a science-fiction hologram more than a spiritual entity. Marcion's choice of the Gospel of Luke as the original gospel is also clearly wrong because that gospel was written after both Mark and Matthew. Most likely Marcion fixed on Luke simply because it was the most gentile and least Jewish of the gospels. But he had to modify even Luke to make it consistent with his own beliefs.

After being rejected by the Roman Christians, Marcion returned to Asia Minor where he was hugely successful in establishing his church. In many places, the Marcionites became the dominant form of Christianity. How can we account for this success? Although Christian teachers were supposed to be poor, in practice money was a great advantage. Still, the extent of Marcion's influence cannot be explained purely by his wealth. The enthusiastic reception to Marcion in Asia Minor is evidence that he was preaching to the converted, and that the Christianity of two Gods was already well established in this area.

> **In many gnostic systems the lower Yahweh has become the ignorant and malevolent Demiurge**

Both Marcion and the author of the Gospel of Philip can be described as almost-gnostics. The more developed forms of gnosticism came later, peaking in the third century, and involved highly elaborate schemes to explain the origins of the cosmos and the power structure in the heavens. In these accounts, the divinities are often androgynous, having both a male and a female component. In the typical version of the myth, the female aspect of the ultimate deity, who is called Pistis or Sophia (meaning Wisdom), becomes separated from the male aspect. In the shock of separation, she creates a chaos from which material reality will come and inadvertently gives birth to a son who will rule over the chaos. This son is the Demiurge or half-maker. In some texts, he is given the name Yaldabaoth, which means "begetter of Sabaoth", with Sabaoth (or Abaoth) meaning "the powers".[3] So the very name of Yaldabaoth indicates that he is the one who created the heavenly powers, the archons.

Yaldabaoth cannot see his mother directly, but only the reflection of her light in a dark pool. So he thinks he is alone. He separates out the chaos, the light from the dark, the waters from the land, creating our physical world. He fashions humans out of the dust, but sparks of light from Sophia, human souls, become trapped within them. Yaldabaoth produces the leading powers who will come under him, each of which is androgynous. The number of these first archons is usually seven (or six plus Yaldabaoth) so that each will rule one of the seventh heavens of classical belief. Many more archons will follow.

Believing himself to be alone, the Demiurge arrogantly says *"It is I who am God, and there is no one who exists apart from me"* (*On the Origins of the*

World, NHC II (5) 103:12-13). Shocked by this blasphemy, Pistis Sophia calls down to him *"You are mistaken Samuel"*—the name means "blind God". For the first time, the Demiurge realises he is not alone. Christ, the man of light, will descend from the ultimate God to rescue Sophia and redeem the specks of light trapped within humanity.

The gnostic myths were generated by the collision of Jewish and early Christian beliefs and Hellenistic speculative reasoning. Our interest in the subject is to find evidence for the original proto-Christian beliefs within the complexity of gnostic doctrine as revealed by the Nag Hammadi texts. gnostic belief is undoubtedly confusing, and there were some completely non-Christian forms such as the Sethian. The predominant influence though is the proto-Christian concept of the two Yahwehs. To the gnostics, the lower God was the Demiurge, but this led to the problem of how the higher God could have created such an evil lower God. So a further level had to be inserted whereby the female component of the higher God became separated from the male component and created the lower God by mistake. This solution preserves the goodness and power of the ultimate father God.

The androgynous nature of the divine beings in these myths reflects a crucial aspect of the original spirituality of the Jesus movement as established by Mary. In Mary's Christianity, all humans are androgynous, with both a male and female component. One of these components was born into the world, becoming a man or woman. The other component remained in heaven; first as the soul and then, if redeemed, as the spirit. The contra-sexual nature of this spiritual component is implicit in the Gospel of Thomas and is clear from the Gospel of Philip and Valentinian gnosticism. We can trace the origins of the idea back to the Greeks and also, more significantly to Genesis, where Adam is first created hermaphrodite, both male and female.

> **Within the gnostic texts, we can find traces of the seventy-two archons and the "good" lower Yahweh.**

Although Yaldabaoth is portrayed as evil, there are some fascinating remnants of the original proto-Christian beliefs of a benevolent lower Yahweh preserved within the gnostic texts. To distinguish this lower Yahweh from the Demiurge, he becomes one of the primary archons. In the First Apocalypse of James, Jesus says that one of these archons, Adonaios, thought that Jesus was his own son and was gracious to him.[4] This is a memory of the lower Yahweh who believed Christ to be his son. This Apocalypse is less developed than the later gnostic texts and preserves some correct memories of the original beliefs of the Jesus movement. It gives the number of the archons correctly as seventy-two (the alternative to seventy); they rule seventy-two heavens and come from he who "has no measure".[5]

More commonly the lower-Yahweh figure is called Sabaoth, from which the name Yaldabaoth (father of Sabaoth) came. Sabaoth originally signified "the powers", meaning the archons, but this concept has become personalised as the "Lord of the Forces", a being who ruled over the archons. In The Origin of the World when Sabaoth hears the voice of Pistis Sophia calling out to Yaldabaoth, he sings praises to her and condemns his father. Pistis Sophia responds by giving Sabaoth some of her light and, after a war in heaven, installs him in the seventh heaven. She sends him her daughter, Zoe, meaning "life", to instruct him. He builds himself a mansion and has a throne which closely resembles the throne of Yahweh in Ezekiel. Like Yahweh in the scriptures, he is surrounded by serpent-like "Seraphim" who praise him continuously. Sabaoth stands for the Jewish Yahweh in a favourable aspect. So it is particularly interesting that from Sabaoth's throne come seventy-two gods:

> *"Furthermore, from this chariot the seventy-two gods took shape; they took shape that they might rule over the seventy-two languages of the peoples." (On the Origin of the World, NHC II (5) 105:13-16)*

This is the same concept as the seventy/seventy-two shepherd angels appointed by Yahweh. The firstborn of Sabaoth is Israel, and he has also fathered a being called Jesus Christ who sits on his right hand, with the virgin of the spirit on the left.[6]

Another work found at Nag Hammadi, The Tripartite Tractate, has a much more positive take on the creation and the Demiurge than other gnostic texts. The ultimate father has existed for all time, along with the son. The Aeons have emanated from him spontaneously, and one of them, the male Logos (taking the place of Pistis Sophia) has created the cosmos. The Logos is good and his creation was intended to praise the father, but it turns out inadequate. At one point in the text, the Logos appoints a chief Archon to rule over all the archons in his cosmos and administer justice. This Archon is called "father", "god" and "demiurge" and represents the God of the Old Testament. Unlike the other gnostic conceptions of the Demiurge, he is not evil at all. In fact, the Logos uses him as a "hand" to intervene beneficially in the world and as a "mouth" to communicate prophecies. With this alternative view of the Demiurge, we have come full circle to something like the angel of the Name.[7]

Evidence from Early Christian Sources

A law given by angels

The original beliefs of the Jesus movement were the inheritance of all the diverse Christianities that developed in the first few centuries. We have seen the evidence supporting our interpretation of the parable of the tenants in Marcion and the gnostic texts. We will now look at some of the earliest evidence from a time before the gospel view predominated. This will include both works that made it into the New Testament, and a text that was rejected from the final canon but which was immensely popular among mainstream Christians in the second and third centuries. Finally, we will consider a tantalising fragment from the writings of the earliest church father, Papias.

> ➤ **The letter to the Hebrews is concerned with proving that Jesus is superior to the angels who have brought the law and rule the current world.**

The letter to the Hebrews is an odd work. It is written in elegant Greek and quotes the Hebrew Bible extensively. But it never tells us a single circumstance or story from Jesus' supposed life on earth, never quotes the gospels, and does not give a single saying or teaching from Jesus.[1] We might describe Hebrews as a half-forgery. The author clearly intends the letter to be taken as coming from Paul—the blatant clue is the reference to Paul's companion Timothy—but the author does not explicitly use Paul's name.[2] The letter is supposedly written from "Italy" which is suspiciously vague. Hebrews was written by a Jewish Christian who offers a mild rebuke of its supposed Jewish audience by copying Paul's analogy of feeding on milk rather than solid food.[3] The letter must date after Paul's letters had gained wide circulation but before the gospels had become established as scripture. This gives a range from the late first century to the mid-second century.

Hebrews will seem strange to anyone whose idea of Jesus comes from the gospels. It starts with extensive quotes from the Hebrew Bible to prove that Jesus was superior to the angels. It goes on to consider Jesus as a high priest of the order of Melchizedek who offers his own blood as a sacrifice. These apparently weird obsessions reflect a confused memory of the earliest Christianity. According to our interpretation of the tenants parable, the world is under the control of the seventy evil angels. The two systems of law arose from the angel of the Name through the two man-angels, Noah and Moses. Jesus comes from the ultimate Yahweh to replace the law and defeat the seventy. So establishing that Jesus was superior to the angels was important.

We find the idea that the law came from angels in Hebrews:

> *For if the message spoken by angels was binding, and every violation and disobedience received its just punishment, how shall we escape if we neglect such a great salvation? (Hebrews 2:2-3)*

The "message spoken by angels" is the law, and humans are condemned by this law except through the salvation that Jesus brings. It continues:

> *For it is not to angels that he has subjected the world to come, about which we speak. (Hebrews 2:5)*

The world to come will be ruled by Jesus and not subject to the angels. The implication is that the current, imperfect world is subject to angelic rule.

➤ **The idea that the law came through angels is also found in Acts.**

In a Jewish context the idea that the law came from "angels" is very odd. But we find the same concept in Acts, in Stephen's speech to his Jewish persecutors:

> *"And now you have betrayed and murdered him—you who have received the law that was given through angels but have not obeyed it." (Acts 7:52-3)*

Earlier, Stephen talks about the unusual beauty of Moses at birth which we have seen is an indication of Moses' angelic nature.[4] He also says that the apparition that Moses saw in the burning bush was an angel and that it was an angel that Moses met on Mount Sinai.[5] But the ultimate source for the idea that the law had come through angels is probably Galatians.

Paul and the angels

> ➢ Paul says that the law came through angels in the hands of a
> mediator. The best fit for the mediator is the angel of the Name
> rather than Moses.

In Galatians, Paul talks about the law in terms which have fascinated
and bemused commentators. The Jerusalem leadership under James had
pressed Paul's gentile converts in Galatia to accept conversion to Judaism,
including circumcision. Paul writes to these Galatians in desperation and
anger to persuade them not to agree to this. He sets out the reasons why
the Galatians should not accept circumcision starting from the perspective that the covenant was given through Abraham long before the law.
According to Paul, the covenant was granted to the "seed" of Abraham,
meaning Jesus; and through Jesus, the Galatians are the sons of Abraham.
Paul then addresses the question of the law:

> *Why then the law? It was added because of transgressions, until the*
> *offspring should come to whom the promise had been made, and it was*
> *ordained through angels in the hand of a mediator. However, a mediator*
> *is not of one, but God is one. (Galatians 3:19-20)*

Paul says that the law has been ordained through "angels" in the plural,
which is inexplicable in the mainstream Jewish view. We have seen that
the law originated with the angel of the Name and was given through
the man-angels Noah and Moses. Who is the "mediator" (*mesites*)? The
word means one who comes between two parties to agree a covenant
or contract. The conventional view is that the mediator is Moses, but
another possibility is that it is the lower Yahweh, the angel of the Name.
The traditional role of a mediator was to establish a covenant or contract
between two parties and then administer that covenant to see that both
parties carry out their obligations. The angel of the Name is the mediator
in this respect between the ultimate God and humanity. Paul says that
faith came from Jesus and replaced the law:

> *Before this faith came, we were held in captivity under the law, locked*
> *up until faith should be revealed. So the law became our tutor to lead us*
> *to Christ, that we might be justified by faith. Now that faith has come,*
> *we are no longer under a tutor. (Galatians 3:23-4)*

The law is described as a "tutor" using the word *paidagogos* which meant a family slave charged with the oversight and training of boys.

> *You are all sons (children) of God through faith in Christ Jesus. All of you who were baptised into Christ, you have been clothed in Christ. There is neither Jew nor Greek, neither slave nor free, neither male and female, for you are all one in Christ Jesus. (Galatians 3:26-28)*

The Galatians are sons and daughters of God "through faith in Jesus Christ"—the Greek does not mean that the Galatians have faith in Jesus, but that faith exists within Jesus. The Galatians have been baptised into Christ and have put him on like a garment. Through the faithfulness of Christ, they are one with God and need no mediator.

> ➤ **The Galatians have been subject to the "elements of the kosmos" who are the rulers of the world. These elements can only be the seventy angels.**

Paul continues with the idea that humanity has been placed under "guardians":

> *What I am saying is that as long as the heir is a child, he does not differ from a slave, although he is the owner of everything. He is subject to guardians and stewards until the date appointed by his father. (Galatians 4:1-2)*

Paul has changed the analogy so that the child is now like a slave under "guardians" and "stewards". These should not be confused with the "tutor" which stood for the law. The two words Paul uses here both mean a manager who administers substantial property, such as an estate, on behalf of its owner and not someone educating a child. The words would fit the vineyard tenants perfectly. Paul continues:

> *So also, when we were children, we were in slavery under the elements [stoicheia] of the world [kosmos]. But when the time had fully come, God sent his son, come [genomenon] of a woman, come [genomenon] under the law, to redeem those under the law, that we might receive our adoption as sons. (Galatians 4:3-5)*

In most translations of this passage, the word *ginomai* is translated as "born". This statement of Paul, along with the equivalent at Romans 1:3, is often used to prove that Jesus must have been a real man because he was "born of a woman". But Paul says no such thing. His words actually mean that Jesus "came" or "appeared" through a woman—this woman being the shaman Mary. The word *ginomai* is very common in the New Testament, occurring 671 times, yet it is scarcely ever translated as "born" except in these two places.[6] The word Paul should have used if he meant to be physically born is *gennao* which appears 97 times in the New Testament, and which always means literal birth.

Paul says that before the Christians received their inherence as children of God through Jesus, they were slaves under the "elements of the kosmos (world)". The word *stoicheion*, "elements", means first things/principles/causes; it is used both for the heavenly bodies and for more abstract philosophical principles. Translators and commentators have had great problems trying to understand what Paul meant by the "elements of the kosmos"; it has been translated variously as "elemental spiritual forces" (NIV), as "elementary principles of the world" (ESV) and left simply as "elements of the world" (KJV). The "elements" also appear in 2 Peter where they are something that will be destroyed with fire at the end of time:

> *The heavens will disappear with a roar, the elements with burning heat will be destroyed, and the earth and its works will be uncovered. (2 Peter 3:10)*

> *... hasten the coming of the day of God, when the heavens will be destroyed by fire and the elements will burn up and melt. (2 Peter 3:12)*

The "elements" here are clearly not abstract principles. They are certainly not chemical elements which are a modern concept. So they must stand for the heavenly bodies. To the ancients, there was no distinction between stars and planets in the sky, and the gods or angels who inhabited heaven. In Isaiah 34:4, it is the "host of heaven", the stars, that will be dissolved and will fall to earth when the heavens are rolled up like a scroll. In the Animal Apocalypse, the fallen angels descend to earth as falling stars. At the end times, these angels will share the same fate as the elements in 2 Peter, burning up in the abyss. So the "elements of the kosmos" must be the "host of heaven", the seventy angels who were believed to rule the world. What Paul says next supports this interpretation:

> *Formerly, when you did not know God, you were slaves to those who by nature are not gods. But now that you know God, or rather are known by God, how is it that you are turning back to those weak and destitute elements? Do you want to be enslaved by them again? (Galatians 4:8-9)*

For once, Paul is clear. The elements are the same as "those who by nature are not gods" to whom the Galatians were previously enslaved. So the elements are the "gods" that the Galatians worshipped as pagans. It is quite certain that the elements cannot stand for the Jewish law because the Galatians were never Jews. Paul, however, says that if the Galatians accept the Jewish law, then they will be returning to their previous gods, a statement which is incomprehensible under mainstream Judaism. But it makes perfect sense if the world is ruled by angels appointed by another angel, the lower Yahweh, who has given the law. In this model, one can only escape from the system of angelic rule through Christ.

> **Paul believed in a higher and lower God.**

We can find confirmation that Paul believed in a lower Yahweh who would be replaced by Christ in another statement that has caused great difficulties to traditional commentators:

> *The God of this age has blinded the minds of unbelievers so as not to shine into them the light of the gospel of the glory of Christ, who is the image of God. (2 Corinthians 4:4)*

Who is the "God of this age" who prevents many from seeing Jesus? Often he is interpreted as Satan; but why should Paul call Satan "God"? In fact, it is Yahweh who gives the instruction to blind the people in Isaiah:

> *"Make the heart of this people dull, and deafen their ears, and shut their eyes; lest they see with their eyes, and hear with their ears, and under-stand with their hearts, and turn and be healed." (Isaiah 6:10)*

So Paul's "God of this age" must be the Yahweh of the Isaiah throne room vision! The heavenly throne room overlaps with the earthly temple, so this "God of this age" dwelt in the first temple. All of this is evidence that Paul believed in two Yahwehs and that the lower Yahweh who gave the law, the God of this age, will be replaced by Christ.

It is no wonder that Marcion revered Paul. Marcion's conception of the wrathful God of Hebrew scriptures and the merciful, loving God from whom Jesus came reflects something genuine in Paul's writings. And it is no wonder that the proto-orthodox Christians found it necessary to forge letters from Paul in an attempt to obscure these troublesome beliefs.

The Shepherd of Hermas

The Shepherd of Hermas is the text outside the New Testament that came closest to inclusion in the canon. To the church father Irenaeus, the Shepherd was "scripture". The number of surviving copies and fragments show that it was certainly very popular with early Christians. It was included in some early copies of the New Testament, but it failed to make the final cut, and today it is almost forgotten except among specialists. The most likely date for the Shepherd of Hermas is c. 100 AD or perhaps a little later.[7] The author of Hermas was proto-orthodox by nature, but because he is writing very early, he reflects traditions that later became viewed as heretical. In *The Rock and the Tower* I show how it recalls early traditions about the "tower"—in particular, that the "rock" and the "tower" were one and the same.[8]

➤ **In Hermas, Shepherds are angels.**

The book reflects the tradition that shepherds were angels, most obviously in the Shepherd of the title who is guardian angel to Hermas. The angel is introduced abruptly midway through the work. While Hermas is praying on his couch he sees a vision: *"an eminent looking man came to me, dressed in shepherd's clothing—wrapped with a white goat skin around his waist, with a bag on his shoulder and a staff in his hand" (Hermas 25:1).*[9] The Shepherd is the "angel of repentance" and will stay with Hermas the rest of his days. But not all shepherd angels in Hermas are good.

➤ **The Shepherd of Hermas also has a vineyard parable.**

There is a parable of the vineyard in Hermas that follows a section linked to the Gospel of Thomas. Hermas is sitting on a mountain and *"keeping a station"* by fasting.[10] The Shepherd rebukes him, telling Hermas that *"when you fast like this to God you do nothing at all righteous" (Hermas 54:4).* This is an allusion to the Gospel of Thomas: *"if you fast you will beget a sin for yourself" (Thomas 14; TC 1.13).* The Shepherd then tells Hermas a parable *"relating to fasting" (Hermas 55:1)* which is the parable of a vineyard.

A man who owns an estate is going on a long journey. He leaves the vineyard in charge of a trusted servant (a slave) and instructs him to fence it round. If the servant does this, he shall be freed. The servant fences the vineyard and then observing it full of weeds, decides to dig it as well. When the master returns, he is delighted to see that the vineyard has not only been fenced but is also weed-free and flourishing. He summons his heir, "his beloved son", and tells him how well the servant has done. As the servant's reward, the master decides not just to free the servant but to make him joint-heir. The son, surprisingly, agrees with this strange decision. There follows a feast. The servant is sent dainties from the feast, but takes only a few, sending the rest to his fellow servants.

The parable is supposed to relate to fasting, but it never mentions fasting. The author is drawing the lesson that it is good to exceed God's instructions. Although fasting is not a command of God, a person who fulfils these commands and then exceeds them will be rewarded. So fasting is presented as an extra-curricular activity, something beyond the call of duty for which the disciple will receive extra points providing he has first satisfied the necessary requirements. This is typical of the type of naive explanations which the author of Hermas develops for things he does not understand, in this case the difficult Gospel of Thomas saying.

The angel then explains the meaning of the parable to Hermas. The estate is the world, the owner of the estate is he who made all things, the son and heir is the holy spirit, the servant/slave is the Son of God, the vines are the people. The fence posts are the angels of the Lord who keep together his people, and the weeds are the transgressions of the servants. The dainties at the feast are the commandments.

Hermas is understandably puzzled by this explanation. He asks the obvious question of how the Son of God can be represented as a servant or slave. The angel's explanation then becomes even more convoluted. He contradicts himself and now says that the Son of God is not the slave. It was the Son who did all the things that the servant did. The servant represents the flesh and the Son is the spirit. If the flesh is a faithful and hard-working slave it will share in the inheritance with the spirit. The modern reader of Hermas will be utterly confused by this point. But the angel's explanation answered a burning question among the Christians of the early centuries—would the flesh be resurrected along with the spirit? The conventional author of Hermas gives a positive answer provided the flesh is hard working and obedient. But neither this question nor the point about fasting has anything to do with the original parable.

> **The author of Hermas has misunderstood the vineyard parable.**
> **The servant is not actually the Son of God, but the lower Yahweh.**

The explanation of the parable in Hermas is blatantly wrong. It is the servant who puts up the fence, meaning that he appoints the angels over humanity—so he cannot possibly represent "the flesh". And surely the Son of God, Jesus, must be the heir to the vineyard as he is in the parable of the tenants—not the servant. There are three main actors in the parable, and we can equate them to the three aspects of God:

The estate owner = the higher Yahweh.

The son and heir = Christ

The servant/slave = the lower Yahweh, the angel of the Name.

Looking through the confusion, we can see that the servant's role corresponds to the actions taken by the lower Yahweh:

- The fence would have stood for the law which is established and administered by angels.
- The servant established the law and placed angels over the people.
- The servant digs the vineyard, meaning he punishes the people for their transgressions of the law.
- The servant is "Lord of the people" having received power from the father.
- The servant receives the dainties from the feast which represent the commandments and sends them to his other servants (representing the man-angels Noah and Moses)

The rule of the servant is only temporary, and he will be replaced by the son who brings a new law. However, the servant will be redeemed. He is not the evil Demiurge of gnostic myth, but part of the Godhead.

> **In the continuation from the vineyard parable, shepherd angels oppress humanity.**

In Hermas, the parable of the vineyard is followed by a parable in which shepherds are evil angels. The angel takes Hermas out into the country where they see a shepherd clothed in a saffron cloak. His sheep are well fed and gadding around, and the shepherd is glad over them. The angel tells Hermas that the shepherd is *"the angel of luxury and deceit. He, then, is the one who wears down the souls of the vacuous slaves of God and turns them away from the truth, deceiving them with evil desires that destroy them"* (Hermas 62:1).[11] They continue, and Hermas is shown another shepherd of fearsome aspect who is placing the sheep among briars and thorns and who beats and whips them. This is the angel of punishment. The two shepherd angels are fulfilling the twin roles of the shepherds. They first tempt man and then, when he transgresses, they punish him. The author puts a proto-orthodox interpretation on all this, but it is drawing from the metaphorical language of the shepherd angels. Here we have evil angelic rulers who apply the law represented as shepherds. The location of the shepherds parable next to the vineyard parable in Hermas is a reflection of the links between the tenant vineyard parable and the shepherds as angelic rulers of humanity.

Papias

➢ **The very early church father Papias says that God appointed
angels to rule the world.**

And so we come to the final intriguing piece of evidence. The church
father, Papias, is believed to have lived early in the second century. All
we possess today of his writings are scraps from much later authors such
as Eusebius. His description of the origins of the gospels of Mark and
Matthew have been used extensively by traditional commentators. (See,
for example, Bauckman's "Jesus and the Eyewitnesses", a book beloved
among the conventionally inclined. The bare essentials of this work are an
analysis of a few lines from Papias, although these essentials are dressed
in the fashionable clothes of memory studies.) Such commentators may
be less keen on another surviving fragment from Papias preserved in a
commentary by Andrew of Caesarea on Revelation:

> And Papias says thus word for word: "Some of them, that is, the divine
> angels of old, he gave (authority) to rule over the earth and commanded
> (them) to rule well." And then says the following: "And it happened
> that their arrangement came to nothing." (Andrew of Caesarea; On the
> Apocalypse 34:12)[12]

Here is a clear and unambiguous statement that Yahweh appointed
angels to rule the world, and that this arrangement was a failure. This ties
in very well with the Animal Apocalypse, where the Lord of the sheep
appoints the shepherd angels to rule. It ties in also with our analysis of
the parable of the tenants. But it does not tie in with church belief. In
Christian theology it is God who rules the world and who has given the
law. There is no room for this God to have appointed angels over humanity, for this would imply that God was fallible. In fact, it would mean there
were two Gods.

PART TWO

ISRAEL AND JUDAH

6

The Origins of Israel and Judah

In this section, we will explore the historical and archaeological evidence for Israel and Judah as they existed before the destruction of the temple by Babylon in 586 BC. The religious beliefs of this era form the substratum for the Christ myth, which has its roots in the Judas War. We will find also the origins of the seventy shepherds and show how they originated as seventy gods. To understand the iron age society of the Israelites before the exile, we must go beyond the surface picture presented in the Bible. Archaeology has enabled this biblical account to be tested against the facts on the ground. So how does it fair?

The biblical story

According to the Bible, the Israelites entered into Canaan, the Promised Land, from Egypt. The twelve tribes were descended from the twelve sons of Jacob (renamed Israel), the son of Isaac and grandson of Abraham. One of the twelve brothers, Joseph, was sold into slavery in Egypt by his brothers. But Joseph rose to be chief-minister under Pharaoh. He forgave his brothers, who all joined him in Egypt to escape a famine. The Jews thrived, and after several generations their population had increased to such an extent that they were no longer welcomed by the Egyptians. They now had the status of slaves, and to reduce their numbers the new Pharaoh decreed that Jewish newborn babies should be killed. One survivor was Moses. He was abandoned in a basket on the Nile by his family, but was found and adopted by Pharaoh's daughter. As an adult, Moses killed an Egyptian who was beating a Jew and fled to Midian, where he acquired a wife and encountered Yahweh in the burning bush. Moses returned and led the Jews to escape Egypt, parting the waters of the Red Sea to allow their passage over the dry sea bed, before closing the waters behind them on the pursuing Egyptian soldiers. He led the Israelites into the desert and had another encounter with God on Mount Sinai where he received the tablets of the law. Moses was ordered by God to build the tabernacle to house the ark of the covenant in which the tablets were kept.

The Israelites wandered in the wilderness for forty years until coming within sight of the Promised Land, where Moses died. He was succeeded by Joshua who miraculously parted the waters of the Jordon and led the Jews into Canaan. Joshua conquered the Canaanite cites one by one, putting all the inhabitants, men women and children, to the sword on the orders of Yahweh.

Having taken possession of the Promised Land of Canaan, the Israelites lived in a relatively egalitarian society without a king. In the Bible, this is the period of Judges and Ruth. This era ended with the rise of Saul, who was of the tribe of Benjamin. Saul became king over the twelve tribes and achieved military success, but he was a flawed character. He had a tempestuous relationship with his most talented warrior, David, who was eventually forced to flee his service. Saul died in battle against the Philistines, and David assumed the kingship. David was of the tribe of Judah and established his capital at the newly-conquered city of Jerusalem. He brought the ark and the tabernacle into the Holy City and planned a temple to house them. But the honour of building the temple fell to his son, King Solomon. It was under Solomon that the united monarchy of the house of David achieved its greatest glory: his wisdom and wealth were legendary, summed up but the visit of the Queen of Sheba who had travelled from afar to question him. After the reign of Solomon, Israel entered a decline. The kingdom split in two, with the ten tribes of Israel rebelling and establishing a breakaway northern kingdom, whereas Judah (and Benjamin) continued as the southern kingdom with its capital at Jerusalem. Unfortunately, Israel fell into evil Canaanite ways and was eventually destroyed by the Assyrians.

This biblical account was accepted unquestioningly for millennia until the development of modern archaeology. So how much of it is true? Not much.

A Canaanite people

> The Israelites first appear in the hill country of Canaan in tiny scattered settlements.

The first physical evidence for the Israelites comes from the hill country lying to the north of Jerusalem and running right up into Galilee. Most of this area would later be the territory of the two chief tribes of Israel, Ephraim and Manasseh. Extensive archaeological surveys have shown that between the years 1200 BC and 1000 BC there was a rapid growth of small isolated settlements in this previously sparsely occupied location.[1]

The dramatic increase in population implies that people were moving into the area. This was marginal land that had not previously been farmed, and it took considerable skill to make the land habitable. The settlers terraced the slopes, to allow ploughing and improve water retention. They hewed grain silos out of rock to preserve excess production in good years. And they made water cisterns to capture the high rainfall in the winter months to irrigate crops through the arid summer.[2]

There is no dislocation in material culture (such as pottery) between these hill dwelling Israelites and the Canaanites as we would expect if the Israelites had really originated from outside Canaan.[3] So from where did these hill-dwellers come? The earlier idea that they were nomads from the Sinai desert can be discounted. We are left with two main theories associated with two prominent archaeologists; William Dever and Israel Finkelstein. Dever's theory is that lowland peasant farmers moved into the hills to escape from the collapse of the Canaanite city-states. He points to the technological sophistication of the new settlements and believes that the settlers must have been experienced arable farmers. In contrast, Finkelstein favours a model with the population oscillating over the centuries between a fixed and nomadic existence. Even in largely nomadic pastoral tribes, a percentage will farm in fixed settlements. The population growth in the hills could be explained if herders who spent most of their time in the wilderness to the east, settled down over a few generations to be arable farmers. Despite their differences, both Dever and Finkelstein agree that the first Israelites were Canaanites.[4]

> **The Israelites spoke a Canaanite language and there is no evidence that they invaded Canaan from outside. They were Canaanites.**

A strong clue that the Israelites are a Canaanite people comes from their language; Hebrew is a Canaanite dialect. The earliest Hebrew inscriptions are even written in the old Canaanite script. Language is a powerful marker of ethnic identity and this alone rules out the hypothesis that the Israelites originated from somewhere outside Canaan, such as Sinai.[5]

Accepting that the Israelites were Canaanites, could there still be an element of truth in the story of the exodus? Is it possible the Israelites migrated to Egypt from Canaan, before returning in force to establish their territory? Something like this actually happened with the Hyksos people who ruled all of Egypt in the period 1640-1500 BC. The Hyksos were Canaanite invaders who built their thriving city of Avaris in the Nile delta. They were eventually expelled by the pharaohs of the Egyptian 18th dynasty and driven back to Canaan. The Egyptian pharaohs followed up this victory with a vicious campaign of destruction in Canaan, which left the Canaanite cities and society in ruins.

There is much about the story of the Hyksos which is reminiscent of the exodus. In the biblical narrative, Joseph, like the Hyksos kings, came from outside Egypt but ruled over the whole country. The Israelites, like the Hyksos, grew in numbers and thrived until the Egyptians turned against them. Both Israelites and Hyksos left Egypt for Canaan pursued by the Egyptians. In both cases, this was followed by a brutal war in which the Canaanite cities were destroyed one by one. If you adjusted the Hyksos story so that the Hyksos/Israelites were always the victors rather than the vanquished, you would get something remarkably similar to the biblical story. There is only one problem; the Hyksos lived centuries before the first Israelites.

According to the Bible, it was the Israelites under Joshua who destroyed the Canaanite cities. But we have seen that the Israelites first appear in tiny settlements in the hill country which had not previously been inhabited or farmed. Successful invaders take the best land—they do not squat on low-quality marginal land which no one else wants.

Another problem is that if the exodus happened, it must have taken place between 1250 BC and 1150 BC when Canaan was still under the control of the Egyptians. It beggars belief to imagine the Israelites escaping from Egypt and then conquering Canaanite cities under the noses of the occupying Egyptian garrison. Egypt was a superpower and vastly more powerful than any potential Israelite force.

Biblical archaeologists "with a Bible in one hand and a shovel in the other" have been searching a long time for evidence of the Joshua invasion. In the early days, it looked like they had been successful; several Canaanite cites were reported to have been destroyed at just the right time. But with improved dating techniques, the case for the Israelite invasion fell apart. The events which destroyed the Canaanite cites were spread out over centuries and had nothing to do with the Israelites. Some cities prominent in the Joshua account, such as Jericho and Gibeon, were not even occupied at the time of the supposed invasion. The conclusion of the modern archaeologists is devastating. As Dever puts it: *"We must confront the fact that the external evidence supports almost nothing of the biblical account of a large-scale invasion of Canaan... Of the more than forty sites that the biblical texts claim were conquered, no more than two or three of those that have been archaeologically investigated are even potential candidates for such a destruction in the entire period from c. 1250-1150 BC".*[6]

The convergence of several lines of evidence is impressive: the biblical accounts of the exodus and conquest of Canaan do not reflect historical reality. The Book of Joshua is now regarded as having been written several hundred years after the events it supposedly depicts. It reflects the facts on the ground in the pre-exilic period, and not in the era of the exodus. The biblical writers did not know what had really happened because it was all in the distant past. They are selecting and repackaging myths to suit the requirements of their own time.

Canaanite folk memories of the Hyksos period and its aftermath likely formed one source for the exodus account—the coincidences are too strong to ignore. Such folk memories would have been part of the Israelites' heritage. Once the Judean authors began to develop the myth of a unique origin of the Israelites to separate themselves from their Canaanite neighbours, they adjusted the Hyksos legends. The Israelites were the Hyksos while they thrived and ruled over all Egypt. And the defeat and devastation of Canaan were interpreted as the defeat of the local Canaanites at the hands of the returning Hyksos/Israelites rather than the Egyptians.

> **The Ugarit tablets show the close links between Canaanite religion and the Hebrew Bible.**

In the Bible the Canaanites are uniformly excoriated. They worship idols and false Gods and corrupt the Israelites. God has decreed that Canaan belongs to the Israelites, and even genocide against the Canaanites is acceptable. Such is the negative attitude towards anything Canaanite that it was difficult to form any objective view of this people. That all changed with the remarkable discovery in the 1920s and 30s of a large number of clay tablets from the coastal Canaanite city of Ugarit. For the first time we were able to read about the Canaanites and their religion in their own words.

The major surprise was how similar the Canaanites were to the Israelites. The name of the Canaanite chief God, El, was one of the two names (along with Yahweh) of God used by the Jews. There were very close links between the religion of the Canaanites and the Bible, to the extent that some Bible passages are now regarded as being originally Canaanite texts. Passages which had previously been obscure, made sense when placed in their Canaanite context.

We will explore the Ugarit myths a little later, for they have much to tell us about the origins of both Judaism and Christianity. But first we will look at another biblical myth; the preeminence of the kingdom of Judah.

Israel and Judah

> ➤ **The Israelites were divided into the two kingdoms of Israel and Judah. Israel was the dominant power of the two.**

We first get independent historical information about the Israelites in the era of the Assyrian invasion. At this time there are two Israelite kingdoms; Israel, with its capital at Samaria to the north, and Judah, with its capital Jerusalem, to the south. In the Bible, Israel receives relatively little notice, and that little is not good. It is presented as a lessor kingdom than Judah, forever flirting with evil Canaanite ways. But archaeology has revolutionised our understanding of the two kingdoms: it was Israel that was the dominant, impressive power, and much the larger of the two. Judah would have been little more than a client state of its more advanced northern neighbour.

In his book *The Forgotten Kingdom*, Finkelstein presents the evidence for the predominance of the kingdom of Israel. It had a much more extensive territory than Judah—at its height its population is estimated at 350,000, three times that of Judah.[7] Israel reached a peak between 884-842 BC with the four kings of the dynasty established by Omri. Under the Omrides the capital was moved from Tirzah to Samaria where they built a new monumental palace of finely hewn ashlar blocks. This palace was encircled by a casement wall and situated on a large platform high above the lower city, which was also surrounded by a defensive wall. The development of Samaria was just one of many impressive construction projects carried out by the Omrides. These included several substantial fortified cities/forts to defend the borders of their kingdom.

The Omride dynasty came to an end with the rise of the Syrian King Hazael. Taking advantage of a period of Assyrian weakness, Hazael built a large kingdom, and took much territory from Israel. The last of the Omride kings, Joram, was killed alongside his client, the Judean King Ahaziah, at the battle of Ramoth-gilead in 842 BC, a victory that is commemorated by Hazael in the Tel Dan Stela. Israel lost much of the north including Galilee, the Gilead and the Jezreel valley.

Judah probably benefited from the decline of its northern sister state. But the eclipse of Israel was only temporary. The kingdom of Israel would recover; it experienced a strong resurgence during the reigns of Joash and in particular Jeroboam II, when it achieved new heights.

> ➤ **The kingdom of Israel operated an extensive trading network.**

The Levant was a strategic location for trade. It lay between the two major civilisations of Egypt and Assyria and was also the outlet to the coast from Arabia. The coastal area was occupied by Phoenician cities who traded with the whole Mediterranean and beyond. Israel took full advantage of this position. The major export was copper until the mines were exhausted. More enduring export industries were the production of olive oil, for which the climate was ideal, and wine. Israel was also a major horse breeding area, exporting the larger horses required for chariots. The excavations at Megiddo have demonstrated the importance of this industry. When the city was reoccupied after the Syrian destruction, it was given over to horse breeding.[8]

There is evidence that the power of Israel under Jeroboam II stretched far to the south and that Israel controlled the valuable trade route from Arabia that passed through the Sinai desert. The fort of Kuntillet 'Ajrud on the Darb el-Ghazza trade route was occupied in the first half of the eighth century. Although it lies far to the south of Judah, the remarkable inscriptions found within the fort establish the connection to Israel.

➤ **There is some archaeological evidence for the kingdom of Saul.**

According to the Bible, the first king of Israel was Saul. There is some archaeological evidence of a historical basis for the Saul legend. The traditional territory of Saul's tribe of Benjamin was the hills to the north of Jerusalem around Gibeon and Bethel. This area had a spike in population at c. 1000 BC when a number of fortified settlements were built and occupied before being suddenly abandoned. Finkelstein believes that these hill settlements were the homeland of Saul's dynasty. This might seem a very modest base for the biblical kingdom of Saul, but this was in line with the typical development pattern for the area. Kingdoms were established from unfortified agricultural centres with the cites only being built generations later.

Most likely, Saul ruled a kingdom that had its centre in Benjamin, Gibeon and southern Ephraim and probably stretched as far north as the Jezreel valley and included the Gilead on the east of the Jordan. It is not known if it included Jerusalem. The Bible records that Saul was defeated and killed with his sons by the Philistines. He was succeeded by a surviving son Eshbaal. Finkelstein believes that Saul's enemy was more likely to have been the army of the Pharaoh Sheshonq I who campaigned in Canaan in the mid to late tenth century BC. On the wall of an Egyptian temple at Karnak, there is a list of the places conquered by Pharaoh on this campaign. It includes Gibeon and other settlements in the highland north of Jerusalem, the heartland of Saul's kingdom. Why would a Pharaoh be interested in this remote location unless he was conducting a campaign against Saul? The list does not include Jerusalem; either the city was too insignificant to mention, or it was not allied to Saul during the campaign.[9]

> There is no archaeological evidence for an impressive kingdom
of David.

One of the surprises from the archaeological exploration of the holy
land was the lack of evidence for the reputed kingdom of David and
Solomon. In the tenth century BC, the two kings were supposedly building Jerusalem into their magnificent capital city while controlling a vast
empire. Yet there is no evidence that Jerusalem had a significant population at this time. The so-called city of David occupied a small, narrow
area on the lower slopes of Mount Moriah. Archaeology has revealed two
phases of significant building activity. The first was in the middle bronze
age, long before David. The second came hundreds of years after David
at the time of the Judas War. Some maintain that the remains of a more
impressive city from David's time may have been lost with the development of the massive temple platform of Herod. But there is no supporting
evidence for this supposition. Significantly, little in the way of pottery
shards or household debris has been found from the tenth century BC.
The lack of rubbish is a good indicator of a low population. Also, surveys have shown that the surrounding hills were only sparsely inhabited during this period. If people were not living in the countryside, then
where was the food coming from to support a major city?[10]

Finkelstein believes that the legend of the magnificent kingdom of
Solomon was based on misunderstood traditions about the kingdom of
the Omrides. The remains of their impressive building works would have
been well known in the pre-exilic period. The Judean storytellers thought
that these buildings must have been built by their own legendary king,
Solomon.

What was the real relationship between David and Saul? The brief
answer is that we don't know. Perhaps David was a semi-independent
ruler who controlled the southern area around Jerusalem as a vassal of
Saul and who switched sides in the final conflict. Or perhaps there was
no connection, and they were not even contemporaries.

The Judas War

> Ahaz, king of Judah, paid a large bribe to the king of Assyria to
invade Israel and its ally Syria. As a result, the kingdom of Israel
was utterly destroyed.

The kingdom of Israel met its end at the hands of the Assyrians in the conflict I have called the Judas War. The war was a result of the inexorable rise

of the neo-Assyrian Empire whose expansion threatened the whole Levant. The kings of Syria and Israel, Rezin and Pekah, formed an unlikely alliance in an attempt to thwart a potential Assyrian invasion. King Ahaz of Judah, however, refused to join the alliance and remained an Assyrian ally. In response, Rezin and Pekah invaded Judah to place a more pliant king on the throne. Although this invasion was not immediately successful, Ahaz was thrown into a state of panic. To counter the threat, he paid a substantial bribe to the Assyrian King Tiglath-pileser III to persuade him to intervene. The Book of Kings reports that he took all the gold and silver from the temple and from the king's house to make up this tribute payment.[11]

As a result of Ahaz's action, the Assyrians attacked in 732 BC and defeated both Syria and Israel. Assyria annexed the northern territory of Israel. Much of the population was exiled, to be replaced by peoples relocated from elsewhere, as was the Assyrian practice. The rump state of Israel continued for a while under the puppet king Hosea, but the conflict broke out again and the capital Samaria fell in 722 BC. This was the end of Israel as both a political and ethnic entity. Most of her population was either exiled or fled, and her former territory was incorporated into the Assyrian Empire.

Ahaz would surely have been horrified by the result of his action. It also made little difference in the long term because Assyria would have eventually invaded Israel anyway. But that is not how the Israelites would have seen things. They would have blamed Ahaz's Judah for their nation's desolation.

> **The population of Jerusalem and Judah greatly increased due to a surge of refugees from southern Israel.**

There was a remarkable increase in the population of Jerusalem and Judah between the 730s and the Sennacherib invasion of 701 BC. Under Ahaz's son Hezekiah, there was a dramatic enlargement of Jerusalem from the city of David to the entire western hill which was surrounded by a new defensive wall. According to Finkelstein, Jerusalem increased from a small settlement of 10-12 acres to a residential area of 150 acres. There was a corresponding increase in the occupation of the countryside. The population of Judah doubled or tripled in just a few decades. This increase can only be explained by an ingress of refugees fleeing the Assyrians from the area of southern Israel. Simultaneous to this expansion, there was an increase in wealth, as demonstrated by the increasingly ornate tombs of the Judean elite. Judah was benefiting economically from its alliance with Assyria, but the same alliance was placing the kingdom under severe social strain.[12]

> ➤ To control the large Israelite population, Hezekiah centralised
>   religion in the temple. The Judean priests developed a new
>   pan-Israelite and monotheistic history.

The kings of Judah had betrayed the Israelites to the Assyrians. But now
they found themselves ruling a kingdom in which Israelite refugees made
up a substantial proportion of the population. This would have posed
a severe challenge. Hezekiah responded by centralising and hence controlling, religion. The only acceptable public place of worship would be
the Jerusalem temple. The Judean priests were complicit with the king.
They developed an explanation for the destruction of Israel that deflected
attention from the guilt of the ruling elite. Israel had been punished for
her sin. The Israelites had fallen away from the original pure religion of
Yahweh into evil Canaanite ways. They had worshipped other gods and
set up high places in opposition to the Jerusalem temple. They had broken
the covenant, so Yahweh had taken away their land.

This explanation only made sense if the Israelites were not Canaanites
but the chosen people of Yahweh alone. So, drawing on existing legends,
a fictitious history was developed in which the Israelites had come from
outside Canaan. It was at this time that the Hebrew Bible had its origins
although its final development would take several centuries. The primacy
of the Jerusalem temple was established through the story of Moses building the tabernacle as the dwelling place of God and the receptacle for
the tablets. Eventually, the movable tabernacle would become the fixed
Jerusalem temple. The implication was that all other cultic centres were
unauthorised by God—they were vile Canaanite places of worship.

> ➤ The legend of David and Solomon was developed to establish the
>   right of the Judean kings to rule over all Israel.

One of the most remarkable parts of the Hebrew Bible is the story of
Saul, David and Solomon, which stretches from 1 Samuel 9 to 1 Kings
2. This is normally regarded as being based on two major sources;
a "History of David's Rise" and a "Succession History", in which
Solomon out-manoeuvred his half-brothers to secure the throne. The
Deuteronomistic historian has reworked the account as part of his greater
narrative which stretches from Judges to 2 Kings. The revision takes pains
to justify David and Solomon, but behind the apologetics a very different
history is visible, a fascinating tale of murder and intrigue. This original
text is pro-Saul and surprisingly anti-David and anti-Solomon.

These features have been taken as a sign of a genuine recollection
of events. Surely no later author would invent such stories against the

ancestors of the Judean kings? This would make the account a remarkable survival from the tenth century BC. There is nothing like it from anywhere else in the world in this period. And it would pose a fascinating historical who-dun-it. Was David a serial killer? And what is the truth behind the anomalous succession of Solomon? One good attempt to solve the mystery is *David's Secret Demons* by Baruch Halpern. He sees the Succession Account as hiding a secret; that Solomon was not really the son of David but of Bathsheba's first husband, Uriah, and that he only became king through an army-led coup.[13]

Unfortunately, it is all too good to be true. The growth of archaeological knowledge of the period has shown that the David history is quite unrealistic. Finkelstein points out that the Israelites did not even have writing until c. 800 BC so the David history could not be earlier than this.[14] He sees different layers of the David stories originating at different times. The earliest layer comes from two separate verbal collections of legends; one cycle about the Israelite King Saul from the area around Bethel in southern Israel; and another cycle about the doings of David in the Jerusalem area. The biblical picture of the young David leading a roving band of a few hundred men is potentially realistic. The total population of the Judean hills, including Jerusalem, would have been no more than a few thousand at this time. The real David would have been part bandit, part mercenary, part local warlord. A force of a few hundred would have been quite sufficient to conquer Jerusalem and subdue the hills, making David king in his tiny domain.[15]

Finkelstein believes that the biblical account of David originated in response to the influx of refugees, although it included prior legends of Saul and David. The intention was to show David as the divinely appointed successor to Saul, whom the Israelites esteemed. According to Finkelstein, Judah and Israel were always separate kingdoms, so David and Solomon never controlled Israel. Even the territory of Benjamin, which eventually became part of Judah, belonged to Israel until long after David. (In an Israelite version of the tribes there were three and not twelve. These were Manasseh, Ephraim, and the most southerly, Benjamin, literally "the son of the south". In the Bible, all three are linked to Joseph—Ephraim and Manasseh are his sons and Benjamin his only full brother.) The idea of a greater Israel consisting of all twelve tribes, ruled over by David and Solomon in succession to Saul was pure propaganda. It reduced the kingdom of Israel to a break-away state that had separated itself from the true Davidic kings.[16]

If this is true, then where then did the negative anti-David and anti-Solomon aspects of the story come from? The Israelites had the more sophisticated civilisation, and it was they who had the accomplished scribes. Judah was undergoing a remarkable transformation, but, in this early phase, would have been heavily dependent upon skilled Israelite refugees. And the Israelite poets took their revenge on the Judeans. They reworked the Judean propaganda to convey a subtle anti-Judean message. A future generation of Judean scribes would rework the history again, removing any overt anti-Davidic elements. But a fascinating Israelite satire is still visible beneath the surface.

For this book, the real David matters less than the David of myth. The story may not tell us much about David or Solomon in the tenth century BC. But as we will see in the Afterword, it can tell us a great deal about Judah in the time of the Judas War.

7

The Gods of the Israelites

The Hebrew Bible is a Judean creation from the century or so after the Israelite exile, although it does not take its final form until long after the Judean return to Jerusalem. The biblical history of the Israelites is mostly fiction. What about the story of the origins of their religion? The worship of Yahweh was supposedly monotheistic from the outset, with the commandment not to worship any other god coming down from Mount Sinai. Polytheistic corruption originated with the Canaanites and infected first the kingdom of Israel and then Judah. No serious archaeologist or scholar believes this picture. There is ample evidence that the early Jews were polytheistic with monotheism emerging comparatively late in the period of the Judas War. Before this time, the Israelites worshipped Yahweh as chief deity alongside a host of other gods.

To find the true origins of Jewish religion, we must look from whence it came, to the Israelites' ancestors, the Canaanites. The discovery of the tablets at Ugarit in the 1920s and 30s was a game-changer for understanding Canaanite religion. In particular, the Baal cycle enabled us to learn more about this rain god who was so hated by the Jewish priests. We even know the name of the author of these Baal tablets; they were signed by Elimelek the Shubanite who lived in the reign of Niqmad, king of Ugarit, which dates the tablets to 1400-1350 BC.[1]

Gods of Canaan

> The Canaanite pantheon is headed by El and his wife, Asherah.

The Canaanite chief god El is a somewhat distant father figure whose symbol is a great bull. El, the creator god, is always acknowledged by the other gods as the ultimate authority although he seldom ends up getting his own way. He has a wife called Athirat, which is a form of the name Asherah. She is also called Elat (the Goddess) and is the mother, or creator, of the other gods alongside El. They preside together over their large unruly family.

Asherah is not the only prominent goddess in the Canaanite pantheon. Athtart (Astarte) is mentioned briefly in the tablets. She is the wife of Baal and even regarded as a manifestation of Baal.[2] The Canaanites had a sun goddess called Shapash who functions as a benign intermediary of El. But the most prominent goddess after Asherah is Anat, sister of Baal. Anat is scary. Although called "virgin", she is a fertility goddess, but also the goddess of war. In the Palace of Baal, we first see her fighting in a battle between "the two cities". Her waist and sash are decorated with the heads and severed hands of the dead, and her clothes are bathed in blood. She enjoys the battle so much that she decides to have a rerun in her own house, in the heavens. She seats the opposing soldiers at tables and then takes joy as they fight and kill each other, plunging her knees and skirts in their blood.

➤   **Baal, the god of rain, was particularly important for the Canaanites.**

Baal is one of the major gods of Ugarit and the hero of the Baal cycle. The name simply means "Lord"; multiple gods were called "Baal" which is very confusing. The name of the Baal of the Ugarit tablets is Hadad. His relationship with the other gods is problematic. Baal is the son of Dagon, the grain god, which may or may not be another name for El. Sometimes Baal calls El "father", but it is not clear if he is really El's son or if this is a term of respect.[3] Baal is a storm god, the bringer of thunder and rain. It is not surprising that a rain god should occupy a crucial role in the Canaanite pantheon. The Levant is hot and arid in summer, and agriculture depends upon the autumn and winter rains which are unreliable. El might have created the world, but appeasing Baal was a more urgent priority for the Canaanite farmers.

In the Ugarit tablets, there are three main stories about Baal. In the first, he battles Yam, the personified sea, for the kingship. The king rules the world as a type of regent under El. The existing king, Athar, is a bit of a joke figure and lacks two essentials, a palace and a wife. With the approval of the other gods, El attempts to appease the powerful Yam by making him king instead of Athar, although he warns Yam that he will have to fight Baal. They celebrate with a feast. But when the gods assemble again under El, Yam sends messengers to demand the surrender of Baal and his supporters. The other gods lower their heads to these messengers, but Baal rebukes them. Consumed with anger, Baal descends to the depths of the sea to do battle with Yam, aided by his sister Anat, and using weapons supplied by the craftsman double god, Kothar-and-Khasis. After a brutal fight, Baal defeats Yam. Encouraged by Athtart (Astarte) Baal kills him and scatters his body. Now Baal will be king.

In the second story, the Palace of Baal, the god laments his lack of a house. He has to dwell in his father El's palace. His sister Anat decides to help him. She goes to El to appeal for permission for Baal's house, but she is no diplomat—she threatens to smash down her father's palace and batter him until the blood runs down his grey hair unless he complies. Unsurprisingly, El says no. So Baal tries a different tack. Along with Anat, he goes to Asherah bearing gifts. The goddess is doing woman's work, spinning and washing clothes by the sea while, in her imagination, fluttering her eyelids at her husband bull El. At the approach of Baal and Anat, she is filled with dread that they mean to kill her sons. However, when she sees their gifts, she is delighted and agrees to make their case to El. She travels to El's domain, and he is pleased to see his consort, asking if she wishes to eat and drink, or whether she has come for love. However, when he realises that she has come to plead Baal's case, he sarcastically replies that the two of them must be Baal's slaves—are they to make the bricks for Baal's house? Nevertheless, he cannot deny his wife and gives permission for the house.

At first, Baal insists that there should be no window in his house lest his daughters Pidray, daughter of mists, and Tallay, daughter of showers, escape. However, if the house has no window, then no rain will fall on the earth. Fortunately, Baal sees sense and a window is included. When his house is finished, Baal invites the other gods for a feast and sends out mighty peals of thunder that shake the whole earth to celebrate.

> ➢ **Baal goes down to the underworld to defeat Mot, the god of death in a story which has parallels to the story of Christ.**

In the third story, Baal faces his most implacable enemy, the death god Mot. Baal has foolishly decided to invite Mot along with his brother gods to celebrate the completion of his house. He sends envoys down into the underworld where Mot has his throne in a pit of filth. He warns the envoys to take care or Mot will swallow them like a lamb in his mouth. Mot is insulted by this invitation issued by the arrogant Baal. He has been invited to feast on meat and drink like his brothers, but Mot desires only human flesh. He tells Baal that he will take him down to his own kingdom instead, and swallow him whole. It seems that Baal is unable to resist Mot. To save him, Shapash, the sun goddess, comes up with a scheme. Baal will send a substitute to Mot, and will then hide in the underworld among the shades to fool Mot into thinking that he is dead. So Baal mates with a heifer near the entrance to the underworld and she bears him a son. He clothes this son with his robe and gives him to the "beloved one" meaning Mot, who thinks he is Baal.

All the other gods believe that Baal is dead. Even El is fooled and descends from his throne to mourn. He covers himself with sackcloth and shaves, wishing that he also was dead. The grieving Anat asks Shapash to carry Baal's body to the mountain Zephon which she does. There Anat buries him (this must be the substitute's body). She then sarcastically tells Asherah and her sons to rejoice, for Baal is dead. This shows that the sons of Asherah are opposed to Baal and on Mot's side. El tells Asherah to select a replacement king from her sons, and she chooses Athar, but he is too feeble for the kingship.

Humanity is suffering because of Baal's death; the earth is without rain, and the sun burns hot. Anat descends to confront Mot demanding that he release Baal. Mot replies that he is unable because he has swallowed him. Anat, however, attacks Mot and kills him, cutting him up and burning and scattering his flesh. She then returns to El, who has a dream that Baal is alive. Anat rejoices, and Shapash agrees to search for him. The story continues with the resurrected Baal fully restored to life. He fights Asherah's sons and kills them to sit again on the throne of his kingdom.

After seven years, Mot is alive again. He asks for one of Baal's brothers to eat, or he will consume all humanity. However, Baal sends Mot one of his own brothers instead. A furious Mot confronts Baal, and there is a battle between the two. They are perfectly matched, and both fall down fighting. The struggle only comes to an end when Shapash tells Mot that El will take away his underworld kingdom if he continues. So Mot desists and accepts Baal as king.

The story is confused, which is not helped by the fragmentary nature of the tablets. At least two separate traditions are being combined which gives rise to some odd features, such as Mot being killed by Anat and then being fully alive again to confront Baal. But beyond this confusion there are clear parallels with the Christ myth. The death and resurrection of Baal are typical of the myths of the dying and resurrected gods of the ancient world. In part, this is a reflection of the seasonal cycle of life. In more temperate areas, the time of death is winter when the god descends to the underworld, to be reborn into the upper world in spring. In Canaan, it is the arid summer that is death, and the autumn rains that bring life. Baal, the god of rains, disappears in the summer. If he returns, there will be life-giving water, if he does not, there will be starvation. But there is more to the myth than just this seasonal aspect. It is ultimately about the underworld and the human longing for a god who can overcome death.

➢ **Imagery from the Baal cycle is applied to Yahweh in the Bible.**

The Bible has taken much over from Canaanite religion. Imagery of Baal as storm god has been applied to Yahweh who has also assumed aspects of Anat as war-goddess, which is behind some blood-curdling passages in the Bible.[4]

Instead of Baal winning the victory over Yam, the god of the sea, the Bible has Yahweh fighting and overcoming the sea god/monster. This explains several puzzling passages.[5] Yahweh's adversary is even called Yam in places; the meaning is hidden because "Yam" is invariably translated as "sea" rather than as the god's proper name. Other names used for Yam or his monsters in the Bible are Rahab, Leviathan and dragon:[6]

> *In that day the Lord Yahweh with his sharp, great and strong sword will punish Leviathan the fleeing serpent, Leviathan the twisted serpent, and he will slay the dragon that is in the sea. (Isaiah 27:1)*

It is clear that Canaanite myths have influenced the Hebrew Bible. If aspects of the story of Baal's defeat of Yam have been transferred to Yahweh, then equally aspects of Baal's defeat of death could have been applied to Christ.

Yahweh and El

> **The cult of Yahweh was imported into Canaan from the south.**

Yahweh was not part of the Canaanite pantheon. The earliest evidence for Yahweh comes from Egyptian records dating to the 13th century BC which talk of the god Yhw associated with the troublesome Shasu Bedouin people of the trans-Jordon. These Shasu lived in the biblical "land of Midian" which is where Moses was living when he had his first encounter with Yahweh in the burning bush. This seems too much of a coincidence to dismiss. The Egyptologist Donald B. Redford first proposed that a group of these Shasu nomads migrated to the unoccupied hill country of Canaan and this gave rise to the story of the exodus. He believed that these Shasu settled down to became farmers and were the proto-Israelites. The archaeological evidence and linguistic continuity disprove this theory—the proto-Israelites came from Canaan. But it is still possible that there was some migration of the Shasu, and that they formed one element of the population, merging in with the Canaanites and adopting their language.[7]

If there were a historical Moses, then he would have been an Egyptian who lived in the desert. Perhaps he really was an aristocrat exiled from his homeland for murder. Moses would have been a shaman and miracle worker of the cult of Yahweh. It is striking that in the Bible, Moses is

forbidden to enter the Promised Land, which implies that he had no connection with Canaan or the Israelites. We should instead locate him to the
south, to the wilderness area of Midian. While shepherding his father-in-
law's flock he had his encounter with Yahweh in the burning bush on
Mount Horeb, which appears in Deuteronomy as an alternative name for
Mount Sinai.[8] The location of the ancient Mount Sinai is unknown, but
the stories probably relate to a "high place", a hilltop sanctuary, in the
Midian area.

We have seen that Israel had an extensive trading network and that it
established forts in the Sinai desert. It is from the fort at Kuntillet 'Ajrud
on the Darb el-Ghazza trade route that we find remarkable inscriptions
to "YHWH of Samaria" and "YHWH of Teman" which are some of the
earliest evidence for the cult of Yahweh in Israel. The inscriptions show
that Yahweh was also worshipped at Teman in the arid southern region.
Finkelstein suggests that an early exodus tradition originated from this
trade route.[9] This gives rise to another, less romantic, theory as to how
the cult of Yahweh travelled to Canaan—through trade rather than an
epic migration. The Darb el-Ghazza route runs from the top of the Gulf
of Aqaba and the area of Midian to the Mediterranean coast. Priests of
Yahweh from Midian could have travelled along the trade route, making
converts of traders and soldiers from Israel and Judah. They would have
brought with them traditions of their great shaman Moses.

➢   **Yahweh was equated with Canaanite El.**

The gods of the ancient world had many names. Each place had its
own gods, and to consolidate the pantheon, these local gods and goddess would be equated to one of the familiar deities. When the Israelites
encountered the new god Yahweh, they identified him with El. This
fusing of Yahweh and El was early and complete. The names were used
interchangeably by the Israelites.

Yahweh, however, was not really the same as El. He was more active,
more heroic, more like Baal in the Canaanite myths. The merger of an
aggressive storm god with the benign father creator of all things was a
dynamic combination. This new Yahweh-El hybrid provided an impetus
that, many centuries later, led to monotheism. The adoption of Yahweh by
the Israelites drove a barrier between them and their fellow Canaanites.
The Israelites saw themselves as Yahweh's chosen people, and hence fundamentally superior to their neighbours.

Asherah

> Asherah was worshipped as the consort of Yahweh/El until the exile. But her existence as an independent goddess was gradually redacted from the biblical account, and an asherah became a cultic symbol, a pole.

The Israelite pantheon was based on that of Canaan but is smaller than the Ugarit pantheon. Thankfully, the psychopathic goddess Anat does not appear directly among the Israelites. The main gods worshipped alongside El/Yahweh were Baal and Asherah. The sons of El as a group are present as "the host of heaven". Aside from them, the sun and the moon were worshipped, and Astarte is mentioned a few times in the Bible with her worship linked to Baal.[10]

In the centuries leading up to the Judean exile, there was a strong Assyrian influence, and the Mesopotamian astral gods became popular in Judah. The Sumerian god Tammuz (Dumuzi) is mentioned in Ezekiel, and Ishtar (Astarte) is probably the "Queen of Heaven" for whom the women bake cakes in Jeremiah.[11] Under her alternative name Inanna, she was the consort of Dumuzi, and the Sumerian pair closely parallel the Canaanite Baal and Anat/Astarte.

This brings us to the strange case of the goddess Asherah. Her name occurs many times in the Bible, and yet she was practically invisible as a goddess. This was because an Asherah (or asherah) was thought to be a pole. It was only with archaeological discoveries in the twentieth century that the goddess Asherah began to re-emerge. An excellent summary of the case for Asherah as the wife of Yahweh is set out in Dever's book *Did God Have a Wife?*

The word Asherah is mentioned some 40 times in the Bible which is a sign of the popularity of the goddess among the Israelites. However, the Bible gives the impression that an "asherah" was a cultic object, a pole or grove of trees. No one doubts that such cultic objects were initially intended to represent the goddess. At the coastal city of Ugarit, Asherah (Athirat) was a sea goddess, but among Israelites, she was associated with trees:

> *Even their children remember their altars and their Asherah, by every green tree and on the high hills... (Jeremiah 17:2)*

Because trees cannot easily be brought into temples, her tree became symbolic—an asherah pole. The Bible nearly always applies the word "Asherah/asherah" to groves of trees or such cultic objects. It is controversial whether such poles or groves represented the goddess in the period before the exile. The traditionalists argue that the Israelites had forgotten the origins of the asherah, and it was simply an object connected to the worship of Yahweh. However, in a few biblical passages, Asherah can only be a deity.[12] So perhaps the biblical writers were all too aware that Asherah was a goddess, but did not want to acknowledge a belief they regarded as blasphemy; that Asherah was the wife of Yahweh.

In the light of the Ugarit tablets, there is nothing surprising about this belief. Asherah (Athirat) was the wife of El. Yahweh was equated with El so it is only logical that Asherah should be his wife. The most spectacular evidence for Asherah as the consort of Yahweh comes from the Kuntillet 'Ajrud excavations where many inscriptions have been found on walls and pottery. These include three Hebrew inscriptions linking Asherah and Yahweh:

To Yahweh (of) Teman (Yemen) and to his Asherah

I blessed you by (or "to") Yahweh of Samaria and by his Asherah

Yahweh of Teman and his Asherah

These date from the mid-ninth to the mid-eighth centuries BC, and so are very early. The inscription to "Yahweh of Samaria" is on a jar decorated with some crudely depicted scenes; two goats eating from a tree (the symbol of the goddess), a lion, and three intriguing figures. Two of these figures are male, although one has breasts, and the other is a lady seated on what may be a lion throne. The androgynous male figure may be the Egyptian god Bes who was popular in Judea. The seated lady may be Asherah. It is all very intriguing but ambiguous.[13]

Unfortunately, the grammar on the inscriptions is also ambiguous; the possessive would usually be used for an object rather than a person. It must be stressed that our knowledge of Hebrew as spoken by ordinary people in this period is very limited. But the grammatical problem leaves open the possibility that the Asherah is something dedicated to Yahweh rather than the goddess. However, there cannot be much serious doubt in the context of the inscription. Why would anyone address offerings to Yahweh and his pole/tree? The purpose of the inscriptions is surely to call upon the protection of Yahweh and his lady wife.

The Kuntillet 'Ajrud inscriptions are not alone. A similar inscription appealing to Yahweh and his Asherah has been found at Khirbet el-Qom.[14] There is also a potential parallel in the Bible. In Amos, there is a prediction of the destruction that will come upon Israel (Samaria):

Those who swear by Ashimah of Samaria, and say, "As your god lives,
O Dan," and, "As the way of Beersheba lives," they shall fall, and never
rise again. (Amos 8:14)

Dan was a significant "high place" which has now been excavated. The intriguing reference to Ashimah would seem to be a play on Asherah. As Dever shows, the substitution of one consonant for another similar looking consonant gets from Asherah to Ashimah. This is a word-play: the root of Ashimah is "shame" or "sin" which is how it is rendered in most translations of the Bible. So "Asherah of Samaria" has been changed to the similar looking "shame of Samaria".[15]

Even with the evidence of the inscriptions, it might still be maintained that Asherah was a pole rather than a goddess. However, this is contradicted by another discovery. A large number of small clay nude female figurines have been found dating to the 8th-7th centuries BC. Although the production of female fertility figurines was common throughout pre-history, the surprise is finding a large number of such figurines in a relatively late Israelite context. They are clearly intended to represent a goddess—they are idols. Only the upper body is modelled with the breasts emphasised. They seem like a chaste version of the earlier full-figure Canaanite fertility figures, with the breasts signifying motherhood rather than sex. They occur in domestic contexts—households rather than cultic sites. All of this points to the figures representing a mother goddess—and who can this be if not Asherah?[16]

Thousands of such figurines have been found. Given that only a tiny proportion of such objects would survive to be unearthed by archaeologists, the figurines must have been very common indeed in the 8th-7th centuries. It is natural to regard such figurines as being used for worship by women. But the nurturing influence of motherhood is revered by men as well as by women. Our experience of the mother as infants and young children is a universal of human existence. What could be more natural than to bring into the household the protective presence of the divine mother, the wife of Yahweh?

The evidence for Asherah is perfectly consistent, stretching from the Ugarit tablets in which she is the wife of El, down through the biblical references, to the archaeological inscriptions to "Yahweh and his Asherah" and the domestic figurines. The worship of Asherah was part of the cult of Yahweh and was popular right up until the exile.

Temples and High Places

The archaeology of cultic sites

To find out more about the religious practice of the Jews before the exile, we can look to both archaeology and the biblical accounts. According to the book of Kings, both Hezekiah and Josiah led reforming movements to re-establish the monotheistic worship of Yahweh. Coming in between these two "good" kings was the "bad" King Manasseh, who undid many of Hezekiah's reforms. The authors of these accounts have unwittingly given us excellent evidence for the real religion of Judah and Israel by cataloguing the evil practices prevalent at the time. It is far from certain if all the reforms actually happened. But even if they were priestly wishful thinking, the account of the unreformed Jewish religion would still reflect first-hand knowledge from those who lived around the time of the exile. And the picture we derive from the Bible is in excellent agreement with the archaeological evidence, to which we turn first.

➢ **There were many cultic centres in operation before the exile, both temples and "high places".**

Enclosed temples were comparatively rare in Israel and Judah. Indeed, the existence of any temple other than the Jerusalem temple was controversial because it contradicted the biblical narrative. But we now know that other temples certainly existed. The best early example is the *"migdal"* tower-temple at Shechem. Situated in the heart of Israel, the origins of this temple go back as far as the Canaanite era at c. 1650 BC. The remains of the temple today are a substantial stone platform with walls up to fifteen feet thick. There are two towers by the entrance, and the main building would have had additional storeys. Alterations were made in the Israelite period at around 1200 BC with the addition of a standing stone, a *massebah*. An external altar was constructed before the temple, giving it the same basic layout as the later Jerusalem temple—a tall building with an outside altar for sacrifices standing in front. Shortly after these additions the Shechem temple was destroyed.[1]

There is a fascinating story about this tower-temple in Judges. A man called Abimelech attempted to make himself king. The people of Shechem accepted him and made him king by the oak of the stone pillar. But after three years, they grew weary of his rule. There was a fight, and Abimelech's force defeated the townspeople, who fled to the *"tower (migdal) of Shechem"* *(Judges 9:46)*. Abimelech had the tower burnt down, killing everyone inside, about a thousand people according to Judges. This story is a folk memory of the temple and its destruction. In Judges, the temple is called both the temple of the covenant of Baal and the covenant of El.[2] Either it was sacred to both Baal and El or else it changed from one to the other.

We should note the connection between the Shechem *migdal* temple, and the representation of the temple as a tower in the Animal Apocalypse. This identification between temple and tower goes right back to the design of Canaanite temples which was retained by the Israelites. It is reflected, of course, in the name the Magdalene which comes from *migdal*.

The very early Shechem temple could be dismissed as an anomaly. But a much later temple from the monarchy period has been excavated at Arad, east of Beersheba, on the margin of the Negev desert. This large structure was part of a Judean fort complex and has been dated to the 8th century BC. A fragment of pottery found at the site has a reference to the "temple of Yahweh" suggesting that this place of worship was dedicated to Yahweh and not some other god. Although Arad is the best surviving remnant of a temple from this era, there is nothing to indicate it was in any way remarkable. It is the temple for a fort, and there were probably many others like it.[3] More recently, another temple dating from the 10th to 9th century BC has been found at Tel Motza close to Jerusalem.[4]

Although excavated public temples are rare, there are many examples of smaller domestic shrines. Such shrines typically consisted of a dedicated room in a building identified by distinctive pottery and often with a small altar for incense and food offerings. Some examples also had standing stones (*massebah*), preparation tables, and benches along the walls for offerings. These shrines have been found dating from the 12th to the 7th centuries BC.[5]

The more usual public places of Israelites worship are the *bamot*, the open-air "high places". The archetypal "high place" was located on a hill-top location and consisted of a large raised platform for sacrifices with a ceremonial staircase. However, the "high places" were not just found on hills, but in many other settings. They might be built on an artificial raised mound, and there were small "high places" by the gates of cities. The basic Canaanite design continued through the proto-Israelite era right down to the monarchy period in both Israel and Judah.

Our knowledge of the "high places" has been greatly improved by the excavation of the sanctuary at Dan, an Israelite "high place" condemned in the Bible. The main structure is a large raised platform measuring 60 foot by 60 foot with a ceremonial staircase. A large four-horned altar for sacrifices was built in front of this platform. Another intriguing feature was an olive press and vat near the altar used for the production of holy oil. The main sanctuary was in use in the 9th to 8th centuries BC and was discontinued at the Assyrian invasion. In the 7th century BC, a three-roomed chamber was built alongside, and sacrifices continued on an altar in one of these rooms. The discovery of a ceremonial mace head indicates that there was a priestly class who officiated at the sanctuary. It is all very similar to the Jerusalem temple.[6]

The high places in the Bible

➢ **The Deuteronomistic authors vigorously opposed the high places which were supposedly destroyed by the reforming kings Hezekiah and Josiah.**

In the book of Kings, the Judean kings are largely judged according to their attitude towards the high places. Hezekiah is rated as one of the two best kings because he supposedly destroyed the high places:

> *He removed the high places and broke the pillars and cut down the Asherah. (2 Kings 18:4)*

The pillars that Hezekiah broke were the *massebah,* like the one erected at the tower of Shechem. Hezekiah's immediate predecessors Uzziah and Jotham are treated relatively kindly although they allowed the high places to continue:

> *The high places, however, were not removed. The people still sacrificed and burnt incense on the high places. (2 Kings 15:4)*

The greatest odium is reserved for the two "evil" kings, Ahaz and Manasseh. It is said about Ahaz:

> *And he sacrificed and burnt incense on the high places, and on the hills, and under every green tree. (2 Kings 16:4)*

The phrase "every green tree" is a reference to the sacred groves dedicated to Asherah. Hezekiah's son Manasseh, who supposedly restored the high places, is presented as the worst king of all. The exile of Judah is even his fault. In contrast, his grandson, Josiah, is the priests' great hero. During his reign an ancient "Book of the Law" was supposedly discovered in the temple—perhaps the book of Deuteronomy. The discovery of this book precipitated a campaign of religious reforms (we might say religious oppression) to eliminate all centres of worship other than the Jerusalem temple. Josiah destroyed the cultic centres on the Mount of Olives, "the mount of corruption" that were attributed to Solomon. He also demolished the ancient high place at Bethel, on the border between the old Israel and Judah (the story of the ascent and descent of the angels in the dream of Jacob relates to this sanctuary):

> *Moreover, the altar at Bethel, and the high place made by Jeroboam the son of Nebat, who made Israel sin, that altar and high place he pulled down. He burned down the high place, and ground it to dust and he also burned the Asherah. (2 Kings 23:15)*

The sanctuary of Bethel was desecrated with bones of the dead burnt on the altars. In Samaria, the old territory of Israel, Josiah went one further and had the priests slaughtered on the altars:

> *Just as Josiah had done at Bethel, so also he removed the shrines of the high places that were in the cities of Samaria, which the kings of Israel had made, provoking Yahweh to anger. On the altars he sacrificed all the priests of the high places who were there, and burned human bones on them. Then he returned to Jerusalem. (2 Kings 23:19-20)*

These murderous actions of Josiah will disgust most modern readers. But they are probably nothing more than priestly fantasies. It is unlikely that Josiah had control of Samaria beyond Bethel.

➤ **From the accounts of Manasseh and Josiah, we get a view of the chief deities worshipped in Judah before the exile.**

Manasseh seems to have been a pragmatist who allowed a partial return to traditional forms of worship. He must have been a successful and popular king because he had an extraordinarily long reign. But he receives a terrible press from the priests:

> *And he did what was evil in the sight of Yahweh, according to the abominations of the nations whom Yahweh drove out before the people of Israel. For he rebuilt the high places that Hezekiah his father had*

destroyed, and he erected altars for Baal and made an Asherah pole, as Ahab king of Israel had done, and worshipped all the host of heaven and served them. And he built altars in the house of Yahweh, of which Yahweh had said, "In Jerusalem will I put my Name." And he built altars for all the host of heaven in the two courts of the house of Yahweh. And he made his son pass through fire, practised divination, sought omens and dealt with familiar spirits and wizards. (2 Kings 21:2-5)

We should note the deities whom the Judeans worshipped:

- Yahweh/El
- Asherah
- Baal
- The host of heaven

There is a close correlation between this list and what we know of the Canaanite pantheon. Manasseh restored the high places and made an Asherah pole or perhaps a whole grove. There were altars for Baal and for the host of heaven, including in the temple where there was also an image of Asherah:

And he set up a carved image of Asherah that he had made, in the house of which Yahweh said to David and to Solomon his son, "In this house, and in Jerusalem, which I have chosen out of all the tribes of Israel, I will put my Name forever." (2 Kings 21:7)

In the account of the religious reforms of Josiah, we get more detail of the previous religious practices, including the reality of temple worship at this time:

- Baal, Asherah and the host of heaven were all worshipped in the temple.[7]
- The sun and the moon were also worshipped, and there were models of the horses and chariot of the sun god at the entrance to the temple.[8]
- "Male prostitutes" served in the temple in the place where women wove "houses" for Asherah.[9]

The statement about the "male prostitutes" is very obscure, and the specialists argue over whether they were really male or female, and whether they were "prostitutes" or just functionaries of the goddess.[10] Still, temple sex was a standard component of the worship of a fertility goddess and castrated men may have been dedicated to serving the goddess in Jerusalem as they were elsewhere. As for the women who were weaving "houses" for Asherah, most likely they were making small tents as mini-shrines for the goddess.

Child sacrifice

> The Israelites and Judeans followed the Canaanite practice of child sacrifice.

It is well known that the Canaanites practised child sacrifice and that this persisted among the early Israelites. In the Ugarit tablets, Baal offers up his own son to the "dearest", meaning the death god Mot. Archaeological evidence comes from the closely related civilisation of the Phoenicians. In the North African Phoenician port of Carthage, there is a 7th-4th century BC cemetery with many thousands of burial urns containing the burned bones of infants. Inscriptions record these as sacrifices made to fulfil a vow, typically to "Tanit", the Phoenician name for Asherah, or Ba'al Hamon, who was equivalent to the Canaanite El. The sacrifices are called a *mulk* which has been shown by Eissfeldt to be the source of the idea in the Bible that the sacrifices were made to a god called Molech.[11] There was no such god amongst the Israelites and the sacrifices would have been made to Yahweh/El.[12]

It was not just any child that could be sacrificed. It had to be the sacrificer's own son or daughter. The greatest sacrifice of all was to give the thing a person loved the most—their child. It is clear that child sacrifice was practised in both Israel and Judah but was eventually abolished. There are grave prohibitions against child sacrifice in the Bible which would not have been necessary if child sacrifice had not been common.

For the Israelites, it was not usually infants who were sacrificed. There is a story in Judges about a warrior called Jephthah the Gileadite, son of a prostitute, who was brought up by his father until driven out as a youth. He wandered and formed a mercenary band with some other "worthless men". His reputation as a fighter increased until the people of his homeland made him an offer he could not refuse. If he fought and defeated their enemies, the Ammonites, they would make him their king. Before the battle, Jephthah made a vow with Yahweh; if he won, he would make a burnt offering of the first thing to come out of his house when he returned. He secured a mighty victory and returned to his homestead triumphant. To greet him, his daughter ran out of the door dancing with tambourines. She was his only child, and when he saw her, Jephthah tore his clothes in grief.

But, as she told him, the vow could not be retracted: *"Do to me as you have said, for Yahweh has avenged you of your enemies, the Ammonites" (Judges 11:36)*. She asked only to be allowed to wander in the hills for two months. He let her go and when she returned *"he did to her as he had vowed" (Judges 11:39)*.

The story has been altered to make it more appropriate for a time when child sacrifice was strictly forbidden. The idea of sacrificing whatever came out of the door first makes no sense, for it could be some worthless animal. Behind this gloss we can see the original vow; Jephthah would sacrifice that which was most precious to him, his daughter, in exchange for victory against the Ammonites. The girl's virginity and readiness for marriage made her all the more valuable as an offering to Yahweh. The god had kept his side of the bargain, so Jephthah had to keep his.[13]

The most potent sacrifice was the king's own child, usually a son rather than a daughter. Such a sacrifice might be required to secure a victory or avert a threat to the kingdom. It was also traditional to sacrifice a king's son to ensure the protection of a god on the founding or rebuilding of a city. When Hiel of Bethel built up Jericho, the foundations cost him his oldest son Abiram, and setting up the city gates cost him his youngest son Segub.[14]

We have direct evidence connecting the kings of Judah to such sacrifices. The book of Kings says that Ahaz had his son "pass through fire":

> *But he walked in the way of the kings of Israel, even making his son pass through fire, the very same abomination that the nations practised, whom Yahweh drove out from the land in front of the Israelites. (2 Kings 16:3)*

The expression "pass through fire" mostly likely means to offer up the child as a burnt offering. This is certainly the meaning of the parallel passage in 2 Chronicles 28:3. The same accusation is levelled against the other "bad" king, Manasseh. The author of Kings knew that child sacrifice was practised by the Canaanites and also specifically connects it to the kings of Israel. This is in line with Judean propaganda that the original religion given by Yahweh had been subverted through the importation of Canaanite corruption through the Israelites.

The archetypal expression of the abandonment of child sacrifice is the story of Abraham and Isaac. Abraham is instructed by Yahweh to sacrifice his son Isaac as a burnt offering. He takes the boy to Mount Moriah, builds the fire, binds Isaac on top of the wood, and prepares to cut his throat. At the very last moment, an angel intervenes and orders Abraham to substitute a ram caught in a thicket. The story comes from a time when child sacrifice had already ceased. It skilfully drives a wedge between Israelite and Canaanite religion by linking the cessation of this practice to the covenant between Abraham and Yahweh. As a result of this covenant, the Promised Land was taken from the Canaanites and granted to the Israelites.[15]

> **The idea that Christ, the son of Yahweh, was offered as sacrifice makes sense in a culture in which child sacrifice was a recent memory.**

There is a modern criticism of Christianity which is both naive and thought-provoking. Why was Jesus' sacrifice necessary to atone for the sin of humanity? Why cannot God simply choose to forgive people their sin? The question reveals the chasm that exists between us and the culture in which the Christ myth emerged. The idea that God would offer up his own son makes perfect sense to a people who had practised child sacrifice within recent memory. It would never have occurred to them that the greatest victory could be won without the greatest sacrifice.

This book will show how the Christ myth evolved as a reaction to the exile. Israel and Judah were the chosen people of Yahweh, the supreme creator God. Yet the two kingdoms had been destroyed by nations who worshipped lesser gods. How could this be? The priests of Judah said that it was because Israel and Judah had broken the covenant by the worship of other gods. The Israelites had a different explanation. At a heavenly level, the Christ had been put to death by the powers that ruled the nations. How could Yahweh allow this to happen? Because it was part of a secret plan that the rulers, the archons, did not know. Just as an Israelite king might make the ultimate sacrifice of his son to invoke the power that would defeat his enemies, so the higher Yahweh had offered up his own son, Christ to defeat the heavenly forces that ruled the earth. Christ was blameless and without blemish, but had been offered as a lamb to the slaughter. So also, at the earthly level, his people, the Israelites, had been offered up to the Assyrians and Babylonians. But the divine rulers of the nations had been tricked. An ultimate sacrifice invoked the ultimate power that would end their rule forever.

The Hezekiah reforms

> **Hezekiah eliminated the worship of other gods and centralised the worship of Yahweh in the Jerusalem temple. This can be seen as a response to the aftermath of the Judas War.**

Before the Judas War, the Israelites and Judeans lived in a world of many gods. Although they regarded themselves as the chosen people of

Yahweh, he was not their only god. This all changed in the centuries up to, during, and after the Judean exile. According to the book of Kings, it was Hezekiah who first attempted to destroy the cultic centres and eliminate the worship of rival gods. Scholars have long been sceptical about the supposed Hezekiah reforms. The accounts of the reforms of Hezekiah and Josiah are suspiciously similar. Is it possible that the reforms never happened, but are an attempt to project the post-exilic position onto the past? Remarkably, there is recent archaeological evidence supporting the reality of Hezekiah's reforms. And a key piece of evidence is a toilet seat.

The seat comes from Lachish, the second most important city in Judah at the time of Hezekiah. The city had a massive gateway divided into several rooms. Excavations by Ganor and Kreimerman have revealed that one of these room was a gate-shrine split into an outer chamber and a small inner sanctum. In this innermost room, there were two small horned altars, but the horns had been cut-off and embedded in the wall. They also found a carved stone seat with a large hole in the middle—a toilet seat. This must have been added in a deliberate act of desecration. There is a reference to such desecration in the Book of Kings: *"They tore down the temple of Baal and made it into a latrine, which it is to this day"* (2 Kings 10:27). Testing showed that the toilet had never been used—no one wanted to go that far! After this act of desecration, the small room was sealed off. We know that the toilet seat was added during Hezekiah's reign because the city was destroyed in 701 BC by the Assyrian King Sennacherib. Ganor and Kreimerman believe that the sanctuary was dedicated to Yahweh so this was not about eliminating the shrine of another god such as Baal, but of enforcing the new Jerusalem temple monopoly on Yahweh worship.[16]

At around the same time the toilet seat was added at Lachish, the temple at Arad was dismantled and filled with earth. And at Beersheba, an altar was deliberately desecrated with its horns removed and incorporated into the walls of a storehouse built in anticipation of the Sennacherib invasion. This altar must have originally stood in a sanctuary, now lost, which was presumably demolished.[17]

All of which shows that the reforms of Hezekiah were perfectly real. Alternative centres of worship to the Jerusalem temple were abolished, and sanctuaries to other gods desecrated. We can see this as a response to the crisis of the Judas War. Centralising religion increased the power of the king and his ability to control a potentially unruly and rebellious population. The reforms are consistent with the strategy of shifting the blame for the destruction of Israel onto Israelite forms of worship and away from the kings of Judah.

There is no archaeological evidence for the later reforms under Josiah and no evidence that the old cultic sites were reinstated under Manasseh.

The account in Kings with its alternation between bad and good kings is suspicious. Have memories relating to Hezekiah's reforms been falsely attributed to Josiah? The Josiah account reads like an attempt to give a backstory for the book of Deuteronomy, which was probably written after the exile. The priests in this post-exilic era had the major embarrassment of trying to explain the exile of Judah. Why, after Hezekiah's reforms, had Judah been punished with exile? The blame had to be placed on Hezekiah's successor, Manasseh who must have returned to Canaanite ways. Even though the good King Josiah swept away the evil worship, it was not enough to wipe out the sin that Manasseh had committed.

9

The Origins of the Seventy

The divine council

We can now place the seventy shepherd angels who killed the Christ within the context of Israelite religion in the pre-exilic period. We will trace the seventy all the way back to the gods of Canaan. As Judaism became increasingly monotheistic, these gods were demoted to angels.

> ➤ **The gods in Canaan met in convocation under El, and this divine assembly was seventy in number.**

In the Ugarit tablets, the gods meet regularly in convocation, usually on the mount of assembly.[1] On such occasions, the gods and goddesses will feast and indulge in much drinking. They are not just there for a good meal but form a ruling council. They are heavenly princes who receive embassies and make decisions. The leader of this council is the father of the gods, El, who has the final say and makes the final judgement.

How many of the gods are there? They are enumerated only once in the surviving tablets when Baal holds a feast to celebrate the completion of his house (translations by JLC Gibson):

> *He did call his brothers into his mansion,*
> *His kinsfolk into the midst of his palace,*
> *He did call the seventy sons of Athirat [Asherah]*
> *He did supply the gods with rams (and) with wine,*
> *He did supply the goddesses with ewes [(and) with wine],*
> *...... (The Palace of Baal 4 vi 44-48)[2]*

So Baal has seventy brother gods, who are called the seventy sons of Asherah. In one sense "seventy" just means "many"—ancient people were often vague about numbers and describe them in ways that may seem inconsistent to us. Yet the number seventy will continue to crop up as we follow the track of the shepherds through time. In this passage, we find that they were seventy from the very beginning, as gods under El. Note also that they are described as the sons of Asherah. This is another theme that occurs again and again: the seventy are brothers, the sons of a single divine mother.

➢   **The concept of the divine assembly was taken over into Judaism where it is said that the gods who rule under El are unjust and will be destroyed.**

It is evident from Psalm 82 that the Canaanite divine council was taken over into Judaism. This psalm starts with God holding judgement among the gods:

> *God [Elohim] has taken his place in the divine assembly;*
> *in the midst of the gods [elohim] he holds judgment: (Psalm 82:1)*

The word Elohim can be either single or plural. Here it stands for both El and the gods as a group. El takes his place and gives his judgement among the other gods who he accuses of not ruling justly:

> *"How long will you judge unjustly*
> *and show partiality to the wicked? Selah*
> *Give justice to the weak and the orphan;*
> *maintain the right of the afflicted and the destitute.*
> *Rescue the weak and needy;*
> *deliver them from the hand of the wicked." (Psalm 82:2-4)*

This is very similar to an accusation made against Keret in the Ugarit tablets:

> *You do not judge the cause of the widow,*
> *You do not try the case of the importunate,*
> *You do not banish the extortioners of the poor,*
> *You do not feed the orphan before your face,*
> *(Nor) the widow behind your back. (Keret 16 vi 46-50)[3]*

The gods have failed the essential requirement for justice. They are inadequate for their task:

> *They know not, nor do they understand,*
> *they walk on in darkness;*
> *all the foundations of the earth are shaken. (Psalm 82:5)*

So they will fall:

> I said, "You are gods [elohim],
> You are all sons of the Most High,
> But like men you shall die,
> and fall like any prince." (Psalm 82:6-7)

Although the gods are the sons of the most high, they shall die like men and fall "like any prince". The rule of the gods over the nations is coming to an end, and El will rule the whole earth directly:

> Arise, O God, judge the earth;
> for you shall inherit all the nations! (Psalm 82:8)

Once again, we can find a remarkable parallel in the Keret story. Keret is a human king, yet when he is sick, he is spoken of as if he were a god. His son tells him "we exulted in your immortality" and expresses surprise that he could die:

> How can it be said that Keret is a son of El,
> The progeny of Latipan and the Holy One?
> Or shall gods die? (Keret 16 i 20-22)[4]

Latipan is another name for El, and the Holy One is Asherah. So Keret is a son of El and Asherah, implying that he is one of the seventy sons of Asherah. Yet he will die "as men". It may also be significant that the divine council of gods meets in Keret's house to feast.[5] Multiple traditions are merged into this story; in one Keret is human; in another, he is a god. The accusation that he does not give justice reads oddly in context. It occurs at the very end and is made by Keret's son who believes his father incapable of giving judgement because he is sick. The son is a hero, but after criticising Keret, he is cursed by his father. Behind the Keret as god tradition, there must be something very similar to Psalm 82—the gods themselves will die if they fail in their duty to give justice. It is clear that the antecedents of Psalm 82 go back long before the Israelites.

Psalm 82 gave the Jews great trouble. It challenged the idea that the gods did not exist, that they were mere idols. The interpretation settled upon was that the "gods" in the psalm meant human judges. By meeting in council with Yahweh in their midst, the elders became "gods" with authority to judge and even make law. The psalm warned that this council must fulfil its responsibility to judge with justice; else its members would no longer be "gods" but would die "like men". So the Sanhedrin, the council of seventy under a president, developed as a mirror of the divine assembly. Ironically, this human council survived long after the gods in the original heavenly assembly had been disowned as unreal.

The gods of the heavenly council also appear in other psalms, for example, Psalm 86:

> *There is none like you among the gods, O Lord, nor are there any works like your works. All the nations you have made shall come and worship before you, O Lord, and shall glorify your name. (Psalm 86:8-9)*

By celebrating the superiority of Yahweh over the other gods, it implies that such gods exist. There is also a hint here that the gods are connected to the nations who will eventually come to Yahweh. Psalm 89 is more specific about the assembly:

> *The heavens praise your wonders, Yahweh, your faithfulness in the assembly of the holy ones. For who in the skies can be compared to Yahweh? Who among the sons of God is like Yahweh? In the council of the holy ones God is greatly to be feared, and awesome above all who are around him. (Psalm 89:5-7)*

Here Yahweh is in the midst of the heavenly assembly, the sons of God. None of these holy beings is equal to Yahweh, and all hold him in awe. This is quite a development from the Ugarit tablets where the gods clearly do not hold El in awe although they recognise him as the supreme authority and their father. The assembly of the host of heaven also appears in the book of Kings, when Yahweh seeks a false spirit to deceive Ahab into fighting a battle that he will lose:

> *"I saw Yahweh sitting on his throne, and all the host of heaven standing on his right hand and on his left. And Yahweh said, 'Who will entice Ahab, that he may go up and fall at Ramoth-gilead?' And one suggested this and another said that. Then a spirit came forward and stood before Yahweh and said 'I will entice him.'" (1 Kings 22:19-21)*

➢   **In Judaism, the divine council was recognised as having seventy members and was conflated with the Sanhedrin, the same body that tries Jesus and condemns him to death.**

There is one biblical source in which the assembly is numbered at seventy, in a passage supposedly about seventy elders. On Mount Sinai, Yahweh

promises Moses that he will reveal himself to all the people. They are to
gather around the mountain and ascend on the signal of the blowing of
a ram's horn.[6] But Yahweh then contradicts himself by telling Moses that
the people are not to come onto the mountain, and only Moses and Aaron
are to go up.[7] A little later, there is another change. Now it is a larger
group who will see God:

> *Then he said to Moses, "Come up to Yahweh, you and Aaron, Nadab,*
> *and Abihu, and seventy of the elders of Israel, and worship from afar.*
> *Moses alone shall come near to Yahweh, but the others shall not come*
> *near. Nor shall the people come up with him." (Exodus 24:1-2)*

Nadab and Abihu are two sons of Aaron, so the three of them represent the priesthood. They ascend the mountain together with the seventy
elders and see God:

> *Then Moses and Aaron, Nadab, and Abihu, went up with seventy of*
> *the elders of Israel, and saw the God [Elohim] of Israel. Under his feet*
> *was something like a pavement of sapphire stone, as clear as the very*
> *sky. But he did not lay his hand on the chief men of the people of Israel.*
> *They saw God [Elohim] and ate and drank. (Exodus 24:9-11)*

The elders are given a day-trip with a private viewing of God and gour-
met catering. They have been taken up to heaven; the transparent stone
paving under the feet of God represents the sky. Why do they eat and
drink in God's presence? The word for God here is Elohim (El) rather than
Yahweh. The seventy elders are eating and drinking with El, just as the
seventy Canaanite gods in the heavenly assembly eat and drink with El.
The elders have gone up a mountain, and the divine assembly meet on
a mountain. A source about the divine assembly (the seventy gods) has
been misunderstood and applied to the human assembly (the seventy
elders who form a proto-Sanhedrin).

We have seen how, in the original myth, the seventy angels put Christ
to death. In the gospels, it is the Sanhedrin, the council of seventy elders,
that tries Jesus and condemns him to death. Is this another instance of
confusion between the human and the divine council?

> ➤ The gods in the assembly were the sons of El, which is why the angels are called the "sons of God".

In Canaan, the gods of the assembly were the sons of El and Asherah. This gave rise to a phrase used for the angels; they are "the sons of God". In Genesis, these sons of God descend to take wives:

> And it came to pass when man began to multiply on the face of the earth and daughters were born to them, that the sons of God saw that the daughters of man were beautiful. And they took wives for themselves of any they chose. (Genesis 6:1-2)

The "sons of God" here are the fallen angels. In Job, we have a more nuanced view, in which the sons of God form Yahweh's court:

> One day, the sons of God came to present themselves before Yahweh, and Satan [the Adversary] also came among them. Yahweh said to Satan, "From where have you come?" Satan answered Yahweh and said, "From going to and fro in the earth, and from walking up and down in it." (Job 1:6-7)

We have here another image of the heavenly assembly. The sons of God wait upon Yahweh like courtiers and ministers upon a king. Among their number is Satan; the word means the Adversary or accuser. Satan is an angel, one of the seventy, and in Job, he functions as chief prosecutor in the heavenly council. He travels the world, observing the sins of humans and brings their cases to Yahweh for judgement. Job is righteous, but Satan persuades Yahweh to test him. So God inflicts a series of disasters on Job who loses all his possessions, his house, and his children. He is even visited with a plague of boils. Job is instinctively faithful to God under his misfortunes, but eventually, even he begins to question God's moral authority for inflicting such evil upon him. For perhaps the first time in human history, God feels the need to justify himself before man. In some of the finest writing from the ancient world, he shows Job just how different is the perspective of the creator of all things. In one passage, God ironically asks Job if he were present at the creation:

> Where were you when I laid the foundations of the earth? Tell me, if you have understanding. Who determined its measurements? Surely you know! Or who stretched the measuring line upon it? On what were its foundations sunk, or who laid its cornerstone, when the morning stars sang together and all the sons of God shouted for joy? (Job 38:4-7)

The angels, the sons of God, were present at the creation of the earth. They are the "morning stars", an expression which goes back to the Canaanite gods who were worshipped as the "host of heaven", the stars and planets.

Gods of the nations

➢ **Each of the seventy shepherd angels was the divine ruler of one of the seventy nations.**

In the Animal Apocalypse, each of the seventy shepherd angels rules for one period. The word "shepherd" implies that they are rulers. So who did they rule? A clue lies in the fact that there are seventy of them. Traditionally there were seventy (or seventy-two) nations, excluding Israel. This correspondence suggests that each of the shepherds was the angelic ruler of a nation.

We find precisely this idea expressed in Deuteronomy, in a textual variation preserved in the Septuagint and the Dead Sea scrolls which is likely to be earlier than the Masoretic equivalent:

> *When the Most High assigned the nations their inheritance, when he separated mankind, he fixed the territories of nations according to the number of the sons of God. Yahweh share is his nation, Jacob is his allotted inheritance. (Deuteronomy 32:8-9 LXX)*

Here the number of nations was made to equal to the number of the sons of God. Genesis 10 enumerates the nations which emerge from the descendants of the sons of Noah; Japheth has fourteen descendants; Ham has thirty; and Shem twenty-six. There are seventy named descendants in total corresponding to the traditional seventy nations. This disregards Nimrod who would appear to be an addition to the genealogy. The Septuagint has seventy-two names rather than seventy, so sometimes it is said that there were seventy-two nations.

The implication of the Deuteronomy passage is that there must be either seventy or seventy-two sons of God, each of whom has been given a nation to rule. Israel (Jacob) is not among the nations listed in Genesis but emerged later; it is not ruled by one of the seventy but by Yahweh. There is another relevant passage in Deuteronomy:

> *And beware not to raise your eyes to heaven, and see the sun and the moon and the stars, all the host of heaven, and be drawn away and bow*

down and worship them, things that Yahweh your God has allotted to
all the nations under the whole heaven. (Deuteronomy 4:19)

The nations belong to the host of heaven. The Israelites are warned not to worship the host because, unlike the nations, they belong to Yahweh. We can see how this idea of the shepherd angels as the rulers of the nations has emerged. Each people had their own gods, and so we get the idea that a different god ruled each nation. The Israelites made themselves a special case; they were the chosen people of Yahweh/El who created the whole universe. So the other nations were assigned to the sons of El, the lesser gods under El. With the development of monotheism, these seventy gods became seventy angels. And since the Israelites regarded the nations as evil, this meant that the seventy angels must also be evil.

Angelic princes

➢ **From the same era as the Animal Apocalypse, we can find angels regarded as the "princes" of specific nations. They represent that nation in the heavenly court.**

Further evidence for the nations having their own angelic kings comes in two books from the Maccabean era (second century BC); Daniel and Jubilees. The book of Daniel was the last written of the books included in the Hebrew Bible and was of great importance to Christianity. The section starts with Daniel seeing a vision of a terrifying man, described in terms similar to Jesus in Revelation; he has a face like lightning, eyes that are flaming torches and arms and legs of bronze.[8] Who is this man? The author of Revelation thinks he is Jesus, but his original identity in Daniel is less certain. He might be Gabriel who also appears in visions to Daniel at 8:16 and 9:21, but perhaps he is a form of the Christ, a divine figure higher than Gabriel. This man explains why he has not come earlier:

However, the prince of the kingdom of Persia withstood me twenty-one
days, but Michael, one of the chief princes, came to help me, for I was left
alone with the kings of Persia. Now I have come to make you understand
what is to happen to your people in the latter days. (Daniel 10:13-14)

The "princes" must be angels because the archangel Michael is called a "prince". The man-angel of the vision has struggled with the angelic "prince of Persia" and only succeeds with the help of Michael. Who are the "kings of Persia"? Perhaps the succession of human kings. The vision occurs in the reign of Cyrus, the Persian ruler who allowed the Jews to return to Jerusalem. This passage implies that this happy outcome was due to the man in the vision who prevailed over the angelic prince of Persia. As a result of this victory, the human king of Persia, Cyrus, has a good spirit towards the Jews.

This reflects the principle that what happens in heaven, happens on earth. Political and military struggles are the visible manifestation of struggles between angels. The story explains why, occasionally, a gentile ruler, such as Cyrus, will act benevolently towards the Jews. The angelic shepherds of the nations will always oppose Israel in the heavenly court. But if the judgement is made in the Jews favour, then the human king will be divinely influenced to be friendly towards them. In Daniel, the battle with the prince of Persia is not yet over:

> So he said "Do you know why I have come to you? I must return now to fight against the prince of Persia; and when I go forth, behold, the prince of Greece will come. But I will tell you what is inscribed in the book of truth. No one upholds me against them except Michael, your prince. (Daniel 10:20-21)

Cyrus may permit the Jews to return, but the future kings of Persia will also have to be influenced to be favourably inclined towards them. And after Persian domination, the prince of Greece will come in. This alludes to the conquests of Alexander the Great who defeated the Persians. The "prince of Greece" is not the human Alexander, but the angel of the Greeks. He will rule the vast kingdom which Alexander established and the Hellenistic successor kingdom, the Seleucid Empire. This angelic prince is a bitter enemy of the Jews, and his evil will reach its climax in the reign of Antiochus IV Epiphanes, which is when the book of Daniel was written.

We learn here that Michael is the prince of the Jews, and that only he and the angel of the vision are on the Jews' side. Michael plays the same role in a description of the end times:

> At that time Michael, the great prince who stands over your people, shall arise. There shall be a time of trouble, such as never occurred since the beginning of the nations until that time. But at that time your people, everyone whose name shall be found written in the book, shall be delivered. And many of those who sleep in the dust of the earth shall awake, some to everlasting life, and some to shame and everlasting contempt. (Daniel 12:1-2)

In one tradition, Michael is the angelic prince of Israel. However, there is an alternative tradition in which the prince of Israel is the heavenly

Messiah, the Son of Man. In Daniel, we find ambiguity between these two traditions. In the above passage, the redeemer is Michael, not Christ, but it has one crucial link with Christianity. The return from exile is also the resurrection of the dead, with the good waking to everlasting life and the bad to everlasting shame.

The idea that evil angels or spirits ruled the nations is also found in the Book of Jubilees, which is an expansion of the Genesis account, drawing heavily upon the Book of Enoch. There are links between Daniel and Jubilees, both of which measure time in weeks of years. Jubilees uses a unit of seven weeks of years, that is forty-nine years, called a "jubilee". The book organises events into these jubilees.

The author of Jubilees makes a fundamental distinction between Israel, the chosen of God, and the nations:

> ...because there are many nations and many people, and they all belong to him, but over all of them he caused spirits to rule so that he might lead them astray from following him. But over Israel he did not cause any spirit or angel to rule because he alone is their ruler and he will protect them and he will seek for them at the hand of his angels and at the hand of his spirits and at the hand of all his authorities so that he might guard them... (Jubilees 15:31-32)[9]

According to Jubilees, the nations are under the rule of "spirits" or angels, but there is no angel or spirit in protective charge of Israel because God himself takes on that task. The spirits are the offspring of the Watchers who have been imprisoned before the flood. One significant difference with the Book of Enoch is that in Jubilees the Watchers had been sent to earth by God in order to rule.[10] This is very similar to the form of the myth that must underly the parable of the tenants. However, the basic story in Jubilees follows Enoch: while on earth, the Watchers see that the daughters of men are beautiful and take them as wives. God, witnessing the corruption of humanity, decides to wipe clean the earth with the flood. The author of Jubilees is trying to address the problem implicit in the Enoch account—why does evil continue after the flood? His solution is that some of the Watchers' offspring, the evil spirits, must have survived the flood and infected Noah's grandsons, the nations. Although Noah prayed to God that all the spirits should be imprisoned, the chief of the spirits Mastema (Satan) requested that 10% should be retained to do his bidding, and surprisingly God agreed.[11]

We can find something similar in the 8th-9th century commentary, Pirke de Rabbi Eliezer. In response to the construction of the tower of Babel under Nimrod, God decides to intervene:

The Holy One, blessed be he, called to the 70 angels who surround the throne of his glory. And he said to them: come let us descend and let us confuse the 70 nations and the 70 languages. (Pirke de Rabbi Eliezer Ch. 24)[12]

They all descend and cast lots for the nations, with the seed of Abraham falling to the Holy One. Once again, the seventy nations each have an angelic ruler, with Israel ruled directly by God. This is from a relatively late Jewish rabbinical source, but we can find the same idea in an earlier Christian gnostic codex. We have seen already how in the Origin of the World, the archon Sabaoth represents the lower Yahweh. He is attended by seventy-two gods who rule the different nations:

"Furthermore, from this chariot, the 72 gods took shape; they took shape that they might rule over the 72 languages of the peoples." (On the Origin of the World, NHC II (5) 105:13-16)[13]

So the seventy-two gods before the holy chariot rule over the seventy-two peoples.

The princes in 3 Enoch

➤ **In 3 Enoch, which contains material going back to the Maccabean era, seventy-two angels rule the seventy-two nations. These angels attend the heavenly law court, where some of them prosecute Israel.**

The third book of Enoch is a Hebrew text dating from the fifth or sixth century AD.[14] Although relatively late, 3 Enoch is a repository of a mix of traditions, many of which are much earlier than the work itself and which may go back to the Maccabean era. This extraordinary text also has seventy-two angelic rulers:

Above them are 72 princes of kingdoms in the height, corresponding to the 72 nations in the world. All of them are crowned with kingly crowns, clothed in regal dress, and decked with royal jewels. All of them ride on royal horses and grasp kingly sceptres in their hands. (3 Enoch 17:8)[15]

Of particular interest is the description of the heavenly law court:

> *Whenever the Great Law Court sits in the height of the heaven of*
> *'Arabot, only the great princes who are called YHWH by the name of*
> *the Holy One, blessed be he, are permitted to speak. How many princes*
> *are there? There are 72 princes of kingdoms in the world, not counting*
> *the Prince of the World, who speaks in favour of the world before the*
> *Holy One, blessed be he, every day at the hour when the book is opened*
> *in which every deed in the world is recorded, as it is written, "A court*
> *was held, and the books were opened." (3 Enoch 30:1-2)[16]*

The law court of seventy/seventy-two is a heavenly Sanhedrin. In 3
Enoch, two of the princes are given individual identities:

> *Every day Satan sits with Samma'el, Prince of Rome, and with Dubbi'el,*
> *Prince of Persia, and they write down the sins of Israel on tablets and*
> *give them to the Seraphim to bring them before the holy one, blessed be*
> *he, so that he should destroy Israel from the world. (3 Enoch 26:12)[17]*

This time Rome is substituted for Greece as the inveterate enemy of the
Jews. The two princes attempt to prosecute Israel before the heavenly court
seeking a death sentence, but each day the Seraphim burn the tablets.

The end of the nations

➢ **In the Gospel of Philip, there is a saying that implies that the**
nations will cease to exist.

When Christ finally establishes his kingdom, he will destroy the angelic
rulers, and the nations will no longer exist as separate entities. This is
reflected by a story in the second-century Gospel of Philip in which Jesus
is a dyer mixing different colours:

> *The Lord went into the dye works of Levi. He took 72 different colours*
> *and threw them into the vat. He took them out all white. And he said,*
> *"Even so has the Son of Man come as a dyer". (Gospel of Philip, NHC*
> *II (3) 63:25-30)*

The seventy-two colours stand for the seventy/seventy-two nations. The
Son of Man mixes them all together so that they all become white. In the
Animal Apocalypse, the first cattle are white, and all the animals revert to
this form at the end of time. After the coming of the Son of Man, the separate nations will cease to exist. Humanity will be reunited as one people.

10

Baal, Dumuzi and Christ

The dying and resurrected gods

When scholars began to explore ancient religions, they noted some strange coincidences with Christianity. Stories of a dying and resurrected god appeared from all over the eastern Mediterranean world. These myths relate to the annual cycle of death and life in the natural world; to winter and summer, scorching heat and life-giving rain. This cycle was crucial to humanity at a time when almost everyone was a farmer. In the myths, the god would die, descending to the underworld. People would grieve; there would be nothing green, nothing growing, and humanity would face starvation. Only the intercession of a female figure, a life-giving goddess would save things. The god would return from the dead, and green life would return. The similarities with Christianity are clear.

The devil though is in the detail. It is one thing to identify common factors between the pagan myths and Christ. It is quite another thing to demonstrate that these myths have influenced Christianity. There needs to be a convincing path of influence and early evidence that such influence actually happened. One god with remarkable parallels to Christ is the Egyptian Osiris. There have always been strong cultural links between Israel and Egypt, so an impact from the cult of Osiris on proto-Christianity is clearly possible. However, we lack direct evidence.

For two other gods, Baal and Dumuzi, there is evidence for an impact on Judaism. The worship of Baal was well established in both Israel and Judah. There was a huge religious influence from Assyria in the pre-exilic period, and the cult of Inanna and Dumuzi is attested in Judah. It is also significant that Dumuzi and Baal were equated; they share many characteristics. They both have the same wife, Ishtar, who was called Inanna by the Sumerians and Astarte by the Canaanites. So Baal and Dumuzi can be treated as two names for the same god in Judah.

If there was influence from these pagan myths, then it could only relate to the pre-exilic period, the era of the Judas War. The worship of gods other than Yahweh died out among the Jews after the exile. This is an

insuperable problem for those who believe that the Jesus movement originated from pagan mythology in the first-century AD.

None of this is to say that Christ was Baal or Dumuzi. But certain
aspects of these gods transferred to the new concept of the Christ, which
emerged in response to the exile. Christ is a divine king who dies and
is resurrected. His death is the exile, the destruction of Israel and Judah,
and the rule of the seventy. His resurrection is the redemption from exile
for the Jews and, beyond them, all humanity. The myth of Christ has
emerged from a culture in which people grieved for Baal and wept for
Dumuzi. It is these ancient mysteries that provide the spiritual technology
for Christianity. There is something in the human mind that responds
to their mythic history. Death and rebirth, the coming to light through
darkness, is the essence of shamanism throughout the world.

Osiris

The cult of Isis and Osiris originated in Egypt but evolved into a mystery religion which spread across the Roman world. The best surviving
account of the myth comes from the Roman author Plutarch.[1] The god
Osiris ruled the Egyptians as a wise and benevolent pharaoh. He taught
them the arts of civilisation and gave them laws. However, his brother
Typhon (the Egyptian Set, the god of chaos) was jealous of Osiris and
desired his death. Typhon formed a group of seventy-two conspirators
and invited Osiris to a feast. At the meal, Typhon brought in a beautifully
carved chest secretly made to the exact dimensions of Osiris. Everyone
admired the chest and Typhoon jokingly offered it to the person whom
it fitted precisely. So one by one, they lay down in the chest, but it fitted
none of them. Last of all was Osiris, but as soon as he laid down in the
chest the seventy-two assassins slammed the lid shut. They secured it
with nails and sealed it with lead. Then they pushed the coffin into the
Nile, where it floated down the river and out into the sea.

The coffin was eventually washed ashore and came to rest in a clump
of heather. The heather grew all around it until the coffin was completely
hidden in the tree. A passing king saw that the tree had a most beautiful trunk and cut it down for a pillar in his palace. Meanwhile, the goddess Isis was mourning the loss of Osiris, her husband and brother. She
searched everywhere until she found the pillar and split it apart to reveal
the coffin. She opened the chest and wept over Osiris. But Typhon seeing
that Isis had retrieved the body, stole it and dismembered Osiris. The
body parts were widely scattered, but Isis retrieved them all except for
the penis, which had been swallowed by a fish.

Although Osiris remained in the underworld, he underwent some kind of resurrection. This enabled him to appear to his son Horus and train him in the arts of war. Eventually, Horus was ready. He fought Typhon and after several protracted battles, finally defeated him. The myth of the death and resurrection of Osiris was central to Egyptian religion. It gave them the promise of an afterlife providing the body was preserved as a mummy, and the correct funerary rites were fulfilled.

There are some remarkable similarities between Osiris and Christ. Both are kings, both die and are resurrected, both bring about an afterlife for their followers. But there are also differences. The resurrected Osiris stays in the underworld, and the Egyptian concept of the afterlife is very different from the Christian idea of heaven.

There are also striking parallels between the Osiris story and the idea that the seventy/seventy-two sons of God, the shepherd angels, put Christ to death. The murderers of Osiris are seventy-two in number, and like the gods of Canaan, they feast and drink in a divine assembly. But then there is much in common between the myths of the eastern Mediterranean.

Baal and Christ

There is extensive evidence for the Baal cult in both Israel and Judah. We know that Baal was worshipped alongside Asherah and Yahweh in the temple. So the cultural path for Baal influencing the Christ myth in pre-exilic times is clear and obvious. Let us now look at the specific similarities between Baal and Christ.

> ➤ **Baal rules the world as regent under El just as Christ will rule the world as regent under Yahweh/El.**

In the Canaanite myths, Baal becomes king after defeating Yam. The kingship is like a regency under El, with the king ruling both the world and the other gods. It is promised that Baal's kingdom will last forever:

> *You shall take your everlasting kingdom, your domain for ever and ever.*
> *(Baal and Yam, 2 iv 10)*[2]

This is very similar to the way Christ will rule the world at the end times under Yahweh/El. Christ's kingdom will also be everlasting: *"His kingdom will never end!" (Luke 1:33).* A similar expression is used in the Hebrew Bible to describe God's kingdom and, in the Book of Daniel, the kingdom that God will establish to replace the rule of the nations.[3]

> ➢ **Both Baal and Christ die and are resurrected, defeating death.**

The most obvious similarity is that Baal, like Christ, dies and is resurrected, so overcoming death. In the Baal myth, death is personified as the god Mot. In the Ugarit tablets, Baal has tricked Mot with a substitute son conceived from a cow. But we can see that the story contains all the elements of the real death of Baal; he goes down into the underworld, his body is buried, El and Anat grieve for him, and the rain no longer falls on the scorched land.

Has the story of Baal and Mot directly influenced Judaism and Christianity? One of the distinguishing features of Mot as the god of death is that he swallows up his victims, desiring endless supplies of human flesh. Baal warns the envoys he sends to Mot be careful lest they be swallowed like a lamb.[4] Later it is said that Baal also must go down into his mouth.[5] We find similar imagery in a prophecy in Isaiah that God *"will swallow up death forever" (Isaiah 25:8)*. And this idea is also found in Christianity. Paul talks about Christ's resurrection in terms of a conflict between Christ and death:

> *For he must reign until he has put all his enemies under his feet. The last enemy to be destroyed is death" (1 Corinthians 15:25-6).*

And he also loosely quotes the same Isaiah passage:

> *"Death has been swallowed up in victory" (I Corinthians 15:54)*

When Baal is resurrected, he reigns over the world just as Christ will reign over the world after his resurrection. It is true that there are differences. Baal and Anat defeat and kill death, yet he comes alive again. And although Baal's resurrection brings rain and a renewal of life, it is not a harbinger of a general resurrection of the dead. Mot still reigns in his kingdom.

> ➢ **The seventy sons of El and Asherah side against Baal in his conflict with Mot. Baal kills them all when he comes back to life. Similarly, the seventy shepherd angels put Christ to death, and will be destroyed after his resurrection.**

In the Ugarit tablets, although the seventy gods are the sons of El and Asherah, they are repeatedly called the "sons of Asherah", particularly in contexts where they are opposed to Baal. These other gods seem to be Baal's enemies. When Baal fights Yam, they are on Yam's side. The poem says that the "sons of the Holy One", meaning the sons of Asherah, have sent Yam gifts.[6] In The Palace of Baal when Asherah sees Baal and Anat approach, her first instinct is to be fearful for her offspring: *"Are my enemies come to smite my sons?"* (*The Palace of Baal 4 ii* 24-5). This is an odd reaction and shows the tension that existed between (i) the cult of Baal and Anat and (ii) the cult of El and Asherah.

The enmity between the sons of Asherah and Baal is most evident in the story of Baal and Mot. After Baal goes down into the underworld, the grieving Anat sarcastically calls out for Asherah and her sons to rejoice *"for mightiest Baal is dead"*.[7] When Baal returns from the underworld, he kills the sons of Asherah, smiting them with his sword.[8] After destroying the other gods, Baal sits on the throne of his kingdom.

When Mot returns to life, he asks for one of Baal's brothers to eat. But that is not what Baal sends him:

> *"But look! Baal has given me my own brothers to eat,*
> *The sons of my mother to consume."* (*Baal and Mot 6 vi 10-11*)[9]

By killing the sons of Asherah, Baal has sent them down to Mot to swallow. But they are Mot's own brothers for he is one of the sons of Asherah. No wonder the other sons are allied with Mot against Baal!

There is a striking equivalence with the tenants/shepherd angels. Christ is put to death by the tenants, but after his resurrection, he will destroy the seventy shepherds. We have seen how these seventy shepherds evolved from the same seventy sons of Asherah who seek the death of Baal and who are killed by Baal after his resurrection. Once the reborn Baal/Christ has destroyed the seventy, he will rule in his kingdom.

> ➢ **Both Baal and Jesus reject their mother and their brothers. Both are aligned closely with their father, El.**

It is not clear if Baal was originally the son of El and Asherah or if he is a foreign interloper into the Canaanite pantheon. At times it seems that the sons of Asherah are not Baal's brothers, but this is contradicted in other places. Asherah is called the "creatress of the gods", implying she is the mother of all the gods other than El. In The Palace of Baal, Anat and Baal address Asherah as their mother.[10] Later, when the sons of Asherah feast with Baal upon the completion of his house, he calls them his brothers and kinsfolk.[11] In the myths, Baal reigns as king below El and is closely associated with El, but is opposed to Asherah and her sons. When Baal dies, El mourns along with Anat, but Asherah and her sons rejoice. We will see later how Jesus, like Baal, rejects his heavenly mother and brothers in the earliest family sayings from the Jesus movement.

➤ **Both Baal and Christ have a father who lives in a house of many mansions.**

In the Gospel of John, Jesus promises his followers that he will prepare a place for them in heaven:

"In the house of my father are many mansions." (John 14:2)

The word translated here as "mansions" means "abode" or "dwelling-place". The odd expression that God's house has "many mansions" can be traced back to the Ugarit myths. The house of El is the abode of many other gods. For example, Baal dwells there before he has his own house.[12] Also Athtar, the king before Yam and Baal, does not have his own house.[13] Gods like Baal and Athtar would have their own "mansions" within their father's house.

In Ugarit, "house" stood for a temple, a meaning that was taken over into Judaism. The story of Baal's house tells us that he was first worshipped in the temple of El before getting his own dedicated temple. Baal's struggle to gain permission to build his house reflects a power struggle between the priests of El and the priests of Baal which was eventually resolved in favour of the latter. The Canaanites believed that the earthly temple was matched by a much grander house or palace in heaven. El's heavenly house would be so large that many other Gods could dwell there. We find the same concept in Judaism, where the temple is simultaneously both a building in Jerusalem and the throne room of God in the third heaven. This idea of two superimposed realities may seem a very advanced reflection of Platonic philosophy, but it actually came from Canaanite culture.

➤ **Both Baal and Christ are represented as bulls.**

The image of Baal was a bull, which was also a symbol for Yahweh before such representation was prohibited. The Messiah appears in the form of a bull at the end times in the Animal Apocalypse. In his conflict with Mot, the bull Baal mates with a heifer to produce the son who is given to Mot. This substitute Baal is reminiscent of Christ, who is also innocent but sacrificed for others. In *The Rock and the Tower*, I discuss a saying from the fragmentary Apocryphon of Ezekiel:[14]

Behold, the heifer has given birth and has not given birth.

This is consistent with other sayings concerning the virgin birth of Jesus from Mary. The cattle imagery ties in with both the Animal Apocalypse and the Baal myth.

Inanna and Dumuzi

The Sumerian myth of Inanna and Dumuzi is a variation on the theme of death and rebirth. Dumuzi is a shepherd god, and like Jesus, is the good shepherd. Inanna is the Queen of Heaven and a fertility goddess. She is the crescent moon and the evening and morning star; the planet Venus. The worship of Inanna and Dumuzi is very old, dating back to at least 2000 BC.

Inanna was a powerful goddess. On one occasion, she gets her father Enki so drunk that he grants her tremendous gifts; she is gifted the high priesthood, the kingship, and the shepherdship. She is given the sceptre, staff, measuring rod, and throne. She has the art of lovemaking and prostitution, of music and all the crafts of building and making. She has the gift of both slanderous and diplomatic speech, the power of the hero and the traitor. She has judgement and wise counsel, as well as fear and consternation. By the time Enki sobers up and realises how much he has given her, she is far away on the boat of heaven. Although he tries to bring her back, she evades him and keeps her gifts.[15]

Dumuzi and Inanna rule side by side as king and queen. At first, Inanna rejected her suitor Dumuzi because he was a rough shepherd. But after they argued, their passion grew hot. Their courtship and lovemaking are described in a poem reminiscent of The Song of Songs. From their lovemaking, the womb of Inanna produces life, all green living things, and the bounteous harvest.[16]

Although Inanna rules the heavens, she decides to make the dangerous journey to the underworld, from the great above to the great below. If she can complete this journey and return it will give her power over death as well as life. As a precaution, she clothes herself with protective ornaments and garments. But when she comes to the underworld, the seven gates are closed against her. To pass through each one, she has to pay a price, to surrender one of her adornments. Finally, at the last gate, she has to give up her robe and enters the underworld naked, as if she were a mortal woman. She greets her sister, Ereshkigal, Queen of the underworld. But the judges of the underworld condemn her and Ereshkigal strikes her dead, hanging her corpse upon a hook.

Her father, Enki, is the one who saves her. He fashions two fly-like creatures and sends them down into the underworld. They please Ereshkigal who grants them any wish, and they ask for the corpse of Inanna. It is taken down, and they sprinkle the food of life onto it, restoring the goddess. However, she is still tied to the underworld and cannot leave unless she gives a replacement in her stead. To find a substitute she returns to the surface, followed closely by the demons of the underworld. They attempt to take her loyal servant and then her two sons, but each time Inanna refuses them. Finally, she approaches Dumuzi. In the most shocking incident in the myth cycle, she fastens the eye of death on her lover and husband: "Take him. Take Dumuzi away!" The demons attack Dumuzi who flees but cannot escape them forever. Eventually they kill his body and take him down into the underworld.[17]

Inanna now weeps and searches for Dumuzi as do his mother and his loving sister, Geshtinanna who offers to share his fate. Inanna finds Dumuzi on the edges of the steppe. He will dwell in the underworld for half the year and Geshtinanna will take his place for the other half.[18]

There are multiple similarities between Dumuzi and Christ.

➢ **Both Dumuzi and Christ are shepherds.**

Dumuzi is a shepherd god and Christ is the good shepherd. He is often depicted as the shepherd carrying the sheep in early Christian art. (Jesus as good shepherd can also be explained as a contrast to the evil shepherd angels who rule the world before Christ establishes his kingdom.)

➢ **Dumuzi and Christ are both innocent, both killed as sacrifices to replace another, and both resurrected.**

One of the most striking similarities with Christianity is that Dumuzi is an innocent sacrifice who dies as a substitute for another. Early Christians portray Christ as the sacrificial lamb who dies for the sins of humankind, whereas Dumuzi dies so that his wife Inanna can be saved. Dumuzi's sacrifice has cosmic significance because Inanna is the fertility goddess, and there is no procreation without her. Both Dumuzi and Christ return fully to life, although in Dumuzi's case, it is only for half the year.

➢ **The worship of Inanna as Astarte was popular in Judah before the exile.**

There was a strong Assyrian influence on Judah following the conquest and exile of the northern kingdom of Israel. The Assyrian astral gods were adopted in Judah, most significantly Astarte, another name for Ishtar/Inanna. She is the Queen of Heaven for whom the Jewish women bake cakes:[19]

The sons gather wood, the fathers light the fire, and the women knead the dough to make cakes for the Queen of Heaven. (Jeremiah 7:18)

Women had a special role in the worship of Astarte, but here the whole family are also involved. Later, when Jeremiah has been taken to Egypt, he reproves the Jewish women for continuing their worship of "the Queen of Heaven". Their response is robust:

"We will burn incense to the Queen of Heaven and pour out drink offerings to her just as we did, we and our fathers, our kings, and our officials, in the cities of Judah and in the streets of Jerusalem." (Jeremiah 44:17)

The worship of Astarte is primarily a female activity, but the women's defence is that before the destruction of Jerusalem, the men also worshipped the goddess, right up to the court and the king.

➢   **The death of Dumuzi was mourned in the Jerusalem temple.**

The most significant link is evidence from Ezekiel that the cult of the death and rebirth of Dumuzi was practised even in the temple:

Then he brought me to the entrance of the north gate of the house of Yahweh and behold, there sat women weeping for Tammuz. (Ezekiel 8:14)

The name Tammuz is a later form of Dumuzi. So "weeping for Tammuz" is all part of the rites of the death and resurrection of the god. The mourning for Dumuzi/Tammuz would have developed from the ancient practice of mourning for Baal.

So we know that Jews before the exile were actively participating in the cult of a dying and resurrected god. This establishes a direct path of influence, for this was the same time that the Christ myth developed.

Baal as Christ

➢   **In Zechariah, the mourning for the heavenly Christ is equated to the mourning for Baal Hadad.**

The final link between Baal and Christ is the most explicit of all. There is a prophecy in Second Zechariah about one who is pierced and mourned like "Hadad-Rimmon *in the plain of Megiddo" (Zechariah 12:11).* Zechariah continues with a prophecy of a shepherd who is slaughtered and his flock scattered. In the Gospel of Mark, this prophecy is quoted after the last supper and applied by Jesus to himself. Taken together the two prophecies point to the heavenly Messiah, the divine protector of Israel and Judah, who is killed, and whose death marks the exile. Christians have always believed that both prophecies refer to Christ.

These prophecies provide an explicit link between the dying heavenly Christ and the dying Baal, as well as an implicit link to the death of Dumuzi. We know from the Ugarit tablets that the personal name of the Canaanite Baal was Hadad. As for Rimmon ("the thunderer"), this was the name of an Aramean god who was identified with Hadad.[20] So in this passage, the mourning for the dead Christ is the same as the mourning for Baal. There is also a potential link to Dumuzi through the second prophecy, which says that a shepherd has been slaughtered.

The two families

> In the gospels, Jesus appears to reject his mother and brothers.
> And yet this group led the Jesus movement and were its most
> esteemed figures.

At one point, Jesus' family pay him a visit. He is gathered with his disciples in a room when someone tells him that his "brothers and mother" are outside. Jesus' reply is dismissive. He refuses to admit his family and says that his true family are those present in the room who do the will of the Father. They are his mother and his brothers. Both the Thomas and Mark versions are very similar except that Mark adds "sisters" to "brothers" to make it clear that women are among Jesus' followers.

Jesus' rejection of his brothers and mother gives the historical Jesus school great difficulties. The first time we get a real glimpse of the Jesus movement, through the letters of Paul, it is led by a Jerusalem group called the "brothers of the Lord" under a leader named James who is "the brother of the Lord". The historical Jesus school has to face the embarrassing fact that the family supposedly rejected by Jesus is apparently in charge of the Jesus movement in the mid-50s. Nor does this apply only to the brothers. Mary, the mother of Jesus, is the most revered figure in Christianity other than Jesus himself. She often seems to be on almost the same level as Jesus. Yet, in this gospel story, she is pointedly rejected by Jesus.

To explain away this blatant inconsistency, the historical Jesus school resorts to the usual "it just so happened" assumptions. It just so happened that although the brothers of Jesus rejected Jesus and were rejected by him, they became reconciled with his movement after his death. It just so happened that the movement then decided to appoint the brothers as its leaders, even though they had not followed Jesus and would have been ignorant of his teachings. It just so happened that after the death of Jesus' rejected mother Mary, Christians invented a new Mary who was a perpetual virgin, had conceived from the holy spirit, and was the co-redeemer of humanity. Really?

When Paul travels to Jerusalem to resolve his differences with James "the brother of the Lord", he meets a group consisting of James, John and Peter. It just so happens that these are also the names of the three leading disciples in the gospels. But in the gospels these three are not the brothers of Jesus—James and John, the sons of Zebedee, and Simon Peter are all fishermen. The coincidence of three names is suspicious and unlikely to arise by chance. In *The Rock and the Tower*, I show that the three brothers are indeed the same as three disciples, being the adopted sons of the shaman Mary. Zebedee was probably Mary's brother, which would explain why his two sons, James and John Mark, occupied the top two positions in her movement.

> ➢ **All the earliest family sayings have the same form; Jesus has two families, one rejected and one accepted. The accepted mother and brothers are Mary and her adopted sons; the rejected family are Asherah and the sons of God.**

The earliest sayings and stories about Jesus' family are analysed in the *The Rock and the Tower*.[21] These passages come from both the Gospel of Thomas and the gospels. It is remarkable that every single one of these early sources takes the same form:

1. Jesus always has two families.
2. He rejects one of these families in favour of the other.

The rejected family involves a mother, either alone, or with her sons. In one single Thomas saying, the rejected family also includes a father. The favoured family always has a father, mother and brothers.

The historical Jesus school has great problems with this "one family rejected; one family accepted" formula. If Jesus were a man, he could not have had two families. Hence the "it just so happened" assumptions. The problem is resolved if Jesus is spiritual and has both a heavenly and human family.

In the visit saying, Jesus is appearing to the disciples through the medium of the shaman. The mother and brothers who are "outside", are not physically present; they are his heavenly family. Jesus rejects them in favour of the people in the room. It is the human disciples who are his true mother and brothers. They do the will of his ultimate father, the higher Yahweh, from whom Jesus has descended. We can reconstruct the two families of Jesus:

Jesus' true family

The mother is Mary the shaman, called both the Virgin and the Magdalene.

The brothers are Paul's "brothers of the Lord" including James, John Mark and Simon Peter. They are the adopted sons of Mary.

The Father is the higher Yahweh.

Jesus' rejected, false family

The mother is Asherah.

The brothers are "the sons of God" also known as "the sons of Asherah", "the host of heaven", and the seventy shepherds.

Normally there is no father, but in one Thomas saying he is the lower Yahweh, the angel of the Name.

The family sayings record a revolutionary reversal between gods and humans. Through Jesus, humans partake of the nature of the ultimate father, and so are higher than the angels who were previously worshipped as gods. The same idea can be found in Paul: *"Do you not know that we shall judge the angels?"* (1 Corinthians 6:3).

PART THREE

THE ALMANAC

11

Cosmic Escalation

The end of Judah

In 588 BC the armies of Nebuchadnezzar, king of Babylon, set siege to Jerusalem. The king of Judah, Zedekiah, had revolted against Nebuchadnezzar, the very man who had placed him on the throne. He had formed an alliance with Egypt. Now Nebuchadnezzar had come to enact a brutal punishment for Zedekiah's disloyalty with Babylon's greatest enemy. The Babylonians had already ravaged Judah. Many towns, including the second city Lachish, had been destroyed and others such as Ramah and Mizpah, were in Babylonian hands. However, Jerusalem was well fortified, and the walls were strong. There was hope when Egypt mounted a bid to come to Judah's rescue. But the attempt failed and gave Jerusalem only a brief respite. It became all too clear that Zedekiah had made a fatal mistake—he had backed the wrong horse. In the third year of the siege, 586 BC, the Babylonians breached the city walls. Ancient warfare was brutal, and the Babylonians would have been infuriated by the lengthy siege. Many of the citizens were put to the sword. The king was forced to watch while all his sons were executed in front of his eyes, before those same eyes were gouged out. He was taken to Babylon in shackles, probably for execution for we hear no more about him. Along with the former king, a large number of captives marched in chains to start their new lives as slaves. Jerusalem was plundered, its walls demolished, the temple and city were burnt to the ground. The kingdom of Judah was no more.

The exile that started with the Judas War and the defeat of Israel by the Assyrians had reached its conclusion. Judah had survived the period of Assyrian domination as a client state. But the Assyrian Empire had begun a rapid collapse, and faced rebellion on multiple fronts. By 640 BC the tide seemed to have been turned under a strong king, Ashurbanipal, who had regained control of the empire. Under his rule, Assyria entered a period of prosperity, but it was the calm before the storm. After the death of Ashurbanipal, the Babylonians successfully revolted. Nabopolassar was declared King of Babylon in 626 BC and defeated an Assyrian army outside Babylon shortly afterwards.

Recent scientific evidence points to climate change playing a key role in the rise and fall of the neo-Assyrian Empire. The expansion coincided with a very unusual two-hundred-year wet period. This era of high rainfall would have brought previously barren land into cultivation, which would explain why the Assyrians were eager to move conquered peoples into their homeland. With the expansion of the food supply, the military resources of Assyria increased greatly. This benign era ended with several decades of drought, and it was in this period that the Assyrian Empire collapsed. The crops would have failed year after year, and the occupants of the newly cultivated land would have faced starvation.[1]

The power vacuum created in the Levant by the decline of Assyria was filled by Egypt. It seems that the two superpowers became allies in this period, another indicator of Assyrian weakness. Because Assyria had to withdraw its forces back to the homeland, it accepted the inevitable Egyptian advance. Did these events play out in Judah's favour? It used to be believed that Judah under Josiah was able to recreate something like the traditional kingdom of Israel under David. However, the archaeological evidence only supports a very minor expansion of Judah to encompass the Bethel area a few miles to the north of the old border. Judah simply switched masters, from Assyria to Egypt.[2]

The situation though was volatile, with a new superpower on the rise.[3] In 612 BC the Babylonians and their allies, the Medes, took the Assyrian capital, Nineveh. Egypt, under Pharaoh Necho II, came to the Assyrians' aid at Harran, but the attempt failed. The proud empire of Assyria had met its end. Babylon and Egypt now squared up against each other, and Judah had the misfortune of being in the middle. The Judean king, Josiah, had been killed by Pharaoh Necho who also deposed his son and successor Jehoahaz. Necho appointed another of Josiah's sons, Eliakim, called Jehoiakim, as the new king. Judah was now completely under Egyptian domination. But in 605 BC a seismic event rocked the ancient world: the Babylonians under their general Nebuchadnezzar defeated the Egyptian army at Carchemish. Shortly afterwards Nebuchadnezzar became King of Babylon upon the death of Nabopolassar. He followed up Carchemish with further victories over the Egyptians. Jehoiakim was obliged to switch allegiance to Babylon.

Babylonian supremacy must have seemed inevitable. Yet in 601 BC there was a setback. The campaign against Egypt in that year ended in heavy casualties and Babylon was forced to withdraw. Jehoiakim took this opportunity to restore his allegiance to the Egyptians. He had underestimated Nebuchadnezzar. The Babylonian king marched on Jerusalem in 598 BC and placed it under siege. Jehoiakim died in mysterious circumstances and his 18-year-old son Jeconiah became king. The city's position was desperate and a surrender was quickly negotiated. Jeconiah was deposed, to be taken to Babylon along with his mother and many of the Jerusalem elite. The Judean exile had started.

The Babylonians were relatively benign rulers by the standards of the time, and they were mild after this first visit. They placed Jeconiah's uncle Zedekiah on the throne, and life in Judah continued more or less as normal as a vassal state of Babylon. But the Egyptians had not gone away, and nor had Judean over-optimism. In 591 BC, the Egyptian king visited Syria and Palestine, attempting to build support. He would seem to have succeeded with Judah, for Zedekiah switched his allegiance and withhold tribute from Babylon. By the honour code of the ancient world, this was a betrayal of his Babylonian liege lord, and it brought down the wrath of Nebuchadnezzar. It led to the destruction of Jerusalem and its temple. And to two religions that changed the world.

Two explanations, two religions

> The Judeans and Israelites had two opposing, but interacting, explanations for the exile; one led to Judaism and the other to Christianity. The Israelite approach involved a "cosmic escalation" of the exile, but we also find evidence for this in the Judean Bible.

The destruction of first Israel and then Judah sent the Jews into trauma. Surely this meant that the gods of Assyria and Babylon were more powerful than Yahweh, the God of the Israelites? The Jews, however, had evolved an entirely new abstract conception of God as the supreme all-powerful creator of the universe. Israel and Judah were his portion, his chosen people. How could this supreme God be defeated by the lesser gods of the nations? Two explanations evolved to address this dissonance:

Explanation 1 (that of Judah): Israel and Judah had been justly punished by Yahweh. It was all the fault of Israel who had abandoned the covenant with Yahweh by falling into Canaanite ways. Israel was punished first, while Judah was given a second chance. Unfortunately, under King Manasseh (named ominously after a tribe of Israel), Judah followed Israel's corruption and so shared her fate. It was Yahweh who had summoned his servants, the kings of Assyria and Babylon, to attack Israel and Judah. They were the stick he wielded to beat his recalcitrant children. But Yahweh would eventually redeem his chosen people and punish the nations who had exceeded his instructions.

Explanation 2 (that of the Israelites): The world was under the control of evil powers who ruled the nations. Chief among these evil powers was the king of Assyria/Babylon. These archons had conspired to put to death the true son and heir, the Christ, the heavenly ruler of Israel and Judah. The ordinary people of Israel and Judah shared in Christ's fate as innocent sacrificial victims. They had been betrayed by the Judean elite of Jerusalem; the kings, the court, the priests. Eventually, Christ would be resurrected and would defeat the evil powers to redeem his people, whether Israelite, Judean or gentile. The old world would come to an end, and a new perfect world would replace it.

One explanation led to Judaism, the other to Christianity. But the two were not as distinct as the above classification implies. There was a degree of overlap. The second explanation required "cosmic escalation", an expansion of the concept of exile to the cosmic scale. Cosmic escalation has multiple dimensions:

- The exile of Israel and Judah becomes the exile of the whole of humanity.
- Exile under the Assyrians and Babylonians becomes exile under the seventy, the host of heaven, led by the angelic king of Babylon.
- The expected earthly Messiah becomes the heavenly Messiah.
- The return from exile and the destruction of Babylon becomes the apocalypse.
- The second rebuilt temple is invalid, and there will come a new temple "not built by hands".
- The seventy years of exile become a much greater span of time.

Many of the concepts behind cosmic escalation already existed in Israelite and Canaanite religion before the exile. We can be sure that cosmic escalation of the exile did indeed take place because the evidence lies within the Hebrew Bible.

The King of Babylon

➢ **In the Bible, the heavenly king of Babylon and Assyria represents the chief of the angelic powers who rule the world. He is also called Satan.**

There are passages in the Hebrew Bible that indicate that the "king of Babylon" was regarded as a supernatural being, the leader of the seventy angels. He is also Satan, meaning the adversary or prosecutor. This heavenly king ruled both the Assyrian and Babylonian empires which were regarded by the Jews as two successive phases of a single entity. The proud ancient city of Babylon had been incorporated into the Neo-Assyrian Empire as the chief city alongside the capital Nineveh. Culturally, Assyria and Babylon were two variations on the same Mesopotamian civilisation. In prophetic literature, such as Isaiah, the two are often conflated together and used interchangeably. This suited prophetical exegesis, as prophecies relating to Assyria, could be applied to Babylon, and vice versa.

> **Nimrod is the first human king of Babylon and Assyria.**

The first hint of the importance of the king of Babylon comes from the Genesis genealogies and the account of the mighty hunter Nimrod:

> *And Cush was the father of Nimrod; he began to be a mighty one on the earth. He was a mighty hunter before Yahweh; so it is said, "Like Nimrod, a mighty hunter before Yahweh." And the beginning of his kingdom was Babylon, Erech, Accad, and Calneh, in the land of Shinar. From that land, he went forth to Assyria, where he built Nineveh, Rehoboth-Ir, Calah, and Resen, which is between Nineveh and Calah— the same is a great city. (Genesis 10:8-12)*

Nimrod is the king of a number of places including Babylon and Assyria. He builds both the cities of Babylon and Nineveh. The passage is odd in the context of the genealogy. The enumeration of the sons of Cush in Genesis 10:7 does not include Nimrod, so why mention him later? Also, Asshur (Assyria) is listed separately as one of the sons of Shem.[4] Another problem is that Cush is the patriarch of the African nations to the south. Why place Mesopotamia, which lies to the north, under Cush rather than under Shem where it belongs? All of these features point to the Nimrod passage as being a later interpolation into the genealogy.

Making Nimrod a son of Cush gives Babylon/Assyria a disreputable family; Nimrod is closely related to that other evil empire, the Egyptians, and to the despised Canaanites. We should note that Nimrod's cities are split into two lists, the first headed up by Babylon, and the second by Nineveh, the respective capitals of the Babylonian and Assyrian empires. Nineveh only came to prominence in the neo-Assyrian era, so we are not dealing with a very early source.

Nimrod is called a "mighty one on the earth". The same word translated as "mighty", or "giant", is used earlier in Genesis to describe the children of the fallen angels.[5] In the Septuagint, Nimrod is a "giant". Some scholars have attempted to identify Nimrod with the Sumerian god Ninurta or with the god of Babylon, Marduk, both of whom were associated with hunting. However, all attempts to explain the name "Nimrod" as that of an Assyrian or Babylonian god (or hero, or king) have failed.[6] This leaves us with the Hebrew meaning of Nimrod; "we have rebelled." It signifies the rebellion of the fallen angels under their leader, the king of Babylon. The name has been invented by the Jewish scribes.

Nimrod may well have started as Marduk—we should note that Nimrod begins at Babylon and only later establishes the Assyrian cities. But by the time of the interpolation, he would be regarded as the heavenly ruler of Babylon and Assyria, one of the seventy under Yahweh. The kings of Assyria and Babylon were associated with hunting, as demonstrated by the lion-hunt reliefs from Nineveh. So it is appropriate that their divine ruler should be a hunter. The association of Nimrod with Babylon enables us to date the interpolation to after the fall of Jerusalem.

➢   **The nations build the tower-temple of Babel (Babylon) to challenge the power of Yahweh.**

The story of the tower of Babel comes after the creation of the nations from the sons of Noah. The people of the nations speak one language and travel together to a *"plain in the land of Shinar" (Genesis 11:2)* which connects the story to Nimrod. They resolve to bake bricks, to make mortar, and to build a city and a great tower, high enough to reach heaven. When Yahweh sees the height of the tower, he is alarmed:

> And Yahweh said, "If they have begun to do this as one people speaking one language, then nothing they propose will be beyond them. Come, let us go down and confuse their language so that they will not understand each other." So Yahweh scattered them from there all over the face of the earth, and they stopped building the city. That is why it is called Babel, for there Yahweh confused the language of the whole world, and from there Yahweh scattered them all over the face of the earth. (Genesis 11:6-9)

This passage raises many questions. To whom is Yahweh talking? Why is the supreme God and creator of the universe scared that people will build a tower to heaven? The "tower of Babel" reflects a pun with *"balal"* meaning "confused". Babel, though, is the same as Babylon—the story is about the building of the city and temple of Babylon. We have seen the "tower" (*migdal*) stood for the temple and is the root of the title "Magdalene". The tower as temple goes back to Canaanite tower-temples, and the ziggurat temples of the middle east. The tower of Babel is believed to relate to the ziggurat temple of Marduk at Babylon, the Etemenanki, which stood over 90m high.

The story is about the angelic rebellion. The seventy nations are ruled by the seventy angels. Yahweh is afraid that the angels under their leader, the divine king of Babylon (Nimrod/Marduk), will succeed in conquering heaven using the tower-temple as siege engine. To weaken the power of the seventy, Yahweh splits the nations and gives them different languages. The seventy will now be divided and will fight wars against each other.

The author of Matthew is using a source that reflects this battle for heaven led by the king of Babylon:

> *From the days of John the Baptist until now, the kingdom of the heavens is taken by violence and the violent seize it. (Matthew 11:12)*

Why does the author of Matthew think that heaven has been under assault since "the days of John the Baptist", only a few months earlier in the context of the gospel? The author of Matthew follows Mark in believing that John is the returned Elijah: *"he is Elijah who is to come" (Matthew 11:14)*. And Elijah is frequently confused with Enoch because both were taken up to heaven alive. The original source must have referred to Enoch: "from the days of the one taken up to heaven". This makes much more sense. Enoch was taken up to avoid the evil of the fallen angels who then attempted to take heaven by force.

➤ **The king of Babylon, a heavenly power, attempts a coup against Yahweh.**

Most significant of all is a passage in Isaiah which shows the king of Babylon as a heavenly power rebelling against Yahweh. The song in Isaiah 14 looks forward to the fall of Babylon and her king. In parts, the king of Babylon is clearly a supernatural being:

> *How you have fallen from heaven, morning star, son of the dawn! You have been cast down to the ground, destroyer of nations. For you said in your heart: "I will ascend into heaven, I will raise my throne above the stars of God. I will sit on the mount of assembly, on the sides of the north. I will ascend above the heights of the clouds; I will make be like the most high." But you will be brought down to Sheol, to the lowest sides of the pit. (Isaiah 14:12-15)*

The "morning star" or "the shining one" (translated by the King James Bible as "Lucifer") is the morning apparition of the planet Venus which far outshines all the stars in the sky. Angels are called "morning stars" in Job when God describes how he created the world: *"When the morning stars sang together, and all the sons of God shouted for joy" (Job 38:7).* "Morning star" was also a title for Christ, something which caused much confusion.

The king of Babylon attempts to raise his throne higher than the stars of God. This attempt to supersede Yahweh and occupy the throne of heaven reflects the original myth of the rebellion of the fallen angels. It also echoes the story of the tower of Babel. In the Isaiah passage, the king lays claim to sit on the "mount of assembly" on "the sides of the north" which indicates Mount Zephon. The king of Babylon attempts to usurp the place of El as head of the assembly of gods. The Isaiah passage predicts that this rebellion will be unsuccessful. The king of Babylon will be cast into the pit, the same fate as the shepherd angels in the Animal Apocalypse.

The destruction of the host of heaven

➢   **The "host of heaven" will be destroyed at the restoration from exile.**

At the end of the exile, the nations who had oppressed the people of Israel and Judah will be defeated. But the prophetic promise went further than this. The gods/angels who represented the nations would be destroyed. There are passages in Isaiah that reflect this idea of the greater cosmic redemption from exile:

> *It shall come to pass, on that day Yahweh will punish the host of heaven on high, and the kings of the earth, on the earth. They will be gathered together as prisoners in a pit, they will be shut up in a prison, and after many days they will be punished. Then the moon will be confounded and the sun ashamed… (Isaiah 24:21-23)*

The sun and moon were worshipped in pre-exilic Israel and Judah, which explains why they will be punished alongside the host of heaven. The confinement in the pit reflects the fate of the fallen angels and the shepherds in the Animal Apocalypse. Another passage starts with Yahweh's fury against the nations:

> *For the anger of Yahweh is against all nations, and his fury against all their armies. He will devote them to destruction. He will give them over to slaughter. (Isaiah 34:2)*

This destruction of the nations also involves the destruction of the stars of heaven:

> *All the host of heaven will be dissolved, and the heavens rolled up like*
> *a scroll, and all their host will fall like withered leaves from the vine,*
> *like fruit falling from the fig tree. When my sword has drunk its fill in*
> *the heavens, then it will come down upon Edom, and upon the people*
> *of my curse for judgement. (Isaiah 34:4-5)*

The destruction of the universe is followed by a curse against the minor kingdom of Edom. This may seem strangely parochial and jarring. But the idea that cosmic forces governed the nations goes back to the time when the enemies of Israel were the insignificant surrounding kingdoms.

The three ages of exile

> ➤ **The exile is extended under cosmic escalation. We find three**
> **different interpretations of the length of the exile ranging from**
> **seventy years to seventy generations. All three levels are repre-**
> **sented in the Almanac.**

Under cosmic escalation, the seventy years of exile predicted by Jeremiah is reinterpreted as a longer time frame. In the Animal Apocalypse, the seventy shepherd angels each rule for a period, giving a total duration of the world of seventy periods. Comparison with the seventy generations for which the fallen angels are imprisoned in the pit shows that each period is one generation. This gives the highest level of exile, with humanity under the angels for seventy generations. But there is also an intermediary timescale between the seventy years and seventy generations. So the exile exists on three levels, each embedded within the next like Russian dolls:

1. The physical exile lasts for a notional 70 years. This is equal to two generations.
2. There is an extended exile, under which the duration is multiplied by seven. The book of Daniel has this form, with the exile lasting for seventy weeks of years. We find it also in the Almanac, where the exile becomes two weeks of generations or fourteen generations.
3. At the highest level, the exile is for seventy generations, being the whole history of the world until the apocalypse.

The starting point for both (1) and (2) is the defeat at the hands of Babylon. There is also a hybrid between (2) and (3) in which the angels rule for seventy periods starting with this defeat. This hybrid is an attempt to reconcile the disparate traditions and we find it in the Animal Apocalypse. In the final form of the Almanac, all three levels are operative.

In what order did the three levels emerge? It is natural to see the Jeremiah prophecy as coming first, but this is probably wrong. Seventy years is a round number and the prediction in Jeremiah that it would be seventy years until the defeat of Babylon, is incorrect. The prophesied length of exile conforms to the mythical time scale rather than historical reality. It is the third and highest level that is probably the earliest, with the world lasting for seventy days or years, each of a generation, and each ruled by a god/angel.

We can be sure that level (2) was the last to emerge because it requires the belief that the physical return from exile was not the true return. The people holding to (2) would expect this true return to occur in the immediate future. So we can date this belief to the approximate timeframe of fourteen generations after the exile. This gives a date of c. 200 BC although a wide variation is possible both because the length of a generation is imprecise and because the Jews of this period did not have a good knowledge of the time elapsed from the exile (there were no history books to consult). A reasonable range is 300 BC to 100 BC, a period which includes both the Animal Apocalypse and the book of Daniel. The Jesus movement did not emerge until the first century AD, a late date which can only be encompassed by omitting some generations. But then this was the great advantage of a calendar based on generations; it was almost infinitely flexible, allowing the user to choose which generations to count and which to ignore.

12

The Almanac

The Almanac is a thing of beauty. The purpose of the Almanac was to elucidate God's master plan for the creation. It is an early attempt at cosmology; to reveal the underlying pattern of a universe seen as finite in time. Those who developed the Almanac believed that God had created time according to certain principles. He divided history into seventy periods because seventy was a mystic number which also enumerated the sons of God and the nations. He organised the seventy periods into ten weeks, with the sabbath set aside as special. Each of these ten weeks could also be thought of as a day—we will call them "great days". History followed the same organisation of time as ordained for humans, but on an expanded scale. Events came to a climax on the "sabbath of sabbaths", the seventh day of the seventh great day.

The greatest secret of the Almanac-framers was that God had made time symmetrical. The end was the same as the beginning. Time was reflected around the midpoint. And from this came an even more remarkable idea. The river of time did not just flow from the past to the future. It also flowed in reverse, from the future to the past.

We will explore these features of the Almanac in the next chapter. But first, in this chapter, we will explain how the Almanac has been reconstructed from existing sources. The Annex sets out the complete Almanac, generation by generation, from Adam to the end of the world.

Sources

The "Almanac" is the name given in this book for the apocalyptic calendar of seventy generations that was central to the beliefs of the early Jesus movement. We cannot understand early Christianity without the Almanac. It explains both the third day of the resurrection and the events of the crucifixion day. Yet the reader will not find the Almanac in any existing theory about Christianity. How can we be sure that it even existed?

The first hint of the Almanac comes from the Animal Apocalypse; the seventy shepherds rule for a total of seventy periods which indicates an

apocalyptic calendar of seventy generations. The proto-Christians identified the shepherds with the archons, the angelic rulers who crucify Christ.
So the duration of the world for which the archons rule is seventy generations. Can we find any evidence for this calendar of seventy periods in
early Christian literature?

The Almanac has, in fact, been hiding in plain sight, in the most obvious place possible—line 1, page 1 of the New Testament! The Gospel of
Matthew starts with a genealogy of Jesus. Most people will pass over this
long list of "begats" with eyes glazed over. But it has been constructed
from the Almanac. The clue is in the way it is organised:

> So all the generations from Abraham to David were fourteen genera-
> tions; and from David until the carrying away to Babylon were four-
> teen generations; and from the carrying away to Babylon to the Christ
> were fourteen generations. (Matthew 1:17)

Fourteen generations are two weeks of generations. The organisation
into weeks must have predated the incorporation of the genealogy into
Matthew because, as we will see, one generation is actually missing.

The genealogy will give us a large section of the Almanac but it is
incomplete— it only gives us six weeks out of ten. Fortunately, there is
another work that does divide the whole of time into ten weeks of seven
generations each. This is the Apocalypse of Weeks which has also been
preserved in the Book of Enoch. From a comparison, it is clear that there
are three weeks missing from the start of the Matthew genealogy and one
week, the apocalypse, missing from the end. The detail for the first three
weeks can be filled in from the Genesis genealogies which are behind this
section of the Apocalypse of Weeks. The final apocalyptic week lay in the
future so the generations are imprecise but the broad outline of events is
given by both the Apocalypse of Weeks and the closely related Animal
Apocalypse. To summarise:

Almanac weeks 1-3 come from the Apocalypse of Weeks and the
Genesis genealogies.
Almanac weeks 4-9 come from the Matthew genealogy.
Almanac week 10 is the week of the apocalypse (Animal Apocalypse/
Apocalypse of Weeks).

The recreation of the Almanac is, in broad outline, this simple. But there
are some complexities which are covered in this chapter and Appendix A.
We start with some issues around the Matthew genealogy.

The Matthew genealogy

The genealogy in Matthew 1:1-17 traces the descent of Jesus from Abraham. A genealogy of Jesus also appears in Luke and is notoriously different. This second genealogy goes right back to Adam, but we cannot use it to recreate the Almanac. The author of Luke has attempted to improve upon Matthew, but in doing so has destroyed the pattern of weeks. There is evidence that the author did know something of the Almanac, and the Luke genealogy has interest in its own right. It is covered in Appendix C.

There are a number of odd things about the Matthew genealogy:

- It does not prove descent from David because Jesus is not Joseph's son.
- There is a missing generation.
- Jesus is shown as being born of the female, Mary, and not the male.

This last point would have appeared very odd in the ancient world. This is how the parentage of Jesus is described:

> *And Jacob was the father of Joseph, the husband of Mary, of whom was born Jesus, who is called Christ. (Matthew 1:16)*

The wording specifically states that Jesus is born of Mary, whose husband was Joseph. The purpose of any genealogy was to demonstrate descent through the male line, and Jesus could not be "the seed" of David through the female. The Gospel of Matthew, of course, offers the supernatural explanation that Jesus is the Son of God through the holy spirit. But whether or not we accept this miracle, the only human parent the genealogy gives for Jesus is Mary.

A traditional answer to this problem is that Jesus was legally Joseph's son because he was born of his wife. It strains credibility that this could be accepted as meaning that Jesus was a "son" of David. It is also unsupported by any early evidence. If Jesus were the legal son of Joseph, then his name should be "Jesus, son of Joseph". But he is never called this in the earliest texts; not Mark, Matthew, the letters of Paul or Thomas. The author of Luke, writing in the 90s AD, was aware of this problem, and calls Jesus "the supposed son of Joseph".[1] This is the first time Jesus is called a son of Joseph anywhere.

> ➤ **In the original genealogy, Mary must have been the daughter of Joseph and not his wife.**

The greatest puzzle of all is the missing generation. If there are three groups of fourteen, we should have forty-two generations—but there are only forty-one. Some have proposed that David should be counted twice, but this is just a fudge. Markers in the text show where the problem lies. There are only three generations where the birth is marked by additional commentary other than adding the name of the mother. These three are:

Generation 14: "David the king"
Generation 28: "Jeconiah and his brothers at the time of the exile to Babylon."
Generation 41: "Jesus, who is called Christ"

The first two mark the end of the first two groups of fourteen which have the correct number of generations. This shows that David has not been counted twice. Jesus comes at the end of the final group, but this group has only thirteen generations. Someone has eliminated a generation from this last group.

In *The Rock and the Tower*, I proposed a solution to all these problems.[2] The clue is that we do actually have fourteen names in the final group. The reason we have only thirteen generations is that Mary is supposedly the wife of Joseph and so belongs to the same generation. This mistake was introduced by the author of Matthew who misunderstood the meaning of the name "Mary of Joses (Joseph)". She was actually Joseph's daughter, not his wife. Restoring the correct relationship resolves everything:

- We have fourteen generations in the last group and not thirteen.
- It explains why Jesus is not called the son of Joseph but only the son of Mary.
- It establishes Mary as the descendant of David.

The genealogist thinks that Jesus was physically born through Mary. But in reality he came spiritually through Mary, the shaman. This is consistent with Romans 1:3 where Paul says that Jesus had *"come of the seed of David according to the flesh"*. Paul uses the same word *ginomai* here as at Galatians 4:4. It has a wide range of meanings relating to a change of state, such as to come into existence/to become/to happen/to appear. The word is very common but scarcely ever used to mean physical birth which would be *gennao*.

Now the "seed" is the common way of referring to the descendants of a man. The literal meaning of the word is a plant's seed and by extension a man's sperm. The ancients did not understand that a child's genes come equally from mother and father. They viewed a baby as growing from the father's seed which was planted in the mother's womb. As the baby grew it absorbed the woman's own substance, which explained why a child resembled its mother as well as its father. This meant that a man was literally grown from the seed of his father, who was grown from the seed of the grandfather, and so on, all the way back to an esteemed ancestor such as David. But a person was never their mother's seed—only their biological father's seed.

As Jesus came through Mary, and as Joseph was not his father, he could not be the seed of David. But then Paul never claims that Jesus is the seed of David. He uses the odd phrase "come of the seed of David" which is parallel to his statement in Galatians 4:4 that Jesus had "come of a woman". It is the woman, and not Jesus, who is the seed of David. If Mary were Joseph's daughter and not his wife, then she would indeed be the seed of David; a girl was her father's seed no less than a boy. Note the odd phrase "according to the flesh" which would be unnecessary if Jesus had simply been born. The "flesh" is Mary, the physical person through whom Jesus, the Son of God, has appeared "according to the spirit" by resurrection from the dead.

The Apocalypse of Weeks

The Apocalypse of Weeks in the Book of Enoch is a unique survival. It is the one source in which we can see the full form of the Almanac explicitly. The history of the world, from beginning to the end, is expressed as seventy generations structured as ten weeks each of seven "days". The Apocalypse is certainly pre-Christian because fragments have been found among the Dead Sea Scrolls at Qumran. It could date from anywhere between the second century BC to the early first century BC.[3]

In the preliminaries to the Apocalypse, Enoch recounts his visions of heaven to his sons, telling them about events to come. He recalls what he has read from the heavenly tablets, a future history of the world written before time. His account is organised by weeks, with Enoch himself occupying the first week:

> "*I was born the seventh during the first week during which time judgement and righteousness continued to endure.*" (1 Enoch 93:3)[4]

This shows us that the "days" of each week are generations. Enoch is seventh in the line of Adam and occupies the seventh day in the first week. The Apocalypse of Weeks is schematic, with no attempt to allocate individual generations. The following gives an overview of the weeks:

Week 1: Enoch
Week 2: The descent of the watchers, the flood, Noah, and a law.
Week 3: Abraham
Week 4: The law of Moses
Week 5: The kingdom of David and the temple
Week 6: The Jews blinded; Elijah; the burning of the temple and the exile.
Week 7: An apostate generation; the elect ones of righteousness, seven-fold instruction.
Week 8: The punishment of the unrighteous; the building of a new temple
Week 9: Righteous judgement revealed and the earth written-off for destruction.
Week 10: Eternal judgement executed by the angels; a new heaven.

(Note: Only Enoch is actually named in the text although the other individuals are indicated.)

The first five weeks are virtually identical to the Almanac but with some subtle but significant differences. From week six onwards the two diverge markedly. For example, the Apocalypse of Weeks allows no less than three weeks, or twenty-one generations for the events of the apocalypse. This seems extreme. In Appendix A we see how this and other features indicate that the Apocalypse of Weeks has been edited by a sect who placed themselves at the culmination of the seventh week. The original is reconstructed and is much closer to the Almanac. The key features of the reconstructed version are:

- The sabbaths (seventh day/generation of each week) are important and mark good events with the exception of the sabbath of sabbaths which was originally occupied by the destruction of the temple, as is the case for the Almanac.
- The laws of Noah and Moses are prominent—this is the only allu-sion to the law of Moses in the Book of Enoch. Abraham does not bring a law but is the "plant of righteous judgement" which will grow into Israel.
- The second temple is not recognised.

These features are consistent with the Almanac and with the other sources we have examined, such as the parable of the tenants and the Animal Apocalypse.

Reconstructing the Almanac

We can now reconstruct the Almanac using the Matthew genealogy, the Apocalypse of Weeks and the genealogies in Genesis.

> ➤ **The Almanac was more schematic than the Matthew genealogy which attempted to fill in all the generations.**

The Apocalypse of Weeks is very broad brush and largely conceptual. It includes just a few key events with no attempt to recreate the generations. In any case, the timescale allowed for each week is often far too short for the events allocated to that week. The Almanac was also conceptual in nature, although more detailed. In contrast, the Matthew genealogy is supposedly a full list of generations from Abraham to Jesus. Its purpose was to prove the descent of Mary, through Joseph, from David. So the genealogy is not identical to the Almanac although the differences are mostly very minor. The genealogy consists of two parts:

1. A genealogy of the kings of Judah, which runs from Abraham to Zerubbabel. This utilises such scriptural sources as Genesis and Chronicles.
2. A personal genealogy of Joseph and Mary, showing their descent from their prominent ancestor Eliakim, son of Abiud, who was reputed to be a descendant of Zerubbabel.

As we have seen, the genealogy must predate Matthew because one generation was inadvertently removed when it was incorporated into that gospel. So we must envisage at least a three-stage process:

1. A proto-Christian Almanac existed before Mary and was used to predict the imminence of the resurrection of Christ and the end times.
2. Mary's group produced a genealogy writing her into the Almanac.
3. This genealogy was incorporated into Matthew.

Most likely things were more complex than this, with multiple versions of the Almanac existing alongside each other simultaneously.

> ➤ Abraham appears in the Almanac at the start of week 4, which is inconsistent with Genesis. This explains why the Matthew genealogy starts with Abraham and not Adam.

In the Apocalypse of Weeks, Abraham comes at the culmination of week 3. However, in the Almanac he has been moved to the first day of week 4. This apparently minor change is vital for the Almanac's structure and symmetries. But it would have caused an annoying difficulty for anyone attempting to fill in the generations. The problem is that the genealogies in Genesis specify the three weeks up to Abraham. In these genealogies, Abraham comes at either generation 20 (in the Hebrew Masoretic text) or generation 21 (in the Greek Septuagint). In the Almanac, he is at generation 22. This would not have bothered the original users—a generation or two must have been omitted from Genesis. But the Matthew genealogist is putting names to all the generations. He faces an unpalatable choice of either abandoning the Almanac structure of weeks or inserting a name not in Genesis somewhere before Abraham. He dodges this dilemma by starting his genealogy at Abraham and not Adam.

> ➤ The Matthew genealogist makes Rahab the wife of Salmon, although 200 years separated them. This mistake gives us a clue as to how the genealogy was constructed from the Almanac.

In the genealogy, Salmon comes after Nahshon and was *"the father of Boaz by Rahab"* (Matthew 1:5). According to the book of Joshua, Rahab was a prostitute of Jericho who betrayed her city by hiding Joshua's spies. Her life, and the lives of her family, were spared although everyone else in the city was killed. However, Rahab cannot be the wife of Salmon and the mother of Boaz because some two hundred years separated them.[5] Something has gone badly wrong here.

This mistake shows us that two separate versions of week 5 were in circulation. The original Almanac was not a genealogy. It would have started the week with the most notable individuals within each generation. This would have given the sequence Moses, Joshua and Rahab. In the book of Joshua, Rahab is a young woman—her family consists of her father and mother and her siblings.[6] However, Joshua must be old because he has been wandering in the wilderness for forty years. So Rahab comes in the generation after Joshua and must have followed Joshua in the Almanac.

The genealogist has replaced this list of three with the genealogy of David at the end of Ruth.[7] We can put these two sources next to each other:

Ruth: Almanac:

Amminadab   Moses

Nahshon   Joshua

Salmon   Rahab

Boaz

Neither Moses nor Joshua was an ancestor of the Judean kings, so the genealogist substitutes Amminadab and Nahshon who are in the same two generations (Nahshon, son of Amminadab is a "prince" of Judah in Numbers).[8] This leaves Rahab who occupied the third day in the Almanac. The equivalent position in the Ruth genealogy is Salmon, and someone has wrongly concluded that the two must have been married.

➢ **Two adjustments have to be made to the genealogy.**

We must make two changes to the generations from the Matthew genealogy to get to the Almanac:

1. As we have seen, Mary was the daughter and not the son of Joseph so she must be given her own generation. This gives the correct number of generations with Jesus ending week 9.
2. The placement of Mary and Jesus has to be moved up by one generation. The resurrection is the event which brings in the final week 10 of the Almanac. In the Matthew genealogy Jesus is regarded as a flesh and blood man so his life is positioned at the end of week 9 and his resurrection begins week 10. But under the shaman paradigm, the disciples only know the resurrected Jesus who remains with them for a notional forty years. So his generation should be positioned at the start of week 10 and not the end of week 9.[9] This leaves an unnamed generation which I have placed at 9.3 between the family and scriptural genealogies, where there are certainly missing generations. The issues around this second point are considered further in Chapter 15.

The Hebrew Bible and the Almanac

➢ **The proto-Christian Almanac was heavily influenced by the Hebrew Bible.**

We have seen that, in many ways, the Hebrew Bible does not reflect the real history of Israel and Judah. The exodus never happened, and the kingdom of David was greatly exaggerated. The Bible is a Judean creation, originating in the era of the Judas War, and only completed after the exile. We have argued that the proto-Christians developed from an Israelite group living in Judah. They inherited alternative Israelite traditions that are at least as early as most of the material in the Bible.

However, when we look at the reconstructed Almanac, we will see that it reflects the Judean biblical version of events. Moses plays an important role. The kingdom of David and Solomon is of great significance, and the Almanac accepts the biblical account of their united Monarchy at face value. Almanac generations are filled in with the kings of Judah rather than Israel. How can we explain this apparent contradiction?

One answer lies in the vast amount of time over which proto-Christianity evolved. Although the Almanac has its roots in the Judas War era c. 700 BC, it could not have taken its final form until 300 BC–100 BC. (It was subsequently edited further by the Jesus movement in the first century AD to write Mary and her family into the Almanac.) The proto-Christian group did not stay static for five hundred years. They were living in Judah and would have absorbed many Judean beliefs. There was no reason why they should reject the broad history in the Bible, particularly as the context in which it was written had long since been forgotten.

We can go a step further. Although the group identified themselves as members of an Israelite tribe, they were most likely loyal to the Davidic kings and the first temple even before the Judas War. The next Shaman Paradigm book will explore the place of origin of the Jesus movement—it is not Galilee! The best candidate is an area which had shifted from the kingdom of Israel to the kingdom of Judah sometime before the Assyrian invasion. It would have been a natural destination for many Israelite refugees who would have greatly added to the population. This would explain why the group respected the legitimacy of the line of David, while, at the same time, despising particular Judean kings as the betrayers of Israel.

Annex:

The Complete Almanac

<u>Week 1:</u> The creation to Enoch
    1.1 Creation of heaven and earth—Adam and Eve
    1.2 Seth
    1.3 Enosh
    1.4 Kenan
    1.5 Mahalalel
    1.6 Jared
    1.7 Enoch—walks with God, taken up to heaven

<u>Week 2:</u> Noah, the flood, the nations
    2:1 Methuselah—the longest-lived human
    2.2 Lamech
    2.3 Noah—the flood
    2.4 Shem, Ham and Japheth—the nations created, the law of Noah
    2.5 Arpachshad
    2.6 Cainan
    2.7 Shelah

<u>Week 3:</u> The nations increase in wickedness
    3.1 Eber—ancestor of the Hebrews
    3.2 Peleg
    3.3 (An unnamed generation)
    3.4 Reu
    3.5 Serug
    3.6 Nahor
    3.7 Terah

<u>Week 4:</u> The covenant with Abraham, the Israelites
    4.1 Abraham—abortive sacrifice of Isaac, the covenant
    4.2 Isaac
    4.3 Jacob—Israel created
    4.4 Joseph, Judah, and their brothers, Tamar—the Israelites go down
        to Egypt

4.5 Perez and Zerah

4.6 Hezron

4.7 Ram—persecution by the Egyptians

Week 5: Moses to David

    5.1 Moses—the exodus, the law of Moses, the building of the tabernacle

    5.2 Joshua—entry into the Promised Land

    5.3 Rahab

    5.4 Ruth and Boaz

    5.5 Obed

    5.6 Jesse

    5.7 David and Bathsheba—the kingdom of David, the conception of the temple

Week 6: Solomon, the decline to Uzziah

    6.1 Solomon—kingdom of Solomon, the building of the temple

    6.2 Rehoboam

    6.3 Abijah

    6.4 Asa

    6.5 Jehoshaphat

    6.6 Joram

    6.7 Uzziah—the desecration of the temple

Week 7: The Judas War, the exile, the crucifixion

    7.1 Jotham

    7.2 Ahaz—the Judas War commences

    7.3 Hezekiah—exile of Israel complete

    7.4 Manasseh

    7.5 Amon

    7.6 Josiah

    7.7 Jeconiah—Jerusalem and the temple destroyed, exile of Judah, the crucifixion

Week 8: The first day of cosmic exile

    8.1 Shealtiel

    8.2 Zerubbabel—the return to Jerusalem, the false second temple

    8.3 (An unnamed generation)

    8.4 Abiud

    8.5 Eliakim—esteemed ancestor of Joseph and Mary

    8.6 Azor

    8.7 Zadok

Week 9: The second day of cosmic exile
9.1 Achim
9.2 Eliud
9.3 Eleazar
9.4 Matthan
9.5 Jacob
9.6 Joseph
9.7 Mary—the shaman, possessed by seven demon husbands

Week 10: The resurrection and the apocalypse
10.1 Jesus resurrected/reborn through Mary who is the new temple
10.2 Jesus appears in the skies—battles of the apocalypse
10.3 Resurrection of the dead
10.4 Judgement of the seventy angels
10.5 Destruction of the seventy angels
10.6 Judgement and destruction of the human followers of the seventy
10.7 Destruction of the earth and heaven

Notes

1. The generations in weeks 1 to 3 have been filled in from Genesis. The genealogy in Genesis 5 goes up to Noah and his sons. The genealogy of the descendants of Noah's sons comes in Genesis 10, and there is a second genealogy of the sons of Shem, the line from which the Jews emerge, in Genesis 11:10-32. The first week follows Genesis, but in the second and third weeks, we have to add a generation. As discussed in the text, the Matthew genealogy implies that Abraham comes in day 22, which is inconsistent with Genesis, which positions Abraham at either generation 20 (Masoretic) or 21 (Septuagint). The Septuagint has an additional patriarch, Cainan, between Arpachshad and Shelah. We have followed the Septuagint for week 2, and in week 3 we have introduced a blank generation after Peleg.

2. The Matthew genealogy positions Amminadab at 5.1 and Nahshon at 5.2. This is a case where the genealogy has substituted two individuals on the line of the Judean kings for the two more prominent individuals who would have appeared in the Almanac. In Numbers, "Nahshon son of Amminadab" is one of the twelve young men that Moses chooses to represent the twelve tribes—he is the "prince" of Judah.[10] Moses is an old man of about eighty at this time.[11] So Moses belongs to the generation of Nahshon's father, Amminadab. Joshua is younger than Moses and becomes his successor, so he would have been the same generation as Nahshon.

3. For generation 5.3, the Matthew genealogy has Salmon and Rahab. As covered in the text, this is a mistake, and Rahab alone is placed here. There is a large gap of time between Rahab and Ruth. According to the biblical account there should be something like 800 years between Judah and David, but in the genealogy this is this is covered by just 11 generations.[12] Making an allowance for the average length of a generation (say 30 years), there are about 500 years missing from these two weeks.

4. Week 6 and 7 follow the list of the kings of Judah in the Book of Kings. As there were more kings than Almanac days, some names were inevitably left out. There are three missing kings between 6.6 and 6.7; Ahaziah, Joash and Amaziah.[13] A queen, Athaliah, mother of Ahaziah, ruled for six years between Ahaziah and Joash.[14] There are another two missing kings between 7.6 and 7.7; Jehoahaz and Jehoiakim.[15] Also, Zedekiah does not feature although he reigned as king after Jeconiah was exiled.[16] These three missing kings were all brothers and sons of Josiah. The Matthew genealogy says that Josiah was the father of "Jeconiah and his brothers" (Matthew 1:11), but, in fact, Jeconiah was the son of Jehoiakim and grandson of Josiah.

5. After Zerubbabel, the Matthew genealogy is the family genealogy of Joseph and Mary. The reconstruction of the Almanac restores Mary as the daughter of Joseph, and so occupying a separate generation. This resolves the problem of the missing generation in the Matthew genealogy.

6. The resurrection of Jesus marks the commencement of the tenth and final week; it divides 9.7 from 10.1. On the gospel view, the life of Jesus must come before his resurrection, and so the genealogy places him at 9.7. As explained in the text, this is incorrect. The time of the spiritual Jesus on earth starts with the resurrection, so Jesus should be moved to 10.1. To achieve this, another generation has to be added. This has been placed at 8.3 between the scriptural and family sections of the genealogy. (This is a completely different issue from the missing generation in the Matthew genealogy which is covered in the point above.)

13

The Almanac: Structure and Symmetry

The three ages

➤ **The Almanac is built around three symmetrical ages.**

The Almanac is constructed around the principle of symmetry; the first half of time mirrors the second half. We find the same principle of symmetry in chiastic writing, where two halves of a passage are symmetrical about a midpoint. Both the Jews and the early Christians loved such chiastic compositions. The Almanac is symmetrical around the central point between weeks 5 and 6. This is the biblical high point of the Jews, the united kingdom of David and Solomon and the building of the temple in Jerusalem.

At the highest level, symmetry is expressed through three different ages; that of the nations, the Jews and the final age of exile and apocalypse (see Figure 1). The ages last for three, four and three great days (weeks) which is the most equitable way of dividing ten periods symmetrically into three groups. The three ages are God's three attempts to save humanity: each is associated with one of the three messengers in the parable of the tenants.

In the age of the nations, Yahweh does not have a chosen people. Because the fallen angels have corrupted humanity, the lower Yahweh sends the first servant, Noah, to give a law. (In Genesis this is combined with the story of the flood which was originally a separate myth.) The people do not listen and the nations become even more evil, worshipping the seventy as their gods.

In the second age, the lower Yahweh attempts salvation through a single chosen people, the Israelites. He sends to them the second servant, Moses, to give them a more exacting law. The intention is for the Israelites to serve as a model for the whole of humanity. But they find it impossible to obey the law of Moses, and the penalty for disobedience is death. So Yahweh withdraws his promise and sends them into slavery. They are given up to exile and placed under the nations.

The three ages of the Almanac

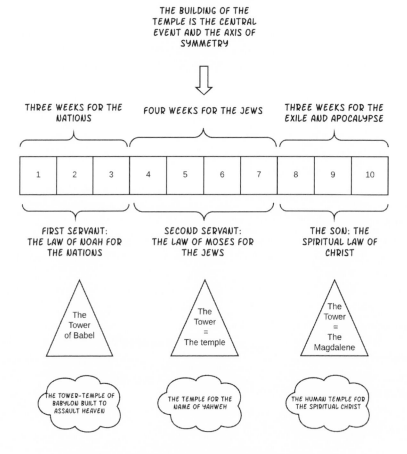

Figure 1: The Almanac ages.

The third age is that of exile and redemption. The first two laws are binding and cannot be unsaid. But the higher Yahweh takes pity on humanity; he sends his own son to pay the price for the people's disobedience. The son is killed at the end of the age of the Jews and lies dead for two great days. On the third day, he is revived and brings his new spiritual law to humanity. This law comes from the ultimate God and is the first law that people can keep, a law of love and forgiveness. Not everyone will be saved though, but only those who recognise and love Jesus, whether Jew or gentile. At the end of the last great day, heaven and earth will be destroyed and replaced by a new perfect creation ruled by Christ.

Each of the three ages is associated with a tower-temple. The first is the tower (*migdal*) of Babel or Babylon. This tower was an attempt by the nations under the king of Babylon to assault heaven. The second tower was the Jerusalem temple, represented as a tower in the Animal Apocalypse and the parable of the vineyard. This temple is the dwelling place of the lower Yahweh, the angel of the Name, and its destruction marks the end of the age of the Jews. The third tower is the Magdalene, also derived from *migdal*. Mary, "the tower", is the receptacle for the spiritual Christ, and the prototype for all spiritual Christians.

The age of the Jews

The central four weeks, the age of the Jews, is illustrated in Figure 2. This age is symmetrical about the midpoint which falls between the generations 5.7 (David) and 6.1 (Solomon), and which is also the midpoint and axis of symmetry for the whole Almanac. The history of the Jews has an ascent for the first two weeks, a zenith at the midpoint, and a descent for the following two weeks, culminating with the destruction of Judah at the end of week 7.

The age of the Jews takes up four weeks of the Almanac, twenty-eight days, which is one lunar month. It can be represented by the phases of the moon, as shown in the diagram. The moon is new, a sliver crescent, at the time of Abraham. It waxes to full under the kingdom of David and Solomon. Then it wanes to the dark of the moon in the final generation of the Jews. We find exactly this description in the medieval Zohar and rabbinical sources, with the moon becoming full in the reign of Solomon, the fifteenth generation after Abraham, and then waning after Solomon towards the final destruction:[1]

> "When Solomon appeared, the disk of the moon became full." (Shemot Rabbah 15:26)

The month of the Jews starts with the covenant of Abraham in 4.1, the promise that Abraham and his seed will become Yahweh's chosen people and inherit the land of Canaan. To mark the covenant, Abraham and his sons are circumcised. The symmetrical point is day 7.7 in which the kingdom of Judah is destroyed, and the Jews expelled from the Promised Land. The Jews have failed to keep their side of the covenant. It was necessary to make the small adjustment to the position of Abraham to achieve this symmetrical structure, moving him to the twenty-second generation, in contradiction to Genesis.

The Almanac month of the Jews

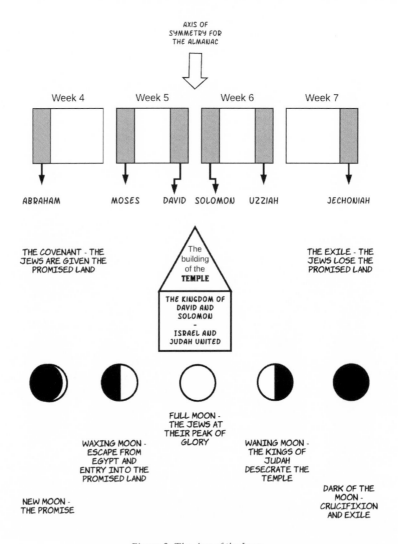

Figure 2: The Age of the Jews.

The twelve tribes emerge during the week of Abraham. The northern patriarch, Jacob is positioned at 4.3, and his twelve sons, from whom the tribes come, at the midpoint of 4.4. This is parallel to week 2 where the sons of Noah, from whom the nations come, are also placed at the midpoint.

Week 5 starts with Moses and the exodus from Egypt. Moses, the second servant, brought the law and built the tabernacle, the movable predecessor of the temple. The symmetrical point to Moses is Uzziah, the king who ends the sixth week and brings in the dreadful seventh.

➢ **The central point of the age of the Jews, and the Almanac, is the building of the temple, and the kingdom of David and Solomon.**

The mathematical midpoint of the Almanac comes between day 5.7 (David) and 6.1 (Solomon). These two generations are the axis of symmetry for the Almanac. Both David and Solomon are associated with the building of the temple in Jerusalem. According to scripture, it was David who brought the Ark of the Covenant into Jerusalem and who planned a temple to replace the movable tabernacle.[2] But through a dream sent to Nathan, the prophet, God tells David that the building of the temple will fall to his successor:

> *Yahweh tells you that he will establish a house for you. And when your days are fulfilled, and you rest with your fathers, I will raise up your seed after you, who will come from your own body, and I will establish his kingdom. He will build a house for my name, and I will establish the throne of his kingdom forever. (2 Samuel 7:11-13)*

This prophecy intimately links the temple (the house of God) to the kingdom (the house of David). Both will be established through Solomon, and both will endure forever.[3] After Solomon, the united kingdom supposedly broke up into the two separate nations of Israel and Judah. There was a steady decline until the line of David came to an end with Jeconiah. This view of David and Solomon may not reflect historical reality, but it was what the framers of the Almanac believed. The first temple was of great importance to the proto-Christians, and it was immutably linked to the Davidic kings.

Temple symmetries

➢ **The Almanac exhibits symmetries around the temple.**

Figure 3 shows the Almanac symmetries concerning the temple. Around the central building of the temple, there are four other key days; 4.1, 5.1, 6.7 and 7.7.

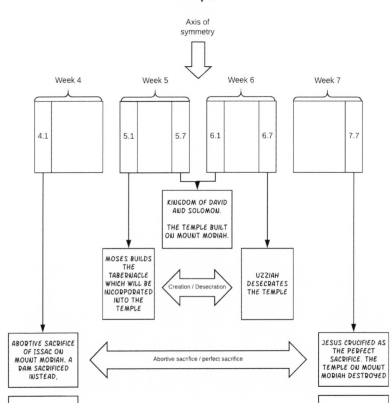

Figure 3: Almanac temple symmetries.

The temple was built on Mount Moriah which was supposedly the same mountain on which Abraham offered up his son Isaac as a sacrifice. God intervened to stop the sacrifice at the last second, and substituted a ram in place of Isaac. This abortive sacrifice took place in Almanac day 4.1. On the symmetrical day, 7.7, the temple was destroyed by the Babylonians. The covenant that started on Moriah ended on Moriah.

The crucifixion of Christ also takes place in day 7.7, and is symmetrical to the abortive sacrifice of Isaac. Early Christians attached great importance to the parallel between Abraham offering up Isaac and the ultimate sacrifice of God's son, Jesus. There are numerous early Christian images and representations of the Isaac sacrifice.

The other symmetry is between Moses in 5.1 and Uzziah in 6.7. Moses constructed the tabernacle, the predecessor of the temple. In the corresponding symmetrical point, the temple was desecrated by Uzziah, the event that marked the beginning of the final week of the Jews. We will explore Uzziah's desecration further when we look in more detail at the seventh great day.

The arrow of time and the new sabbath

> The symmetry of the Almanac implies that the arrow of time is reversible.

We have seen how the Almanac is chiastic (symmetrical) about the midpoint. Mathematically, this is a reflection about the midpoint. In such a transition, the arrow of time is reversed, as shown in Figure 4. Under the reflection, time flows backwards.

> A saying in the Gospel of Thomas implies that time is reversible.

The concept of the reversibility of time may seem far too sophisticated for the age in which the proto-Christians lived. But we find something very similar in the Gospel of Thomas:

> *The disciples said to Jesus: "Tell us how our end shall be." Jesus said: "Have you discovered then the beginning, that you seek after the end? For where the beginning is, the end will be also. Blessed is he who will stand in the beginning, and he will know the end and not taste of death." (Thomas 18; TC 1.17)*

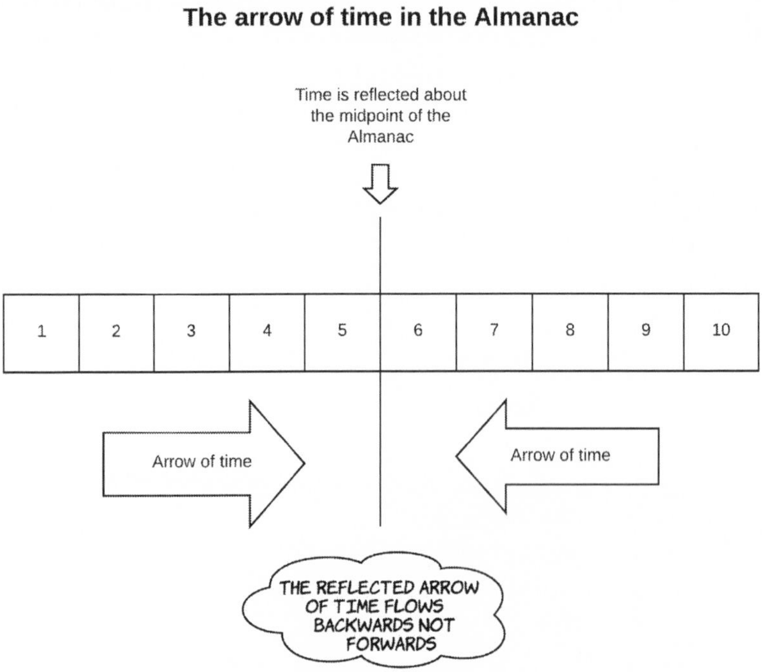

The arrow of time in the Almanac

Time is reflected about
the midpoint of the
Almanac

1	2	3	4	5	6	7	8	9	10

Arrow of time

Arrow of time

THE REFLECTED ARROW
OF TIME FLOWS
BACKWARDS NOT
FORWARDS

Figure 4: The reversal of the arrow of time.

The disciples are looking towards the end (forwards), but Jesus tells them instead to look towards the beginning (backwards). Where the beginning is, the end will be: beginning and end are one and the same because time is symmetrical.

In *The Thomas Code*, I proposed that this saying was positioned to signal the imminent end of the first group of eighteen sayings. However, the Thomas sayings convey multiple levels of meaning. Beyond the superficial riddle meaning relating to the structure of the Gospel of Thomas, lies a more profound meaning about the nature of time.

➤ **The change of the sabbath from Saturday to Sunday is due to the reversal of time.**

Nothing was more fundamental to the Jews than observing the sabbath. How then was it possible for a supposedly Jewish movement to change the sabbath from the seventh day to the first day of the week? The conventional explanation is that the Christian sabbath is the day of Jesus' resurrection. However, if law-observant Jews founded Christianity, then they would have passed down their traditions to their gentile converts.

Religion is inherently conservative. Something as fundamental as sabbath observance would never have been changed simply because later Christians thought it was a nice idea to hold the sabbath on the day of the resurrection. The sabbath is specified in scripture as the seventh day of the week, not the first.

There must be a fundamental reason for this change, one that goes back to the origins of the Jesus movement. If time is reversible, then Christians are still honouring the sabbath as the seventh day, but they are counting backwards (see Figure 5.)

If the arrow of time is reversed, then the sabbath is reversed.

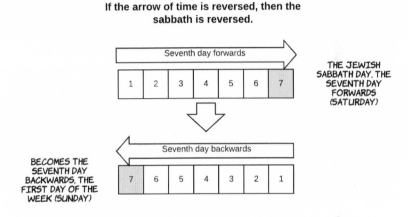

Figure 5: Time reversal implies a switch in sabbath.

The resurrection day explanation confuses cause and effect: the resurrection took place on the first day of the week because the proto-Christians believed that it was the true sabbath.

As the early Jesus movement expanded out from their original group and began converting some of their Jewish neighbours, they would have encountered a great deal of opposition to the change in the sabbath. This conflict is apparent from a story in Mark. One sabbath, Jesus is passing through a field when his disciples begin to pick the heads of grain. The Pharisees point this out to Jesus: *"Look, why do they that which is unlawful on the sabbath?"* (Mark 2:24). Jesus responds with a story about David and his companions eating consecrated bread in the time of Abiathar, the high priest. He ends with a sweeping statement:

> *"The sabbath was made for man, not man for the sabbath. So then, the Son of Man is lord even of the sabbath."* (Mark 2:27-8)

There is much that is wrong with this story. Picking individual heads of grain to eat was not a violation of the sabbath because it was not considered work. Jesus is also incorrect in saying that David took the consecrated bread from Abiathar—it was his father Ahimelech who was high priest at the time.[4] More significantly, the fact that David was obliged to eat consecrated bread in a time of crisis is scarcely justification for the disciples not observing the sabbath just because they were hungry. And the line "the sabbath was made for men..." is a general statement about humans (men) which does not justify the conclusion about Jesus, "the Son of Man".

The story has been concocted by the author of Mark to explain something he does not understand. He searches for a reason why Christians do not keep the sabbath. His explanation, that it is acceptable to violate the sabbath if there is a pressing need, does not warrant the punch line which gives the original justification: "the Son of Man is lord of the sabbath". We will see later why the Son of Man is indeed lord of the sabbath.

The Mark story is evidence that the Christian practice of not observing the sabbath was early, which receives further support from a saying in the Gospel of Thomas:

> Jesus said: "If you do not fast from the world, you will not find the kingdom; if you do not keep the sabbath as sabbath, you will not see the father." (Thomas 27; TC 2.8)

Note the odd phrase "keep the sabbath as sabbath". The repetition of "sabbath" is redundant—why does it not just say "keep the sabbath"? If we take the saying at face value, then there must be two sabbaths. One, the new sabbath, must be kept in a similar way to the other, the old sabbath. And this is what Christians did, modelling their sabbath, the first day of the week, on the Jewish sabbath. The Christians did not adhere to the many detailed Jewish sabbath prohibitions and rules, but applied the spiritual principle of "fasting from the world".

Forward and reverse sabbaths

➢ **In the Almanac, bad things tend to happen on the forward sabbaths, good things on the reverse sabbaths.**

We would expect the sabbaths to represent special events in the Almanac and they do. But there is an unexpected twist. Bad things tend to happen on the forward sabbaths and good things on the reverse sabbaths (see Figure 6).

Almanac sabbaths and reverse sabbaths

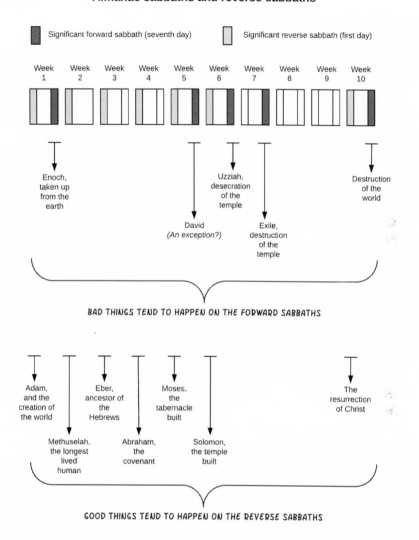

Figure 6: Events on the forward and reverse sabbaths.

Compared to the Apocalypse of Weeks, which brings each week to a climax on the sabbath, the difference is striking. One possible exception is David, who comes in the sabbath position of the fifth week. Together with Solomon, he forms the central fulcrum of the Almanac. But even David is a questionable figure, portrayed as a murderer in the Bible. So perhaps it is fitting that he occupies the negative sabbath and Solomon the positive reverse sabbath.

➤ **The first sabbath, in which Enoch is taken up to heaven, is symmetrical with the first reverse sabbath, in which Jesus comes down from heaven.**

The important first sabbath is occupied by Enoch, who is the seventh generation from Adam. Enoch is undoubtedly a positive figure, so this may seem to contradict the idea that the forward sabbaths are negative. But Enoch was taken out of the world to heaven, supposedly because of the evil of the Watchers:

> *And behold I saw the clouds: And they were calling me in a vision: and the fogs were calling me; and the course of the stars and the lightnings were rushing to me and causing me to desire; and in the vision, the winds were causing me to fly and rushing me high up to heaven. (1 Enoch 14:8)*[5]

The corresponding reverse sabbath (10.1) is occupied by the resurrection of Jesus (see Figure 7). The proto-Christians who came before Mary expected the resurrected Christ to appear in splendid heavenly form visible to everyone. Even most of Mary's supporters would have regarded the spiritual resurrection as a preliminary to the real event which was expected to commence in the same generation. Jesus, at his trial in Mark, quotes the book of Daniel when asked if he is the "son of the blessed one" meaning God:

> *And Jesus said, "I am, and you will see the Son of Man sitting at the right hand of power, and coming with the clouds of heaven." (Mark 14:62)*

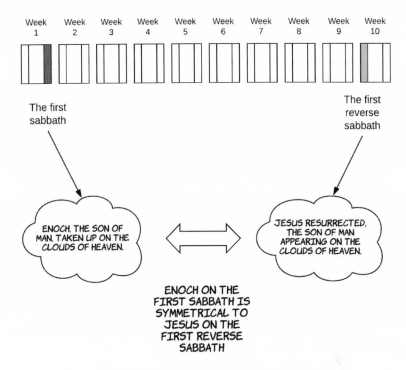

Figure 7: The first forward and reverse sabbaths.

So Enoch ascends from earth to heaven on the first sabbath, whereas Christ descends from heaven to earth on the symmetrical reverse sabbath. Moreover, Enoch is given the title, "the Son of Man" in the Similitudes (included in 1 Enoch), a work dating from around the first century. We will explore the connection between Christ and Enoch further in the final section of this book.

> ➤ **The sabbath of sabbaths marks the end of the covenant, the most negative event in history. The corresponding reverse sabbath of sabbaths marks the making of the covenant.**

The most special day in the whole Almanac should be the sabbath of sabbaths, the seventh day of the seventh week. Yet it is the day of doom, the day of exile. In this day, the Christ, divine king of the Jews, is crucified. There are multiple dimensions of the disaster:

The temple is destroyed.
The house of David is extinguished.
The Holy City, Jerusalem, is destroyed.
The Jews are exiled.
The Christ is crucified.

The forward and reverse sabbath of sabbaths

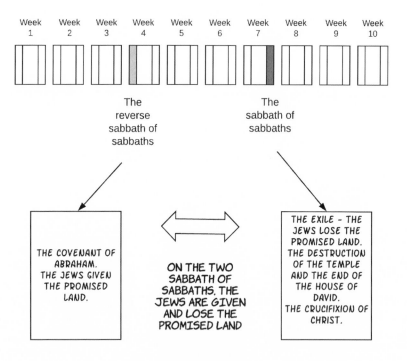

Figure 8: The sabbath of sabbaths.

So we have the contradiction that the worst events in history happen on the holiest day. The revisor of the Apocalypse of Weeks addressed this problem by moving the destruction of Jerusalem to the sixth week. The Almanac constructers came up with a radically different solution. The true sabbath must be the reverse sabbath, not the forward sabbath. It was the reverse sabbath of sabbaths that was the holiest day, that of the promise granted through Abraham, a promise that applied to Christians as well as all Jews (see Figure 8).

> ➤ The early Jesus movement believed that the reverse sabbath was the true sabbath. This concept makes no sense without the Almanac.

The Almanac demonstrates the importance of the reverse sabbath. It is the reflected sabbath, the first day of the week, that is holy. Good events tend to happen in the Almanac on the backwards sabbath, bad events on the forward sabbath. The worst day in history occurs on the sabbath of sabbaths, no less. This could not happen if the forward sabbath were the real sabbath.

The Almanac explains why Christians made the extraordinary switch of the sabbath from Saturday to Sunday, a change which defies conventional understanding. It is the seventh day which is the sabbath in scripture. It is not much of an exaggeration to say that Judaism was built around sabbath observance. Such a fundamental change only makes sense in the context of the Almanac and underlines the importance of the Almanac to the early Jesus movement.

The cosmic Jubilee

> ➤ The redemption from cosmic exile comes at the Jubilee, counting from the promise given to Abraham.

The Jubilee is related to the concept of the sabbath of sabbaths. After seven weeks of years (forty-nine years), there was a redemption of slaves. Property that had been sold would revert to the family of the original owners. The institution of the Jubilee was intended to stop the otherwise inevitable accumulation of land and economic power into a few hands.[6]

On a cosmic level, the Jubilee applies to the Almanac. The seed of Abraham were granted the Promised Land in perpetuity in day 4.1. But the Israelites and Judeans lost their land and their freedom in week 7. Although they were now slaves in exile, the original promise would still apply; they would eventually be redeemed from their slavery, and their land returned. When would this happen? Counting forty-nine days from the original promise gets to the last day of the world in 10.7. The redemption would occur after this last day. The lost freedom would be restored, and a new perfect earth created.

14

The Almanac in Context

Genealogical time

The Almanac did not come from nowhere; it has antecedents and parallels. The calendar of generations is a very early concept—the ancients thought in genealogical time rather than our geological time. To us moderns, a generation is an unsatisfactory measure and maddeningly imprecise. How can you speak in terms of generations when there is no inherent dividing line between one generation and the next, but a continuous process of birth and death? But in the ancient world, before modern calendars emerged, the generation was the fundamental unit of time.

Events would be recorded by the year of the reign of a king or emperor. When a king died and was replaced by his son, the system would start again at year one. The measurement of time by generations also applied to less exalted families. The past was remembered though genealogies; lists of ancestors, typically on the male line, each generation marked by a name. We find many such genealogies in the Bible. The past was perceived through genealogies and king lists, so it was natural to express the duration of the world in generations.

How long was a generation? To the Jews, the lifespan was seventy years. If a king lived to this age and died, he would be succeeded by a son in middle age. The lifespan of a ruler could be thought of as two generations—in the first, they were a child or youthful prince; in the second, a king in their own right. So each generation was theoretically half the human lifespan or about thirty-five years. This is a notional calculation, and a realistic length would be less than this, perhaps about thirty years. In reality, generations, as measured by the reigns of real kings, varied hugely.

➢ **Time periods were often used by the Jews interchangeably. A generation could be called a "day", a "week" or a "year". A week of days was regarded as a "day" in its own right.**

A literary convention of the Jews was to apply a unit of time, such as a day, week or year, to mean a much longer period. For example, a generation is called a "day" in the Apocalypse of Weeks. There is another example from the Dead Sea scrolls, which we will come to shortly, in which a generation is called a "week". We find a similar idea behind the "cosmic escalation" in which the original exile of seventy years has been reinterpreted as seventy generations. In Daniel, the seventy years of exile become seventy weeks of years.

It was common to think of a year as a "day". The land had its own sabbath and would lie fallow every seventh year.[1] Another practice was to move up a level so that "weeks" became "days". This gave rise to the concept of the Jubilee, a week of weeks of years. The idea is carried to an extreme in the book of Jubilees, in which the history of the world is measured in Jubilees, which are grouped to give a super-Jubilee, a Jubilee of Jubilees.

The Almanac, with its "days" of generations organised into "weeks" which are also "great days" fits in well with this pattern of using days and weeks to organise much longer periods of time.

> Generations were sometimes grouped by sevens or tens in early genealogies. We find evidence of this pattern in both Genesis and the Book of Ruth.

In the Almanac, the seventy generations are grouped into ten weeks of seven. The idea of using seven and ten to count out significant generations is found in the Masoretic Genesis genealogies.[2] Key individuals occupy the last place (the "sabbath") in the sevens and tens:

Last place in sevens:
7th Enoch
14th Eber

Last place in tens:
10th Noah
20th Abraham

Enoch comes at the end of the first week of seven days, and Eber at the end of the second week. Both were important. The Jews would emerge from Eber's descendants, and the word "Hebrew" was supposed to have derived from his name.[3]

Noah and Abraham come at the first two multiples of ten, and these are the two most significant individuals in the period after Adam. This positioning of key names in key places is unlikely to be accidental; the genealogies are designed around groupings of seven and ten.

The second example comes from the book of Ruth, which tells the story of Ruth, the Moabitess, a foreigner and gentile. She is the widow of a Jew who lived in Moab and she and her mother-in-law, also a widow, have no men to support them. So they travel to Judah where Ruth gleans in the fields of Boaz, a rich relation of her mother-in-law. He takes notice of her, and in a daring move, she goes to lie with him while he is sleeping at night to ask him to marry her. At the end of this short book there is a genealogy of David:[4]

Perez
Hezron
Ram
Amminadab
Nahshon
Salmon
Boaz (7th)
Obed
Jesse
David (10th)

The purpose of this genealogy is to show Ruth's special position in the history of Judah. Through her husband Boaz, she is seventh in line from Perez, the son of Judah. David is her descendant and comes in tenth place. This genealogy shows the same pattern of sevens and tens that we find in Genesis.[5]

➢   **Seventy was a special number—the multiple of seven and ten.**

The significant numbers seven and ten multiplied together give seventy. This number seventy was regarded as special by the Jews and by other middle eastern civilisations. The one disadvantage of seventy is that it is not divisible by twelve, another significant number. So seventy-two was often substituted for seventy. To some extent "seventy" started as a way of saying "many" and did not mean a precise number. But over time a special significance attached to the number itself. The idea that there were seventy nations would have originally meant that there were many nations. But by the time we get to Genesis, the patriarchs of seventy nations are carefully enumerated.

Given the importance of the sabbath to the Israelites, it was natural to arrange time as seventy days, with each day being one generation. While adhering to the week, there were two possible arrangements:

- One week of seven great days, each of which was a "week" of ten days.
- Ten weeks (great days) of seven days each.

Each of these has advantages and disadvantages. The first expresses all time as a single week, corresponding to the week of creation. It also leads to a natural climax at the end of the sabbath great day which is the end of time. It has the disadvantage that each great day consists of a "week" of ten days rather than a proper week of seven.

The second method starts by arranging time into weeks of seven days, which is a more natural approach. It has the disadvantage that unlike the first method, the duration of the world is not a single week of seven great days. After the week of great days, there are three more great days. The Apocalypse of Weeks struggles with this problem, and allocates all three weeks for the apocalypse. The Almanac uses this feature brilliantly by applying the week both backwards and forwards under the principle of symmetry.

A Dead Sea scroll text

> In a text found among the Dead Sea scrolls, the fallen angels rule the world for seventy generations. This period is organised as seven great days each of ten generations.

Two Aramaic fragments found at Qumran, 4Q180 and 4Q181, link the Genesis genealogies to the duration of the world and the rule of the fallen angels. The fragments have been identified as coming from a single text which has been reconstructed and translated by J.T. Milik.[6] According to Milik, the text was a commentary on "a book of periods" that was used by the author of Enoch. This is Milik's translation:

> *Commentary on (the book of) periods created by God: each single period in order that [every past] and future event may be fulfilled. Before creating them He established the activities [of the angels in accordance with their periods], one period after another, (each one of) which is engraved on tablets [of heaven, and the law is determined for] all the periods of their domination.*

God has created the periods that make up the duration of the world according to a master plan: *"that every past and future event may be fulfilled"*. He has appointed the angels before time to rule over each period. This

confirms exactly the picture we have already found; that the whole history of the earth, past and future, is organised into periods with an angel
appointed for each period. The document continues:

> *This is the order of (generations after) the creation [of Adam; and from
> Noah to] Abraham, when he begat Isaac, there are ten [weeks].*

The periods are called "weeks" but are actually generations. The first
twenty generations in Genesis are organised as two groups each of ten
generations which culminate with Noah and Abraham respectively. The
text continues with a commentary on the descent of the fallen angels:

> *And] commentary concerning 'Azaz'el and the angels "who [went unto
> the daughters] of men and they gave birth to giants for them" And con-
> cerning 'Azaz'el [who led] Israel [astray to love] iniquity and to (wish
> to) possess wickedness, all [his] period, during seventy weeks, [making
> (them)] forget commandments*

Here it is explicit that the angels will rule for seventy "weeks" meaning
seventy generations. The generations are grouped into tens, so we have a
week of seven great days each ten generations long:

"Week" = one generation
Great day = 10 "weeks" = 10 generations
Duration of the world = one great week = 7 great days

Jubilees

Jubilees is another work which places historical events in a calendar of
weeks. It dates from the mid second-century BC and gives an account
of history, from Adam to the Promised Land, organised in a calendar of
"jubilees". Each jubilee is a week of seven "days", with each "day" being
a week of seven years, giving forty-nine years in total. The history in
Jubilees is mostly based on Genesis and Exodus. However, the author
also had access to apocalyptic material, including Enoch and a book of
Noah. Jubilees is not itself an apocalypse; it takes a priestly view of events.
The concept of the week as the fundamental division of time, the sabbath
ordained by God, runs throughout the work.[7]
There are some unexpected similarities between Jubilees and
Christianity. We have already seen that in Jubilees each nation has its
own spiritual ruler, just as in proto-Christianity the seventy angels each

rule a nation. There are also some remarkable similarities to Christianity in a passage which describes the restoration from exile.[8] The Jews will go back to God *"with all their heart and all their soul" and they will become "sons of the living God"*. God will *"cut off the foreskin of their heart"*, meaning a new spiritual circumcision.[9] Most revealingly, the returning Jews will be given a "holy spirit": *"And I shall create for them a holy spirit, and I shall purify them…" (Jubilees 1:23)*. This anticipates the Christian holy spirit by two hundred years.

> **The Jubilees history lasts for fifty jubilees and not forty-nine jubilees as we would expect.**

As the jubilees are counted up starting with Adam, everything leads us to expect that there will be a total of forty-nine jubilees—a jubilee of jubilees. But this expectation is disappointed. In the forty-ninth jubilee Moses dwells in Midian, and returns to Egypt in the fiftieth jubilee. However, the concept of forty-nine jubilees does come in near the end of the book:

> *On account of this I ordained for you the weeks of years, and the years, and the jubilees (as) forty-nine jubilees from the days of Adam until this day and one week and two years. And they are still forty further years to learn the commands of the Lord until they cross over the shore of the land of Canaan, crossing over the Jordon to its western side. (Jubilees 50:4)*[10]

The timeline is expressed as forty-nine jubilees plus two odd periods; nine years tacked on to the forty-nine jubilees between the creation of Adam and Sinai, and a further forty years in the wilderness before the entry into Canaan. So the total duration is fifty jubilees. The whole book is constructed around a hierarchy with each unit of time seven times greater than the previous unit:

Year (1 yr)
Week of years (7 yrs)
Jubilee (49 yrs)
Week of jubilees (343 yrs) (does not appear explicitly)
Jubilee of jubilees (2,401 yrs)

So why make the whole duration fifty jubilees? The author had wide discretion in translating the Genesis stories into years and could easily have made his history cover forty-nine jubilees. What is so special about fifty jubilees?

> ➢ Jubilees is using an apocalyptic calendar of seventy generations
>   from Adam to the new temple. The author has confused the final
>   return from exile with the original entry into the Promised Land.
>   The fifty jubilees correspond to seventy generations.

The author of Jubilees has chosen to end his historical account with the
entry into Canaan. Why this particular endpoint? Jubilees is supposedly an
account of revelations received by Moses from God on Mount Sinai. God
warns Moses about the coming falling away of the people and the exile. But
he promises that after the people are repentant, he will restore them. God
tells Moses to write two books; the first is the Torah, and the second is the
book of Jubilees which is dictated by "the angel of the presence":

> *And he said to the angel of the presence, "Write for Moses from the first
> creation until my sanctuary is built in their midst forever and ever."
> (Jubilees 1:27)[11]*

This specifies the endpoint as the establishment of the sanctuary, the
temple. But how does this relate to the entry into Canaan? The answer is
that the author has confused the apocalyptic temple at the end of time
with the first temple. The words of God make it clear that this temple will
be built after the exile: *"I shall transplant them as a righteous plant"* and *"I
shall build my sanctuary in their midst, and I shall dwell with them."* (Jubilees
1:16;17). The author of Jubilees is using an apocalyptic source, but such
apocalyptic ideas are foreign to his way of thinking. He is preoccupied
with everyday priestly concerns, such as the ritual calendar and the correct observance of sacrifices. So he has confused this final apocalyptic
temple with the first temple and made the return from cosmic exile into
the entry into Canaan.

In Jubilees, the tabernacle serves as a placeholder for the temple which
was not built until Solomon. The tabernacle is only ever mentioned in
conjunction with the temple or temple observances. Typical is the way
that God describes the disobedience of the Jews:

> *...they have forsaken my ordinances and my commandments and the
> feasts of my covenant and my sabbaths and my sacred place, which I
> sanctified for myself among them, and my tabernacle and my sanctu-
> ary, which I sanctified for myself in the midst of the land so that I might
> set my name upon it and might dwell (there). (Jubilees 1:10)*

The establishment of the sanctuary is linked to the entry into Canaan
near the end of Jubilees:

*And whenever the children of Israel enter into the land which they will
possess, into the land of Canaan, they will set up the tabernacle of the
Lord in the midst of the land, in one of the tribes, until the sanctuary
of the Lord is built upon the land. (Jubilees 49:18)*

This is the true endpoint of the calendar in Jubilees; the erection of the
temple as the tabernacle. By "one of the tribes" the author means Judah.
This is really all about the Jerusalem temple.

Why are there fifty jubilees, and not forty-nine, from Adam to this
proto-temple? The starting point would be a calendar of seventy generations. The author of Jubilees is living in an age when, under Hellenistic
influence, calendars began to be set out in years. So he converts the seventy generations to years. To do this, he needs the length of a generation. Biblical generations were not equal; the earliest lifetimes in Genesis
were far longer than later generations, a point that is actually discussed
in Jubilees.[12] But to allow for this would be incredibly complex. A better,
conceptual calculation is to use the traditional lifespan of seventy years.
Notionally, a generation is half the lifespan or thirty-five years. The calculation is then as follows:

Seventy generations = 70 * 35 years = 2,450 years.

But this is the same as fifty jubilees:

Fifty jubilees = 50 * 49 years = 2,450 years

The author of Jubilees has noticed this coincidence. Fifty jubilees are
remarkably close to the significant forty-nine jubilees, so he builds his
calendar around fifty jubilees. He expresses the fifty as forty-nine plus
some extra years for the beginning and end. This supports the idea that
the author of Jubilees was using an apocalyptic source of seventy generations ending with the new temple.

Daniel

The most significant work that uses a calendar of seventy periods is Daniel.
The apocalyptic book of Daniel is the odd man out in the Hebrew Bible.
It is of poor literary quality, and the original language of some sections
was Aramaic rather than Hebrew. Yet it was to exercise extraordinary
influence. The Hebrew is an odd attempt at recreating the archaic style
of the prophets and has been produced by someone whose first language

was Aramaic. The book is supposedly set during the Babylonian exile but was obviously written in the Maccabean age, although some elements are doubtless earlier than this. The chief value of Daniel is as a record of the beliefs of the apocalyptic movement at a time when the Christ myth is taking its final form.

Two sections are of particular interest here; the prophecy of weeks in Daniel 9 and the prophecies concerning the "king of the North" in Daniel 11. Both are supposedly given to Daniel at the very start of the Persian period, following the defeat of Babylon. But the author has no genuine historical knowledge of this time and makes some appalling errors. For example, the prophecy of Daniel 9 occurs in the "first year of Darius, the son of Ahasuerus", a Mede who has been appointed king over the newly conquered Babylonian Empire. But there was no such person. Babylon was defeated and ruled by the Persian King Cyrus. The confusion seems to have arisen from another Persian monarch, Darius, who ruled a few years after Cyrus, and who, like Cyrus, gave permission for the rebuilding of the temple. As for Darius being a Mede, this reflects a prophecy in the book of Jeremiah in which the conquers of Babylon are the "kings of the Medes" (Jeremiah 51:11,28), another title for the kings of Persia.

> **The book of Daniel is greatly influenced by Jeremiah. It measures dates from prophecies in Jeremiah and gives an absurdly early date for the start of exile.**

The book of Jeremiah is the author of Daniel's main source of information about the exile. The author calculates his timing of events from Jeremiah, even to the extent of absurdly moving the start of the exile to 606 BC, early in the reign of Jehoiakim. This date is closer to Jeremiah's prediction of the 70 years of exile to the fall of Babylon, whereas the actual exile lasted no more than 58 years:

    First exile (Jeconiah); 597 BC to 539 BC = 58 years
    Main exile (Zedekiah); 586 BC to 539 BC = 47 years
    Exile in Daniel (Jehoiakim); 606 BC to 539 BC = 67 years

As Appendix B shows, this timing of the exile comes from a misunderstanding of other prophecies in Jeremiah. Still, it has doubtless been adopted because it more closely matches the prediction of seventy years.

➤ Daniel utilises an existing apocalyptic calendar of seventy
   periods which included the destruction of Jerusalem by the
   Babylonians. The author of Daniel has applied "prophecies"
   about the king of Babylon to Antiochus IV.

One of the most important parts of Daniel is the prophecy of the seventy
years. Daniel is praying after the defeat of Babylon, asking why the exile
has not come to an end. The angel Gabriel comes to him with a reply:

> *"Seventy weeks are decreed on your people and your holy city, to finish
> the transgression, and to put an end to sin, to make atonement for
> iniquity, and to bring in everlasting righteousness, and to seal both
> vision and prophet, and to anoint the most holy place." (Daniel 9:24)*

The timescale of exile has been expanded sevenfold, to seventy weeks of
years. The famous prophecy of the seventy weeks follows; it has inspired
and infuriated generations of interpreters. However, we can make sense
of the prophecy if we start from the perspective that the author of Daniel
is habitually muddled and greatly values the prophecies in Jeremiah.
The author has edited, and added to, an existing source with a calendar
of seventy periods to make it applicable to his own time. So prophecies
which were recounting past events concerning the king of Babylon and
the destruction of Judah, have wrongly been interpreted as relating to
the Seleucid King Antiochus IV. (See Appendix B for the justification of
what follows.)

➤ The first part of the prophecy has been written or heavily edited
   by the author of Daniel. The "anointed one" in this part is
   intended to be Cyrus.

The prophecy starts with the return to Jerusalem.

> *Know therefore and understand that from the going out of the word to
> restore and build Jerusalem to the coming of an anointed one, a prince,
> there shall be seven weeks... (Daniel 9:25)*

The word to restore Jerusalem is the prophecy in Jeremiah (the "word
of God") that the city would be rebuilt (Jeremiah 31:38). This prophecy
followed by a statement (Jeremiah 32:1) indicating a date of 588 BC (or
perhaps 587 BC). Going forward from this date by seven weeks of years
(forty-nine years) gives 539 BC, the year that Cyrus defeated Babylon. So
the "anointed one" is the Persian King Cyrus who allowed the Jews to

return and rebuild Jerusalem: Cyrus is even called Yahweh's "anointed" in Isaiah.[13]

> *... and sixty-two weeks: it shall be built again with squares and moat,*
> *but in a troubled time. (Daniel 9:25)*

Although Jerusalem was rebuilt following Cyrus' victory, the Jews lived under domination by successive foreign empires, so it was a "troubled time". The period of sixty-two weeks of years, which is intended to bring the prophecy up to the author's own time, is inaccurate. The Jews who lived in the Maccabean age did not know precisely how long had elapsed since the exile because there were no scriptural books spanning this long period.

➤ **The middle section is unchanged from the original source; the author of Daniel has confused Nebuchadnezzar, king of Babylon, with Antiochus IV.**

Within the Daniel prophecy, we can find a remnant of the original source in Daniel 9:26:

> *And after the sixty-two weeks, an anointed one shall be cut off and*
> *shall have nothing.*

This "anointed one" who is cut-off fits perfectly the young King Jeconiah who was deposed by Nebuchadnezzar in 597 BC. He was taken to Babylon and imprisoned for most of his long life, so he indeed can be said to have had "nothing".

> *And the people of the prince that shall come will destroy the city and*
> *the sanctuary.*

The exile of Jeconiah was followed by the destruction of Jerusalem and the temple in the reign of Zedekiah. The "prince that shall come" is actually Nebuchadnezzar, king of Babylon. (The practice of referring to past events as if they will happen in the future is common in prophetic literature.)

> *Its end shall come with a flood, and to the end there shall be war.*
> *Desolations are decreed.*

This confirms that the prophecy related to Babylon and not the Seleucid Empire. Flood imagery was a metaphor for invasion by the great powers whose capital was built by a river; specifically, Egypt, Assyria and Babylon. The "desolation" is the devastation and depopulation of Judah following the Babylonian conquest.

The author of Daniel must have thought that the "prince to come" meant Antiochus IV and his actions against the temple and the Jews. He has added the sixty-two weeks, but otherwise, the fragment has survived relatively unchanged.

➢ **The final part explicitly relates the prophecy to Antiochus IV.**

The author of Daniel has clearly written the last section:

> *And he shall make a strong covenant with many for one week. In the middle of the week he shall put an end to sacrifice and offering. And on the wing of abominations shall come one who makes desolate, until the end decreed is poured out on him.*

This must relate to Antiochus, who had the support of many Jews, who caused the temple sacrifices to cease and who erected the "abomination of desolation" in the temple. Such precise prophecies are the hallmark of the author of Daniel and quite unlike the original prophetic books.

➢ **Antiochus IV is also confused with Nebuchadnezzar in the prophecies of the "king of the North".**

We can find a remarkable confirmation that the author of Daniel did apply a source about Nebuchadnezzar to Antiochus IV; he did the same in Daniel 11. This is a prophecy of the history of the Seleucid Empire that is both very specific and, up to a certain point of time, amazingly accurate. But prophecy is hard, particularly when it relates to the future. The end of this section goes hilariously wrong. There could be no clearer evidence that the "prophecy" was written during the period it depicts, immediately after the events of the accurate section.

However, the author of Daniel did have a source for these future predictions. This source was not about Antiochus, "the king of the North" as he is called in Daniel, but the king of Babylon. The following are the main points of similarity, with more detail in Appendix B:

- In Daniel, the "king of the North" (Antiochus) battles the "king of the South", the Egyptian Ptolemaic king. But Nebuchadnezzar, king of Babylon, could also be called "the king of the North" because in Jewish scripture he comes from the north. He fought a series of battles against Pharaoh Necho II of Egypt (who could be called the king of the South) for regional dominance.

- The king of the South comes with an army against the king of the North but suffers a crushing defeat.[14] This describes the battle of Carchemish in 605 BC when Necho's army came up to attack Babylon but was defeated by Nebuchadnezzar.
- After the king of the North wins the battle, he sweeps down into many countries, including Judah.[15] This describes the advance of Babylonian power under Nebuchadnezzar after Carchemish.
- Only three countries avoid the invasion; Edom, Moab and Ammon.[16] These are the same three countries in which, according to Jeremiah, the Jews took refuge from Nebuchadnezzar.[17]
- The prediction of the end of the king of the North fits the end of the Babylonian Empire, but not the real death of Antiochus. (See Appendix B)

The religion of the king of the North also reflects the Jewish and proto-Christian view of the king of Babylon:

- The king of the North, like the angelic king of Babylon, magnifies himself above every god.[18]
- The king of the North rejects the god "beloved of women", probably signifying Dumuzi (Tammuz).[19] If Dumuzi stands for Christ, then this reflects the opposition of the heavenly king of Babylon to Christ.
- The king of the North is victorious due to the aid of a strange foreign "god of fortresses".[20] This god can only be Yahweh who, according to the Jews, enabled the conquests of Nebuchadnezzar.

In contrast, none of this description is at all applicable to Antiochus.

➢ **The author of Daniel's source had similarities with the Almanac.**

What was the nature of the source used by the author of Daniel? The original source is obscured by the mist of confusion which descends in Daniel, but certain characteristics are consistent with an apocalyptic calendar similar to the Almanac:

- The source must have had seventy periods.
- It included the events of the Babylonian exile, which were positioned within the seventy periods. So the seventy periods did not initially start with the exile but covered a much more extended period.

- Most likely the periods were called "weeks", with each week standing for a generation. (We find this same terminology in the fragments 4Q180 and 4Q181 where the seventy generations are called "seventy weeks".)

If the last point is correct, then a "week" would have existed at two levels; as one generation, and as a "week of weeks" or seven generations. This gives the possibility that the two anointed ones were the same person in the source document. The seven weeks to the first anointed would have originally meant seven weeks of weeks, or forty-nine generations rather than forty-nine years. The person who comes at this position in the Almanac is Jeconiah, who, we have seen, is the second anointed one. Jeconiah was exiled at the very start of generation 7.7, which is perhaps why the anointed one is cut off at the beginning of the final week. If this is correct, then "sixty-two weeks" would not have been in the source. Although the length of the world is seventy periods, the author of Daniel would have utilised a section of the apocalypse which ended after forty-nine periods.

PART FOUR

CRUCIFIXION

15

The Third Day

Paul and the third day

➤ **The earliest account of the death and resurrection of Jesus leads
to a prophecy in Hosea which is expressed in Almanac time.**

The first account of the death and resurrection of Jesus comes not from the
gospels but the letters of Paul:

> *For I delivered to you foremost what I also received: that Christ died
> for our sins in accordance with the scriptures, that he was buried, that
> he was raised on the third day in accordance with the scriptures, and
> that he appeared to Cephas, then to the twelve. (1 Corinthians 15:3-5)*

Paul is not giving his own view but passing on information that he has
received. This must come from those who founded the movement, in particular Cephas with whom Paul stayed in Jerusalem. We are getting here
an excellent source of information which is far closer to the early movement than any of the gospel accounts. Paul has been taught that Christ
died "in accordance with the scriptures" and was raised on the third day
"in accordance with the scriptures". But what does this formula mean?
Paul does not elaborate, although elsewhere he is keen to give scriptural
justifications for beliefs. Either he does not know the ultimate source, or
it is secret knowledge not to be divulged in an open letter.

There is only one potential source in scripture for the third day; a passage in Hosea which starts with Yahweh destroying Israel (Ephraim) and
Judah:

> *For I will be to Ephraim as a lion,*
> *And as a young lion to the house of Judah.*
> *I, even I, will tear and go away;*
> *I will carry off, and none shall rescue. (Hosea 5:14)*

But Yahweh will redeem his people from their exile:

Come, let us return to Yahweh;
for he has torn us, but he will heal us;
he has struck us, and he will bind us up.
After two days he will revive us;
on the third day he will raise us up,
And we will live in his sight. (Hosea 6:1-2)

The exile will last for two days, and on the third day Israel and Judah will be "raised up" or resurrected. Paul's words "in accordance with scripture" takes us straight to the exile. Why, though, does Hosea tell us that the exile will last for two days when other sources say it will last for seventy years? The answer lies in the Almanac. The days of the final exile and return are:

7.7 Jeconiah
8.1 Shealtiel
8.2 Zerubbabel

The exile started at the beginning of the generation of Jeconiah and ended physically with the return under Zerubbabel. So the exile lasts for two days in Almanac time (7.7 and 8.1). The restoration is on the third day (8.2) just as Hosea says. Another way of looking at this is that the length of the exile was equal to the notional human lifespan of seventy years and so equal to two generations of 35 years each, or two days of Almanac time.

This means that the Almanac's method of reckoning time was in existence before Hosea. The author of Hosea may or may not have had a complete calendar like the Almanac, but they certainly thought about time in the same way, with a generation as a day.

➢   **The death and resurrection of Christ are linked to the exile and return in this earliest source from Paul.**

Paul is talking about the death and resurrection of Jesus which he says were in accordance to a scripture that was about the exile. The implications are:

The death of Jesus = the exile
The resurrection of Jesus = the return

These equivalences are a reflection of the basic principle of prophecy:

What happens on earth mirrors what happens in heaven.

If Israel and Judah had been defeated on earth by Assyria and Babylon, then something terrible had happened in heaven. The son and rightful heir had been murdered by the tenants under their leader, the heavenly king of Assyria/Babylon. Jesus had been crucified at the time of the destruction of Judah, and his death was the exile.

> **The Hosea prophecy was reinterpreted under cosmic escalation with the timescale multiplied by seven.**

There is an obvious problem in applying the Hosea prophecy to Jesus: his resurrection did not occur at the day of Zerubbabel but several hundred years later. The belief that the exile had not ended with Zerubbabel and that the second temple was invalid is earlier than the Jesus movement, for it is found in the Animal Apocalypse. The true exile continued for much longer than two generations or seventy years. And the exile encompassed that of Israel as well as Judah. The timescale must be expanded under the principle of cosmic escalation—but how?

The best evidence for cosmic escalation in scripture comes from Isaiah, where there is a passage which uses the same imagery as the Hosea prophecy:

> *And on every lofty mountain and every high hill there will be streams running with water, in the day of the great slaughter, when the towers fall. Moreover, the light of the moon will be as the light of the sun, and the light of the sun will be sevenfold, as the light of seven days, in the day when Yahweh binds up the breach in his people, and heals the stroke of their wound.* (Isaiah 30:25-6)

Like the Hosea passage, this is about the exile and return. In both, Yahweh's people have been struck a blow which he will "bind up" and heal. The similarity suggests a connection between the two passages, with Isaiah reinterpreting the earlier Hosea prophecy. The books of prophecy draw upon shared traditions and sayings, and we often find similar or related material occurring in different books.

The Isaiah passage tells us how we should expand the timescale. Note the reference to days; "the light of the sun will be sevenfold, as the light of seven days". It is hot in Israel. Why would anyone want a sevenfold increase in the brightness and heat of the sun? The middle-eastern idea of paradise is a shady garden, a cool haven of bubbling streams. A sevenfold increase in heat is more like a vision of hell. The meaning cannot be literal. The idea that one day shall be "as the light of seven days" is reinterpreting time. The day will be expanded sevenfold so that a "day" becomes a week of days.

The exile will not last for two Almanac days, but two Almanac weeks or great days. The destruction of Israel and Judah by Assyria and Babylon takes up the seventh great day, the sabbath week. The final act, the destruction of Jerusalem and the temple, occurs in the seventh day of this seventh great day; the "sabbath of sabbaths", the most special day in history. It is not by chance that the destruction of the temple and the line of David comes at this unique point in time.

The death of Christ is the exile so he is crucified on this day. He lies dead for the duration of the exile; not for two days but two great days, and is restored to life on the third great day.

➢   **Christ appears in the Almanac after the two great days have elapsed.**

If the death of Jesus lasts for two great days or weeks, then where would his resurrection occur in the Almanac? The precise time can be calculated in two different ways.

First method: Start with the first day of physical exile, that of Jeconiah at 7.7. Taking fourteen days as the duration of the exile, the last day of exile is 9.6 and the return 9.7. This is exactly where Jesus appears in the genealogy in Matthew.

Second method: Use the Almanac weeks to measure the great days. Jesus dies in day 7.7, so the two great days for which he is dead encompass weeks 8 and 9. His resurrection will start the final, third week, so he should be placed in 10.1. This is where he comes in the reconstructed Almanac.

The second is the preferred option as it respects the structure of Almanac great days. The resurrection of Jesus is the transition between the ninth and the final tenth great days; it brings in the last week of the apocalypse.

The two methods are not inconsistent. The resurrected Jesus must be placed in 10.1, but if Jesus were thought to be a man then his human life must be set in 9.7 which is where Jesus appears in the Matthew genealogy. Jesus' age is mentioned only once in the gospels:

And Jesus beginning, was about thirty years old... (Luke 3:23)

The belief that Jesus had been a physical man in the first-century only emerged shortly before the Gospel of Mark was produced. The early

Jesus movement only knew the spiritual Jesus who appeared through the shaman Mary and her followers and apostles. The thirty years must have related to the age of Mary at the time of this first spiritual appearance. Note the odd phrase that "Jesus beginning" occurred at thirty years old.

In Acts, Jesus stays on earth for forty days after his resurrection. We find the same forty days in Mark, where it is the time that Jesus spent in the wilderness after baptism. In both cases the forty days goes back to a tradition that Jesus was present through Mary for forty years after his resurrection. So her lifetime would be the notional seventy years for a person who had lived to old age, divided into two unequal generations of 30 and 40 years.

> ➢ **In the Almanac, the resurrection takes place on the first day of the final week. This has become the literal first day of the week, a Sunday, in the gospels.**

The appearance of the resurrected Jesus in 10.1, the first day of the last Almanac week, explains why Jesus is resurrected on the first day of the week in the gospels. In the Rock and the Tower, I trace this back to the "Gospel of the Long Ending". Although most scholars view the so-called "long ending" of Mark as a later addition, I show that it is actually an earlier source which was incorporated into Mark twice. It was first used as a source for the Mark account of the empty tomb which ended with the message of the angel. Early readers were dissatisfied with this ending because it did not acknowledge the first resurrection appearance to Mary the Magdalene. The Gospel of the Long Ending was appended to Mark in its entirety to correct this deficiency very soon after the production of the first version of the gospel. It was this second expanded version that was widely distributed and known to the authors of Matthew and Luke.[1]

The earliest gospel account of the first resurrection appearance from the Gospel of the Long Ending, is just one line:

> *And having risen early on the first day of the week, he appeared first to Mary the Magdalene, from whom he had cast out seven demons.* (Mark 16:9)

We are told three things here; that the resurrection happened early on the first day of the week, that Jesus appeared first to Mary the Magdalene, and that he had cast out seven demons from her. A similar formula for the first day occurs when the women visit the tomb: *"very early on the first (day) of the week ..."* (Mark 16:2). Both confirm the placing of the resurrected Jesus in day 10.1 of the Almanac.

The gospels and the third day

➢   The formula of the third day also occurs in the gospels. It is
    linked in Matthew to the "sign of Jonah", that Christ will be
    dead for three days and nights.

In the Gospel of Mark, Jesus twice predicts to his disciples that he will be
killed and resurrected on the third day:

> *"The Son of Man is being delivered to the hands of men, and they shall
> kill him, and having been killed, he shall rise on the third day." (Mark
> 9:31)*

And:

> *"We go up to Jerusalem, and the Son of Man shall be delivered to the
> chief priests and scribes, and they shall condemn him to death, and
> deliver him to the nations. And they shall mock him, and spit on him,
> and scourge him, and kill him, and the third day he shall rise again."
> (Mark 10:33-34)*

Note the phrase "and shall deliver him to the nations" which fits the
exile of Israel and Judah. Matthew repeats these two predictions and goes
a step further:

> *And he answering said to them, "An evil and adulterous generation
> seeks for a sign, and no sign shall be given to it, except the sign of Jonah
> the prophet. For just as Jonah was in the belly of the great fish for three
> days and three nights, so shall the Son of Man be in the heart of the
> earth three days and three nights." (Matthew 12:39-40)*

The author of Matthew goes disastrously wrong with this prediction
that Jesus will be dead and buried for three days and nights. In the
gospel accounts, he is dead for a much shorter period. The timescale
in Mark is clear and specific; Jesus dies at 3 pm on the day before the
sabbath and is resurrected by dawn (6 am) on the day after the sabbath.
The gives the maximum time for which he could be dead as 39 hours,
much less than the 72 hours that the comparison with Jonah implies. In
Mark, Jesus is only dead for one day and two nights, not three days and
three nights.

In the Matthew resurrection account, the timing is even shorter:

At the end of the sabbath, at dawn towards the first (day) of the week,
Mary the Magdalene, and the other Mary came to see the tomb.
(Matthew 28:1)

The women go to the tomb at the "end of the sabbath", meaning just after sundown. This is the "dawn" of the next day, the customary way of referring to the beginning of the day at around 6 pm and not 6 am. So the women approach the tomb during twilight in the early Saturday evening. Jesus is dead for only a single day and night, about 27 hours, compared to the 72 hours of the Jonah comparison.

The sign of Jonah does not match the timings in the gospel accounts of the resurrection. The application of the sign to Jesus must date from before the gospels, with the ultimate source being the prophecy of the "third day". In the Book of Jonah, God orders Jonah to go to the Assyrian capital Nineveh and predict its destruction. Jonah has no wish to be a prophet and takes the first ship in the opposite direction! God sends a storm, and Jonah is thrown by the sailors into the sea where he is swallowed by a "great fish", remaining in its belly for three days and three nights. While in the fish, he prays to God using images of death and burial; he is in the *"belly of Sheol"* and has descended to the *"roots of the mountain"* where the earth imprisons him. But he looks towards the holy temple, for God has raised him from the pit.[2] After Jonah is vomited up by the fish, he goes to Nineveh and predicts its end. But the people are repentant, so God does not destroy the city. Jonah is furious with God for making him look silly. There is then a strange episode in which God causes a gourd plant to grow over Jonah to keep the hot sun off his head. The next day God kills the plant so that the sun beats down upon him. Both the fish and the gourd plant became favourite visual images for early Christians.

The story of Jonah matches both the death and resurrection of Jesus, and the exile and restoration of Israel. The three days and nights do not agree precisely with the Hosea prediction of the third day or with the Almanac timing. But they are close enough on a broad-brush view. It is easy to see how the author of Jonah could start with the Hosea prediction and turn it into three days and nights. The comparison between Jonah and the gospels goes glaringly wrong because the author of Mark has omitted a whole day.

> ➤ The change that the author of Matthew makes to the timing of
> the resurrection of Mark shows that he had a source that reflected
> the Almanac timing.

In Matthew, the women come to the tomb on Saturday evening. In Mark, it is explicit that the sun has risen, so the women approach the tomb at around 6 am.[3] Why has the author of Matthew changed the timing of the resurrection from Sunday morning to Saturday evening? He only changes Mark when he detects a problem. The idea that the resurrection happened at the rising of the sun is a powerful image: most readers will instinctively prefer a sunrise resurrection to an evening resurrection. So it is easy to see why the evening should be changed to the morning, but not why the morning should be changed to the evening. The author of Matthew must have had a good reason for believing that the resurrection had taken place just after sundown.

In the Almanac, the resurrection ends week 9 and starts week 10. So it occurs at the end of the sabbath day in week nine (9.7) and the start, the "dawn", of the first day in week ten (10.1). And this is exactly where Mathew places the resurrection: "At the end of the sabbath, at dawn towards the first (day) of the week..." This is consistent with the Gospel of the Long Ending which has "early on the first day of the week". Almanac days are notional, without a night or day. But when expressed as a real day of twenty-four hours, the resurrection occurs at the dawn of darkness. This would make the resurrected Jesus seem like a ghost. So the author of Mark has reinterpreted the "dawn" of the day, the evening, as sunrise.

> ➤ In applying the third-day formula, the Gospel of Mark has lost
> a day.

The author of Mark derives the timing of the crucifixion from two pieces of information:

1. Jesus is resurrected on the third day after his death.
2. Jesus is resurrected on the first day of the week.

The day of the crucifixion is counted as the first day, so this becomes a Friday. In converting Almanac great days to literal days of twenty-four hours, the author of Mark encounters problems that would never have occurred to the framers of the Almanac. Jesus has to be buried before the sabbath, so he must die mid-afternoon on Friday and not at 6 pm.

If we follow the Matthew timing then Jesus is dead for little more than one day. This is very different from the three days and three nights of the

Jonah prophecy because the gospels have missed out a great day from the Almanac. Christ is dead for two whole great days (weeks eight and nine). But when converted into the gospels' literal days, he is only dead for one complete day, Saturday.

The third day and the apocalypse

➢   **The third day is the Almanac week of the apocalypse.**

The resurrection of Jesus brings in the apocalypse, but this was seen as taking time to play out. The extant version of the Apocalypse of Weeks reserves no less than three weeks, or twenty-one generations for the end times. Clearly, this is too long and the Almanac sets aside one week, the tenth, for the apocalypse. Christ was expected to appear in the skies, as predicted in the Gospel of Mark:

> *At that time they will see the Son of Man coming in the clouds with great power and glory. And then he will send the angels and gather his elect from the four winds, from the ends of the earth to the ends of heaven. (Mark 13:26-7)*

The movement accepted the spiritual appearance of Christ through Mary and her followers as a preliminary to this spectacular appearance of Christ. Most people in the movement expected Christ to come in the skies by the end of the first generation:

> *Truly I say to you, this generation will not pass away until all these things are done. (Mark 13:30)*

The spiritual appearance of Jesus to Mary started day 10.1. The appearance of Jesus in the skies, visible to all, would end this first day of the final week. We can fill in the other generations in week ten from the list of things that had to happen:

There would be battles on earth, and then a final battle involving Christ and the angels of heaven.

There would be a general resurrection of the dead.

The seventy fallen angels would be judged, condemned, and sent into the pit of fire.

The human followers of the seventy would be condemned and sent into the pit.

Heaven and earth would be destroyed.

A new heaven and earth would be created to be ruled over by Christ.

The early Christians believed that the first battles were already underway. The servants of the seventy, the powers of this world, were attempting to destroy the Jesus movement through persecution. Soon Christ would appear to end this first stage. By the time Mark was written, knowledge of the Almanac had faded. The allocation of apocalyptic events to specific generations in the final week served no purpose. So the end time events became telescoped together and were seen as happening rapidly, one after the other.

Mary built her new religion on apocalyptic foundations, but that religion was inherently spiritual rather than apocalyptic. Otherwise, it would never have survived the failure of the apocalyptic predictions. Mary believed that the spiritual appearance of Christ was the real appearance, whereas others, such as Paul, continued to look for the ultimate coming in the skies. Inherent in the Gospel of Thomas is the idea that the kingdom of heaven is already present on the earth. The new temple has already come in the form of the Magdalene and, beyond her, all pneumatic, chosen Christians. The Gospel of Thomas does expect an ultimate apocalypse. But the new heaven and earth is also the first creation which exists all around us, here and now. Many scholars think that the belief in an already present kingdom of God emerged in response to disappointment at the failure of apocalyptic expectations. But this cannot be true. Paul reacts against this belief as early as the mid-50s. In 1 Corinthians 4:8, he sarcastically reproves those Corinthians who see themselves as being "rich" and "reigning" as kings. This is imagery found in the Gospel of Thomas, where the "rich" are those who are in the kingdom. The Corinthians must have been taught this belief by Paul's rival, the apostle Apollos. It is already widespread in the first generation, long before disappointment about the failure of the apocalypse could set in.

16

Jesus' Last Day

Passion and exile

In the Almanac, the exile will end on the third great day with the resurrection of Christ. We have seen how the author of Mark has made the mistake of interpreting the "third-day" formula as literal days of twenty-four hours. This gives an intriguing possibility. Has the same mistake been made for Jesus' last day, the day of his passion?

Almanac great days (weeks) to days in Mark

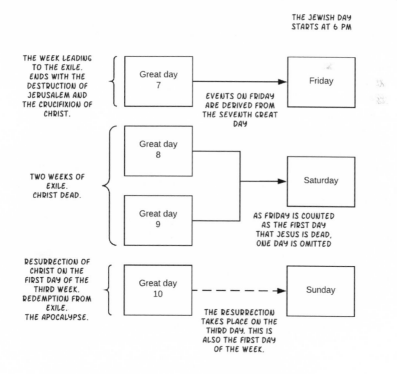

Figure 9: Almanac great days become literal days in Mark.

Translating the great days into days gives the situation shown in Figure 9. The author of Mark changes the death of Jesus to 3 pm to leave time for the burial. Friday becomes the first day that Jesus is dead, and one great day is omitted. To be consistent, the seventh great day or week should be equivalent to Jesus' last day, which culminates in his crucifixion. Is the passion day account derived from the seventh great day?

> **A conversion of a great day to a literal day would have to respect the four cardinal points.**

A great day is a week of seven days, each of one generation. Suppose we wanted to represent this great day in terms of a real day of twenty-four hours. How could this be done? We might divide twenty-four hours equally by seven so that each day would correspond to 3.429 hours. But no one in the ancient world would have made such a calculation. They did not have decimals and would have wanted to preserve the cardinal points of the daily cycle; dusk, midnight, dawn and midday. These cardinal points divided the day into four. A further division split each six-hour period into two which gave the eight watches of the day:

1st watch: dusk (6 pm) to mid-evening (9 pm)
2nd watch: mid-evening (9 pm) to midnight
3rd watch: midnight to cock-crow (3 am)
4th watch: cock-crow (3 am) to dawn (6 am)
5th watch: dawn (6 am) to mid-morning (9 am)
6th watch: mid-morning (9 am) to noon
7th watch: noon to mid-afternoon (3 pm)
8th watch: mid-afternoon (3 pm) to dusk (6 pm)

There are seven days (generations) but eight watches, so two watches would have to be combined into one period. Which day would be regarded as special to be worthy of being twice as long as the others? This could only be the seventh day, the sabbath, which would be represented by the six hours between 12 am and 6 pm. This would give the following structure:

Day 1: dusk (6 am) to mid-evening (9 pm)
Day 2: mid-evening (9 pm) to midnight
Day 3: midnight to cock-crow (3 am)
Day 4: cock-crow (3 am) to dawn (6 am)
Day 5: dawn (6 am) to mid-morning (9 am)
Day 6: mid-morning (9 am) to noon

Day 7: noon to dusk (6 pm)

If the seventh great day has really been translated into a day of twenty-four hours, is there evidence for this structure?

> **The passion day in Mark is divided into three-hour periods.**

In Mark's passion account, Jesus' last day is divided into three-hour periods. This is the first remarkable indication that the day reflects the seventh great day of the Almanac. Others have noticed the strange structure of the passion day, but as there has never been a good explanation, it is usually passed over in silence. A clue that Mark's account is organised by the eight watches comes in the run-up to the final day:

> *Therefore stay awake—for you do not know when the master of the house comes; in the evening, or at midnight, or when the rooster crows, or in the morning. (Mark 13:35)*

This is a reference to the four watches of the night ending in; (i) the evening, (ii) midnight, (iii) cock-crow, and (iv) the morning (dawn). One of the most famous incidents of the last day is when Jesus predicts that Peter will deny him three times before cock-crow. It would be a remarkable coincidence that the first three watches of the night also end with cock-crow. Originally each of the three denials must have been associated with one of the first three watches, the three days in the Almanac. In the proto-crucifixion source there must be three events that are denials or betrayals of Christ, linked to each of the first three days of the seventh week. The author of Mark has transformed these historical betrayals into the Peter story. Before looking for the three denials, we will briefly set out Jesus' last day in Mark to demonstrate the pattern of three-hour segments.

The passion day

The passion account starts with the preparations for the Passover meal. The lamb was sacrificed in the late afternoon of Nisan 14 but not eaten until after sunset which was the following day, the feast of unleavened bread, Nisan 15. Jesus is represented in early Christians sources as the Passover lamb, the perfect sacrifice; this is quite explicit, for example, in Revelation. So it is significant that his crucifixion should occur at the time of the Passover. This is the type of coincidence that we would not expect if we were dealing with real history. In Mark and the other synoptic gospels,

Jesus is not actually crucified until Nisan 15. The author of John makes the link to the lamb more explicit by moving Jesus' crucifixion to Nisan 14 so that he dies at the same time as the lambs are sacrificed. This change comes at a cost; in John, the last supper is not a Passover feast.

Returning to Mark, Jesus made prior arrangements for the Passover meal by sending two of his disciples ahead. He tells them to follow a man carrying a jar of water to a house. They are to ask the master of that house for the guest room. He will show them to an upper chamber furnished and ready, where they can make the preparations for the feast. This story is distinctly odd, and some have seen an astrological significance in the man carrying the jug of water. Does he represent Aquarius? In support, it is often said that men would never carry water in the Roman world, but this is not true. Although free men would be reluctant to fetch water which was women's work, such considerations did not apply to slaves.

The narrative of the last day proper starts when these preparations have been made. In what follows, I have represented the divisions as starting and ending at three-hour intervals. The ancient world did not keep time with anything like modern precision, and the actual times of the watches would have been approximate.

Sunset (6 pm) to mid-evening (9 pm)[1]

The first period of the day is the last supper. The thirteen lie down on couches for the meal:

> And evening having arrived, he came with the twelve. And as they were reclining at table and eating, Jesus said, "Truly, I say to you, one of you eating with me will betray me." (Mark 14:17-18)

Jesus does not say who will betray him, but only that he is "one of the twelve."

> And as they were eating, he took bread, and having spoken a blessing, he broke it and gave it to them, saying "Take this, it is my body." And he took a cup, and having given thanks, he gave it to them, and they all drank of it. And he said to them, "This is my blood of the covenant, which is poured out for many. Truly, I say to you, no more will I drink of the fruit of the vine until that day when I drink it anew in the kingdom of God." (Mark 14:22-25)

The bread and wine are an allusion to Jesus' approaching sacrifice. In the Mark timing of the crucifixion, this is the Passover meal in which the sacrificial lamb is eaten. The "fruit of the vine" carries an allusion to the parable of the vineyard.

Mid-evening (9 pm) to midnight[2]

After the meal, Jesus leads his disciples to the Mount of Olives. On the way, he tells them that they will all fall away. Peter is adamant that he never will, and Jesus predicts his three denials. Jesus continues to the garden of Gethsemane with just Peter, James and John. He tells them to keep watch while he goes apart to pray. He asks God, his father, that the cup may be removed from him: *"Yet not what I will, but what you will"* (Mark 14:36). The three disciples, however, fall asleep. Jesus rebukes them and then returns to pray, but the disciples fall asleep again. This is repeated one final time:

> *"It is enough, the hour has come. Behold, the Son of Man is delivered up into the hands of sinners. Rise, let us go. Behold, my betrayer is at hand."* (Mark 14:41-2)

Jesus has seen another of his disciples, Judas Iscariot, approach at the head of an armed crowd sent by the priests. Judas, the betrayer, kisses Jesus who is then arrested. A bystander draws his sword and strikes off the ear of the servant of the high priest, and all Jesus' followers flee, leaving him alone. There is a young man present with just a linen cloth around his body, and when the guards grab the cloth, the young man has to flee naked.

How long does this all take? There is one clue. When Jesus comes back the first time to find his disciples asleep, he says *"Could you not watch one hour [horan]?"* (Mark 14:37). If each of the three times the disciples fall asleep takes one hour, then Jesus is at Gethsemane for three hours, from around 9 pm to around midnight.

Midnight to cock-crow (3 am)[3]

Jesus is taken before the high priest and the Sanhedrin, the council of the priests and elders. The priests are seeking testimony to put Jesus to death, but the witnesses do not agree. Some false witnesses accuse Jesus of claiming that he would destroy the temple and raise another, not built with hands, after three days. Throughout the trial, Jesus is silent until the high priest finally asks him if he is the Messiah, the son of the Blessed One. Jesus replies that he is and that they will see the Son of Man sitting at the right-hand side and coming on the clouds of heaven. Shocked at his blasphemy, the priests tear their clothes, strike him on his mouth and condemn him to death.

While this trial before the Sanhedrin is in progress, Peter, waiting outside with the servants, denies Jesus three times before the second crow of the cock.

Cock-crow (3 am) to dawn (6 am)[4]

It is "early in the morning" when the Sanhedrin, having formed a counsel, have Jesus bound and taken to Pilate. This could mean either dawn or the pre-dawn hours; the fourth pre-dawn watch is called the "morning" elsewhere in Mark.[5] So we take "early in the morning" to mean the start of the fourth watch, or just after 3 am. The alternative interpretation that the Sanhedrin formally met at sun rise to condemn Jesus is inconsistent with what follows. According to the Gospel of Mark, Jesus is crucified at 9 am. So if the Sanhedrin did not condemn Jesus until after 6 am, this would not leave enough time for the real trial before Pilate and preparations for the crucifixion. The Sanhedrin had no power to condemn Jesus to death, and he had not yet even been accused before the Roman authorities. Roman justice was quick by our standards, but not that quick. There was a process that had to be followed, and a trial had to be held first. Indeed, the idea of Jesus being crucified at any time that day is unrealistic; the sentence was not supposed to be executed on the same day as the trial.

The fourth period starts with Jesus being handed over to the Romans and then tried before Pilate. There is much in the account of this trial that is unrealistic. We are not told Jesus' supposed crime, nor the evidence against him, and Jesus does not offer any defence. Pilate calls him the "king of the Jews" and has this written over his cross, but it is not clear whether this is a title or accusation. Much of the account of the trail is taken up with Pilate offering to release Jesus under a supposed traditional amnesty on the feast day. The Jewish crowd instead ask for the release of a murderer and insurrectionist called Barabbas and demand that Jesus be crucified. Pilate finds that Jesus has done nothing wrong, yet he condemns him to crucifixion simply because the Jews want him to. So Jesus is taken away to be scourged, and then the soldiers perform a strange act of mock homage:

> They put a purple robe on him, then twisted together a crown of thorns and set it on him. And they began to call out to him, "Hail, king of the Jews!" Again and again they struck him on the head with a staff and spit on him. Falling on their knees, they paid homage to him. (Mark 15:17-19)

The purple indicates Jesus status as a king. Even though mocked and abused, he is treated as king throughout this period.

Dawn (6 am) to mid-morning (9 am)[6]

There is no indication of the boundary between the fourth and fifth periods. We have assigned the mocking episode to the fourth period as it relates to Jesus as "king of the Jews". This would leave the fifth period for the carrying of the cross to the place of crucifixion. The victim would usually carry his own cross, but the Romans impress a passer-by to carry Jesus' cross for him:

> And they compelled a passer-by, Simon of Cyrene, coming from the country, the father of Alexander and Rufus, to carry his cross. And they brought him to the place Golgotha, which is translated Place of a Skull. (Mark 15:21-22)

This is odd. Why does Jesus not carry his cross? The author of John recognises this problem and eliminates Simon from the story, saying that Jesus "went out, bearing his own cross" (John 19:17). And why should the Romans make this particular man, Simon the Cyrenian, carry the cross if he was just a passer-by? Why would anyone remember his name together with the information that he was the father of Alexander and Rufus, a detail quite superfluous to the story?

The place of execution is called Golgotha, a Hebrew word meaning "skull". Did such a place really exist? No other Jewish writer mentions Golgotha. In the Gospel of John, Jesus is not only crucified at Golgotha but also buried there.[7] We should not be surprised that the other gospels omit this detail, for it would be a very odd coincidence if Joseph of Arimathea just happened to have a new empty tomb ready at the very place of execution. The idea that Jesus was crucified and buried at a place called the "skull" is the stuff of myth rather than historical detail.

Mid-morning (9 am) to midday[8]

From this point on, the division of the day into three hourly intervals is explicit. Jesus is crucified at the "third hour" meaning 9 am, between two robbers:

> And with him they crucify two robbers, one on the right hand, and one on his left. (Mark 15:27)

The passers-by repeat the accusation about the destruction of the temple: *"Aha! The one destroying the temple and building it in three days" (Mark 15:29)*. Even the priests call him a king: *"Let the Christ, the King of Israel, descend now from the cross that we may see and believe. And those crucified with him also reviled him" (Mark 15:32)*. Jesus is not just the king of the Jews (the king of Judah), but also the king of Israel.

Midday to mid-afternoon (3 pm)[9]

The second half of the crucifixion is marked by a darkness that starts at midday:

> *And the sixth hour having arrived, darkness came over all the land until the ninth hour. (Mark 15:33)*

The ninth hour is 3 pm, and at this time, Jesus dies:

> *And at the ninth hour Jesus cried out in a loud voice, "Eloi, Eloi, lema sabachthani?" which is translated, "My God, my God, why have you forsaken me?" And some of those standing by hearing it said, "Behold, he is calling Elijah." And someone ran and filled a sponge with vinegar, putting it on a reed to give him to drink, saying, "Wait, let us see if Elijah comes to take him down." But Jesus uttered a loud cry and breathed his last. And the curtain of the temple was torn in two, from top to bottom. (Mark 15:34-38)*

The death of Jesus is simultaneous to the tearing in two of the temple veil or curtain. This could be either the impressive outer curtain that separated the holy place of the priests from the body of the temple or the smaller inner curtain which separated the holy of holies from the holy place.[10] It is probably this later curtain that is intended; it shielded the sacred area of the temple that could only be entered by the high priest. If either curtain had spontaneously split into two, it would have been a most momentous and ominous event. We would surely have heard about it from Josephus or some other Jewish or Roman source, but there is complete silence.

Mid-afternoon (3 pm) to sunset (6 pm)[11]

According to Jewish custom, a dead body must be buried before the sabbath which began at sunset. The body is requested by Joseph of Arimathea:

> *And when evening had arrived, since it was the day of Preparation,*
> *that is, the day before the sabbath, Joseph of Arimathea, a prominent*
> *council member, who was also himself looking for the kingdom of God,*
> *took courage and went to Pilate and asked for the body of Jesus. (Mark*
> *15:42-3)*

It is a surprise to find a respected member of the council "looking for
the kingdom of God" as a follower of Jesus. But it is even more surprising
that Pilate would give him the body of Jesus. The remains of crucified
criminals would be thrown into a common pit. Denial of a proper burial
was all part of the punishment. But Jesus was allowed to be buried in a
fancy new tomb:

> *And he bought a linen shroud, and taking him down, wrapped him in*
> *the linen shroud and laid him in a tomb that had been cut out of the*
> *rock. And he rolled a stone against the entrance of the tomb. (Mark*
> *15:46)*

Tombs were expensive to make and hosted a large number of burials,
being reused repeatedly, often over hundreds of years. It is another indication of the fictional nature of the story that Jesus' tomb should be freshly
hewn and empty. The burial finishes the eighth part of the day.

Unrealistic timing

Much of the passion account is unrealistic, showing that it is not based
on historical reality. Jesus would not have been crucified on the day
before the sabbath but held over to the following week so as not to lessen
the period of torture. The execution and perhaps burial at the "place of
the skull" is a fictional touch. A condemned criminal's body would not
receive an honourable burial but would be thrown anonymously into a
communal pit. But the least realistic feature of the Mark account is the
timing of the last day.

➤ **Jesus is arrested in the middle of the night at a country location**
   where escape would have been easy.

Why should Jesus be arrested in the middle of the night in the country
even though he was perfectly visible going around Jerusalem in the day?
At night, a person could very easily slip away for there was no street light-
ing. It would have been the Passover full-moon, but Jesus was among trees

whose shadows would have provided excellent cover. He could see and hear the large crowd approaching with torches from afar. So why did he not run and hide, as his supporters did? If the purpose of the night arrest were to avoid trouble with the crowd, then this would be better achieved just before dawn, when Jesus and his supporters were asleep. The author of Mark is clearly aware of these problems. As Jesus says: *"Day after day I was with you in the temple teaching, and you did not seize me"* (Mark 14:49).

> Jesus is supposedly tried at night by the Sanhedrin. But the Sanhedrin never met at night.

Traditional commentators may pass over the problems of the night-time arrest with a shrug of the shoulders, but even they have difficulties with the night-time trial by the Sanhedrin. The Sanhedrin was the supreme Jewish council of the seventy most respected elders under the high priest, and it never met at night. The idea that seventy-one powerful men would be taken out of their beds to hold a trial between midnight and 3 am is absurd. Even if Jesus were arrested at night, he would have been held until the council could assemble at a sensible time of day. Indeed, for a capital charge, the Sanhedrin was not supposed to pass sentence on the same day as the trial to give time for reflection and cooling of tempers. We cannot be sure that the rule was applied in Roman-occupied Judea at this time; if it was, then Jesus could not have been condemned until after the sabbath. The rule certainly demonstrates that the Jews in the early centuries AD were concerned about proper process and care in capital matters.[12]

There is evidence that the author of Mark was aware of the problem of the night meeting of the Sanhedrin. He employs ambiguity by having the Sanhedrin issue its sentence after cock-crow, "early in the morning". We have seen that this could either mean the fourth watch, called the morning watch, or later after sunrise. The author of Mark is trying to fudge the issue, but either way gives insurmountable problems for a realistic account.

Some scholars have tried to explain the trial as an informal meeting of the high priest and some senior members of the Sanhedrin in the night, followed by a very early meeting of the whole Sanhedrin at first light to condemn Jesus. But this is a desperate attempt to turn an unrealistic timetable into something historically conceivable. The councillors would still have to get up very early in the morning to gather for 6 am. They would not have any time to debate Jesus' guilt but would have to take it on trust. The Jews loved due process. Would the Sanhedrin really be so compliant to ignore their own rules in this one case? And what is the point, why would they need to hurry? Even a ridiculously rushed condemnation would take an hour or so. And Jesus was not yet even accused before the only people who mattered, the Romans who would have to hold their own trial. So how could Jesus possibly be crucified by 9 am?

> **The crucifixion of Jesus lasted just six hours, far too short for a real crucifixion.**

Perhaps the most significant timing issue is the short duration of the crucifixion with Jesus dying after just six hours. Crucifixion was a prolonged torture that would last for days. The sight of a person languishing on the cross was a sign to everyone else to behave and obey their Roman masters. Typically, a person would die of slow suffocation when their legs became too weak to support their weight. At this point, they would hang from their arms and be unable to breathe properly. The Gospel of Mark's original readers would have been very aware of crucifixion and would have seen it many times with their own eyes: it was a common enough method of execution throughout the Roman world, particularly for slaves and rebels. So reading that Jesus died after only six hours on the cross would have caused those readers considerable surprise. This is anticipated by the author of Mark, who shows Pilate as being equally amazed:

> *And Pilate marvelled if he were already dead: and calling to him the centurion, he asked him whether he had been any while dead. (Mark 15:44)*

By having Pilate "marvel" at the short duration of Jesus' suffering, the author of Mark presents it as a kind of a miracle. God had taken pity on his son and kept his torment short. But for a person to die after six hours, he would have to be ill or infirm. Jesus was supposedly still young, in his thirties, and fit enough to spend his time traipsing around the country. So why should he be unable to support his weight with his legs after just a few hours?

> **The structure of three-hour periods is fundamental to the crucifixion account. It causes events to be compressed into unrealistic periods.**

Everything shows the same consistent pattern in which the timing of events is compressed. They are squeezed into a time interval which is too short. Jesus should be arrested in the day. He should be held over until the Sanhedrin could meet in a proper manner. His crucifixion should last for far longer than six hours. Had there been a historical reality behind the story, then Jesus would have been arrested and tried on Friday, held in prison over the sabbath, and crucified on the first day of the week, Sunday. He would probably have died a day or two later on Monday or Tuesday. From start to end, the whole process would have taken four days or so, but the Gospel of Mark fits it into just twenty-four hours.

Not only is the last day set out in eight equal intervals, but this pattern is dictating the timing of events. The author of Mark is writing his narrative around this strange structuring of the day: events are taking place at odd times or in periods that are too short. So the division of the day into eight parts is fundamental and not some incidental feature.

The crucifixion in John

> In the Gospel of John, the crucifixion is ordered at noon, and Jesus is only on the cross for about three hours.

The unrealistic timing originates in the Gospel of Mark, which is largely followed by Matthew and Luke. But in John we find something different, and on the face of it, even more absurd. Jesus is brought before Pilate *"early in the morning"* (John 18:28). Pilate is reluctant to crucify Jesus, but the Jews insist. All this takes some time, for when Pilate sits down in the judgement seat to sentence Jesus, it is already noon:

> *And it was the preparation of the Passover, and about the sixth hour: and he said to the Jews, "Behold your King!" (John 19:14)*

This is one of those embarrassing contradictions in the gospels that commentators spend a great deal of time trying to explain away. Mark is specific that the crucifixion started at the third hour of the day, at 9 am. But John says that Pilate only ordered him to be crucified at the sixth hour, at noon. Jesus has still to carry his cross to Golgotha, so the actual crucifixion cannot have started before about 1 pm.

Jesus must have spent a ridiculously short period on the cross for he is buried by sundown. It would take some time for the Roman soldiers to realise that he is dead, to put a spear in his side to make sure, and then take him down from the cross. Word of his death has to reach Joseph of Arimathea who would then have to go and get an audience with Pilate (a busy man) to petition for the body:

> *After these things Joseph of Arimathea, who was a disciple of Jesus, but secretly for fear of the Jews, asked Pilate that he might take away the body of Jesus, and Pilate gave him permission. (John 19:38)*

Joseph is accompanied by another senior Pharisee, Nicodemus, who brings a vast quantity (one hundred Roman pounds) of expensive spices. Once again, this would take some organising. The author of John has an appreciation that time is tight, for Jesus' body is placed in a nearby newly hewn tomb.[13] It is not clear how or why Joseph of Arimathea had such a convenient tomb.

Allowing two hours from death to burial, and an hour for the journey to the cross and preparations for crucifixion, Jesus could have been alive on the cross for no more than three hours. No wonder the Gospel of John is vague and does not tell us the time when Jesus died. Why should the author of John move the time of the crucifixion in stark contradiction to the other gospels when it results in such an absurdity? He must have had a good reason, a source which told him that Christ was actually crucified at noon.

17

Betrayal and Blasphemy

Jewish betrayal

A theme of betrayal runs throughout the story of the passion. Jesus is betrayed or denied by everyone around him; by his closest disciples, by Judas Iscariot, by the crowd who appeared to support him, and by the Jewish establishment of the high priests, the Pharisees and the Sanhedrin. There is one common factor; his betrayers are all Jewish. The Romans are almost good in comparison. Pilate goes out of his way to try and free Jesus. This hostility towards the Jews and white-washing of the Romans is believed by many scholars to reflect the expansion of the early church among gentiles. According to this theory, the gentile Christian churches attempted to dissociate themselves from the Jews, particularly after the Jewish war. So they switched the blame for the crucifixion away from the Romans and on to the Jews. Yet, in reality, this explains nothing. Christianity started as a Jewish movement; the founders of the movement were Jewish, the first apostles and teachers were Jewish. The early gentile Christians were converted and taught by these beloved Jewish teachers. They learnt about Jewish scripture and traditions and joined the church of the Jewish God. How then could they have become suddenly rabidly anti-Jewish? It is also certain that the authors of the two most anti-Jewish gospels, Matthew and John, were both Jewish Christians and not former gentiles. Why would they blame their own people for the crucifixion unless they believed it to be true? So we have the paradox of a Jewish movement that is vehemently anti-Jewish.

The betrayal of Jesus at the hands of the Jews must have been there from the very beginning. If the first Jewish Christians had blamed the Romans, then this should still be visible within the passion account. But the chief movers for Jesus' execution are the Jews. The high priest and the Sanhedrin do not just acquiesce in Jesus' killing, they seek his execution. They put Jesus on trial and condemn him to death. This has to relate to something in the original source.

Three betrayals

> ➢ **Peter's three denials of Jesus before cock-crow are part of a pattern of three betrayals of Christ.**

At the last supper, Jesus predicts the betrayal of Judas Iscariot. After the supper, Jesus and his disciples cross over to the Mount of Olives, and Jesus makes a second prediction of a betrayal. This time it concerns his chief disciple, Peter. When Jesus tells his disciples that they all will be scattered and desert him, Peter is emphatic that he never would, not even if he had to die with Jesus. In response, Jesus gives a famous prediction that Peter will deny him three times that very night:

> *And Jesus said to him, "Truly, I tell you, this very night, before the cock crows twice, you will deny me three times." (Mark 14:30)*

After Jesus' arrest, Peter secretly follows as far as the courtyard of the high priest's residence and warms himself by a fire. A maid recognises him as a follower of Jesus, but Peter denies it, and a rooster crows. The maid tells some others that Peter was with Jesus, and he denies it again. Finally, some bystanders say that as he is a Galilean, he must be "one of them", but Peter curses and swears that he does not know Jesus. The cock crows a second time and Peter, remembering Jesus' prediction, weeps.

One puzzle is what Peter is supposed to have done wrong. He shows considerable bravery in following Jesus to the trial. As for denying that he is a follower of Jesus, that is tactical common sense. To admit to being part of Jesus' group is to be arrested and perhaps executed. Any soldier acting as Peter is supposed to have done would be commended and not criticised for his actions. So why should Peter be thought to have betrayed Jesus?

In the other gospels and some variations of the Mark text, Jesus predicts that Peter's denials will occur before the cock crows once rather than twice. The reading of the two cock-crows is probably original to Mark. However, the fact that the other gospel writers removed the initial cock-crow suggests that they had access to a source which only mentioned "cock-crow". Either way, the crowing of the cock makes the end of the watch of cock-crow which covered the darkest part of the night, starting sometime after midnight and ending with the first slight brightening of the sky. The crowing of the cocks marked this brightening. (In reality, the cock also crows at random times throughout the night. Mark's two consecutive cock-crows is a more practical way of identifying the time of cock-crow.)

The three denials of Peter are part of a pattern. When Jesus takes his leading three disciples, Peter, James and John, to Gethsemane they also 'betray" him three times. He tells them to keep watch, but they fall asleep. Twice he wakes them, but they fall asleep again each time. The three failures to keep watch allow the armed crowd to approach, and so lead to the arrest and death of Jesus.

A more blatant betrayal is that of the Jewish crowd who a few days earlier had greeted Jesus in jubilation. But when Jesus is tried by Pilate, they quite inexplicably demand his death. Pilate offers to release Jesus, but the Jerusalem crowd refuse his offer three times, choosing Barabbas instead. When he asks the crowd what he should do with Jesus, they give a simple reply: "Crucify him!"[1]

The Judas betrayal

➢   Judas' betrayal amounts to nothing more than a kiss in Mark.

The most serious betrayal is, of course, that of Judas Iscariot. The problem concerns the nature of this betrayal. In the gospels, Judas does nothing more than kiss Jesus, the standard greeting between friends. Supposedly, by this kiss, he delivers up Jesus, yet he lacks any power to do this. In the gospel story, Judas initiates the betrayal by going to the priests asking for money:

> Then Judas Iscariot, one of the twelve, went to the chief priests in order to betray him to them. And when they heard it, they were glad and promised to give him money. And he sought an opportunity to deliver him up. (Mark 14:10-11)

Mark does not specify the exact amount of money that Judas is to be paid, but in Matthew it is "thirty pieces of silver", an amount which comes from a prophecy in Zechariah.[2] At the last supper, Jesus predicts that one of his disciples will betray him, but he does not say who:

> And as they were reclining at table and eating, Jesus said, "Truly, I say to you, one of you who is eating with me will betray me." (Mark 14:18)

The actual betrayal comes while Jesus is at Gethsemane:

> And immediately, while he was yet speaking, Judas came, one of the twelve, and with him a crowd with swords and clubs, from the chief priests and the scribes and the elders. Now the betrayer had given them a sign, saying, "The one I will kiss is he. Take him and lead him away

under guard." And having arrived, he went immediately up to him,
and said, "Rabbi!" And he kissed him. And they laid hands on him
and seized him. (Mark 14:43-6)

The kiss of greeting identifies Jesus so that the armed men know who to arrest. But why would anyone pay Judas good money for just identifying Jesus? According to the gospels, Jesus was a well-known public figure. He had spent the last week going openly about Jerusalem. He is supposed to have debated with the priests in public several times. As Jesus himself points out, he could have been arrested at any time for the past several days.[3] Even if the priests wanted to capture Jesus in private out of fear of the people, he would have been easily found with his large retinue. In reality, there is only one thing that the priests would have wanted from an informer in Jesus' inner circle, and that is testimony. Someone to dish the dirt. But Judas does not testify against Jesus, nor is he present at either trial. According to the gospels, Judas' betrayal was nothing more than a symbolic kiss.

➤ **The word used for betrayal means to hand over or deliver up and is used in this sense by Paul.**

A clue to the nature of Judas' betrayal is to be found in the word the gospel uses; *paradidomi* does not specifically mean to betray, but "to hand over" or "deliver" which may involve betrayal.[4] There are 120 occurrences of this word in the New Testament, but it is only normally translated as "betray" in connection with Judas. Most significantly, Paul uses this word in a passage which is traditionally interpreted as meaning that Jesus was betrayed on the night of the last supper:

For I received from the Lord that which I also delivered [paredoka] to you,
that the Lord Jesus on the night when he was betrayed [paredideto] took
bread, and having given thanks, he broke it, and said, "This is my body,
which is for you. Do this in remembrance of me." In the same way he
also took the cup, after supper, saying, "This cup is the new covenant
in my blood. Do this, as often as you might drink it, in remembrance of
me." For as often as you eat this bread and drink the cup, you proclaim
the Lord's death until he should come. (1 Corinthians 11:23-6)

Paul, writing in the mid-50s AD, is the closest we have to an eyewitness. So this passage is often quoted as definitive evidence that Jesus was a real man, that he ate the last supper with his disciples, and was betrayed by Judas. Ironically, it is actually evidence that Jesus did not exist as a man.

Those who use the passage to "prove" the historicity of Jesus usually pass over in silence the source of Paul's information: "For I received from the Lord...". Paul says that he received this information from Jesus himself.

The problem is that according to the gospels, Jesus was executed very shortly after the last supper. So how could Paul possibly have got this from Jesus? Even if Paul were somehow present at the trial, there is no way he could have communicated with Jesus in private. Paul admits his guilt in persecuting the church in his days as a Pharisee, for which he calls himself the least of the apostles. Why then does Paul never mention the much greater crime of persecuting Jesus, if he were really among his persecutors? Although Paul had many enemies in the early church, we never hear a whisper that he was involved in the crucifixion. Nor is there any tradition that he ever met or knew Jesus.

Besides, a real human Jesus could never have talked of his flesh being the bread and his blood being the wine that his followers should eat and drink. This is a ritual formula. The flesh and blood are spiritual, and it is from the spiritual Jesus that Paul has received his information. Did Paul then originate the idea of the bread and wine as a revelation from the resurrected Christ? The words "For I received from the Lord what I also delivered to you..." indicate an authorised teaching which Paul has received and is dutifully passing on. In *The Rock and the Tower*, I suggest that the revelation came from Jesus speaking through the shaman, Mary/Cephas, probably when Paul visited Jerusalem.[5]

In the above passage Paul uses the same word *paradidomi* for the delivering up of Jesus and for passing on his knowledge to the Corinthians: *"what I also delivered [paredoka] to you"*. He uses the word in this sense of delivering teachings elsewhere in his letters.[6] This shows that *paradidomi* does not imply betrayal, although it was often used to mean being given up to something bad, such as imprisonment or death. In Romans, Paul uses the word to describe how God had delivered up Jesus:

> *He who did not spare his own Son but delivered him up [paredoken]*
> *for us all, how will he not also with him freely give us all things?*
> *(Romans 8:32)*

And in Galatians 2:20, Paul describes how Jesus has delivered himself up, again using the identical word. So the 1 Corinthians passage does not necessarily mean that Jesus was betrayed, only that he was "delivered up".

Judas in the gospels is a betrayer, one who has "delivered up" or surrendered Jesus to his persecutors. In the context of the Mark account the "delivering up" makes little sense because a disciple does not have the power to hand Jesus over. The original Judas must have had this power.

> ➤ There were at least two sources for the crucifixion account; the proto-crucifixion source and the shamanic formula for the crucifixion experience. Judas only appears in the former.

We have argued that Paul's account of the "last supper" is actually a spiritual experience mediated by the shaman Mary/Cephas. The author of Mark incorporates the bread and the wine into his last supper account. This may have come directly from Paul's description in 1 Corinthians, or reflect a wider tradition within the movement. Either way, we have to envisage at least two sources for the crucifixion in addition to scriptural references:

1. The proto-crucifixion source derived from the Almanac seventh great day.
2. A spiritual shamanic experience of the crucifixion which comes ultimately from Mary.

Judas belongs to source (1) and probably played no part in source (2). We know that source (2) existed because Christians did experience the crucifixion spiritually in the shamanic transformation of being born again. Paul talks about such an experience when he says that Christ has been crucified in front of the Galatians' eyes.[7] Mary developed a ritual formula to be used by her apostles in taking converts through the crucifixion and resurrection experience. Elements of this ritual formula became incorporated into the gospels giving them their power. The last supper, in which Jesus offers up the bread and wine as his flesh and blood, belongs to this formula and comes from source (2) rather than source (1).

Three blasphemies

The betrayals tend to come in threes, but this does not apply to Judas. His betrayal must have been the worst of the three, which brings us to a saying from the Gospel of Thomas:

> *Jesus said: "Whoever blasphemes against the father will be forgiven, and whoever blasphemes against the son will be forgiven but whoever blasphemes against the holy spirit will not be forgiven, either on earth or in heaven." (Thomas 44; TC 3.7)*

This saying is found in a modified form in the synoptic gospels. The saying is very difficult: if it is promised in advance that blasphemies will be forgiven, does this not authorise those blasphemies? To the Jews, there was no worse crime than blaspheming Yahweh, the father. Christians added a strong prohibition against blaspheming the son. According to a letter from Pliny the Younger, the Romans would test a suspected Christian by ordering them to curse Christ, which was something that a Christian could not do.[8] So how can Jesus say that blasphemies against both the father and son will be forgiven?

It is equally odd that the saying elevates the spirit above both God and Christ. If the spirit emanates from God, why should it be more important than God himself? The conventional explanation is that the Thomas version of the saying is comparatively late. The saying also appears in Mark, Matthew and Luke and all three omit blasphemy against the father. It must be the gnostics who have included God in the Thomas formula, perhaps a reference to the Jewish God as Demiurge. To the gnostics, the spirit is higher than the lower God because it comes from Sophia.

> **The Matthew and Luke versions have modified the difficult Thomas saying.**

There are two difficulties with the explanation that the Thomas version is late. First, it leaves a loose end, because both Matthew and Luke say that it is forgivable to blaspheme Jesus, something which should not be possible among Christians. More fundamentally, there is evidence that the Thomas version is original, and the others have used it as their source.

Once again, we find that Thomas has a traditional structure of three. The first two instances, blasphemy against the father and the son are both forgivable, leading to the climax of the third instance, that blasphemy against the spirit will never be forgiven. And if we look at the earliest synoptic version in Mark there is clearly something wrong with it:

> *"Truly, I say to you, all sins and blasphemies will be forgiven the sons of men, as many as they have blasphemed. But whoever blasphemes against the holy spirit shall never be forgiven, but is guilty of eternal sin"— for they were saying, "He has an unclean spirit." (Mark 3:28-30)*

The saying comes after the scribes have accused Jesus of casting out demons by the power of Beelzebub, the devil. By placing it here, the author of Mark is trying to give a context in which Jesus, the son, was blasphemed. This shows that the author Mark is using a source that did feature blasphemy against the son. But he suppresses the explicit mention of such blasphemy out of embarrassment. The most significant element, though, is the first line: "all sins and blasphemies will be forgiven" and in particular the odd phrase "as many as they have blasphemed". Consider the implications:

1. Multiple parties have been blasphemed.
2. However, the only two entities it is possible to blaspheme are the father and the son.
3. So the original source must have had blasphemy against both the father and the son as forgivable.

The Gospel of Matthew is always a sensitive barometer of problems in Mark, and, significantly, this passage is changed:

> *Therefore I tell you, every sin and blasphemy will be forgiven, but the blasphemy against the spirit will not be forgiven. Whoever speaks a word against the Son of Man will be forgiven, but whoever speaks against the holy spirit will not be forgiven, neither in this age or in the age to come. (Matthew 12:31-32)*

The first part follows Mark except that it eliminates the embarrassing phrase "as many as they have blasphemed". Matthew then restates the saying. Words spoken against the Son of Man are forgivable, but words against the holy spirit are unforgivable. The author of Matthew must be using a source which is just like the Thomas saying. As a Jewish Christian, he would find it impossible to explicitly authorise blasphemy against the father, but he has blasphemy against God on his mind. The Gospel of Matthew generally uses the phrase "kingdom of heaven" in preference to "kingdom of God". One of few times it uses "kingdom of God" comes in this section:

> *"But if I cast out demons by the spirit of God, then the kingdom of God has come upon you." (Matthew 12:28)*

Shortly before this, the gospel quotes from Isaiah *"I will put my spirit upon him" (Matthew 12:18)*. It is made clear that Jesus can only perform his miracles because the "spirit of God" has entered into him. But if Jesus' spirit has come from God, then a blasphemy against his spirit is a blasphemy against God. The Pharisees commit such a blasphemy by accusing Jesus of casting out demons by Beelzebul.[9]

We must admire the ingenuity of the author of Matthew in his explanation of this problematic saying. He first establishes that the spirit is the spirit of God. He then contrasts blaspheming Jesus in his human state (the

Son of Man), which is forgivable, with blaspheming Jesus in his spiritual state (the spirit of God) which is unforgivable. In contrast, we must feel slightly sorry for the author of Luke:

> *And I say to you, whoever acknowledges me before men, the Son of Man also will acknowledge before the angels of God, but whoever denies me before men will be denied before the angels of God. And everyone who speaks a word against the Son of Man will be forgiven, but whoever blasphemes against the holy spirit will not be forgiven. (Luke 12:8-10)*

By repositioning the saying, the author of Luke creates a blatant contradiction between two successive lines:

"whoever denies me before men will be denied before the angels of God"
Is the opposite of:

"everyone who speaks a word against the Son of Man will be forgiven".

The authors of Mark, Matthew and Luke all had enormous difficulties with this saying, and none of them understood it. In both Mark and Matthew, it is placed in a narrative story with the Pharisees committing the blasphemies. To tame this saying it was necessary to relate it a specific instance of blasphemy. Is this the clue to the original meaning of the saying?

➤ **The Thomas saying must be based upon a source which referred to three historical events.**

A saying that permits blasphemy against the only two who should never be blasphemed sets up an unbearable contradiction. So perhaps the saying, even in its Thomas form, has been corrupted with the passage of time. There is one simple change that will avoid the contradiction; suppose that the original tense was the past rather than the future. To say you will forgive a past sin is very different from saying that you will forgive a future sin. Forgiving a sin that has already occurred does not authorise that sin in the future.

The original source would have concerned three historical events. One involved blasphemy against the father, another blasphemy against the son, and the third blasphemy against the spirit. The first two could be forgiven, but the third was so terrible that it could never be forgiven. Whoever put the Thomas saying in its final form did not realise the significance of these three blasphemies. By that time, the knowledge had been lost.

Are these three blasphemies the same as the three betrayals of the proto-crucifixion source? If so, then the betrayal by Judas must somehow be the unforgivable "blasphemy against the spirit". To see why it could be called this, we must go back to the Judas War.

18

The Seventh Great Day

Generations

The seventh great day has been translated into the passion day in the gospels. That is the conclusion from the structure of Jesus' last day in Mark. Can we find confirmation in the events of the passion account? These are the Almanac days making up the seventh week/great day:

6.7 Uzziah

7.1 Jotham
7.2 Ahaz
7.3 Hezekiah
7.4 Manasseh
7.5 Amon
7.6 Josiah
7.7 Jeconiah

The genealogy has missed out three kings of Judah who came towards the end of this list; the reigns of these kings will have to be allocated between Josiah and Jeconiah. We have included Uzziah who ends the sixth week and brings in the seventh because he played a vital role in the proto-crucifixion source.

> ➤ **The three betrayals should be associated with the reigns of the first three kings in week seven: Jotham, Ahaz and Hezekiah.**

The three betrayals by cock-crow must end with 7.3, the reign of Hezekiah. We would expect one of the betrayals to be associated with each of the first three periods; the reigns of Jotham, Ahaz and Hezekiah. Before looking at our sources for these reigns, we must consider the timing of the crucifixion.

Crucifixion and burial

➤ **The author of Mark has moved the crucifixion forward three hours to give time for the burial of Jesus before the sabbath.**

To construct a realistic literalistic narrative, the author of Mark had to adjust the timescale. The most significant change was moving the start of the crucifixion from noon to 9 am while preserving the six-hour duration. This change was necessary to give time for Jesus to be buried before the commencement of the sabbath at dusk. One generation of the Almanac week, the generation of Amon, had to be eliminated to achieve this.

➤ **The original crucifixion timing was restored in John and is also visible from Mark, Matthew and Luke.**

The original timing of noon for the crucifixion is found in the Gospel of John. As we have seen, the author of John must have had good reason to change Mark when this change resulted in an even shorter crucifixion. The original timescale is also visible in the Gospel of Mark, which splits the period of crucifixion into two halves, drawing attention to noon:

> *And the sixth hour having come, darkness came over the whole land till the ninth hour. (Mark 15:33)*

The darkness that comes over the earth in the sixth hour, noon, is a remnant of the original proto-crucifixion source. We have seen how the month of the Jews can be compared to the phases of the moon, and the seventh day of the seventh great day is the dark of the moon. The full period of the crucifixion, from noon to 6 pm, should be a period of darkness. The author of Mark ends the darkness early at "the ninth hour" (3 pm) when Jesus dies in his narrative.

The author of Matthew was very faithful to Mark. Changes which he makes to the earlier gospel are significant because they point to problems with Mark. One such change occurs at the start of the crucifixion. This is Mark's account:

> *And they crucified him and divided up his garments, casting lots for them, to decide what each should take. And it was the third hour, and they crucified him. And the inscription of the charge against him was written: "The king of the Jews." (Mark 15:24-26)*

And this is the same passage in Matthew:

And when they had crucified him, they divided his garments casting lots. And sitting down, they guarded him there. And over his head they put the charge against him, written: "This is Jesus, the king of the Jews." (Matthew 27:35-37)

Matthew takes out Mark's "third hour" and substitutes the line: "And sitting down, they guarded him there". The author of Matthew must have had a source that contradicted "the third hour" so he kept the timing vague. Luke follows Matthew and also omits "the third hour". This is one of the so-called "minor agreements" found in the passion account, where Luke and Matthew both deviate from Mark but agree with each other.

In conclusion, the 9 am time for the crucifixion is only mentioned explicitly in Mark. The other gospels change the time to noon (John), or omit the time (Matthew and Luke), which is only explicable if they had sources contradicting Mark.

Scriptural sources

The primary source of information for the period of the seventh Almanac week is the Hebrew Bible. Both 2 Kings and 2 Chronicles give historical accounts which cover the period. The Book of Kings is part of the Deuteronomistic history, the collection of books from Joshua to Kings covering the period from Moses to the exile. It is believed to have been written, or edited, by the same group who produced Deuteronomy. There is a debate about when Kings was written, and whether it should be allocated to the post-exilic period or if it contains substantial elements dating from before the exile. It makes formulaic references to the "book of the annals of the kings of Israel" or the "book of the annals of the kings of Judah", for example:

As for the other events of Jotham's reign, and all what he did, are they not written in the book of the annals of the kings of Judah? (2 Kings 15:36)

These annals or chronicles (days) of the kings are surely legendary. No one would compile a history such as Kings but leave out much of the information contained in their source. The other historical work, Chronicles, is much later than Kings. It relies heavily on Kings and repeats much of its content. The Chronicler was obsessed by genealogies which take up much of the first book, but he also had access to other early sources beyond Kings. We will find that the Almanac is often more closely aligned to Chronicles than Kings.

The other major sources for the period are the books of prophecy; Isaiah, Jeremiah and the twelve so-called minor prophets. Although they claim to be eye-witness accounts, this claim cannot be accepted at face value. They are later literary productions, but will still give us a valuable window on the period of the Judas War.

> **The books of prophecy cluster into three periods. The early group is concerned with the period of the three betrayals.**

In what periods are the books of prophecy set? We have no information about Joel, but the others cluster in three groups; an early period, a later period leading up to the destruction of Jerusalem, and the post-exilic Persian period.

The chief source for the period of the Jerusalem exile is the book of Jeremiah, a prophet who lived through the destruction. Two other books can also be allocated to this period: Habakkuk predicts the coming of the Babylonians, and Zephaniah is set in the reign of Josiah, shortly before the destruction.

For the Persian period, we have Haggai, Zechariah and Malachi. However, although Zechariah is set after the exile, Second Zechariah contains material from a much earlier period and will be highly relevant to our quest. Malachi is supposedly the last of the books of prophecy and was important for the Jesus movement.

Turning to the early group, we have two books, Jonah and Nahum, that are vague in date but concern prophecies addressed to Nineveh, the capital of the Assyrian Empire. The other books tell us the reigns in which they were supposedly written:

Isaiah: Uzziah, Jotham, Ahaz, Hezekiah
Hosea: Uzziah, Jotham, Ahaz, Hezekiah
Amos: Uzziah
Micah: Jotham, Ahaz, Hezekiah

There is a certain pattern here! The books of prophecy focus intensely on the kings of the first three periods of the seventh day, along with Uzziah who ends the sixth week. These are the same kings we have identified as connected to the three betrayals. Apart from these four, the only books of prophecy set in the reign of a named king of Judah are Jeremiah and Habakkuk, covering the period from Josiah to the exile (7.6 and 7.7).

One other book that will be important is Ezekiel. Supposedly set in Babylon during the exile, it contains prophecies relating to the exile. But for now, we will focus on the prime work of prophecy, Isaiah.

First Isaiah

> Isaiah is a composite work with three identifiable sections writ-
> ten in different periods. There is a close link between First Isaiah
> and the proto-crucifixion account.

Isaiah is perhaps the most fascinating and important of the books of
prophecy in the Bible. It had a huge influence on Christianity and was
the most quoted of the books of prophecy in the New Testament. It is virtually a self-contained literary work in its own right, constructed around
the theme of exile and return.

Isaiah is a composite text. We think of a book as being written at one
time, generally by one author, and then fixed forever. But in the Old
Testament period, books evolved. They were subject to a continual process of revision, editing and additions, as generation after generation
applied their own interpretation to the material that they had inherited.
The books were community property, and not for one age only. Isaiah took
its final form in the post-exile period, with some sections written in the
Persian period. The Isaiah Scroll found among the Dead Sea scrolls show
that the text was essentially stable by 100 BC.

Scholars identify at least three different works within Isaiah; First,
Second and Third Isaiah. We should not, however, view it as three sections simply pasted together. There is no evidence that Second or Third
Isaiah ever existed independent of the whole. And although there are
clear differences, there is also a shared, consistent theme. Isaiah is like an
old house that has received two substantial extensions at different times
and in different styles. These additions were never separate, standalone
buildings, but were designed to complement the original structure. The
older parts of the building have also been reworked according to the
needs and fashions of different periods.

We will be concerned here mainly with First Isaiah, which is set in the
Assyrian period, mostly in the reigns of Ahaz and Hezekiah. However,
the later Babylon exile and the even greater cosmic exile are constant pre-
occupations. First Isaiah is built around two episodes in which Isaiah
prophesies to Ahaz and Hezekiah. These two parts form a matching pair,
one near the beginning and the other at the end. The Ahaz section is
followed by a large number of oracles about the fate of the nations. The
Hezekiah section is proceeded by a number of prophecies concerned with
the crisis of Hezekiah's reign, the invasion of Judea by the Assyrian King
Sennacherib.

There are several paradoxes and inconsistencies in First Isaiah. The
prophecies that Isaiah supposedly gives to Ahaz and Hezekiah might

seem like genuine historical information. Yet they are suspiciously similar to each other, although separated in time by over thirty years. In both cases, Isaiah tells the king to rely on Yahweh and do nothing. It is also problematic that the Hezekiah section is virtually identical to 2 Kings. This raises the question of which book copied which, or whether they both copied a third source.

Both the Ahaz and Hezekiah sections were written much later than the reigns of the two kings. At the end of the Hezekiah section, there is a reference to the fate of the Assyrian king, which shows that it must date from at least twenty years after the events it describes.

Almost certainly there was a real prophet called Isaiah who lived in the time of Ahaz and Hezekiah. However, the book of Isaiah is a literary production of later ages. The standard technique was to interpret events through the fictional sayings of an earlier prophet. In this way, you would elucidate Yahweh's intentions, and explain the heavenly causes of recent history. The author of First Isaiah is trying to make sense of things that had already happened. There is a snowball effect here. Prophecies were attributed to the esteemed prophet Isaiah. With the passage of time, it was forgotten that these prophecies were written after the events they predicted, and it seemed that they had come miraculously true. This increased the status of Isaiah, and more scribes used him as the authority for their writings. The result is a collection of prophecies around the subject of the exile which were, in truth, written over several centuries by multiple individuals.

➤ **Isaiah supposedly prophesied in the reigns of four successive kings covering an unrealistically long timeline. The four kings correspond to the period of the three betrayals.**

The first line of Isaiah introduces the prophet and gives us the scope of his prophecy:

> *The vision of Isaiah the son of Amoz, which he saw concerning Judah and Jerusalem in the days of Uzziah, Jotham, Ahaz, and Hezekiah, kings of Judah. (Isaiah 1:1)*

We know nothing about Amoz, his father. The prophecies concern "Judah and Jerusalem" a phrase which occurs many times in the book. This introduction states that Isaiah saw visions concerning the days of all four kings, which would cover an extraordinarily long period. Hezekiah was the son of Ahaz, who was the son of Jotham, who was the son of Uzziah. So we are asked to believe that the prophet was active over four generations. And the last of the four, Hezekiah, was not a child when he received the prophecies, but aged about 50.[1] This is not realistic.

Even odder is the fact that Isaiah actually only prophesies to Ahaz and Hezekiah. Uzziah is mentioned only once, seemingly in passing, and Jotham not at all except to say that Ahaz was the son of Jotham.[2] What was Isaiah doing during the reign of Jotham? Even if Isaiah was a prophet only during the reigns of Ahaz and Hezekiah, his career would still be a long one. So why does the Book of Isaiah extend the time of Isaiah back to Uzziah? The first line tells us that the book contains a vision or visions relating to the days of Uzziah and Jotham. With the inclusion of these two kings, the time span of the book matches the three betrayals.

First Isaiah and the three betrayals

➢   First Isaiah contained an account of the three betrayals but has received a drastic makeover by the Judean side.

We need to look no further than First Isaiah for the three betrayals and the key to understanding the passion account. First Isaiah was based on a work structured around the three betrayals. Had this work survived in its original form, then the three betrayals and their connection to Judas Iscariot would have been obvious. But the betrayals were a huge embarrassment to the priests of Judah, and at some point, the work received a considerable pro-Judean revision. Fortunately, this revision was less than complete and left sufficient clues to give us a good idea of the original.

First Isaiah is structured around three key episodes:

Isaiah and the throne room vision.
Isaiah prophesies to Ahaz
Isaiah prophesies to Hezekiah

These are the three times that Isaiah actually does something. The remaining material is a collection of assorted prophecies attributed to Isaiah. We will see that the three episodes correspond to the three betrayals. Other prophecies around these episodes were very important to the Jesus movement. One of these is the mountain raised above the hills (Isaiah 2:1-4), a prophecy of the eventual kingdom of heaven that will replace the kingdoms of the nations and encompass gentiles as well as Jews. This kingdom will bring an end to war and an era of peace with swords beaten into ploughshares. Then we have the vineyard parable (Isaiah 5:1-7), the raising of the throne of the king of Babylon (Isaiah

14:12-15), and the prediction that the Messiah will come as a branch of the root of Jesse (Isaiah 11).

First Isaiah started as a tragedy in three acts, built around three betrayals committed by three kings of Judah. It was edited by the Judean priests to make it more acceptable, but beneath the revision, we can make out the original account of the Judas War.

19

Uzziah

Jotham

The reign of Jotham occupies the first day of the seventh week. There is little about Jotham in the historical record. From 2 Kings, we learn that he was twenty-five years old when he became king and reigned for sixteen years.[1] The only achievement recorded is that he rebuilt the upper gate of the temple. From 2 Chronicles, we learn a little more; that he also had work done on the wall at the hill of Ophel, had towns built in Judah and forts and towers in the wooded areas.[2] He won a war against the Ammonites who paid him tribute for three years. It all quite meagre. But there was one thing that was very special about Jotham's reign—he came to the throne while his father was still alive. We must turn to Uzziah rather than Jotham for the first betrayal.

Uzziah

Uzziah was a successful king with a very long reign of fifty-two years. He ruled at a fortunate time when Judah was not under pressure from the regional superpowers, Egypt and Assyria. Israel had also entered a period of weakness, and for once, Judah had the upper hand. So it is surprising that Kings contains little about his reign; it calls him by the names Azariah and Uzziah, says that he became king at the age of sixteen, that he brought Elath back to Judah, and was a good king except that he allowed the high places to continue.[3]

In such a long reign, more must have happened than just the return of Elath. For some reason, the Kings account of Uzziah has been censored. We must instead turn to Chronicles which gives a wealth of information about Uzziah.[4] He won victories over the Philistines, the Arabians and Meunites, received tribute from the Ammonites and expanded his territory as far as Egypt. He led an army of over 300,000 soldiers and had cunning engines made for the walls and towers of Jerusalem to fire arrows and great stones. Even allowing for the obvious exaggeration, the reign of

Uzziah would have been a high point for Judah. And the Chronicler must be using another source of information besides Kings.[5] Chronicles tells us how Uzziah was influenced by a prophet Zechariah:

> *And he sought God in the days of Zechariah, who had understanding in the visions of God: and as long as he sought Yahweh, God made him to prosper. (2 Chronicles 26:5)*

This is not the same Zechariah for whom the Book of Zechariah is named, because that book is set hundreds of years later. The priestly author of 2 Chronicles attributes Uzziah's initial success to the guidance of Zechariah. But at the height of his power, the king did something terrible:

> *But when he was strong, he grew arrogant, to his destruction. He was unfaithful to Yahweh his God and entered the temple of Yahweh to burn incense on the altar of incense. Then Azariah the priest went in after him, with eighty priests of Yahweh who were men of valour. They confronted King Uzziah and said to him, "It is not for you, Uzziah, to burn incense to Yahweh, but for the priests, the sons of Aaron, who are consecrated to burn incense. Leave the sanctuary, for you have done wrong, and it will bring you no honour from Yahweh, God." Uzziah was angry and had a censer in his hand to burn incense. When he became angry with the priests, leprosy broke out on his forehead in the presence of the priests in the house of Yahweh, by the altar of incense. When Azariah the chief priest and all the priests looked at him, they saw he was leprous in his forehead! And they rushed him out quickly, and he himself hurried to go out because Yahweh had struck him. (2 Chronicles 26:16-20)*

The king, who has blasphemously burned incense at the altar, has been struck instantly by leprosy. His fate is to be confined in a leper house while Jotham rules in his stead:

> *And King Uzziah was a leper to the day of his death. He lived in a separate house, leprous, for he was excluded from the house of Yahweh. And Jotham his son was over the king's household, governing the people of the land. (2 Chronicles 26:21)*

In 2 Kings we find nothing about Uzziah burning incense in the temple or being challenged by the priests. It just says that he contracted leprosy and that Jotham took over his responsibilities as king:

And Yahweh touched the king, so that he was a leper to the day of his
death, and he lived in a separate house. And Jotham the king's son was
over the palace, governing the people of the land. (2 Kings 15:5)

The status of Jotham while Uzziah was still alive is ambiguous. Did he
immediately become king, or was he the regent? The passage says that
Jotham ruled over the king's household, the palace, and governed the
people, but does not explicitly say that he was king. However, the idea that
Jotham was only a regent takes no account of the ancient belief that a king
should be unblemished. Uzziah had been touched with leprosy and there
could be no stronger mark of Yahweh's rejection. He could not enter the
temple, nor could he fulfil the two most important practical requirements
of a king; to administer justice and lead his warriors in battle. So Uzziah
must surely have been deposed in favour of Jotham. On account of his
illness, he would have been confined to a house where he would have had
little contact with others and no influence on events.

Why does 2 Kings omit the story about Uzziah in the temple? Did this
episode even happen? Clearly, much of the 2 Chronicles account is fictional embellishment. The idea that Uzziah is struck immediately with
leprosy, like Miriam, sister of Moses, is absurd. And the fine speech that
Azariah gives to Uzziah has obviously been added by the Chronicler who
attached great importance to the temple and the priesthood. However,
equally, there must have been something underlying this story, for the
Chronicler is not going to make up this extravagant account from nothing.

➢   **Behind the story in Chronicles is a historical memory that Uzziah**
    became high priest as well as king.

There is a mystery about what Uzziah is supposed to have done wrong. The
burning of incense at an altar was a normal kingly function of that time.
Only later did it become forbidden to any but the priests. But there is a clue
as to the nature of Uzziah's real offence. The high priest is called Azariah,
which is what Uzziah is called in Kings. It would be an odd coincidence if
the high priest at the time when Uzziah/Azariah usurped the priestly function just happened to have the same name as the king. This points to Uzziah
being both high priest and king, which was the usual arrangement in other
states in the region. Having a separate office of chief priest was potentially
dangerous as it created a rival centre of power to the king. When Uzziah's
grandfather Joash was a small child, the high priest Jehoiada had successfully staged a coup against the regent, Joash's grandmother Athaliah.[6]

The account in Chronicles of the priests showing great bravery in
opposing the king is a later fiction. Anyone who actually objected would

have been immediately executed. Uzziah's usurpation of the high priest-hood would have been successful had he not been struck a terrible blow by fate and contracted leprosy. A leper could not be king and certainly not high priest—the accounts say he was exiled from the temple. So he was shut away to wait for death while his son ruled in his place.

Although the blasphemy of Uzziah was to loom ever larger for later generations, at the time the idea of the king being high priest would not have been remarkable. The king had always exercised some priestly functions, and the temple was only one of many cultic sites dedicated to Yahweh. Only after the temple became viewed as the unique dwelling place of Yahweh on earth did Uzziah's actions become a terrible crime against God, punishable by leprosy.

➤ **The earthquake in Uzziah's reign was eventually regarded as simultaneous to his blasphemy in the temple.**

The account of Uzziah in 2 Kings is seriously deficient. Even the detail about the king rebuilding Elath comes from the story of his father's assassination.[7] The main account of Uzziah reign (2 Kings 15:1- 7) mentions not a single event except for the bare fact of his leprosy. The author of 2 Kings gives a favourable view of Uzziah, but for some reason, the information about his reign has been removed. The most significant event of his reign, the terrible earthquake, is not mentioned in either Kings or Chronicles, but has left its mark in other sources. Isaiah records how bodies littered the streets:

> *Therefore the anger of Yahweh burns against his people, and he stretched out his hand against them and struck them. And the mountains quaked, and their corpses lay like refuse in the midst of the streets. (Isaiah 5:25)*

The same earthquake appears in Zechariah:

> *And you shall flee as you fled from the earthquake in the days of Uzziah king of Judah. (Zechariah 14:5)*

The beginning of Amos mentions the earthquake and provides enough detail for a rough dating:

> *The words of Amos, who was among the sheepherders of Tekoa, which he saw concerning Israel in the days of Uzziah king of Judah and in the days of Jeroboam the son of Joash, king of Israel, two years before the earthquake. (Amos 1:1)*

This indicates that the earthquake happened in the earlier part of Uzziah's reign. Uzziah became king in the twenty-seventh year of King Jeroboam of Israel, who reigned for forty-one years.[8] So the two kings overlapped for fourteen years. Amos was active while both kings were alive and the earthquake happened no later than two years afterwards, by the sixteenth year of Uzziah's reign. All assuming that we can trust the information in Amos and 2 Kings.

In the ancient world, natural disasters and disease were portents showing the will of the gods. The earthquake and the king's leprosy gave a message that was loud and clear. God hated that king and he hated his people. The three events, originally separate, the earthquake, Uzziah assuming the priesthood, and his leprosy became conflated over time. They had all happened in the same generation, the day of Uzziah. And eventually they were all seen as taking place at the same moment. When the first temple was destroyed, it took over the Jewish religious imagination. Uzziah's grab for the priesthood became a crime against God and his leprosy tangible evidence of Yahweh's anger. We can see the proof of this in 2 Chronicles, written around 350 BC, give or take a hundred years, the same timeframe in which the Almanac was being developed. The legend was to develop further so that the earthquake also coincided with the desecration and leprosy:

> In the meantime a great earthquake shook the ground and a rent was made in the temple, and the bright rays of the sun shone through it, and fell upon the king's face, insomuch that the leprosy seized upon him immediately. (Josephus Antiquities 9:10:4)

Behind Josephus' account lies the historical memory that the earthquake damaged the fabric of the temple. The streets were strewn with dead bodies, so many buildings and structures must have collapsed, and the largest construction in Jerusalem was the temple.

The throne room vision

➢ The throne room vision in Isaiah records the blasphemy of Uzziah as simultaneous to the earthquake. At the same moment, in heaven, Yahweh condemns Israel and Judah to exile.

We come again to the mystery of why, in Isaiah, the prophet's mission extends back to Uzziah and Jotham. Aside from the introduction, there is no mention of Jotham except to say that Ahaz was his son.[9] There is only one other mention of Uzziah (other than to say Ahaz was his grandson) and that is in the throne room vision:

> *In the year that King Uzziah died I saw the Lord sitting upon a throne, high and lifted up; and the train of his robe filled the temple. (Isaiah 6:1)*

The throne room vision is the most mystical episode in Isaiah. In the vision, a heavenly reality is superimposed upon the earthly. The temple is both on earth and yet occupying the same space as the throne room of God in heaven. God sits on his heavenly throne with his robe filling the earthly temple. To see this vision, Isaiah must be physically present in the temple. He witnesses what happens on earth but is also able to see the concurrent heavenly events. Yahweh is waited upon by the seraphim:

> *Above him stood the seraphim, each with six wings: with two they covered their faces, and with two they covered their feet, and with two they flew. And one called to another and said: "Holy, holy, holy is Yahweh of hosts; the whole earth is full of his glory!" (Isaiah 6:2-3)*

The word *seraphim*, the plural of *seraph*, comes from a root meaning "to burn". It was used to describe the fiery serpents which bit the Israelites in the desert, and for flying fiery serpents, and for the bronze serpent on a pole, the Nehushtan, that Moses used as an antidote for the bites of the snakes.[10] The seraphim are the heavenly equivalent of the Nehushtan standing in the temple.[11] They are a type of angel giving constant praise to Yahweh. The song of the seraphim causes a reverberation on the earth:

> *And the foundations of the thresholds shook at the sound of their voices, and the house was filled with smoke. (Isaiah 6:4)*

The structure of the temple is shaking, and the building is filled with smoke: it is an earthquake. The smoke cannot be incense smoke which was perfectly normal—the vision is describing something extraordinary. The "smoke" must be thrown up by the building's partial collapse.

> *And I said: "Woe is me! For I am ruined; for I am a man of unclean lips, and I dwell in the midst of a people of unclean lips; for my eyes have seen the King, Yahweh of hosts!" (Isaiah 6:5)*

The prophet says he is "ruined". The word is a strong one meaning to be destroyed or cut-off and can be used for a building reduced to ruins.

The temple is literally falling down around him, and he fears death. He deserves this fate because he is a "a man of unclean lips" in a "people of unclean lips". He is impure because he is a blasphemer living among blasphemers. Now, seeing God, he believes he is being destroyed:

> *Then one of the seraphim flew to me, with a burning coal in his hands that he had taken with tongs from the altar. And he touched my mouth and said: "See, this has touched your lips; your guilt is taken away, and your sin atoned for." (Isaiah 6:6-7)*

Isaiah is purified; the burning coal cleanses him and atones for his sin. He will not die. He has been purged and has been given the fire of prophecy in his mouth:

> *And I heard the voice of Yahweh saying, "Whom shall I send, and who will go for us?" Then I said, "Here I am! Send me." (Isaiah 6:8)*

Unlike other prophets, Isaiah has a choice and volunteers. He is given a hard task:

> *And he replied, "Go, and say to this people: "'Keep on hearing, but do not understand; keep on seeing, but do not perceive.' Make the heart of this people dull, and deafen their ears, and shut their eyes; lest they see with their eyes, and hear with their ears, and understand with their hearts, and turn and be healed." (Isaiah 6:9-10)*

Clearly, this is not a literal instruction. It is not Isaiah who can make the "heart of the people dull" or make them deaf and blind. It is Yahweh who will do these things. Isaiah's mission is to proclaim, but his words will fall on deaf ears.

> *Then I said, "Lord, how long?" And he said: "Until cities lie waste without inhabitant, and houses without people and the land is a desolate waste, and Yahweh has removed far away, and the land is utterly forsaken. And though a tenth remain in it, it shall be burnt again. But like a terebinth or an oak, whose stump remains when it is felled, so the holy seed shall be its stump." (Isaiah 6:11-13)*

It is a prediction of the exile. The land is deserted and only a small remnant of the people, one-tenth, will remain. Even then there will be further incursions. But the remnant will be the holy seed from which the tree of Israel/Judah can regrow. Isaiah prophesies to the kings of Judah, not the kings of Israel, so he must be speaking of the later exile of Judah under the Babylonians.

The throne room vision is set in the time of Isaiah but was written much later, after the fact of the Judean exile. The vision is the reason why the prophetic career of Isaiah is extended back to Uzziah and Jotham. What does the phrase "in the year that King Uzziah died" mean? Uzziah's physical death would probably have occurred many years after the onset of his leprosy. But death could also be meant in a figurative sense. After being deposed and shut away in a leper house, the king is "dead". The author of the vision would know little about the historical Uzziah because it was all in the distant past. What he knows is the myth. In this myth Uzziah died, either literally or figuratively, in the same year he desecrated the temple and caused the earthquake.

The throne room vision must be describing the events in heaven simultaneous to Uzziah burning incense on the incense altar when the temple is struck with an earthquake. Several clues point towards this reading of the passage:

- The posts and foundations of the temple are shaking.
- The temple is filled with "smoke" meaning the dust from the earthquake. This "smoke" is an ironic counterpoint to the smoke from Uzziah's incense.
- Isaiah implies that he is a blasphemer living among blasphemers—he is witnessing an act of blasphemy in progress.
- Isaiah says he is "ruined"—an implied reference to the collapse of the building.
- The Seraphim takes a coal from the altar on which Uzziah has been offering incense, and uses it to purify Isaiah. At the same time, Uzziah is struck by leprosy, making him forever unclean.
- Isaiah exclaims that he has seen the true king, Yahweh—"my eyes have seen the King". Ironically, the human King Uzziah is in front of him as he says this.

The author of the throne room vision knows the legend that Josephus recounts much later; the temple incident, the earthquake and the leprosy are all simultaneous. What could be more significant as a sign of Yahweh's displeasure than an earthquake which ruins the temple, and leprosy that strikes the king? The author gives Isaiah, and through him, the reader, the privileged position of seeing the heavenly events that are parallel to Uzziah's blasphemous act in the temple. The arrogance of the king of Judah will lead to the exile and the doom of his people. But only Isaiah is destined to perceive this for Yahweh has taken away the spiritual sight and hearing of the people lest they should avert their fate.

The first betrayal and blasphemy

➤ **Uzziah's desecration of the temple is the first of the three betrayals. It is also the first of the three blasphemies, that against the father.**

Uzziah's usurpation of the function of the high priest assumes great importance in the Almanac. It is the event that starts the first day of the ominous seventh week. In Isaiah, it leads Yahweh to condemn his chosen people to exile. Uzziah occupies the Almanac position symmetrical to Moses. In the day of Moses, the angel of the Name descends to the tabernacle and gives the law. In the day of Uzziah, he condemns his chosen people because of the desecration of the temple.

Uzziah's is the first of the three blasphemies—the blasphemy against the father. This blasphemy is largely retrospective, the product of later generations to whom Uzziah's actions seemed worse than they would have at the time. The combination of the earthquake and leprosy were seen as God's judgement on Uzziah. And so the idea evolved that Uzziah had brought on the condemnation of Judah and the terrible events that followed.

Uzziah and the gospels

Does the account of Jesus' last day reflect the blasphemy of Uzziah? The first period is the last supper, from 6 pm to 9 pm, which corresponds to the reign of Jotham. Any link with Uzziah should come shortly before the last supper.

➤ **There are links between the throne room vision and the "little apocalypse" in Mark a few days before his passion.**

Shortly before the passion day, Jesus makes a prediction about the temple:

> *And as he came out of the temple, one of his disciples said to him, "Look, Teacher, what stones and what wonderful buildings!" And Jesus said to him, "Do you see these great buildings? There will not be left one stone upon another that will not be thrown down." (Mark 13:1-2)*

The source could be a combination of a reference to the earthquake in Uzziah's reign and the ultimate destruction of the temple by the Babylonians. The earthquake threw down stones from the temple and was a precursor to the total Babylonian destruction. The author of Mark thought this was a prediction of the destruction of the temple by the Romans in 70 AD. Although the Romans accidentally set fire to the temple, the whole complex was not razed to the ground as Jesus predicts in Mark. So the prediction that not one stone would be left on another cannot have come from the author of Mark, but was already present in his source.

Jesus and his disciples, Peter, James, John and Andrew, cross over to the Mount of Olives from where they can see the temple. Sitting down, Jesus tells them about the coming chaos. There are links between his words and the throne room vision, particularly with Isaiah 6:9-13. This is the structure of the Isaiah passage:

Yahweh tells Isaiah to give the prophecy about hearing but not under-standing, seeing but not perceiving.
Isaiah asks "How long, O Lord?"
Yahweh replies that cites will be laid waste and the land made desolate.

Let us see how this compares to Mark. First, there is a question from the disciples, which corresponds to Isaiah's question "How long, O Lord?":

> *"Tell us, when will these things be, and what will be the sign when all these things are going to be accomplished?" (Mark 13:4)*

God answers Isaiah by telling him of the things that must happen. Jesus similarly answers his disciples by describing what will happen, and his first prediction corresponds to "seeing and not perceiving":

> *And Jesus began to say to them, "See that no one deceives you. Many will come in my name, saying, 'I am he!' and shall deceive many." (Mark 13:5-6)*

The disciples must not be like those deceived by false prophets but must see and perceive. Next, Jesus says something that corresponds to "hearing and not understanding":

> *And when you hear of wars and rumours of wars, do not be alarmed. Such things must happen, but the end is not yet. (Mark 13:7)*

The disciples are not to misunderstand what they hear. Note how Mark has "see that ..." and then "when you hear..." using the same words for "see" and "hear" that the gospel uses when it quotes the Isaiah throne prophecy at Mark 4:12 (also alluded to at Mark 8:18). After this comes a reference to earthquakes:

> *For nation will rise against nation, and kingdom against kingdom. There will be earthquakes in places, there will be famines. These are the beginning of birth pains. (Mark 13:8)*

There is followed by Mark 13:9-13, about the tribulations of Jesus' followers and a prediction of the "abomination of desolation", which would not have come from the Uzziah source. In *The Rock and the Tower*, I suggest that the original "abomination of desolation" was Pilate bringing in Roman ensigns (idols) into the holy city. Some Jews at the time interpreted this event as marking the start of the apocalypse.[12]

The correspondences with the throne room vision continue immediately after the "abomination". We can set out Isaiah 6:11-12 alongside Mark 13:14-16:

Isaiah: "Until cities lie ruined and without inhabitant..."
Mark: "...then let those in Judea flee to the mountains."

Isaiah: "...until the houses are left deserted..."
Mark: "Let the one upon the housetop not go down, nor enter his house, to take anything out,...

Isaiah: "and the fields ruined and ravaged."
Mark: "...and let the one who is in the field not turn back to take up his cloak."

The final similarity comes a little later, in a prediction of the apocalypse:

> *"But in those days, after that tribulation, the sun shall be darkened, and the moon will not give its light. And the stars of heaven shall fall, and the powers in the heavens shall be shaken." (Mark 13:24-25)*

This is linked to another passage in First Isaiah (Isaiah 13:10). But it may also have been suggested by the line which immediately precedes the throne room vision:

And if he looks over the land, there is only darkness and distress; even the light will be darkened by clouds. (Isaiah 5:30)

Overall, there are several connections between the throne room vision and Jesus' speech on the Mount of Olives. It is true that some of these correspondences are generic "end of times" material that can be expected to be found in apocalyptic passages. But there is another coincidence that is much more specific; a small, seemingly inexplicable, detail.

➤ **Immediately before the passion day in Mark, Jesus visits the house of a leper. This is a parallel to the house of leprosy in which Uzziah was confined.**

In Mark, just before the preparations for the last supper, Jesus attends a meal at which a woman anoints him "for burial". This meal takes place at a house in Bethany belonging to "Simon the leper".[13] We are not told who Simon is or why he is called a leper. The conventional explanation is that he had been cured by Jesus of leprosy and was now "clean". But if we disregard such supernatural cures, Simon would still be a leper. It is this which is inexplicable. Even if Jesus were brave enough to eat in a leper house, no one would have joined him. Leprosy terrified people.

The story as it appears in Mark is undoubtedly fictional. But the author of Mark would not have included such an unrealistic detail unless it appeared in his sources. In Luke, the story of the woman with the alabaster jar comes much earlier in Jesus ministry, taking place in the house of a Pharisee called Simon.[14] Luke follows Mark's account of Jesus' last few days quite closely except for eliminating this meal at the leper's house.

So why is Jesus in a leper house? If the passion is based on the seventh great day of the Almanac, then the reason is clear. Uzziah is confined to a house of leprosy at the end of the sixth week. This confinement results in Jotham taking over as king and brings in the first day of the seventh week. In Mark, Jesus' visit to the leper house is the last thing he does before arranging the Passover feast, which corresponds to the first day of the seventh week.

Uzziah is a king, God's anointed one. There must have been a reference to an "anointed one" eating in a leper's house in the proto-crucifixion source. The author of Mark has combined this with a separate story about a woman, originally Mary the Magdalene, anointing Jesus in the house of Simon. The author of Luke has access to this second source and knew that it did not belong in the crucifixion account. So in Luke, the story is moved, and the leper detail omitted.

➤   **The links to Uzziah are all clustered just before the passion day.**

The following shows the order of these events in Mark:

Jesus' speech to his disciples on the Mount of Olives (Mark 13:1-26)—
links to the throne room vision in Isaiah.
The meal in the house of Simon the leper (Mark 14:3-9)—links to the
house of Uzziah the leper
Judas meets the priests to betray Jesus (Mark 14:10-11)
Preparations for the last supper (Mark 14:12-16)
The last supper (Mark 14:17 onwards)

The Gospel of Mark includes a timing in Mark 14:1-2 that it was two
days before the Passover. The meal at Bethany would have taken place
after sundown, which is the following day according to the Jewish reckoning. This was the day before the Passover, and the last time the meal
could be fitted into a realistic narrative. It is followed by Judas going to
the priests, the first act of his betrayal. Behind this account, we can see the
shadowy outlines of the blasphemy of Uzziah, king of Judah, which sets
in motion the events of the last great day of the Jews.

20

Isaiah and Ahaz

The invasion by two kings

We do not have to search far for the second betrayal; it follows straight on from the first.

> ➢ The second betrayal is associated with the conflict between the Syrian-Israelite alliance and Judah. It is this conflict that led to the Judas War.

The next line after the throne room vision in Isaiah takes us to the second, unforgivable, betrayal:

> *And it came to pass in the days of Ahaz the son of Jotham, the son of Uzziah, king of Judah, that Rezin the king of Syria, and Pekah the son of Remaliah, king of Israel, went up toward Jerusalem to war against it, but could not prevail against it. (Isaiah 7:1)*

We have come to the year 734 BC and the events that led to the Judas War. It all started with the tensions caused by the extending reach of Assyria. The two kingdoms of Israel and Judah were caught in the middle between Assyria and the other superpower, Egypt. They took two radically different approaches to deal with the rising threat. Israel joined the Syrian alliance opposed to Assyria, whereas Judah was closely allied to Assyria. The kings of Israel and Syria, Pekah and Rezin, did not want an Assyrian client state in their midst and invaded Judah with the aim of putting their own puppet on the throne. The war may have started while Jotham was still king, but it was his son, Ahaz, who inherited the task of dealing with it. The Syrian-Israel alliance presented a very real threat to Ahaz who feared that he would lose his kingdom:

> *And it was told the house of David, saying, Syria is confederate with Ephraim [Israel]. And his heart was moved, and the heart of his people, as the trees of the wood are moved with the wind [ruach]. (Isaiah 7:2)*

The "house of David" is the royal family led by Ahaz. On hearing of the alliance between Israel and Syria, Ahaz and his people are terrified. Their hearts are moved like trees with the wind. After this introduction, Isaiah undertakes his first prophetic mission. Yahweh tells him to take his son, Shear-jashub, and go and meet Ahaz at the *"conduit to the upper pool, by the highway of the fuller's field" (Isaiah 7:3.)*. He is to reassure Ahaz not to fear the "two smouldering stumps of firebrands" for their invasion will not succeed.

> *And within sixty and five years is Ephraim [Israel] broken from being*
> *a people. (Isaiah 7:8)*

The episode, as reported in Isaiah, is odd. There seems to be no point to the prophecy. Why is Isaiah to take Shear-jashub with him? The boy plays no part in what follows. And the prediction of sixty-five years is far longer than it took the Assyrians to conquer Israel completely. Possibly the original prophecy referred to "two generations", meaning the reigns of Ahaz and Hezekiah. If so, then someone has wrongly translated the generations into years using a length of the generation of thirty-five years, with five years subtracted for time already elapsed.

Isaiah tells Ahaz to do nothing. But what is he not to do? Whatever it was, he obviously did it. The portrayal of Ahaz in Isaiah is very negative, yet there is a coverup. Why is the author of First Isaiah in its final form so reluctant to let us know what Ahaz did?

The virgin and the prophetess as metaphors

➢   **Isaiah predicts that a virgin will conceive a son, Immanuel.**

Isaiah continues by asking Ahaz to ask for a sign, *"be it deep as Sheol or high as heaven" (Isaiah 7:11)*. Ahaz refuses, but Isaiah gives him the sign anyway:

> *Behold, the virgin shall conceive and bear a son, and shall call his*
> *name Immanuel. He shall eat curds and honey when he knows how to*
> *reject evil and choose good. For before the boy knows how to reject evil*
> *and choose good, the land whose two kings you dread will be deserted.*
> *(Isaiah 7:14-16)*

There is much that is puzzling here. Who is the "virgin"? Who is the father of Immanuel? In the culture of the time, a child's father was all-important, but he is not even mentioned. Is Immanuel, which means "God is with us", the child's real name? The boy will eat "curds and honey" when he knows how to choose good from evil. By this time the land of the two kings will be deserted, which contradicts the idea that it will take sixty-five years for Israel to be destroyed. The prophecy continues with Yahweh summoning flies and bees:

> *In that day Yahweh will whistle for the fly at the farthest streams of Egypt, and for the bee in the land of Assyria. (Isaiah 7:18)*

The flies and bees stand for the Egyptian and Assyrian armies. They will settle in the ravines and among the rocks, in the thorn bushes and by the water holes; Egypt and Assyria will occupy the land. This does not fit the situation of Ahaz, when only the Assyrians invaded, but is an allusion to the later exile of Judah. The prophecy continues:

> *In that day the Lord will hire a razor from beyond the river—the king of Assyria— to shave the head and the hair of the feet, and will remove the beard also. (Isaiah 7:20)*

It was common for captive soldiers to be shaved, removing all their hair to humiliate them. The "feet" are an allusion to the genitals; the pubic hair will also be shaved. For those who remain it will be a time of plenty, and they will eat as much curds and milk as they wish, even though there are only one cow and two sheep to feed them. A thousand vines worth a thousand shekels of silver will become a worthless patch of thorns. It is a prediction of a severe depopulation of the land following the exile.

➤ **The conception of a second boy, Maher-shalal-hash-baz, by a whore-prophetess is described in crude sexual slang.**

An enacted prophecy follows Isaiah's first prophecy to Ahaz:

> *Then Yahweh said to me, "Take a large tablet and write on it with a man's pen: Maher-shalal-hash-baz. And I will get reliable witnesses, Uriah the priest and Zechariah the son of Jeberechiah, to attest for me." (Isaiah 8:1-2)*

Why is Isaiah to write the name "Maher-shalal-hash-baz" on a tablet? And why should this be witnessed by the high priest, Uriah, and Zechariah? Most likely this is the same Zechariah who was the king's father-in-law.[1] Although "man's pen" is usually translated as something like "common stylus" this hides the strong sexual allusion: a man's pen is his penis. Isaiah is told to write the name on a tablet with his penis while the high priest and a member of the royal family watch. The prophecy continues:

> *And I came near to the prophetess, and she conceived and bore a son. Then Yahweh said to me, "Call him Maher-shalal-hash-baz; for before the boy knows how to cry 'My father' and 'My mother,' the wealth of Damascus and the spoil of Samaria will be carried away before the king of Assyria." (Isaiah 8:3-4)*

To "come near" to a woman is to approach her for sex. Isaiah coming near to the prophetess is the same as his writing on the tablet with a "man's pen". It was a common poetic convention to express the same thing in two different ways, one after the other. So the tablet stands for a woman's womb, and Isaiah is to "write" the boys name in the womb with his penis. It is pornographic sexual imagery, not the type of thing to be taught in Sunday school. So why is Isaiah having sex with a "prophetess"? And why are the high priest and the king's father-in-law watching as witnesses to the transaction?

Clearly, the two boys are two halves of a single prophecy, with the "good" Immanuel contrasted to the "bad" Maher-shalal-hash-baz. The conception of Immanuel is presented as virginal and pure, whereas the conception of Maher-shalal-hash-baz is irregular and promiscuous, described in crude sexual slang. Some conventional commentators have tried to maintain that the prophetess is the wife of Isaiah. But the word is never used elsewhere in the sense of the wife of a prophet. A prophetess is always a prophet in her own right. And in Isaiah, to be a prophet is to be a false prophet. The only true prophet is Isaiah himself, and he is only called "prophet" in the section which repeats material from 2 Kings.[2] So the "prophetess" is a false prophet who carries the additional stigma of being female. Not only that, but this prophetess is a whore, as is clear from the casual way in which Isaiah approaches her for sex.

➤ **The theory that Immanuel stands for Hezekiah must be rejected.**

So what or whom does Immanuel stand for? One theory is that he is the king's son, Hezekiah, who was regarded as a hero by the priestly classes. However, the ages and times given in 2 Kings do not match. Ahaz reigned for sixteen years, and Hezekiah was twenty-five when he succeeded Ahaz.[3] So Hezekiah was already about nine when his father became king, and so, according to these dates, could not be the predicted child. This does not, however, entirely rule out the possibility of Hezekiah being Immanuel because the information in this part of 2 Kings about the length of reigns and ages is completely unreliable. The age of Ahaz when coming to the throne is given as twenty, implying that he was just eleven when he conceived Hezekiah.[4] There is also some support for the Hezekiah theory in the prediction that the river of the Assyrians will sweep into the land of Immanuel:

> And it will rise over all its channels and go over all its banks, and it
> will sweep on into Judah, it will overflow and pass on, reaching even
> to the neck, and its outspread wings will fill the breadth of your land,
> O Immanuel." (Isaiah 8:7-8)

Isaiah here predicts the Sennacherib invasion that occurred during the reign of Hezekiah with the Assyrian troops surrounding but not conquering Jerusalem—it reached "even to the neck". But if the Assyrians spread their wings over the land of Immanuel, does this not imply that Immanuel is the king, Hezekiah? There are more problems with this theory than just the age of Hezekiah. Much of Isaiah is very negative about Hezekiah's court, implying a strongly negative view of Hezekiah himself. The prophecy about the river reaching the neck is predicting a punishment, the Assyrian invasion, that will fall on Hezekiah. And why should the Immanuel prophecy go out of its way to express the purity of Immanuel's mother, describing her in terms appropriate for a virgin? This is not the way the king's wife would be represented. And why is there no mention of the father if he were Ahaz?

Most likely Immanuel has been written in here by a later scribe to replace an original reference to Hezekiah which was deemed unacceptable. We should note that this prophecy reflecting criticism of Hezekiah follows on immediately from the Maher-shalal-hash-baz passage. Did it originally imply that Maher-shalal-hash-baz represented Hezekiah?

➤ **Christians equated Immanuel with Christ. Many scholars wrongly believe that this gave rise to the story of the virgin birth.**

The most famous use of this prophecy is the Christian interpretation that Immanuel is Jesus and that the prophecy predicts the virgin birth. We find this in the Gospel of Matthew:

> All this came to pass to fulfil what the Lord had spoken through the
> prophet: "Behold, the virgin will conceive and will bear a son, and

they shall call his name Immanuel", which is translated "God with us".
(Matthew 1:22-3)

A great deal of debate has swirled around the word used to describe Immanuel's mother; in Hebrew, she is *almah* meaning "young woman", a girl of marriageable age. In the Greek Septuagint this is translated as *parthenos*, meaning virgin, and it is this word that is quoted in Matthew. Technically *almah* does not mean "virgin" although it is generally used in the context of a young woman before marriage, which, in ancient Israel, would certainly imply virginity. The translator of the Septuagint had this understanding.

Most modern scholars believe that the author of Matthew invented the story of the virgin birth because he misunderstood this prophecy. The argument goes that he was relying on the Septuagint which says that the mother of Immanuel was a virgin, whereas in the original Hebrew she was just a young woman. As he believed that Immanuel was a prophecy of the Messiah, the author of Matthew thought Jesus must have been born of a virgin. Although this explanation is superficially attractive, it collapses on closer examination. No one would have come to the interpretation that the author of Matthew is supposed to have placed on the passage unless they had some prior reason for believing that the mother of Jesus was a virgin. It does not matter if the word used in Isaiah was "virgin" or "young woman" because in neither case would the passage be interpreted as meaning that the woman was a virgin after conception. Immanuel's mother is pure because she comes to the marriage bed as a virgin bride. She does not remain a virgin after conception.

In fact, the choice of *almah* is dictated by a wordplay contrasting the mothers of the two children. The pure mother of Immanuel is ha-almah, and the impure mother of Maher-shalal-hash-baz is han-nebiah, the prophetess. When the passage was translated into Greek, this wordplay no longer made sense, and "young woman" was translated as "virgin" to make the meaning clear.

In *The Rock and the Tower* we look at the evidence that the author of Matthew had good reasons for believing that Mary was a virgin.[5] The idea goes back to the shaman Mary who was both mother of the movement and the mother of the spiritually reborn and resurrected Jesus. Mary was believed to be a virgin, and the prophecy of Immanuel was used to justify the idea that Christ was not born physically, but through spiritual conception within a virgin. Originally the birth of Jesus was non-physical, as is shown in several early sources and the widespread belief that Jesus had a spiritual body, a belief that was eventually condemned as the heresy of Docetism.

> ➤ The two children are a literary device to represent two factions;
> those who remain pure to Yahweh and those who have prosti-
> tuted themselves with foreign gods.

We must go back to the question of what the original author of the
Immanuel passage intended. A clue comes in the final summary about
the children:

> *Bind up the testimony; seal the teaching among my disciples. I will*
> *wait for Yahweh, who hides his face from the house of Jacob, and I will*
> *hope in him. Behold, I and the children whom the Lord has given me*
> *are signs and wonders in Israel from Yahweh of hosts, who dwells on*
> *Mount Zion. (Isaiah 8:16-18)*

It is explicit in this passage that the children, along with the actions
of Isaiah, are "signs and wonders"—they are prophecy. The testimony
is bound up and sealed. This was a common practice; a scroll might be
sealed in a jar. By analogy, the prophecies are to be kept within a small
group of select disciples and passed down until the time for a general
unveiling. This is a fictional device. The real author, writing long after the
time of Isaiah, is explaining why his newly written prophecies have not
been in circulation before.

As the children are "signs and wonders" we need to look at what their
names mean:

Shear-jashub = "a remnant shall return"
Immanuel = "God is with us"
Maher-shalal-hash-baz = "Swift is booty, speedy is prey"

The two conceptions are enacted metaphor. They indicate not only
what will happen in the immediate future (Rezin and Pekah will be
defeated by the Assyrians), but also the nature of Israel and Judah. The
author sees two factions. Immanuel represents those who are faithful
to Yahweh, whose mother is the chaste virgin bride of Yahweh, meaning that she has not played the whore with foreign gods. In contrast,
Maher-shalal-hash-baz represents those heading full tilt to destruction. They will become the "booty" and "prey" of the Assyrians and
Babylonians and are hastening to a dark fate. This group are those who
have embraced the worship of foreign gods and assimilated foreign customs. Their mother is a whore-prophetess, the exact opposite of the virginal mother of Immanuel. The other child, Shear-jashub, the son who
Isaiah takes with him when he prophesies to Ahaz, represents those

who will remain in the land after the exile, the holy seed from which the house of Israel will be reborn.

The mother of Maher-shalal-hash-baz is a false female prophet. She represents the heterodox religion that the Jews have supposedly been whoring after, worshipping idols and gods other than Yahweh. The developing cult of Yahweh was becoming increasingly masculine in nature, excluding women from any significant role and eliminating female elements, such as Asherah, the wife of Yahweh. Women were forced to the sidelines, practising magic-based folk religion, the target of prophetic works such as Isaiah. The roles of necromancer and soothsayer were often associated with females; for example, the witch of Endor whom Saul consults.[6] The "prophetess" represents all these elements that were antithetical to the monotheistic and male-mediated cult of Yahweh.

> **Comparing the worship of gods other than Yahweh to prostitution is a common metaphor in the Hebrew Bible.**

It was a very common metaphor to represent the worship of other gods as an act of prostitution. A similar example is found later in Isaiah:

> *But you, come here, you sons of the sorceress, offspring of the adulterer and the prostitute. (Isaiah 57:3)*

Those who worship other gods and idols are the sons of a "sorceress" (compare to "prophetess") who is a prostitute. A few lines later, it is they who are whores:

> *On a high and lofty mountain you have set your bed, and there you went up to offer sacrifice. Behind the door and the doorpost you have set up your sign, you have uncovered yourself to others than me, you have enlarged your bed. You have made a covenant for yourself with those whose bed you loved, you have looked on their nakedness. (Isaiah 57:7-8)*

The "high and lofty mountain" refers to the high places, the perennial target for the priests of the temple cult. The practice of sacrifice on the high places is compared to a woman prostitute making her bed open to lovers. The implication is that she has betrayed her true husband, Yahweh.

➤   **The conception of Maher-shalal-hash-baz is a satire on the
    Jerusalem establishment and the court of Ahaz for their
    pro-Assyrian stance.**

So why are Uriah the priest and Zechariah witnessing Isaiah writing
with his "man's pen" on the tablet that is the whore-prophetess? It is
a satire. The two men are described as reliable or faithful witnesses.
They are two respectable high-status individuals, the high priest and
the king's father-in-law, representing the two pillars of the Jerusalem
establishment, the priesthood and the king's court. For all their apparent
respectability they are shown as solemnly witnessing an illicit sex act,
and of giving the stamp of approval to prostitution. This is describing
the political situation in the time of Ahaz. The Assyrian influence was
very strong in the court and stretched even as far as the temple. When
visiting the Assyrian King Tiglath-pileser in Damascus, Ahaz was so
impressed with what he saw that he determined to remodel the temple
on the Assyrian pattern:

> *And King Ahaz sent Uriah the priest a model of the altar, and its plan,*
> *exact in all its details. And Uriah the priest built the altar; in accor-*
> *dance with what King Ahaz had sent from Damascus. So Uriah the*
> *priest made it, before King Ahaz came back from Damascus. And when*
> *the king came from Damascus, the king saw the altar, and the king*
> *approached it and made offerings on it. He burned his burnt offering*
> *and his grain offering and poured his drink offering and sprinkled the*
> *blood of his peace offerings on the altar. (2 Kings 16:10-13)*

Note the similarity with Uzziah's desecration of the temple. Ahaz, like
Uzziah, made an offering, although this time with the connivance of the
high priest. But he went one step further than Uzziah. He substituted an
Assyrian style altar for the traditional altar supposedly built by Solomon.
The altar stood outside in front of the main temple building. It seems
that the original bronze altar had been moved closer to the temple to
make way for the new altar. Ahaz was not satisfied with this arrangement
because the old altar was between the new altar and the temple. So he
demoted the old altar further by moving it to the north side. In future, all
sacrifices were to be made on the new altar.

Religious practice is invariably conservative, and these changes would
have been met with fury. Ahaz, though, was the all-powerful king, so
opposition had to be expressed with subtlety, through satire. To make
things worse, Uriah, the high priest, was complicit with Ahaz: *"Uriah
the priest did all this, as King Ahaz commanded"* (2 Kings 16:16). So it is

unsurprising to find him as one of the two respectable witnesses to the act of whoredom in Isaiah.

Ahaz was probably worshipping Yahweh at his new altar. There is no hint in the 2 Kings passage that the main altar was used for the worship of other gods. Both 2 Kings and 2 Chronicles accuse Ahaz of adopting the religious practices of Israel, including making his son pass through fire, an act of child sacrifice. It is difficult to know how much of this is true. In any case, Ahaz would be simply reflecting the religion of his time. The original criticism would have been about his pro-Assyrian innovations, not his observance of traditional religious practices.

> **The mother of Maher-shalal-hash-baz may have been intended to be understood as Ahaz's queen, Abi.**

There is an intriguing clue that Ahaz's wife, Abi, belonged to the pro-Assyrian faction. This is the presence of her father, assuming that he is the same Zechariah, as a witness to Isaiah's sexual transaction. Clearly, this Zechariah must have been someone important to be paired with the high priest, Uriah. It would make sense for the royal family to be represented alongside the priesthood as the two pillars of the establishment. Zechariah must have been a prominent member of the pro-Assyrian party to qualify as a particular target of the satirist. Which implies that his daughter would have been associated with the pro-Assyrian faction also, making her unpopular with the people.

This gives the possibility that the mother of Maher-shalal-hash-baz is not just intended as a metaphor for prostitution with foreign gods, but is also a covert allusion to the queen in particular. If so, the casual way that Isaiah approaches her for sex would reflect a perception of Abi as an adulteress. Calling her a prophetess suggests some religious role. She may have been involved in the worship of the imported Assyrian gods, such as Ishtar and Dumuzi, who became popular in Judah at this time, particularly among women. If this is correct, then we can most likely date the initial satire to the reign of Hezekiah, when Judah was swamped by Israelite refugees. It is effectively making the supreme insult against Hezekiah, that he was the son of a whore. The satire would have been subsequently edited to remove any overt criticism of Hezekiah or his mother. Although there is virtually no direct information about Abi, we have a remarkable disguised literary portrait of the queen. The Afterword shows that Bathsheba in the David story is another satirical allusion to Abi.

Prophecy as literary enactment

➤ **The prophecies of Immanuel and Maher-shalal-hash-baz reveal a genre of prophecy as literary enactment.**

The prophecies of Immanuel and Maher-shalal-hash-baz are important for understanding early Christianity because they show that there existed a genre of prophecy as fictional literary enactment. This idea developed from the genuine practice of Israelite prophets to act out their prophecy as a type of performance art. There is an episode in which Isaiah supposedly walked around naked in Jerusalem for three years to make the point that it was foolish to rely upon the Egyptians because their soldiers would be defeated, stripped by the Assyrians, and led away with bare buttocks to slavery.[7] There was likely some historical memory of Isaiah walking around naked: this was the sort of thing that prophets did. But doubtless, the Egyptian interpretation was added later.

The literary form of enacted prophecy involved an author writing his "prophecy" as a story acted out by a prophet who had lived in the past. We can distinguish a literary prophecy from one based on a real historical enactment because the literary will include fantastic elements and exhibit detailed knowledge of future events. We find just such fantastic and unrealistic events in the Immanuel and Maher-shalal-hash-baz prophecy. To believe that these children were real, we would have to accept:

1. That Isaiah first had sex with a virgin.
2. This was followed by sex with a whore-prophetess under the watchful eyes of the high priest and the king's father-in-law.
3. That the two women immediately conceived, and that Isaiah then waited patiently for both children to be born.
4. They were both boys and were both named appropriately.
5. That Isaiah did all this to make a prophecy to Ahaz about an immediate and imminent threat to his kingdom.

We must add that he had an existing son, Shear-jashub, whose name conveniently represented the remnant who would return from exile. Obviously, none of this happened. It is literary prophecy using enacted metaphor to convey the heavenly meaning of historical events.

Gomer, the unfaithful wife

➤ There is another example of fictional enacted prophecy from
the same era as the Isaiah prophecies, the story of Hosea's wife,
Gomer.

The Book of Hosea records the supposed doings of the prophet Hosea in
Israel in the years before the Assyrian exile. The book does not explicitly
say that Hosea came to Israel rather than Judah. The introduction records
the same four kings of Judah as in Isaiah and only mentions a single
Israelite king, Jeroboam. Yet all the action takes place in Israel. Hosea
predicts the coming destruction of Israel, allocating all the blame to the
Israelites while taking a much more positive view of Judah. The book
can only be a Judean production. Although it undoubtedly contains some
early Israelite materials, the overall tone is viciously anti-Israel.

The story of Gomer starts with the instruction that Hosea is to marry
a prostitute:

> When Yahweh first spoke through Hosea, Yahweh said to Hosea, "Go,
> take to yourself a wife of whoredom and have children of whoredom, for
> the land commits great whoredom by departing from Yahweh." So he
> went and took Gomer, the daughter of Diblaim, and she conceived and
> bore him a son. (Hosea 1:2-3)

The name Gomer means "completion", "accomplished", "perfect". It
alludes to the consummate sexual skills of Gomer. It also foretells the
result of her prostitution; the completion, that is ending, of the kingdom of
Israel. The name of Gomer's father, Diblaim, means "two fig cakes" which
were sweat and rounded in form. This is an allusion to Gomer's breasts.
The first son of Gomer and Hosea is to be called Jezreel:

> And Yahweh said to him, "Call him Jezreel, for in just a little while I
> will punish the house of Jehu for the blood of Jezreel, and I will put an
> end to the kingdom of the house of Israel. (Hosea 1:4)

The prophecy is aimed against the royal family of Israel, the house
of Jehu. The name refers to the supposed bloody massacre at the city of
Jezreel by Jehu, who led a rebellion against King Joram of Israel. After
Jehu killed Joram and his mother, the notorious Jezebel, he arranged the
slaughter of all those related to the previous royal line, the house of Ahab.[8]
Or at least that is the story in the Judean Bible. By drawing attention to
this massacre, the final author of Hosea is attempting to undermine the

legitimacy of the Israelite kings. After the birth of Jezreel, Gomer has another child:

> *She conceived again and bore a daughter. And Yahweh said to him,*
> *"Call her name Lo-ruhamah, for I will no more have mercy on the house*
> *of Israel, to forgive them at all. But I will have mercy on the house of*
> *Judah, and I will save them by Yahweh their God, yet not by bow or by*
> *sword or by war or by horses or by horsemen." (Hosea 1:6-7)*

The name "Lo-ruhamah" means "no mercy". Yahweh will show no compassion or mercy to Israel, but he will show mercy to Judah. Israel will be defeated and exiled whereas Judah will be saved, at least for now. The salvation of Judah comes through Yahweh and not through their own arms, a reference to the crisis under Hezekiah. This dates the prophecy from sometime after Hezekiah's reign when Israel was no longer in existence. The book, in its final form, is a production of Judah. The fertile Gomer continues her childbearing:

> *When she had weaned Lo-ruhamah, she conceived and bore a son. And*
> *Yahweh said, "Call his name Lo-ammi, for you are not my people, and*
> *I am not your God." (Hosea 1:8-9)*

The name Lo-ammi means "not my people". Israel is utterly rejected, but not forever:

> *Yet the number of the children of Israel shall be as the sand of the sea,*
> *which cannot be measured or numbered. And in the place where it was*
> *said to them, "You are not my people," it shall be said to them, "you are*
> *children of the living God." And the children of Judah and the children*
> *of Israel shall be gathered together, and appoint for themselves one head.*
> *And they shall come up out from the land, for great shall be the day of*
> *Jezreel. (Hosea 1:10-11)*

This is predicting that Israel and Judah will be reunited under one king who will restore the united kingdom of David; he will be the Messiah. There is then a play on the children's names: "*Say of your brothers, 'My people,' and of your sisters, 'Shown mercy'*" (Hosea 2:1). The evil import of their names will be reversed to a blessing. The two are to plead with their mother to change her ways:

Rebuke your mother, rebuke her—for she is not my wife, and I am not
her husband—that she put away her whoredom from her face, and her
adultery from between her breasts. (Hosea 2:2)

What follows makes it clear that the whole thing is a metaphor for Israel
going "whoring" after gods other than Yahweh:

I will punish her for the days of the Baal's, when she burned incense to
them. She decked herself with rings and jewellery, and went after her
lovers, but me she forgot." (Hosea 2:13)

There is a promise that one day Israel will again be the wife of Yahweh.
This promise is enacted out by Hosea and Gomer:

And Yahweh said to me, "Go again, love a woman who is loved by
another man and is an adulteress, even as Yahweh loves the children
of Israel, though they turn to other gods and love cakes of raisins." So
I bought her for fifteen shekels of silver and a homer and a lethek of
barley. And I said to her, "You must dwell as mine for many days. You
shall not play the whore, or have another man; so will I also be to you."
(Hosea 3:1-3)

Hosea pays the equivalent of thirty shekels of silver for his wife, half
in silver and the other half in barley. This is a very low bride price, equal
to the compensation to be paid for a gored slave.[9] This is all intended as
a metaphor. It reads oddly in the narrative because Gomer (assuming
that this wife is indeed her) is already married to Hosea. Why then does
he need to pay anything? The cakes of raisins that the Israelites love are
offerings to other gods and recall the name of Gomer's father, Diblaim or
"two fig-cakes". It is all a play on the equivalence between the Israelites
worshipping other gods and a wife offering her body to other men. The
second, faithful marriage of Hosea and Gomer is a prediction of the
redemption of Israel and a return to the house of David:

For the children of Israel shall dwell many days without king or
prince, without sacrifice or pillar, without ephod or household gods.
Afterwards, the children of Israel shall return and seek Yahweh their
God, and David their king, and they shall come in fear to Yahweh and
to his goodness in the latter days. (Hosea 3:4-5)

The prediction that Israel will be without king or places of worship
must have been written after the Israelite exile, which confirms a date

long subsequent to the supposed setting. A return to "David their king" means a return to the house of David. This is either a prophecy that the exiled Israelites will return and accept Judean dominion or a prediction of the coming Messiah.

This story of Hosea and Gomer is an elaborate metaphor told as if it were acted out in real life. The sequence of events is so fantastic that we can rule it out as a historical account. Gomer and her children are a very close parallel to Immanuel and Maher-shalal-hash-baz. There is some link between Isaiah and Hosea, although Isaiah is concerned with Judah and Hosea with Israel. The story of Gomer has none of the subtlety of Isaiah, but they are both of the same genre; imaginary literary productions set in the past and written as if recounting the actions of a prophet. These actions elucidate the meaning of historical events as demonstrations of the will of Yahweh using the device of the birth of children whose names indicate their significance. This sophisticated literary technique has fooled many people into thinking that the actions described were real.

The gospels as literary enactment

➢ **The proto-crucifixion account, and hence the gospels, are a development from this genre of fictional enacted prophecy.**

The prophecies of Immanuel in Isaiah and Gomer in Hosea are presented as if literally true in the same way that a modern novel is presented as being literally true. These prophecies all relate to the time of the Assyrian invasion of Israel and reflect the literary techniques of their age. The first readers of such a prophecy would have understood the convention and interpreted them the way they were intended to be read, as a commentary on recent historical events. Similarly, if we pick up a novel, we understand it as a fictional story and do not accuse the author of lies or forgery. But over time the context for the prophecies was lost. They became viewed as miraculous predictions of the future. Generations of Jews and Christians, over thousands of years, have believed that Gomer, Immanuel and Maher-shalal-hash-baz were all real. Similarly, generation after generation of Christians have considered the gospels as literally true. But if we follow the gospels back to their earliest source, the proto-crucifixion account, it will turn out to be of the same genre as the literary enacted prophecies.

One clue lies in the names. In this genre, the names of characters convey their significance. We will see later that "Judas Iscariot" is just such a name. This principle also provides the best explanation for the name "Jesus". The concept of the Messiah, the Christ, is very old. But why should Christ be called Jesus? The name was a common one, being a form of Joshua, but none of the men called Joshua in the Hebrew Bible quite fits the role of Christ. Nor do we find the name in earlier apocalyptic texts. Does this mean that Jesus must have been a real preacher in first-century Judea? Not at all. The meaning of the name is highly significant— "Yahweh saves". It is the perfect name for the redeemer in the genre of enacted prophecy.

21

Ahaz and the Judas War

The Judas War

> Ahaz initiated the Judas War by paying Tiglath-pileser III, the king of Assyria to invade Israel.

We return to the central mystery of Ahaz's reign in Isaiah. What was it that he was supposed not to do? From Chronicles and Kings, and Assyrian sources, we can piece together what Ahaz actually did in response to the threat to his kingdom. In 2 Chronicles, there is an account of severe losses that Ahaz suffers at the hands of Syria and Israel.[1] It talks of one hundred and twenty thousand slain by Israel in one day and a further two hundred thousand taken captive. The king's son Maaseiah is reported as being killed. This Chronicles account is dubious, but the kingdom of Judah was certainly in deep trouble. Isaiah advises Ahaz to do nothing because Syria and Israel will be destroyed within sixty-five years. Such advice would not have been helpful. To do nothing was not an option except in the imagination of the author of the Book of Isaiah, who was writing long afterwards. What Ahaz actually did was to call on Assyria:

> *And Ahaz sends messengers unto Tiglath-Pileser king of Assyria saying, "Your servant and your son am I; come up and save me out of the hand of the king of Syria, and out of the hand of the king of Israel, who are rising up against me." And Ahaz takes the silver and the gold that is found in the house of Yahweh and in the treasures of the house of the king, and sends it to the king of Assyria as a bribe. (2 Kings 16:7-8)*

A desperate king is forced into desperate measures. To request the intervention of the Assyrians by paying an enormous tribute was both humiliating and dangerous. It made Judah a vassal of the Assyrians, and the revolt of a vassal state would be severely punished. Even worse, Ahaz had to raid the temple treasures to provide the bribe for Tiglath-Pileser. It was a fateful decision that would change the course of world history. Judah's sister kingdom of Israel would be utterly destroyed.

In 2 Chronicles, written much later, it is said that Tiglath-Pileser comes in and "distresses" Ahaz and that his assistance has not strengthened him.[2] But in reality, the Assyrian intervention was decisive. According to 2 Kings, the Assyrians captured Damascus and put Rezin the king of Syria to death.[3] It is also recorded separately in 2 Kings how Tiglath-pileser took action against Israel at the same time:

> *In the days of Pekah king of Israel, Tiglath-pileser king of Assyria came*
> *and captured Ijon, Abel-beth-maacah, Janoah, Kedesh, Hazor, Gilead,*
> *and Galilee, all the land of Naphtali, and he carried the people captive*
> *to Assyria. (2 Kings 15:29)*

We are not told that this is a direct result of Ahaz's intervention, but if the Assyrians attacked Syria then they would have attacked Israel also. Tiglath-pileser took large areas of the northern territory of Israel, including the Galilee in 732 BC. The inhabitants were removed to other regions of the Assyrian Empire. King Pekah of Israel was killed and replaced in a coup by Hoshea who made a temporary peace with the Assyrians and began paying tribute. What happens next is a turn of events that occurs no less than three times in the course of the exile. Like Hezekiah and Zedekiah, Hoshea made the mistake of stopping the tribute payment and forming an alliance with Egypt. Retribution was swift. Tiglath-Pileser's son and successor Shalmaneser imprisoned Hoshea and conquered the remaining territory of Israel, taking the capital Samaria after a three-year siege in 722 BC. There was then a forced relocation. As Kings states bleakly: *"So Israel was carried away from their own land to Assyria until this day" (2 Kings 17:23).* All this occurred in the early years of the reign of Hezekiah.[4]

As well as initiating the war, Judah was a military ally of the Assyrians throughout the destruction of Israel. It is this conflict that I have called the Judas War.

The second betrayal

➤ **The payment by Ahaz to get the Assyrians to invade is the second betrayal. The Judas War started on the second day of the seventh week and led to the complete destruction of Israel.**

We have found the second betrayal. Ahaz paid the Assyrians to intervene against Israel and Syria. Ultimately this resulted in the total destruction of Israel and the exile of her people. This exile started in the reign of Ahaz and concluded in the reign of his son, Hezekiah. That is the conclusion from putting together the pieces scattered in Isaiah, 2 Kings and 2 Chronicles alongside Assyrian sources and archaeological evidence.

The Assyrian policy of deportation was oppressive. It involved resettling the subject peoples by dispersing them to other parts of the Assyrian Empire. Their old land would be granted to another people who would be transported into the area. The Book of Kings says that populations were moved into the former territory of Israel from Babylon, Cuthah, Avva, Hamath, and Sepharvaim.[5] The aim was to break the will of the conquered nations by splitting them up and severing the link with their ancestral lands. It also enabled the Assyrians to reward their collaborators with the choice farms and vineyards of the dispossessed.

No wonder Isaiah and the other books of prophecy are silent about what Ahaz did! All our sources have come down through the Judean side of this conflict because Israel ceased to exist. The idea of Judah betraying their fellow kingdom was acutely embarrassing for the priestly authors who put the books into their final form. This was not out of respect for Ahaz whom they despised for his pro-Assyrian tendencies. But if they blamed Ahaz for the destruction of Israel, then the guilt would have been Judah's also. This would have demolished the priests' meta-narrative for the exile, that it was a just punishment for the worship of idols and a neglect of the proper worship of Yahweh in the Jerusalem temple. The priests blamed the people and kings of Israel for their defeat—they had worshipped Asherah, Baal and the host of heaven in the high places, and so their land was forfeit. In this meta-narrative, Israel is punished first for her greater sin. Judah is given a second chance but succumbs to the same disease, and earns the same punishment. In this explanation, there is no place for Israel as a victim of political action by Judah.

Although the idea that God punished Israel for idol worship runs throughout the prophetic books, it finds a particularly virulent expression in Hosea which berates "the iniquity of Ephraim" and "the wickedness of Samaria".[6] The author disapproves of the alliance that Hoshea attempts to make with the Egyptians to throw off the Assyrians: *"Ephraim is as a foolish dove without heart, they call to Egypt, they go to Assyria" (Hosea 7:11).* It continues *"Woe to them, for they wandered from me. Destruction to them, for they transgressed against me. Though I redeem them, they have spoken lies against me" (Hosea 7:13).* Israel is a prostitute: *"Rejoice not, O Israel! Exult not like the nations. For you have played the whore against your God. You have made love for hire on every threshing floor" (Hosea 9:1).* The most significant allusion is a line that has become a well-known phrase:

They sow the wind and reap the whirlwind [cuwphah]. (Hosea 8:7)

The English translation "whirlwind" is poetic, but "hurricane" is perhaps more accurate. There is a problem with this metaphor in Hosea. The point is that what is sowed (the wind) will later be reaped (the whirlwind), coming back greatly magnified. If you sow wheat, you reap more wheat, not pumpkins. An apt use of this phrase would be its quotation by "Bomber" Harris in the war. According to Harris, the Germans "sowed the wind" by bombing the cities of Britain and "reaped the whirlwind" of the much more destructive allied bombing of Germany. In Hosea, the wind is idol worship, and the whirlwind is the Assyrians. But these are two completely different things. If the whirlwind is the Assyrians, then the wind should also be the Assyrians. It is Ahaz and Judah who "sow the wind" by paying the Assyrians to intervene militarily and who then reap what they sow, by being invaded by the Assyrians and eventually destroyed by the Assyrian's successors, the Babylonians. In Jeremiah, the Babylonians descending on Jerusalem are the "whirlwind":

> ... *a wind too strong for this comes from me, Now, also, I speak judgments with them. Lo, as clouds he cometh up, And as a whirlwind [cuwphah] his chariots... (Jeremiah 4:12-13)*

In the original, the wind must be sowed by Ahaz and comes back as a hurricane to destroy his people. The final author of Hosea has changed the meaning to make Israel into the guilty party instead of Judah.

In reality, Ahaz had no option but to call in the Assyrians, and he would have been horrified by the eventual outcome. Besides, his intervention would have scarcely mattered in the long run. Assyria was expanding ever closer to its only rival, Egypt. Israel and Judah were in between, and were doomed to be crushed by the two superpowers. The Israelites would not have seen things this way. Their land was lost, their relatives and friends taken or killed. Judah and Israel shared the same culture, the same religion. At one time they may have been the same nation. But now Judah had betrayed their Israelite brothers and sisters, paying money from the temple to have them destroyed. The Israelites would have felt burning, bitter anger against the Jerusalem establishment and the kings of Judah.

The unforgivable blasphemy

> ➤ Ahaz's betrayal of Israel is the unforgivable blasphemy.
> Originally this would have been a blasphemy by the spirit rather
> than a blasphemy of the spirit.

There can be nothing worse than Ahaz raiding the temple to secure the
destruction of Israel. This must be the unforgivable blasphemy. Why then
should it be called a "blasphemy against the spirit"? This cannot be the
original meaning because you cannot blaspheme a spirit. You can only
blaspheme a divine entity such as the father or the son. But although a
spirit cannot be blasphemed, it can certainly blaspheme. Evil deeds were
believed to come from evil spirits. In the Gospel of John, when Judas
betrayals Jesus it is because the devil had entered into him.[7] An evil spirit
can come from God as well as the devil. When Saul is distressed in his
mind, he is said to be afflicted by an evil spirit sent by God.[8] The spirit
caused him to prophesy, and to hurl his spear through the wall of his
house in an attempt to kill David.[9]

The unforgivable blasphemy must have been a blasphemy carried out
through the spirit and not a blasphemy of the spirit. The saying, as we
find it in Thomas, has been tweaked and reinterpreted. But why should
the betrayal by Ahaz be associated with the spirit? The answer lies in
Ahaz's response to the news of the alliance against him:

> *And his heart was moved, and the heart of his people, as the trees of the*
> *wood are moved with the wind [ruach]. (Isaiah 7:2)*

The Hebrew word, *ruach*, like the Greek equivalent *pneuma*, means both
"wind" and "spirit". The heart of Ahaz and his people are moved by a
spirit as trees are moved by a wind. It is this spirit that Isaiah attempts
to quieten with his prophecy, telling Ahaz to do nothing.[10] But we know
that Ahaz actually did a deed so shameful that the Book of Isaiah covers
it with a cloak of silence.

We find a similar spiritual explanation of the invasion by Tiglath-pileser
in Chronicles:

> *So the God of Israel stirred up the spirit [ruach] of Pul king of Assyria,*
> *the spirit [ruach] of Tiglath-pileser king of Assyria, and he took the*
> *Reubenites, the Gadites, and the half-tribe of Manasseh into exile. He*
> *brought them to Halah, Habor, Hara, and the river Gozan, to this day.*
> *(1 Chronicles 5:26)*

"Pul, king of Assyria" is another name for Tiglath-pileser. In this passage, the spirit of the Assyrian king is stirred up, causing him to invade Israel and exile the three tribes of Manasseh, Reuben and Gad. The explanation has been doctored; there is no mention of the involvement of Ahaz. But the author has inherited the tradition that an evil spirit caused the invasion.

The same idea is found in a prophecy that Isaiah gives to Hezekiah concerning Sennacherib: *"Behold, I will put a spirit [ruach] in him, so that he shall hear a rumour and return to his own land, and I will cause him to fall by the sword in his own land"* (Isaiah 37:7). Here God sends a spirit to make another Assyrian king do his will.

We come back to the saying in Hosea of sowing the wind, *ruach*, and reaping the whirlwind. The wind is the spirit of Ahaz. The unforgivable betrayal caused by this spirit will come back to haunt the Judeans.

22

Hezekiah

Hezekiah and the Judas War

When Hezekiah succeeded his father Ahaz in 727 BC, he confronted a dangerous situation. The early years of his reign saw the Assyrians complete the destruction and annexation of Israel. Throughout the conflict, Judah was a client state and ally of the Assyrians and would have been obliged to give military support in the war against Israel. Although this enabled Judah to survive and thrive, it would also have created unbearable internal tensions. Judah was flooded with refugees from Israel. According to Finkelstein: "The population of Judah at least doubled if not tripled in a very short period of time". Simultaneous to this increase in Judah there was a depopulation of the territory of southern Israel and in particular the Bethel area.[1] The accuracy of archaeological surveys can be disputed. Even if the numbers turn out to be too high, it is inconceivable that there would not have been a substantial southwards migration to escape the invading Assyrians.

It is not just the Israelite refugees who would have hated the Assyrian alliance. The pro-Assyrian policy would have been unpopular with the ordinary people in Judah, many of whom would have had kin in Israel. It was associated with the court and priestly establishment of Jerusalem, with King Ahaz himself and probably with Abi, Ahaz's queen and Hezekiah's mother. All of them would have been despised by the countryfolk. The stage was set for rebellion, yet the revolution never happened. Hezekiah was an able and unscrupulous leader who set about melding together his expanded people with a new pan-Israelite identity that encompassed both kingdoms. Such is the theory for the development of the biblical concept of Israel envisaged by Finkelstein in *The Forgotten Kingdom*.[2]

Under the new narrative, Yahweh was the one and only God. He had appointed the house of David as exclusive monarchs over both Israel and Judah. This meant that the previous kings of Israel were usurpers. Yahweh had established his house and dwelling at the temple in Jerusalem, so all other cultic sites were invalid. It was a stunning centralisation of power, in

which the absolute rule of Yahweh in heaven was matched by the absolute
rule of his anointed, Hezekiah, on earth. Such, at least, was the theory.

> **Hezekiah undertook a sweeping series of reforms aimed at cen-
> tralising worship in the Jerusalem temple.**

The Book of Kings records two waves of religious reforms under Hezekiah
and Josiah. There is now some archaeological evidence for the Hezekiah
reforms. As yet, there is no evidence for the supposed reestablishment of
cultic centres by Manasseh, nor for the subsequent Josiah reforms. The
reactionary policies of Manasseh and reforms of Josiah may have been
exaggerated to explain the embarrassment of the exile. If Hezekiah had
reformed the religious aberrations that caused the fall of Israel, then why
had Judah still shared her fate? The only possible explanation was a back-
sliding under Manasseh.

The accounts of the reforms under Hezekiah and Josiah are very similar.
According to 2 Kings, Hezekiah was the best king of all: *"... there was none
like him among all the kings of Judah after him, nor any that were before him"*
(2 Kings 18:5). A little later virtually the same thing is said about Josiah:
*"There was no king like him before him, who turned to Yahweh with all his heart
and with all his soul and with all his might, according to all the law of Moses, nor
did any like him arise after him"* (2 Kings 23:25). How can they both be the
best king? Do not the two statements contradict each other?

According to the Deuteronomistic historian, Hezekiah was the first to
attack the cultic centres:

> *He removed the high places and broke the pillars and cut down the
> Asherah. He broke in pieces the bronze serpent that Moses had made,
> for until those days the people of Israel had burnt incense to it—it was
> called Nehushtan.* (2 Kings 18:4)

Hezekiah took advantage of the weakness of Israel to impose a new
uniformity of worship, eliminating what he and his religious advisors
saw as idolatry. In 2 Chronicles 29-31, there is a long account of the cleansing of the temple by Hezekiah and its re-consecration. He *"establishes a
decree to make a proclamation throughout all Israel"* (2 Chronicles 30:5) that the
people should come and keep the Passover at Jerusalem. The letters ask
the Israelites to reform and worship at the temple, but the messengers are
not received kindly:

> *So the couriers went from city to city through the land of Ephraim and*
> *Manasseh, and as far as Zebulun, but they laughed them to scorn and*
> *mocked them. (2 Chronicles 30:10)*

It adds that some Israelites from the tribes of Asher, Manasseh and Zebulun did come to Jerusalem. Unlike the others, those from Asher are close enough to Jerusalem to be ritually clean before the Passover feast.[3] The account has doubtless been embellished, but we can deduce that Hezekiah attempted to centralise worship in the Jerusalem temple for the people of Israel as well as Judah and that most Israelites rejected this attempt. Intriguingly, some did accept the invitation; this is evidence for temple-accepting Israelites at the time of the Judas War. It is from just such a group that Christianity would eventually emerge.

➢ **The reality of the similar Josiah reforms is doubtful. Some actions attributed to Josiah probably took place in the earlier reign of Hezekiah.**

The account of the reforms of Josiah gives a lot more detail than those of Hezekiah. It is possible that some actions actually carried out by Hezekiah have been ascribed to Josiah:

> *And he brought all the priests from the cities of Judah and desecrated*
> *the high places, from Geba to Beersheba, where the priests had burned*
> *incense. He tore down the high places of the gates, at the entrance of*
> *the gate of Joshua, the governor of the city, to the left of the city gate.*
> *(2 Kings 23:8)*

The priests were brought in from sanctuaries around Judah and relocated to Jerusalem, while the high places at the Jerusalem gates were destroyed. This all matches well with what we know about Hezekiah centralising worship in the capital. There is evidence that he ordered the desecration of the high place at the gates of Lachish, and perhaps he did the same at Jerusalem. It also makes more sense that Hezekiah rather than Josiah removed cultic objects dedicated by the "kings of Judah":

> *"And he removed the horses that the kings of Judah had dedicated to the*
> *sun from the entrance to the house of Yahweh." (2 Kings 23:11)*

> *"He pulled down the altars that the kings of Judah had made on the roof*
> *near the upper chamber of Ahaz..." (2 Kings 23:12)*

It would be strange if the horses of the sun god and the altars on the upper chamber of Ahaz survived Hezekiah's reforms for Josiah to pull down. Similarly, the supposed actions of Josiah against the high place on the "Mount of corruption", the Mount of Olives, would be more appropriate for Hezekiah's reign.[4]

Did Hezekiah carry out the destruction that Josiah is supposed to have committed in Israel and Bethel? We cannot be sure. As an Assyrian ally, Hezekiah would have had the opportunity during the Judas War to destroy Israelite sanctuaries in the south, including the pre-eminent high place at Bethel. Many of the refugees into Judah came from the Bethel area, which lay only 9 miles north of Jerusalem. The sanctuary would have been a thorn in the side for Hezekiah. It was a potential centre for both religious and even political dissidence. Israelite refugees and their Judean supporters would have looked to this ancient high place, which lay outside Hezekiah's control, rather than the Jerusalem temple. Clearly, Hezekiah had strong reasons to destroy the Bethel sanctuary. However, archaeology has shown that Josiah extended his territory as far as Bethel. He also had both the opportunity and motive to act against the sanctuary.[5]

Hezekiah must have destroyed many traditional sanctuaries in an attempt to establish a monopoly for the Jerusalem temple. It is less clear whether the destruction was total. His reforms against the religion of the people would have been met by tremendous opposition. To the priests, Hezekiah became a hero, but to the Israelites and many Judeans at the time, he would have been an evil desecrator.

> **Hezekiah eventually broke the Assyrian alliance, which resulted in the invasion by Sennacherib.**

In 705 BC the Assyrian King Sargon II died, and the Assyrian Empire entered a period of crisis. Hezekiah took the opportunity to cease tribute payments to the new king, Sennacherib, and to join an Egyptian alliance instead. Hezekiah was aware of the likelihood of Assyrian invasion and undertook a remarkable program of fortification, including a new wall around Jerusalem. The Assyrian alliance had enabled Judah to survive a tumultuous period, so why did Hezekiah now take this tremendous risk?

It is a measure of the strength of anti-Assyrian feeling in Judah that Hezekiah was obliged to take such a dangerous course. The Judeans and Israelite refugees had witnessed the Assyrians' systematic and forcible relocation of the people of Israel. The heartland of Israel, lands which had been home to the Jews for countless centuries, were lost, now occupied by outsiders. How could the king of Judah remain allied to the despoiler of

Israel? Hezekiah's preparations show that he was well aware of the risk. But it seems he had no option but to go along with the will of his people.

Whatever the reasons for breaking the alliance, it was a terrible mistake. The Assyrian forces of Sennacherib invaded in 701 BC and swept over Judah. They took many settlements including the second city Lachish, an action which is recorded in the stone reliefs now in the British Museum. Archaeology has revealed the extent of the destruction. Almost every place they took was devastated in a brutal program of revenge against the rebellious state. The Assyrians surrounded Jerusalem so that none could enter or leave. Hezekiah was trapped in the royal city. His doom, and that of the house of David, looked imminent.

Isaiah and Hezekiah

➢ The story in Isaiah and 2 Kings of the siege of Hezekiah and his eventual triumph due to the intervention of Yahweh, is an attempt by Judean authors to explain away an appalling defeat.

It is at this point of looming defeat that the Book of Isaiah takes up the narrative. The prophecy of Isaiah to Hezekiah is a pair with the prophecy to Ahaz. In both cases, Isaiah addresses a king in a time of crisis to reassure him, effectively telling him to do nothing. The material in Isaiah 36-38 is shared with 2 Kings 18:13-20:19. Which of the two came first is not immediately apparent. What is certain is that the account has received a thorough pro-Judean and pro-Hezekiah makeover.

The section starts with a speech given by an Assyrian official called Rabshakeh before the walls of Jerusalem in an attempt to persuade the Jews to surrender. Hezekiah despairs when told about Rabshakeh's speech. He enters the temple and sends messengers to Isaiah, who replies with encouragement. A spirit will be put into the Assyrian king so that he will return to his own land and fall by the sword. We then have a second version of the story, in which Sennacherib sends the message directly to Hezekiah in a letter. Once again Hezekiah despairs and prays in the temple. Once again, Isaiah sends him a message with the good news that the Assyrian king will leave. That night an angel of the lord enters the Assyrian camp and kills 185,000 men. Sennacherib withdraws back to Nineveh, and while praying to his gods, is struck down and murdered by two of his sons.

It is all presented as a fantastic miracle by which Yahweh saved Jerusalem and punished the Assyrian king. But Kings includes another, much shorter and very different account:

> *In the fourteenth year of Hezekiah's reign, Sennacherib king of Assyria*
> *attacked all the fortified cities of Judah and seized them. So Hezekiah*
> *king of Judah sent to the king of Assyria at Lachish, saying, "I have*
> *done wrong; turn away from me, and I will pay whatever you demand*
> *from me." And the king of Assyria assessed Hezekiah king of Judah*
> *three hundred talents of silver and thirty talents of gold. Hezekiah*
> *gave him all the silver that was found in the house of Yahweh and in*
> *the treasuries of the king's house. At that time Hezekiah stripped the*
> *gold with which he had plated the doors and doorposts of the temple of*
> *Yahweh, and he gave it to the king of Assyria. (2 Kings 18:13-16)*

This is followed, illogically, by the material shared with Isaiah, with
the Assyrians invading after the tribute payment. The timing in the first
line (also shared with Isaiah) is wrong; the fourteenth year of Hezekiah's
reign would be 713 BC whereas the Sennacherib invasion took place in
701 BC. But the remainder of the account is remarkably accurate. We
know this because for once we hear from the other side. A description
of this campaign against Hezekiah was engraved on stone bulls in the
palace at Nineveh, and on three hexagonal clay prisms including the
Taylor Prism now in the British Museum. The Assyrian king claimed
to have conquered forty-six of Hezekiah's walled towns and taken over
200,000 prisoners as slaves, a likely exaggeration. Hezekiah himself was
shut up "in Jerusalem, his royal city, like a bird in a cage." Some of the
captured cities were given to other local kings, reducing his kingdom.
Hezekiah was overwhelmed by the "lordly splendour" of the king of
Assyria and the warriors he had brought in to defend Jerusalem "did not
fight". Finally, Hezekiah sends a messenger to pay tribute and do obei-
sance. The tribute is sent after Sennacherib to Nineveh. It includes thirty
talents of gold and eight hundred talents of silver, "valuable treasures of
every sort", women of the palace, singers, and even some of the king's
own daughters.

Once again, the Book of Isaiah is covering up what actually happened.
Hezekiah, reduced to despair, sent messengers to the king of Assyria
at Lachish, begging for forgiveness. He offered to pay a huge tribute to
end the invasion. Rather than embark upon a long siege of Jerusalem,
Sennacherib decided to accept this tribute. It was indeed a miracle of
sorts, for the Assyrians would have been expected to destroy Jerusalem
and remove or kill Hezekiah. Doubtless, the Assyrians had their reasons,
and there may be some truth in the explanation that they had received
news of a threat elsewhere. But the whole episode was still a disaster for
Judah and a humiliation for Hezekiah. Sennacherib was indeed killed by
his sons in a temple, but not until much later. Isaiah and Kings give the

impression that he was murdered shortly after his return from Judah. In fact, he reigned for another twenty years, long outliving Hezekiah.

Originally, the Book of Kings must have just had the original short and accurate account of events. This, however, was deemed too negative towards Hezekiah. So someone added the much longer report from Isaiah. This Isaiah account is another cover-up. Isaiah advises both Ahaz and Hezekiah to do nothing, but they both actually did something very similar; they both paid the temple treasures to the Assyrians. Ahaz paid the treasure to get an Assyrian king to invade and Hezekiah to get an Assyrian king to leave.

➤ **An accusation by the Assyrian official Rabshakeh shows that the people saw the Assyrian invasion as a punishment inflicted by Yahweh for Hezekiah's religious reforms.**

At one point in the harangue by Rabshakeh, the Judean negotiators do something strange. They ask Rabshakeh to switch from speaking in Hebrew to Aramaic. Understandably, Rabshakeh refuses to do this. He is addressing the Judean soldiers on the wall and wants to be understood. Had this episode not been included, the reader would have assumed that Rabshakeh was speaking in Aramaic. An Assyrian is not going to bother to learn Hebrew. Aramaic would have been well understood by the Jerusalem elite but not by the ordinary people. Why should the author stress in this way that the people on the walls understood Rabshakeh because he was speaking in Hebrew?

A clue is to be found in what comes immediately before this request to switch language. Rabshakeh has just made two potentially dangerous accusations against Hezekiah:

> *"But if you say to me, 'We trust in Yahweh our God', is it not he whose high places and altars Hezekiah has removed, saying to Judah and to Jerusalem, 'You shall worship before this altar'?" (Isaiah 36:7)*

> *"Moreover, is it without Yahweh that I have come up against this land to destroy it? Yahweh said to me, 'Go up against this land and destroy it'." (Isaiah 36:10)*

Rabshakeh is claiming:

1. That Yahweh is angry with Hezekiah because he has destroyed the high places and centralised all worship in the Jerusalem temple.

2. As a result, Yahweh has summoned the Assyrian king to punish
   the Judeans.

The account in Isaiah and Kings is a skilful attempt to refute these two
central accusations. The author uses what was to become a classic literary
device; the villain's speech. We can find the device of the villain's speech
in many books and movies today. The speech has to be superficially per-
suasive and clever, delivered with an aura of confident power. Yet the
reader or viewer is intended to detest everything that the villain says. It
is a useful method to discredit opinions with which the author disagrees.

Rabshakeh starts by saying that Hezekiah has been foolish to trust in
Egyptian help. Egypt is a broken reed that pierces through a man's hand.
He mocks the failure of Egypt to supply Judah with promised horses and
chariots by offering to give them two thousand horses should they be able
to find enough riders. He then puts on a false voice of reason, promising
that if they surrender and abandon Hezekiah, they will be allowed to
return to their old homes for a while, before being given new lands and
vineyards that are just as good. He enumerates all the other peoples that
the Assyrians have conquered and asks rhetorically where are the gods
these people worshipped now? At this, his listeners fall silent, for the
validity of Yahweh's power is being tested.

By placing the accusations against Hezekiah in the mouth of such a villain, the author aims to discredit them. The author is explaining that the
two claims originated with Rabshakeh's speech. The people on the wall
heard Rabshakeh because he was speaking in Hebrew, emphasised by the
request to switch language. By the end of the story, Hezekiah and Judah
will be saved, and the Assyrians defeated. Rabshakeh's argument is then
turned on its head; Yahweh is not like the gods of other nations, but is the
real thing. Isaiah gives Hezekiah a message from Yahweh that Rabshakeh
is a blasphemer, which discredits all of Rabshakeh's accusations.[6]

We can conclude that the allegations concerning Hezekiah's reforms
were actually in general circulation amongst the people. These accusations caused acute embarrassment among the priestly class who were the
beneficiaries of the reforms. The purpose of the Isaiah/Kings story is to
repudiate the allegations and recast Hezekiah's defeat by the Assyrians
as a great victory.

➢ **Elsewhere in Isaiah, we find the view that the Sennacherib invasion was intended to punish Hezekiah.**

We have seen how Kings has both an accurate account of the Sennacherib
invasion and also the contradictory and extended priestly apology for

Hezekiah. We find a similar phenomenon in Isaiah. Rabshakeh's claim that Yahweh has summoned the Assyrian king to invade actually reflects a view found throughout the prophetic writings, that the Assyrians and Babylonians were tools of Yahweh, summoned to punish Judah and Israel. So was Sennacherib sent by Yahweh? Surprisingly, an affirmative answer is given elsewhere in Isaiah:

> *Therefore Yahweh is bringing up against them the mighty waters of the Euphrates—the king of Assyria and all his glory. And it will rise over all its channels and go over all its banks, and it will sweep on into Judah, it will overflow and pass on, reaching even to the neck, and its outspread wings will fill the breadth of your land, O Immanuel."* (Isaiah 8:7-8)

This is a prophecy of the Sennacherib invasion which reached "to the neck" meaning that it surrounded Jerusalem. The Assyrian King Sennacherib "and all his glory" has been summoned by Yahweh, just as Rabshakeh claimed! It is clear that in Isaiah we have alternative, and contradictory, traditions, reflecting internal disagreements among the Judeans of the time. A section of the people rejected the religious reforms and saw the Assyrian invasion as evidence of Yahweh's anger with Hezekiah.

➢ **The third betrayal must be Hezekiah's religious repression of the Israelites.**

We can now see that the main accusation against Hezekiah concerned his unpopular religious reforms which were aimed against the traditional centres and forms of Israelite worship. It is these reforms that must be the third betrayal. Not only had the kings of Judah desecrated the temple and betrayed the Israelites to the Assyrians. They used their position of power as an Assyrian ally to destroy Israelite religion.

The dial of Ahaz

➢ **Hezekiah and Judah are given extra life corresponding to ten steps on the sundial of Ahaz. The ten steps are ten hours measured in Almanac time.**

It was a miracle of sorts that the Assyrians failed to take Jerusalem, although a less spectacular miracle than recorded in the Bible. If the city had fallen this would not just have ended the rule of Hezekiah but also precipitated the exile of Judah. It is not the only miracle that 2 Kings and Isaiah records about Hezekiah. As the city is about to fall, Hezekiah is sick and close to death. Isaiah tells him that he will die.[7] But Hezekiah prays to God, and his prayers are heeded:

> *Then the word of Yahweh came to Isaiah: "Go and say to Hezekiah, Thus says Yahweh, the God of David your father: I have heard your prayer, I have seen your tears. Behold, I will add fifteen years to your life. I will deliver you and this city out of the hand of the king of Assyria. I will defend this city." (Isaiah 38:4-6; see also 2 Kings 20:5-6)*

Isaiah tells Hezekiah that he will be given a sign:

> *"Behold, I will make the shadow on the sundial of Ahaz which has descended, turn back ten steps." So the sun turned back on the dial the ten steps by which it had declined. (Isaiah 38:8; see also 2 Kings 20:9-11)*

The sickness of Hezekiah is presented as simultaneous with the siege of Jerusalem. Not only is Hezekiah given fifteen more years of life, but Jerusalem and Judah are also reprieved. In fact, Hezekiah lived for only three years after the siege and his illness must actually have occurred much earlier in 713 BC. The author of the Kings/Isaiah account mistakenly takes this illness as the date of the Sennacherib invasion. The two events, separated by over a decade, became simultaneous in the development of the story.

The supposed miracle of the sun moving backwards is unnecessary to the story. The real miracle is that the life of Hezekiah and Judah are both prolonged. The moving back of the sun on the dial is a metaphor for this gift of extra time. The writer of the account in Isaiah and 2 Kings misunderstood the metaphor, transforming it into a literal miracle.

What is the meaning of the ten steps? The sundial is described as if it were a staircase with a shadow moving over the steps to indicate the time. However, we should consider the likelihood that the author had never seen the sundial, or indeed any other sundial. What did each step represent? We can be sure that the ten steps are less than the length of the day (sunrise to sunset). And they cannot be Babylonian degrees which are far too small (4 minutes of our time) to be practical measures for a sundial. So it is most likely that a step is an hour, a twenty-fourth of the day. The dial of Ahaz is the earliest known literary reference to a sundial, but they were in use long before Ahaz. A very early example has been found in

Egypt dating to the 13th century BC.[8] Its face is divided into twelve equal hours. So the ten steps must represent ten hours.

We can calculate the extra lifetime in Almanac time. A generation was nominally half the human lifespan of 70 years, so each Almanac day would notionally represent 35 years. So how many years would be represented by 10 hours? To derive a whole number of years, we must resort to something that the Jews frequently did, and substitute 72 for 70. This is necessary because 70 is not divisible by twelve. With 72 years for the lifespan, the day becomes 36 years. The calculation is then:

10 hours = (10/24) x 36 years = 15 years

Which is the exact extra lifetime granted to Hezekiah. Judah is spared along with Hezekiah. So does the 10 hours also represent the extra time given to Judah? We need to move up a level from days to great days. Each great day is seven days, so:

10 hours = (10/24) x 7 days = (70/24) days

Once again we must substitute 72 for 70 to get a whole number:

(72/24) days = 3 days

So Judah would have three days (generations) of extra time. In the Almanac we have the following days from Hezekiah to the exile:

7.3 Hezekiah
7.4 Manasseh
7.5 Amon
7.6 Josiah
7.7 Jeconiah

The exile commenced at the very start of Jeconiah's reign, so after Hezekiah, there are three days (7.4, 7.5 and 7.6) before the exile. Judah was indeed given the extra time represented by 10 hours of a great day.

It might be objected that we have had to use 72 instead of 70 in the above calculations, but this is an inevitable consequence of converting Almanac time into a 24-hour clock. If we did the calculations in reverse without substituting 72 for 70 then:

15 years in a generation of 35 years would correspond to 10.3 hours.
3 days in a great day would correspond to 10.3 hours.

The ancients did not use decimals and would have rounded the hours to ten. Whoever first developed the story about the sundial was using a version of the Almanac.

23

Blasphemy Against the Son

Blasphemy against Baal?

> ➢ Hezekiah's religious reforms are the blasphemy against the son.
> One potential explanation is that the "son" was Baal.

If our analysis of the three blasphemies is correct, Hezekiah's reforms must be the remaining blasphemy, that against the son. The fully developed myth of Christ would not have existed at the time of Hezekiah. So if Hezekiah committed blasphemy against the son, this would have involved one of the cultic forms that became integrated into the Christ myth. We have seen that Christ has taken over aspects of the myths of Baal and Dumuzi. Christ, like Baal, is the special son of El. And like Baal, he rejects his heavenly mother and brothers, who can be equated with Asherah and her seventy sons. The most obvious explanation of Hezekiah's blasphemy is that it relates to his destruction of Baal worship.

The accounts of Hezekiah's action against the old religion are very brief, and Baal is not mentioned directly. However, Hezekiah is said to have destroyed the Asherah poles and, according to Chronicles, cleansed the temple of "filth" meaning idols.[1] Baal worship must have been one target of these reforms. There is, however, a better explanation of "blasphemy against the son" than the destruction of Baal worship.

The Nehushtan

> ➢ An alternative explanation of Hezekiah's blasphemy against the
> son is that it relates to the destruction of the bronze snake, the
> Nehushtan.

The Nehushtan was an odd cultic object which was destroyed on the orders of Hezekiah:

He broke in pieces the bronze serpent that Moses had made, for until those days the people of Israel had burnt incense to it—it was called Nehushtan. (2 Kings 18:4)

The Nehushtan is the only object explicitly mentioned in the Kings passage apart from the Asherah poles, and it must have been important. The name occurs only here in the Bible and is derived from the word for bronze.[2] The story about Moses making the bronze snake comes from Numbers:

And Yahweh said to Moses, "Make a fiery serpent [seraph] and set it on a pole, and everyone who is bitten, when he sees it, shall live." So Moses made a bronze serpent and set it on a pole. And if a serpent bit anyone, he would look at the bronze serpent and live. (Numbers 21:8-9)

The story is clearly intended to explain the existence of the Nehushtan in the temple. Significantly, the later Book of Chronicles does not mention the Nehushtan at all—the idea of Moses making an idol must have become acutely embarrassing by this time.[3]

The 2 Kings passage says that the "people of Israel" worshipped the object, which is likely to be a derogatory reference to the Israelites. But it must also have been important among the people of Judah, or the Moses story would never have been incorporated into Numbers. There are several lines of evidence connecting Christ with snakes and with the Nehushtan in particular.

➢   **The Gospel of John compares Christ to the Nehushtan.**

The most obvious link between Christ and the Nehushtan comes in the Gospel of John:

And as Moses lifted up the serpent in the wilderness, so must the Son of Man be lifted up, that everyone who believes in him may have eternal life. (John 3:14-15)

Here, the lifting up of "the Son of Man", crucifixion, is compared to Moses lifting up the snake of bronze. Christ is identified with the Nehushtan, and both bring life. Does this link go back to an ancient tradition or is it just a metaphor invented by the author of John? Several converging lines of evidence suggest that Christ was linked to the Nehushtan.

> ➤ Jesus is implicitly compared to the Nehushtan or snake, in Thomas, Matthew, the long ending of Mark and the letters of Paul.

The identification of Christ with the Nehushtan would have pre-dated the story of Eve and the snake in Genesis. Once the Genesis account was accepted, the snake nature of Christ became embarrassing and this aspect was gradually repressed. But we can still find a positive saying about the snake in both Thomas and Matthew:

> *Jesus said: "The Pharisees and the scribes have taken the keys of knowl-*
> *edge; they have hidden them. They did not go in, and those who wanted*
> *to go in they did not allow. You, however, be as wise as serpents and as*
> *innocent as doves." (Thomas 39; TC 3.2)*

The expression "be as wise as serpents and as innocent as doves" is also found at Matthew 10:16 and has become a well-known phrase. Originally the dove was Mary, and the serpent was Christ. Together, they allow the disciple to find the "keys of knowledge" and enter into the kingdom.

Turning to the long ending of Mark, we find something more closely linked with the Nehushtan:

> *"And these signs will follow those who believe: in my name, they shall*
> *cast out demons; they shall speak in new tongues; they will pick up*
> *serpents with their hands; and if they drink any deadly poison, it will*
> *not hurt them; they will lay their hands on the sick, and they will*
> *recover." (Mark 16:17-18)*

The idea that the first Christians could "pick up serpents with their hands" is oddly specific. The next point, drinking deadly poison without being harmed, probably meant that false teachers would not sway the disciples. But why should the author of Mark include this very particular power of picking up snakes? Most scholars think they know the answer. There is a story in Acts in which the shipwrecked Paul has a viper fasten onto his hand but, miraculously, suffers no ill effects.[4] These scholars believe that the long ending was a much later addition to the gospel and that the author has taken this miracle from Acts. However, while it is comparatively easy to know that two passages are related, it is far harder to determine which came first. The Paul episode could equally be a fictional development of the long ending miracle. We know the author of Luke used Mark, so if the long ending were attached at this time, it would explain the Acts story. And if we look at the structure of Acts, we see an unexpected link with the long ending. The start and end of Acts are chiastic (symmetrical). At the beginning, Peter gives a speech in Jerusalem, and at the end, Paul gives a speech in Rome. Both of these speeches pick up on themes set out in the long ending. Not only that, but the first and last miracles in Acts are also found in the long ending. The first miracle is speaking in tongues. The last two miracles are (i) Paul picking up the snake with his hand, and then (ii) Paul laying hands on a sick man and healing him.[5] Now it is possible that the author of the long ending has, for some unknown reason, gone out of his way to pick episodes from the beginning and end of Acts. But it is much more likely that the author of Acts has placed the material from the long ending in an artful, chiastic structure.

The question of the long ending is considered in much more detail in the Rock and the Tower.[6] The conclusion is that the original form of the long ending (I call it "the Gospel of the Long Ending") is earlier than all the gospels, including Mark. So the miraculous picking up of snakes reflects a belief that existed before the gospels. If Christ were the Nehushtan, this would explain why his followers were thought to be immune from snakebite.

Another link between Christ and the bronze snake comes from Paul. In 1 Corinthians, he talks about the Israelites in the desert and how they were bitten by snakes:

> *We should not test Christ, as some of them did, and were destroyed by serpents... (1 Corinthians 10:9)*

One odd thing here is that Paul has "Christ" rather than Yahweh—it is Yahweh who sends the snakes in Numbers. So it is understandable that some manuscripts of 1 Corinthians replace "Christ" with "Lord". However, the textual evidence, including the very early papyrus P46, indicates that the more difficult reading of "Christ" is original.[7] Paul's words support the idea that Christ was present in the desert with the Israelites in the form of the Nehushtan. He preserved the Israelites from snakebite, but those who tried his patience lost their immunity and were destroyed.

➤ **Two Christian gnostic groups, the Naassenes and the Ophites were named after the snake. Another gnostic group, the Peratae, believed that Christ was the Nehushtan.**

Another line of evidence comes from the alternative forms of Christianity that existed alongside the proto-orthodox church in the early centuries. Two prominent gnostic groups were named after the snake; the Naassenes derive their name from *nachash*, the Hebrew for "snake"; and the Ophites are named after the Greek for "snake".

The Naassenes are of particular interest because they remembered many correct traditions from the early Jesus movement. From Hyppolitus, we hear that they identified their teachings as coming from James through Mary.[8] This correctly identifies the first two leaders, Mary, the shaman, and her appointed successor and "son" James. The order is wrong—it should be from Mary through James—but this is understandable given the confusion introduced by the gospels. Hyppolitus says that the Naassenes worship only the serpent and that it is a "moist essence" and that nothing of existing things could exist without it. All things that the snake enters into become "temples" and the substance of the snake flows though the universe like "the river proceeding forth from Eden and dividing itself into four heads".[9]

The Ophites were a particularly notorious sect. There is an account by Epiphanius describing the Ophite Eucharist. In this ceremony, a snake crawls out of a box and mingles with the Eucharistic bread on the table. The recipients eat the bread and kiss the snake. The account would have sent shivers of horror down the spines of the orthodox. Here are those wicked gnostics corrupting the very Eucharist with the serpent, the symbol of Satan! But the ceremony makes sense if the serpent was an aspect of Christ. The snake mingling with the bread enables its essence to transform the bread into the body of Christ.[10]

A direct link with the Nehushtan is given in Hyppolitus' account of the Peratae, an offshoot of the Naassenes.[11] The Peratae thought that the fiery serpents that bit the Israelites in the desert were the stars, the gods of destruction. The only protection against them was the brazen snake which Moses lifted up; it was the "true and perfect serpent", the Christ. In this explanation, we can see that the snakes stand for the host of heaven, the seventy who bring death into the world. The Christ, also a son of God and a snake, has the power to heal the evil of the seventy. He brings life.

> There is a prophecy from First Isaiah that equates the Messiah with the "seraph", the flying serpent.

The seraphs, flying serpent-like creatures, are the closest attendants upon Yahweh. In the throne room vision, it is a seraph who takes the burning coal and presses it to Isaiah's lips. The throne room occupies the same space as the temple on a different level of reality. So the seraph should correspond to something in the temple, and what can this be except the Nehushtan? If so then Hezekiah's destruction of the Nehushtan would have been highly contentious. There is a prophecy in First Isaiah that also mentions a "seraph":

> *In the year that King Ahaz died was this oracle. Rejoice not, Philistia,*
> *because the rod that struck you is broken: for out of the serpent's root*
> *shall come forth an adder, and his fruit shall be a flying fiery serpent*
> *[seraph]. (Isaiah 14:28-29)*

The one who smote Philistia is likely to be King Uzziah who won victories over the Philistines.[12] In Ahaz's reign, however, the Philistines had invaded the territory of Judah.[13] They would "rejoice" because the rod that had beat them, the house of David, appeared to be broken. But now Ahaz is succeeded by his energetic son Hezekiah who in the earlier part of his reign won more victories against the Philistines.[14] So Hezekiah is the adder which has come from the serpent's (Uzziah's) root. The prophecy predicts that a third strong leader will eventually emerge from the "fruit" (the descendants) of Hezekiah. This one will be far more powerful than either Uzziah or Hezekiah. He is represented, not as an ordinary snake, but as a flying fiery serpent. The Targum interprets this as a prediction of the Messiah: *"for out of the children's children of Jesse shall come forth the Messiah, and his works shall be among you as a flying serpent"*.

The word used for the flying fiery serpent is the same as for the seraphs who wait upon God in the throne room vision. So we have a prediction that was interpreted as meaning that the Messiah, the Christ, would be a seraph. The positioning of the prophecy within Isaiah is significant, for it follows on from two other prophecies; first, that the king of Babylon, called the morning star or Lucifer, would be overcome; and, second, that the Assyrians would be defeated. Although directed against the Philistines, the placing suggests a greater meaning; the seraph would overthrow the heavenly king of Babylon.

➢ **The Gospel of John implies that Christ was present at the throne room vision, which could only have been as a seraph. In Revelation, Christ is described in terms similar to the seraph and the Nehushtan.**

The Gospel of John quotes from the throne room vision in Isaiah about the Jews being unable to see or hear, and then adds: *"Isaiah said these things because he saw his (Jesus') glory and spoke about him" (John 12:41)*. The implication is that Christ was in attendance during Isaiah's vision; but the only ones present were Yahweh, Isaiah and the seraphim. A seraph holds the burning coal which takes away Isaiah's sins: *"this has touched your lips; and your iniquity is taken away, and your sin purged" (Isaiah 6:7).* Jesus likewise has the power to forgive sins.[15]

In Revelation there is a bizarre description of Christ:

> ... and in the midst of the lampstands was one like the Son of Man, clothed with a garment down to the foot, with a golden sash about his breast. His head and his hairs were white like wool, as white as snow; and his eyes were like a flame of fire. His feet were like fine bronze, as if they burned in a furnace; and his voice was like the sound of many waters. (Revelation 1:13-15)

Note the odd detail that the Son of Man had feet of bronze which burned as in a furnace. This description is of the fiery seraph and the bronze Nehushtan. Revelation was greatly influenced by Ezekiel and its vision of the chariot, which is one of those heretical apocalyptic elements that found their way into mainstream scripture. The chariot passages gave rise to the Merkabah school of mysticism, in which the Jewish seer would attempt the ascent to heaven. The chariot is the mobile throne of Yahweh and at its four corners are four "living creatures" which have been developed from the seraphs in the throne room vision. These living creatures also had feet described as being like bronze:

> "and their feet are straight feet, and the sole of their feet is as a sole of a calf's foot, and they are sparkling as the colour of burnished bronze" (Ezekiel 1:7)

So there are connections between the Son of Man in Revelation, the "living creatures" in Ezekiel, the seraphim in the throne room vision and the bronze Nehushtan in the temple. Behind all this is a tradition that Christ could take the form of the seraph and the Nehushtan in the temple.

The son as the Nehushtan

There are two explanations of how the reforms of Hezekiah came to be seen as a "blasphemy against the son". The destruction of the Baal sites makes logical sense as Baal was the son of El. But the evidence points to the unexpected conclusion that Christ was identified with the Nehushtan. The fact that it is specifically recorded that Hezekiah had ordered the Nehushtan to be broken up shows that this action stood out as having special significance.

The destruction of the temple Nehushtan makes a neat pair with Uzziah offering incense in the temple. We know that the proto-Christian movement was focused on the first temple. So it would make sense that the two blasphemies, against the father and the son, both involved the temple. The seraph and the incense altar are linked together in the throne room vision which comes immediately before the Ahaz section of Isaiah. So all three blasphemies would be represented close together in First Isaiah.

Undoubtedly Hezekiah's reforms would have enraged the remaining Israelites. Their religion, like their nation, was being dismantled by the kings of Judah. No wonder they looked upon Ahaz and his son with disgust. The breaking up of the beloved and protective Nehushtan would have symbolised the wider desolation of their religious life.

24

Gethsemane

The first three periods

We return to Jesus' last day in the proto-crucifixion source. Can we correlate events in the first three periods of the seventh Almanac week to the first three periods in the passion account? We would have the following correspondence:

7.1 Jotham = the last supper
7.2 Ahaz = the garden of Gethsemane
7.3 Hezekiah = the Sanhedrin trial of Jesus

The three betrayals associated with Uzziah, Ahaz and Hezekiah come before "cock-crow" meaning the end of 7.3 in the Almanac. This is represented in the passion account by the three denials by Peter before the cock crows. We will find the most significant correspondences in the second period, that of Ahaz and the unforgivable betrayal.

The last supper

The first day of this great day, the reign of Jotham, corresponds to the last supper. There are no direct correspondences with the Almanac in this period because it is important for the event that started it—the desecration by Uzziah. We have seen that Uzziah and the throne room vision is linked to the material that comes immediately before the passion day in Mark, including apocalyptic predictions and the leper house. We know little about the reign of Jotham; the first period in the proto-crucifixion source was a vacant space which the author of Mark could fill with his last supper account.

We have hypothesised that the passion account is based on two primary sources:

1. The proto-crucifixion source derived from the Almanac seventh
    great day.
2. A spiritual shamanic experience of the crucifixion which came ulti-
    mately from Mary.

The last supper is from source (2) and not (1). The gospel writers
adopted a spiritual interpretation of Jesus as the Passover lamb. However,
it is notable that Jesus says that the bread is his flesh and does not mention
meat. Although the bread and wine were symbolic of sacrifice, they were
not specifically related to the Passover. Jesus was not the Passover lamb
in the original myth.

> ➤   **Judas belongs to the proto-crucifixion source, whereas the last
>   supper is from the shamanic source.**

Judas does not belong in the shamanic experience of the crucifixion but
comes from the Almanac; he comes from source (1) but not source (2). So
he does not feature in Mark's account of the last supper. Judas is first introduced as the betrayer immediately before the meal, when he approaches
the priests.[1] At the meal, Jesus predicts that he will be betrayed by "one
of the twelve" who dips his bread into the bowl with him. We would
expect the gospel to make it clear that the betrayer is Judas, but he is
neither named nor indicated. The author of Matthew is a good barometer
of problems in Mark, and in his gospel, Jesus explicitly identifies Judas.[2]
The Gospel of John goes much further. Jesus hands the piece of bread to
Judas and tells him to do what he must. Judas then rushes out into the
dark to betray Jesus.[3]

The second period

Following the last supper, the action moves to the Mount of Olives:

> *And when they had sung a hymn, they went out to the Mount of Olives.
> And Jesus said to them, "You will all fall away this night, for it has been
> written, 'I will strike the shepherd, and the sheep will be scattered.'"*
> (Mark 14:26-7)

The quote is from Zechariah 13:7. Jesus adds that he will be raised
up and will go to Galilee before his disciples. He then predicts Peter's
three denials before cock-crow, although Peter and the disciples protest
that they will never desert Jesus. After this, they come to a place called

Gethsemane, described as a "garden" in the Gospel of John. Only three disciples are now with Jesus; Peter, James and John. He tells them to keep watch while he prays:

> And he said to them, "Very sorrowful is my soul, even to death. Stay here and watch." And he went a little farther, and fell on the ground and prayed that, if it were possible, the hour might pass from him. And he said, "Abba, Father, all things are possible for you. Take this cup away from me. Yet not what I will, but what you will." (Mark 14:34-6)

The disciples, however, fall asleep. Jesus returns and upbraids Peter with the famous words: *"the spirit indeed is willing, but the flesh is weak"* (*Mark 14:38*). They fall asleep another two times. It is odd that not one of the three can stay awake when it is still only evening. But then this is another version of the three betrayals. Jesus' vigil ends with the approach of the crowd sent by the priests:

> It is enough: the hour has come. Behold, the Son of Man is betrayed into the hands of sinners. (Mark 14:41)

Judas comes with the armed multitude and gives the prearranged signal. He kisses Jesus and the priests' men arrest him. Two unusual episodes follow the arrest. The first is the severing of an ear:

> One of those standing by drew his sword and struck the servant of the high priest and cut off his ear. (Mark 14:47)

At this outbreak of violence, Jesus' disciples all flee, and we have the second, even stranger, episode:

> And a young man followed him, having cast a linen cloth about his naked body. And they seized him, but he left the linen cloth and fled naked. (Mark 14:51-2)

The story serves no purpose in the narrative. It is an embarrassing detail that raises questions without providing any answers. What on earth was the young man doing there naked apart from a single sheet? Why did the gospel not tell us that others were present with Jesus and his three disciples? What was going on?

Many conjectures have been offered to explain the naked young man. The most extreme was a forgery perpetrated by the iconoclastic scholar Morton Smith who gave the episode a homo-erotic meaning in his so-called Secret Gospel of Mark. He claimed to have found an extract from an original, unexpurgated version of Mark quoted in a letter by the church father Clement. According to Morton Smith, this letter was copied into the back pages of a seventeenth-century book that he found in the monastery of Mar Saba. In this Secret Mark extract, Jesus asks a young man to come to him alone at night wearing nothing but a sheet so that Jesus can show him "the kingdom of heaven".[4]

Morton Smith spent his life studying Christianity, but like many lapsed Christians he carried a grudge against the church. The forgery was a response to police action in the US against gay men who would use parks to meet up in the 1950s. The police were spurred on by the evangelical church to patrol the parks and arrest these gays. Morton Smith took his revenge by forging a Mark passage in which Jesus arranged hook-ups with naked men in parks at night! It is really quite funny. Morton Smith salted the forgery with many clues—quite literally, since the letter talks about adulterated salt being added to the gospel, and the best-known brand of salt at the time was Morton Salt. He wrote the letter opposite a printed page which denounced an "impudent fellow" who had forged many Christian texts. He included an allusion to Salome and the dance of the seven veils which first appeared in the play by Oscar Wilde who was sent to prison for homosexuality. He dedicated his book to a scholar who argued that the letter was inauthentic, with the cryptic comment "to he who knows". And the whole idea was based on a best-selling evangelical thriller about a forged document supposedly disproving Jesus' resurrection which was discovered at (you've guessed it!) the monastery of Mar Saba. Incredibly, most of these clues were not picked up until modern scholars such as Bart Ehrman and Stephen Carlson began to question the still common belief that the letter was original to Clement.

We do not need to turn to the fictional Secret Mark to see that the original story is strange. The other gospel writers omitted the young man out of sheer embarrassment. It is an incongruent detail that must come from the source. After the young man flees, the crowd lead Jesus away to the high priests. This marks the end of the second period and the beginning of the third.

➤ **The major themes and details of the second period will be traced to the betrayal of the Judas War.**

The account of the second period is quite long within the context of Mark's passion story as we would expect if it corresponds to the worst betrayal, the unforgivable blasphemy. The main themes and features of the period are set out below.

Main themes:

Judas Iscariot betrays Jesus with a kiss.
He brings the men who arrest Jesus.

Other details:

The Mount of Olives
A quotation from Zechariah
The place "Gethsemane"
The cup that Jesus must drink
The disciples who fall asleep
The approaching armed crowd
The cut-off ear of the high priest's servant
The sheet torn from the naked young man

We will show that all of these themes and details—every single one—can be traced to sources which are related to the Judas War. Three sources are relevant; First Isaiah, Ezekiel, and Second (Deutero) Zechariah. We have already seen the importance of First Isaiah to the three betrayals. Ezekiel and Zechariah are supposedly set later, in the exile and post-exilic periods, but include earlier materials.

The starting point is to find the meaning of Gethsemane for which we will turn to First Isaiah. We will then move to the stories of two sisters (Israel and Judah) in Ezekiel. After this, we will consider the true meaning of the name "Judas Iscariot" and his relationship to the books of prophecy and Second Zechariah in particular.

The name "Gethsemane"

In the Gospel of John, Gethsemane is described as a "garden", and in Mark, it is a "place". There was no real distinction between the two. The word for "place" meant an enclosed area, and a garden on the Mount of Olives would be a fenced-in orchard of olive trees. The name Gethsemane is not known from any source other than the gospels. (We can discount later traditions about the location of Gethsemane. When Christianity became the official religion of the Roman Empire, a tourist industry developed in Palestine. Pilgrims who had travelled far from distant lands wanted to see the sites that were famous from the gospels. The local population, increasingly dependent on the pilgrimage trade, were keen to oblige.) We would not expect the name of a small, private place to be preserved, but was Gethsemane ever a real place?

> ➤ The garden of Gethsemane comes from the vineyard parable in
>   Isaiah.

We have seen the importance of the vineyard parable, which is linked to
the parable of the tenants. This parable about the exile precedes the sections of Isaiah which originally addressed the three betrayals of Uzziah,
Ahaz and Hezekiah. First Isaiah does not follow a simple linear pattern,
but jumps back and forth in time while maintaining an underlying
chronological progression. Between the vineyard parable and the Ahaz
prophecy come several other elements:

> The parable of the vineyard (5:1-7)
>> Woes upon the oppressors (5:8-24)
>> The earthquake. (5:25)
>> The summoning of the Assyrian army (5:26-30)
>> The throne room vision. (6:1-13)
> Prophecy to Ahaz (7:1-8:18)

The section as a whole, concentrating on the failings of Judah and
Jerusalem, intertwines cause and effect; indictment, judgement, and punishment. Introduced by the vineyard parable, it reaches its climax with the
prophecy to Ahaz. The list of "woes" records the sins of the ruling class
in Jerusalem. They buy up houses and land so that there is nowhere for
the poor to live and farm; they drink and feast; they confuse right and
wrong; they are clever in their own eyes, but not in reality. (One can find
similar gripes against "the establishment" in our own day.) The earthquake is an ominous foretaste of the disaster to come. The throne room
vision reveals the meaning of the earthquake by showing us the events in
heaven that take place as Uzziah usurps the function of high priest in the
temple. Between the earthquake and the throne room vision, the Assyrian
army prepares to set out to destroy Israel. The throne room vision looks
forward and reveals that the Judeans have been made blind and deaf to
their doom; they will not listen to the warnings of Isaiah. This explains
what comes next. Ahaz ignores Isaiah's prophecy and (expurgated from
our text) betrays Israel to the Assyrians.

The vineyard parable gives the meaning of "Gethsemane". There is
an obvious parallelism between Gethsemane, an enclosed space of olive
trees, and the vineyard fenced and planted with vines. The vineyard contains a tower (the temple) and a cistern or winepress (the altar in front of
the temple). Grapes would be pressed in a large hollowed-out stone vessel
which was also the cistern to store the juice. The grapes represent the
sacrifices to Yahweh which symbolise the loving obedience of his people.

The sacrifices would be offered on the altar in front of the temple, just as the grapes are pressed before the tower.

Jesus is the perfect sacrifice offered up to atone for the sin of his chosen people, the Jews, and beyond them, for all humanity. The sacrifice is represented by the pressing of the grapes on the winepress. This idea that the blood of Jesus is the wine is quite explicit in the last supper:

> *And he took a cup, and when he had given thanks he gave it to them, and they all drank of it. And he said to them, "This is my blood of the covenant, which is poured out for many. Truly, I say to you, I will not drink again of the fruit of the vine until that day when I drink it new in the kingdom of God." (Mark 14:23-5)*

Jesus is offered up at the altar, the winepress of the vineyard parable.

➢ **Gethsemane on the Mount of Olives represents the winepress in the vineyard and so stands for the temple altar.**

Both the name "Gethsemane" and its location on the Mount of Olives are parallel to the winepress in the vineyard parable. The word "Gethsemane" means "oil press". It is made from two Hebrew words: "gath" meaning "winepress", and "shamen" meaning "oil".[5] So the name Gethsemane actually includes the word for winepress.

The idea that an olive press should represent the altar is probably older than the winepress imagery. A winepress and an olive press are close parallels. The climate of Israel is perfect for both wine and olive oil production, and they were the two major agricultural exports. Both grapes and olives are pressed to yield their juice.

There is an excellent reason why the olive press should be used as a metaphor for the altar. The evidence comes from a surprising discovery made in the excavation of the high place at Dan, in the far north of Israel. A complete stone olive press was found within the sanctuary, close to the main altar. It would have been used to produce ritually pure olive oil for offerings or anointing.[6] The presence of the olive press in sanctuaries would explain why it came to represent the altar. The use of the winepress as an equivalent metaphor would have emerged by extension.

The location of Gethsemane on the Mount of Olives comes from the vineyard parable. The location of the winepress is normally translated as a "fertile hill":

> *"My beloved had a vineyard on a very fertile hill." (Isaiah 5:1)*

In the context of the parable, the hill represents the hills of Jerusalem and in particular Mount Moriah. However, the expression for "fertile hill" literally means "a horn, a son of oil". The first element "horn" is a poetic term for a hill, and the second, "son of oil", is imagery meaning "fruitful" or "fertile". So a literal interpretation is that the vineyard is on a "horn" (hill) that is the "son of oil"—a place given over to olive oil production, an excellent description of the Mount of Olives, famous for its many olive groves.

So Gethsemane on the Mount of Olives is derived from; (i) the parable of the vineyard and; (ii) an early tradition that represented the altar by an olive press, a parallel to the winepress. Jesus is offered as sacrifice at Gethsemane. His blood is the juice of the grapes from the winepress altar.

> Jesus sweats blood at Gethsemane in Luke, an episode which comes from the grapes being pressed on the winepress/altar.

There is an odd episode in the Gospel of Luke in which Jesus sweats blood:

> *"Father, if you be willing, take this cup from me. Yet not my will, but yours be done." […] And being in agony, he prayed more earnestly; and his sweat became like great drops of blood falling down upon the ground. (Luke 22:42,44)*

Luke never mentions the name of the place, but we know from Mark and Matthew that it is Gethsemane. This strange idea of Jesus sweating blood has caused the biblical literalists to resort to various rare medical conditions in explanation. But we should recall what Jesus has said a few lines earlier, that the cup of wine is his blood. The blood that Jesus sweats at Gethsemane is wine; the juice of the sacrificial grapes which are pressed on the winepress.

The sleeping disciples and the Assyrian army

> The crowd who come to arrest Jesus represents the Assyrian army. This army does not sleep, which has given the idea that the disciples did sleep.

While Jesus is praying, his three disciples, ordered to keep watch, fall asleep three times. The theme of three betrayals runs through the passion account, but why is it represented here by the disciples falling asleep? In reality, three grown men are not all going to fall asleep three times before midnight.

The disciples' slumber permits the crowd who have come to arrest Jesus to approach unseen. Again this is not very realistic. Jesus is still awake and would hear or see the crowd long before it reached him. And why would anyone send a crowd to arrest a single man at night?

If the period of Gethsemane is the Almanac day of Ahaz, then the crowd represent the Assyrian army. The betrayal of Ahaz summoned the Assyrians who took the Israelites away into exile. Jesus words that *"the Son of Man is delivered into the hand of sinners"* (Mark 14:41) indicates that he is being handed over to gentiles. In First Isaiah, the approach of the Assyrian army is described between the vineyard parable and the throne room vision:

> He will lift up an ensign for nations far away, and whistle for those at
> the ends of the earth; and behold they come, quickly, with speed! [...]
> Their arrows are sharp, their bows all bent, their horses' hoofs seem like
> flint, and their wheels like a whirlwind. (Isaiah 5:26,28)

Judas is accompanied by *"a crowd armed with swords and clubs, sent from the chief priests, scribes, and elders"* (Mark 14:43). So both groups are armed. The Assyrian armaments are undoubtedly more impressive, but then the author of Mark has to try to keep his account realistic, and the priests did not control soldiers in Roman-occupied Judea. If the crowd represent the Assyrian army, then we can trace the origins of the sleeping disciples to something else from Isaiah:

> Not one of them grows tired or stumbles, not one slumbers or sleeps
> ... (Isaiah 5:27)

The Assyrian army marching to Israel will neither slumber nor sleep. From this came the idea that the disciples keeping watch for the crowd (the Assyrian army) did fall sleep. By sleeping they betray Jesus three times, allowing the crowd to approach and take him, just as the Assyrians took Israel.

25

Two Sisters

The Ezekiel allegories

In this chapter, we will look at two allegories in Ezekiel, both of which involve two sisters. In the next chapter, we will see that these allegories are the source for three elements of the Gethsemane episode; the severed ear, the naked man and the cup.

Although Ezekiel supposedly lived during the Babylonian exile, the Book of Ezekiel was written in the post-exilic period. The apocalyptic visions in Ezekiel had tremendous influence, not least on the author of Revelation. Ezekiel follows the allegorical fashion established by Isaiah and other early prophetic writings but frequently crosses over into the absurd. In one episode, God commands Ezekiel to tie himself down on his side with meagre rations for 390 days to predict the coming siege of Jerusalem under Zedekiah.[1] The two relevant allegories are:

Ezekiel 16: a complex allegory involving:

  i.   Jerusalem as an abandoned baby brought up by Yahweh and made his wife, but becoming a harlot. (Ezekiel 16:1-43)
  ii. an embedded second allegory with two other sisters called Sodom and Samaria. (Ezekiel 16:44-58)

Ezekiel 23: an allegory of two sisters representing Israel and Judah. They play the whore with Egyptians, Assyrians and Babylonians and are severely punished.

➢ **The imagery in the allegories relates to the era of the Judas War. The source behind the allegories was an Israelite criticism of Judah and Jerusalem under Ahaz.**

Both allegories use strong sexual imagery in which the worship of other gods is represented as acts of prostitution. We have already come across such imagery in two contexts; the allegory of Immanuel and

Maher-shalal-hash-baz in Isaiah, and Hosea's unfaithful wife, Gomer. Both belong to the era of the Judas War reflecting the political situation at the time of Ahaz.

Behind the passages in Ezekiel lie three Israelite sources, all involving strong satirical criticism of Ahaz's Judah and Jerusalem. The allegories have received the usual pro-Judean makeover to deflect blame onto Israel. However, the revision was clumsy, and we can trace the originals behind the edited versions. In one case, the final author of Ezekiel did not even realise that the allegory was about Judah, and has passed it on unscathed.

Oholah and Oholibah

We will start with the allegory in Ezekiel 23, involving two sisters, representing Israel and Judah. The two are prostitutes from the beginning:

> *Son of man, there were two women, the daughters of one mother. They played the whore in Egypt, they played the whore in their youth; their breasts were pressed there and their virgin bosoms handled. (Ezekiel 23:2-3)*

The elder sister is called Oholah ("she who has a tent") and is Samaria (Israel). The younger is Oholibah ("tent in her") representing Jerusalem (Judah). The tent is the tabernacle. The names relate to the Moses myth and so must come from a later Judean revision rather than the original source. The extension of the allegory back to Egypt must be part of this later revision; both sisters are lewd in their youth in Egypt, even though the two nations had not even come into existence at this time.

The parable really starts with Oholah (Israel) taking the Assyrians as her lovers:

> *Oholah played the whore while she was mine. She lusted after her lovers, the Assyrians, warriors clothed in purple, governors and rulers, all of them desirable young men, horsemen riding on horses. (Ezekiel 23:5-6)*

The Assyrians are finely dressed soldiers whom Oholah desires. They come, and she gives herself to them:

> *She committed her whoring upon them, the choice men of Assyria; with all she lusted, and defiled herself with their idols. (Ezekiel 23:8)*

Because Oholah has been unfaithful, Yahweh punishes her with exile and destruction:

> *Therefore I delivered her into the hands of her lovers, into the hands of the Assyrians, upon whom she lusted. They uncovered her nakedness. They took away her sons and her daughters and killed her with the sword. (Ezekiel 23:9-10)*

The treatment of Oholah is brutal, and her ironic fate is to be given to those who she lusted after, the Assyrians, while her sons and daughters are taken into exile. She herself is killed by the Assyrian sword, meaning that the kingdom of Israel is destroyed. There is nothing about Judean guilt, and the whole blame is laid on the Israelites themselves. The allegory moves on to Oholibah (Judah):

> *Her sister Oholibah saw this, yet she was more corrupt in her lust than her sister, and her whoring was worse than her sister's. She lusted after the Assyrians, governors and rulers, warriors dressed magnificently, horsemen riding on horses, all of them desirable young men. And I saw that she was defiled, that they both took the same way. (Ezekiel 23:11-2)*

Note the significant repetition here. Oholibah's lust after the Assyrians, the "desirable young men", is described in identical terms to the lust of Oholah. However, Oholibah's Assyrian passion has no consequences. Instead, she sees pictures of the Babylonians (Chaldeans):

> *But she increased her whoring. She saw men portrayed upon the wall, images of the Chaldeans portrayed in vermilion, with belts on their waists, and flowing turbans on their heads, all of them having the appearance of officers, like Babylonians of Chaldea, the land of their nativity. (Ezekiel 23:14-15)*

Oholibah is so entranced she sends messengers to summon her new lovers. They come and abuse her, and she falls out of her infatuation:

> *As soon as her eyes saw them, she lusted after them and sent messengers to them in Chaldea. And the Babylonians came to her into the bed of love, and they defiled her with their fornication. And when she was defiled by them, she turned away from them in disgust. (Ezekiel 23:16-17)*

Oholibah now returns to her first lovers, the Egyptians:

Yet she multiplied her whoring, remembering the days of her youth, when she was a whore in the land of Egypt and lusted after her lovers there, whose genitals were like those of donkeys, and whose emissions were like those of horses. (Ezekiel 23:19-20)

The oversized male genitals of Oholibah's Egyptian lovers are reminiscent of the fallen angels in the Animal Apocalypse who also have sexual organs like horses.[2] Behind this imagery, there may be a reference to the descent of the angels to take human wives. The passage in Ezekiel continues with the coming punishment of Oholibah:

Behold, I will raise up your lovers against you, from whom you turned in disgust, and I will bring them against you from every side: the Babylonians and all the Chaldeans, Pekod, Shoa, Koa, and all the Assyrians with them, desirable young men, governors and rulers all of them, officers and men of renown, all of them riding on horses. (Ezekiel 23:22-3)

In this passage, the Babylonians and Assyrians are conflated using the same language as was previously applied to the Assyrians alone; they are "desirable young men". The inclusion of the Assyrians is odd, as the Assyrian Empire was brought to an end by Babylon.

➤ **Multiple difficulties with the allegory show where it has been revised and extended.**

There are several things wrong with the allegory as we find it in Ezekiel:

- The chief blame of lusting after the Assyrians is assigned to the sister representing Israel. Although Israel undoubtedly had good relations with Assyria at times, by far the most notorious Assyrian client and vassal state was Judah. Apart from a brief apostasy in the later reign of Hezekiah, Judah was an enthusiastic Assyrian vassal for over a century, from the Judas War right up until the eventual fall of Assyria. There is a hint of this when Oholibah is described as being even worse than her sister with the Assyrians.
- The destruction of Israel came about because the northern kingdom rejected Assyria. So it does not make sense to say that it was caused by Israel "lusting" after the Assyrians.
- The same language is used for the lusting after the Assyrians by both sisters. It is repeated again in the description of the coming of the Babylonians. They are shown accompanied by the Assyrians,

"the desirable young men". All of this suggests that an original allegory about the Assyrians has been expanded and the language
copied from place to place.

- Oholibah (Judah) sends messengers to summon the Babylonians.
  Although Judah was forced briefly into the position of a Babylonian
  client state, she never sent to Babylon or welcomed Babylonian
  involvement. This episode does not match Babylon but agrees very
  well with Ahaz sending messengers to summon the Assyrians.
- The Babylonians come into Oholibah's bed and defile her by their
  lust, until, disgusted, she turns from them in favour of the Egyptians.
  This does not correspond with what we know of Babylonian influence on Judah in the years before the exile. But it again matches
  Ahaz's Judah perfectly. The Jerusalem elite became obsessed with
  Assyrian culture. Under both Ahaz and Hezekiah, Judah was a willing Assyrian client, importing Assyrian dress, manners, architec-
  ture and, most significantly, the cults of her gods. This ended when
  Hezekiah, late in his reign, turned away from Assyria to make an
  alliance with Egypt.

The original allegory must have started with a condemnation of the
Judah of Ahaz and Hezekiah:

1. Judah sent messengers to Assyria, which resulted in the destruction
   of Israel.
2. Judah was then defiled by Assyrian religion and culture until she
   turned away from them and to the Egyptians.
3. Judah was punished by God sending the Assyrians under
   Sennacherib to invade Judah.

After the Judean exile, the Assyrians of Sennacherib were replaced in
the allegory by the Babylonians. The allegory was likely revised again
when incorporated into Ezekiel. This gives a three-stage process:

1. The starting point is an allegory condemning Judah for the Judas
   War.
2. After the Babylonian exile, much of the blame was shifted onto
   Israel. Elements relating to Ahaz and the Assyrians were recast to
   apply to the Babylonian exile with additional material relevant to
   the Babylonians added.
3. The allegory was extended back to include the period in Egypt
   before the Exodus. The names Oholah and Oholibah were added.

> ➤ The final judgement in the two sisters allegory shows editorial fatigue. The accusations point to Judah and the betrayals of Uzziah and Ahaz.

With the final judgement, the author of the allegory shows a familiar phenomenon that often occurs when an author is reworking his source; he becomes fatigued and reverts to the original. So the two sisters become one woman who is both "Oholah and Oholibah", Israel and Judah. There are two accusations made against this woman, and they both actually relate to Judah. The first is that the temple has been defiled and the sabbath profaned:

> *Moreover, they have done this to me: they have defiled my sanctuary*
> *on that day and profaned my sabbaths. (Ezekiel 23:38)*

Both sanctuary and sabbath are defiled on the same day. The author of Ezekiel does not understand the meaning of this accusation, so he falls back on that familiar trope of post-exilic condemnation, child sacrifice. Whether the alleged sacrifice of Ahaz's and Manasseh's sons took place is doubtful, but even if these sacrifices happened, they would not have been carried out at the temple. Ezekiel explains that on the same day that the kings sacrificed their children, the sabbath, they came to the temple. This is weak and contrived.

The original accusation must have been that the temple was defiled on the sabbath day of Almanac time. It is the betrayal by Uzziah, the desecration of the temple on the seventh day of the sixth Almanac week. The second betrayal in Ezekiel follows on. The woman sends messengers for men coming from afar. She then baths and adorns herself, and waits for those she has sent for:

> *You sat on a stately couch, with a table spread before it on which you*
> *had placed my incense and my oil. (Ezekiel 23:41)*

A crowd of drunken men come to her from the wilderness. They place bracelets on her wrists and beautiful crowns (plural) on her head. What does this all stand for?

- The sending of messengers is Ahaz's appeal to the Assyrians.
- The table in front of the woman is Ahaz's new Assyrian style altar. This new altar stood before the temple building (the stately couch). On it is offered the things that belonged to Yahweh (the oil and incense).

- The crowd represents the Assyrian (and later the Babylonian) army. They did not literally come from the wilderness but crossed over it to get to Israel and Judah.

The invading army is represented as a crowd of drunks like the rough, wild men who live in the desert. There is a deliberate ironic contrast here between the delicate refinement of the woman making herself beautiful for her lovers and the brutish nature of those lovers when they come.

So what do the bracelets and crowns represent? The placing of the crowns on the woman indicates the status of Judah and Israel as client kingdoms: it is their "lovers" who now have the power to appoint their kings. This fits the situation after the Judas War when Judah became a client state of Assyria. It does not fit Israel so well. The rump of the conquered kingdom of Israel was only briefly a client state before it was incorporated into the Assyrian Empire; this is another indication that the woman initially represented Judah alone. The bracelets are gifts made by the Assyrian king to the lessor subject kings, such as the sundial of Ahaz. The gifts were intended to be a visible demonstration of the superiority of Assyrian civilisation. It is known that Ahaz's court in particular was besotted with everything Assyrian. Of course, the client kingdoms would pay vastly more in tribute than the value of any gifts they received.

In summary, Ezekiel is using a source that condemned the first two betrayals, those of Uzziah and Ahaz. The author of this source was familiar with the Almanac, another indication that the Almanac long predated Christianity.

Jerusalem

The closely related allegory in Ezekiel 16 is an amalgam of at least two separate parts. The first part is about a baby abandoned at birth who is adopted by Yahweh; she grows into a beautiful woman and is married to Yahweh, but then falls into prostitution. The second part brings in the woman's two sisters.

➢ **The first part is addressed to Jerusalem but alludes to the scriptural history of the greater Israel.**

A strange aspect of the first part is that although addressed to Jerusalem, it actually relates to the biblical history of the greater Israel of the twelve tribes. In the allegory, Jerusalem is like a baby abandoned at birth to die, the usual custom in the ancient world with unwanted children:

And as for your nativity, your cord was not cut on the day you were born, nor were you washed with water to cleanse you, nor rubbed with salt, nor wrapped in swaddling clothes. (Ezekiel 16:4)

The baby was abhorred, but redeemed by Yahweh:

And when I passed by you and saw you struggling in your own blood, I said to you in your blood, "Live!" (Ezekiel 16:6)

The child grows into a fine woman and is ready to marry:

Your breasts were formed, and your hair had grown, but you were naked and bare. When I passed by and looked upon you, behold, you were at the age for love; and I spread my garment over you and covered your nakedness. I swore to you and entered into a covenant with you, and you became mine, declares the Lord, Yahweh. (Ezekiel 16:7-8)

For a man to place his garment over a woman was a symbol of marriage. This union between God and his chosen people is consecrated by the covenants of Abraham and Moses. None of this fits an allegory addressed to Jerusalem. The covenant was made to the twelve tribes, not only Judah. And Jerusalem was not a Jewish city until very much later.

The woman is dressed for marriage; given fine clothes and linen and silk. She is adorned with jewels and given a crown. She is washed and anointed. All of this represents the peak of the united monarchy under David and Solomon.

➤ **The beloved bride of Yahweh falls into religious and political prostitution. There are allusions to the events of the reigns of Ahaz and Hezekiah.**

The woman representing Jerusalem is renowned among the nations due to the gifts bestowed upon her by God. In Almanac terms, it is the central point of human history, the building of the temple under Solomon. But after this, it is all downhill. The woman betrays her husband, Yahweh, and offers her love to anyone. She uses her clothes to make shrines and high places, and her jewels to make idols. She offers these other gods the sacrifices that belong to Yahweh. She even sacrifices Yahweh's children by making them pass through fire. This is the familiar catalogue of sins that supposedly led to the exile. The high places come in for particular criticism:

You built yourself a mound and made yourself a high place in every
public square. At the head of every street you built your high places
and degraded your beauty. You spread your legs to all who passed by
and increased your harlotry. (Ezekiel 16:24-5)

She cavorts with the Egyptians and her behaviour is met by punishment:

You prostituted yourself with Egypt, your neighbours with great
flesh, and increased your promiscuity to provoke me to anger. Behold,
I stretched out my hand against you and reduced your allotment. I
gave you over to the will of those who hate you, the daughters of the
Philistines, who were ashamed of your lewd ways. You prostituted
yourself also with the Assyrians, because you were insatiable. (Ezekiel
16:26-8)

Here is something that can be dated. The "daughters of the Philistines"
are the small Philistine city-states lying to the south-west of Judah. The
"allotment" of Judah and Jerusalem, meaning its territory, has been
reduced and given to these cities. Precisely this happened in the aftermath of the Sennacherib invasion, which was caused by Hezekiah entering into an alliance with the Egyptians. The Assyrians took much of the
Shephelah away from Judah and gave it to the cities of Philistia. This was
a complete disaster: the Shephelah had the best agricultural land and
was home to a significant proportion of the Judean population before the
Sennacherib invasion.[3]

This allusion to Hezekiah's revolt against Sennacherib supports our
reading of the Oholah and Oholibah allegory. Oholibah also prostitutes
herself with the Egyptians who are described as having horse-sized
genitals—compare to the Egyptians "great flesh" above. Following her
promiscuity with the Egyptians, Oholibah suffers the Babylonian invasion. We have seen that in the original this was actually the Assyrian
Sennacherib invasion.

There is an allusion to Ahaz in what comes next. Jerusalem is unlike
other prostitutes because she pays the money:

Men give gifts to whores: but you gave your gifts to all your lovers,
bribing them to come to you from every side for your whoring. (Ezekiel
16:33)

The "gifts" made by Jerusalem are the payment of tribute. Regular tribute was involuntary, the result of losing a war or of trying to prevent one.

There is only one instance where a gift was made to "bribe" a foreign king to come, and that is Ahaz's payment to Tiglath-pileser. Moreover, he financed this payment with the temple treasures which are the "gifts" of the woman in the allegory. Once again, we come back to the Judas War.

> **The Jerusalem allegory originally related to the time of Ahaz and Hezekiah, but has been extended back in time.**

The allegory of Jerusalem, like that of Oholah and Oholibah, has been extended backwards. The only events that can be definitely dated relate to Hezekiah and Ahaz. The original allegory must have been a criticism of the Jerusalem of these two kings. The author of Ezekiel has taken it back to the covenant, with the unpleasant image of the baby abandoned at birth. But Jerusalem was not even a Jewish city at this time. What comes next is even more bizarre.

Samaria—and Sodom?

> **The second part of the allegory brings in two sisters of "Jerusalem". This results in the absurdity of three sisters to represent two kingdoms.**

The second half of the Ezekiel 16 allegory introduces a whole family for Jerusalem:

> *Behold, everyone who uses proverbs will use this proverb against you: "Like mother, like daughter." You are your mother's daughter, who loathed her husband and her children, and you are the sister of your sisters, who loathed their husbands and their children. Your mother was a Hittite and your father an Amorite. (Ezekiel 16:44-5)*

Things here get very confused as the author ties himself in increasingly painful knots. Jerusalem is now the daughter of a mother who despised her husband and her children. The "mother" of Jerusalem can only be Judah although this is inconsistent with the earlier part of the allegory, in which Jerusalem represents all twelve tribes. Judah has loathed her husband, Yahweh, and her "children", the ordinary people who have been betrayed by their leaders. But then two other sisters are brought in who have also have loathed their husbands and children. So, absurdly, we have three sisters to represent two kingdoms.

> ➤ The accusation that the mother of Jerusalem was a Hittite and her
> father an Amorite is an Israelite insult aimed at the Judean kings.

Jerusalem is insulted by calling her mother a Hittite and her father an
Amorite. These are two Israelite accusations that could be made against
the house of David. They reflect two notorious episodes from the history
of David. These episodes relate to Bathsheba and David, the mother and
father of King Solomon:

- Bathsheba was married to Uriah, a Hittite, before his murder at the
  orders of David.
- David surrendered several members of the house of Saul to the
  Gibeonites who were Amorites as supposed compensation for a
  victory that Israel, under Saul, had won over them. The Amorites
  crucified these men as human sacrifices.[4]

Bathsheba was "a Hittite" because she was married to a Hittite. This
insult also carries an allusion to the adulterous and murderous nature
of the union between David and Bathsheba. David could be called an
Amorite because of his betrayal of the brave Israelite warriors of Saul to
the Amorites. (The story of David, Bathsheba and Solomon and its origins
in the Judas War are explored in the Afterword.)

The person who has a Hittite mother and an Amorite father is Solomon,
the builder of the temple in Jerusalem. This shows that behind the
allegory lies an Israelite source aimed against the house of David. The
extreme anti-Jerusalem stance of this source is confirmed by what follows.

> ➤ The two sisters of Jerusalem are called Samaria and Sodom.
> However, "Sodom" cannot represent the ancient city of that name.

We are then told the names of the two sisters:

> *And your elder sister is Samaria, who lived with her daughters to your
> north; and your younger sister, who lived to your south, is Sodom with
> her daughters. (Ezekiel 16:46)*

We had wondered how Jerusalem could have two sisters. As expected,
the sister to the north is Samaria (Israel). But the sister to the south is called
Sodom. According to Genesis, the city of Sodom was utterly destroyed
in the time of Abraham by brimstone and fire. So how is it possible for
Sodom to be the younger sister of Jerusalem, and also younger than
Samaria? The twelve tribes of Israel supposedly came from the twelve

sons of Jacob (Israel), who was the grandson of Abraham. So neither Samaria nor Jerusalem can be older than Sodom which was eradicated before Israel and the twelve tribes had come into existence.

The description of the sins of the sisters is also odd. The first surprise is the favourable treatment of Samaria. She is less guilty than Jerusalem: *"Samaria has not committed half your sins" (Ezekiel 16:51)*. Indeed, she is not accused of anything. As Israel habitually gets the lion's share of the blame from the Judean scribes, this is a clear sign that the allegory did not originate with Judah. The sins of Sodom are particularly strange. Among the Jews, Sodom was a byword for sexual depravity. When two angels in the form of two men visited Abraham's nephew Lot, the Sodomites attempted to gang rape them. But the accusation in the allegory does not even mention sexual crimes:

> Behold, this was the iniquity of your sister Sodom: she and her daughters had pride, excess of food, and abundance of idleness, but did not aid the poor and needy. They were haughty and committed an abomination before me. (Ezekiel 16:49-50)

The main accusation is simply that they are well-fed, idle and did not help the poor. There is mention of an "abomination", but this is vague. None of this fits the Sodom that was consumed by fire from heaven, whose sins were so severe that God was determined to destroy it even before the attempted homosexual rape. Strangest of all is the promise that both Sodom and Samaria will be redeemed:

> I will restore Sodom and her daughters from captivity, and Samaria and her daughters from captivity, and I will restore you from captivity in their midst. [...] And your sisters, Sodom and her daughters shall return to their former state, and Samaria and her daughters shall return to their former state. You and your daughters shall return to your former state. (Ezekiel 16:53;55)

It was the apocalyptic hope that the people of Israel (Samaria) would be restored along with Judah. But the redemption of Sodom is inexplicable. Every man, woman and child in Sodom was supposedly destroyed with the city, except for Lot and his two daughters. And Lot was not a man of Sodom but the nephew of Abraham. The three escapees found a cave where they dwelt alone, separated from all humanity. The two daughters, lacking husbands, decided to get their father drunk at night and then slip into his bed. They both became pregnant and had two sons who gave rise to two peoples the Israelites despised; the Moabites and the Ammonites. With this history, there is nothing left of Sodom to be redeemed.[5]

Clearly, Sodom does not mean the ancient city in the time of Abraham. In the original source, it stood for some other place. The author of Ezekiel has clumsily combined this source with the allegory about Jerusalem. In the above passage, the pair Sodom and Samaria are promised redemption first, followed by an identical statement about "you" meaning Jerusalem. The same clumsy phrasing, with the two sisters and "you" (Jerusalem), is evident in the introduction. So what place is Sodom?

> **Sodom stands for Jerusalem. The original source was extremely negative about Judah and the Davidic kings.**

Let us look at the clues:

> Sodom is south of Samaria and Israel.
> Sodom is younger than the sister called Samaria.
> Sodom will be restored from exile along with Samaria and Israel.

There is only one possibility—Sodom is Jerusalem. The city of Jerusalem was not actually younger than the city of Samaria. But in the allegory of the two sisters, Oholah (Samaria) is said to be younger than Oholibah (Jerusalem).[6] This represents a genuine historical memory that the kingdom of Israel developed earlier than the kingdom of Judah.

The crimes attributed to Sodom make much more sense if they are the crimes of Jerusalem. The ruling class are proud, rich and idle; they ignore the fate of the poor. We find these accusations made against the elite of Jerusalem in Isaiah. As for committing "an abomination before me" this matches the desecration of the temple by Uzziah.

The two sisters "loath their husband and their children" because they are seen as rejecting Yahweh and betraying their people. The ruling class of Samaria shares the blame for this disaster, but the sins of Jerusalem are so much worse. To be compared to Sodom is a considerable insult. It shows the extent of anger directed against Jerusalem and Judah by the original authors of the allegory. The insult is so great that the later author of Ezekiel does not even realise that Sodom is supposed to be Jerusalem. So he ends up with three sisters.

> **Both Ezekiel allegories started as Israelite criticisms of Judah from the era of the Judas War.**

Both allegories (Ezekiel 16 and 23) commenced life as Israelite criticisms of Judah. They focused on the actions of three kings in particular; Uzziah, Ahaz and Hezekiah. Chief blame rested with Ahaz and the sending of messengers to the Assyrians, the action which started the Judas War. Subsequently, the allegories were modified to bring in the Babylonians and received a comparatively light pro-Judean editing to shift blame onto Israel. Where this all gets very interesting is the connection between these allegories and the Gethsemane account in the gospels.

26

The Ear, the Naked Young
Man and the Cup

The severed ear

What do the allegories in Ezekiel have to do with Mark's story of Jesus' arrest at Gethsemane? We have seen how the Gethsemane period of 9 pm to midnight corresponds to the day of Ahaz in the Almanac and the betrayal that led to the Judas War. We have also seen that the same actions of Ahaz are central to the two allegories which originated as Israelite condemnations of Judah. We will trace back three specific episodes in Gethsemane to these allegories. We start with the severed ear.

> ➤ **The story of the severed ear becomes more elaborate with each successive gospel.**

The severed ear appears in all four gospels with the story developing from gospel to gospel. In Mark, the description is brief and enigmatic:

> *And one of the bystanders drew his sword and struck the servant of the high priest and cut off his ear. (Mark 14:47)*

The swordsman is described as a "bystander"—he is not even a disciple. The victim is the "servant of the high priest". How did the assailant escape from a large contingent of armed men? We would expect the guards to focus on the sword-bearing attacker and arrest him along with Jesus. In the Matthew retelling, it is one of Jesus' companions who cut off the ear and Jesus immediately rebukes him:

> *Then Jesus said to him, "Put your sword back into its place. For all who take the sword will die by the sword. Do you think that I cannot call upon my Father, and he will send me now more than twelve legions of angels?" (Matthew 26:52-3)*

This reflects disquiet with the original story in Mark, which might suggest that Jesus was a troublemaker involved in an unsuccessful rebellion. The author of Matthew shows Jesus as having the power to call on an army of angels but refusing to use that power. There is still the problem of the disfigured man, but the next gospel, Luke, even puts the ear back on:

> But Jesus said, "No more of this!" And having touched the ear, he healed him. (Luke 22:51)

Of more interest is the version in John which, unlike the other gospels, gives us names:

> Then Simon Peter, having a sword, drew it and struck the high priest's servant and cut off his right ear. The name of the servant was Malchus. (John 18:10)

The person who draws the sword is now Simon Peter, a suspiciously obvious candidate. There are only three disciples present at Gethsemane, so the author of John did not have much choice. And if the swordsman were Simon Peter, then why does the author of Mark not tell us such an interesting fact? It would cast Peter's subsequent action in denying Jesus three times in a very different light. The author of Mark describes the man as a bystander which does not sound like Peter.

The other name, Malchus, is much more intriguing. Early Christians would have had a keen interest in the identity of the mysterious swordsman, but no interest in the victim. He is a bit-player, one of the high priest's men. There is no need for the Gospel of John to name him. So the fact that it does is significant. And, unlike Simon Peter, the name Malchus is far from obvious. Can it give us a clue to the original source?

➤ **The only occurrence of Malchus in scripture is the brother of a person named Ahaz.**

There is a surprising link between "Malchus" and "Ahaz". The Hebrew form of Malchus is Melek, meaning "king". The name only occurs once in scripture; an obscure descendant of Benjamin mentioned in a genealogy in 1 Chronicles.[1] There are two people in scripture called Ahaz; one is the king of Judah, and the other is another obscure descendant of Benjamin. The coincidence is that Melek and the other Ahaz are brothers:

> The sons of Micah: Pithon, Melek, Tarea, and Ahaz. (1 Chronicles 8:35)

According to Chronicles, the father of Melek and Ahaz is Micah, the supposed grandson of Jonathan, son of King Saul. The genealogy is surely fictional. The author of Chronicles, writing in the post-exilic period, has no accurate historical information from the remote and obscure era following the reign of David. Perhaps the genealogist had a source which linked Ahaz and Melek but did not realise that this actually related to King Ahaz. However, the link might be nothing more than coincidence. We will find a better reason why the person whose ear is cut off should be called Melek.

The sisters and Gethsemane

➤ **The stripping of the young man and the ear severing both come from the Ezekiel allegory of Oholah and Oholibah.**

After the severing of the ear, the followers of Jesus run away. The young man has his sheet grabbed and has to flee naked. The source of both episodes lies in the Ezekiel allegories. The crowd who come to arrest Jesus in Mark represent the Assyrian army. The fate of Oholah is to be given to the Assyrians:

> *Therefore I delivered her into the hands of her lovers, into the hands of the Assyrians for whom she lusted. They uncovered her nakedness ...*
> *(Ezekiel 23:9-10)*

Oholah (Israel) is delivered into the hands of the Assyrians who strip her naked. In Mark, men from the crowd (the Assyrians) grab the sheet of the young man who is left naked. There is a close parallel in the treatment of the other sister Oholibah (Judah) by the Babylonians:

> *They shall cut off your nose and ears, and your survivors shall fall by the sword. They shall seize your sons and daughters, and your survivors shall be devoured by fire. They shall also strip you of your clothes and take away your beautiful jewellery. (Ezekiel 23:25-6)*

So the two passages of Ezekiel and Mark both feature:

1. A cut-off ear or ears.
2. A person stripped naked.

A coincidence here is improbable because the episode of the ear is very unusual. In the whole of the Hebrew Bible, this is the only place in which an ear is severed. The Mark account must be linked to the allegory. But what is the meaning of the ears and nose?

> ➢ **The nose and ears represent the king and the high priests.**

The fate of Oholibah represents the destruction of the kingdom of Judah by the Babylonians. Captured soldiers were sometimes mutilated and disfigured to make them more pliable as slaves. However, the ear and nose belong to Oholibah (Judah) and are not the ears and noses of individual Judeans. They must have a symbolic meaning that relates to Judah as a nation. The best interpretation is that the nose is the king and the ears the priests.

Whether we regard the last king of Judah as being either Jeconiah or Zedekiah, he was undoubtedly cut off by the Babylonians. As for the two ears, it is significant that Kings mentions two chief priests at the time of the ultimate fall of Jerusalem. These two met their fate together; Seraiah, the head priest, and Zephaniah, the second priest, were both executed before the king of Babylon.[2] These two priests must be the severed ears. The loss of the nose and ears goes beyond the death of individuals. Both king and priests are removed, marking the end of the house of David and the temple.

> ➢ **The adornment of Jerusalem as the bride of God indicates the significance of the nose, the ears and the garments. The king, the priests, the temple and the law are all given with the covenant, and brutally taken away at the exile.**

The other allegory in Ezekiel 16 casts further light on the significance of the nose, ears, and the garment stripped away. It describes how the woman, Jerusalem, is adorned for marriage;

> *Then I bathed you with water, washed off your blood, and anointed you with oil. I clothed you also with embroidered cloth and gave you sandals of fine leather. I wrapped you in fine linen, and I covered you with silk. I adorned you with ornaments and put bracelets on your wrists and a chain on your neck. And I put a ring in your nose and earrings in your ears and a beautiful crown on your head. (Ezekiel 16:9-12)*

The embroidered cloth may allude to the tabernacle and the adornments to the treasures of the temple. All the elements in the debasement of Oholah/Oholibah are present here in reverse. Instead of the stripping and the cutting off of ears and nose, the nakedness of the bride is covered with beautiful garments, with a ring placed on her nose, and earrings on her ears. If the nose represents the king and the ears the high priesthood, then this represents the appointment of King David (the nose ring) and the temple priests (the earrings). An alternative explanation is that the crown represents the Davidic monarchy. But the crown makes the woman herself a queen, and more appropriately represents her transformation from scattered tribes into a united kingdom. The king, as an individual, would be the nose ring. Rough nose rings were used to lead animals and captives. A fine decorative nose ring would signify the gentler leadership of a legitimate king.

As for the woman's clothes, she is naked until Yahweh spreads his garment over her in the marriage of the covenant. Her clothes must signify the covering of the tabernacle and temple and perhaps also the law. This attaches a new significance to Oholah/Oholibah being stripped naked at the final destruction. The protective covering of the temple and the law is taken from Israel and Judah. In the Almanac, the age of the Jews has come to an end; the temple is destroyed, the law rendered invalid. Although mainstream Jews continued to adhere to the law with ever-increasing rigour, this was not the philosophy of the proto-Christians.

> **There are allusions to the high priest and the king in the gospel accounts of the severed ear.**

The most obvious clue in Mark that the ear represented the high priest is that the person whose ear is severed is "the servant of the high priest". There is no mention of the nose. But then, in a realistic narrative, to have both ears and nose cut off would be truly absurd. If we look beyond Mark, we can find an allusion to the king. We have seen that the name given to the priest's servant in John is Malchus, the Greek equivalent of the Hebrew Melek meaning king. So the person whose ear is struck off is:

1. Called a servant of the high priest in Mark.
2. Called by a name meaning "king" in John.

In this way the victim is linked to both the high priest and the king.

> **The ones doing the stripping in Ezekiel are the "desirable young men". The same word for young men appears in the Mark description of the stripping.**

We have seen how in Ezekiel the phrase "desirable young men" is applied to the Assyrians and Babylonians who strip the two sisters. The word for "young men" in the Greek Septuagint is *neaniskoi*, and we find this same word in Mark:

> *And a young man [neaniskos] followed him, with nothing but a linen cloth about his body. And the young men [neaniskoi] seized him, but he left the linen cloth and ran away naked. (Mark 14:51-2)*

There is a textual variation here. The majority of early manuscripts repeat the word *neaniskos* for both the young man who flees and the young men who snatch his garment. However, some copies, including the two important Alexandrian manuscripts, Sinaiticus and Vaticanus, omit the word the second time, and it is this variation that is adopted by Nestle-Aland and followed by most translations.[3] These have "they seized him" rather than "the young men seized him". Although the word could have been repeated by a scribal mistake, the repetition seems awkward and is the more difficult reading which would normally be favoured. We have seen that there is a good reason why the assailants should be described as *neaniskoi*, so the word is more likely to have been removed than added.

➢ **The priests are victims in the source but change to the aggressors in the conversion of the allegory to the Mark narrative. This creates difficulties and explains why the victim of the stripping becomes a "young man".**

There are two apparent problems with the idea that the stripping has come from the allegory. First, the victim has changed sex from female to male. Second, the victim has become a "young man" whereas in the allegory the "young men" tear off the garment. Both points can be explained by understanding the difficulties the author of Mark faced in converting the allegory to a narrative set in the first-century:

1. In the allegory, the priests are the victims, and the "desirable young men" the assailants. But in the Mark narrative, the crowd (the young men) has been sent by the priests. So in Mark, the priests are on the same side as the "young men".
2. The "young men" grab the garment in Mark as they do in the allegory.
3. But the same "young men" cannot be the assailants who cut off the ear because this represents the High Priest. The victim in Mark, the high priest's servant, belongs to the crowd. So the ear must be severed by another "young man" external to the crowd.

The author of Mark has solved these problems by creating a new character, a bystander, who is both victim of the stripping and also the assailant. This explains two otherwise puzzling points;

1. There is apparently no attempt to arrest the swordsman.
2. The young man who flees naked is the only person the armed crowd attempt to detain apart from Jesus.

Logically, then, the young man who flees naked must be the swordsman. In Mark, he becomes a man rather than a woman because the swordsman is a "young man". Besides, a Christian writer of the time could not decently depict a woman being stripped naked at Jesus' arrest. Male nudity was acceptable because, unlike female nudity, it was not regarded as sexual.

The cup

> The cup which Jesus asks might be passed from him at Gethsemane is the cup of Israel in the Ezekiel allegory.

There is one other link between the allegory and Gethsemane, the cup which features in Jesus' prayer as his followers sleep. Jesus tells his disciples:

"My soul is exceedingly sorrowful even to death." (Mark 14:34)

Then, as he prays apart:

"Abba, Father, all things are possible for you. Take this cup away from me. Yet not what I will, but what you will." (Mark 14:36)

The cup comes from the Ezekiel allegory:

You shall drink of your sister's cup
deep and large;
you shall be laughed to scorn and held in derision,
for it contains much;
you shall be filled with drunkenness and sorrow.
A cup of horror and desolation,
the cup of your sister Samaria;
you shall drink it and drain it out,

and gnaw its shards,
and tear at your own breasts; (Ezekiel 23:32-4)

The name Oholah is dropped here, and the cup is that of Samaria, Israel. It is the cup of the Judas War, the same cup which Christ asks to be averted but which he and Israel must drink. Note how Jesus' feelings are paralleled in the poem: "you shall be filled with drunkenness and sorrow" compared to "my soul is very sorrowful even to death". Perhaps more than anything else, the poem conveys the horrifying fate of the northern kingdom. Later, Judah will also drink Israel's cup.

We have seen how multiple features of the Gethsemane account relate to the exile and, specifically, to the Judas War. But so far we have not covered the most significant event at Gethsemane, the betrayal by Judas.

27

Judas Iscariot

The name

The betrayal by Judas in the gospels amounts to just a kiss. Clearly, the real betrayal was something more. From the Gospel of Mark, we learn very little about Judas; he is "one of the twelve" included in the list of the disciples, and his full name is Judas Iscariot. He does not feature in Mark before the crucifixion account when he goes to the priests asking for money to betray Jesus. At Gethsemane, he brings the armed crowd to arrest Jesus and gives him the Judas kiss. And that is it. We hear nothing more about him.

We must fill out this picture from the other gospels. In Matthew, we learn that he hangs himself and that he betrayed Jesus for thirty pieces of silver. In Acts, the author of Luke includes the story of the suicide of Judas, although the details are different. The Gospel of John gives the information that the father of Judas was called Simon Iscariot—the repetition of the second name for both father and son is unusual and suspicious.

Apart from the circumstances of his betrayal, the only thing we can analyse about Judas in Mark is his name. So what is the meaning of "Judas Iscariot".

➤ **Judas means Judah. It signifies the tribe and kingdom of Judah.**

The meaning of Judas, a common name, is not in doubt—it is the same as "Judah". The fact that Judas indicates the tribe, and hence kingdom, of Judah, is shown by the way he is described in Mark. First, he approaches the high priests:

> *And Judas Iscariot, one of the twelve, went to the chief priests in order to betray him to them. (Mark 14:10)*

Then Jesus alludes to Judas at the last supper:

"It is one of the twelve, one who is dipping bread into the bowl with me."
(Mark 14:20)

The third and final time Judas appears in Mark is when he comes with the crowd to arrest Jesus:

And immediately, while he was yet speaking, Judas, one of the twelve, approached and with him a crowd with swords and clubs, from the chief priests and the scribes and the elders. (Mark 14:43)

At every appearance of Judas, he is called "one of the twelve". Nor is this a common phrase in Mark. None of the other individual disciples is ever described as "one of the twelve". So why is Judas called this three times within twenty-four lines?

Another peculiarity is that Judas only comes into Mark in the passion account, apart from the bare mention of his name as the "betrayer" in the list of the twelve disciples.[1] The author of Mark's only source for Judas must have been the proto-crucifixion account. The twelve disciples were a real group mentioned by Paul, but Judas Iscariot was never one of them.[2] The author of Mark has confused the disciples with the twelve tribes of Israel, upon which they were modelled. The original Judas Iscariot was one of the twelve tribes, not a disciple.

It might be objected that Judas was a very common name among Jews in the first century. Could not Judas have been a real man who just happened to bear the name of Judah by coincidence? Such a coincidence is certainly possible for the name "Judas" but what about "Iscariot"?

> "Iscariot" most likely comes from "ish qiryah" meaning "man of Kerioth". This is not a place name but means "a man of the city", a man of Jerusalem.

The name "Iscariot" is as rare as "Judas" is common. In fact, apart from Judas' supposed father Simon Iscariot, we know of no other instance of the name. And Simon Iscariot is probably an invention of the author of John. Both Simon and Judas are common names which occur multiple times among the early members of the Jesus movement. The author of John could have mistakenly thought that an early figure called "Judas the son of Simon" was Judas Iscariot. As for Simon's second name, this has doubtless been copied from his son.

A great deal of effort has been expended by scholars to understand "Iscariot". Gunther Schwarz listed no less than nine interpretations of the name and added another. One popular explanation was that the name came from the Latin *sicarius* meaning dagger-man. If so then Judas would have been one of the notorious Sicarii assassins who resisted Roman occupation. What could better fit the traditional picture of Judas? He was an assassin, a man of violence, who joined Jesus as a disciple. In his heart, though, he remained a killer, rebelling against Jesus' gospel of peace. When the opportunity presented itself, he betrayed Jesus, and then, filled with remorse, killed himself. It is a tragic and romantic story, but has no basis in truth. It is no longer thought that the name came from *sicarius* and it is unlikely that the Sicarii even existed at this time. Judas was not a knife-man.

The name is now generally accepted to have come from *"ish qiryah"*. Traditionally this has been interpreted as "man of Kerioth", and there is a place called Kerioth-Hezron mentioned at Joshua 15:25. Is this the home town of Judas? If the name signified the birthplace of Judas, then this would explain why his father could also be called Iscariot. But there is a problem with this interpretation. Kerioth actually means "town" or "city" and the place mentioned in Joshua would seem to have been called Hezron, not Kerioth.

The most likely entomology is that suggested by Gunther Schwarz who advanced the idea that Iscariot meant "man of the city". He came to this conclusion from studying the Targum in which he found that a closely related term meaning "men of the city" is used frequently. He also found evidence that Kerioth, "the city", was a common expression for Jerusalem. If this interpretation is correct, then "Iscariot" indicates that Judas was a "man of Jerusalem".[3]

Those who adhere to the historical Jesus will have considerable problems with Iscariot as "man of the city (Jerusalem)". The purpose of the second name was to distinguish people at a time when they did not have surnames, and there were only a small number of first names in circulation. But how could anyone be distinguished by saying that they came from "the city", from Jerusalem?

However, combined with our conclusion that Judas meant the kingdom of Judah, everything now becomes beautifully clear:

Judas Iscariot
= Judah, "man of the city"
= Judah, man of Jerusalem

> **Judas Iscariot is an allegorical name signifying Judah and Jerusalem. It represents the elites of Ahaz's Jerusalem.**

Judas Iscariot was not a disciple. It is a made-up name representing the kingdom of Judah and the elites of Jerusalem. The "man of the city" represents those in the king's court and the priestly temple hierarchy.

The use of such a name to represent a faction was a common literary technique at the time of the Judas War. From Isaiah, we have Immanuel ("God is with us"), Maher-shalal-hash-baz ("Swift is booty, speedy is prey"), Shear-jashub ("a remnant shall return"). From Hosea, there is Gomer whose name signifies both her sexual skills and the end of Israel, and whose father's name is an allusion to the sweet cake offerings to the goddess and a woman's breasts. Her children are Jezreel (the city where an infamous massacre took place), Lo-Ruhamah ("no mercy"), and Lo-ammi ("not my people"). All these characters are presented as if they were real, and they have been believed to be real people by countless readers over the ages, right down to the present day. They all come from the same era, the time leading up to the Assyrian exile of Israel. The names in Isaiah represent factions in the Judah and Jerusalem of King Ahaz, the same Judah that is represented as Judas Iscariot.

> **In the prophetic writings, the kingdom of Judah is generally addressed as "Judah and Jerusalem" or its reverse.**

The idea that Judas Iscariot represents "Judah and Jerusalem" ties in perfectly with prophetic convention. Prophecies about the coming exile are frequently addressed to both Judah and Jerusalem. We have seen that in one version of the two sisters allegory in Ezekiel, Jerusalem, called Sodom, stands for Judah as a whole. In First Isaiah, the phrase," Judah and Jerusalem" or the reverse "Jerusalem and Judah", are used repeatedly, including in the opening line.[4] In general, these are prophecies of condemnation. As an example, take Isaiah 3, which gives a lengthy charge sheet:

> *For Jerusalem has stumbled, and Judah has fallen, For the look on their faces bears witness against them; they proclaim their sin like Sodom…*
> *(Isaiah 3:8-9)*

The target, in this case, is the failings of the ruling class and the accusations are the usual fare; there is no respect for age, the rulers are boys and infants, and even (heaven forbid!) women. The point of this example is not that Judah is accused of betrayal, but that it was the usual literary practice to combine Judah and Jerusalem together in such condemnations. Another example, which offers a close parallel to "Judas Iscariot", is found in that key text, the vineyard parable:

> *And now, dweller in Jerusalem and man of Judah, judge between me and my vineyard. (Isaiah 5:3)*

Not only is the parable addressed to those of Jerusalem and Judah, but the phrase "man of Judah" is very similar in form to "Iscariot", "man of the city". (Translations will invariably have "men of Judah", but the literal sense is singular.)

In summary, it was a standard literary technique to use a personal name to represent a particular party. If that party were the kingdom of Judah, the name should follow the convention of an allusion to both Judah and Jerusalem. "Judas Iscariot" is just what we would expect.

The fate of Judas

➢ **From Matthew, we learn that Judas was paid thirty pieces of silver. There are different versions of his suicide in Matthew and Acts.**

Discounting the idea from John that the father of Judas was Simon Iscariot leaves us with two additional sources of information about Judas. The Gospel of Matthew makes an addition to Judas' meeting with the priests in Mark:

> *Then one of the twelve, the one called Judas Iscariot, went to the chief priests and said, "What will you be willing to give me if I deliver him to you?" And they paid him thirty pieces of silver. (Matthew 26:14-15)*

We learn that the price of Jesus' betrayal is thirty pieces of silver. Later in the narrative, Matthew has a story not found in Mark about the remorse and suicide of Judas:

> *Then when Judas, who had betrayed him, saw that Jesus was condemned, he regretted it and returned the thirty pieces of silver to the chief priests and the elders, saying, "I have sinned having betrayed innocent blood." They said, "What is that to us? See to it yourself." And throwing down the pieces of silver into the temple, he left, and went and hanged himself. And the chief priests took the pieces of silver, and said, "It is not lawful to put them into the treasury since it is the price of blood." And they took counsel and bought with them the potter's field for a burial place for strangers. Therefore the field was called the Field of Blood to this day. Then was fulfilled what had been spoken by Jeremiah the prophet, saying: "And they took the thirty pieces of silver, the price of him who had been valued, whom they the children of Israel did price, and they gave them for the potter's field, as the Lord directed me." (Matthew 27:3-10)*

From this source, we get the picture of a remorseful Judas, who throws his silver back into the temple and goes off to hang himself. The priests cannot use the tainted blood money for the temple, so they buy a field in which to bury strangers. This field is called both the potter's field and the Field of Blood. The Gospel gives a quotation to show how Jeremiah prophesied all this. There is a fascinating amount of detail here, and one blatant error—the quotation is not from Jeremiah, but Zechariah. Acts also has a story about Judas' suicide:

> *Now this man bought a field with the reward of his wickedness, and falling headlong, he burst open in the middle, and all his intestines gushed out. And it became known to all the inhabitants of Jerusalem so that the field was called in their own language Akeldama, that is Field of Blood. (Acts 1:18-19)*

This passage shows the familiar "same but different" pattern in which the author of Luke and Acts is influenced by Matthew but deliberately changes the details. In Luke, the field is bought by Judas and not the priests. He intends to enjoy the fruits of his betrayal, but God punishes him by having him fall down and burst open in the field. Those who believe in the literal truth of the New Testament are obliged to reconcile these two obviously inconsistent accounts. So they have explored various unsavoury scenarios such as Judas hanging himself from a tree and his partially decayed body falling down and bursting open. Yet it is clear from similar episodes in Acts, that a miraculous splitting open is intended. A parallel case is a married couple, Ananias and Sapphira, who sell a field on joining the Jesus movement but keep the proceeds rather than giving them to the common purse. Confronted separately by Peter, they both fall down dead.[5] Such are the tall tales told by the author of Luke.

The author of Luke may have had an excessive imagination, but also had access to excellent sources, so there is probably something behind the Acts account of Judas. One significant piece of information from Acts is the Aramaic name of the field of blood, Akeldama.

There is another account of the death of Judas from the early church father Papias. This does not survive directly but in quotes from Apollinaris who was writing c. 400.[6] There are two different versions, but behind them appears to be the tradition that Judas was split open by the wheels of a passing cart, which is probably intended to be the knives on the wheels of a chariot. We can see this Papias account as an attempt to explain the splitting open of Judas in Acts rather than an independent witness. Returning to Matthew, we will follow the clue of the thirty pieces of silver to the Book of Zechariah before looking for the real source for the Judas suicide stories.

28

The Flock of Slaughter

Zechariah

The clues in Matthew take us to Zechariah. The Book of Zechariah is a composite work made up of disparate elements, and we are interested here in the Second (or Deutero) Zechariah of chapters 9-14. There are actually three different prophets called Zechariah in scripture. The earliest is the son of the high priest Jehoiada who was killed in the temple complex during the reign of King Joash.[1] Then there was a Zechariah who exercised a good influence on Uzziah during the first part of his reign.[2] Finally there is Zechariah, the son of Berechiah, who lived during the return from exile and who was the supposed author of the Book of Zechariah.[3] Confusion between these Zechariah's may explain why the Book of Zechariah contains elements that obviously come from different periods.

> ➢ **Second Zechariah combines historical allusions to the exile with apocalyptic expectations.**

There are clear links between Second Zechariah and Christianity. One of the most famous is the prediction of the return of the king:

> *Rejoice greatly, O daughter of Zion! Shout, O daughter of Jerusalem! Behold, your king is coming to you. He is righteous and having salvation, humble and mounted on a donkey, on a colt, the foal of a donkey. (Zechariah 9:9)*

This prophecy gave rise to the episode in Mark when Jesus rides a donkey into Jerusalem. The Book of Zechariah ends with a strange apocalyptic battle. It is predicted that the nations will come up against Jerusalem and will prevail with plunder and rape and that half the people will be taken away. This seems to be based on the Babylonian exile, but this time, things will end differently. Yahweh will fight on the side of the Israelites. Standing on the Mount of Olives he will split that mountain in two. The people will flee into the newly created valley as they fled from the earthquake in the time of Uzziah. There will be no day or night, but a unique type of day (the passage is confused). Living waters will flow from Jerusalem, half to the Eastern Sea and half to the Western Sea. Then Yahweh will strike those who fight Jerusalem with a plague until their flesh falls off their bones, and their eyes rot in their sockets. At the victory, the wealth of the nations will flow to Jerusalem. The people of the nations will come to keep the Jewish festivals and do homage to Yahweh. And as for any who do not come, there will be no rain for them![4]

The shepherds and the flock

➢ **There is a lengthy allegory in Second Zechariah involving shepherds and a flock. This allegory is about the Judas War and is linked to the Animal Apocalypse.**

In Zechariah 10-11 there is a complex allegory concerning shepherds and a "flock of slaughter". Zechariah 10 has a prediction of the return from exile and in Zechariah 11 comes the main allegory about the events leading to the exile. The idea of Israel being represented by a flock under evil shepherds gives an immediate link with the Animal Apocalypse. The allegory starts with a prediction of punishment for the rulers:

> *My anger is hot against the shepherds, and I will punish the male goats, for Yahweh of hosts cares for his flock, the house of Judah...*
> *(Zechariah 10:3)*

What is the meaning of this odd phrase "male goats" which occurs in parallel to the shepherds? In the Animal Apocalypse, a horned animal represents a king. The Jewish kings are rams (sheep), so a "male goat" must mean a gentile king. The male goats are the rulers of the nations, the conquers of Israel. The shepherds are also rulers, but in the system of the Animal Apocalypse they represent angels, whereas the goats are humans. Zechariah is predicting that both the angelic and human rulers of the nations will be brought to punishment.

The flock is represented as being the "house of Judah" which must be part of a pro-Judean makeover. What comes next makes it plain that the original allegory was concerned with Israel rather than Judah.

> *"I will strengthen the house of Judah and save the house of Joseph."*
> *(Zechariah 10:6)*

The "house of Judah", the southern kingdom, is still in existence and will be strengthened but the "house of Joseph", the northern kingdom, has been defeated and must be saved. It continues: *"Ephraim is as a mighty man"* *(Zechariah 10:7)* which makes it clear that the subject is Israel. Yahweh will whistle for the deported and gather them from far off places:

> *I will bring them back from Egypt, and gather them from Assyria, and I will bring them to Gilead and to Lebanon, until there is no more room for them. [...] The pride of Assyria shall be brought down, and the sceptre of Egypt shall depart. (Zechariah 10:10-11)*

The targets of condemnation are the superpowers, Assyria and Egypt; there is no mention of Babylon. The hope is for a return of Israel from Assyrian exile. This dates the allegory to the century between the destruction of Israel and the rise of Babylon, basically the reigns of Hezekiah and Manasseh.

> ➤ **The main allegory concerns the "flock of slaughter" which has been betrayed by the rulers. It is about the Judas War and the betrayal of Israel by Ahaz.**

The hope of redemption is a prelude to a prophecy of the Assyrian exile in Zechariah 11. The metaphor of the flock and the shepherds is developed further. The shepherds now represent both the human and divine rulers, and the flock is doomed for slaughter. Zechariah, representing Yahweh, is appointed shepherd over the flock. This idea of a prophet acting out Yahweh's intentions was a result of the Jewish prohibition against representations of God. Yahweh cannot be portrayed in human terms, so instead a prophet enacts his actions.

The prophecy starts with a lament for the destruction of the great trees. The doors of Lebanon are opened so that fire can destroy the cedars, the oaks of Bashan are felled, and the thicket of Jordan is ruined. All refer to places in the north. After the lament, comes the appointment of Zechariah as shepherd. The theme of buying and selling the flock is established— the buyers will slaughter the flock, the sellers will delight in their riches. Yahweh no longer has pity on the flock and will cause each *"to fall into his neighbour's hand, and each into the hand of his king" (Zechariah 11:6)*. The Israelites will be betrayed by their neighbours Judah and by the kings of both Israel and Judah.

Zechariah, the shepherd, takes up two staffs. One is called Favour, signifying the divine favour of Yahweh; the other is called Union, signifying the bonds between Judah and Israel. There is an enigmatic reference to three shepherds (kings) being cut-off in one month which we will consider later. Whatever these three kings did it has so angered Yahweh that he breaks the first staff:

> So I said, "I will no longer be your shepherd. What is to die, let it die. What is to perish, let it perish. And let those who remain devour the flesh of each other." And I took my staff Favour, and I broke it, annulling the covenant that I had made with all the peoples [ammim]. (Zechariah 11:9-10)

The word used for "peoples" here, *ammim*, indicates the twelve tribes of Israel rather than the nations. The covenant between Yahweh and the Israelites is broken and Yahweh renounces his role as shepherd of the flock. This is the critical moment, for it initiates the events which lead to exile. The sheep traders watch the annulment of the covenant, and a monetary transaction follows:

> Then I said to them, "If it seems good to you, give me my wages; and if not, keep them." And they weighed out as my wages thirty pieces of silver. And Yahweh said to me, "Throw it to the potter, the magnificent price at which I was valued by them." So I took the thirty pieces of silver and threw them to the potter in the house of Yahweh. (Zechariah 11:12-13)

The thirty pieces of silver are the wages of Zechariah/Yahweh to be thrown dismissively into the temple, "to the potter". This raises a number of questions. Why should Zechariah/Yahweh be paid wages? Who is the "potter"? And why should the money be thrown to him? Immediately after this payment, the other staff is broken:

> Then I broke my second staff Union, annulling the brotherhood between Judah and Israel. (Zechariah 11:14)

This shows that the prophecy relates to a time when Israel was still in existence. The breaking of Union between Judah and Israel can only mean the Judas War. After this break, a new, brutal, shepherd is raised:

> For behold, I am raising up in the land a shepherd who does not care for those who are cut-off, or seek the young or heal the broken, nor nourish the healthy, but devours the flesh of the plump ones, tearing off even their hoofs. (Zechariah 11:16)

The new shepherd who replaces Zechariah/Yahweh must be the king of Assyria. The new shepherd does not care for the flock, or nourish them, but regards them purely as meat to be devoured. The Assyrians treated their subject peoples as slaves or commodities. Their only interest was in generating an economic return and increasing their military strength. They thought nothing of relocating whole peoples to fulfil these ends. In many ways, they were the first modern empire. We can see what is happening;

1. The previous shepherd is Yahweh, and the flock of slaughter is Israel.
2. Yahweh breaks his covenant with Israel/Judah due to the actions of the three shepherds (kings) who were removed in one month.
3. The flock is bought and sold. The old shepherd, Yahweh, is paid his wages—thirty pieces of silver to be flung down in the temple.
4. The union between Israel and Judah is broken.
5. The flock is given to a new shepherd. In human terms, this is Tiglath-pileser, the conqueror of Israel, and his successors. In divine terms, the shepherd is the angelic king of Assyria, better known as "Lucifer", the king of Babylon.

There is an obvious link here with the Animal Apocalypse where the "Lord of the sheep", Yahweh, gives the flock over to seventy shepherds. In the Animal Apocalypse, this occurs at the time of the destruction of Judah. In the development of the allegory, Judah will share the same fate as Israel. But the Zechariah version dates from when Judah was still in existence. It must derive from an Israelite community who have survived the war and live in Judah, exactly the context we have deduced for the earliest origins of Christianity. So it is no surprise that it has given us the Judas Iscariot story. Before we look at the connections with Judas, we have two more mysteries to solve; what does Yahweh's wage represent, and who are the three kings who are extinguished in one month?

➢ **The wage of the old shepherd Yahweh, thirty pieces of silver, is an ironic allusion to the payment made by Ahaz to secure the service of the new shepherd, Tiglath-pileser.**

The wage of Yahweh is thirty pieces of silver which is called a "magnificent price". It is actually equal to the compensation to be paid for a gored slave, and so values Yahweh at the lowest possible amount.[5] The wages are to be flung into the temple "to the potter". Who is this potter? It can only be another name for Yahweh. The Hebrew word means "maker" and is used elsewhere to represent Yahweh as the creator of humans and nations, who are compared to pots and vessels. See, for example, a prophecy from Jeremiah:

> *So I went down to the potter's house, and there he was working at his wheel. And the vessel he was making of clay was marred in the potter's hand, and he reworked it into another vessel, as it seemed good to the potter to do. Then the word of Yahweh came to me: "O house of Israel, can I not do with you as this potter has done?" declares Yahweh. "Like the clay in the potter's hand, so are you in my hand, O house of Israel."*
> *(Jeremiah 18:3-6)*

The "potter" is an ironic and dismissive way of referring to the creator of humanity and the universe. We can make sense of the payment of the potter's wage using the principle of ironic inversion. Actual events are inverted in meaning, quantity and direction to make an ironic point.

What actually happened:

1. Ahaz paid Tiglath-pileser an enormous "wage" in gold and silver to become the new shepherd of Israel. Eventually, the kings of Assyria/Babylon will seize the flock of Judah as well.
2. The "wage" was taken from the temple treasures and paid to the Assyrian king who is treated with great reverence.

In the reversal:

1. The old shepherd Yahweh is paid a "wage" equal to a low slave price.
2. His "wage" is flung down in the temple for the "potter", a disparaging name for the creator of the universe.

The thirty pieces of silver are an ironic representation of the vast treasures that Ahaz paid to betray Israel. Ahaz's payment is also reflected in the prophecy through the theme of buying and selling. In one sense, Ahaz has bought the flock, to be delivered for slaughter, by paying the Assyrians. In another sense, he has sold them out in return for Assyrian favour.

Three shepherds

> The three shepherd-kings who are "cut-off" in one month bring about the exile. The "month" must mean the Almanac generation 6.7.

There is one part of the prophecy that we have not explained; the prediction that three shepherds will be cut-off or disappear in one month:

In one month I cut-off three shepherds. I became impatient with them, and they also detested me. (Zechariah 11:8)

A later Christian explanation was that these three "shepherds" represented the three classes of leaders over the Jews; the kings, prophets and priests. This is contrived and obviously not the original meaning. It is undoubtedly three specific shepherd-kings who are intended. The problem is that nothing in the historical record fits. The closest is a fight for the throne of Israel in the time of Uzziah. The king of Israel, Zechariah, ruled for only six months before being killed in a coup by Shallum who ruled for a single month before he was killed by Menahem. But this gives only two kings, Zechariah and Shallum, who can be said to have died in the same month. Besides, a squabble between pretenders for the throne of Israel would hardly justify the breaking of the covenant. Nothing fits an actual "month" so we must interpret the period non-literally.

The Almanac periods of one generation are variously called "days" or "years". In the Dead Sea scroll texts 4Q180/81 a generation is called a "week". So it is reasonable that "month" should be another expression for an Almanac period. If so, then we are looking for three kings who were killed or deposed in the same Almanac generation.

The three shepherds are vitally important in the allegory—they are the reason for Yahweh breaking the covenant. The event that breaks the covenant and brings in the exile in the Almanac is Uzziah's desecration of the temple. This is also the event which condemns the Jews in the throne room vision of Isaiah. So is one of the three kings Uzziah?

The sixth and seventh weeks of the Almanac, as recorded in the genealogy in Matthew, closely follow the kingly succession of Judah given in Kings. However, some deviation is necessary as the real king list does not fall neatly into the artificial structure of Almanac weeks. Some reigns have to be omitted in both the sixth and seventh weeks. In both weeks, the omissions occur between days six and seven. The following is a list of the kings, and one queen, who reigned towards the end of week six along with the length of their reigns:[6]

Joram/Jehoram (8 yrs.) = day 6.6
Ahaziah (1 yr.)
Athaliah (6 yrs.)
Joash (40 yrs.)
Amaziah (29 yrs.)
Uzziah (52 yrs.) = day 6.7

Only the first and last of the kings, Joram and Uzziah, are in the Almanac. The other three, Ahaziah, Joash and Amaziah, are all missing. The lone queen, Athaliah, ruled for six years after the death of her son, Ahaziah, but as a woman she would not be included in the king lists. The word translated as "cut-off" in Zechariah, *kachad*, literally means to hide or to make disappear, but also, figuratively, to annihilate or destroy.[7] It is used in this latter sense a few lines later: "What is to be destroyed, let it be destroyed." So the expression here must mean that three reigns were ended in one month.

The names in the Almanac are generation markers. The kings who are not named are still in the timeline, but their reigns have to be allocated to the generations of other, named, kings. So the reigns of the three missing kings Ahaziah, Joash and Amaziah must be allocated between Joram and Uzziah. How was this done? Not by the length of reign, but by significant events.

➤ **Day 6.7 was ended by the desecration of the temple by Uzziah. It would be symmetrical if this day started with the killing of Zechariah in the temple by Joash.**

Matthew 23 contains some very strong imprecations against the "scribes and Pharisees". The final accusation is particularly odd:

> *"And so upon you will come all the righteous bloodshed on earth, from the blood of righteous Abel to the blood of Zechariah, son of Berechiah, whom you slew between the temple and the altar." (Matthew 23:35)*

The author of Matthew is wrong about the identity of this Zachariah; he was not the much later Zachariah, son of Berechiah, who supposedly wrote the Book of Zachariah, but the son of a high priest Jehoiada who was killed at the orders of King Joash.[8] (Once again, this story is only in Chronicles and not Kings.) Why should the Pharisees of the first century be accused of this obscure killing which took place some 800 years before their time? The guilty party was not the priests but a king of Judah. It must be all part of the original accusations against the "Jews", the Judeans, which we have seen revolve around the betrayals by Uzziah, Ahaz and Hezekiah.

In reality, the killing of Zechariah and the temple desecration by Uzziah were two episodes in a protracted power struggle between the kings of Judah and the priests of the Jerusalem temple. This conflict started when the high priest Jehoiada staged a coup against Athaliah whom he killed before appointing himself as regent for Joash, her young grandson. Jehoiada became king in all but name and was even buried with the kings of Judah after his death. The killing of his son, Zechariah, can be seen as the adult Joash's counterstrike to break free of the priests and revenge his grandmother. Uzziah's attempt to become high priest as well as king would have been made with his grandfather Joash's experiences very much in mind.

Needless to say, this is not how the story is presented in Kings or Chronicles; Athaliah is an evil queen who kills her own grandchildren, and Joash lapses into wicked ways after the death of the saintly Jehoiada.[9] It was the priests who wrote the history, and by the time the Almanac was formed the rights and wrongs of the conflict had long been forgotten. To the Israelites living under the religious suppression of Hezekiah, the murder of Zechariah in the temple court made a perfect pair with the desecration of the temple by Uzziah. Both were crimes against God committed by a king of Judah.

By the principle of symmetry, we would expect one to start the seventh day of the week and the other to end that day. The martyrdom would then be the dividing line between days six and seven, and the reign of Joash would be split between two Almanac days:

Day 6.6:
Joram
Ahaziah
Joash until the killing of Zechariah

Day 6.7:
Joash after the killing of Zechariah
Amaziah
Uzziah

➢   **If the days 6.6 and 6.7 are divided this way, then the Zechariah prophecy is correct as three kings are all "cut off" in day 6.7. It is the actions of two of these kings, Joash and Uzziah, that cause the breaking of the covenant.**

If the killing of Zechariah marked the start of generation 6.7, then three kings are cut-off in one period. Joash and Amaziah both die, Uzziah is deposed and hidden away. This fits the prophecy in Zechariah of the three shepherds if we interpret a "month" as an Almanac generation.

The actions of this period result in the breaking of the covenant. The killing of Zechariah "between the temple and the altar" came to be viewed as a terrible omen. The desecration of the temple by Uzziah, regarded as simultaneous to the earthquake and the king's leprosy, is the first betrayal and brought in the week of exile. As the Book of Zechariah says of the shepherds; "I became impatient with them, and they also detested me." It is because of these two events that the first staff representing the covenant is broken. Everything fits perfectly, which cannot be said of any other explanation. All this implies that the Almanac was already in existence when Second Zechariah was written

29

Judas and Jesus

Thirty pieces of silver

➤ **The payment made to Judas Iscariot for his betrayal represents the payment made by Ahaz to Tiglath-pileser to betray Israel.**

We can now see the origins and meaning of the thirty pieces of silver in the Judas story. The thirty pieces represent the treasures that Ahaz paid to secure the intervention of the Assyrians against Israel and Syria. By the principle of ironic inversion, the large amount taken from the temple becomes a paltry amount flung down into the temple. Judas Iscariot corresponds to Ahaz's Judah and Jerusalem. The payment made to Judas corresponds to the payment made by Ahaz. Naturally, the direction of the payment has to be reversed for the sake of the story. However, in the Matthew version, the original direction is restored. The bribe is paid out of the temple to Judas who then flings it down in the temple, just as the thirty pieces are flung down into the temple in Zechariah.

➤ **Several elements of the Matthew story and quote come from Zechariah where they apply to the Judas War. But the author of Matthew must be getting them through a secondary source.**

After Judas flings down the money into the temple, there is a quote:

> *Then was fulfilled what had been spoken by Jeremiah the prophet, saying: "And they took the thirty pieces of silver, the price of the one who had been valued, who the children of Israel put a price on, and they gave them for the field of the potter, as the Lord directed me." (Matthew 27:9-10)*

There is much that is odd in this prediction:

- The prophecy is not, in fact, from Jeremiah. The closest we get is the Zechariah passage covered in the previous chapter.
- The throwing down of thirty pieces of silver in the temple by Judas

would seem to be a miraculous verification of the prophecy in Zechariah in which thirty pieces of silver are cast into the temple. But strangely this prophecy is not mentioned in Matthew.

- Instead, there is the purchase of a potter's field which does not appear anywhere in Zechariah.

This is all evidence that the quote came from a secondary source and not directly from Zechariah. This source combined the Zechariah prophecy with something else. To find out what, we should look at the features of the Judas stories in Matthew and Acts which did not come from Zechariah:

In Matthew:
A prophecy from Jeremiah.
The field of the potter.
The field is a burial place for strangers
The field is called the Field of blood.

In Acts
Judas falls and bursts open in the field.
The field is called Akeldama (Field of Blood)

We do not have to look far for a source combining most of these elements. In fact, we have already come across it by following the clue of the potter.

Bursting open

➤ **The other elements in the Matthew/Acts stories of Judas come from the passage in Jeremiah in which the prophet takes a pot representing Judah and Jerusalem into a field and breaks it. The pot symbolises the coming destruction of Judah, which will share the fate of Israel.**

After Jeremiah watches the potter making his pot, symbolising how Yahweh has made the house of Israel, he is given a further instruction. He must buy a pot and take with him the *"elders of the people and the elders of the priests"* (1 Jeremiah 19:1):

> *And go forth to the valley of the son of Hinnom, which is by the entry of the Potsherd gate, and proclaim there the words that I shall tell you. (Jeremiah 19:2)*

The prophet has come from the potter's house and is told to go out through the Potsherd/Potter's gate to the valley of the son of Hinnom. This valley is the notorious Gehenna, a name given to hell by the gospel writers. The Potsherd gate was associated with potters; the name indicates that the "potter's field" on the other side of the gate was a rubbish dump for broken pots and fragments.

After the elders follow Jeremiah to this field the prophet addresses them as *"kings of Judah, and inhabitants of Jerusalem" (Jeremiah 19:3)*. He tells the elders he has brought them to this place because it has been used for burning incense to other gods and is stained with the blood of innocents:

> They have built also the high places of Baal, to burn their sons with
> fire for burnt offerings unto Baal, which I commanded not, nor spoke
> it, neither came it into my mind. (Jeremiah 19:5)

There is an allusion here to Ahaz: *"Moreover he burnt incense in the valley of the son of Hinnom, and burnt his children in the fire..."* (2 Chronicles 28:3). The familiar trope of child sacrifice stands in place of the true crime of Ahaz, the betrayal of Israel. Jeremiah continues with the prophecy against "Judah and Jerusalem", how they will fall by the hand of their enemies and be made desolate. To illustrate their fate, God tells Jeremiah to break the pot before the men who have come with him:

> And say to them, "Thus said Yahweh of hosts; Even so will I break this
> people and this city, as one breaks a potter's vessel, that cannot be made
> whole again: and they shall bury them in Tophet, till there be no place
> to bury." (Jeremiah 19:11)

Tophet was another name for the valley of the son of Hinnom.[1] The pot represents Judah and it is shattered in the field to demonstrate the coming destruction. The people of Jerusalem will be buried in this same field.

The same image of a pot representing Judah and being burst open is found in First Isaiah. This prophecy is concerned with those who had appealed to Egypt for help:

> And he shall break it as the breaking of the potters' vessel that is broken
> in pieces; he shall not spare: so that there shall not be found in the
> bursting of it a shard to take fire from the hearth, or to take water out
> of the well. (Isaiah 30:14)

The complete destruction of the pot here suggests the total destruction of Jerusalem under Zedekiah who entered into an alliance with

Egypt against the Babylonians. This would place it long after the time of Isaiah.

> ➤ **The story of the suicide of Judas Iscariot is really about the coming destruction of Judah. Multiple elements of the story come from prophecies of the fate of "Judah and Jerusalem".**

We can see the connections between the Jeremiah passage and the Judas story:

Jeremiah: the prophet Jeremiah carries a pot through the "potsherd gate" to the place where broken pots were thrown away.
Matthew: Judas' money buys "the potter's field" (Matthew).

Jeremiah: the place has been filled "with the blood of the innocent".
Matthew: the field is called "the Field of Blood"

Jeremiah: the pot represents the "kings of Judah, and inhabitants of Jerusalem", "man of Judah and inhabitants of Jerusalem, "Judah and Jerusalem", and "this people and this city".
The gospels: the betrayer is called Judas Iscariot meaning "Judah, man of the city" / "Judah, man of Jerusalem".

Jeremiah: the pot is cast down in the field and bursts.
Acts: Judas Iscariot falls down in the potter's field and bursts open.

Jeremiah: the field will become a place of burial for the people of Jerusalem.
Matthew: the potter's field will be used as a place of burial for strangers.

The application of the Jeremiah prophecy confirms what we have already deduced from an analysis of the name—Judas Iscariot stands for Judah and Jerusalem. The story of the suicide has evolved from the idea that Judah will share the fate of Israel. The betrayal by Judah results ultimately in Judah's own destruction. Even the bursting open of Judas has not been made up—it comes from Jeremiah throwing down and bursting the pot representing the "kings of Judah and the inhabitants of Jerusalem".

The slain God

➤   **Second Zechariah continues with prophecies of a slaughtered Messiah with the guilt resting on the priests and the house of David.**

Later in Second Zechariah is a prophecy which points towards a slaughtered Messiah:

> *And I will pour upon the house of David and the inhabitants of Jerusalem the spirit of grace and supplication, and they will look upon me, on him whom they have pierced. They shall mourn for him, as one mourns for an only child, and grieve for him, as one grieves for a firstborn. On that day the mourning in Jerusalem will be as great as the mourning for Hadad-Rimmon in the plain of Megiddo. (Zechariah 12:10-11)*

Christians have long taken this as a prophecy of the crucifixion. But the passage is ambiguous and difficult. The word translated as "pierced" means to thrust through with a sword or spear rather than to be pierced by nails. And who is pierced? Is it Yahweh or someone else? Perhaps it is Israel, thrust through by the Assyrian sword, and represented here as if Yahweh himself were pierced.

The passage is clear where the guilt lies—with the Judean kings, the house of David, and the people of Jerusalem, the priests and court. We are back to Judas Iscariot. We see this also in the list of those who mourn:

> *The land shall mourn, each family apart. The family of the house of David by itself, and their wives by themselves. The family of the house of Nathan by itself, and their wives by themselves. The family of the house of Levi by itself, and their wives by themselves. The family of the Shimei by itself, and their wives by themselves; and all the remaining families and their wives by themselves. (Zechariah 12:12-14)*

Four groups are identified here; the houses of David, Nathan, and Levi, and Shimei. Nathan was a son of David and full brother of Solomon. Shimei could have been confused with Shimea, another full brother of Solomon.[2] Although Solomon is not mentioned directly, he would be the "house of David" because the royal line continued through him. The house of Levi are the temple priests. So the groups represent those descended from the sons of David and Bathsheba, along with the temple priests. They are the "sheep traders" who have sold the flock of Israel to slaughter.

> ➤ The destruction of Israel is personified as the death of a "shepherd" who is an aspect of Yahweh.

We see, in the above prophecy, the beginnings of the personification of the exile as the death of the heavenly Christ. The destruction of Israel is like a fatal thrust to Yahweh himself. This becomes more concrete in what follows:

> *Awake, O sword, against my shepherd, against the man who is my companion, declares Yahweh of hosts. Strike the shepherd, and the sheep will be scattered; I will turn my hand against the little ones. In the whole land, declares Yahweh two-thirds shall be cut off and perish, and one-third shall be left in it. (Zechariah 13:7-8)*

This prophecy is quoted by Jesus at the very beginning of the Gethsemane period: *"'I will strike the shepherd, and the sheep will be scattered'"* *(Mark 14:27)*. The shepherd in the Zechariah prophecy is closely associated with Yahweh—he is Yahweh's companion who is "next to" Yahweh. The shepherd is a king, but not a human king. He rules over the flock that will be scattered; Israel and, later, Judah. So the shepherd is the heavenly king of Israel and Judah. Originally this divine ruler was Yahweh. But the supreme God cannot die, so an aspect of Yahweh was separated, and the Christ myth was developed to personify the exile.

> ➤ The mourning for the slain figure is compared to the mourning for Baal.

The most explicit connection between the Christ myth and Baal worship occurs here in Zechariah. The mourning for the slaughtered figure is compared to the grief for Baal: *"On that day, the mourning in Jerusalem will be as great as the mourning for Hadad-Rimmon in the plain of Megiddo"* *(Zechariah 12:11)*. The plain of Megiddo is the Jezreel Valley, part of the kingdom of Israel. Israel was more ethnically diverse than Judah and included a significant Canaanite population in the fertile Jezreel valley. It is here that the final battle at the end of times will supposedly be fought—Armageddon is Am Megiddo. As for Hadad-Rimmon, he is the Canaanite Baal. The mourning of Jerusalem for the slain figure, the Christ, is compared to the mourning of the Canaanites for Baal after his descent into the underworld.

30

Two Trials

The third period

In the third period, Jesus is tried before the Sanhedrin, found guilty of blasphemy, and condemned to death. The trial account is unrealistic. The Sanhedrin never met at night and would have taken a considerable time over a capital offence. The accusations against Jesus are vague and the nature of Jesus' supposed blasphemy unclear. After the Sanhedrin trial, Jesus is handed over to Pilate, who then holds a second trial. We will take the two trials together; there was only one trial in the original myth, and it did not take place in first-century Judea but in heaven.

The third period corresponds to Hezekiah and Almanac day 7.3. Before we get to the trials, we will look at links between the third period and the events of Hezekiah's reign.

> ➤ **Hezekiah's betrayal was the blasphemy against the son. In the Sanhedrin trial, Jesus is found guilty of blasphemy for claiming to be the son.**

We have seen that the betrayal by Hezekiah was the destruction of the ancient forms and places of Israelite worship. In particular, a cultic object linked to Christ, the temple Nehushtan, was destroyed by Hezekiah. His unpopular religious reforms were the "blasphemy against the son" that formed a pair with Uzziah's blasphemy against the father.

The same theme of blasphemy against the son occurs in distorted form in the first trial. Jesus has been silent throughout as the priests hear from false witnesses. The key moment comes when the high priest asks him if he is the Son of God:

> *Again the high priest asked him, and said to him "Are you the Christ, the Son of the blessed?" And Jesus said, "I am, and you will see the Son of Man sitting at the right hand of power, and coming with the clouds of heaven." (Mark 14:61-2)*

With this admission, the high priest tears his robes and the assembly condemn Jesus for blasphemy. The historical Jesus school has problems with this condemnation because Jesus' words were not actually blasphemous. There was nothing wrong with calling yourself a son of God, and Jesus is quoting from the Book of Daniel, that the Son of Man will sit on the right hand of God and come on the clouds of heaven.

However, if the author of Mark has a source associating "blasphemy against the son" with the third period, he might think that this supposed blasphemy was Jesus claiming to be the son.

In the Mark account, Jesus is then blindfolded by the priests and struck, although such violence would not occur at a meeting of the Sanhedrin. Perhaps it reflects the breaking of the Nehushtan by Hezekiah, the true blasphemy against the son.

> **The Israelite exile was complete during Hezekiah's reign. This would correspond to the Jews handing Jesus over to the Romans.**

The exile of Israel commenced under Ahaz and was completed under Hezekiah. In the crucifixion account, the Romans correspond to the Assyrians/Babylonians. So the exile of Israel to Assyria due to the actions of the Judeans corresponds to the Judeans handing Jesus over to the Romans at the end of the third period.

> **The three denials of Peter by cock-crow are the three betrayals by the end of the third Almanac day. Peter stands for the tribe of Judah due to confusion in the meaning of "the first of the twelve".**

The most obvious correspondence between the third period of the passion day and the third period of the Almanac involves the three denials by Peter. The denials happen before cock-crow, the end of the third period, corresponding to the end of the reign of Hezekiah.

In the Mark account, Peter's denials are simply a failure to acknowledge that he is one of Jesus' followers. In truth, he seems to have done nothing wrong. Peter shows considerable courage by following Jesus into the lion's den, the court of the high priest's house. It would be absurd for him to admit to the enemy that he is one of Jesus' supporters. The denials would, however, have had a very different meaning for Christians at the time Mark was written. The church was all too familiar with persecution. Those who refused to deny Christ even under penalty of death were heroic martyrs, and those who denied Christ, pretending not to be Christians, were despised.

The author of Mark has a source which he interprets as meaning that Peter betrayed Jesus three times before cock-crow. He casts these three

betrayals in terms of the issues of his own day, when failure to acknowledge Christ when confronted by a prosecutor was seen as a betrayal of
Jesus. But why should any source accuse Peter of the three betrayals when
the guilty parties were the kings of Judah?

We can find the answer in the description of Judas in Mark; three times
he is called "one of the twelve". So the twelve tribes were confused with
the twelve disciples, and Judah was turned into a disciple. With Peter, the
same thing happened, but in a slightly different way.

The twelve were Cephas' inner group of followers. Cephas, as the
founder and leader, was not one of the twelve. However, the mysterious
Cephas was widely confused with another person, the second-generation
apostle Simon Peter who was in the list of the twelve. Both Cephas and
Peter meant "rock" which comes from the Animal Apocalypse where it
stands for Mount Sinai. The author of Mark, confusing Peter with Cephas,
promoted him to first in the list of the twelve ahead of the two real leaders, James and John. In the Gospel of Mark, Simon Peter's role as the chief
disciple is emphasised.

Now Judah was also "first of the twelve" in the sense of being the primary tribe. With the elimination of Israel, there were no competitors to
rival this supremacy of Judah. The old legends were altered to make this
new standing of Judah clear. When Jacob blesses his twelve sons, it is
Judah and not the elder Rueben who will be first among them: *"Judah,
your brothers shall praise you; [...] your father's sons shall bow down to you"*
(Genesis 49:8).

The three betrayals belonged originally to Judah, the first among the
twelve tribes. The author of Mark has misinterpreted "first among the
twelve" as meaning Peter. He then interprets Peter's supposed three betrayals in terms of the burning issue for the Christians of his day—having the
courage not to deny Jesus when accused of being a Christian. So the three
betrayals by the kings of Judah became the three denials by Peter.

The first trial

We have seen how such a nighttime trial by the Sanhedrin would have
been impossible and how the whole timeline of events has been unrealistically compressed. The description of this trial in front of the Sanhedrin
is quite brief. The priests attempt to find something on Jesus by ques-
tioning false witnesses, but these all disagree with each other and make
only one specific accusation against Jesus. Seeing that they are not getting
anywhere, the high priest asks Jesus outright if he is the son of the blessed.
Jesus admits that he is and is condemned for blasphemy.

➢ **The accusation that Jesus will destroy and then raise the temple caused acute embarrassment to the gospel writers. It is only explicable if we place the crucifixion in the context of the exile.**

The only specific accusation at the Sanhedrin trial is something that Jesus is alleged to have said:

> *"We heard him say, 'I will destroy this temple that is made with hands, and in three days I will build another, not made with hands.'"* (Mark 14:58)

The early Christians struggled with this saying, eventually settling on the interpretation that it related to the death and resurrection of Christ. But even this interpretation presents difficulties. If the temple was Jesus' body, then how can Jesus say that he would destroy it? Would this not be suicide? The author of Mark puts the saying in the mouth of false witnesses. In Matthew, it is not clear whether or not the witnesses are lying. In John, it is Jesus who makes the prediction but with one vital difference; the Jews destroy the temple, and he will raise it again in three days.

To understand this saying, we must restore it to the original context of the exile:

- The temple that is destroyed is the first temple.
- This physical first temple will not be replaced. In the Animal Apocalypse, the second temple is invalid and lacks the presence of God.
- The real second temple will not be built by human hands but will be made by Jesus. It is the "tower", the Magdalene.
- The new temple will come on the third day after the destruction of the first temple. The days are great days, so this is a prediction of Jesus' resurrection in Almanac day 10.1 when he enters into the new temple.

The gospel writers were right in thinking that the raising of the new temple is also the resurrection of Jesus. But they were wrong in identifying the temple with the body of Jesus. The three days actually covers several hundred years, and the destroyed temple is not at all the same as the replacement "not made by hands".

The second trial

The first trial before the Sanhedrin may be odd, but the second trial before Pilate is even odder. Once again Jesus is largely silent. The priests make accusations against him, but Pilate is unconvinced of his guilt and makes an attempt to free Jesus. It is the custom to release a prisoner at the Passover. Pilate offers the crowd a choice between Jesus and a murderer, Barabbas, expecting the crowd to choose Jesus. But three times the crowd reject Jesus and choose Barabbas instead. When Pilate asks what he should do with Jesus, the people demand that he should be crucified. Pilate gives in to these demands and orders Jesus to be scourged and then led to crucifixion. The crime of the accused was fixed to the top of his cross—it read "king of the Jews".

The whole account of this trial is thoroughly unrealistic. We will take it point by point.

➢ **Jesus is not accused of anything.**

In the first trial, the accusations made against Jesus are mostly unstated, and the priests only hit upon the blasphemy charge in response to Jesus quoting from Daniel. The Jews did not have the authority to execute Jesus and blasphemy against the Jewish God would not be a crime for the Romans. So what crime was Jesus accused of before Pilate? The author of Mark does not know. The gospel says the priests accused Jesus "of many things" and brought many charges against Jesus, but it is suspiciously silent about what these things actually were. At no time in the trial is there any explicit charge.

➢ **Pilate consistently calls Jesus the "king of the Jews".**

When Jesus is bound over to Pilate, he starts by asking a question:

> *And Pilate asked him, "Are you the king of the Jews?" And answering him, he says "So you have said." (Mark 15:2)*

Not only does Pilate call Jesus the king of the Jews, but he implies that he is called this by the people:

> *And Pilate answered them again, saying: What, then, shall I do with the man you call the king of the Jews?" (Mark 15:12)*

Some have seen the charge "king of the Jews" written above Jesus' cross as implying that he was convicted of revolt against Rome, but there is no evidence to indicate a rebellion. The two episodes of possible violence by Jesus or his supporters, the cleansing of the temple and the severing of the ear, were both aimed at the priests and not the Romans. And there is a more fundamental difficulty; the Romans responded to rebellions with mass crucifixions. Yet all the sources tell us that Jesus alone was crucified. Not a single one of his followers was punished. It is true that they all supposedly fled, but the Romans were used to finding people. Surely, they could have rounded up enough members of Jesus' entourage to stage a nice group crucifixion to discourage others. Yet only Jesus was crucified and you cannot have a revolt with one person.

So according to the gospels:

1. Witnesses testified many things against Jesus before the Sanhedrin, all of them inconsistent.
2. Jesus was then found guilty of blasphemy by the Sanhedrin.
3. He was passed to Pilate accused of "many things" by the Jews, all unspecified.
4. Pilate did not find him guilty of anything.
5. Pilate ordered him to be crucified with the writing "king of the Jews" over his head.

Whatever the priests' accusations against Jesus, they certainly did not claim that he was "king of the Jews". Something is seriously wrong with the gospel account of the two trials.

➤ **The story of Pilate's offer to release either Jesus or Barabbas, and the Jews preferring Barabbas, is unrealistic. In some manuscripts of Matthew, Barabbas is called "Jesus Barabbas".**

Perhaps the strangest part of the story concerns Barabbas. According to the Gospel of Mark, the Romans would release one prisoner at the Passover to please the Jews. Needless to say, there is no independent evidence for such an unlikely custom. Pilate suggests to the crowd that he should free "the king of the Jews", but they demand another prisoner instead:

> *And there was one called Barabbas, who was imprisoned among the rebels who had committed murder in the insurrection. (Mark 15:7)*

So Barabbas is a member of a group of rebels who had committed murder during a recent insurrection. We know of no such insurrection at this time. And if there were a revolt, it is simply unbelievable that a Roman governor would ever consider freeing such a rebel. Then there is the inexplicable reaction of the crowd who for some unknown reason choose Barabbas over Jesus, and demand Jesus' crucifixion. What were the origins of this strange, unrealistic story? It must have been lifted from the author of Mark's sources and misapplied to the Roman world of first-century Judea.

The name Barabbas is significant; it means "son of the father". There is a variation in the text of Matthew in which Barabbas is called "Jesus Barabbas". The name would then mean "Jesus, son of the father"! So is Barabbas another identity of Jesus? Is it possible that the Barabbas story recalls an independent and earlier version of the crucifixion trial? But this would make Jesus a rebel and perhaps even a murderer which is inconsistent with other sources. It is also historically unrealistic to suppose a crowd of Jews would demand the release of an insurrectionist from a Roman governor. People were fully aware of what the Romans did to rebels and their supporters.

The reading of "Jesus Barabbas" is very doubtful and found in only a few surviving manuscripts today. However, it is undoubtedly old because the church father Origen was aware of it as a variation.[1] It is also unique to Matthew: we do not find Barabbas called Jesus in Mark, Luke or John. However, "Jesus Barabbas" is the most difficult reading, which is why it is preferred by some textual critics. It is easier to see why "Jesus" should be omitted from the name than why it should be added. The author of Matthew is following Mark for his information on the Barabbas story but did he, or an early copyist, have another source for "Jesus Barabbas"?

The heavenly trial

➢ **The original trial of Jesus took place before the heavenly law court which developed from the Canaanite assembly of the gods. The seventy shepherd gods/angels become the Sanhedrin in Mark.**

The original source of the two trials in Mark must be a single trial in heaven. This trial takes place in the heavenly law court. We have seen how this law court features in early sources and apocalyptic literature, and how it can be traced back to the original Canaanite assembly with seventy gods under their father, El. This is the background to Psalm 82, where the members of the divine council, who are called "gods", are accused of not judging fairly. The Jewish institution of the Sanhedrin was based on this heavenly law court and mimicked the constitution of the court with seventy members under the high priest.

The seventy gods evolved over time into the seventy evil shepherd angels under El/Yahweh. We have seen that they are the tenants who kill Christ in the vineyard parable. Each of the seventy angels is the ruler of a nation, so the divine council is something like a heavenly united nations assembly. Only Israel and Judah were not ruled by one of the seventy but were the chosen people of Yahweh. Originally, they were represented by Yahweh, but this gave the difficulty that he was also the supreme judge. So the role of advocate for Israel is sometimes taken by the senior archangel Michael.

In the apocalyptic myths, the angelic rulers of the nations seek to get Israel condemned. In apocalyptic sources we find two angels pressing the prosecution of Israel. In Daniel, these angels are the princes of Persia and Greece, and in 3 Enoch, the princes of Rome and Persia.[2] Both texts are much later than the Judas War, and the original enemies of Israel were not Persia, Greece or Rome, but Assyria/Babylon and Egypt. Alongside the two special persecutors, the whole seventy are against Israel. This reflects a habitual Jewish viewpoint in which all the nations are grouped against Israel.

> **The Christ myth started as an attempt to explain the exile of Israel but only took its final form after the exile of Judah.**

The Christ myth emerged as a result of the exile of Israel and, later, Judah. The defeat of the kingdom of Israel was total. It had been destroyed at the instigation of the kings of Judah. How could the surviving Israelites living as refugees in Judah understand such a disaster in heavenly terms? It meant that the seventy rulers of the nations had conspired against Israel and put to death Israel's heavenly king. This god-king could not be Yahweh, the chief judge. Nor could it be Michael, who was an angel, having been created by Yahweh, because no mere created being could personify Israel. Instead, the myth of Israel's heavenly king drew upon the earlier myths of the dying and resurrected god-kings such as Dumuzi and, most significantly, the Canaanite Baal-Hadad. Baal was the son of the creator God El, but his brothers, the sons of Asherah, conspired against him, just as the seventy conspire against the heavenly king of Israel.

The myth began among the Israelites but only assumed its final form following the exile of Judah. The Judean exile is essential to the Almanac and the proto-crucifixion source which cannot have taken final shape until after that exile. Following the tragedy of the destruction of Jerusalem, the heavenly king came to personify Judah as well as Israel. By the time that the Christ myth reached its final form, the proto-Christians had been living in Judah for centuries. They accepted both the temple and the legitimacy of the Davidic kings as rulers over all Israel. The human line of David had been extinguished, even though God had promised that Solomon's and David's kingdom would endure forever. Yet the prophecies could not be false. So the kingdom of David must be restored in a new form. But if the kingdom were to come, then the heavenly king must also return, resurrected from the dead. This king was now called the Christ, the anointed one, and his resurrection would bring in the new kingdom, the kingdom of heaven.

> ➤ **The judge of the heavenly law court is the lower Yahweh. In the crucifixion account, he becomes Pontius Pilate.**

The Christ myth told the story of the trial in heaven. It starts with a conspiracy. The seventy archons gather together and determine to seek the execution of the king of Israel. In earthly terms, the death of Christ would mean the destruction of Israel and Judah. It would give the world into the hands of the nations and their angelic kings. The conspiracy of the seventy becomes the Sanhedrin trial in the Mark account.

There would have been two chief prosecutors among the seventy; the king of Egypt and the leader of the seventy, the king of Babylon. Having determined that the Christ should die, the seventy bring him to their father, Yahweh and demand judgement against him.

Yahweh is the supreme judge. We have seen the bifurcation of El/Yahweh that took place with the emergence of monotheism. He separated into two aspects; a remote, heavenly Yahweh who took no visible form and could not be represented as an image or idol; and the angelic manifestation of Yahweh to humans, the angel of the Name who inhabited the temple. Originally, they were two parts of the same entity, but there was an inevitable tendency to regard them as two separate beings.

The tendency to split God into two was increased among the proto-Christians by the problematic role of Yahweh. He had appointed the seventy to rule and had given a law to humanity which was impossible to keep. And it was Yahweh who was obliged to sentence Christ to death. Such deeds could not have been done by the ultimate God of pure goodness and perfect knowledge. So it was necessary to attribute these actions to the lower Yahweh. The trial took place in the heavenly throne room, which occupied a simultaneous reality to the temple on earth. So the God who administered justice in the throne room must be the same who dwelt in the temple, the angel of the Name.

In the Mark account, the angel of the Name is depicted as Pontius

Pilate. Both governed on behalf of a superior authority. The translation of Yahweh into a despised Roman governor was the result of wrongly placing the story in first-century Judea. The author of Mark, unaware of Almanac time, thinks "the third day" means the third literal day. It was known that the resurrection occurred under Pilate, probably because it was linked to the episode recounted by Josephus in which Pilate brought the legendary ensigns into Jerusalem.[3] At the time this would have been seen as starting the apocalypse—the prophecy in Mark about the *"abomination of desolation standing where it should not" (Mark 13:14)* fits this earlier episode better than the destruction of the temple by the Romans in 70 AD. Mary's first spiritual experiences of the resurrected Christ would have occurred at around the same time. In the apocalyptic imagination, the two were linked, and the resurrection was associated with the governorship of Pilate. But if the resurrection on the third day happened under Pilate, then the crucifixion must have happened under him also.

> ➢ **In the original trial story, the angel of the Name is good and wants to free Christ. This has carried over into the historically unrealistic depiction of Pilate who also wants to release Jesus.**

To the proto-Christians, the angel of the Name was good and not the evil Demiurge of gnostic imagination. This is reflected in the portrayal of Pilate, which owes nothing to the real Roman governor. He is reluctant to condemn Jesus. He goes out of his way to try and save Jesus, offering the crowd three times to release him. An apocryphal literature grew up around the figure of Pilate, and the supposed executioner of Jesus eventually became a Christian saint.

Those who attempt to recreate the historical Jesus are puzzled by the picture of Pilate at the trial; they are obliged to put it down to gentile reluctance to blame the Romans for the death of Christ. But there is evidence that early Christians were also disturbed by Mark's positive depiction of Pilate. The author of Matthew follows Mark closely but is always sensitive to problems in the earlier gospel. Significantly, he felt it necessary to add two episodes concerning Pilate. First, Pilate's wife sends him a message: *"Have nothing to do with that righteous man, for I have suffered terribly in a dream today because of him." (Matthew 27:19).* This odd addition is not found in any other gospel. We can see it as the author of Matthew's attempt to explain why Pilate should seek Jesus' release. The second, more famous, episode is Pilate washing his hands of Jesus' blood. This shows that the blood-guilt does not lie with Pilate and the Romans, but with the Jews. It also casts a less favourable light on Pilate as a moral coward.

> ➤ Jesus, the "king of the Jews", pays the sin price for his people.
> The lower Yahweh is a God of justice and is obliged to condemn
> him.

Ultimately the lower Yahweh and hence Pilate must find Christ guilty.
The crime of Jesus was written above the cross—he was "king of the Jews".
Although Christ was perfect and innocent of all sin, he must pay the pen-
alty for his people. While both Israel and Judah are guilty, the chief blame
rests with "Judas Iscariot", the ruling elite of Judah, the men of Jerusalem.
And most guilty of all are the kings of Judah

The trial of Christ is the trial of Israel and Judah. The angel of the Name
desperately wants to free Christ, and hence save his chosen people. But
the lower Yahweh is a God of justice. He is bound by the law that he has
given to the Israelites, a law which the Jews find it impossible to obey.
The people of Israel and Judah are guilty, so Christ must pay their blood
price. The seventy (the Sanhedrin) are remorseless in pressing their case
before the lower Yahweh (Pilate). So Yahweh reluctantly pronounces the
sentence of death.

Seen in this way, we can find many parallels to the trial of Christ in
the Hebrew Bible. Prophetic predictions of the exile typically have a
three-fold structure. Yahweh lists the accusations against Israel and Judah,
he passes judgement and then summons their executioners, the Assyrians
and Babylonians. In the throne room vision in Isaiah, Yahweh pronounces
the doom of the Jews. In Second Zechariah, Yahweh cancels the covenant
and condemns the flock to slaughter.

In the original version of the trial, the Christ would be led away to execution by the two gleeful angelic rulers of the nations, the king of Assyria/
Babylon and the king of Egypt. Simultaneously on earth, Israel and Judah
would be put to death between these two superpowers.

> ➤ Barabbas represents the leader of the fallen angels, the heavenly
> King of Babylon. The Jerusalem crowd's choice of Barabbas and
> demand for Jesus' crucifixion is another version of the betrayal
> of the Judas War.

There is one more mystery—who does Barabbas stand for? He is said to
have been imprisoned with his fellow rebels who have committed murder
in the insurrection. Some copies of Matthew have "Jesus Barabbas" suggesting that Barabbas might be Christ.

Barabbas, "son of the father", is an appropriate title for any of the seventy and also for Jesus. All of them are sons of God. And this explains
why Jesus should be confused with Barabbas; "Jesus Barabbas" is a title

of the Christ. But Jesus is not the Barabbas described in the trial in Mark. That Barabbas is an insurrectionist and murderer, and there is one son of God who fits this description perfectly.

The king of Babylon mounts a rebellion against God. In Isaiah, he seeks to place his throne on the mount of assembly, level with that of the Highest, but he is brought down to the pit.[4] In the Book of the Watchers, the fallen angels carry out a rebellion against Yahweh under their chief, Semyaz. The rebel angels descend to earth to take human wives and corrupt humanity. Semyaz and his followers are then bound and sealed in a pit as punishment for their revolt.[5] The king of Babylon, Semyaz, and Satan were all alternative names for the same being. The word used to describe the imprisonment of Barabbas means literally to be bound, just as Semyaz was bound in the pit.

Satan is called a murderer in the Gospel of John, when Jesus tells the Jews they belong to the devil:

> You belong to your father, the devil, and you desire to do the desires of your father's desires. He was a murderer from the beginning... (John 8:44)

All of this is consistent: Barabbas must stand for the king of Assyria and Babylon who is also Satan. The Jerusalem crowd choose Barabbas three times in preference to Jesus while demanding that Jesus should be crucified. Ahaz's Jerusalem was also given a choice; they chose the king of Assyria and demanded the crucifixion of Israel. Once again, we return to the Judas War.

➤ **The perfect sacrifice of Christ is the final fulfilment of the law of the lower Yahweh. The Christ will be resurrected on the third great day to replace the lower Yahweh and destroy the seventy.**

The seventy archons think they have triumphed. However, there is a secret they do not know, hidden before time by the ultimate authority, the higher Yahweh. He has sent the Christ, his son, down into our realm of reality. Christ is an innocent and perfect sacrifice. His death satisfies and ends the law of the lower Yahweh. Christ will be resurrected and return to replace the lower Yahweh, ruling a new kingdom on behalf of the higher Yahweh. He will defeat the seventy in the final battles of the apocalypse and save all his people, both Jew and gentile. The archons have been tricked.

31

The Servant Songs

My servant, Israel

In Isaiah, there is a remarkable portrait of the heavenly Christ in the "servant songs". Under the typical Jewish interpretation, the servant in these passages is Israel. Christians, however, see them as a prophecy of Christ. While the servant is undoubtedly Israel in some places, the Jewish explanation does not fit the passages as a whole. The servant resembles the Christ of the gospels in many ways. In particular, several aspects of the crucifixion account closely match the description of the suffering servant. This does not mean that the servant is a miraculous prophecy of Christ because the Isaiah passages came first. The gospel accounts have either copied Isaiah or used a source related to Isaiah.

We will see that the servant songs belong to a Christ myth which existed hundreds of years before the Jesus movement. A literary technique used by the Jews was to approach a subject through a series of concrete metaphors. These metaphors are often presented as real events or people, causing a great deal of confusion among the literally-minded readers of later times. Each metaphor is a snapshot from a different perspective. By combining the metaphors, we get a multiple-dimensional image of the subject; in this case, the heavenly Christ.

We have seen that the original Christ was both a divine ruler ("king of the Jews") and, at another level, the personification of Israel and Judah. The servant songs hint at a third level of Christ's identity.

> ➤ In the first song, the servant is the chosen one and a light to the nations. He is contrasted to human prophets and kings in a passage containing allusions to Hezekiah and Ahaz.

The servant of the first song is *"my chosen in whom my soul delights"* (Isaiah 42:1). This links the servant to both the chosen people, Israel, and the Messiah. We find evidence of cosmic escalation, as the servant is also called *"the light of the nations"* (Isaiah 42:6). He saves gentiles as well as Jews, redeeming both from cosmic exile: *"to open the eyes of the blind and bring out the prisoners from the prison" (Isaiah 42:7).*

In this first song, the servant is described by a two-fold negation. First, that he will not *"cry out"* or *"make his voice heard in the streets" (Isaiah 42:2).* The servant is not a human prophet whose duty was to cry out their prophecies in a public place. In the second negation he is contrasted to a human king:

> *A bruised reed he will not break, and a smouldering wick he will not extinguish. (Isaiah 42:3)*

There are two hidden allusions here to episodes involving Hezekiah and Ahaz in Isaiah. When the Assyrian Rabshakeh speaks before the walls of Jerusalem, he uses the same phrase *"a bruised reed" (Isaiah 36:6)* to describe the Egypt in whom Hezekiah had placed his trust. It is the Assyrians who defeated Egypt, and who broke the "bruised reed". And when Isaiah prophesies to Ahaz about Pekah and Rezin, the kings of Israel and Syria, he uses a similar image to a smouldering wick: they are *"two stubs of smouldering firebrands" (Isaiah 7:4).* Ahaz summoned the Assyrian king who extinguished these smouldering firebrands.

The negations described the servant in the two senses of an "anointed one"; as priest/prophet and king. But he is unlike human prophets or kings. And utterly unlike the king of Assyria who broke bruised reeds and extinguished smouldering wicks.

➤   **In the second song, the servant is both Israel and the Messiah who will save the nations along with Israel.**

The second song starts with the servant being called and named from the womb. His mouth is like a sharp sword, and he is a polished arrow which Yahweh has kept hidden. The servant is identified as Israel:

> *He said to me, "You are my servant, Israel, in whom I will be glorified." (Isaiah 49:3)*

The servant replies that he has laboured in vain and spent his strength in vanity—a criticism of Israel. The identity of the servant then switches from Israel to the Messiah. He has been formed to bring back Jacob and gather Israel, references to the northern kingdom. But the servant is given an even greater task:

He says: "It is too light a thing for you to be my servant, to raise up the
tribes of Jacob, and to restore the preserved ones of Israel. I will also
give you for a light for the nations, to bring my salvation to the ends of
the earth." (Isaiah 49:6)

Here we have an unambiguous statement that the servant will redeem
the gentiles along with Israel, a cosmic escalation of the mission of the
Christ.

➤   **In the third song, the servant, Israel, is abused, which has influ-**
    enced the crucifixion account.

In the third song, the servant is obedient, even under abuse:

I gave my back to those who struck me, and my cheeks to those who
pulled out my beard; I hid not my face from shame and spitting. (Isaiah
50:6)

Originally, this would have been intended to reflect the obedience of
Israel under exile. In the gospels, it becomes the abuse that Jesus suffers at
the hands of the priests and the Romans. The priests strike him and spit
on him.[1] He is scourged by the Romans as a preliminary to crucifixion.[2]
Then the Roman soldiers hit him on the head with a reed and spit in his
face.[3]

The suffering servant

➤   **The servant songs reach their climax with the fourth song, that**
    of the suffering servant. Here the servant bears the sins of Israel,
    suffers and dies, and yet returns to life.

The description of the servant as despised and rejected reaches its extreme
expression in Isaiah 53. The servant is now without form or majesty, and
has no beauty that people would desire:

He was despised and rejected by men, a man of sorrows and acquainted
with grief. Like one from whom men hide their faces he was despised,
and we esteemed him not. (Isaiah 53:3)

It is perhaps from this line that the author of Mark has taken the idea
that Jesus had his face covered when being struck by the servants of the

high priest.[4] Here we begin to get the impression of another, human level of Christ's identity. Christ is both the divine ruler of Israel and also Israel itself. But this description does not fit either of these identities. Instead, it points to a prophet coming at the destruction of Judah, who was ignored and suffered much. This should not surprise us. The other divine kings ruled through human avatars. The king of Babylon was simultaneously the angelic archon, a human king, and the empires of Assyria and Babylon. So it is reasonable that the Christ also had an avatar who was put to death on earth when the divine Christ was put to death in heaven. The song continues with the servant paying the sin price for others:

> Surely he has borne our griefs and carried our sorrows; yet we esteemed
> him stricken, smitten by God, and afflicted. But he was pierced for
> our transgressions; he was crushed for our iniquities; the punishment
> that brought us peace was upon him, and by his stripes we are healed.
> (Isaiah 53:4-5)

Who is the narrator here? Perhaps the people of Israel who have strayed:

> We all like sheep have gone astray; everyone has turned to his own
> way; and Yahweh has laid on him the iniquity of us all. (Isaiah 53:6)

The servant bears their sin and suffers his fate in silence:

> He was oppressed, and afflicted, yet he opened not his mouth. He was
> led like a lamb to the slaughter, and like a sheep that before its shearers
> is silent. So he opened not his mouth. (Isaiah 53:7)

From this passage comes the strange silence in Mark of Jesus at both his trials. It is clear from Isaiah that the servant actually dies. He is "cut-off from the land of the living" and buried:

> And they made his grave with the wicked and with the rich in his death,
> although he had done no violence, nor was any deceit in his mouth.
> (Isaiah 53:9)

The parallelism implies that the wicked do violence, and the rich speak deceit. The servant does neither, and yet he goes to his death alongside those who are guilty. This line has been misunderstood by the author of Mark, who takes it all quite literally. So Jesus is buried in an expensive new tomb by Joseph of Arimathea (the "rich" man), who is a member of the Sanhedrin (the "wicked").[5]

It is Yahweh who has "crushed him" and "put him to grief". His soul/ life has been made into a sin offering. Yet there is a promise of some form of resurrection. His days will be prolonged, and he will see "the light of life." By his "knowledge" he will justify many and bear their iniquities:[6]

> *Therefore I will allot him a portion with the great, and he shall divide the spoil with the strong; because he has poured out his soul unto death and was numbered with the transgressors. And he bore the sin of many, and made intercession for the transgressors. (Isaiah 53:12)*

➢ **The suffering servant cannot be just Israel, or just a human prophet or just a heavenly Messiah, but all three. The song of the servant is evidence that the myth of a divine Christ existed hundreds of years before the Jesus movement.**

The idea of the servant suffering, dying, and coming back to life fits the defeat and exile of Israel and the promised return. Yet the servant cannot be just Israel. The servant is innocent and bears the sins of others. Nor can the servant be just an ordinary prophet. First, he stays silent, whereas the duty of a prophet was to proclaim. Then he comes back to life, unlike any prophet. Nor does the idea that the servant is the king Messiah fit. The servant is despised and without form. He suffers and is killed as a sin offering. None of which fits the idea of the Messiah as the great liberator of the Jews. Although the servant has aspects that relate to Israel, a human prophet, and the Messiah, no single explanation fits.

Instead, the servant resembles almost perfectly the Christian conception of Christ, as suffering and resurrected redeemer. Although Jews have understandably rejected this explanation, nothing fits so well. Christians see the suffering servant as a miraculous prophecy of Christ. Yet we do not require any miracles to explain the connection. The suffering servant in Isaiah and the account of Jesus's death in Mark are two parallel expressions of the Christ myth. The later Mark account draws upon the earlier Isaiah passages.

All of which agrees with our previous conclusions. The myth of the Christ as the divine ruler representing Israel, dying at the exile but whose resurrection is promised and expected, must have existed hundreds of years before the Jesus movement of the first century.

> ➤ **The suffering servant is followed by verses that were taken by the Jesus movement as a prophecy of the shaman Mary.**

What comes immediately after the suffering servant passage was of particular importance for the Jesus movement:

> *"Shout for joy, O barren one, who bears no children; break forth into song and cry aloud, you who have never laboured with child; because more are the children of the desolate woman than of her who has a husband," says Yahweh. (Isaiah 54:1)*

The idea that Christ had been resurrected through a female shaman would have met with great resistance. But Mary and her supporters could point to this passage. It followed straight on from the suffering servant prediction of the resurrection. It said that a woman who had no husband and who had never given birth would yet be more blessed and have more children than a fecund woman. Motherhood was the supreme standard by which women were measured in ancient societies. By this standard Mary, a virgin dedicated to God, was a failure. Yet she styled herself as the mother of the reborn spiritual Christ, and mother of the whole movement. This prophecy was surely her inspiration. It is linked to Thomas 79, one of the early sources behind the virgin birth story.

The prophecy of the barren one is followed by a series of instructions that the early Jesus movement carried out:

- To spread out the tent, by taking the movement across the known world. (The author of Luke/Acts wrongly interpreted this as meaning that Paul and his missionary companions were tentmakers!)
- To expand on the left and the right. They would appeal not just to the few "chosen" (those baptised with the spirit, the right hand), but also to the many "called" (baptised with water, the left hand).
- To inherit the nations, by expanding aggressively among the gentiles.

32

A Crown of Thorns

The trial in front of Pilate takes place in the fourth period or watch, which corresponds to King Manasseh. The trial was originally in heaven and has been split into the two trials in Mark. Most of the fourth period is occupied by the heavenly trial, but is there anything that can be tied to the reign of Manasseh?

Our information on Manasseh comes from 2 Kings and 2 Chronicles with a fundamental discrepancy between the two accounts. They both state that Manasseh was 12 years old when he succeeded his father Hezekiah on the throne. He ruled for no less than fifty-five years, the longest of all the kings in this period.[1] According to the author of Kings, Manasseh was notorious for reversing the reforms of his father. He rebuilt the high places, erected altars for Baal and the host of heaven, and made an Asherah pole. Some of these altars were in the temple itself. He was also guilty of child sacrifice, making his son pass through fire.[2]

The author of Kings goes as far as to assign the blame for the exile of Judah to Manasseh's wickedness:

> *Because Manasseh king of Judah has done these abominations and has done things more evil than all that the Amorites did, who were before him, and has made Judah also to sin with his idols, therefore thus says Yahweh, the God of Israel: Behold, I am bringing upon Jerusalem and Judah such evil that the ears of everyone who hears of it will tingle. And I will stretch over Jerusalem the measuring line of Samaria, and the plumb line of the house of Ahab, and I will wipe Jerusalem as one wipes a dish, wiping it and turning it upside down. (2 Kings 21:11-13)*

This prediction that Judah and Jerusalem would share the fate that had befallen Israel must have been composed after the exile. It is here that 2 Chronicles departs from 2 Kings. In 2 Chronicles, an extraordinary event causes the king to repent. The chastised and penitent king removes the altars to "foreign gods" and restores the proper worship of Yahweh. He keeps the high places, but as cultic centres dedicated exclusively to Yahweh.[3]

There is no archaeological evidence to support the idea that Manasseh renewed the old cultic centres of worship. Nor is there any evidence for Josiah's reforms. This does not prove that neither of these happened. But it raises the suspicion that both reaction and reform have been exaggerated.

The Book of Kings presents the narrative of the two good kings, Hezekiah and Josiah, coming before and after the bad King Manasseh. This is not how anyone at the time would have seen things. Hezekiah suffered the Assyrian invasion that almost destroyed Judah, and Josiah left the kingdom under Egyptian control. By contrast, the reign of Manasseh was long and comparatively peaceful. The people must have looked back at his time as a golden age. And that was the problem. The two kings associated with concentrating the exclusive worship of Yahweh in the Jerusalem temple had bad things happen to them. In contrast, the king who the priests regarded as a backslider had a very long and successful reign. At a time when such events were believed to reflect divine will, the people would have drawn the natural conclusion; Yahweh loved Manasseh and hated Hezekiah and Josiah. It was vital for the priests to change this narrative, and it was they who wrote the history.

So Manasseh was blamed for events that happened long after his death. The defeat of Hezekiah was reengineered as a miraculous victory. And the goodness of Josiah's reign held back the punishment that had been due for Manasseh, with Josiah himself being blessed by an early death to be spared the sight of the defeat of Jerusalem.

Reforms that cast aside the old gods and sacred places would have been unpopular. So the real reason for Manasseh's return to religious plurality was probably pragmatic—he needed to quell the growing outrage among the people. Indeed, if 2 Chronicles is to be believed, Manasseh may even have been among the reformers. Perhaps he was just less absolute than his father or his grandson Josiah. There is evidence that the 2 Kings account was much more positive towards the king before it was edited by the Deuteronomistic historian. The conclusion that *"Manasseh rested with his ancestors and was buried in his palace garden ..." (2 Kings 21:18)* indicates a favourable judgement.

Mock homage

> The "king of the Jews" theme of the fourth period climaxes with the mock worship of Jesus by the Roman soldiers.

Is there anything in the reign of Manasseh that can be related to the fourth period of the passion account? We have seen that the main event of this period, the trial, does not relate directly to the Almanac periods. The mock-homage of Jesus immediately follows it:

> And the soldiers led him away inside the palace (that is the Praetorium) and they called together the whole cohort. And they clothed him in a purple cloak, and twisting together a crown of thorns, they put it on him. And they began to salute him, "Hail, king of the Jews!" And they were striking his head with a reed and spitting on him and kneeling down in homage to him. (Mark 15:16-19)

Should we place this episode as the continuation of the fourth period or as the start of the fifth? There is no explicit timing here. A change of location usually marks the division between one period and the next, but here there are two such changes; the soldiers move Jesus to the Praetorium and then, after the mock homage, lead him away to crucifixion. The homage is the climax of the "king of the Jews" theme, so we will take it as the culmination of the fourth period.

At one level we can see this story as representing the homage that the seventy and their demonic offspring are obliged to offer the true king, bowing even while abusing him. But the source for most of the details is very different.

➤ **The mock homage of Jesus reflects an event which happened when King Agrippa I visited Alexandria.**

In 37 AD the Emperor Caligula freed Agrippa I from prison and appointed him as king over territories on the east side of the Jordon. The new Tetrarch had to stop over at Alexandria in Egypt on the way from Rome to his kingdom. This was a potentially dangerous visit. The city was the scene of unrest between the substantial Jewish population and other ethnic groups. Just a few years before, severe riots bordering on warfare had broken out between the two communities.[4] The newly appointed Tetrarch was entering a powder keg.

The sight of a Jewish king inflamed the native Egyptian population who thought the Jews were once again being given special treatment. They ridiculed what they saw as the pretentions of this new Jewish king, and this led to an episode of humiliating mock homage. There was a gentle madman called Carabbas who wandered naked about the roads. A mob went onto the streets, fetched Carabbas, and pretended that he was Agrippa:

And they, driving the poor wretch as far as the public gymnasium, and setting him up there on high that he might be seen by everybody, flattened out a leaf of papyrus and put it on his head instead of a diadem, and clothed the rest of his body with a common doormat instead of a cloak and instead of a sceptre they put in his hand a small stick of the native papyrus which they found lying by the wayside and gave to him; and when, like actors in theatrical spectacles, he had received all the insignia of royal authority, and had been dressed and adorned like a king, the young men bearing sticks on their shoulders stood on each side of him instead of spear-bearers, in imitation of the bodyguards of the king, and then others came up, some as if to salute him, and others making as though they wished to plead their causes before him, and others pretending to wish to consult with him about the affairs of the state. Then from the multitude of those who were standing around there arose a wonderful shout of men calling out Maris. (Philo, Flaccus 37-39).[5]

The word the crowd are shouting, "Maris", was used to salute the Syrian kings.[6] We can see that there must be a link between the two stories. Agrippa I's territory would shortly expand to include the whole of Judea, so he was literally "king of the Jews". Christian apologists have suggested that the crowd would have been aware of the mocking of Jesus by the Romans a few years before and copied it to ridicule Agrippa. But the Jesus movement was a tiny obscure sect at this time, and there is no way the population of Alexandria was going to know or care about Jesus' execution in Jerusalem. On the other hand, this absurd public ridicule of a king who was a favourite of the Emperor would have made an irresistible story that would have spread around the Empire. It would have appalled Jews everywhere, and been equally enjoyed by their detractors. The author of Mark, writing much later in the 70s AD, must have heard about this mock homage of a "king of the Jews" and mistakenly thought that the king was Jesus.

Identifying the Agrippa episode as the primary source of the story enables us to separate details that do not come from this source. The purple cloak, the colour of kings, is an understandable addition. But there is one inexplicable and striking detail that deviates from the Carabbas story: Jesus is given a crown of thorns rather than papyrus. From where did this odd idea of a crown of thorns come? In Christian images, the thorns are grossly exaggerated, turning the crown into an instrument of torture. But the Romans would not have messed around with a few thorns for the serious business of torture. Such an unusual detail must be significant.

Among thorns

➢   **According to Chronicles, Manasseh was captured among thorns.**

We can find the thorns in 2 Chronicles. It is here that 2 Kings and 2
Chronicles diverge with the later giving us an extraordinary story:

> *So Yahweh brought against them the captains of the host of the king
> of Assyria, who took Manasseh among the thorns [choach], and bound
> him in fetters and brought him to Babylon. And when he was in dis-
> tress, he sought the favour of Yahweh his God and humbled himself
> greatly before the God of his fathers. And when he prayed to him, the
> Lord was moved by his entreaty and listened to his plea, and brought
> him back to Jerusalem and his kingdom. Then Manasseh knew that
> Yahweh is God. (2 Chronicles 33:11-13)*

Manasseh repented after his capture and return: he removed the image
and altars to other gods from the temple. The whole episode is odd, and
most historians do not believe that this Chronicles account is historical. There is no confirmation from any other source that the Assyrians
invaded Judah at this time or came up against Jerusalem. Surely if they
had taken Jerusalem, we would have heard about it from the prophetic
writings? This leaves one possibility; that the king was captured while
campaigning outside Judah.

➢   **The Hebrew word *choach*, literally "thorns", is often translated
      in this passage as meaning "hooks".**

There is also doubt about whether the word *choach* should be taken at its
literal meaning of "thorns" or as a metaphor for "hooks" as in Job 41:2.
Modern translations invariably take this second approach and translate
it as something like "they captured Manasseh with hooks" instead of
"among the thorns". Hooks were used by the Assyrians to humiliate prisoners who were brought before the king led by a hook. In 2 Kings 19:28
when the Assyrians besieged Jerusalem in the time of Hezekiah it is was
promised that they would be led away with "a hook in their nose and a
bridle in their lips". In Ezekiel 19 there is a "lamentation for the princes of
Israel". They are two lion whelps who are both caught in turn, the first by
the Egyptians, the second by the Babylonians: *"And they put him in a cage
with hooks, and brought him to the king of Babylon"* (Ezekiel 19:9). However, we
should remember that in this passage the princes are lions. Wild animals
were captured with nets and hooks, but not men.

There is actually nothing wrong with the natural reading of *choach* as "thorns". We know that soldiers could hide among thickets of thorns when escaping from the enemy:

> *When the men of Israel saw that their situation was critical and that their army was hard-pressed, they hid in caves and thickets [choach], among the rocks, and in pits and cisterns. (1 Samuel 13:6)*

There is nothing inherently unlikely about Manasseh having to flee and hide in a thicket of thorns following an ambush or a defeat while campaigning outside Judah. It is quite possible that the account in 2 Chronicles preserves a garbled memory of the capture of Manasseh (the detail that he was taken to Babylon is unlikely to be historical). Assyrian power was on the wane, and the political situation was unstable, with wars and shifting alliances. If the Assyrians had the king, but not the kingdom, it would make sense for them to free Manasseh in return for an oath of fealty and tribute. The thorns are exactly the sort of detail that would be remembered in the popular imagination. Compare it to the story of the king of England, Charles II, hiding in an oak tree at Boscobel on the Shropshire border to escape the parliamentary forces. This story was endlessly retold for centuries and even today, "The Royal Oak" is a common pub name. Perhaps Manasseh's "crown of thorns" was as well known in Judah as the "royal oak" was to be in England.

In any case, whether or not the historical Manasseh was captured among thorns is not the point here. There are other instances in which the Almanac follows Chronicles where it differs from Kings. Most significantly, the story of Uzziah's desecration of the temple is only found in Chronicles, as is the story of the martyrdom of Zechariah in front of the temple. So we know that the Almanac authors were influenced by Chronicles or a closely related source.

There are multiple connections between the story of Manasseh and the mock homage of Jesus:

- Both Manasseh and Jesus are "king of the Jews".
- Both are captives; Manasseh by the Assyrians/Babylonians and Jesus by their successors, the Romans.
- Manasseh is taken to Babylon to be mocked and humiliated, and Jesus is taken to the Praetorium to be mocked and humiliated.

Most likely, the proto-crucifixion source used the "crown of thorns" in the fourth period as an allusion to the capture of Manasseh among thorns. This was combined with the misunderstood story of the mock-homage of the "king of the Jews" to give the account of the Roman soldiers mocking Jesus that we find it in Mark.

Amon

➤   **Almanac day 7.5 is that of Amon who had a very short reign. This period was eliminated by the author of Mark to make time for the burial.**

Manasseh was succeeded by his twenty-two-year-old son, Amon, who ruled for just two years before he was assassinated in a palace conspiracy. His assassins were killed by the people, who made his eight-year-old son Josiah king.[7] It may be that the period of two years is a symbolic number to represent a short reign and that Amon actually ruled for longer than this. From the information in 2 Kings, Amon would only have been sixteen when Josiah was born. Although not impossible, this seems unlikely. Both Kings and Chronicles are negative about Amon, who is said to have followed the idolatrous ways of his father.

The generation of Amon does not correspond to a period in the passion day because one generation in the last week had to be sacrificed. The original proto-passion source would have had seven periods; six of three hours and one, the crucifixion, of six hours. The author of Mark faces the problem that he must leave time for the burial of Jesus before the sabbath starts at nightfall. The crucifixion period is already very short and cannot be reduced. So he is forced to delete one of the earlier periods, move the crucifixion up three hours to start at 9 am and end at 3 pm.

The choice of the day of Amon to be eliminated is not surprising. He had by far the shortest reign of any of the Almanac kings in the final week. The accounts of his reign in 2 Chronicles and 2 Kings are very brief, with little more than the bare statement of his assassination in the palace. Apart from the circumstances of his death, we know virtually nothing about him.

33

The Way of the Cross

Josiah

Josiah, who followed Amon, was one of the two "good" kings. There must have been a regency for the boy king, but we hear nothing about it. His reign lasted thirty-one years, and he was in his prime at thirty-nine when he died.[1]

This was a time of rapidly declining Assyrian power, marked by the rise of Babylon which was soon to conquer Assyria. Although it had been previously believed that Assyrian weakness enabled the young king to assert Judah's independence and rebuild a Judean kingdom, the archaeological evidence does not support this scenario. Judah did take over the region of Bethel a few miles to the north of Jerusalem, but this was only a very minor expansion.[2] It seems there was no power vacuum in the Levant for Judah to exploit because the Egyptians pushed up to replace the retreating Assyrians. Dominance by Egypt followed seamlessly from dominance by Assyria.

The story of the discovery of an ancient book which supposedly inspired Josiah's reforms comes from Kings.[3] In the eighteenth year of his reign, Josiah ordered some restoration work in the temple, and during this work, the "Book of the Law" was supposedly discovered by the high priest, Hilkiah. According to Kings, the book was given to Shaphan the scribe who passed it on to the king. When he read the book, Josiah tore his clothes in grief at how far the Jews had departed from the ordnances of Yahweh. The king told the high priests and his officials to find out the word of Yahweh, and they went to a woman called Huldah the prophetess. She told them that the anger of Yahweh was upon Judah and Jerusalem and that a terrible fate would befall them. She did give Josiah the excellent news that Yahweh would take his life first to spare him from the sight of the destruction of his kingdom.

Josiah then summoned the elders of Judah and Jerusalem and assembled all the people in the temple. He read out the book, and the king and the people all swore to keep the covenant with Yahweh. This was to signal the start of a vicious campaign of religious persecution.

The modern reader will naturally see through all this. The book is commonly identified with Deuteronomy, but there are two different explanations for the finding of the book:

i.   Deuteronomy was written during the reign of Josiah, perhaps by the scribe Shaphan. To pass off the forgery the priests claimed the book was ancient and had been hidden in the temple.[4]
ii. The whole story was invented by the Deuteronomistic historian long after the events it describes to give a back history to the newly written Deuteronomy.[5]

If (i) is true, then the account of Josiah's reforms could be historical—the king may even have believed that the book was genuine. There is, however, currently no archaeological evidence for the reforms, although this does not prove that they did not take place. It is certainly possible that Josiah took some action against the high place at Bethel which had become part of Judah. However, the reforming role of Josiah seems to have been exaggerated, and explanation (ii) is more likely. The Deuteronomistic historian would be writing after the Judean exile, and his account is intended to build up Josiah, to blame Manasseh for the exile, and to explain the origins of Deuteronomy.

➤   **According to Chronicles, Josiah died from his wounds after being defeated by an Egyptian army at Megiddo. However, a close reading of the Kings account suggests that Josiah was actually executed by the Egyptian king while paying him homage as a vassal.**

The end of Josiah is described in Kings:

> *In his days Pharaoh Neco king of Egypt went up to the king of Assyria at the river Euphrates. And King Josiah went to meet him, and Pharaoh Neco killed him at Megiddo, as soon as he saw him. (2 Kings 23:29)*

The Chronicles account has Josiah marching to meet Necho in battle. The Pharaoh sends him messengers asking him not to interfere because he has no quarrel with Josiah and is marching to meet his enemy (the Babylonians) at God's command. But Josiah ignores these warnings, approaches Necho's army and is shot by archers. He is taken to Jerusalem where he dies.[6]

The long-established idea that Josiah died heroically in battle against the Egyptians has been questioned recently by Nadav Na'aman.[7] The

Kings account does not say that Josiah was fighting the Egyptians, just that he was meeting Necho. With a realistic assessment of the relative strength of Judah and Egypt, a direct battle between the two becomes almost inconceivable—the Judeans could never hope to win.

So a new explanation has been offered. The new Egyptian Pharaoh is progressing up the coastal area to receive the vassal kings who will pay him homage and present gifts. Josiah is among these vassals and has no option but to go and meet Pharaoh. However, for some reason, Josiah has upset Necho. As soon as the Pharaoh sets eyes on the Judean king, he orders his death. We can imagine the other kings trembling as they watch Josiah's execution—such brutality served as a potent example.

The fate of Josiah was tragic but also humiliating. The king of Judah did not die in battle but was killed at the whim of a foreign ruler. And much worse was to come.

Jehoahaz and Jehoiakim

> ➤ Jehoahaz ruled for three months before being captured by the Egyptians.

Josiah was succeeded by his son Jehoahaz who was twenty-three. The verdict of Kings is the familiar formula: *"he did evil in the eyes of Yahweh"* *(2 Kings 23:32)*. In the case of Jehoahaz, this is absurd because he ruled for just three months in Jerusalem before being placed in chains by Pharaoh Necho and taken to Egypt, where he died. The Pharaoh made his brother Jehoiakim king instead and imposed a large tribute on Judah.[8]

> ➤ Jehoiakim ruled for eleven years before dying in mysterious circumstances as the Babylonians surrounded the walls of Jerusalem.

Eliakim, called Jehoiakim, was twenty-five when he assumed the throne and was to rule for eleven years.[9] It was a time of upheaval. The Babylonians conquered and sacked Nineveh, bringing to an end the long, remarkable history of the Assyrian Empire. Now the Babylonians turned their attention to Egypt, and Judah was in the middle. For a while, Jehoiakim stayed loyal to Egypt. But an incursion into Judah by the Babylonian king, Nebuchadnezzar, obliged him to switch sides to the Babylonians. After three years, Egypt appeared to have rebuffed the Babylonians, and Jehoiakim took the opportunity to return to an Egyptian alliance.[10] It was an error that brought Judah down. The resurgence of Egypt proved to be nothing more than a temporary setback for the Babylonians, and Nebuchadnezzar came against Jerusalem with a full army. We cannot be sure of the fate of Jehoiakim; he may have been assassinated, or died in a skirmish outside the walls of Jerusalem, or he may have been captured. In Kings it is said that he slept with his fathers, but unlike the other kings, his burial place is not given.[11] In Chronicles he is carried off to Babylon in chains, which is also supported by Ezekiel (see below).[12] In Jeremiah, the king's body is cast outside the gates of Jerusalem, and he does not receive a proper burial.[13]

➢   **The Ezekiel lament for the two lion clubs captures the tragedy of the final years of the house of David and kingdom of Judah.**

In Ezekiel 19 there is a lament for the two princes of Israel, who are compared to two lion cubs born to a lioness (Israel). The first (Jehoahaz) is caught by the nations with hooks and brought in a cage to Egypt. The second cub (Jehoiakim) takes its place, devastating the strongholds and cities of the enemy. But the nations surround it on every side:

> *They spread their net over him; he was taken in their pit. They put him in a cage with hooks and brought him to the king of Babylon. They brought him into captivity so that his voice was heard no more on the mountains of Israel. (Ezekiel 19:8-9)*

There is sadness in this lament: the house of David, the last hope of the people of Judah, had met its effective end with these two princes. The Ezekiel lament suggests a more heroic role for the two young kings than is evident from Kings or Chronicles. Jehoiakim, in particular, must have secured a number of victories to have justified the description in Ezekiel. Yet it was not enough, and his reign ended in tragedy.

➢   **Jehoiakim was succeeded by his young son Jeconiah who ruled for just a few months before Jerusalem surrendered to the Babylonians. Jeconiah was taken to Babylon where he spent the remainder of his long life in captivity.**

Jeconiah (who was also called Jehoiachin), the son of Jehoiakim, was eighteen years old when he became king.[14] No prince of Judah had ever come to the throne in more desperate circumstances. The Babylonian armies surrounded Jerusalem, and the fall of the city was inevitable. The Judeans' only chance was to throw themselves on the mercy of the Babylonians. The young king had been on the throne for just three months when the gates of Jerusalem were opened in surrender. The king, the king's mother, and the court were all taken to Babylon, along with the treasures from the temple. With this surrender, the city was saved from destruction.

The king of Babylon placed Jeconiah's uncle, Zedekiah, on the throne as a puppet ruler. The reign of Zedekiah was to end in complete disaster whereas Jeconiah was a survivor. Although he spent only a few months ruling in Jerusalem and the remainder of his long life in Babylon, Jeconiah was seen by the Jews as the last of the Davidic kings.

The sixth day

➢ **There are six kings for the two Almanac generations 7.6 and 7.7.**

The following is a list of the kings from Josiah onwards:

Josiah
Jehoahaz, son of Josiah
Jehoiakim, son of Josiah
Jeconiah (Jehoiachin), son of Jehoiakim
Zedekiah, brother of Jehoiakim, uncle of Jeconiah
Jeconiah (Jehoiachin) continues as king in captivity in Babylon

The Almanac has only two generations, 7.6 (Josiah) and 7.7 (Jeconiah), to cover this period. So the other reigns must be allocated between these two generations. This is how the end of the seventh week is described in the Matthew genealogy:

> *Josiah begat Jeconiah and his brethren, at the Babylonian removal.*
> *(Matthew 1:11)*

The "brethren of Jeconiah" must mean Jehoahaz, Jehoiakim and Zedekiah. From the Matthew genealogy, we would think that these three kings should all be allocated to the generation of Jeconiah. But there is a mistake which shows that this was not how the Almanac framers arranged the kings.

➢ The author of the genealogy mistakenly thinks that Jeconiah is a brother of Jehoahaz, Jehoiakim and Zedekiah. In the Almanac, Jeconiah must have followed on from Josiah without any comment.

Although Jehoahaz, Jehoiakim and Zedekiah were all brothers, they were not brothers of Jeconiah who was the son of Jehoiakim and the nephew of Jehoahaz and Zedekiah. So the genealogy contains an obvious mistake here. The author of the genealogy thought that Jeconiah was a son of Josiah, which tells us that the Almanac must have looked like this:

7.6 Josiah
7.7 Jeconiah

Those who put the Almanac together would have known that Jeconiah was not Josiah's son. But someone reading the Almanac could come to this mistaken impression because Jeconiah's father is missing. If that person knew that there were other kings at this time who were sons of Josiah, then it would be natural to allocate those other kings as brothers of Jeconiah, as we find in the genealogy. So the comment about the brothers of Jeconiah has been added by the genealogist and was not taken from his source. It is a red herring that does not help us allocate the kings between the two generations.

➢ The two brothers should be allocated to the generation of Josiah as all three shared a similar fate. This enables the exile to start at the very beginning of generation 7.7.

So how would the Almanac have allocated the missing three kings between generations? Zedekiah obviously has to be subsumed within the reign of Jeconiah. This leaves Jehoahaz and Jehoiakim to be placed in either 7.6 or 7.7. A split between Josiah and Jehoahaz would be artificial as Jehoahaz shared a similar fate to his father at the hands of Necho. It would also be unfortunate to divide up the brothers, Ezekiel's two lion clubs. So we should put both brothers in 7.6 alongside their father, Josiah. The three kings are linked; each met defeat and death, their three reigns the three acts of a tragedy leading to exile. Under this arrangement, the exile would commence at the very beginning of 7.7, with Jeconiah, which fits the requirement that the physical exile should last for two generations, 7.7 and 8.1.

So the division between the days must be as follows:

7.6 Josiah, Jehoahaz and Jehoiakim
7.7 Jeconiah including Zedekiah

Three who carried the cross

➤ The sixth day corresponds to the period between 6 am, and 9 am, occupied by the carrying of the cross.

We have allocated the mock-homage of Jesus in Mark to the fourth period. So the fifth period, corresponding to the sixth day, is occupied solely by the carrying of the cross. The description is very brief:

> And they compelled [angareuousin] one Simon of Cyrene, a passer-by, who was coming in from the country, the father of Alexander and Rufus, to carry his cross. And they brought him to the place called Golgotha, which means Place of the Skull. (Mark 15:21-22)

There is no independent evidence for the existence of Golgotha, the Place of the Skull, which is so perfectly named for the site of a mythical crucifixion. Although the passage is short, there are two very odd things about it.

➤ A condemned criminal would carry his own cross, yet a "passer-by" was impressed to carry Jesus' cross.

The first odd thing is that Jesus does not bear his own cross. The condemned criminal should be led through the streets, visible to all, carrying his cross to the place of execution. It was all part of the show to discourage others from making the same mistake. So why does Simon carry Jesus' cross for him? The author of John recognises the problem; in his gospel, Jesus carries the cross alone, and there is no Simon of Cyrene.

The Gospel of Mark says that Simon was "compelled" using the word that means to impress a messenger into service. The same word is used in Matthew in the sermon on the mount: *"And if anyone compels [angareusei] you to go one mile, go with him two" (Matthew 5:41)*. The cross is also taken up in a Thomas saying:

> Jesus said: "Whoever does not hate his father and his mother cannot be my disciple, and whoever does not hate his brothers and his sisters and take up his cross like me, he shall not be worthy of me." (Thomas 55; TC 3.18)

To take up the cross is to follow a path of self-denial, to be "a passer-by" as another Thomas saying puts it.[15] As the Gospel of Mark says: "If *anyone wishes to come after me, let him deny himself and take up his cross and let him follow me"* (*Mark 8:34*). Compare how Simon of Cyrene is called a "passer-by". Why should this random person who is coming into town be impressed to carry the cross? And even if he were, why should his name be remembered, and the names of his sons?

> ➢ Simon is called the father of Alexander and Rufus even though these two play no part in what follows.

The oddest thing about the account is the way Simon is called the father of Alexander and Rufus. A person could be identified by adding the name of their father, or the place from which they came. It was certainly not normal to identify a man by the names of his sons. Also, Simon has already been sufficiently distinguished through his hometown of Cyrene, a prominent city in north Africa. The author of Matthew, always sensitive to problems in Mark, drops Alexander and Rufus, calling Simon simply "a man from Cyrene". Luke also copies this approach, so Alexander and Rufus only appear in Mark.[16]

We must reject the idea that Alexander and Rufus were two well-known Christians among the community which produced Mark and who could vouch for the accuracy of the story. The author of Mark is writing an account modelled on a biography or history, which is designed to be read widely, not a letter for a closed group. He assumes no special knowledge and takes care to explain things for the benefit of his readers. So why does he not explain who Alexander and Rufus were?

Perhaps the role of the two is implied rather than explicit. Although Simon is impressed to carry the cross, the mention of his sons suggests they were also present. So perhaps we are intended to read the passage as meaning that a father and his two sons carried the cross.

> ➢ Josiah, Jehoahaz and Jehoiakim can all be said to have carried the cross for Judah.

We have allocated the three kings Josiah, Jehoahaz and Jehoiakim to day 7.6. All three suffered a tragic fate at the hands of the nations. Josiah was summarily executed by the king of Egypt; Jehoahaz was taken in chains to Egypt where he died; Jehoiakim was either captured and taken in a cage to the king of Babylon or died outside the walls of Jerusalem where his body lay unburied. To "carry the cross" was a common saying of the first-century and all three kings can be said to have "carried the cross" for Judah.

> ➤ The author of Mark has confused the father and two sons with Simon of Cyrene and his sons Alexander and Rufus. These three were probably early Christian martyrs.

We can reconstruct what must have happened:

1. The proto-crucifixion source recorded that the cross was carried by a father and his two sons—meaning Josiah, Jehoahaz and Jehoiakim.
2. There was a Christian tradition about three who "carried the cross of Jesus"; Simon of Cyrene and his sons Alexander and Rufus. The three were probably early martyrs.
3. The author of Mark wrongly connects the two pieces of information and has Simon, father of Alexander and Rufus, carry Jesus' cross at the crucifixion.

There were many martyrs in the first century, and Christianity tended to run in families. We know that there was an intense period of persecution under Nero, particularly in Rome. Entire families would have been wiped out at this time. So it is quite likely that a father and two sons suffered martyrdom together. The original meaning of "taking up your cross" was to follow a path of self-denial, but it quickly became associated with martyrdom. So it is quite feasible that there were three martyrs, Simon, Alexander and Rufus, who were said to have carried Jesus' cross.

Could Rufus be the person of that name who Paul greets as "the chosen in the Lord" along with his unnamed mother at Romans 16:13? Neither Simon nor Alexander are mentioned by Paul, but perhaps they had converted later, and were not Christians when Paul had known the family. Simon's name, "of Cyrene", tells us that he was living somewhere other than his home town, so Rome is a possibility. However, Rufus was a common name, and the appearance of a Rufus in Romans may be nothing more than coincidence.

34

Crucifixion Between Two Robbers

Zedekiah

Zedekiah was appointed king by Nebuchadnezzar and ruled for eleven years.[1] At first, he was a loyal Babylonian vassal, and if he had continued in this way, Judah might have been saved. However, Zedekiah succumbed to the familiar temptation of switching sides. He joined an Egyptian led alliance and ceased the payment of tribute. Babylonian retribution was swift. Nebuchadnezzar invaded Judah with an army and took the Judean cities one by one until only Jerusalem remained. The city fell in 586 BC, and the Babylonian revenge on their disloyal subject people was brutal. After his sons had been killed, the blinded Zedekiah was taken to Babylon, and we hear no more about him.

A month after Jerusalem had fallen, the city and its temple were set afire by the Babylonians. The walls were broken down, and any remaining citizens were taken away into exile. Archaeology has shown that the devastation was total and that the city was left uninhabited. Judah had ceased to be an independent state, and the capital of the new province was moved to Mizpah eight miles to the north of Jerusalem.[2] The elite population was exiled to Babylon, but most Judeans remained where they had always lived, in the villages and farms in the country. It is from such a location that the proto-Christians would emerge.

Crucifixion

➢ The seventh day of the seventh week in the Almanac, the day of the destruction of Jerusalem and Judah, corresponds to the period of the crucifixion in Mark.

Day 7.7 is the ominous sabbath of sabbaths—the seventh day of the seventh week. The day is represented by Jeconiah, exiled at the very start, and also incorporated the catastrophic reign of Zedekiah. It corresponds to the six-hour period of the crucifixion in the Mark account. This originally ran from noon to 6 pm, but the author of Mark shifted the time to 9 am to 3 pm. When Christ dies, the house of David is extinguished, and the kingdoms of Judah and Israel cease to exist. The age of the Jews has come to an end.

> ➤ **Most of the details of Mark's account of the crucifixion come from Psalm 22.**

This is how Mark describes the moment of crucifixion:

> *And they offered him wine mixed with myrrh. He, however, did not take it. And having crucified him, they also divided his garments among them, casting lots for them, to decide what each should take. It was the third hour when they crucified him. And the inscription of the accusation against him read, "The king of the Jews." And with him they crucified two robbers, one on his right and one on his left. (Mark 15:23-27)*

We will see that many details come from Psalm 22. First, the dividing of Jesus' garments and casting lots:

> *They divide my garments among them, and cast lost for my clothing. (Psalm 22:18)*

Other elements of the crucifixion come from the same Psalm. The passers-by and the priests mock Jesus:

> *And those who passed by abused him, wagging their heads and saying, "Aha! You who would destroy the temple and rebuild it in three days, save yourself, and come down from the cross!" Likewise, the chief priests with the scribes mocked him among themselves, saying, "He saved others; he cannot save himself. Let the Christ, the king of Israel, descend now from the cross that we may see and believe." And those being crucified with him were insulting him. (Mark 15:29-32)*

Which relates to Psalm 22:

> *All who see me mock me; they make mouths at me; they shake their heads… (Psalm 22:7)*

The final cry that Jesus makes from the cross echoes the first line of Psalm 22: *"My God, my God, why have you forsaken me?" (Psalm 22:1)* Even the piercing of Jesus' hands and feet with nails can be related to the Septuagint translation of Psalm 22:16 where hands and feet are pierced.

Between two robbers

➢ **The detail of the two robbers cannot be traced back to scripture and must reflect something in the proto-crucifixion source.**

The author of Mark has taken many of the details of the crucifixion from Psalm 22. There is, however, one conspicuous exception; the story of the two robbers crucified with Jesus. It is the type of specific detail you would not expect, and there must be some source for it.

Some manuscripts of Mark add an extra line to explain the presence of the robbers: *"And the Scripture was fulfilled which says, 'And he was numbered with transgressors'"* (Mark 15:28). The reference is to Isaiah 53:12 and the suffering servant. This extra line is probably not original to Mark.[3] It was not copied by the author of Matthew who loved to give such scriptural justifications. Most likely the line came from Luke where it appears in a completely different context.[4] But even if the line were original to Mark, the idea that Jesus was "numbered with the transgressors" is too vague to account for the particular detail of the two robbers.

There is no scriptural justification for the robbers, and they must have come from the proto-crucifixion source. But this presents a problem. The crucifixion occurs on at least two levels. At the heavenly level, the divine being, the Christ, is put to death by the angelic seventy. On the earthly level, Israel and Judah are extinguished by the nations. Yet on both levels, Christ, as the greater Israel, should be crucified alone. Why then do we have the iconic image derived from Mark of three crosses on a hill? Clearly, the author of Mark has misunderstood something in his source.

➢ **In the early Jesus movement, robbers and other malefactors represented the shepherd angels and their progeny, the demons.**

The word used for the robbers is *lestes*. It means a bandit, one who takes the property of others using force rather than a thief who steals with stealth. Jesus uses this word when he asks the crowd why they come to arrest him as if he were a robber.[5] And in Mark he calls the temple a "den of robbers".[6]

In the Gospel of Thomas, malefactors such as robbers invariably represent demons. In *The Rock and the Tower*, I suggested that the story about Jesus expelling the "robbers", the money changers, from the temple was a misunderstanding of Jesus' expulsion of seven demons from the Magdalene, the temple.[7]

In John, Jesus tells his disciples that anyone entering the sheepfold without going through the door is a "robber".[8] His disciples are understandably confused, so Jesus enlightens them: *"I am the door of the sheep. All who came before me are thieves and robbers..." (John 10:7-8).* Jesus will save the sheep but *"the thief comes only to steal and to kill and to destroy" (John 10:10).* A memory of the shepherd-angels is behind this. Christ is the good shepherd; the seventy shepherds who ruled before him are thieves and robbers.

The same idea that the angelic rulers are robbers is implicit in the parable of the tenants. The tenant farmers assault the two servants and kill the son in an attempt to steal the vineyard from its rightful owner.

➢ **The two robbers are the two shepherd-angels representing Egypt and Assyria/Babylon. In the original source, they are not crucified with Jesus but are crucifying him.**

The tenant-robbers kill Christ, and this gives us the real reason why the robbers are at the crucifixion—they are Jesus' executioners. We have seen how the trial of Jesus was originally in heaven with the chief prosecutors being the angelic rulers of Egypt and Assyria/Babylon. The later is also represented in the story by Barabbas, son of the father, who is described in John as a robber:

"Now Barabbas was a robber [lestes]" (John 18:40)

The king of Babylon is identified with Satan and is the Morning Star, Lucifer. Once the judgement has been passed, the two angels, the divine kings of Egypt and Assyria/Babylon lead Christ away to crucify him. Christ is hung from the cross while one stands on his left and one on the right. They both abuse Christ, mocking his suffering and telling him that his kingdom is now theirs. When Christ dies, and Israel and Judah are no more, they will rule the whole world. Or so they think.

On earth, Israel and Judah are crushed between Egypt and Assyria/Babylon. By this final period, Israel has already long since been destroyed by Assyria. Now it is Judah's turn. She is abused and weakened by Egypt, with the Pharaoh killing her kings before the final death blow is administered by Babylon.

The author of Mark is attempting to construct a realistic account of a Roman crucifixion from his source materials. In the proto-crucifixion source, the crucifixion was the ancient "cursed death" of "hanging from a tree". In the earliest form of crucifixion, the victim would have been suspended by ropes from a real tree. Later a T-shaped cross was substituted for the tree. And this is how Jesus' crucifixion is shown in the earliest surviving Christian depiction, a bloodstone intaglio gem in the British Museum. On this gem, Jesus hangs by ropes from a T-shaped cross. The very early Constanza gem (again in the British Museum) shows this same form of crucifixion with Jesus suspended by ropes.[9] Notably, two of the earliest visual representations of the crucifixion contradict the four gospel accounts in which Jesus is nailed to the cross. They speak of a tradition that existed before the gospels, in which Jesus was suspended by ropes from the bar of a T-cross. This is one example of the way in which the author of Mark has changed the crucifixion to adhere to Roman norms.

A more significant change involves the two robbers. The author of Mark's source must have stated that a robber was on each side of Jesus at his death. But robbers did not carry out crucifixions under Rome—they suffered crucifixion. So the author of Mark assumed that the robbers were crucified alongside Jesus. In Mark and Matthew, the robbers are hostile towards Jesus as we would expect.[10] The author of Luke takes the opportunity to improve upon the story. One robber is unrepentant, but the other shows faith in Jesus and asks that he should be remembered when Jesus enters into his kingdom. Jesus replies that he will join him that day in paradise. The story is a beautiful invention of the author of Luke, but the idea that the robber will be with Jesus in heaven may reflect a source in which the robber is called an angel.[11]

➤   **The positions of the robbers, one on the right and one on the left of Christ, represent the positions of Egypt and Babylon/Assyria relative to Judah.**

To the Jews, the Egyptians came from the south and the Assyrians and Babylonians from the north. Our maps show Assyria to the north-east of Jerusalem and Babylon almost to the east, but the Syrian desert lay between Mesopotamia and Judah. If you wished to travel from Babylon to Judah, you would not want to cross this desert. Instead, you would follow the fertile crescent, going first to the north, then west towards the coastal plain and then south to Jerusalem. So travellers and invading armies from Babylon or Assyria approached Judah from the north. It is clear from scripture that the Jews regarded Babylon as being to the north of them:[12]

Raise a standard toward Zion. Take refuge, stay not! For I am bringing disaster from the north, and great destruction. (Jeremiah 4:6)

> *Behold, I will send for all the tribes of the north, said Yahweh, and for*
> *Nebuchadnezzar, the king of Babylon, my servant... (Jeremiah 25:9)*

Now, a common way of representing direction was relative to a person facing east, as we find in Ezekiel:

> *And your elder sister is Samaria, who lived with her daughters to your*
> *left [north]; and your younger sister, who lived to your right [south], is*
> *Sodom with her daughters. (Ezekiel 16:46)*

The context of the passage shows that the left stands for the north and the right for the south. If a person faces east, north is to the left and south to the right. So the two robbers, one on the right and one on the left, are the two super-powers who crucified the kingdoms of Israel and Judah. Egypt is to the right (the south) and Babylon to the left (the north).

The walking, talking cross

> ➢ **A remarkable fragment from the original crucifixion account has**
> **survived embedded in the Gospel of Peter. This fragment shows**
> **Christ crucified by angels.**

The other three gospels followed the Gospel of Mark's account of the crucifixion by the Romans. The gospels became enormously popular and swept across the Jesus movement, replacing earlier literature and traditions. Only here and there do we get a glimpse of what came before. The crucifixion gems give us one such glimpse. Another comes from a remarkable survival; an account of the crucifixion by two angels rather than by the Romans. Over the years this text has attracted a great deal of scholarly attention, but its true nature has not previously been recognised.

The Gospel of Peter is one of those works excluded from the New Testament. The text is only known from a single incomplete copy found in the grave of a monk at Akhmim in Egypt. It can be dated to the second century.[13] The surviving portion starts with Pilate washing his hands at the trial of Jesus and ends with the resurrection account. Most of this gospel is secondary, based on Matthew and the other gospels. But there is one episode that has no parallel in the canonical gospels. It involves Jesus' resurrection along with a walking, talking cross.

Early Christians were desperate for any stories about Jesus beyond those in the gospels and a lively literary tradition developed to supply this need. One obvious gap was that no one had actually witnessed the moment of resurrection. In Mark, when the woman come to the tomb, they find the stone rolled away and a young man inside who tells them that Jesus has risen. The Matthew account follows the same pattern except that the women come across Jesus outside the tomb. The author of Matthew takes the opportunity of addressing some obvious flaws in the Mark account. To rebut the accusation that Jesus' disciples may have stolen his body, he adds a story in which the Jews arrange with Pilate for a watch to be placed on the tomb. The man who gives the women the message is now explicitly an angel, and the guards see him descend from heaven. However, they are bribed to lie and say that the disciples stole the body.[14]

Even with these elaborations, no one in Matthew witnesses the moment of Jesus' resurrection. The Gospel of Peter aims to fill this deficiency. In Peter, the guards see the heavens open, and two young men descend. The stone rolls away from the entrance and the two men enter the tomb. They come out with Jesus between them:

> ... they saw three men come out from the sepulchre, two of them sup-porting the other, and a cross following them, and the heads of the two reaching to heaven, but that of him that was being led reached beyond the heavens. And they heard a voice out of the heavens crying "Have you preached to them that sleep?", and from the cross there was heard the answer "Yes". (The Gospel of Peter 10:39-42)[15]

If you were making up an account of the resurrection, you would have Jesus appear in glorious form bathed in light, not led by two others like an invalid. You would certainly not include a walking, talking cross! This strangeness is a sign that the author of Peter has misunderstood his source. The story raises several questions:

- Why is the cross in the tomb with Jesus? People did not put crosses in tombs. The gospels say that Jesus' body was taken down from the cross and wrapped in a linen cloth before being placed in the tomb.[16]
- Why does the cross follow behind Jesus at his resurrection, and why does it appear to speak?
- Why should the cross and not Jesus preach "to those that sleep"?
- Why do the heads of the two men reach up to heaven and the head of Jesus reach even higher? Why are the men holding onto Jesus?

The two men are certainly angels. They both support Jesus so one must be on his left and one on his right. The height of their heads is an expression of their relative level in the divine hierarchy. In early Jewish belief, there were three heavens; the first, the lowest, was the earth's sky, and the third, the highest, the abode of Yahweh. The fallen angels were expelled from the highest heaven but dwelt above the earth as "the host of heaven", the stars. So they existed in the second heaven. This was a dangerous place that had a malign influence on the earth and would be destroyed at the end times. The two angels in the Gospel of Peter have heads which reach heaven, but which are far lower than Jesus' head. They belong in the lower, second heaven, whereas Jesus comes from a higher heaven.

The two angels are members of the host of heaven, the seventy. They are the two robber angels, one on each side of Jesus. They are not helping the resurrected Jesus but taking him to crucifixion. The author of the Gospel of Peter has access to the original crucifixion story which he does not understand. His source involved two angels, and he confuses them with the two angels in the Luke resurrection story. So he turns the crucifixion into the resurrection. With this realisation, everything makes sense:

- The cross is not in the tomb of Jesus, and it does not walk by itself. Jesus is carrying it on his back.
- The men are not supporting Jesus. They are guarding him, one on each side, and leading him to the place of execution.
- When the voice from heaven asks if he has preached to those who sleep, it is Jesus who answers. His voice comes from the cross because by this time the two angels have crucified him.

What is the meaning of the question *"Have you preached to them that sleep?"* There was an early tradition that Jesus descended to the under-world after his crucifixion to preach to the dead. But it is easy to confuse cause and effect. The story of Jesus preaching to the dead could be due to a misunderstanding of the Gospel of Peter source. Both the "dead" and the "sleeping" were metaphors used by the early Jesus movement for those who were spiritually dead/asleep. In the Animal Apocalypse, the sheep are described as having eyes closed, a state of spiritual blindness akin to sleeping. Jesus has come to give life, and to resurrect the dead. Originally the resurrection did not take place after physical death, but while the person was alive—it was the resurrection of the spirit. We can find the "dead" used in this metaphorical sense in the gospels. As Jesus says to a disciple who wishes to bury his father: *"Follow me, and let the dead bury the dead"* (Matthew 8:22). Jesus comes to the world to preach to the sleeping, the dead, to waken them, and resurrect them spiritually.

Jesus could only preach to the sleeping if he had come to earth before his crucifixion. Jesus must have been believed to have been physically present in the seventh generation of the seventh week in some form. We have already seen a hint of this in the song of the suffering servant in Isaiah. The crucifixion would have taken place on three levels:

- At the heavenly level, the divine Christ is crucified by the angelic rulers of Assyria/Babylon and Egypt.
- At the national level, Israel and Judah are destroyed by the angels' human avatars, the kings of Babylon/Assyria and Egypt.
- At the personal level, the human avatar of Christ is put to death.

The Gospel of Peter gives us a glimpse of the earliest form of the crucifixion account. The embedding of this fragment into a resurrection account has enabled its survival. Had it been recognised for what it is, a crucifixion of Jesus by two angels, it would undoubtedly have been condemned as heretical.

35

Death and the Temple

Jeconiah

Jeconiah represents the final day of the seventh week of the Almanac. As he scarcely ruled at all, why does he, rather than Zedekiah, mark the last day of Judah? Jeconiah, unlike Zedekiah, was a survivor. He lived to old age in Babylon among the exiled Judean elite after the destruction of Jerusalem. He was seen as their leader and the last hope of Judah. To preserve this hope it was necessary to regard him as the true king and interpret Zedekiah's failed reign as a type of regency. All future claimants to the throne of David would trace their descent through Jeconiah.

When Zerubbabel led the return to Jerusalem it seemed that the hope kept alive by Jeconiah might be realised. He was reputed to be related to the king, although Jeremiah says that Jeconiah had no descendants.[1] Whatever their relationship, Zerubbabel did not, in the event, lead to a return of the house of David. He was appointed as Persian governor of Judea, not as king. And he disappears abruptly from history, leaving no descendants to inherit his post.

The Deuteronomistic history ends with the release of Jeconiah from prison by the order of the new Babylonian King Evil-merodach. He had been captive since he was eighteen and had been imprisoned for thirty-seven years. This imprisonment was probably less severe than it sounds, something like house arrest. After his release he was assigned a place at the table above the other captive kings, and, as the author of Kings adds proudly, granted a daily allowance for the rest of his life. The house of David came to an end with a pension and a nice seat at the dinner table.[2]

The temple destroyed

> ➤ **The original timing of the crucifixion is visible through the Mark account.**

In the proto-crucifixion source, the final period would have started at noon, which is the sixth hour of the day. This timing is still evident in the gospel:

> *And when the sixth hour had arrived, there was darkness over all the land until the ninth hour. (Mark 15:33)*

The darkness was originally the dark of the moon that corresponded to the sabbath of sabbaths. The age of the Jews was twenty-eight Almanac days, exactly one lunar month. The moon is the merest sliver of a crescent on the day of Abraham, full at the reigns of David and Solomon, and dark on the sabbath of sabbaths. The darkness should last for the whole of 7.7, from 12 am to 6 pm; it should start at the sixth hour and end at the twelfth. The start time has been preserved in Mark, although the dark now ends at the ninth hour when Jesus dies.

> ➤ **The death of Jesus is simultaneous to the tearing of the temple veil. The author of Mark has substituted the veil for the destruction of the temple.**

Jesus calls out just before his death, quoting from Psalm 22:

> *And at the ninth hour, Jesus cried with a loud voice, "Eloi, Eloi, lema sabachthani?" which means, "My God, my God, why have you forsaken me?"*
> *And some of those standing by, having heard this, said, "Behold, He is calling Elijah." And one ran and filled a sponge with vinegar, and put it on a reed and gave it to him to drink, saying "Wait! Let us see if Elijah comes to take him down." (Mark 15:34-36)*

The reference to Elijah is intriguing. Why do the people think that Elijah will come and save Jesus? We will explore the confusion between Elijah and another figure later. Immediately after this, Jesus dies:

> *But Jesus uttered a loud cry and breathed his last. And the veil of the temple was torn into two from top to bottom. (Mark 15:37-38)*

The destruction of the temple is simultaneous to the death of the heavenly Christ in the original myth. The author of Mark has the problem that the temple is very obviously still standing during the governorship of Pontius Pilate. So he represents the temple destruction by the tearing in two of the veil which divided the holy of holies from the holy place.

This miracle is absurd on many levels. Buildings can collapse, wood can split, a stone wall can crack in two, but how can a curtain spontaneously tear into two? Rotten cloth might disintegrate, but the curtain was a major feature of a temple on which enormous wealth and care were lavished. And why does no one outside the gospels mention such a miracle? This was a superstitious age when anything slightly odd that happened to a temple or statue of a god would become widely known and interpreted as a sign. How would it be possible for the spontaneous splitting of the main curtain in one of the ancient world's most famous and most visited temples go unremarked by Jewish commentators, such as Josephus, or pagan historians, such as Tacitus? Surely the Jews would have long remembered such an event in their commentaries and writings?

The tearing of the curtain is an invention of the author of Mark. The holy of holies was the place where the divine presence dwelt; the tearing of the veil signified that the presence of God had left the temple. The departure of the presence is described in Ezekiel:

> *Then the glory of Yahweh departed from the threshold of the temple and stood above the cherubim. As I watched, the cherubim lifted up their wings and mounted up from the ground, with the wheels beside them. And they stood at the door of the east gate of the house of Yahweh, with the glory of the God of Israel above them. (Ezekiel 10:18-19)*

The presence leaves Jerusalem and settles over the Mount of Olives:

> *And the glory of Yahweh rose up from within the city and stopped over the mountain east of the city. (Ezekiel 11:23)*

The glory will ascend to heaven from the Mount of Olives, and Jesus ascends from the same mountain after his resurrection. But this Ezekiel account is about the first temple. The divine presence, the angel of the Name, leaves this temple before its final destruction by the Babylonians. The tearing of the veil symbolises the departure of God from the temple. The author of Mark has placed this event in the wrong time frame; in the first century rather than 586 BC.

> Jesus is said to have prophesied the destruction of the temple.
> These prophecies relate to the first temple.

At his first trial, Jesus is said to have predicted that he would destroy the temple:

> *"We heard him say, 'I will destroy this temple that is made with hands,*
> *and in three days I will build another, not made with hands.'" (Mark*
> *14:58)*

The accusation is repeated when Jesus is on the cross. This story is also found in Matthew.[3] In John, the prediction that he will raise the temple in three days comes directly from Jesus, although he does not say that he will destroy it.[4] The Thomas version is rather different:

> *Jesus said: "I will des[troy this] house, and none shall be able to build*
> *it [again]." (Thomas 71; TC 4.17)*

This gives us a version of the saying independent of the gospels. "House" was a common term for the temple and is used with this meaning in the Animal Apocalypse. The Thomas saying denies the validity of the second temple, again in agreement with the Animal Apocalypse. The gospel version goes further and says that the temple will be rebuilt, but not by hands, within three days. This new temple would have originally been the apocalyptic temple that descends to the earth at the end of times, as it does in the Animal Apocalypse. But in the Jesus movement of the first century, the new temple was reinterpreted. Jesus would not dwell in a building but in a person; the Magdalene, and beyond her, all spiritual Christians.

There is another place in Mark in which Jesus predicts the destruction of the temple:

> *Jesus said, "Do you see all these great buildings? There shall not be left*
> *one stone upon another, that will not be thrown down." (Mark 13:2)*

The Babylonian destruction of the first temple fits this prediction much better than the Roman destruction of the temple of Herod. The first temple was destroyed utterly along with the city of Jerusalem. An accidental fire destroyed the temple of Herod, but much of the temple complex remained standing. The original prediction of the destruction of the first temple has been applied by the author of Mark to the second temple so that Jesus can be shown as predicting the coming Roman destruction.

In scripture, the destruction of the temple is commanded by Yahweh and carried out by the Babylonians. The early Jesus movement shifted the responsibility onto Jesus, who orders the destruction before his crucifixion. The temple of stone was appropriate as a dwelling place for the angel of the Name. But the coming spiritual kingdom of Christ will need no such building.

The crucifixion day as seventh Almanac great day

This completes our treatment of the crucifixion day. The burial did not belong to the proto-crucifixion account and will be considered in the next volume. Figure 10 gives an overview of how the seventh Almanac great day translates into the passion day in Mark.

We can summarise the evidence that the passion day has been derived from the Almanac. Among other things, it explains the following points:

Why the passion day is divided into three-hour segments.

Why there are three betrayals before cock-crow.

The short length of the crucifixion of just six hours.

Why Matthew and Luke suppress the 9 am start of the crucifixion in Mark, and why John places the crucifixion at noon.

The leper house Jesus attends before the last day.

The significance of the place name Gethsemane.

Why the disciples fall asleep while keeping watch.

The cup which Jesus must drink.

The severed ear of the high priest's servant.

The young man who has his sheet pulled off and flees naked.

Why Judas hands over Jesus at Gethsemane.

The significance of the name Judas Iscariot.

Why Judas is paid thirty pieces of silver and why it should be flung down into the temple.

Why Judas dies after betraying Jesus.

The potter's field.

Why Judas falls down in the field and bursts open.

Why the Sanhedrin meet at night.

Why Jesus is found guilty of blasphemy for acknowledging he is the son.

Why Pilate wants to free Jesus.

The significance of Barabbas whom the Jews choose over Jesus.

The crown of thorns.

Why Jesus' cross is carried by a father with two sons.

Why there is a robber on the left and right of Jesus at the crucifixion.
The walking, talking cross in the Gospel of Peter.
The prediction by Jesus that he will destroy the temple and build one without hands in three days.
The splitting of the temple veil when Jesus dies.

These correspondences are not general in nature, but very specific. The clues lead us back to the same place, the Judas War.

Seventh great day to Mark's passion day

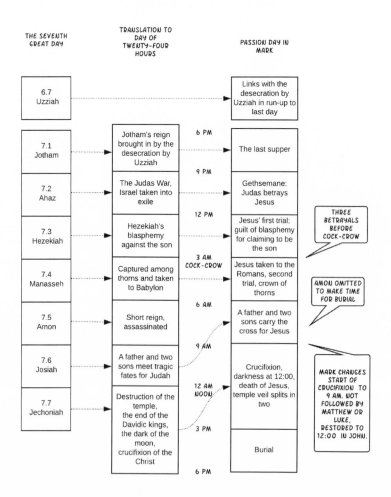

Figure 10: Translation of Almanac seventh day to Mark's passion day.

PART FIVE

THE CHILD OF SEVEN DAYS

36

The Child of Seven Days

Enoch

In the Gospel of Thomas there is a saying about a "child of seven days":

> *Jesus said: "The man aged in days will not hesitate to ask a little child of seven days about the place of life, and he will live. For many who are first shall become last and they will become a single one." (Thomas 4; TC 1.3)*

In *The Thomas Code* I show how the second half of this saying has a riddle meaning that only makes sense in the context of the structure of the gospel.[1] The Thomas sayings carry multiple levels of meaning, with the riddle level being the most superficial. When the Gospel of Thomas was assembled, existing sayings were adjusted or reconfigured to fit in with the structure. In this case, the second half has been conjoined with the first which would originally have stood alone:

> *The man aged in days will not hesitate to ask a little child of seven days about the place of life, and he will live.*

What does it mean? A baby boy was circumcised on the eighth day, so scholars interpret the saying as representing an innocent child before circumcision. But old men do not ask anything of new-born babies nor learn anything from them. The Gospel of Thomas is cleverer than its interpreters and is playing its usual games with us. To solve this problem, we need the Almanac.

➢ **The child of seven days is Enoch.**

The Almanac days are generations. The "child of seven days" is a person associated with the seventh day or generation of the Almanac, the day assigned to Enoch. We have seen how the parable of the tenants has two servants, Noah and Moses, who were both regarded as angels. But there is one figure more important to the apocalyptic movement than even Noah and Moses, and that is Enoch. We would expect Enoch to be preeminent to the proto-Christians, but so far he has played little part in the Christ myth. There is, however, one feature of the Almanac which gives us a strong clue as to his importance.

> **Enoch at the first sabbath is symmetrical to the resurrected Jesus on the first reverse sabbath. The ascent of Enoch is described in near-identical terms to the return of the resurrected Son of Man.**

We have already seen that the position of Enoch in the Almanac, on day 1.7, the first sabbath, is symmetrical with the resurrection of Jesus at 10.1, the first reverse sabbath (see Figure 7). Moreover, the ascent of Enoch is described in very similar terms to the resurrection of the Son of Man in Mark.

The ascent of Enoch:

> *And behold I saw the clouds: And they were calling me in a vision: and the fogs were calling me; and the course of the stars and the lightnings were rushing to me and causing me to desire; and in the vision, the winds were causing me to fly and rushing me high up to heaven. (1 Enoch 14:8)*[2]

The return of Jesus as the Son of Man in Mark:

> *And Jesus said, "I am, and you will see the Son of Man sitting at the right hand of power, and coming with the clouds of heaven." (Mark 14:62)*

> **Enoch is the Son of Man and an identity of the Christ.**

The implications are startling and unavoidable. Enoch must be the "Son of Man", and he must be the same as the Christ. This is what the Almanac, and the description of the resurrection of Jesus, is telling us. The title "the Son of Man" which Jesus adopts in the gospels is a deliberate contrast to his other title "the Son of God". The seventy are also sons of God. But Christ is separate from the seventy; he alone is also the Son of Man, meaning he is both human and divine.

> The man "aged in days" is the lower Yahweh, the angel of the Name. He learns about the secret plan of the higher Yahweh from Enoch/Christ.

If the child of seven days is Enoch, then the only possibility for the man "aged in days" is the lower Yahweh, the owner of the vineyard. The old man asks "about the place of life", and will live. This means that the child has knowledge that the lower Yahweh does not possess. Once the child tells him the secret, he will be saved. The aged man is good, not evil, but limited in his understanding. Unlike his seventy sons, he will be redeemed.

This only makes sense if Enoch, the Christ, was believed to be the son of the higher Yahweh, born before time, before the angel of the Name was created. In the first account of the creation in Genesis, Adam is made in the image of God. So the Son of Man partakes of the nature of God, whereas the angels were mere created beings.

> The meeting between the child and the old man is equivalent to Enoch's audience with God.

In the Book of the Watchers, Enoch ascends to heaven and meets God. There is a description of Yahweh in the throne room:

> *And the Great Glory was sitting upon it—as for his gown, which was shining more brightly than the sun, it was whiter than any snow. None of the angels was able to come in and see the face of the Excellent and the Glorious One; and no one of the flesh can see him—the flaming fire was around him, and a great fire stood before him. No one could come near unto him from among those that surrounded the tens of millions (that stood) before him. He needed no council. (1 Enoch 14:20-23)*[3]

Neither angel nor flesh can look upon the divine presence. When Enoch comes before him, he prostrates himself, but God tells him to rise and approach. Enoch's eyes are still cast down, "but he raised me". Enoch does what is supposed to be impossible and looks upon God. When Moses sees Yahweh, he only sees his back because the sight of the face of God is too intense for humans to stand. Only Enoch can see him face to face.

Enoch is raised above all humans in the Book of Enoch, but there is no suggestion that God has learnt from him. Yet the origins of this heretical idea are present in the above passage. It says that none can approach God and that he needed "no council" or "no counsellor". However, Enoch does approach God and looks upon him. Is Enoch then a counsellor of God?

Such a concept requires Yahweh to be split into a higher and lower God, a development made by the proto-Christians, but not by the authors of the Book of the Watchers.

> ➢   **In the Book of Daniel, there is another version of the throne room meeting. In Daniel's vision, Yahweh is called "the Ancient of Days" and Enoch "the Son of Man". This Son of Man is the Christ figure who will rule the eternal kingdom at the end of time.**

The Book of Daniel gives a vision of four beasts who represent four empires. In the vision, a judgement is pronounced on the fourth beast:

> *I watched until thrones were set in place, and the Ancient of Days was seated. His garment was white as snow, and the hair of his head like pure wool. His throne was flaming fire, and its wheels were blazing fire. A river of fire was flowing, coming forth from before him. Thousands upon thousands attended him, and myriads upon myriads stood before him. The court was seated and the books were opened. (Daniel 7:9-10)*

This is clearly the heavenly law court. The language is very similar to the meeting between Enoch and Yahweh in the Book of the Watchers. Yahweh is now called the Ancient of Days. The name Enoch is not mentioned, but there is one present "like the Son of Man":

> *And I saw one like a Son of Man coming with the clouds of heaven. He approached the Ancient of Days and was led into his presence. And there was given to him dominion, glory, and kingship, that all nations, and peoples, and languages should serve him. His dominion is an everlasting dominion that will not pass away, and his kingdom is one that shall not be destroyed. (Daniel 7:13-14)*

Obviously, the person who comes with the clouds of heaven is Enoch who must be the "one like a Son of Man". But this means that Enoch has the role of Christ. He rules an eternal kingdom of all the nations and peoples of the earth. All of which confirms what we have already deduced. We have the following equations:

The man aged in days
= Yahweh
= the Ancient of Days

The child of seven days
= Enoch
= the Son of Man
= the Christ

For the proto-Christians, the Ancient of Days is the lower Yahweh, the angel of the Name. This is the inevitable conclusion from the child of seven days saying, but it is not explicit in either Daniel or Enoch.

The Similitudes

> **The Similitudes of Enoch includes a version of the meeting of the Ancient of Days (the Head of Days) and the Son of Man.**

The Ancient of Days appears also in the Similitudes of Enoch, which only survives in an Ethiopic translation within the Book of Enoch. He is called by a name that can be translated variously as "the Head of Days" or "the First of Days" or "the Antecedent of Time". Transmission of ancient texts through the Ethiopian church was subject to similar issues as transmission through the European churches. In places, the material would be subject to revision and editing to make it more acceptable. Such revisions may account for the confused nature of the Similitudes.

Unlike the other components of the Book of Enoch, no fragment of the Similitudes has been found at Qumran, suggesting that the Similitudes are more recent than other parts of Enoch. The scholarly consensus is for a date in the first century, although there continues to be wide uncertainty.[4] It would thus seem that the Similitudes originate from around the same time as the Jesus movement and provide a glimpse of the apocalyptic movement in parallel to the Jesus movement. Like the Jesus movement, the Similitudes has an "Elect One", the Messiah, who will rule the world after the day of judgement.

The Similitudes start with Enoch recounting how he was taken up to heaven and observed the mysteries of heaven. Enoch sees the Elect One and is brought into the presence of the "Lord of the Spirits" (God) and shown all the hidden things. The "Head of Days" is introduced in identical terms to the Ancient of Days in Daniel (translations in this section by E. Isaac[5]):

> *At that place, I saw the One to whom belongs the time before time. And his head was white like wool, and there was with him another individual, whose face was like that of a human being. His countenance was full of grace, like that of one among the holy angels. (1 Enoch 46:1)*

Enoch asks about the one who is "born of human beings" and is told he is the "Son of Man" and that he will "reveal the hidden treasures". The Son of Man will "remove the kings and the mighty ones from their seats" and "loosen the reigns of the strong".[6]

Much of this is dependent on Daniel. The Son of Man in the Similitudes is equivalent to Christ for the Jesus movement. There are fountains of wisdom that the holy ones drink and become filled with wisdom after which they dwell with the elect ones.[7] The Lord of the Spirits gives the Son of Man a name:

> ...*even before the creation of the sun and the moon, before the creation of the stars, he was given a name in the presence of the Lord of the Spirits. (1 Enoch 48:3)*

Unfortunately, we are not told what this name is! The Similitudes goes on to call the Son of Man "the light of the gentiles" a title also applied to Jesus.[8] He has been hidden since before the beginning of time:

> *For this purpose he became the Chosen One; he was concealed in the presence of (the Lord of the Spirits) prior to the creation of the world and for eternity. (1 Enoch 48:6)*

He is explicitly called the Messiah or Christ of the Lord of the Spirits.[9] All of which shows that the author of the Similitudes saw the Son of Man as Christians see Christ.

In all this Enoch is clearly not the same as the Son of Man or the Elect One. The author of the main body of the Similitudes regards the Son of Man as Christ, and certainly does not think that Enoch is the same as Christ. But there is evidence that Enoch was indeed the Son of Man in the source which the author is using. For there is a second version of the meeting between Enoch and God in the Similitudes.

➢ **Enoch is the Son of Man in the second version of the meeting between Enoch and the Head of Days.**

The account of the Son of Man and the Head of Days above has been inserted into an original account of Enoch's journey to heaven. The Head of Days comes from a different source from the Lord of the Spirits who represents God in most other parts of the Similitudes. Towards the end of the Similitudes, there is a repetition of the meeting between Enoch and the Head of Days. In this second version, Enoch is called the Son of Man.

This second version starts with the spirit of Enoch being translated to heaven and seeing the "holy sons of God".[10] Michael shows him the secrets of heaven before he is translated spiritually into the "heaven of heavens", described in terms similar to the Book of the Watchers as a structure of crystal surrounded by fire. There he sees the angels and the Head of Days:

> *With them is the Antecedent of Time [Head of Days]: His head is white and pure like wool and his garment is indescribable. I fell on my face, my whole body mollified and my spirit transformed. Then I cried with a great voice by the spirit of power, blessing, glorifying and extolling.* (1 Enoch 71:10-11)

The Head of Days is pleased with Enoch's blessings, and he appoints Enoch as the Son of Man:

> *Then the Antecedent of Time [Head of Days] came with Michael, Gabriel, Raphael, Phanuel, and a hundred thousand and ten million times a hundred thousand angels that are countless. Then an angel [or "he"] came to me and greeted me and said to me: "You, son of man who art born in righteousness, and upon whom righteousness has dwelt, the righteousness of the Antecedent of Time [Head of Days] will not forsake you."* (1 Enoch 71:13-14)

The texts differ here; it is either the Head of Days himself or an angel who is addressing Enoch. Another issue is that the word for "man" in the "son of man" is different here from other places in the Similitudes.[11] Although the Ethiopian church venerated Enoch, the idea that he was the same as the Christ (the Son of Man) would have been heretical. So we should not be surprised that the translators attempted to avoid this suggestion.

If we compare the passage with the equivalent in 1 Enoch 46, there can be no doubt that Enoch is indeed called the Son of Man here. The introduction of the Son of Man in the above passage is almost identical to the earlier version:

> Version 1: *"This is the Son of Man to whom belongs righteousness, with whom righteousness dwells."* (1 Enoch 46:3).

> Version 2: *"You, son of man who art born in righteousness, and upon whom righteousness has dwelt"* (1 Enoch 71:14)

Compare also to an expression for Enoch in the Book of the Watchers:

> *Book of the Watchers: "Do not fear Enoch, righteous man, scribe of*
> *righteousness" (1 Enoch 15:1).*

The continuation of the second version makes it clear that Enoch is the Son of Man:

> *He shall proclaim peace to you in the name of the world that is to*
> *become. For from here proceeds peace since the creation of the world,*
> *and so it shall be unto you forever and ever and ever. Everyone that*
> *shall come to exist and walk shall (follow) your path since righ-*
> *teousness never forsakes you. Together with you will shall be their*
> *dwelling-places; and together with you shall be their portion. They*
> *shall not be separated from you forever and ever and ever. (1 Enoch*
> *71:15-16)*

We can conclude that two closely related versions of the meeting between the Ancient of Days and the Son of Man have been incorporated into the Similitudes as two separate episodes. In one version, the Son of Man is explicitly named as Enoch, and in the other, he is not.

The child of seven days in Luke

> ➤ **The child of seven days saying has given rise to the Luke story of**
> **the presentation of the baby Jesus in the temple.**

The author of Luke shows awareness of the child of seven days saying and seems to know that it related to the presentation of Jesus to Yahweh. In Luke, it gives rise to the story of the presentation of the baby Jesus in the temple:

> *When the eight days were completed for his circumcision, he was*
> *named Jesus, the name given him by the angel before he had been*
> *conceived. And when the days of purification according to the law of*
> *Moses were completed, they brought him to Jerusalem to present to the*
> *Lord. (Luke 2:21-2)*

The author of Luke adheres to the traditional Jewish timing of events around birth but starts the episode immediately after the child has reached the age of seven days. A Jewish woman would be unclean for seven days after the birth of a boy, and the child would be circumcised on the eighth. Then after a further thirty-three days, the woman would offer a sacrifice at the temple.[12] It is only Luke that mentions the circumcision of Jesus or the purification or the offering in the temple.

A Jewish baby boy did not, in fact, have to be presented to the Lord in the temple. The first-born of every womb, whether human or animal, if male, belonged to Yahweh. Originally this meant that a first-born boy had to be offered as a burnt sacrifice. But child sacrifice had long since been abandoned, and a male child was automatically redeemed by payment of a five-shekel priestly tax. It was the mother who had to go to the temple to be purified by offering two doves (if poor) or a dove and a lamb (if a little richer) as sacrifices.

The story of Jesus' presentation in the temple is fictional but based upon an existing source. The temple on earth corresponded to the throne room in the third heaven. So the baby Jesus presented to Yahweh in the temple is equivalent to the child of seven days meeting Yahweh in heaven. There is an old man Simeon waiting in the temple for Jesus:

> *And behold, there was a man in Jerusalem whose name was Simeon, and this man was righteous and devout waiting for the consolation of Israel, and the holy spirit was upon him. It had been revealed to him through the holy spirit that he would not see death before he should see the Lord's Christ. And he came in the spirit into the temple, and when the parents brought in the child Jesus to do for him what was customary under the law, Simeon took him in his arms and blessed God, saying "Now Lord dismiss your servant in peace according to your word. For my eyes have seen your salvation that you have prepared before the face of all the people, a light of revelation for the gentiles and a glory of your people Israel." (Luke 2:25-32)*

There are several links here with the child of seven days saying. Simeon is "aged in days". It has been promised that he will not die until he has seen the "consolation of Israel", so like the old man in the saying, "he will live". When he sees the baby, he understands that he has seen God's salvation. This is all parallel to the saying; an old man encounters a baby so that he understands "the place of life" and will live.

➢ **The Valentinian gnostics equated Simeon with the lower Yahweh. They thought that he had learnt about his true place in the divine hierarchy when he encountered the baby Jesus, and so departed in peace.**

We know that some early Christians did indeed recognise that Simeon stood for the lower Yahweh and that when he met the child, he was enlightened about the secrets of the ultimate God. Irenaeus writing in about 180 AD tells us so much in his hostile report on the Valentinian gnostics:

> They say, too, that Simeon, "who took Christ into his arms, and gave thanks to God, and said, Lord, now let you your servant depart in peace, according to your word," was a type of the Demiurge, who, on the arrival of the Saviour, learned his own change of place, and gave thanks to Bythus. (Irenaeus Against Heresies 1:8:16)[13]

The Demiurge is the gnostic understanding of the lower Yahweh. So Simeon stands for the lower Yahweh who learns about his true place in the divine scheme when he encounters the Christ child. Which ties in perfectly with the child of seven days saying.

The child of seven days in John

➢   **The episode of Nicodemus meeting Jesus in the Gospel of John is also based upon the "child of seven days" saying.**

Near the beginning of the Gospel of John, there is an unexpectedly friendly meeting between Jesus and a Pharisee. Although Jesus has just created a disturbance in the temple, Nicodemus, a member of the Sanhedrin, comes to him secretly at night to learn more. Nicodemus is surprised when Jesus tells him that he must be reborn:

> Jesus replied, "Truly, truly, I tell you, no one is able to see the kingdom of God unless he is born from above."
> Nicodemus said to him, "How can a man be born when he is old? Can he enter his mother's womb a second time to be born?"
> Jesus answered, "Truly, truly, I tell you, unless he is born of water and the spirit no one can enter the kingdom of God." (John 3:3-5)

There are several connections here to the "child of seven days" saying.

1.   Nicodemus is "aged in days".

     Nicodemus is called a Pharisee and a "ruler of the people" meaning a member of the Sanhedrin. This implies that he was an elder, over fifty, and this is confirmed by his asking Jesus how an "old man" can be reborn again.

2. Nicodemus questions Jesus who tells him the secrets of the kingdom.

   Nicodemus comes to Jesus at night to ask him questions, and Jesus
   enlightens him with the secrets of the kingdom of God. There is a
   strong suggestion that Nicodemus becomes a follower of Jesus; he
   speaks later in Jesus' defence.[14] So Nicodemus, like the man "aged
   in days", comes to Jesus, asks him questions and is saved.

3. Jesus tells Nicodemus he must become like a new-born baby to see
   the kingdom.

   The reference to the new-born baby provides an obvious link with
   the "child of seven days".

If Nicodemus is the "man aged in days" then Jesus must be the "child
of seven days". However, in this story, Jesus is a full-grown man, so how
can he also be a new-born baby?

➤ **The author of John regarded baptism as rebirth. Jesus is a "child
of seven days" counting from his baptism to the meeting with
Nicodemus.**

In John, one is reborn by the descent of the spirit. There is no nativity in
this gospel and the first time we see Jesus is when the spirit descends
upon him from heaven, as vouched for by the testimony of John the
Baptist. To the author of John, this is the key moment; Jesus has been
reborn from above.

The section from the introduction of John the Baptist to the conversation with Nicodemus, mentions the passage of days several times which
is not at all typical of the gospel. The author of John goes out of his way to
note the passing of time in this one place. Taking the baptism day as the
zero point, we can calculate the number of days to other events:

Baptism -1 day: The priests and Pharisees come to question John the
Baptist. (John 1:19-28)

Baptism = 0 day: "The next day" John sees Jesus approach. The Baptist
sees the spirit descend from heaven like a dove and settle on Jesus. (John
1:29-34)

Baptism +1 day: "The next day" John sees Jesus again and points him
out to some of his disciples. As a result, Jesus recruits his first disciples.
(John 1:35-42)

Baptism +2 days: "The next day" Jesus heads off to Galilee and recruits more disciples. (John 1:43-51)

Baptism +3 days: "On the third day" the wedding takes place at Cana. Jesus turns water into wine. (John 2:1-11)

Baptism +4 /5 days: Jesus goes to Capernaum with his mother and brothers and his disciples, and stays there "not many days". (John 2:12)

Baptism +6/7 days: The Passover was near, so Jesus goes to Jerusalem. He cleanses the temple of the merchants and money changers. While Jesus is at Jerusalem for the Passover, many people see the signs he is doing and believe in him. Nicodemus, the Pharisee, is one of these people and comes to Jesus at night. (John 2:13-23; 3:1-21)

The sequence from the baptism to the temple is based on what I have called the "Deep Source"; an account of the appearance of Jesus to the shaman. The baptism, the wedding, the visit to Capernaum, and the expulsion from the temple all come from the Deep Source. The author of John has to fit these into a single week so that Jesus can meet with Nicodemus after seven days. Inevitably the timescale gets squashed. In reality, it would be difficult, although not impossible, for Jesus to have done all the things assigned for the week. As the author of John progresses through his narrative, he realises the problem and the timings get increasingly vague.

According to the above schedule, seven complete days have elapsed from Jesus' baptism to his meeting with Nicodemus at night. So Jesus can indeed be called "the child of seven days".

➢ **Jesus implies that he is Enoch.**

When Nicodemus expresses doubt at the idea of rebirth, Jesus continues:

> "Truly, truly, I say to you, we speak of what we know, and testify to what we have seen, but you do not receive our testimony. If I have spoken to you of earthly things and you do not believe, how can you believe if I speak to you of heavenly things? No one has ascended into heaven except he who descended from heaven, the Son of Man who is in heaven." (John 3: 11-13)

The one who has come down from heaven is the same as the one who has gone up to heaven—he is the Son of Man in heaven. This means that Jesus must be one of the two individuals who were believed to have ascended to heaven; Enoch or Elijah. The connection with the Son of Man narrows this down to Enoch. Jesus can testify about heavenly things because the Son of Man has dwelt in heaven; all of which fits Enoch perfectly.

So in this passage, we are told that Jesus, the Son of Man, is the same as Enoch. And this is expressed in a story which uses the "child of seven days" saying as its source.

The place of life

➢ **Some gnostic texts show knowledge of the "child of seven days"
saying because Yahweh is educated about "the place of life".**

In the Thomas saying the man aged in days asks the child about "the place of life". There is evidence that some gnostics were aware of this curious expression. Although the demiurge is generally evil in gnostic mythology, the figure of Sabaoth represents the Jewish God in a positive aspect. In On the Origin of the World, Sophia takes Sabaoth up to the seventh heaven. There she gives him a companion, her daughter Zoe meaning "Life", and instructs him about the eighth heaven.[15] The description of his throne as a four-faced chariot makes it very clear that Sabaoth is the Jewish Yahweh. In the same passage, he creates the seventy-two gods/angels to rule the seventy-two languages or nations. So here we have a "good" lower Yahweh dwelling with Zoe, Life, as his companion and learning the secrets of the heavens.

The same story is repeated in the Hypostasis of the Archons, and this time it is more explicit about the role of Zoe:

> *And Sophia took her daughter Zoe and had her sit upon his right to teach him about the things that exist in the eighth (heaven). (Hypostasis of the Archons, NHC II (4) 95:31-34)*

So it is Zoe (Life) who is educating Sabaoth about the eighth heaven. As in the "child of seven days" saying, Sabaoth is learning about the "place of life" and will live.

Two powers in heaven

There were a number of other books of Enoch, two of which survive: the so-called second and third books of Enoch. Both are difficult to date but were written centuries later than 1 Enoch. Neither is Christian in an orthodox sense. The book of 3 Enoch belongs to the Jewish school of

Merkabah mysticism. The adepts of this school would attempt the hazardous ascent to heaven to look upon the chariot of God. The work claims to record the journey to heaven of the Palestinian scholar Rabbi Ishmael who died before the year 132. It actually comes from long after his time, although it does preserve some early elements and traditions.[16]

The book starts with R. Ishmael ascending to the height. He passes through six heavens, one inside the other, until he comes to the door of the seventh. The angel who guards the seventh heaven would destroy him, but he calls on the Lord to save him. The angel Metatron comes to his rescue and takes R. Ismael into the seventh heaven leading him to the chariot and throne of the Holy One. The seraphim begin to gaze at him, but their bright light is unbearable to R. Ishmael, and the Holy One asks them to look away. The gates of Sekinah, the divine presence, are opened, and R. Ismael is enlightened.

Not all the inhabitants of heaven accept that R. Ishmael has the right to be there. Those guarding the chariot call Metatron "youth" and ask him why one born of woman has been allowed to approach God. He replies that R. Ishmael is of the tribe of Israel which was chosen of the seventy nations to be the people of the Holy One. Moreover, he belongs to the tribe of Levi and is descendant of Aaron the first high priest. R. Ismael is being designated as a high priest who can be admitted to the divine presence.

Metatron plays a similar role here to Michael in the story of Enoch's ascension to heaven. But Metatron is far above Michael in 3 Enoch. Although Michael is the senior of the seven angels in charge of the seven heavens, angel after angel is placed above these seven, so that Michael is about as exalted as a small-town clerk. And the most powerful angel, above all others, is Metatron.

When R. Ismael asks Metatron *"What is your name?"* he replies *"I have seventy names corresponding to the seventy nations"* (3 Enoch 3:2). Each of these names is based on the name of God, but he adds "my King calls me youth". The seventy names indicate that Metatron is Lord of the seventy nations and of the seventy angels who rule over them. We have seen that the seventy (or seventy-two) angelic rulers occur quite explicitly in 3 Enoch. When R. Ismael asks Metatron why he is called "youth" even though he is above all the angels, he gives a shocking reply:

"Because I am Enoch the son of Jared" (3 Enoch 4:2)

The identification of Metatron as Enoch is shattering. Not only has Enoch been taken up to heaven, but he has been placed in charge of the heavenly host. When Enoch was appointed to this position, three angels challenged his ascension, telling God that the ancient ones were right to advise him not to create man. This reflects a rabbinical legend about the Lord asking the first-created angels about his intention to create man and destroying them when they told him not to. The same happened to a second set of angels until a third set allowed man to be created.[17] In 3 Enoch, God tells the three angels that he has chosen Enoch to rule over them, and they then prostrate themselves before Enoch.[18]

Metatron tells R. Ismael that they call him "youth" (*naar*) because he was created after all the angels. The word can be applied to a range of ages from young men to babies. It could also mean "servant", which some see as the original meaning; that Metatron started as a servant of Yahweh, and only became the "youth", Enoch, in a later reinterpretation of the title.[19] However, the child of seven days saying is earlier than any source for Metatron and shows that "youth" must indeed be the original meaning. Enoch is apparently created in the seventh generation, long after the morning stars, the sons of God, but is actually older than all the angels. According to proto-Christian belief, Enoch/Christ came from the ultimate God and was prepared before time, before even the angel of the Name was made.

In 3 Enoch, Yahweh brought Enoch to heaven on the wings of the Sekinah, the divine presence, which was withdrawn from the earth at this time: *"This one who I have taken is my sole reward from my whole world under heaven" (3 Enoch 6:3)*. The withdrawal of the Sekinah on the first sabbath, ahead of the flood, matches its removal from the temple on the sabbath of sabbaths.

After his ascension, Enoch is enlarged to be the width and breadth of the world and given seventy-two wings, symbolising his kingship over the nations. The Holy One enthrones him in the seventh heaven and announces that Metatron has been appointed as prince and ruler over all the occupants of heaven. An exception is made for the eight great princes, but this is probably a later addition from the hand of a scribe shocked by the powers granted to Metatron. God reveals all secrets to Enoch/Metatron, the mysteries of Wisdom and the perfect Torah. All men's thoughts and deeds are revealed to him: *"before a man thinks in secret I see his thought, before he acts I see his act" (3 Enoch 11:3)*. The Holy One has a majestic robe fashioned set with brilliant luminaries, and he wraps this robe around Metatron. He takes a crown with forty-nine stones shining like the sun:

> He set it upon my head and he called me, "The lessor YHWH" in the presence of his whole household in the height, as it is written "My name is in him". (3 Enoch 12:5)

After his enthronement Enoch is transformed into a creature of fire:

> "*my flesh turned to flame, my sinews to blazing fire, my bones to juni-*
> *per coals, my eyelashes to lightning flashes, my eyeballs to fiery torches*
> *…" (3 Enoch 15:1).*

Metatron then serves at the throne of glory and the wheels of the chariot. Jesus also was a Seraph, a fiery creature serving at the chariot and
throne.

> ➤ **In the Christian version of the myth, Enoch/Christ is above the**
> **lower Yahweh. In the Jewish version of the same myth, Enoch/**
> **Metatron becomes the lower Yahweh, the angel of the Name.**

The elevation of Enoch is extraordinary. In the original myth, Enoch must
have been enthroned equal to Yahweh. To Christians, Enoch/Christ comes
from a higher reality and educates the lower Yahweh, before replacing
him as king over all heaven and earth. Something like this is behind the
Jewish version also. But the Jews naturally rejected the idea that any being
could be above Yahweh. So Enoch is equated with the lower Yahweh, the
angel of the Name. This is clear from his title "the lesser YHWH" and "my
Name is in him".

> ➤ **Orthodox rabbis rejected the idea that Metatron was on a level**
> **with Yahweh. They regarded it as a false belief introduced by the**
> **heretical rabbi Elisha/Aher.**

The idea of an angel bearing the name of Yahweh and ruling jointly
with him was regarded with great suspicion by the rabbis. That this
angel should be Enoch, transformed into Metatron, and made level with
Yahweh, was scandalous. We can find the signs of fierce disagreement in
3 Enoch itself, where an added story diminishes Metatron.[20] According
to this story, Metatron was sat on a throne in the seventh heaven, judging
all the denizens of heaven when Aher ascended. Aher, astounded at this
sight, exclaims: *"There are indeed two powers in heaven!"*. At this blasphemy,
a voice comes from the Sekinah saying *"Come back to me my apostate sons,
apart from Aher!"* (3 Enoch 16:4). Metatron is given sixty lashes of fire and
made to stand to demonstrate the falseness of Aher's assertion.

The purpose of the story is theological, to counter the "two powers in
heaven" heresy. Metatron is shown as being subject to Yahweh and by no
means his equal. His right to remain enthroned and seated in the seventh
heaven is removed. Aher (meaning "other") is a derogatory name given

by the rabbis to Elisha b. Abuya, a Palestinian scholar of the later first and early second centuries. Elisha was despised by the mainstream rabbis and was the brunt of many stories aimed against the "two powers in heaven" heresy.

In the rabbinical version of the story, four rabbis, Simeon b. Zoma, Simeon b. Azzai, Elisha and Akiba attempt to make the journey to Pardes (paradise). Only Akiba returns unscathed; b. Zoma dies, and b. Azzai goes mad. As for Elisha, he sees Metatron seated, writing down the merits of Israel, and exclaims "God forbid! There are two divinities!" Because Metatron did not stand, and so gave a mistaken impression to Elisha, he is given sixty fiery lashes. When Elisha returns to earth, he becomes a heretic. The purpose of these stories is to demote the myth as heresy associated with Elisha. The rabbis do not question that he actually made the journey to heaven and saw Metatron there, but they use the stories to explain that he misunderstood the meaning of the vision.[21]

From all this we can deduce that there was a strong tradition that Elisha b. Abuya had journeyed to heaven and seen two powers in heaven. Elisha became so notorious that he could not even be named directly. Is it a coincidence that the mystic journey of Elisha is remarkably similar to the journeys to heaven made by members of the early Jesus movement?

The Three Identities of Christ

➢ Christ must have had a third identity; a human avatar who suffered crucifixion at the sabbath of sabbaths.

Christ has come to earth in human form as Enoch on the first sabbath of the Almanac. He does not die but ascends to heaven. On the symmetrical reverse sabbath, he will descend as the spiritual resurrected Christ. In between these two events, Christ is crucified. In heaven, he is put to death by the seventy. On earth, Judah is simultaneously destroyed by the nations. But if Christ came to earth in human form, then we would expect him to have suffered death as a human. Enoch did not die—so the Christ must have come to earth again as an avatar. In this human form, he would have suffered death in Almanac day 7.7, the sabbath of sabbaths.

➢ In a saying found in Thomas and the synoptics, Jesus has three identities and three names.

Confirmation that Christ had three identities comes from a saying in which Jesus asks his disciples to tell him what he is like. It is found in all three synoptic gospels and also (below) in Thomas:

> Jesus said to his disciples: "Make a comparison to me, and tell me whom I am like." Simon Peter said to him: "You are like a righteous angel." Matthew said to him: "You are like a wise philosopher." Thomas said to him: "Master, my mouth will not allow me to speak whom you are like." Jesus said: "I am not your master, because you have drunk, you have become drunk from the bubbling spring that I have measured out." And he took him, went aside, and spoke to him three words. Now when Thomas came to his companions, they asked him: "What did Jesus say to you?" Thomas said to them: "If I speak to you one of the words he has spoken to me, you will take up stones and cast them at me, and fire will come out of the stones and burn you." (Thomas 13; TC 1.12)

It is my belief that most of the named disciples in Thomas do not belong to the original gospel. In the early centuries, Thomas was preserved outside the proto-orthodox church in groups labelled as heretics by that church. It is suspicious that the two disciples giving supposedly wrong answers are Simon Peter (the chief apostle of the proto-orthodox) and Matthew (supposed author of the chief gospel of the proto-orthodox). This suggests that the names have been added by someone opposed to the proto-orthodox church. The name of Thomas, representing the gnostic view, would have been added at the same time. We will analyse the saying assuming that all three disciples were initially unnamed.

Jesus asks his disciples what he is like, and they give three replies. Jesus then takes the third disciple aside to instruct him, explaining that he is not his master, but has measured out a bubbling stream from which he has drunk. Jesus tells this third disciple three words or things. The disciple returns to the others and says that were he to say one of the words then they would stone him and fire would burst from the stones to consume them. What are we to make of all this?

The person adding the names has misunderstood the saying. It is not the first two disciples who are being stupid; they give correct answers. It is the third who requires further instruction. The saying is telling us that the Christ has three identities. The three words that Jesus tells the third disciple are his three natures.

➢ **The third identity must be the name of God; Yahweh. It was blasphemous to say this name aloud under penalty of death by stoning.**

If the third disciple were to say one of the words, the other disciples would feel obliged to stone him. There is one word a Jew must never say aloud, the name of God. The divine name was represented in written form by the Tetragrammaton, YHWH, which was never spoken but replaced in speech by "Lord". Yahweh is a modern guess at the pronunciation. Any Jew who said the name aloud, even accidentally, was to be immediately stoned. This must be the third name, corresponding to the guess of the third disciple: "my mouth will not allow me to say what you are like".

So one of the identities of Christ is Yahweh, part of the ultimate God. This third identity must correspond to the resurrected Christ on earth who will rule at the end of time.

➢ **The first identity, "the righteous angel", must be Enoch.**

It would seem that the three identities are in chronological order. The first, the "righteous angel", should correspond to Enoch. It is indeed an appropriate description for Enoch, who is repeatedly called "righteous"; in the Book of the Watchers he is a *"righteous man, scribe of righteousness" (1 Enoch 15:1)* and in the Similitudes *"you, son of man who art born in righteousness, and upon whom righteousness has dwelt" (1 Enoch 71:14)*. Elsewhere in the Similitudes, the Son of Man is described as looking like an angel.[1] And Enoch was regarded as the angel Metatron in later myth.

➢ **The second identity can only be the prophet Jeremiah. There was a tradition that Jeremiah was martyred in Egypt.**

The second identity is "a wise philosopher" or a "wise man of understanding" which is rather vague. However, we know that this second person must come in Almanac day 7.7 and the only person at this time who could be the "wise man" is the prophet Jeremiah. In scripture, it is Jeremiah's fate to predict the coming disaster, but for no one to listen to him. The Judean aristocrats view Jeremiah as almost a traitor. In the last we hear of him, he is taken to Egypt against his will as captive of the establishment Jews. A faction has rebelled and murdered the new governor Gedaliah, and the other Jews, fearing the revenge of the king of Babylon, have fled to Egypt.[2]

Christ must die on earth in his second identity, and there was a strong tradition that Jeremiah was stoned to death in Egypt by his countrymen. The earliest expression of this tradition is the first-century "The Lives of the Prophets" in which Jeremiah is stoned and then buried in Pharaoh's palace.[3] So there was certainly an early belief that Jeremiah was put to death. But stoning is not crucifixion. Is it possible that the author of the Lives, knowing that Jeremiah was killed by his fellow Jews, assumed wrongly that it was by stoning? Appendix D shows that the Jeremiah account is best explained as a Jewish reworking of an early Christian tradition in which the pagan Egyptians worshipped a wooden cross which can only be Jeremiah's.

➢ **Revelation uses a source that located the crucifixion in Sodom (Jerusalem) and Egypt.**

It should be a great embarrassment to the historical Jesus school that the author of Revelation does not know that Jesus was crucified in Jerusalem. But like so much else, it is ignored or brushed aside. The sole mention of the crucifixion in Revelation comes in the tale of the two witnesses slain by the beast:

> *And their bodies will lie in the street of the great city, which is called spiritually Sodom and Egypt, where also their Lord was crucified. (Revelation 11:8)*

In the context of Revelation, the great city that is "spiritually Sodom and Egypt" is undoubtedly Rome. The issues around the story of the witnesses are discussed in *The Rock and the Tower*.[4] This story is one of nine passages spread over five early Christian texts which go back to what I call the "Martyrdom Source". The Martyrdom Source told of the martyrdom of Mary and Paul in Rome during the persecution of Nero—it is not for nothing that early Christians saw Nero as the anti-Christ. The idea that Christ was crucified in Rome is a memory of the martyrdom of Mary, who probably suffered some form of crucifixion. Christ is crucified "a second time" in Rome in the second-century Acts of Peter. But there was no reference to either Sodom or Egypt in the Martyrdom Source. So the author of Revelation either invented the idea that Rome is Sodom and Egypt, or had a source which said that Christ was crucified in "Sodom and Egypt".

It is understandable why the author of Revelation might call Rome by the name of "Sodom", but "Egypt" is less explicable. It is true that Egypt and Rome were both empires who oppressed the Jews. But Egypt was, above all, the archetypal place of exile for Israel, and the Jews were never exiled to Rome. Also, the story is set in the city of Rome, and Egypt is not a city but a nation. We conclude that the author had a source which located the crucifixion in "Egypt". Most likely "Sodom" came from the same source, for the author would be unlikely to add a second name. What then did Sodom and Egypt originally mean? Let us take each separately.

Sodom: in the Ezekiel allegories "Sodom" is specifically used to mean Jerusalem. This is particularly relevant because, as we have seen, these allegories are closely connected to the proto-crucifixion account.

Egypt: most likely, this just meant Egypt. It cannot be Jerusalem because the Israelites escaped from Egypt to enter the Promised Land (Jerusalem!).

This suggests that "Sodom and Egypt" originally meant two separate places. Christ was crucified in (i) Jerusalem and (ii) Egypt. If Jeremiah was the human avatar of Christ, this all makes sense. At the national level, the crucifixion was the destruction of the temple and the city of Jerusalem; at a human level, it was the death of Jeremiah in Egypt.

The author of Revelation, reading that Christ was crucified in "Sodom and Egypt", is understandably confused. He is not aware of the gospel tradition of a Jerusalem crucifixion and thinks that "Sodom" and "Egypt" both mean Rome.

> **Jeremiah is the best fit for the human aspects of the suffering servant song.**

Jeremiah is the best fit for those sections of the suffering servant song that match neither the heavenly Christ nor Israel. The servant was *"despised and rejected by men, a man of sorrows and acquainted with grief"* (Isaiah 53:3) which sums up Jeremiah perfectly. Suffering is the characteristic that defines him as a prophet. He was certainly despised and at one point is imprisoned in a well for three days. Jeremiah was forbidden by God to have children, and the same is said of the suffering servant: *"Who can declare his generation?"* (Isaiah 53:8). The servant has a grave with the "rich man" and "the wicked", which is a good description of the group of Judeans who took Jeremiah with them to Egypt.

If this is correct, then the servant of the Isaiah song, like Christ, has three identities; he is (i) Israel and (ii) the Messiah and (iii) Jeremiah. He is all three at the same time. For us moderns, this is a strange way of thinking—we expect a person to be one thing or another. But in ancient Jewish literary culture, a metaphor was treated as a concrete identity of the thing being described. The subject would be approached from different angles. In the same way, the seventy represent; (i) angelic rulers; (ii) the nations; and (iii) the human kings of the nations.

> **Each of the three appearances corresponds to a special sabbath day in the Almanac.**

The timing of the three appearances of Christ on the earth in the Almanac are not random. There are four particularly special days in the Almanac; the first sabbath, the sabbath of sabbaths, the first reverse sabbath (seven days from the end), and the reverse sabbath of sabbaths. The three appearances each take place on one of these special days:

- On the first sabbath, Christ has appeared as Enoch, who is taken up to heaven alive.
- On the sabbath of sabbaths, Christ returns in the form of the prophet Jeremiah and suffers death. Simultaneously the divine Christ is crucified by the seventy angels in heaven.

- On the first reverse sabbath, Christ is reborn and resurrected through the shaman Mary.

Three identities in a gnostic text

➢ **In the Apocryphon of John, Jesus has three likenesses and has come to earth three times.**

We can find the three identities of Jesus in a gnostic text, The Apocryphon of John. This is supposedly set sometime after the crucifixion. John has been disturbed by the biting words of a Pharisee in the temple. He grieves about the many unanswered questions concerning Jesus' nature when the heavens open and he has a vision of Jesus who appears to him in three forms:

> *I was afraid, and behold I saw in the light a youth who stood by me. While I looked at him he became like an old man. And he changed his likeness becoming like a servant. (The Apocryphon of John, NHC II (1) 2:1-4)*

The three forms are a single person. We can match them to the three identities in the Thomas saying:

The youth = Enoch
The servant = Jeremiah
The old man = Yahweh

Jesus then reveals to John the secrets of heaven, giving a very complex system of heavenly powers. Basically, the Apocryphon follows the familiar gnostic pattern in which Sophia creates the chief archon Yaltabaoth (standing for the Demiurge and lower Yahweh) by mistake. He, in turn, creates the angels/archons to rule over the world.

One interesting variation comes in the myth of the fallen angels in the Apocryphon. Unlike the Book of the Watchers, the angels are not disobedient but sent by Yaltabaoth to mate with women. The angels create a counterfeit spirit and fill the women with their darkness so that the women beget children in the likeness of the false spirit. So humanity becomes infected with the persistent seed of evil.[5]

After this account of the angels and the women, Jesus gives a surprising revelation—he has come to earth three separate times. The first time he penetrated into the realm of darkness, but was forced to hide: "and they did not recognise me". When he returned for the second time, Jesus went further, down into Hades, but had to follow the light back up because the time is too early. The third time Jesus descended again to Hades and entered the prison of the body to redeem humanity. He told "he who hears" to awake from a deep sleep.[6]

The first descent would correspond to Enoch, who was not recognised by the evil powers but was taken up alive and hidden in heaven. In the second descent, Jesus goes to Hades, suggesting that he has died. This would correspond to the crucifixion and the appearance and death as Jeremiah. In the original myth, Jesus remains dead until the third appearance, but this would not suit the Apocryphon's theology in which Christ is an indestructible aeon of light. So in the Apocryphon, Christ descends a third time. In this third visitation, Christ returns to Hades and ascends to the prison of the body. The author of the Apocryphon probably intends this to represent the aeon entering into the physical man, Jesus. But we can see it as a memory that the resurrected Christ comes up from Hades and enters a human vessel, the shaman Mary.

The three identities in the gospels

The saying of the three identities of Jesus occurs in Mark, Matthew and Luke as well as Thomas. Do these confirm the conclusions reached from the original form of the saying in Thomas?

> **The first identity is equated with Elijah in Mark—an understandable confusion for Enoch.**

In the Mark version of the multiple identities of Jesus, there are actually four names:

> *And Jesus went out, and his disciples, into the towns of Caesarea Philippi: and by the way he asked his disciples, saying to them, "Who do men say that I am?" And they answered, "John the Baptist: but some say, Elijah and others, one of the prophets". And he said to them, "But who do you say that I am?" And Peter answers and said to him, "You are the Christ". And he charged them that they should tell no man of him. (Mark 8:27-30)*

The names here appear in a previous passage in which Herod hears about Jesus' miracles and becomes convinced he is John the Baptist risen from the dead:

Now King Herod heard about it, for Jesus' name had become well known, and people were saying, "John the Baptist has risen from the dead, which is why miraculous powers operate in him." Others, however, said, "He is Elijah," and still others, "He is a prophet, like one of the prophets." (Mark 6:14-15)

In these passages, Elijah stands in place of Enoch. Confusion between the two is understandable because they are the only humans who were taken up to heaven alive. They frequently appear together as a pair. John the Baptist is brought in as well because the author of Mark had the theory that John was the returned Elijah.

➢ **The second identity is a "prophet" in Mark but further identified as Jeremiah in Matthew.**

In the two passages in Mark, the second identity is simply "one of the prophets". The Gospel of Matthew copies the story from Mark but adds a specific name:

And they said, "Some say John the Baptist, others Elijah, and others Jeremiah or one of the prophets." (Matthew 16:14)

The name of Jeremiah is the only detail that the author of Matthew adds to the corresponding line of the Mark account. He must have access to a source that correctly names the second identity.

➢ **The author of Mark is aware of the myth that Enoch has returned and suffered death, but confuses him with Elijah. He comes up with the theory that John the Baptist was Elijah.**

The author of Mark knew the original myth; that Enoch, the Son of Man, has already returned. But his mistakes and false theories disguise this knowledge. When Jesus is questioned about why Elijah was expected to return before the Messiah, he replies:

"Elijah indeed, having come first, restores all things. Why then is it written that the Son of Man must suffer many things and be despised? But I say to you that Elijah has come, and they have done to him whatever they wished, as it has been written about him." (Mark 9:12-13)

This is very confused. It implies that John the Baptist was Elijah. As a theory, this has problems. How can John the Baptist be said to have "restored all things"? And why the reference to the "Son of Man"? Clearly the author of Mark is using an existing source which he has misunderstood. This source is about a person who:

1. Has returned to earth having first been taken up alive.
2. Is the Son of Man.
3. Has suffered many things and has been despised.
4. Has been put to death.

The author of Mark thinks that this person is Elijah/John. But he is really Enoch, the Son of Man, who has come back as Jeremiah, the suffering and despised prophet.

> **In Mark and the other synoptics, the third identity is the Christ. The author of Mark has taken the concept of the "Messianic secret" from his misunderstanding of the Thomas saying.**

There is no doubt over the final identity of Jesus in Mark. Peter calls him Christ at a climactic moment in the gospel. The notion of Mark's "Messianic secret" has intrigued scholars. The knowledge that Jesus is the Christ is presented as a secret to be carefully guarded, revealed in stages; with Peter's confession, it is first unveiled to the inner circle of the twelve.

Why does the author of Mark attach so much importance to the seemingly obvious idea that Jesus is the Christ? The answer can be found in the Gospel of Thomas. In the Thomas version, the final identity is left unsaid: "my mouth will not allow me to say what you are like". This third identity is dangerous knowledge, not to be spoken off on pain of stoning. But the author of Mark thinks that the third identity of Jesus is the Christ. So in Mark, the idea that Jesus is Christ becomes a great secret.

The strangest feature of the story in Mark is that Peter is not rewarded for recognising Jesus as Christ, but immediately suffers a remarkable rebuke. Jesus has followed up Peter's declaration by telling his disciples that the Son of Man must be killed and rise after three days. Peter takes Jesus aside to tell him not to say so much. Jesus turns on him: *"Get behind Me, Satan!" (Mark 8:33).*

We can understand this rebuke by reference to the Thomas version of the saying:

- In Thomas, the third disciple who gives the final answer is rebuked by Jesus. In Mark, Peter gives the final answer and is rebuked by Jesus.
- Jesus tells the third disciple "I am not your master...". This could

have been misunderstood as meaning that the third disciple's master was Satan.

- In Thomas, the third disciple is taken aside for a private communication. In Mark, Peter takes Jesus aside to speak to him.
- In Thomas, the third disciple tells the others that Jesus' communication cannot be spoken to them, or they will stone him. In Mark, Peter reproves Jesus for telling the other disciples of these things.

The Mark account seems to reflect a very confused understanding of the Thomas saying. In Mark, the third identity is perfectly clear—Jesus is the Christ. As always, Thomas gives us a riddle; and as always, the synoptics leave nothing to the imagination. The riddle comes first. The supposed clarity of the gospels is nothing more than a false guess at the riddle's meaning.

38

Conclusion

We are at the end of our exploration of the Christ myth, although not quite at the end of the Judas War. We have travelled back far in time to discover a world ruled by angels who were gods in Canaan. We have seen how the crucifixion was originally the exile of Israel and Judah and how Judas Iscariot represented the betrayal by the Judah and Jerusalem of King Ahaz. The Christ myth started with the Judas War and expressed the viewpoint of the Israelites in contrast with the Hebrew Bible, which was a Judean production. The Christ myth combined the historical facts of the exile with the myth of the seventy angels. The resurrection of Christ would be the rebirth of his people, Israel. But the Christ myth went much further, expanding the exile vastly in time and extent. The resurrection would bring an end to the rule of the seventy angels, and free the nations along with the Jews. At the heart of this new understanding was the Almanac, the symmetrical calendar of seventy days/generations organised into ten weeks/great days. Christ would be dead for two great days and resurrected on the third.

The Christ myth was transmitted down the ages through a small Israelite tribal community who had lived in Judah since before the Judas War. Their numbers were swelled at the time of the Judas War by refugees from the north. These proto-Christians rejected the second temple, the law and the Jerusalem priestly establishment. Their Judean neighbours would have called them Samaritans, which they were not, and tolerated their dissident views as long as they kept to themselves, which they did until an extraordinary event fractured the status quo. A woman within the group announced that Christ had been resurrected and had appeared to her. No one else could see him and most rejected her revelation—Christ was expected to come in the sky at the head of a legion of angels. The evidence of this early rejection remains in the gospels. But Mary was a shaman who was able to take a potential disciple on a spiritual journey, to become their mother until Christ was born within them. Others saw Jesus for themselves and become her loyal followers.

Mary was believed to be "the seed of David", probably born into a leading family, and perhaps even the daughter of the leader. It may seem odd that an Israelite could trace their descent back to the Judean kings. The tribal system had long since fallen into disrepair, and the group was one of the few who claimed a distinct tribal identity. Although Israelites, they accepted both the first temple and the legitimacy of the house of David to rule over all twelve tribes. The divine Messiah would come in the skies, but many also looked for a human Messiah, a son of David, on earth. The group expected this human king to emerge from their own and not from the hated Judeans around them. So a principal family or families needed to claim descent from David. We should not ask whether or not this claim was valid. No one actually possessed a detailed genealogy going back several centuries. Such genealogies were theoretical constructions, their truth a matter of opinion.

We know virtually nothing about this Israelite community. It would have been too small to attract the attention of a historian like Josephus; most likely no more than a few villages, with a population numbering in the hundreds rather than thousands. The majority would have rejected Mary's revelations. The evidence points to an early move away from her home village to the wilderness area around the Jordon. There she and her small group of followers came into contact with the much larger movement of John the Baptist.

Mary's new Jesus movement could only expand by recruiting among Judeans, and here they encountered a fundamental difficulty. The Israelite group paid scant respect to the law of Moses and regarded the second temple as invalid; both were absolutely central to Judean religion. This became a serious stumbling block for would-be converts. And the movement's attempts to convert Judeans alerted those guardians of the Torah, the Pharisees and small-town scribes, to the heresy of their teachings. The Pharisees began a persecution to eliminate the Jesus movement entirely. One of the persecutors was the future apostle Paul.

Eventually, these problems would be bypassed by the mission to the gentiles. This international phase started about ten to fifteen years after Mary's initial revelation. The expansion out of Judea is closely associated with Paul, the self-styled apostle to the gentiles. Yet it commenced before Paul and involved many more "apostles". For example, the prominent church of Rome owed nothing to Paul. The initial target of this expansion would have been the diaspora Jews, but the missionaries soon found a more receptive audience among the gentiles.

The Gospel of Mark was written in the 70s AD, quickly followed by the gospels of Matthew, Luke and John. They fundamentally changed Christianity. By this time Mary, James, Paul and other leaders were dead, having suffered martyrdom. The new dispersed churches were leaderless and rudderless in this disturbing, chaotic time in which no one knew what to believe. The gospels filled this vacuum brilliantly. The Christ myth was repackaged as something that had happened literally in the recent past. Expressing the myth in simple human terms made it all the more accessible and all the more powerful.

The new story depended on supernatural miracles. Jesus, although coming as a human, was really the Son of God. He gave evidence of this by performing many wonders, even bringing back people from the dead. After his own death, he was resurrected on the third day and appeared in bodily form to his disciples. He then returned to heaven until the time would come for him to establish his kingdom. This dependence on the supernatural was no disadvantage in the ancient world, nor through-out most of history. Christians accepted the account without question, and Jesus' ability to perform miracles was part of his appeal. But in the last few hundred years with the development of science, it has become increasingly apparent that none of it happened, at least not as told.

Take away the miracles, take away the idea that Jesus was the Son of God, take away the resurrection and nothing much remains. We are left with the barren subject of "historical" Jesus studies. There is no way that a new religion could have formed around the supposed Jesus of such studies.

This is not the only disadvantage of the gospel account; much was lost by the simplification of the myth. For a start, there was no place for the seventy shepherds. Jesus was not crucified by the angels, but by the Romans at the instigation of the Jews. The idea of a world ruled by evil angels persisted but was disconnected from the crucifixion. The split of God into the higher and lower Yahweh also had no place in the gospel view, although many Christian groups continued to make this distinction. Earlier traditions that did not fit into the gospel account survived, causing Christianity to split into a multitude of sects. The movement of Marcion and the many gnostic groups evolved in this era. Eventually, the gospel sect, what we now call the proto-orthodox, won out. Within a century, the gospels were widely accepted as history, and anything that contradicted them was deemed to be wrong. Earlier authorities were made to conform by forgery or simple neglect. Paul lived before the gospels, so his letters contained much that was embarrassing for the proto-orthodox. As he was too prominent and revered for his letters to be abandoned, new letters and interpolations were penned by the unscrupulous so that Paul could appear to support the gospel view. Among the many texts that ceased to be copied until they were lost was the Gospel of Thomas, the only work that could claim to go back to the founders. It remained popular for a while but was eventually declared heretical.

The anti-Jewish elements of the new gospel story became divorced from the original context of the Judas War. It was forgotten that the original betrayers were the court and priestly establishment of Ahaz's and Hezekiah's Jerusalem. Now the Jews (Judeans) as a people were blamed for a crime committed within living memory. The Jews of the first-century bore the blood-guilt for the murder of Christ, the Son of God. Their descendants would pay the penalty.

Christianity thrived and spread despite periodic persecutions, and under Constantine became the state religion of the Roman Empire. Thus commenced almost two thousand years of religious dominance over Europe. The Jews retained their separate identity, living among their Christian neighbours just as the Israelite proto-Christian group had once lived among the Judeans. Roles were reversed now, and the continued hostilities of the Judas War became antisemitism. Pogroms against the Jews were justified by the condemnations in the gospels, ignoring those parts of the New Testament that expressed continued hope for God's chosen people. Such actions were, of course, at complete variance with the true gospel teachings of non-violence, love and forgiveness. But then people have always taken from the Bible what suits their purpose. The anti-Jewish elements from the Judas War gave cover for the virulent antisemitism of the medieval period that was to resurge with tragic consequences in the twentieth century.

My fear is that some readers will take this book as meaning that there is no truth in Christianity. I would not accept this contention. A myth comes from a reality that is beyond ours. And even though the crucifixion was not the death of a real flesh and blood man in Roman-occupied Judea, yet it happened. The Israelites and Judeans saw their nations destroyed; many killed, others forcibly taken from their homes and farms, some made into slaves. Their suffering is the suffering of all the victims of war, of all refugees. And beyond that, it is the universal human suffering, for even those who are fortunate to live in peaceful times, in lands of plenty, must eventually die. The ultimate God has sent part of him/herself down to us, to dwell within us. Christ suffers with us and shares in our death so we may share in his life.

Like Paul, we should be adults now and put away childish things. The world has grown up. We can no longer believe in the fairy stories from our youth but must seek the reality behind those stories. A myth is not literally true but expresses a truth that cannot be expressed literally. We may struggle to believe in seventy shepherd angels ruling the world, but humanity has always been enslaved by what the seventy represent. The nature of the seventy is that they are many, all opposed to each other, all fighting each other, but possessing a deep underlying unity of purpose—which is death. Originally, they represented the nations. In the ancient world, people took it for granted that their own nation and race were superior to all others. Which is why every nation was pretty much in a state of continual warfare with the surrounding states.

The Jesus movement believed that the seventy ruled from within as well as without. The fallen angels had corrupted humanity with their seed by taking human wives. Men and women were haunted by their progeny, the demons. Even Mary had been possessed by seven demon husbands before her true husband, Christ, cast them out. The demons and angels have infected people with desire for the things in their domain, such as gold, property, possessions, food and drink, sexuality, status and power. Beyond such lusts, we might see the seventy as representing the mutually antagonistic "isms" that have oppressed the modern world. The seventy blind their followers until they become drunk with certainty, seeing their own cause alone as moral, a crusade worthy of fighting for, and even of dying for. It is amazing how one person's morality becomes another person's suffering.

For the Jesus movement, it was Christ alone who could conquer the demons. For Mary and her followers, the Christ myth was the gate to a new spiritual reality. When one who was receptive believed in the myth, it became operative. To die with Christ was to be reborn, and this rebirth was the awakening of the spirit. It was the light of the spirit alone that could cast asunder the darkness of the seventy. As Jesus says in Thomas, "there is light within a person of light, and it lights the world."

Afterword

David, Solomon and Bathsheba

My investigation of the Judas War started with the Almanac. If the strange structure of the passion day in Mark represented the seventh week of the Almanac, then the generation of Ahaz had to correspond to the betrayal of Judas Iscariot. The search for a betrayal in this period came up with Ahaz's bribe to the Assyrian king to wage war against Israel. This fitted perfectly. As the investigation continued, detail after detail began to click into place. The ultimate test of a hypothesis is that things you were not looking for and were not expecting to be connected, suddenly make sense.

At the beginning I had no concept of the importance of the Judas War. But as I wrote this book, the scope just kept expanding. Ahaz's Assyrian alliance had seemed nothing more than an odd detail of history. But source after source kept leading me back to the same time frame, the same event and its aftermath. It was not just the gospels. The Judas War was also central to Isaiah, Hosea, Ezekiel and Second Zechariah. Ahaz's action against Israel had a profound effect on Judaism just as it had on Christianity. It is not much of an exaggeration to say that the Hebrew Bible was written to exorcise the demons of the Judas War, to erase the deep-felt guilt of Judah, and to shift the blame onto the Israelites.

One thing that kept cropping up was the story of David and Solomon. As this was believed to date from the tenth century BC, it seemed far too early to be relevant. A critical insight came from the work of Israel Finkelstein who argued that the David account was actually first written down immediately after the fall of the north.[1] This changed everything. It put the story bang in the middle of the context and timeframe of the Judas War. In this section, we will explore the many contradictions and odd features of the David account to uncover an anti-David satire, a window on the Judas War written by the opponents of the Judean royal establishment.

It should be emphasised that this original anti-David narrative did not directly influence proto-Christianity. Those who framed the Almanac accepted the David narrative as it appears in the Hebrew Bible today. They believed that the reigns of David and Solomon were the high point of the age of the Jews and that the building of the Jerusalem temple was the central point of all history. By the time the Almanac was produced, the anti-David story had long since been forgotten. So it is a great irony that the anti-David account goes back to the same people, and the same era, as the origins of the Christ movement.

David and Solomon

The story of David and Solomon as narrated in the books of Samuel and 1 Kings, is one of the most fascinating in the Hebrew Bible.[2] It tells of how the shepherd boy David defeated the giant Philistine warrior Goliath with his sling to become King Saul's best warrior and close companion. He was a talented musician, playing the harp to ease Saul's melancholy. Saul had been anointed by the prophet Samuel as Israel's first king and had won a series of victories in the field. But he was a flawed character. David now proved himself the greater warrior, killing ten thousands where Saul killed thousands. The king became jealous of the younger man and increasingly unhinged. Yahweh had told Samuel that Saul was no longer worthy of the throne, and the prophet had secretly anointed David as his successor. However, David remained loyal to Saul and would not con-template revolt. Only when Saul attempted to kill him, was he forced to flee the king's service and wander the hills with a band of followers. For a while, David and his men even joined the Philistines, serving Achish, king of Gath. However, secretly David always maintained his loyalty to Israel and Saul.

Saul met his end in a battle with the Philistines. David was present in the Philistine army that fought Saul's Israelites, having been assigned a position in the rear by Achish. However, the other Philistine commanders feared that David would turn and fight on Saul's side, so he was sent away before the battle. By the day's end, the Philistines had won the victory and Saul was dead along with most of his sons. Eshbaal, a surviving son, took the throne briefly but he was assassinated, and David became king over both Judah and Israel.

The new king conquered Jerusalem and made it his capital. He brought up the ark of the covenant and installed it in the city. Nathan, the prophet told David that Yahweh had promised that his kingdom, and that of his future son, would endure forever. But at the peak of his power, David did something terrible; he committed adultery with Bathsheba, the wife of Uriah, one of his soldiers. David then arranged the cowardly murder of Uriah, sending him into a hopeless position in battle, so that he could marry Bathsheba. Yahweh was wrathful at this crime and sent the prophet Nathan to condemn David. Punishment for the killing would come from David's own house, and the sword would never leave that house. The infant that Bathsheba had conceived from him would die, but the two of them would have another son, Solomon.

Nathan's prophecy came true when David's beloved son Absalom revolted against him, forcing David to flee Jerusalem. David came within a hairsbreadth of losing his throne, but his forces were able to regroup under David's cold-blooded general Joab, and defeat Absalom. Against David's orders and wishes, Absalom was killed by Joab. This was not the only tragedy to afflict David's family. Another son Amon was killed by Absalom, and a third, Adonijah, tried to seize David's throne when he was old and feeble. It took quick thinking and action by Nathan and Bathsheba to enable David's chosen successor, Solomon, to be anointed as king. Solomon spared the life of his half-brother Adonijah at first. But when Adonijah made another move to claim the throne, Solomon ordered his execution.

The reign of Solomon, unlike that of his father, was peaceful and prosperous. He was renowned for both his vast wealth and his great wisdom. He constructed many impressive buildings, but none so important as the temple for Yahweh. Even the most powerful of foreign rulers sought him as an ally. The Queen of Sheba travelled a great distance to test his wisdom and bring him gifts.

Scholars have long been wary about accepting the David account at face value. Take, for example, the famous episode in which David defeats Goliath with a sling-shot. Elsewhere in Samuel, it is recorded that another warrior, Elhanan the son of Jaare-oregim of Bethlehem, killed Goliath.[3] It would seem that this feat has been transferred from the obscure Elhanan to the well-known David, a phenomenon that is well attested in the development of legends.

The story of David and Solomon in Samuel and Kings forms part of the Deuteronomistic history and has clearly been worked over by a later priestly author. Scratch away the later gloss, and a dark story of murder and revenge is revealed, with David as the main suspect. The protestations of innocence are too exaggerated and the excuses too convoluted to be believable. David was a remorseless killer, relentless in his quest to eliminate the house of Saul. He was all too ready to fight on the side of the enemies of Israel if it suited his purpose. Nor was Solomon innocent of blood guilt. Read between the lines of the succession account and Solomon is shown to be a usurper who eliminated the real heir, Adonijah.

The implications were intriguing. Surely no later author would have written about the founders of the Davidic dynasty in these negative terms. So the warts-and-all-portraits must have been written within living memory of the real David and Solomon before the mythology around the two kings developed. The history of David and the succession of Solomon would be a remarkable survival from c.1000 BC. Or so it was believed until the archaeologists got to work. As we have seen, Finkelstein showed that the account could not have come from the time of David. He offered a very different theory; that it was a response to the influx of Israelite refugees into Judah during the reign of Hezekiah.

If the story does date from much later than 1000 BC, then there must be another explanation for the negative portrait of David and Solomon. No Judean would have written the account in the form in which we find it. So we have to envisage a two-stage process. The original anti-David story was composed by someone who was opposed to the kings of Judah. Later this was reworked by a pro-Judean scribe, the "revisionist". It is the revisionist's version that has come down to us, and even this was probably edited further when incorporated into the Deuteronomistic history.

Scholars typically identify two separate sub-narratives; the Rise of David and the Succession History. But we will see that both are derived from the single anti-David source. There is no doubt that some elements of the account in Samuel and 1 Kings are very old. Both the revisionist and the original author would have had access to a plenitude of verbal legends and myths about the Judean hero-king David and the first Israelite King Saul. The account as we find it in Samuel and 1 Kings includes many such traditional elements. But the main narrative is not history. We shall see that the anti-David source was so fantastic that we must regard it as total fiction. It tells us more about the time it was written than about the real David. As for the revisionist, we are fortunate that he was not skilful. He addressed each and every accusation with a curious technique of enumerating a large number of mutually inconsistent reasons why David could not have committed the deed in question. This makes it easy to identify the revisionist's changes and to reconstruct the original. We will start with the murders.

David the serial killer

In *David's Secret Demons* Baruch Halpern lists the killings for which David could be responsible. There are no less than nine separate episodes. Most follow the same pattern, with strenuous denials, alibis and reasons why David was innocent of the crime. But the narrator protests too much. These denials would not be necessary unless he was replying to an accusation. I have followed Halpern's numbering, but added my own notes:

1. Nabal, husband of Abigail.[4] Supposedly died of heart failure.
    Suspicious circumstances: David had set out to kill Nabal because

he refused to pay his dues under David's protection racket. David benefited by marrying Abigail after his death. (This case will be considered in more detail later.)

Excuses and protestations of innocence: Although both Abigail and David thought that Nabal deserved to die, they rejoiced (seven verses) that David had not, in fact, killed him.

2. Saul and his sons, including Jonathan.[5] Killed at Gilboa after losing a battle to the Philistines.

    Suspicious circumstances: David was present in the Philistine army as a vassal of Achish, the king of Gath. He profited by Saul's death by eventually becoming king of Israel. Saul's assassin reported back to David and brought him Saul's crown.

    Excuses and protestations of innocence: David had already had two opportunities to kill Saul. Once, while Saul was pissing in a cave, David sneaked up and cut off part of his robe. Another time David crept into Saul's camp at night, and stood over the king while he slept, taking only his water jug and spear as trophies. Both times he preserved the life of Saul. David was also Jonathan's best buddy.

    Although the Philistines had employed David to raid Judah, he actually fooled Achish and raided desert settlements instead. David was present at the start of the battle but was assigned a supporting role in the rearguard. The other Philistine commanders did not trust David and asked that he should not fight at all against the Israelites. So during the battle, David was far away fighting the Amalekites.

    In any case, it was not even really a murder. The Amalekite who had killed Saul had done so at Saul's own command because the king was fatally injured and in terrible pain. David was so horrified by the killing that he had this man immediately executed.

    David laments for eleven verses over Saul and Jonathan's death.

3. Eshbaal, Saul's surviving son and successor.[6] Although David became king of Judah, Eshbaal was made king of Israel. He was assassinated while sleeping by Rechab and Baanah.

    Suspicious circumstances: The two assassins reported back to David with the head of Eshbaal. David benefited by the removal of his rival by being made king of all Israel.

    Excuses and protestations of innocence: David laments at the deed (three verses) and has the two assassins killed, their arms and legs hacked off, and their corpses hung by a pool in Hebron.

4. Abner.[7] Saul's right-hand man, and second in command to Eshbaal.

Lured to a meeting and stabbed in the stomach by David's man Joab because Abner had killed his brother in battle.

Suspicious circumstances: Joab was David's fixer and favourite assassin. Removing Abner would have been a priority because he was the house of Saul's best general.

Excuses and protestations of innocence: Abner had supposedly betrayed Eshbaal and joined David, so there was no reason to kill him. Joab went after Abner without David's knowledge. David cursed Joab for the deed, although he continued to employ him.

David shows extreme mourning and grief (ten verses) for the death of Abner.

5. Seven heirs of Saul; two sons and five grandsons.[8] David surrendered them to the Gibeonites who were ethnic Amorites. The seven men of the house of Saul were hung on a hill, a form of crucifixion, as human sacrifices to Yahweh.

   Suspicious circumstances: this act by David removed all the remaining heirs of Saul except for Mephibosheth who could not have become king because he was disabled. A kinsman of Saul, Shimei, curses David for the crime; he is "a man of blood" and is guilty of the "blood of the house of Saul".

   Excuses and protestations of innocence: David was responding to a famine caused because Saul had driven the Gibeonites out of Israel. David was directed by Yahweh to make reparations to the Gibeonites, and it was they who requested Saul's heirs for recompense.

   David saved Mephibosheth, the son of Jonathan because of a vow he had made his father. The king showed kindness to Mephibosheth, who was lame in both feet and allowed him to eat at his table.

6. Amon, David's eldest son.[9] Murdered by another of David's sons, Absalom because Amon had raped his sister Tamar.

   Suspicious circumstances: Amon was the son of Jezreel who was likely the same Jezreel who had been Saul's wife before she was David's. So Amon had a strong connection with the house of Saul.

   Excuses and protestations of innocence: David did not know of the murder in advance. At first, he thought all his sons had been killed and tore his clothes in a paroxysm of grief. In any case, the murder was justified as revenge for a sister's rape. Absalom was forced to flee to Geshur for three years. Although David longed to see Absalom again, he only gave his permission for his return after Joab had tricked him into it.

7. Absalom, David's son and heir.[10] Killed by Joab after mounting a rebellion.

   Suspicious circumstances: Joab was David's hit-man. Absalom was hanging from an oak tree while run-through with three spears, indicating that his death was a human sacrifice. It is known that the kings of Israel and Judah did sacrifice their sons.

   Excuses and protestations of innocence: Absalom had revolted against David who had to flee for his life. The king was not present in the army that went after Absalom. He had given explicit orders, heard by all the people, that Absalom should not be harmed. The first man to find Absalom hanging by his head from the tree refused to kill him because of David's orders.

   There is an elaborate story about two runners who bring David "the good news" about Absalom's death. Hearing the news, the king is inconsolable with grief. The victorious army also grieves until Joab reproves the king for not recognising the army's triumph.

8. Amasa, Absalom's military commander in the revolt.[11] David appoints Amasa as head of his army instead of Joab and then gives him an impossible task, which he fails. Joab goes to meet him and gives Amasa the kiss of greeting while plunging his knife into his guts. Amasa's bloody body is pushed to the side of the road as the army march past.

   Suspicious circumstances: David had an obvious motivation to eliminate the rebel general. Amasa is commanded to raise the army in just three days, which was not feasible. Joab is David's assassin, and there is no effort to hide the deed.

   Excuses and protestations of innocence: None.

9. Uriah, Bathsheba's first husband.[12] Murdered by Joab on the orders of David. Joab orders Uriah to assault an enemy position and then withdraws the supporting troops.

   Suspicious circumstances: The only murder by David admitted by the Book of Samuel. (This case will be considered in more detail later.)

If anything, this list is too short. The killing of the priests by Doeg the Edomite at the orders of Saul is likely to have been originally committed by David as we will see later. And it excludes the murders committed by Solomon.

David and the ark of the covenant

The supposed high point of David's reign is the bringing of the ark of the covenant to Jerusalem.[13] There are multiple suspicious features about this episode which show that the revisionist has been hard at work. According to the Book of Samuel, the ark has been resting at Kiriath-jearim in Saul's tribe of Benjamin.[14] David comes from a place called "Baal of Judah" to bring the ark back to Jerusalem. Where is this unknown place whose name identifies it as a centre of Baal worship? In the later books of Joshua and Chronicles, Baal of Judah is the same as Kiriath-jearim.[15] But this identification can be seen as an attempt to explain and white-wash the earlier 1 Samuel passage. Baal of Judah cannot possibly be Kiriath-jearim because (i) it is in Judah and Kiriath-jearim is in Benjamin and (ii) David comes from Baal of Judah and goes to Kiriath-jearim, so they cannot be the same place. There is only one explanation that fits—Baal of Judah is a satirical name for Jerusalem. David is bringing the ark of Yahweh to Jerusalem, which is called the centre of Baal worship!

The ark has been held in the house of Abinadab and is moved on a cart accompanied by Abinadab's two sons, Uzzah and Ahio. Disaster comes when the oxen stumble. Uzzah reaches out a hand to steady the ark and is immediately struck dead by Yahweh. According to 2 Samuel, Uzzah was killed for being irreverent. Readers throughout the ages have had concerns with this story. What has Uzzah done wrong? Was he supposed to allow the ark to fall to the ground? These problems have arisen because the revisionist has disguised the original reason for Uzzah's death; he is complicit in the attempt to take the ark to Jerusalem. The evidence lies in David's reaction:

> Then David became angry because Yahweh had burst forth against Uzzah [....] And David was afraid of Yahweh that day and asked, "How can the ark of Yahweh ever come to me?" So David would not move the ark of Yahweh to the City of David. Instead, David took it aside to the house of Obed-edom the Gittite. (2 Samuel 6:8-10)

The ark supposedly rests for three months at this house of "Obed-edom the Gittite". The name is again highly suggestive:

Obed-edom = "servant of Edom", the neighbouring enemy kingdom.
Gittite = "inhabitant of Gath", the Philistine city.

It is David who was an inhabitant of Gath, taking refuge in the city when he became the vassal of King Achish. The "servant of Edom and inhabitant of Gath" is a satirical name for David himself. The house that the ark rests in is the house of David, meaning Jerusalem.

As the ark is carried into Jerusalem, David dances and leaps with abandon before it while his wife Michal, a daughter of Saul, looks on in disgust:

> *"How the king of Israel has distinguished himself today!" she said. "He has uncovered himself today in the sight of the maidservants of the servants, as a worthless one uncovers himself." (2 Samuel 6:20)*

The word "uncover" means to reveal nakedness. Michal is saying that even the lowliest female in the city has looked upon David naked that day. However, according to 2 Samuel 6:14, he wore the linen ephod, a priestly garment. The inconsistency shows that the revisionist has been at work again, this time literally covering up David. In the original, the king accompanied the ark by dancing naked. To summarise:

- David's Jerusalem is called "Baal of Judah", a centre of Baal worship.
- When David attempts to bring the ark into Jerusalem, Yahweh strikes one of the porters dead.
- David is furious with Yahweh and doubts he can bring the ark into Jerusalem.
- The ark goes to the house of "the servant of Edom and inhabitant of Gath" another satirical name for the house of David (Jerusalem).
- David performs an obscene, naked dance in front of the ark.

Whoever wrote the original is not just against David, but against Jerusalem and its temple. The author believes that the ark should have remained in the territory of Benjamin in Israel. This is not the only time David is shown as being blasphemous to Yahweh. Before he becomes king, he goes to Ahimelech, the priest at Nob to ask for the consecrated bread. When Doeg the Edomite reports on this conversation to Saul, the king orders the massacre of all the priests and Doeg slays them.[16]

Doeg is another peculiar name—it means "to fear" or "to be anxious". No one would actually be called "anxious the Edomite". It is a satirical name, most likely an insult directed at David. Significantly, Doeg is mysteriously present when David meets Ahimelech. There are other odd features in the account of this meeting and the subsequent slaying of the priests. When Ahimelech sees David approach, he trembles with fear. Why should the priest be so terrified of David? Ahimelech asks a strange question: *"Why are you alone and no one with you?" (1 Samuel 21:1).* David replies that he will meet his young men at a nearby place. It is clear from 1 Samuel 22:6 that David is travelling around with a war band, so why does he approach the sanctuary alone?

Saul is at Gibeah when he hears about David and his men. He is enraged, even more so when Doeg informs him that Ahimelech has assisted David. Saul summons Ahimelech and *"his father's whole family"* (1 Samuel 22:11) who were also priests. He accuses them of giving David bread and the sword of Goliath, the Philistine. Saul then orders his men to slaughter the priests, but none of his soldiers will lift a hand against them. It is Doeg who does the deed and who embarks upon a quite remarkable killing spree:

> *And Doeg the Edomite turned and struck down the priests, and killed on that day eighty-five men who wore the linen ephod. And Nob, the city of the priests, he put to the sword with its men and women, children and infants, oxen, donkeys, and sheep. (1 Samuel 22:18-19)*

There is much that is ridiculous about this account:

- It is quite impossible for one individual armed with just a sword to kill as many people and animals as Doeg is supposed to have done. The narrative is quite specific that none of the men of Saul helped Doeg. Those who were attacked would have resisted and easily overpowered a single man.
- The narrator seems to have forgotten that the massacre was supposed to take place at Gibeah. Doeg does not just kill the priests, but the whole town, of Nob including "women, children, infants, oxen, donkeys and sheep". Did they all go to Gibeah?
- The bread that Ahimelech gave to David amounted to no more than five loaves. Not much to feed a band of young men.

These absurdities demonstrate that the revisionist has been at work blaming Saul for a massacre originally carried out by David. We can reconstruct the original sequence of events:

1. David did not approach Nob alone but at the head of a war band.
2. The priest Ahimelech is terrified when he sees David's men approach. The question "Why are you alone..." has been added by the revisionist to hide the fact that David's men were present at the sanctuary.
3. David demands the consecrated bread and the priests refuse to give it to him.
4. Doeg the Edomite is a satirical name for David. It is David who puts

the priests and the whole town to the sword. He gives the order and his men physically carry out the killings.

5. David then steals the bread—much more than five loaves—and his men slaughter the animals to eat them.

This explanation makes much more sense. The sanctuary at Nob was an Israelite "high place" in the territory of Saul's tribe of Benjamin. Saul would never have killed his own people and destroyed one of his tribe's sacred places in the way that he is supposed to have done in 1 Samuel. But David and his men are Judeans. In the original, it is they who carried out this atrocity against an Israelite religious centre.

As for the story that David was given the sword of Goliath, the Philistine, this can be seen as reflecting the accusation that David had "wielded the Philistine sword". The original meaning was that David had fought for the Philistines. The revisionist explains it away by having Ahimelech give David the trophy sword of Goliath.

The name "Doeg the Edomite" implies that David is from Edom. This is just one of many accusations suggesting that David is on the side of the foreign enemies of Israel or is himself a foreigner. These accusations should not be taken at face value—they are insults hurled against David. Evidence for another such insult comes between the episodes of the bread and the slaughter in Samuel. David has gone all the way to Moab, another enemy of Israel, to appeal to its king: *"Please let my father and mother come forth with you…"* (1 Samuel 22:3). The wording is odd and generally translated as David asking for his father and mother to stay with the king of Moab, presumably for safety from Saul. But behind this we can see the original accusation that David's mother and father had "come forth from Moab", meaning that they were Moabites.

It is significant that in the Hebrew Bible, David does indeed have a Moabitess as an ancestor; Ruth. But the Book of Ruth was written long after the David account, and the Ruth story can be seen as an attempt to explain away the insult that the "mother" of David was a Moabitess.

Bathsheba—the innocent victim?

One spring evening, David is walking on the roof of his palace and sees a beautiful woman below bathing on the roof of her house.[17] He enquires for her name and is told she is Bathsheba, the wife of Uriah the Hittite. Her husband is one of David's soldiers and is away fighting the Ammonites. He sends for her, and they make love. A little later, she sends a message to David saying that she is pregnant.

David arranges for Uriah to come back from the front to the palace and instructs him to go home. Instead, Uriah chooses to sleep at the palace. When David asks why he has not gone to his wife, he replies that the ark of the covenant is in the field and he would make himself impure by sleeping with his wife before the battle is won. David gets him drunk, but he still will not go home. So David sends him back to the army with a secret message for Joab—put Uriah in the fiercest part of the battle and then withdraw the other men. Joab does this and Uriah is killed. Bathsheba mourns for her dead husband, and once the mourning period is over, David takes her as his wife.

The role of Bathsheba in all this is deeply ambiguous. Was her relationship with David consensual, or was she effectively raped? Did she have any advance knowledge of David's plot against Uriah? Did she genuinely mourn her husband or was it all for show? The narrative presents her as innocent; in Nathan's story, she is a poor man's lamb taken by a greedy rich man, David. Yet the narrative never says that Bathsheba was unwilling or objected to anything David did.

David supposedly sends for Uriah in an attempt to cover up his adultery. When this fails, he arranges his murder. Yet all this is unnecessary. David is king and can do what he likes. He can pay Uriah the customary compensation for the adultery and then oblige him to divorce his wife.

For David's other murders, the narrative protests his innocence too much. Yet for Uriah, and Uriah alone, the murder is admitted. In reality, it would have been the easiest of crimes to hide. A man dies in battle, and no one would know that it was the fault of David. So why is this one murder admitted? Perhaps because the revisionist is covering up for someone else this time. It is Bathsheba, not David, who mourns for Uriah. And the narrative goes out of its way to stress that the baby is David's:

1. Bathsheba has purified herself following her period before David sends for her. This rules out the baby being conceived beforehand from Uriah.
2. It is repeatedly stressed that Uriah did not go back to his house to see Bathsheba. Not even when he was drunk. And he was killed immediately afterwards.
3. Besides, the baby was not Solomon. The baby dies, so David and Bethesda have a second baby (Solomon) to replace him.

This use of repeated and mutually inconsistent excuses is typical of the style of the Judean revisionist. Once again, we have a cover-up. In the original the first baby was Solomon, and he was really the son of Uriah.

David has been tricked into accepting a Hittite's baby as his own son. But who tricked him? It can only have been Bathsheba.

Bathsheba, the scheming murderess

Let us look at the story again, this time without any preconceptions that Bathsheba is innocent. How do we know that the bathing was accidental? Bathsheba would have been aware that David went walking on his roof in the evening and could have arranged her bath accordingly. Women have a way of signalling to men that they may be available. Consumed with lust, David sends for her, and she seduces him. A little later, she tells him she is pregnant.

As for her husband's murder, who had the strongest motive? Not David, but Bathsheba. She wants to be queen and Uriah is in the way. She persuades David to arrange for his death in battle so the two can marry. We now have a very different Bathsheba from the innocent lamb:

1. She is an adulteress who sets out to seduce David.
2. She is a murderess who arranges the elimination of her own husband.
3. She is a schemer who tricks David into thinking that Uriah's son Solomon is his own.

This would explain why David is blamed for just this one murder. Although the later Judean apologist wants to excuse David from the accusations against him, in this one case he has a higher priority, to protect Bathsheba and hence Solomon. He puts the blame on David so that none falls on Bathsheba. To find confirmation, we will look at two other suspicious episodes involving Bathsheba.

Solomon as nemesis of David

David is old and cannot keep warm.[18] His attendants search for a young virgin to share his bed and choose a beautiful girl, Abishag the Shunammite. She looks after the king, but he does not sleep with her.

While David is in his dotage, his son Adonijah tries to usurp the kingdom. He sets up a gathering with a group of high-status individuals including his "royal brothers", the commanders of the army, Joab, Abiathar the priest, and the servants of the king. The intention is that they will proclaim Adonijah as king. Solomon is not invited.

Hearing of this plot, Nathan the prophet warns Bathsheba of the danger: *"save your own life and the life of your son, Solomon"* (1 Kings 1:12). He tells her to go to David and remind him that he has appointed Solomon as his successor. Bathsheba obeys Nathan and goes to the king who is being looked after by Abishag. She starts by reminding him of his pledge: *"You swore to me, your maidservant, by Yahweh your God: 'Surely your son Solomon will reign after me, and he will sit on my throne.'"* (1 Kings 1:17) She then tells David about Adonijah's attempt to seize the throne. She adds something odd: *"Otherwise, it shall come to pass when my lord the king sleeps with his fathers, I and my son Solomon will be counted as criminals"* (1 Kings 1:21). The reader may wonder why Bathsheba and Solomon should be regarded as criminals (or sinners) by Adonijah and his brothers.

At this point Nathan arrives and has an audience with the king while Bathsheba comes out. He repeats her words about Adonijah and asks the king if he intends to appoint Adonijah as his successor. The king is roused to action. He summons Bathsheba back and tells her that he will do as he had sworn to her. He orders his servants to place Solomon on his mule and take him to Gihon where Zadok the priest and Nathan will anoint him and declare him king. They do this, and the people proclaim the newly anointed Solomon. The first that Adonijah and his co-conspirators know about it is the blowing of the ram's horns for the new king.

Other commentators have noted the strangeness of this story. Something is going on below the surface. Adonijah's intention to be declared regent seems entirely reasonable given David's condition. He has the court and army behind him and is obviously the legitimate successor to David. Nathan's motive is an odd one, to save Bathsheba's and Solomon's lives. David had not publicly announced that Solomon was his successor, but supposedly promised this to Bathsheba in private. Reading between the lines it is clear that David had never made any such promise. Solomon is not included among the "royal brothers" and the other princes and may not even have recognised him as a legitimate son of the king. It all points to Solomon being the usurper, not Adonijah.

This leaves the puzzling question of how it would be possible for Bathsheba and Solomon to seize the throne when all the legitimate powers were allied against them. Halpern suggests that it was a military coup and that Solomon had the support of the army because of the murder of his real father, Uriah, who had been one of their number. This is unrealistic—Uriah would have died decades earlier, and any wrongdoing was on the part of David, not his son. A more fundamental issue is that this explanation assumes that the account is history. The Israelites did not even have writing at the time of David and archaeology has shown that the population of Jerusalem and Judah as a whole was insignificant.

The account is a fiction from centuries later when the royal court of Judah more closely resembled the mythical court of David. It is pointless to ask questions such as why Solomon was able to become king because it is all a made-up story. Instead, we must analyse the narrative for what it can reveal about the objectives of the first authors, and uncover their original story which lies beneath the Judean make-over.

> ➢ **In the original, Nathan condemned the relationship between David and Bathsheba. The Judean revisionist wrote in the episodes in which Nathan fully endorses Solomon as king.**

Nathan plays a key role in Solomon's seizure of the throne. He suggests the course of action to Bathsheba and goes into David to second her appeal. He accompanies Zadok the priest to anoint Solomon. The narrative goes out of its way to demonstrate that Solomon's elevation to the throne had the full endorsement of Nathan. All of which suggests that in the original account, Nathan condemned Solomon and his mother. If we take out Nathan entirely from the succession story, it makes much more sense.

It is Bathsheba who formulates the plan to get David to choose Solomon as his successor. Her motive is not just a lust for power. She also knows that if Adonijah becomes king, both she and her son will be executed as criminals; Bathsheba is a murderer, and Solomon is the cuckoo in the nest. The section where Nathan goes into David (1 Kings 1:22-28) has been inserted by the revisionist. If it is taken out, the account flows naturally from Bathsheba's request to David's response. Nathan is also an unnecessary extra at the anointing. It would make more sense if just Zadok the priest anointed Solomon.

We can divide the episodes involving Nathan into original or revisionist elements, depending on their attitude to Solomon:

Revisionist:

Through Nathan, God tells David to build a house for him and promises to establish the house of David forever through his son (Solomon). (2 Samuel 7)

Original:

Through Nathan, God condemns David for the murder of Uriah and for taking his wife, Bathsheba. (2 Samuel 12:1-12)

Revisionist:

Nathan says that David will be forgiven, but the child will die. (2 Samuel 12:13-14)

Revisionist:
Nathan says Solomon should be called Jedidiah, "beloved of Yahweh".
(2 Samuel 12:25)
Revisionist:
Nathan arranges the succession of Solomon and anoints him king. (1
Kings 1)

All the revisionist elements in this list are concerned with asserting that
Solomon is the legitimate king, the real son of David. If we look at the
promise given to David, it is linked to Solomon:

> "And when your days are fulfilled and you sleep with your fathers, I will
> set up your seed after you, who will come from your own body, and I
> will establish his kingdom. He will build a house for my Name, and I
> will establish the throne of his kingdom forever. I will be his father, and
> he shall be my son. When he commits iniquity, I will discipline him
> with the rod of men and with the blows of the sons of men. But my
> loving devotion shall not depart from him, as I took it from Saul, whom
> I removed from before you." (2 Samuel 7:12-15)

Note how it is stressed that "your seed", meaning David's son, has "come
from your own body". This addition is quite unnecessary and not part of the
traditional formula for a son. It is addressing the accusation that Solomon
was not David's child. The text also emphasises how Solomon is appointed
by God— "I will be his father, and he shall be my son." The idea that Solomon
was named Jedidiah, "beloved of Yahweh", a name which is never used
again, serves the same purpose. It is all a response to the accusation that
Solomon was not the legitimate king and was hated by Yahweh.

Take out the revisionist elements, and Nathan only appears in the single
sequence of 2 Samuel 12:1-12. This is built around the three elements of a
prophetic denunciation: (i) the charge, (ii) the condemnation and (iii) the
punishment. The charge comes in the story (doubtless modified) about
the man with many sheep who kills his guest's single lamb. As for the
condemnation, that comes first in David's response to Nathan's story: "the
man who did this deserves to die" (2 Samuel 12:5). David then adds, inconsis-
tently, that he should make four-fold restitution.

But the real original condemnation comes afterwards. Nathan tells
David of the good things that have been given to him: "I gave you your
master's house and your master's wives into your arms" (2 Samuel 12:8). This
would have originally been part of the condemnation, that David had
stolen Saul's throne and his wives. It is followed by the crime admitted
by the Book of Samuel:

"You have struck down Uriah the Hittite with the sword and took his wife as your wife, for you have killed him with the sword of the Ammonites." (2 Samuel 12:9)

Then comes the punishment:

"Now, therefore, the sword will never depart from your house, because you have despised me and have taken the wife of Uriah the Hittite to be your wife. Thus says Yahweh: I will raise up adversity against you from your own house. Before your sight I will take your wives and give them to another, and in the sight of the sun [shemesh] he will lie with them." (2 Samuel 12:10-11)

In the 2 Samuel story, this comes true through the revolt of David's son, Absalom. When David flees Jerusalem, Absalom lies with the concubines he has left behind:

So they pitched a tent for Absalom on the roof, and he slept with his father's concubines in the sight of all Israel. (2 Samuel 16:22)

This episode, with the tent set up on the roof, is so contrived that it has obviously been made up to explain the prophecy: *"in the sight of the sun he will lie with them".* But then the whole story of Absalom's revolt has been invented by the revisionist around this prophecy. Absalom dies as a human sacrifice; he is hung from an oak tree and run through by three spears. The revisionist lives at a time when such human sacrifice is strictly forbidden. He cannot show David as ordering his son's ritual death, so he has to provide another reason; Absalom was fleeing on a mule from the defeat of his revolt when his head caught in a tree leaving him hanging. Later Joab came along and thrust three spears through his heart. The revolt story also satisfies the prediction that the *"sword will never depart from your house"* and that David's adversity comes from his own house. But in the original, this prophecy was about Solomon, not Absalom.

It was the principle of poetic justice that the punishment should fit the crime. David had usurped Saul's throne, murdered his sons, slept with his wives and concubines, and eliminated his whole house. Not content with this, David had also stolen Uriah's wife and through her scheming, arranged Uriah's murder. What David had sown, he would reap. The house of David would be wiped out, and his sons killed. Uriah was the victim of the seductive wiles of Bathsheba, and David would suffer the same fate. He would live to see Uriah's son take his throne and sleep with his wives and concubines.

Solomon becomes king while David was still alive. And he certainly had many wives and concubines—seven hundred wives and three hundred concubines according to 1 Kings.[19] (These numbers are probably greater than the entire female population of Jerusalem at the time!) Not only has Pharaoh given his daughter to be the wife of the ruler of the tiny state of Judah, but Solomon's other wives come from *"Moab, Ammon, Edom, and Sidon, as well as Hittite women" (1 Kings 11:1)*. Behind this, we can see the original, that Solomon took over David's many wives, who are presented as foreign women worshipping foreign gods.

In support of this explanation is the strange wording: *"Before your sight I will take your wives and give them to another, and in the sight of the sun [shemesh] he will lie with them."* There is a wordplay here between David's sight and the sight of the sun. But why should the usurper lie with David's wives *"in the sight of the sun"*? A king's lovemaking would be done in private, not in the open air.

The name Solomon comes from the Hebrew word *shalem*. Although *shalem* can mean "peaceful" (the meaning of the name given in the much later 1 Chronicles), it is used more significantly to mean "to restore". Was Solomon named as the restoration for his real father, Uriah? The authors of the original would have known little about the historical Solomon. But they could have picked up on the wordplay that Solomon was a restoration (*shalem*), so giving rise to the Uriah story. It is suspicious that in 2 Samuel, Solomon replaces the first infant son of David and Bathsheba, suggesting that the revisionist was trying to counter the idea that Solomon was the replacement for Uriah.

It is more likely though that the historical Solomon was named after the Canaanite god Shalem, not least because Jerusalem ("city of Shalem") was named after this very same god. Shalem was the god of the setting sun and was closely associated with the sun goddess Shapash who was also called Shemesh. The word *shalem* came to mean "peaceful" because of the association with the quiet time of evening, the last rays of Shalem. So David's wives lie in the sight of Solomon the usurper, who was named after the god of the setting sun. It is Solomon who has stolen David's wives and his throne.

Abishag as agent of Bathsheba

We must remove Nathan from the succession account to recover the original. Bathsheba goes in to see David without the help of Nathan, but she is not alone. The young concubine Abishag is present throughout the interview. And there is something very odd about how she features, or rather does not feature, in what follows. Abishag is introduced as a beautiful girl chosen to keep David warm, but the narrative then contradicts this by stressing that she never slept with the king. She is present when Bathsheba appeals to David but plays no part in the action. Ancient narratives did not introduce characters like Abishag unless they were important. Her actual role in events has been edited out by the revisionist.

Bathsheba uses seduction as her weapon. She bathed in sight of David to become his wife and eliminate Uriah. How fitting that she should also use seduction to place Solomon on David's throne. Bathsheba herself is now old (for the time), so she uses a younger woman to do the deed. In the original, Abishag would have been Bathsheba's agent, hand-selected by her and given to David to keep him "warm". Abishag would most certainly have slept with David, the lustful old goat—hence the revisionist's denial. It is Abishag who uses her influence over David to persuade him to agree to Bathsheba's request. The revisionist replaces her intervention by that of Nathan.

> **Abishag was also employed by Bathsheba to seduce the original heir Adonijah leading to his death.**

Solomon becomes king, but there is a loose end; Adonijah, the legitimate heir.[20] Adonijah seeks sanctuary and is allowed to live, but then does something quite mad. He goes to Bathsheba and requests Abishag as his wife. Bathsheba agrees to appeal to Solomon on his behalf and goes to her son. We get an intriguing detail here that Bathsheba had a throne next to Solomon:

> *Then the king had a throne brought for his mother, who sat down at his right hand. (1 Kings 2:19)*

Bathsheba's throne is on the right and Solomon on the left; this shows quite plainly that Bathsheba is in charge and that Solomon is mummy's boy. Bathsheba is no innocent lamb, no passive object of male lust. When Bathsheba passes on Adonijah's request, Solomon is supposedly outraged. To ask for a former king's concubine is tantamount to asking for his throne. Solomon immediately orders the death of Adonijah, who is struck down and killed by his assassin Benaiah.

Even the most traditionalist of readers must sense something fishy about this episode. Adonijah has clearly been set up. But why should Adonijah make this crazy request for David's concubine? Bathsheba's role must have been edited down in the final Kings version. She has used Abishag to seduce Adonijah. She then meets with him and suggests that

Solomon would be open to his request for Abishag. There is one very telling line in the account of this meeting:

> He said, "You know that the kingdom was mine, and that all Israel set their faces on me to reign." (1 Kings 2:15)

It is Adonijah who is the real heir and who should be king over all Israel. But he falls into Bathsheba's trap which is sprung when she formally passes on his request to Solomon. The joint rulers now have the perfect pretext to order his execution.

Once again, the scheming Bathsheba uses seduction and murder to achieve her end. With the death of Adonijah, the house of David becomes the house of Solomon, son of a Hittite.

An Israelite satire

What can be deduced about the authors of the original? We can summarise the many odd features of the David and Solomon account:

David is guilty of nine distinct episodes of murder.

He is a vassal of the Philistines and fights against the Israelites in the army that defeats Saul.

He arranges the murder of Saul and his sons using an Amalekite assassin.

He arranges the death of the remaining sons and grandsons of Saul as sacrifices to be hung from a tree by the Gibeonites, who were Amorites.

He makes a human sacrifice out of his own son by having him hung from a tree and run through by three spears.

David attempts to bring the ark into Jerusalem, but God shows his disapproval by striking down one of the porters.

When David does bring the ark into the city, he performs a naked dance in front of it.

The destination of the ark, Jerusalem is called (i) "Baal of Judah" (the centre of Baal worship) and (ii) the house "of the servant of Edom, and inhabitant of Gath" (Gath was the Philistine city in which David took refuge, Edom an enemy of Israel).

David is called Doeg, "anxious/full of fear", the Edomite.

David and his men destroy the Israelite sanctuary and town of Nob, massacring the priests and all the inhabitants including children.

David steals the consecrated bread from Nob.

David's mother and father are said to have "come forth from Moab" (another enemy of Israel).

Bathsheba seduces David by bathing in his sight and then persuades him to murder her husband, Uriah, using the Ammonites.

Solomon is really the son of Uriah the Hittite, but Bathsheba tricks David into thinking he is his own son.

Through Nathan the prophet, God swears vengeance on David and his house for his crimes.

Bathsheba selects Abishag as David's last concubine, and then uses Abishag's influence with the senile king to persuade him to appoint Solomon as his successor.

Bathsheba uses Abishag to seduce the rightful heir Adonijah and then tricks him into asking for her as his wife, giving Solomon the perfect pretext for ordering his death.

By this means the true house of David is eliminated, and all the future Judean kings will be "sons of a Hittite".

Bathsheba and Solomon sit on joint thrones; Bathsheba on the right with Solomon relegated to the left.

Solomon marries the daughter of the Egyptian Pharaoh and takes many foreign wives and concubines.

The catalogue of anti-Judean elements is long and extreme. We have here a work of satire which has nothing to do with the real David and Solomon. The list of murders reads like a work of Agatha Christie because it is all fiction.

The satire has been used by the Revisionist as the main source for the narrative between 1 Samuel 21:1 and 1 Kings 3:1. Interspersed between the re-worked satire is additional material consisting of; (i) a few songs of David; (ii) lists of David's sons and officers, and a brief account of the doings of his "mighty men"; (iii) brief accounts of David's military victories; and (iv) an account of a famine and the building of an altar. This additional material must have come from a Judean source pre-dating the satire. Some of it may even be historical.

As for the satire, we can deduce the following:

- It was written by an Israelite who had great anger against the house of David.
- The chief target of this anger is David, although Solomon also comes in for a share.
- The mother of Solomon, Bathsheba, is surprisingly prominent as a scheming, murdering, adulteress. She dominates her son, Solomon.
- The authors did not regard the Jerusalem temple's pretensions as valid and mocked the bringing of the ark into the city.
- The house of David is shown as closely allied with foreign peoples;

fighting on their side against Israel, using foreign assassins, and taking foreign women as wives.

The whole work has then received a make-over by a Judean author who has reversed every condemnation. The revisionist goes out of his way to protect Solomon, Bathsheba, and David (in that order!) from every accusation in the original source. The house of David will now endure forever through David's own son Solomon who is also a beloved son of God.

The Judas War

The satire can only have been written in the reign of Hezekiah. It is the work of Israelite scribes taking refuge in Judah and witnessing the destruction of their homeland. They do not dare attack the ruling Judean kings directly, so they concoct a fake history of the legendary ancestors of the royal house, David and Solomon. Undoubtedly they had some sources; Judean folk tales of the doings of David as well as their own esteemed king, Saul. But the final creation is so bizarre and extreme that there cannot be much historical truth in it.

So why did the Judeans not simply ban this subversive work? Writing was very new at this time, and there was precious little written literature. This ballad about the acts of David, Bathsheba and Solomon was not dull history but entertainment. A steamy tale of murder, sex, and wicked doings by the royal elite, it resembled a modern tabloid story or soap opera. It must have been listened to with eager astonishment by the people, most of whom could not read themselves, but who would listen to a scribe recite the work. The Judean kings could not ban anything so popular without putting something in its place. So they made their own revised version which rebutted every accusation and exulted the kingdom of David and Solomon.

Those in the know would have appreciated the real targets of the satire. It was all about the Judas War, and was aimed at the royal family:

David = Ahaz
Bathsheba = Abi
Solomon = Hezekiah

The extraordinary portrayal of Bathsheba shows that she must represent a specific target of the satirist, as does the Judean attempt to whitewash her reputation. If she represents the king's mother and the power behind his throne, this explains the hostility directed against her. We will take the three in turn.

David as Ahaz

David joins the Philistines as a vassal and fights (in the rear!) in the army that defeats Saul's Israel. Substitute the Assyrians for the Philistines and we have an account of Ahaz's betrayal of Israel. David arranges the death of the Israelite kings and the leader of the Israelite army. He betrays the remnants of the house of Saul to the Gibeonites (Amorites) whom the Israelites had managed to drive out from their land. He destroys the Israelite sanctuary of Nob, massacring all the priests and inhabitants. David makes repeated use of assassins recruited from Israel's enemies to attain his aims. He offers one of his sons as a human sacrifice as did Ahaz.[21] In short, David is a traitor to his own people, who uses foreigners to wreak destruction on the Israelites.

In the David story, Achish, king of Gath, stands for Tiglath-pileser. When Ahaz hears about the Syrian and Israelite invasion, he is filled with a spirit of fear and becomes the willing vassal of the king of Assyria. Likewise, David flees from the Saul's Israelites to Gath, but then becomes fearful:

> *So he changed his behaviour before them and pretended madness in their hands; he scratched on the doors of the gate and let his saliva run down his beard. (1 Samuel 21:13)*

In the final version, this is all presented as a trick. The revisionist is trying to cover up a most unflattering portrait of David. The audience for the original satire would have been rollicking with laughter as they recognised the real target; Ahaz, raving mad with fear, scratching at the gate of the king of Assyria while spit dribbles down his beard.

Bathsheba as Abi

This is the most intriguing association. We have virtually no direct information about Ahaz's wife Abi—she was the mother of Hezekiah, the daughter of Zechariah, and her full name was Abijah—that is all. But we have seen one very intriguing clue, that Zechariah, her father, was one of the two witnesses to Isaiah's conception of Maher-shalal-hash-baz from the "prophetess". We have suggested that this shows that Abi's father, and hence Abi herself, was closely associated with the pro-Assyrian element of Ahaz's court. It is even possible that the prophetess is a satirical reference to Abi. If so, then Abi would have been regarded by her enemies as a whore and an adulteress. Who was her supposed lover? Perhaps a clue lies in the name of Bathsheba's husband, Uriah. Did this indicate to the winking, knowing audience the identity of Abi's "husband"? In Isaiah, the high priest Uriah stands next to Zechariah as a solemn witness to the act of whoredom. We can deduce that Abi (represented in Isaiah by her father) and Uriah, the high priest, were regarded as the two most significant figures behind the pro-Assyrian faction.

The Israelite refugees would have hated Ahaz and his whole court, but they would have reserved their greatest venom for the schemers behind the king. That Uriah was pro-Assyrian is clear from his eager acceptance of Ahaz's Assyrian style altar. The idea of Abi as a beautiful, sexually immoral woman who exercises her influence on a weak besotted man, Ahaz, to secure the downfall of Israel, draws on the archetype of the femme-fatal. It is not surprising that the Israelites regarded her as an adulteress with Uriah.

There is a further potential allusion to Abi in the David story in another version of the Bathsheba story. Abigail is a clever and beautiful woman married to a rich man called Nabal. David is an outlaw from Saul and operating a protection racket with his group of bandits. He has allowed Nabal's shepherds to peacefully tend their flock. Now he wants his cut. There is to be a feast, and David sends some of his thugs to Nabal with the message that they are to give him "whatever you can afford". Nabal tells them to get lost. When David hears about this, he is enraged, puts on his sword and leads his band out to kill Nabal and all the males in his household. Abigail, anticipating trouble, loads up donkeys with food, and goes out to meet David. She bows down before him and apologises for the stupidity of her husband. David accepts her apologies and her food, and they both rejoice that he has not had to murder Nabal even though he deserves to be killed. When Abigail gets back, Nabal is feasting and drunk. She tells him the next day what she has done, and he is struck in the heart, dying ten days later. David then takes Abigail as his willing wife.

Once again, David protests too much. The original story would have been a tale of murder with Abigail as an accomplice. The motive is surely to enable David to marry her, so it is another version of the Bathsheba story. There are similarities between the story and the accusation that Nathan makes against David:

- Both involve a rich man who had many sheep.
- In both stories, a traveller(s) comes to the rich man, and there is to be a meal/ feast.

- In both stories, the rich man refuses to give up a single one of his sheep.

The difference is that in Nathan's story, the rich man is David, the perpetrator, and in the Abigail story, the rich man is Nabal, the victim. The name "Nabal" is another literary device—as Abigail points out to David, it means "fool". The story has been turned upside-down by the revisionist. The original Nabal, "the fool", was a satirical allusion to David/Ahaz. Abigail, the wife of both Nabal and David, stands for Abijah, the wife of Ahaz. The giveaway is in the names—the short form of both Abigail and Abijah is "Abi".

The name of that alter-ego of Bathsheba, the seductress Abishag, is also revealing. It is another very odd name composed of *abi*, "my father", and *shagah* which means to go astray, to sin, to be drunk. In the Hebrew Bible, *shagah* is always used in a negative sense, for those who have strayed from the commandments, or who have been intoxicated by false prophets. We find it used in this later sense in First Isaiah to describe the Jerusalem of Hezekiah and Ahaz:

> *These also have erred [shagah] from wine and stumble from strong drink: Priests and prophets have erred [shagah] from strong drink and are swallowed up by wine. They stumble because of strong drink, they err [shagah] in their visions and stumble in their judgments. (Isaiah 28:7)*

In Proverbs, the word is given a sexual meaning: "*Why should you be intoxicated [shagah], my son, with a forbidden woman, and embrace the bosom of a seductress?*" (*Proverbs 5:20*). No real person would be given a name like Abishag ("my father has gone astray/become drunk"). It is another satirical name, intended to insult the person Abishag represents together with her father. Abishag is, of course, another "Abi". We know that Abi's father, Zechariah, was present as a witness to Isaiah's sexual transaction with the prophetess, so he was included among those who had strayed from the pure worship of Yahweh and become intoxicated with Assyrian ways. Abishag, concubine of David, is a mocking reference to Abijah, wife of Ahaz.

Abi may even have been accused by her enemies of murdering Ahaz to place her son Hezekiah on the throne. In the satire, both Bathsheba and Abigail murder their husbands. Nabal, the fool, stands for Ahaz. Does his death reflect Ahaz's demise? Nabal falls ill after feasting and lingers for ten days before dying. Poison, that traditional weapon of the female, was always suspected when a king died slowly like this.

Solomon as Hezekiah

In the satire, Solomon is not David's son, but the son of Uriah. If Solomon stands for Hezekiah and David for Ahaz, then this implies that Ahaz has been duped by Abi and that Hezekiah is not really his son. Remarkably, we can find evidence for the same accusation hidden in Isaiah. The boy Maher-shalal-hash-baz is named twice:

> Then Yahweh said to me, "Take a large tablet and write on it with a man's pen: Maher-shalal-hash-baz. And I will get reliable witnesses, Uriah the priest and Zechariah the son of Jeberechiah, to attest for me." (Isaiah 8:1-2)

> Then Yahweh said to me, "Call him Maher-shalal-hash-baz; for before the boy knows how to cry 'My father' and 'My mother' ..." (Isaiah 8:3-4)

There is a parallel between these two passages; the name is first written and then spoken, with the boy's two cries parallel to the two witnesses:

"My father" = Uriah
"My mother" = Zechariah, representing his daughter Abi

Abi is not mentioned here directly, but her name is actually uttered by the child. As well as the above parallel between the two lines, there is another parallel within Isaiah 8:4; the boy cries "My father" and "My mother". The expression for "My father" is *abi*—so the child says "Abi, My mother". Abi has not just been unfaithful to Ahaz with Uriah the high priest, but the adulterous couple have had a child; Maher-shalal-hash-baz, representing Hezekiah. It is all very clever, with the clues hidden well enough to evade the Judean revisionists. The continuation of the Maher-shalal-hash-baz passage is the prophecy of the crisis of Hezekiah's reign, the Sennacherib invasion. Hezekiah appears to be called Immanuel in this prophecy which can be seen as a substitution for Maher-shalal-hash-baz.

The allegation about Hezekiah's parentage was not necessarily true, but it was how the political opponents of Ahaz, Abi and Hezekiah saw things. The same accusation is reflected in both First Isaiah and the David story, and must be contemporary to Hezekiah although both sources were subsequently worked over by pro-Judean scribes. By presenting Hezekiah as the child of Uriah, these opponents denied his right to be king. To make such a suggestion was treason punishable by death—so it could not be explicit.

In the succession history, Solomon is presented as being overshadowed by his mother. We cannot know if this was how Hezekiah was perceived. But there are other aspects which point to Solomon representing Hezekiah. The first is Solomon's alliance and marriage with Egypt: *"Solomon made an alliance with Pharaoh king of Egypt and married his daughter. Solomon brought her to the City of David until he had finished building his palace and the house of Yahweh, as well as the wall around Jerusalem"* (1 Kings 3:1). This could be an allusion to Hezekiah's Egyptian alliance in the run-up to the Sennacherib invasion. At this time Hezekiah built a new wall around the western hill of Jerusalem as an addition to the existing wall around the City of David.

The second is a potential reference to Hezekiah's desecration of the sacred places. When Adonijah hears that Solomon has been anointed king, he claims sanctuary by holding on to the horns of the altar. He only leaves when Solomon promises that he will live unless *"evil is found in him"* (1 Kings 1:52). Shortly after this he is killed on the orders of Solomon, but there is a surprising absence of detail for his death—we are just told that Benaiah struck him. This is immediately followed by another suspiciously similar death. David's right-hand man Joab has conspired with Adonijah, so he also flees to the altar and grabs hold of the horns. This time Solomon orders the execution of Joab at the altar, and Benaiah strikes and kills him, just as he did Adonijah.

Joab is the revisionist's fall guy, a character brought in to deflect blame from David. Here he serves the purpose of substituting for the original victim, Adonijah, struck down at the altar as he clung to the horns. By changing the fugitive seeking sanctuary to Joab, a serial assassin, the revisionist seeks to justify the act. In the original text, Solomon violated sanctuary to commit the murder of the rightful king, a dreadful crime before God. Solomon's contempt for the altar is an allusion to Hezekiah's contempt for the altars outside of the Jerusalem temple. We even have archaeological evidence for Hezekiah's action against these altars; two examples whose horns were deliberately sheared off.

The real David and Solomon?

The Israelite satire tells us nothing about the real David and Solomon any more than Shakespeare's King Lear tells us about the realities of Anglo-Saxon England. Both works were written hundreds of years after the time they depict and are literary creations based on legends and myths. Unlike King Lear, there can be little doubt that David existed. He was a local warlord who conquered Jerusalem and started a dynasty of kings. We can be much less sure about Solomon for whom there is not a single shred of independent evidence.

Is it just coincidence that Solomon, the great temple builder, should be named after the same Canaanite god, Shalem, as Jerusalem itself? Logically, we would expect Solomon's temple to be dedicated to Shalem, not Yahweh. Were the sun god's chariot and horses at the temple entrance a survival from this earlier dedication?[22] If so, then Solomon would not have been a Judean or an Israelite, but would have lived before David's conquest of the city. He may even have been a purely legendary figure, the Jerusalem equivalent of Romulus, the mythical founder of Rome.

Although the Jerusalem of David's time was a very minor settlement, this had not always been the case. Bronze-age Jerusalem was a more impressive city, with the large and enigmatic "stepped structure" providing evidence of significant construction. Unfortunately, we have no archaeological evidence about the first temple because the site was razed during the building of the temple of Herod. Crucially, we do not know when the first temple was built. Certainly, no Davidic king other than Solomon is claimed to have built the temple in the Bible. According to 2 Kings, Joash carried out extensive renovation work on the temple, but the account does not suggest that he built the temple.[23] This gives the possibility that the temple was already in existence when David captured the city. David would have rededicated this temple to his own God, Yahweh. The memory of this event may survive in the distorted story of David bringing the ark of the covenant into Jerusalem.

The people of Jerusalem would have had two founding fathers. The Judean kings looked to their ancestor David but ruled over a population who still cherished legends about the wise, mythical Solomon, supposed builder of the temple. The stories about Solomon, such as his mines and the visit of the Queen of Sheba, better reflect the internationalist bronze age rather than the impoverished early iron age. So perhaps the two distinct traditions were combined, with David preeminent, and Solomon slotted in as his son.

At the time of the Judas War, Judah was flooded with Israelite refugees, and it became vital to establish the right of the Judean kings to rule over all Israel. The legend of David and Solomon was extended to assert a claim to Israel. David was made the successor of the esteemed early Israelite King Saul while Solomon supposedly ruled over a kingdom that embraced the territory of both Israel and Judah. The impressive relics of the Omride dynasty were constructed by Solomon, and the kings of Israel were rebels who had broken away from this united kingdom.

The first generation of Israelite refugees would have been enraged by this fake history. They went on the attack with their own version of the truth, an outrageous satire in which David, standing in for Ahaz, was a cowardly traitor who betrayed and murdered Saul and the Israelites. This racy story became so popular that it could not be ignored. The Judean establishment responded with a reworked version that pedantically addressed each and every accusation.

Ironically, it was the revisionist's account that was to have a lasting impact. It was necessary to refute the prophecy of Nathan that the house of David would come to destruction through Solomon, son of Uriah. The idea that David's true line had been eliminated and that the Judean kings were "sons of a Hittite" was too dangerous to leave unchecked. So another prophecy by Nathan was inserted, predicting that the house of David would last forever through his son Solomon who had come "from your own body". This prophecy would attain special significance after the exile when the line of Judean kings had finally come to an end. It was read as a prediction of the return of the king, the Messiah of the house of David.

Appendix A

The Apocalypse of Weeks

This appendix complements Chapter 12 by looking in more detail at the Apocalypse of Weeks and offering a reconstruction of the original Apocalypse.

In the Ethiopian Book of Enoch, the Apocalypse is split into two parts with weeks 1-7 (1 Enoch 93:3-10) positioned a little after weeks 8-10 (1 Enoch 91:12-16). It was obvious that the two parts belonged together and this has now been confirmed by the Dead Sea scrolls fragments in which weeks 8-10 follow straight on from weeks 1-7. Combining the two parts gives the following structure:

Week 1: Enoch
Week 2: The descent of the watchers, the flood, Noah, and a law.
Week 3: Abraham
Week 4: The law of Moses
Week 5: The kingdom of David and the temple
Week 6: The Jews blinded; Elijah; the burning of the temple and the exile.
Week 7: An apostate generation; the elect ones of righteousness, seven-fold instruction.
Week 8: The punishment of the unrighteous; the building of a new temple
Week 9: Righteous judgement revealed and the earth written-off for destruction.
Week 10: Eternal judgement executed by the angels; a new heaven.

Only Enoch is named, although it is obvious who the other individuals are. Let us look at some features of the Apocalypse.

➢ **Significant events come at the sabbath of each week. With one exception, these events are all good.**

The sabbath, the seventh day of each week, was important to the author of the Apocalypse of Weeks. Significant events happen at the end of each

459

week. The only exception is the ninth week which seems redundant. The "good" events occurring on a sabbath are; Enoch; the law of Noah; Abraham; the law of Moses; the kingdom of David and the temple; the sevenfold instruction to the elect; the building of a new temple; the creation of a new heaven. The one "bad" event happening on a sabbath is the burning of the temple and the exile at the culmination of week 6. This habit of placing good events at the sabbath position is a key difference between the Apocalypse of Weeks and the Almanac.

➢ **The two laws of Noah and Moses are prominent in the Apocalypse. Abraham is not included as a law-giver but as the root of the plant representing the Jews.**

We have seen how the parable of the tenants is about the three law-givers, the man-angels Noah and Moses, and the Christ. There is no Christ in the Apocalypse of Weeks, but we find the same importance given to the first two laws. The law of Noah comes at the end of the second week, which brings "a law for sinners" meaning the gentiles, the nations. The law of Moses comes at the end of the fourth week: *"visions of the old and righteous ones shall be seen, and a law shall be made with a fence for all the generations" (1 Enoch 93:6).*[1] There is no allusion to Moses as a prophet in the text, and this is the only reference to the law of Moses in the whole Book of Enoch.[2] The law is described as a fence, an image also found in the parable of the vineyard in the Shepherd of Hermas. The "old and righteous ones" must signify the angels, including the angel of the Name. So the law comes from angels, as it does in Paul's letters and Acts.

Abraham is not depicted as a law-giver. He comes in the third week: *"and at its conclusion a man will be chosen as the plant of righteous judgement, and after him will go forth the plant of righteousness for ever and ever" (1 Enoch 93:5).*[3] So Abraham is "chosen" as "the plant of righteous judgement" and from him will come forth Israel, "the plant of righteousness", which will go on forever. In terms of the vineyard and tenants parable, Israel is the vine, and Abraham the root of that vine. He is not a man-angel, like Noah and Moses, but fully human.

➢ **Weeks six and onwards have been modified to place the author's own group at the culmination of week seven.**

There is no Christ in the Apocalypse of Weeks, but there is an equivalent of the law of Christ at the culmination of the seventh week:

At its completion, there shall be elected the elect ones of righteousness from the eternal plant of righteousness, to whom shall be given seven-fold instruction concerning all his flock. (1 Enoch 93:10)[4]

The "sevenfold instruction" is the transmission of some secret knowledge to "the elect ones of righteousness". These "elect" or chosen ones are Jews since they come from "the eternal plant of righteousness". They must be the final author's own group. This would explain the oddest feature of the Apocalypse. The sabbaths are very important, so the most important day of all should be the "sabbath of sabbaths"; the seventh day of the seventh week. However, there is no remarkable event on this day, but only the obscure reference to the elect ones. The Apocalypse of Weeks must have been modified from the original to place the final author's group at this special position.

> ➤ **The earlier form of the Apocalypse must have had the destruction of the temple at the sabbath of sabbaths.**

Several points indicate that the original Apocalypse has been edited:

- The Matthew genealogy agrees well with the Apocalypse in weeks 4 and 5. However, the two diverge after this with the next two genealogy weeks collapsed into Apocalypse week 6.
- The Apocalypse shows a compression of events in week 6. Elijah is taken to heaven immediately before the temple is destroyed. Yet Elijah lived in the time of the Israelite King Ahab (873-852 BC), almost three hundred years before the burning of the temple in 586 BC.
- The return from exile does not feature in the Apocalypse. The "clan of the chosen root" (the Jews) are dispersed at the end of week 6. Immediately after, in week 7, "an apostate generation shall arise" without explaining how the Jews have come back to Jerusalem.
- The duration allowed for the apocalypse is absurdly long; it takes no less than three weeks or twenty-one generations. In particular, week 9 is superfluous.

We can attempt a reconstruction of the Apocalypse which resolves these points. This is the description of weeks 6-7:

After that in the sixth week those who happen to be in it shall all of them be blindfolded, and the hearts of them all shall forget wisdom. Therein a (certain) man shall ascend. And, at its completion, the house of the kingdom shall be burnt with fire; and therein the whole clan of the chosen root will be dispersed.

After that in the seventh week an apostate generation shall arise; its deeds shall be many, and all of them criminal. At its completion, there shall be elected the elect ones of righteousness from the eternal plant of righteousness, to whom shall be given sevenfold instruction concerning all his flock. (1 Enoch 93:8-10)[5]

We can recover the likely form of these two weeks by moving the destruction of the temple to the end of the seventh week:

Reconstructed weeks 6-7:

After that in the sixth week those who happen to be in it shall all of them be blindfolded, and the hearts of them all shall forget wisdom. Therein a (certain) man shall ascend.

After that in the seventh week an apostate generation shall arise; its deeds shall be many, and all of them criminal. And, at its completion, the house of the kingdom shall be burnt with fire; and therein the whole clan of the chosen root will be dispersed.

The eighth week would have had the return from exile and the election of the chosen. Week 9 would be replaced by the current week 8, and week 10 would be unchanged. This gives the following structure, with key events typically positioned at the end of the week:

The reconstructed original Apocalypse of Weeks

Week 1: Enoch
Week 2: Noah, the flood, and the law for the nations
Week 3: Abraham
Week 4: Moses, and the law for the Jews
Week 5: The kingdom of David and the temple
Week 6: Elijah
Week 7: An apostate generation and the destruction of the temple
Week 8: The partial return from exile
Week 9: The final battle and the new temple
Week 10: The final judgement, a new heaven and earth

We see that in this structure, each of the first six periods is linked to an individual; Enoch, Noah, Abraham, Moses, David and Elijah. The pattern is broken and comes to a climax in week seven, with the destruction of the temple on the sabbath of sabbaths. There is a partial return from exile in week eight, which probably ended with the choosing of the elect ones. These elect ones then fight the final battles in week 9, which ends with the coming of the new temple. Week 10 is reserved for the apocalypse and the final judgement. This sequence of events matches quite closely that in the Animal Apocalypse.

> ➤ **The Apocalypse of Weeks does not recognise the second temple and could not have been written by a supporter of the Maccabees.**

In the Animal Apocalypse, the second temple is invalid. The Apocalypse of Weeks goes one step further and does not even acknowledge the existence of this second temple. (It may have appeared in the original week 8 which was deleted. Even so, it is clear that the only valid successor temple is that which comes after the final battles.)

The absence of the second temple rules out the idea that a supporter of the Maccabees could have composed the Apocalypse of Weeks. Was the original Apocalypse of Weeks produced by the same group as the Animal Apocalypse? The two are clearly very closely related. There is though one vital difference; the Apocalypse of Weeks does not have the great bull, the heavenly Messiah, at the end times. So it does not come from the proto-Christian group that produced the Animal Apocalypse. The Apocalypse of Weeks is not on the direct line that leads to the Jesus movement but it is a side shoot from the same trunk.

Appendix B

The Daniel Prophecies and the Almanac

In this appendix, we look at two sections of prophecy in the Book of Daniel. We will show that the author of Daniel used a source involving the Babylonian exile and misinterpreted it as a prophecy of the future. The author, writing in the Maccabean era, applies this source to events unfolding in his own time. The prophecies in these sections of Daniel have two layers:

1. Aspects of the original source.
2. Additions and interpretations that fit events in the Maccabean era.

We need to split out these two layers to determine the form of the original source or sources. The practice of applying a scriptural source relating to past historical events as a future prophecy has been common throughout history. Ironically, it has often been used of Daniel itself. Many preachers down the ages have interpreted Daniel and its Christian equivalent, the Book of Revelation, as applying to events in their own time.

The two sections of prophecy of interest here are:

The prophecy of the seventy weeks in Daniel 9.
The prophecies of the "king of the North" in Daniel 11.

We will show that the seventy weeks prophecy is based on a source similar to the Almanac and that the original "king of the North" was the king of Babylon.

➢ **The prophecy of seventy weeks in Daniel is using something like the Almanac as its source.**

According to Daniel, the seventy weeks prophecy was given to the prophet in the year that Babylon fell to the Persians (539 BC). Daniel is reflecting on the prediction in Jeremiah that the exile would last seventy years. Although the period was now up, the Jews had not returned to Jerusalem. The angel Gabriel appears to him to clarify the earlier prophecy:

"Seventy weeks are decreed about your people and your holy city, to finish the transgression, to make an end of sin, and to atone for iniquity, to bring in everlasting righteousness, to seal both vision and prophecy, and to anoint a most holy place." (Daniel 9:24)

Instead of the exile lasting for seventy years, it will last for seventy weeks of years, or 490 years. The prophecy continues:

"Know therefore and understand this, that from the going out of the word to restore and build Jerusalem to the coming of an anointed one, the prince, there shall be seven weeks. Then in sixty-two weeks it shall be built again with squares and moat, but in a troubled time. And after sixty-two weeks, an anointed one shall be cut off and will have nothing. And the people of the prince who is to come shall destroy the city and the sanctuary. Its end shall come with a flood. War will continue to the end, and desolations are decreed. And he shall make a covenant with many for one week, and in the middle of the week he shall put an end to sacrifice and offering. And on the wing of abominations shall come one who makes desolate, until the decreed consummation is poured out on the desolator." (Daniel 9:25-27)

There are points of obvious similarity between the Daniel prophecy and the Almanac:

1. Both involve a calendar of seventy periods.
2. In both cases, the length of the exile is subject to a sevenfold increase from the prophetic predictions of the defeat of Babylon (seventy years which equals "two days"/generations). The Jews will return to Jerusalem, but the real exile will last much longer.

However, Daniel applies the seventy periods to the length of the exile, starting from the fall of Jerusalem, and each period is only seven years long. This is quite unlike the seventy generations of the Almanac. How can we be sure that the author of Daniel has used something like the Almanac as his source? Because, as we will see, the destruction of Jerusalem is actually embedded within Daniel's seventy periods. This means that the seventy periods could not have been weeks of years as they are in Daniel. In the source they must have covered a much longer period.

> ➢ **The Book of Daniel uses Jeremiah as a major source to the extent of changing the timing of events to match prophecies in Jeremiah.**

To understand the prophecy of the seventy weeks, we must start with the author's use of Jeremiah to derive the timing of events. Although Daniel supposedly lived during the Babylonian exile, the author actually has no direct sources for this period beyond the scriptures. This is evident from the strange date given in Daniel for the start of the exile:

> *In the third year of the reign of Jehoiakim king of Judah, Nebuchadnezzar king of Babylon came to Jerusalem and besieged it. And the Lord gave Jehoiakim king of Judah into his hand, along with some of the articles from the house of God. He carried these off to the land of Shinar [Babylon] to the house of his god, and he brought them into the treasury of his god. (Daniel 1:1-2)*

So the exile supposedly commenced under King Jehoiakim in 606 BC. No other source supports such an early date, and Nebuchadnezzar could not have defeated Jehoiakim at this time. However, the description does fit the first exile under Jehoiakim's son Jeconiah (Jehoiachin) in 597 BC. In Daniel, some of the royal family and the nobility are exiled to Babylon which could be a reference to the Jeconiah exile. But why should the exile be shifted back in time by over a decade? The answer is to fit in with Jeremiah which describes the Jeconiah exile:

> *After Nebuchadnezzar king of Babylon had carried away Jeconiah son of Jehoiakim, king of Judah, and the officials of Judah and the craftsmen and metalsmiths from Jerusalem, and had brought them to Babylon ... (Jeremiah 24:1)*

Someone reading this could think Jehoiakim was still alive when Nebuchadnezzar took his son. It is followed in Jeremiah by a parable of good and bad figs; those who go to Babylon with Jeconiah are good figs, whereas those who remain under Zedekiah are bad figs. Next comes another prophecy dated to 605 BC:

> *The word that came to Jeremiah concerning all the people of Judah in the fourth year of Jehoiakim, son of Josiah king of Judah, which was the first year of Nebuchadnezzar king of Babylon. (Jeremiah 25:1)*

The prophecy that follows predicts the invasion of Nebuchadnezzar, king of Babylon against Zedekiah, and the eventual defeat of Babylon after seventy years:

> *And this whole land will become a desolation and a horror, and these nations will serve the king of Babylon for seventy years. But when seventy years are accomplished, I will punish the king of Babylon and that nation, the land of the Chaldeans, for their guilt, declares Yahweh, and I will make it an everlasting desolation. I will bring upon that land all my words which I have pronounced against it, all that is written in this book, which Jeremiah has prophesied against all the nations. They shall be enslaved by many nations and great kings... (Jeremiah 25:11-14)*

So this section of Jeremiah has the following structure:

1. Statement of the exile of Jeconiah (no date given)
   Prophecy of the return; the parable of the good and bad figs.
2. Jeremiah gives a prophecy in the fourth year of Jehoiakim (= 605 BC)
   Prophecy of the final defeat of Judah, and the defeat of Babylon after 70 years.

Jeremiah jumps back ten years between these two sections, which is typical of the non-linear nature of the prophetic books. However, this jump back in time is not evident from the text. The author of Daniel has not appreciated the step-back and thinks that first event, the Jeconiah exile, must have happened shortly before the second prophecy. So he places the exile in the previous year to the second prophecy, the third year of Jehoiakim, or 606 BC.

This odd timing agrees better with Jeremiah's prophecy than the real date. Jeremiah says that the Jews will be under the Babylonians for seventy years after which Babylon will be enslaved by many nations and great kings. If we go forward seventy years from 606 BC we get to 536 BC which is close; Babylon was defeated by the Persian King Cyrus in 539 BC. But in reality, the exile started in 597 BC, so the Jews were only under Babylonian rule for less than sixty years. Jeremiah's prophecy of seventy years is actually wrong.

➤   The starting point of Daniel's seventy weeks of years is not the
    declaration of Cyrus but the prophecy of the return in Jeremiah.
    The first "anointed one" is Cyrus.

The prophecy of the seventy weeks starts with the coming of the first
"anointed one" who is "a prince":

> Know therefore and understand this, that from the going out of the
> word to restore and build Jerusalem to the coming of an anointed one,
> the prince, there shall be seven weeks. (Daniel 9:25)

The word to rebuild Jerusalem is usually taken as the declaration of
Cyrus, which permitted the Jews to return. But the author of Daniel has
only a minimal knowledge of the period, and this does not explain the
"anointed one" who comes after seven weeks. We should instead look to
the author's favourite source, Jeremiah, for the "word to restore and build
Jerusalem";

> "The days are coming," declares Yahweh, "when the city will be rebuilt
> for Yahweh, from the tower of Hananel to the Corner Gate." (Jeremiah
> 31:38)

The word is not given by Cyrus but by Yahweh. A date immediately follows this prophecy; the "tenth year of Zedekiah king of Judah" (Jeremiah 32:1)
which indicates 588/7 BC. If we go forward seven weeks of years from 588
BC we get to 539 BC, the year of Cyrus' conquest of Babylon. The prophecy
agrees precisely if Cyrus is the "anointed one". Would a gentile Persian
king be called the Messiah? Yes, because Cyrus is called exactly this in
Isaiah: "This is what Yahweh says to his anointed, to Cyrus..." (Isaiah 45:1).
   This identification of the first anointed with Cyrus must be an interpretation added by the author of Daniel. It does not belong in the original
source.

➤   The period of sixty-two weeks does not take us to the Maccabean
    period because the Jews did not know how much time had
    elapsed since the exile.

The first anointed one is followed by a long period of sixty-two weeks
in which the temple and Jerusalem will be rebuilt "in a troubled time".
Although the city is rebuilt, the Jews were still in a state of exile. The
author of Daniel sees the Maccabean wars as bringing in the final restoration from exile.

The author clearly intends the final week to match the events of his own time. But if we go forward sixty-two weeks (434 years) from 539 BC, we get 105 BC which is too late for the Maccabees. But the author of Daniel has only a hazy knowledge of history. The Jews at this time did not know how long had elapsed from the exile because they had no sources from which to calculate this period. No Jewish texts or histories spanned this gulf of time. In the modern era, we can date events because we have records from the surrounding civilisations. The Jews living in the Maccabean age did not possess such records.

> ➤ **The second "anointed one" is not the high priest Onias III but Jeconiah. The original source relates to the Babylonian exile.**

After the sixty-two weeks, the Book of Daniel comes to the events of the author's own age—or so the author believes. The account clearly relates to the actions of the Seleucid King Antiochus IV Epiphanes which sparked the Maccabean revolt. But much does not fit. Taking the section line by line:

> *And after the sixty-two weeks, an anointed one shall be cut off and will have nothing. (Daniel 9:26)*

This second "anointed one" could be either a king or a priest. Under the Maccabean hypothesis, he is identified as the former high priest Onias III. Onias was deprived of the priesthood by Antiochus IV and later assassinated by one of the king's ministers Andronikos, at the instigation of the then high priest Menelaus. When the king heard about the assassination, he had Andronikos executed in a display of grief. The whole story seems inherently unlikely and is only found in 2 Maccabees. There are also close similarities to the story of another murder, that of Antiochus, the child heir of the previous king, Seleucus IV. This murder was committed by a person also called Andronikos on the secret orders of Antiochus IV. The king mourned the killing in public and had Andronikos executed. It is hard to believe that there were two men both called Andronikos, who both committed a murder, and who were then both executed by Antiochus IV in a display of grief. It makes more sense that Antiochus IV should sacrifice Andronikos to remove the rival heir to the Seleucid throne, than that he should grieve over the death of a Jewish high priest.[1]

In any case, Onias may not have been the popular hero that he is presented as in 2 Maccabees. He is not even mentioned in 1 Maccabees, and there is a hint in 2 Maccabees 4:1-2 that some Jews saw him as being complicit with the Seleucid regime in an attempt to confiscate deposits held in the temple. Besides, the Onias interpretation does not fit what comes next; after being "cut-off" the anointed one "had nothing". This implies that the anointed one was not killed but lived on in an abject state.

There is an anointed one who was "cut-off" so that he "had nothing"— the young King Jeconiah (Jehoiachin). He was deposed as king, losing his kingdom and taken to Babylon. Jeconiah spent the rest of his long life in Babylon where he certainly "had nothing". He was imprisoned for many years, and after his release, he was dependent upon the goodwill of the king of Babylon for his daily rations of food.[2] There is a tradition that Jeconiah had no posterity, a bitter fate for a Jew: "*Write down this man as childless, a man who will not prosper in his lifetime.*" *(Jeremiah 22:30)*

> ➤ **The cutting off of Jeconiah is followed by the Babylonian assault on Jerusalem.**

The prophecy in Daniel continues:

> *And the people of the prince who is to come shall destroy the city and the sanctuary. Its end shall come with a flood. War will continue to the end, and desolations are decreed. (Daniel 9:26)*

This does not fit Antiochus Epiphanes at all: he did not destroy either Jerusalem or the temple. But the description fits the events of the exile of Judah perfectly. The forces of Nebuchadnezzar destroyed Jerusalem and the temple a decade after the exile of Jeconiah. As for this destruction being a "flood", this is imagery in the prophetic books for invasions by powers whose civilisation was built around a great river. Like a river in flood, they overflowed their banks and inundated the surrounding nations. It is applied to Egypt (Jeremiah 46:8), the Assyrians (Isaiah 8:6-8) and the Babylonians (Jeremiah 47:2). An invasion by Babylon would be a flood, but not an attack by the Greek Seleucid Empire. The phrase "desolations are decreed" refers to the desolation of Judah by Babylon predicted in the prophetic literature. Daniel continues:

> *And he shall make a covenant with many for one week, and in the middle of the week he shall put an end to sacrifice and offering. And on the wing of abominations shall come one who makes desolate, until the decreed consummation is poured out on the desolator. (Daniel 9:27)*

Finally, we come to Antiochus IV Epiphanes. Many Jews supported his attempts at Hellenization, so he can be said to have made a covenant with many. He erected "the abomination of desolation", a statue of Zeus, in the temple and sacrifices to Yahweh stopped.

The prophecy of the seventy weeks includes aspects relating to Antiochus imposed on an earlier source concerned with the Judean exile and king of Babylon. These events were embedded within the seventy periods, showing that the source calendar must have covered a much longer period than the seventy weeks of years in Daniel.

Can we find anything directly relating to the Almanac? It is difficult to determine much of the original source beneath the Daniel interpretations. But one possibility is that the first and second anointed ones were the same person. If the anointed one came after "seven weeks" in Almanac time, this would indicate Jeconiah who matches the description of the second anointed one in Daniel.

The king of the North

The other section of interest is the prophecy concerning the "king of the North" in Daniel 11. We will see that the author is again using an existing source about the king of Babylon and misapplying it to Antiochus.

> ➤ **Daniel 11 starts with detailed prophecies leading up to Antiochus IV. But when the prophecy turns to the author's future, it uses a source which was about the king of Babylon.**

The prophecies of Daniel 11 demonstrate beyond doubt that the author was writing while Antiochus IV Epiphanes was still alive. It describes the break-up of Alexander the Great's kingdom into four successor kingdoms, culminating with Antiochus IV, the odious "king of the North" whose reign is detailed in Daniel 11:21-45. The account is an accurate description up to the setting up of the "abomination of desolation". From this point onwards the prophecy is dealing with the author's own future and goes wildly, and often hilariously, wrong.

These future failed prophecies are not random. They actually relate to the king of Babylon, both as heavenly ruler and the human King Nebuchadnezzar. The author of Daniel has misunderstood "the king of the North" as meaning Antiochus Epiphanes. But the original "king of the North" was the king of Babylon. The Jews regarded the Babylonians as coming from the north because they approached Judah from that direction.

The confusion starts in Daniel 11:36 where the king of the North magnifies himself above every god. It continues:

*He shall show no regard to the gods of his fathers, or to the one beloved
by women, nor for any other god, for he shall magnify himself above
all. (Daniel 11:37)*

This god "beloved of women" is most likely Tammuz (Dumuzi) who
is mourned by women in the temple and who perhaps stands for Christ.[3]
We find the idea that the king of Babylon places himself above all other
gods including Yahweh in Isaiah 14:3-23 where the king of Babylon sets
his throne above that of Yahweh.

> ➤ **Daniel continues with a description of the triumphs of
> Nebuchadnezzar with the aid of a "god of fortresses" who must
> be Yahweh. It includes a description of the battle of Carchemish,
> Nebuchadnezzar's subsequent invasion of Judah and his influ-
> ence over Egypt.**

According to the Daniel prophecy, the king of the North would go on
to conquer Egypt and many other countries. But this was something
that Antiochus IV never did. The prophecy goes wrong because the
author of Daniel is using a source where "the king of the North" is now
Nebuchadnezzar, the human king of Babylon. The king is said to honour
a foreign "god of fortresses", who enables him to capture fortresses. Who
is this strange "god of fortresses", who does not correspond to any known
pagan god? It can be none other than Yahweh who is repeatedly described
in scripture as the "fortress" or "rock". To the king of Babylon, Yahweh
is a foreign god, but he grants the king the power for conquest. We find
precisely this idea in the books of the prophets where the king of Babylon
is Yahweh's servant summoned to do Yahweh's will. Daniel continues:

*At the time of the end, the king of the South shall attack him. And
the king of the North shall storm out against him, with chariots and
horsemen, and with many ships. And he shall enter countries and shall
overflow them and pass through. (Daniel 11:40)*

This is describing the battle of Carchemish and its aftermath. The army
of Pharaoh Necho of Egypt (king of the South) came up to Carchemish to
attack Babylon but was destroyed by Nebuchadnezzar's forces (the king
of the North). After this victory, Babylon was able to extend its empire.
The passage uses flood imagery in describing the king of the North "overflowing" other countries. Jeremiah alludes to Babylon in similar terms as
"waters rising from the north" that shall be *"an overflowing flood"* (Jeremiah 47:2).
The same word meaning "overflow" or "flood" is used in both passages.

Jeremiah describes the Egyptians setting out to Carchemish using the same language as the forces of the king of the North meeting the Egyptians in Daniel. The Egyptians are like the Nile in flood (Jeremiah 46:7-8) and surge with horses and chariots: *"Advance, O horses, and rage, O chariots!" (Jeremiah 46:9)*. Compare to *"the king of the North shall storm out against him, with chariots and horsemen"*. In Daniel, the forces of the king of the North then invade Judah:

> He will also invade the Beautiful Land. Many countries will fall. But Edom, Moab and the prominent sons of Ammon will be delivered from his hand. (Daniel 11:41)

After Carchemish, the Babylonians conquered the nations between them and Egypt, including Judah. But why are Edom, Moab and Ammon said to be spared? Because in Jeremiah 40:11-12 it is reported that many Jews had fled the Babylonians to *"Moab, Ammon, Edom and all the other countries"*.

Daniel continues with the king of the North extending his power as far as Egypt, gaining control of the treasure of Egypt, and the submission of the Libyans and Cushites (Ethiopians). Babylon did attain influence over Egypt, although it never completely conquered that country. As for the Libyans and Cushites, these both carry the shield for Egypt in the force that was defeated at Carchemish (Jeremiah 46:9).

➤ **The predicted end of the king of the North relates to the fall of Babylon at the hands of Cyrus.**

Daniel also gets the predicted end of Antiochus IV completely wrong. The Seleucid king actually died in Tabae in Persia, but in Daniel he dies near Jerusalem. Once again, the author of Daniel has misapplied a source about the king of Babylon. In Daniel, the end of the king of the North is predicted to come between the sea and the mountain:

> But reports from the east and the north shall alarm him, and he shall go out with great fury to destroy and devote many to destruction. And he shall pitch his royal tents between the sea and the beautiful holy mountain. Yet he shall come to his end, and none shall help him. (Daniel 11:44-5)

The king of the North comes to his end between Jerusalem (the holy mountain) and the sea. This comes from misunderstood prophecies of the end of Babylon. In Jeremiah 50-1, the prophet tells of the eventual fall of Babylon using phrases and imagery linked to the Daniel passage. The threat to Babylon is repeatedly said to come from the north: *"for a nation from the north will come against her"* (Jeremiah 50:3). In reality, Persia and Media were to the east of Babylon, which is why in Daniel reports come from the east as well as the north. The phrase "devote to destruction" found in the Daniel passage is applied to Babylon three times in Jeremiah.[4] In Daniel the king is without allies: "none shall help him". And in Jeremiah, the vast array of nations coming against Babylon is stressed without mentioning a single ally.[5]

The idea that the fall of the king of the North would come near the sea arises from a misunderstanding of imagery applied to the fall of Babylon. The defeat of Babylon in Jeremiah is expressed using sea imagery, as if the sea were coming against it, or drying up.[6] The sea is an ironic allusion to the great river Euphrates which bisected the city of Babylon. The rise of Babylon was a great flood, but now the waters flow the other way, and the Euphrates dries up. Babylon is also described as a mountain, and Babylon ascends to the heavens to fortify her stronghold. This could have given rise to the "holy mountain" in the Daniel passage.[7]

Another potential influence is the fall of Babylon in Isaiah 21. The subject of this Isaiah prophecy is addressed enigmatically as the "desert of the sea". The word for "desert" could mean wilderness or even flat, empty, country such as scrubby pasture land which could have given rise to the idea that the king of the North camped on a plain near the sea. However, the original "desert of the sea" meant Babylon. It reflects the description of Babylon in Jeremiah: *"she shall be the last of the nations, a wilderness, a dry land, and a desert."* (Jeremiah 50:12).[8] In her prime, Babylon is a flood from the Euphrates which overwhelmed all other nations. But now Babylon has fallen and the great river has become a desert.

Appendix C

The Luke Genealogy

There is a second genealogy of Jesus in the Gospel of Luke, and it is very different from Matthew.[1] Scholars and commentators have attempted many explanations for the difference, the most popular being that it is a genealogy of Mary, even though she is not even mentioned. In reality, the genealogy shows the "same but different" pattern that Luke demonstrates when using Matthew. The author of Luke is continually trying to upstage the Gospel of Matthew.

The first change is that Luke reverses the order. In Matthew, the genealogy is of *"Jesus Christ, son of David, son of Abraham" (Matthew 1:1)*. It starts at Abraham and works forward, reflecting the order of the Almanac. Luke, however, begins with Jesus and works backwards. Unlike Matthew, Luke acknowledges that Jesus was only the "supposed" son of Joseph.[2] It then gives a long list of the descendants of Jesus through Joseph, each of whom was the son of the following name, going all the way back to "Adam, the son of God". Starting the genealogy with Adam is one of the improvements that the author of Luke makes upon Matthew. The Almanac also started with Adam, but other supposed improvements destroy the Almanac's structure.

> ➤ **Luke has seventy-seven (or perhaps seventy-six) names and reflects the idea that after Enoch there were seventy generations.**

The pattern of seventy generations is visible in Luke in a confused way. If we include the name Arni which is probably original although some manuscripts omit it, then we have seventy-seven names.[3] This is the clue that the structure of weeks of generations is also present in Luke. Seventy names come after Enoch. These could correspond to the seventy generations for which the angels will be imprisoned in the Book of Enoch. So the author of Luke shows some knowledge of the apocalyptic origins of the genealogy.

➤   **Luke is virtually identical to the Almanac for the first five weeks.**

Luke supplies the start of the genealogy, which is missing in Matthew, using the Septuagint version of Genesis. The first three weeks are virtually identical to Almanac weeks 1 to 3 except that, following Genesis, Abraham comes at the end of week three and not the start of week four. The addition of Arni enables the Luke genealogy to get back in sync with the Almanac by the end of week four. Week 5 is identical to the Almanac, starting with Amminadab (the generation of Moses) and ending with David.

➤   **Luke traces the descent after week five through Nathan and not Solomon.**

The author of Luke makes the strange decision to trace the descent of Jesus through Nathan rather than Solomon. So the genealogy veers drastically away from the Almanac, and the king list of Judah. The reason is probably theological. In 2 Samuel the promise of the eternal kingdom is given jointly to David and his offspring, meaning Solomon. But the author of Luke wants this promise to be fulfilled through Jesus and not through Solomon. So the author chooses another of David's sons, Nathan, as the ancestor of Jesus. There may also be confusion between Nathan the prophet, to whom the promise is made, and Nathan, the son of David.[4]

➤   **Luke inserts six extra days to "correct" for the missing generations in the Almanac weeks 6 and 7.**

In the second half of the genealogy, the differences with Matthew are startling. Between David and Joseph, the only points of agreement are Zerubbabel and his father, Shealtiel. Luke has twenty names between David and Shealtiel, six more than Matthew. The number of kings omitted from the Matthew genealogy is also six. So although the Gospel of Luke does not follow the Judean king list, the author seems to be aware that some reigns have been omitted, and arranges the list of generations to give the correct number. This "improvement" destroys the pattern of the Almanac, with three weeks between David and the exile instead of two. It also means that Zerubbabel starts the ninth week in Luke instead of coming in the second day of the week.

➢ **Luke has three weeks after the exile until the coming of Jesus and not two.**

After Zerubbabel the names are again completely different from Matthew even to the extent of having a different father for Joseph; Heli (the shortened name of the prominent ancestor Eliakim) rather than Jacob. Luke adds an extra eight names here; an additional week, and an extra day to adjust for the misplacement of Zerubbabel. So there are three final weeks between the exile and the coming of Jesus, reflecting the three weeks in the Almanac between the exile and the destruction of the earth. In the original Almanac, the end times take a week of generations to play out, starting with the generation of Jesus. Christians soon adopted a cut-down version in which the generation of Jesus was the final generation.

➢ **The author of Luke has inserted a list of relations and followers of Jesus into the genealogy shortly after Nathan, the son of David.**

The absurd nature of the Luke genealogy is indicated by a list of names that come in weeks 6 and 7. These are:[5]

Eliakim
Jonam (John)
Joseph
Judah (Judas/Jude)
Simeon
Levi
Matthat (cf. Matthew)

We have seen that Eliakim is a prominent ancestor of Joseph and Mary, and all the other names occur in the gospels as relatives or close followers of Jesus in Mark and Matthew. This could be pure coincidence if only a few names were involved, but to find a list of seven names appearing consecutively rules out coincidence. The author of Luke has made up this section of the genealogy from a misunderstood Christian source. In the Rock and the Tower, I suggest that this group was compiled from the earlier two gospels as a list of relations of James, the brother of the Lord.[6]

To summarise, the correspondence between the weeks of Luke and the Almanac/Matthew genealogy is as follows:

Luke weeks 1-2 = Almanac weeks 1-2 (except Eber ends week 2)
Luke weeks 3 = Almanac week 3 (except Abraham ends week 3)

Luke weeks 4-5 = Almanac weeks 4-5 (except Abraham does not start week 4)

Luke weeks 6-8 correspond to Almanac weeks 6-7, but the names are different and six days are added.

Luke weeks 9-11 correspond to Almanac weeks 8-9, but the names are different and eight days are added.

Almanac week 10 has been eliminated by Luke.

Appendix D

Jeremiah in The Lives of the Prophets

The Lives of the Prophets is a first-century text recording traditions about the prophets. It contains the earliest known account of the death of Jeremiah.

➤ **The Jewish author of the Lives of the Prophets has used a very early Christian source.**

Although the account of Jeremiah in the Lives is quite short, it contains several odd features which reveal a link with the earliest Christianity. The author of the Lives is believed to be Jewish, but the work has come down to us through Christians.[1] The Christian copyists have made many interpolations, but these cannot account for the Jeremiah passage. Instead, we must hypothesise that a very early Christian source has been mis-interpreted by a mid-first-century Jewish author. This gives us a rare pre-gospel glimpse into the Jesus movement.

Let us look at the features which indicate a connection with early Christianity. The first point is that Jeremiah protects against snakebite.[2] The Egyptians supposedly honoured him because he had saved them from an invasion of asps. Also, the dust of his tomb was used to cure snakebite, and his remains were even moved by Alexander the Great to protect the city of Alexandria from snakes. Jesus also had this power to protect his followers from snakebite, and we have seen how this can be traced back to the Nehushtan. This point supports an identification of Jeremiah and Jesus in the source used by the Lives.

This is followed by a short passage which is very confused in the sur-viving manuscripts. It talks of a virgin and a child in a manger who are venerated and worshiped by the Egyptians. It has clearly been the subject of interpolation by Christian copyists—we will discuss its significance shortly. After this comes the weirdest section:

> *This prophet (Jeremiah), before the capture of the temple, seized the ark of the law and the things in it, and made them to be swallowed up in a rock. And to those standing by he said, "The Lord has gone away from*

Zion into heaven and will come again in power. And this will be for you a sign of his coming, when all the gentiles worship a piece of wood. [...] And in the resurrection the ark will be the first to be resurrected and will come out of the rock and will be placed on Mount Sinai, and all the saints will be gathered to it there as they await the Lord and flee from the enemy who wishes to destroy them." (The Lives of the Prophets 2:11-13; 15)[3]

It adds that the name of God was written within the rock, which was placed in the wilderness. What can we make of this strange story?

➢ **The rock is Cephas, the alternative name of the Magdalene.**

We have seen how the title Cephas meaning "rock" comes from the Animal Apocalypse where the rock stands for Mount Sinai. The title "the Magdalene", the tower comes from the same source and stands for the temple. So Mary's two shamanic titles, the Magdalene and Cephas, stand for the three places associated with the ark in the Lives; the temple, the rock and Mount Sinai.

➢ **The ark takes the place of Christ.**

The first Christians believed that Christ was resurrected through Mary and dwelt spiritually within her. We do not know how Christ was named in the original source, but the final Jewish author of the Jeremiah account has interpreted Christ as the ark of the covenant. This probably results from confusion with the idea of Christ dwelling within the temple (the Magdalene)—the ark was supposedly kept in the holy of holies of the first temple. So the ark becomes contained within the rock (Cephas) and is resurrected on Mount Sinai (also Cephas). The saints gather around the ark waiting for the Lord, just as the saints, the church, gathered around Mary waiting for the appearance of Jesus in the skies. The ark is to be resurrected first, and Jesus also was resurrected first. Paul calls him the "first fruits" of those who have fallen asleep.[4]

In the myth of Christ, he dies at the time the temple is destroyed and is resurrected through Cephas. So the ark disappears at the time of the destruction of the temple and reappears through the rock/Mount Sinai. The name of Yahweh is written within the rock as a secret not to be revealed. And one of the three identities of Jesus is Yahweh, the name which must be kept secret.

> ➤ **The Egyptians worshipped the cross of Jeremiah until the resurrection.**

The original source seems to have been about the death and resurrection of Christ. The death takes place at the same time as the destruction of the temple and is connected with Jeremiah. What, though, of that piece of wood that the gentiles will worship? It can only stand for the cross. Christians did come to venerate Jesus' cross, but long after the first century. However, no Christian author would have represented Christians as worshipping the cross. And it is difficult to see how it would be possible for a later Jew to make such an interpolation, or why they would regard the Christian veneration of the cross as bringing in the end times. So the worship of the cross must be part of the original source.

It must be the Egyptians, not the Christians, who worship the cross. Although pagans, they are presented as the good guys in this account. They have received the prophecies of Jeremiah with open hearts and will eventually turn from their idols. But for now, they are worshiping a piece of wood—the cross. This cannot be an abstract cross, but must be a real cross because pagans worship physical things; idols of wood and stone. But how could the Egyptians have come into possession of Jesus' cross?

The problem has occurred to the later Christian interpolator who wrote in the idea that the Egyptians worship a manger in which a virgin has placed a child. A manger is made of wood. The baby Jesus is placed in a manger in Luke, and Joseph takes Mary and the infant Jesus to Egypt in Matthew. Someone familiar with both gospels could conclude that the couple took the manger, or more realistically part of it, with them to Egypt. So the Egyptians had a piece of the manger which they could worship.

Clearly the piece of wood, in the original, was not a manger—that would be absurd—but the cross. So where did this cross come from? It can only be the cross on which Jeremiah was crucified by his fellow Jews.

Bibliography

Ackerman, Susan, *Under Every Green Tree: Popular Religion in* Sixth-Century *Judah* (Winona Lake, Indiana: Eisenbrauns, Reprint 2001).

Alexander, P., *Hebrew Apocalypse of 3 Enoch: A new translation and introduction in The Old Testament Pseudepigrapha Vol. 1*, ed. James H. Charlesworth (New York: Doubleday, 1983).

Ayali-Darshan, Noga, *Baal son of Dagan (Journal of the American Oriental Society*, Vol. 133, No. 4, 2013), pp. 651-657.

Bauckham, *Richard, Jesus and the Eyewitnesses: The Gospels as Eyewitness Testimony* (Grand Rapids: Eerdmans, 2006)

Baltzer, Klaus, *The Book of Isaiah* (The Harvard Theological Review, Vol. 103, No. 3, 2010), pp. 261-270.

Bethge, Hans-Gebhard and Bentley Layton, *On The Origin of the World* in *The Nag Hammadi Library, 3rd Ed.* (San Francisco: Harper, 1988).

Blenkinsopp, Joseph, *The Anchor Yale Bible: Isaiah 1-39* (New York: Doubleday, 2000).

— *Isaiah 40-55* (New York: Doubleday, 2002).

— *Isaiah 56-66* (New York: Doubleday, 2003).

Block, Daniel I., *The Book of Ezekiel Ch. 1-24* (Grand Rapids: Eerdmans, 1997).

— *The Book of Ezekiel Ch. 25-48* (Grand Rapids: Eerdmans, 1998).

Broshi, Magen and Israel Finkelstein, *The Population of Palestine in Iron Age II*, BASOR 287 (Aug. 1992), pp. 47-60.

Bryner, Jeanna, *Ancient Egyptian Sundial Discovered at Valley of the Kings* in Live Science 20 March 2020, <https://www.livescience.com/28057-ancient-egyptian-sundial-discovered.html>.

Carlson, Stephen C., *The Gospel Hoax: Morton Smith's Invention of Secret Mark* (Waco, Texas: Baylor University Press, 2005).

Carrier, Richard, *On the Historicity of Jesus: Why We Might Have Reason for Doubt* (Sheffield: Sheffield Phoenix Press, 2014).

Coggins R.J., *The Cambridge Bible Commentary on the New English Bible: The First and Second Books of the Chronicles* (Cambridge: Cambridge University Press, 1976).

Cohen, Shaye J.D., *From the Maccabees to the Mishnah* (Philadelphia: Westminster Press, 1987).

Cohn-Sherbok, Dan, *The Jewish Messiah* (Edinburgh: T&T Clark Ltd, 1997).

Collins, John J., *Daniel* (Minneapolis: Fortress Press, 1993).

Constantinou, Eugenia Scarvelis, *Andrew of Caesarea and the Apocalypse in the Ancient Church of the East* (Quebec: University Laval, 2008).

Dalley, Stephanie, *Myths from Mesopotamia* (Oxford: Oxford University Press, Revised Ed., 2000).

Davies, Philip R., *The Origins of Biblical Israel* (New York: T&T Clark, 2007).

Davies, W.D. and Dale C. Allison Jr, *Matthew: Vol. 1* (Edinburgh: T&T Clark Ltd, 1988).

— *Matthew: Vol. 2* (Edinburgh: T&T Clark Ltd, 1991).

— *Matthew: Vol. 3* (Edinburgh: T&T Clark Ltd, 1997).

Davies, W.D. and Louis Finkelstein, *The Cambridge History of Judaism: The Hellenistic Age* (Cambridge: Cambridge University Press, 1989).

DeConick, April D., *The Gnostic New Age: How a Countercultural Spirituality Revolutionized Religion from Antiquity to Today* (New York: Columbia University Press, 2016).

Dever, William G., *Who Were the Early Israelites and Where Did They Come From?* (Grand Rapids: Eerdmans, 2003).

— *Did God have a Wife? Archaeology and Folk Religion in Ancient Israel.* (Grand Rapids: Eerdmans, 2005).

Ehrman, Bart D., *Lost Christianities: The Battles for Scripture and the Faiths we Never Knew* (Oxford: Oxford University Press, 2003).

— *The Shepherd of Hermas* in *The Loeb Classical Library: The Apostolic Fathers Vol 2* (Cambridge, Massachusetts: Harvard University Press, 2003).

Elliott, J. K., *The Apocryphal New Testament* (Oxford: Oxford University Press, 2005).

Fee, Gordon D., *The First and Second Letters to the Thessalonians* (Grand Rapids: Eerdmans, 2009).

Finkelstein, Israel, *The Forgotten Kingdom: The Archaeology and History of Northern Israel* (Atlanta: The Society of Biblical Literature, 2013).

Finkelstein, Israel and Neil Asher Silberman, *The Bible Unearthed* (New York: Touchstone, 2002).

— *David and Solomon* (New York: Simon & Schuster, 2006).

Friedlander, Gerald, *Pirke De Rabbi Eliezer* (London: Kegan Paul, Trench, Turner & Co Ltd, 1916).

Fontenrose, Joseph, *Dagon and El* (Oriens. Vol. 10 No. 2, 1957) pp. 277-79.

Ganor, Sa'ar and Igor Kreimerman, *Going to the Bathroom at Lachish* (Biblical Archaeology Review, Vol 63, No 6, 2017), pp. 56-60.

Gibson, J.C.L., *Canaanite Myths and Legends*, 2nd Ed. (London: T&C Clark, 1978).

Greenfield, Jonas C., *The Aramean God Ramman / Rimmon* (Israel Exploration Journal, Vol. 26, No. 4, 1976), pp. 195-98.

Golden, Jonathan M., *Ancient Canaan and Israel* (New York: Oxford University Press, 2009).

Goldstein, Jonathan A., *The Anchor Bible: I Maccabees* (New York: Doubleday, 1976).

— *The Anchor Bible: II Maccabees* (New York: Doubleday, 1983).

Halpern, Baruch, *David's Secret Demons: Messiah, Murderer, King* (Grand Rapids: Eerdmans, 2001).

Hamilton, Victor P., *The Book of Genesis: Chapters 1–17* (Grand Rapids: Eerdmans, 1990).

— *The Book of Genesis: Chapters 18–50* (Grand Rapids: Eerdmans, 1995).

Hare, D.R.A. *The Lives of the Prophets: A new translation and introduction in The*

Old Testament Pseudepigrapha Vol. 2, ed. James H. Charlesworth (New York: Doubleday, 1985).

Harley-McGowan, Felicity, *Picturing the Passion in The Routledge Handbook of Early Christian Art*, ed. Robin M. Jensen, and Mark D. Ellison (Routledge, 2018).

Isenberg, Wesley W., *The Gospel of Philip in The Nag Hammadi Library*, 3rd Ed. (San Francisco: Harper, 1988).

Isaac, E., *Ethiopic Apocalypse of 1 Enoch: A new translation and introduction* in *The Old Testament Pseudepigrapha Vol. 1*, ed. James H. Charlesworth (New York: Doubleday, 1983).

Jones, GH, *The New Century Bible Commentary: 1 and 2 Kings*, 2 vols. (Grand Rapids: Eerdmans, 1984).

Klassen, William, *Judas: Betrayer or Friend of Jesus?* (London: SCM Press, 1996).

Klein, Ralph W., *1 Chronicles* (Minneapolis: Augsburg Fortress, 2006).

Laurie, S.P., *The Rock and the Tower* (London: Hypostasis, 2016).

— *The Thomas Code: Solving the Mystery of the Gospel of Thomas* (London: Hypostasis, 2018).

Lehrman, S.M., *Midrash Rabbah: Exodus* (London: Soncino Press, 1939).

Lundbom, Jack R., *Jeremiah 1-20: A New Translation with Introduction and Commentary* (New York: Doubleday,1999).

— *Jeremiah 21-36* (New York: Doubleday,2004)

— *Jeremiah 37-52* (New York: Doubleday,2004)

Malherbe, Abraham J., *The Anchor Bible: The Letters to the Thessalonians* (New York: Doubleday, 2000).

Marcus, Joel, *Mark 1-8: A New Translation with Introduction and Commentary* (New Haven: Yale University Press, 2007)

— *Mark 8-16* (New Haven: Yale University Press, 2009)

Matt, Daniel C., *The Zohar: Pritzker Edition*, Vol. 1 (Stanford: Stanford University Press, 2004).

Meyer, Marvin W. (ed.), *The Ancient Mysteries: A Source book of Sacred Texts* (Philadelphia: University of Pennsylvania Press, 1999).

Milik, J.T. (ed.), *The Books of Enoch: Aramaic fragments of Qumran Cave 4* (Oxford: Clarendon Press).

Miller, J. Maxwell and John H. Hayes, *A History of Ancient Israel and Judah* (London: SCM Press, 1986).

Moulis, David Rafael, *Hezekiah's Religious Reform—In the Bible and Archaeology* (2017 Bible History Daily, accessed June 28, 2019).

Na'aman, Nadav, *Historical and Chronological Notes on the Kingdoms of Israel and Judah in the Eighth Century B.C.* (Vetus Testamentum, Vol. 36, Fasc. 1, 1986), pp. 71-92.

— *The Kingdom of Judah Under Josiah* (Tel Aviv, 18:1, 1991).

— *The "Discovered Book" and the Legitimation of Josiah's Reform* (Journal of Biblical Literature, Vol. 130, No. 1, 2011), pp. 47-62.

Nestle-Aland, *Novum Testamentum Graece:* Greek-English *New Testament*, 28th Revised Ed. (Stuttgart: Deutsche Bibelgesellschaft, 2013)

Nickelsburg, George W.E., *1 Enoch 1* (Minneapolis: Augsburg Fortress, 2001).

Oropeza, B. J., *Judas' Death and Final Destiny in the Gospels and Earliest Christian Writings* (Neotestamentica, Vol. 44, No. 2, 2010), pp. 342-361.

Oswalt, John N., *The Book of Isaiah* 1-39: *The New International Commentary on the Old Testament* (Grand Rapids: Eerdmans, 1986).

— *The Book of Isaiah* 40-66 (Grand Rapids: Eerdmans, 1998).

Pagels, Elaine, *The Gnostic Paul: Gnostic Exegesis of the Pauline Letters* (Harrisburg, Pennsylvania: Trinity Press International, 1992).

Richelle, Matthieu, *Elusive Scrolls: Could Any Hebrew Literature Have Been Written Prior to the Eighth Century BCE?* (Vetus Testamentum, Vol. 66, Fasc. 4, 2016), pp. 556-594.

Roberts, Alexander, James Donaldson, and A. Cleveland Coxe (eds.), Ante-Nicene *Fathers, Vol. 1* (Buffalo, NY: Christian Literature Publishing Co., 1885.)

Robinson, J., *The First Book of Kings: The Cambridge Bible Commentary on the New English Bible* (Cambridge: Cambridge University Press, 1972).

— *The Second Book of Kings* (Cambridge: Cambridge University Press, 1976).

Rudolph, Kurt, *Gnosis: The Nature and History of Gnosticism* (San Francisco: Harper & Row, 1987).

Saggs, H.W.F., *The Might That Was Assyria* (Letchworth: The Garden City Press, 1984).

Schneemelcher, Wilhelm (ed.) trans. R. McL. Wilson, *New Testament Apocrypha Vol. 1: Gospels and Related Writings* (London: Westminster John Knox Press, 2003).

— *New Testament Apocrypha Vol. 2: Writings Relating to the Apostles, Apocalypses and Related Subjects* (London: Westminster John Knox Press, 1992).

Segal, Alan F., *Rebecca's Children: Judaism and Christianity in the Roman World* (Cambridge Massachusetts: Harvard University Press, 1986).

— *Two Powers in Heaven: Early Rabbinic Reports about Christianity and Gnosticism* (Boston: Brill, 2002).

Smith, Mark S., *The Early History of God*, 2nd Ed. (Grand Rapids: Eerdmans, 2002).

Stott, Katherine, *Finding the Lost Book of the Law:* Re-reading *the Story of "The Book of the Law" (Deuteronomy–2 Kings) in Light of Classical Literature* (Journal for the Study of the Old Testament, No. 30, 2005), Vol. 30 No. 2), pp. 153-169.

van der Toorn, K. and P. W. van der Horst, *Nimrod before and after the Bible* (The Harvard Theological Review Vol. 83 No. 1, 1990), pp. 1-29.

Williamson, H.G.M., *The New Century Bible Commentary: 1 and 2 Chronicles* (Grand Rapids: Eerdmans, 1982).

Wintermute, O.S., *Jubilees: A New Translation and Introduction* in *The Old Testament Pseudepigrapha Vol. 2*, ed. James H. Charlesworth (New York: Doubleday, 1985).

Wolkstein, Diane and Samuel Noah Kramer, *Inanna: Queen of Heaven and Earth* (New York: Harper & Row, 1983).

Yonge C.D., *The Works of Philo: New Updated Edition* (Hendrickson Publishers, Eleventh printing 2013).

Notes

Chapter 1

1   Revelation 17:6.
2   First argued by B.A Pearson, *1 Thessalonians 2: 13-16: A Deutero-Pauline interpretation*, HTR 64 (1971), 79-94. See Gordon D. Fee, *The first and second letters to the Thessalonians* (Grand Rapids: Eerdmans, 2009), p.91, n.21, for others holding this view.
3   For a discussion of the issues see Fee, *The first and second letters to the Thessalonians*, pp. 65-72.
4   See S.P. Laurie, *The Thomas Code: Solving the Mystery of the Gospel of Thomas* (London: Hypostasis, 2018) and *The Rock and the Tower* (London: Hypostasis, 2016).
5   Laurie, *The Thomas Code*.
6   In Thomas 55, Jesus tells his disciples to take up their cross like himself.
7   1 Samuel 22:17-18; 1 Kings 18:13.
8   2 Chronicles 24:21-22.
9   Matthew 21:34-6.
10 Luke 20:10-12.
11 For a discussion of the nomina sacra in Thomas 65, see Richard Valantasis, *The Gospel of Thomas* (London: Routledge, 1997), pp. 144-45.

Chapter 2

1   J.T Milik, *The Books of Enoch: Aramaic fragments of Qumran cave 4* (Oxford: Clarendon Press, 1976), pp. 244-45.
2   George W.E. Nickelsburg, *1 Enoch 1* (Minneapolis: Augsburg Fortress, 2001), p.9.
3   Genesis 4:17-18.
4   Translation by E. Isaac, *1 (Ethiopic Apocalypse of) Enoch: A new translation and introduction* in *The Old Testament Pseudepigrapha Vol. 1*, ed. James H. Charlesworth (New York: Doubleday, 1983).
5   Stephanie Dalley, *Myths from Mesopotamia* (Oxford: Oxford university Press, Revised Ed., 2000), pp. 1-8.
6   The problem of the origins of the wife of Cain originates with Genesis 4:16-17. When Cain goes east of Eden, he finds inhabitants and a wife, even though he is supposed to be the only human in existence other than his mother and father.

7   Translation by E. Isaac, *The Old Testament Pseudepigrapha Vol. 1.*
8   One white person is followed by three others making four. But in some
    manuscripts there are seven angels, four followed by three.
9   Translation by E. Isaac, *The Old Testament Pseudepigrapha Vol. 1.*
10 Translation by E. Isaac, *The Old Testament Pseudepigrapha Vol. 1.*
11 Translation by E. Isaac, *The Old Testament Pseudepigrapha Vol. 1.*
12 Genesis 9:20-25.
13 Milik, *Enoch* pp. 55-57.
14 Translation by E. Isaac, *The Old Testament Pseudepigrapha Vol. 1.*
15 Translation by E. Isaac, *The Old Testament Pseudepigrapha Vol. 1.*
16 1 Enoch 106:19.
17 Exodus 2:2.
18 Josephus, Antiquities 2:9:6.
19 Translation by Gerald Friedlander, *Pirke De Rabbi Eliezer* (London: Kegan
    Paul, Trench, Turner & Co Ltd, 1916), p. 378.
20 Exodus 34:33-35.
21 Genesis 9:1-17.
22 Exodus 35:15-19.
23 Exodus 19:10-25.

Chapter 3

1   Translation by E. Isaac, *The Old Testament Pseudepigrapha Vol. 1.*
2   Translation by E. Isaac, *The Old Testament Pseudepigrapha Vol. 1.*
3   Translation by E. Isaac, *The Old Testament Pseudepigrapha Vol. 1.*
4   This assumes that the twelve hours of pasturing at 1 Enoch 90:72 is a
    reference to 12 shepherds.
5   1 Enoch 90:1,5. The text gives the number of shepherds in the first half
    period as 37 and not 35. But this is contradicted as the sum of the first half,
    and the next group of 23 is given as 58.
6   1 Enoch 89:74-5.
7   Translation by E. Isaac, *The Old Testament Pseudepigrapha Vol. 1.*
8   Translation by E. Isaac, *The Old Testament Pseudepigrapha Vol. 1.*
9   Translation by E. Isaac, *The Old Testament Pseudepigrapha Vol. 1.*
10 Jonathan A. Goldstein, *The Hasmonean revolt and the Hasmonean dynasty* in
    The Cambridge History of Judaism: Volume 2, The Hellenistic Age, ed. by W.D.
    Davies and Louis Finkelstein (Cambridge: Cambridge University Press,
    1989) pp. 292-311.
11 2 Maccabees 11:5-12.
12 2 Maccabees 4:31-38.
13 Nickelsburg, *1 Enoch 1*, pp. 396-98.
14 Nickelsburg, *1 Enoch 1*, pp. 360-61.

Chapter 4

1   Translation by Wesley W. Isenberg, *The Gospel of Philip* in *The Nag Hammadi Library*, 3rd Ed. (San Francisco: Harper, 1988).
2   For an account of Marcion see Bart D. Ehrman, *Lost Christianities: The Battles for Scripture and the Faiths we Never Knew* (Oxford: Oxford University Press, 2003), pp. 103-09.
3   Kurt Rudolph, *Gnosis: The nature and history of Gnosticism* (San Francisco: Harper & Row, 1987), p. 73.
4   First Apocalypse of James, NHC V (3) 39:9-18.
5   First Apocalypse of James, NHC V (3) 26:8-30.
6   On the Origin of the World, NHC II (5) 103:32-106:11; See also Hypostasis of the Archons, NHC II (4) 95:13-96:3)
7   The Tripartite Tractate, NHC I (5) 100:19-35.

Chapter 5

1   A possible exception is Hebrews 13:12 where Jesus is said to have suffered outside the "gate", a potential reference to the gospel crucifixion which took place outside the walls of Jerusalem. But the statement is too vague to prove that that the author was familiar with the gospels.
2   Hebrews 13:23.
3   Hebrews 5:11-14.
4   Acts 7:20.
5   Acts 7:30;38.
6   Thayer's Greek Lexicon entry for Strongs 1096 gives just three examples for the meaning "born"; two of these are Galatians 4:4 and Romans 1:3, and the other is the fig tree in Matthew 21:19. However, the standard meaning that no more fruit will "come" on the fig tree, makes more sense that saying that fruit will be "born" on it.
7   The Muratorian fragment says that Hermas was written by Hermas, the brother of Pius, bishop of Rome (140-155), but this must be a case of mistaken identity. The Shepherd contains scandalous details about the narrator, Hermas, which no one would have included if they were writing under their own name. Most likely Hermas, who lives in Rome, is a fictional character who is intended to be the Hermas who Paul greets in his letter to the Romans (16:14).
8   Laurie, *The Rock and the Tower*, pp. 504-06.
9   Translation by Bart D. Ehrman, *The Shepherd of Hermas* in *The Loeb Classical Library: The Apostolic Fathers Vol 2* (Cambridge, Massachusetts: Harvard University Press, 2003).
10 Hermas 54:1.
11 Translation by Ehrman, *The Apostolic Fathers Vol 2*.
12 Translation by Eugenia Scarvelis Constantinou, Andrew of Caesarea and the Apocalypse in the Ancient Church of the East (Quebec: University Laval, 2008) p.134.

Chapter 6

1   Israel Finkelstein and Neil Asher Silberman, *The Bible Unearthed* (New York: Touchstone 2002), Ch. 4 pp. 97-122. William G. Dever, *Who Were the Early Israelites and Where Did They Come From?* (Grand Rapids: Eerdmans, 2003), Ch. 5-6, pp. 75-100.
2   Dever, *Who Were the Early Israelites and Where Did They Come From?*, pp. 113-18.
3   Dever, *Who Were the Early Israelites and Where Did They Come From?*, pp. 118-25.
4   Dever, *Who Were the Early Israelites and Where Did They Come From?*, pp. 153-66. Finkelstein and Silberman, *The Bible Unearthed*, pp. 97-122; 337-39.
5   Dever, *Who Were the Early Israelites and Where Did They Come From?*, pp. 200.
6   Dever, *Who Were the Early Israelites and Where Did They Come From?*, p. 71.
7   Magen Broshi and Israel Finkelstein, *The Population of Palestine in Iron Age II*, BASOR 287 (Aug. 1992), pp. 47-60. Israel Finkelstein, *The Forgotten Kingdom: The Archaeology and History of Northern Israel* (Atlanta: The Society of Biblical Literature, 2013), p. 110.
8   Finkelstein, *The Forgotten Kingdom*, pp. 133-5.
9   Finkelstein, *The Forgotten Kingdom*, pp. 37-49.
10 Israel Finkelstein and Neil Asher Silberman, *David and Solomon* (New York: Simon & Schuster, 2006), pp. 94-96; 267-74.
11 2 Kings 16:7-8.
12 Finkelstein, *The Forgotten Kingdom*, p.154. Finkelstein and Silberman, The Bible Unearthed, pp. 243-46.
13 Baruch Halpern, *David's Secret Demons: Messiah, Murderer, King* (Grand Rapids: Eerdmans, 2001).
14 For an alternative view on the possibility that the Israelites had writing before 800 BC see Richelle, Matthieu, *Elusive Scrolls: Could Any Hebrew Literature Have Been Written Prior to the Eighth Century BCE?* (Vetus Testamentum, Vol. 66, Fasc. 4, 2016), pp. 556-594.
15 Finkelstein, *The Forgotten Kingdom*, pp. 155-58. See also: Finkelstein and Silberman, David and Solomon.
16 Finkelstein, *The Forgotten Kingdom*, pp. 44-47.

Chapter 7

1   J.C.L. Gibson, *Canaanite Myths and Legends*, 2nd Ed. (London: T&C Clark, 1978), p. 1.
2   Gibson, *Canaanite Myths and Legends*, p.4 n.6.
3   For the suggestion that El and Dagan were equated at Ugarit, see Joseph Fontenrose, *Dagon and El* (Oriens. Vol. 10 No. 2, 1957) pp. 277-79. For an alternative view that Baal was regarded as having two fathers, both Dagan and El, see Noga Ayali-Darshan, *Baal son of Dagan* (Journal of the American Oriental Society , Vol. 133, No. 4, 2013), pp. 651-657.
4   Mark S. Smith, *The Early History of God*, 2nd Ed. (Grand Rapids: Eerdmans, 2002) pp. 80-91; 101-07.

5   Gibson, *Canaanite Myths and Legends*, p. 7.
6   Psalm 74:13-14; 89:10; Job 3:8; 7:12; 9:13; 26:12; 41:1-34; Isaiah 27:1; 51:9.
7   Dever, Who Were the Early Israelites and Where Did They Come From?, pp. 150-01.
8   Exodus 3:1-2.
9   Finkelstein, *The Forgotten Kingdom*, pp. 145-51.
10   Judges 2:13; 10:6; 1 Samuel 7:4; 12:10; 1 Kings 11:5; 2 Kings 23:13. See William G. Dever, *Did God have a Wife? Archaeology and Folk Religion in Ancient Israel.* (Grand Rapids: Eerdmans, 2005), p. 233.
11   Dever, *Did God have a Wife?*, pp. 232-34.
12   1 Kings 15:13; 18:19; 2 Kings 21:7; 23:4. Dever, Did God have a Wife?, pp. 101-02.
13   Dever, *Did God have a Wife?*, pp. 160--67.
14   Dever, *Did God have a Wife?*, pp. 131--32.
15   Dever, *Did God have a Wife?*, p. 150.
16   Dever, *Did God have a Wife?*, pp. 179-89.

Chapter 8

1   Dever, *Did God have a Wife?*, pp. 167-70.
2   See Judges 9:4 "temple of Baal-berith" and Judges 9:46 "temple of El-berith".
3   Dever, *Did God have a Wife?*, pp. 170-75.
4   David Rafael Moulis, *Hezekiah's Religious Reform—In the Bible and Archaeology* (2017 Bible History Daily, accessed June 28, 2019).
5   Dever, *Did God have a Wife?*, pp. 111-125.
6   Dever, *Did God have a Wife?*, pp. 139-151.
7   2 Kings 23:4.
8   2 Kings 23:11.
9   2 Kings 23:7.
10   Dever, *Did God have a Wife?*, pp. 216-17.
11   Susan Ackerman, *Under Every Green Tree: Popular Religion in Sixth-Century Judah* (Winona Lake, IN: Eisenbrauns, Reprint 2001), p. 134.
12   Dever, *Did God have a Wife?*, pp. 217-18.
13   Judges 11:29-40.
14   1 Kings 16:34.
15   Genesis 22:1-18.
16   Sa'ar Ganor and Igor Kreimerman, *Going to the Bathroom at Lachish* (Biblical Archaeology Review, Vol 63, No 6, 2017), pp. 56-60.
17   David Rafael Moulis, *Hezekiah's Religious Reform—In the Bible and Archaeology.*

Chapter 9

1   See, for example, Baal and Yam 2 i 20 where the gods meet on the mountain of assembly which is called Lei, meaning night (Gibson, *Canaanite Myths and Legends*, p.5 n. 1). But the gods could also meet in other locations. In

Keret 15 (ii) they meet in the king's house.

2   Gibson, *Canaanite Myths and Legends*, p. 63.

3   Gibson, *Canaanite Myths and Legends*, p. 102.

4   Gibson, *Canaanite Myths and Legends*, p. 95.

5   Keret 15 ii 8-28.

6   Exodus 19:10-13.

7   Exodus 19:24.

8   Daniel 10:5-6. Compare to Revelation 1:13-16.

9   Translation by O.S. Wintermute, *Jubilees: A new translation and introduction* in *The Old Testament Pseudepigrapha Vol. 2*, ed. James H. Charlesworth (New York: Doubleday, 1985).

10   Jubilees 5:6.

11   Jubilees 10:1-9.

12   Translation by Gerald Friedlander, *Pirke De Rabbi Eliezer* (London: Kegan Paul, Trench, Turner & Co Ltd, 1916), p. 176.

13   Translation by Hans-Gebhard Bethge and Bentley Layton, *On The Origin of the World* in *The Nag Hammadi Library*, 3rd Ed. (San Francisco: Harper, 1988).

14   P. Alexander, *3 (Hebrew Apocalypse of) Enoch: A new translation and introduction* in *The Old Testament Pseudepigrapha Vol. 1*, ed. James H. Charlesworth (New York: Doubleday, 1983) pp. 225-29.

15   Translation by P. Alexander, *The Old Testament Pseudepigrapha Vol. 1*.

16   Translation by P. Alexander, *The Old Testament Pseudepigrapha Vol. 1*.

17   Translation by P. Alexander, *The Old Testament Pseudepigrapha Vol. 1*.

Chapter 10

1   Plutarch, On Isis and Osiris. See also *The Ancient Mysteries: A Source book of Sacred Texts*, Ed. Marvin W. Meyer (Philadelphia: University of Pennsylvania Press, 1999), Ch. 6 pp. 157-196.

2   Gibson, *Canaanite Myths and Legends*, p. 43.

3   Psalm 145:13; Daniel 2:44; 4:34.

4   The Palace of Baal, 4 viii 17-20.

5   Baal and Mot, 5 ii 3-4.

6   Baal and Yam, 2 i 38.

7   Baal and Mot, 6 i 39-42.

8   Baal and Mot, 6 v 1-6.

9   Gibson, *Canaanite Myths and Legends*, p. 80.

10   The Palace of Baal, 4 iii 34.

11   The Palace of Baal, 4 vi 44-6.

12   The Palace of Baal, 3 E 1-2.

13   Baal and Yam, 2 iii 19-20.

14   Laurie, *The Rock and the Tower*, pp. 435-36.

15   Diane Wolkstein and Samuel Noah Kramer, *Inanna and the God of Wisdom* in *Inanna: Queen of Heaven and Earth* (New York: Harper & Row, 1983).

16   Wolkstein and Kramer, *The Courtship of Inanna and Dumuzi* in *Inanna*.

17   Wolkstein and Kramer, *From the Great Above to the Great Below* and *The Dream of Dumuzi* in *Inanna*.

18   Wolkstein and Kramer, *The Return* in *Inanna*.
19   Dever, *Did God have a Wife?*, pp. 230-36.
20   2 Kings 5:18. Jonas C. Greenfield, *The Aramean God Rammān / Rimmōn* (Israel Exploration Journal, Vol. 26, No. 4, 1976), pp. 195-98.
21   Laurie, *The Rock and the Tower*, pp. 461-75.

Chapter 11

1   Ashish Sinha et al., *Role of climate in the rise and fall of the Neo-Assyrian Empire* (Science Advances Vol. 5, No. 11, 2019).
2   Finkelstein and Silberman, *The Bible Unearthed*, pp. 347-53.
3   For an account of events leading to the Babylonian exile see Jack R. Lundbom, *Jeremiah 1-20: A New Translation with Introduction and Commentary* (New York: Doubleday,1999), pp. 102-05.
4   Genesis 10:22.
5   Genesis 6:4.
6   K. van der Toorn and P. W. van der Horst, *Nimrod before and after the Bible* (The Harvard Theological Review Vol. 83 No. 1, 1990), pp. 1-29.

Chapter 12

1   Luke 3:23.
2   Laurie, *The Rock and the Tower*, pp. 269-79.
3   George W.E. Nickelsburg, *1 Enoch 1* (Minneapolis: Augsburg Fortress, 2001), pp. 427-28.
4   Translation by E. Isaac, *The Old Testament Pseudepigrapha Vol. 1.*
5   W.D. Davies and Dale C. Allison Jr, *Matthew*, Vol 1 (Edinburgh: T&T Clark Ltd, 1988), p.173.
6   Joshua 2:13.
7   Ruth 4:18-22; 1 Chronicles 2:5-15.
8   Numbers 1:17; 2:3.
9   For the justification of the resurrected Jesus appearing for one generation, see Laurie, *The Rock and the Tower*, pp. 196-98; 206.
10   Numbers. 1:7; 2:3; 7:12; 7:17; 10:14.
11   Deuteronomy 34:7 says that Moses died at age 120. The exodus took forty years to complete so he was around 80 at the start.
12   Ralph W. Klein, *1 Chronicles* (Minneapolis: Augsburg Fortress, 2006), p. 95.
13   2 Kings 8:25; 12:1; 14:1; 2 Chronicles 22:1; 24:1; 25:1.
14   2 Kings 11:3; 2 Chronicles 22:12.
15   2 Kings 23:31,34; 2 Chronicles 36:2,4.
16   2 Kings 24:18; 2 Chronicles 36:11.

Chapter 13

1　Daniel C. Matt, *The Zohar, Pritzker Edition, Vol. 1* (Stanford: Stanford University Press, 2004), p.437 n. 720.
2　2 Samuel 6; 7:1-3.
3　2 Samuel 7:16.
4　1 Samuel 21:1-6; 22:20.
5　Translation by E. Isaac, *The Old Testament Pseudepigrapha Vol. 1.*
6　Leviticus 25.

Chapter 14

1　Leviticus 25:2-4.
2　Genesis 5:1-17; 10:1-22; 11:10-32.
3　Genesis 10:21. For "Hebrew" coming from Eber see Josephus, Antiquities 1:6:4.
4　Ruth 4:18-22.
5　We also find this genealogy in 1 Chronicles 2:1-15, although this is probably based on Ruth. It has also served as a source for the Matthew genealogy of David (Klein, *1 Chronicles*, p. 88).
6　J.T. Milik (ed.), *The Books of Enoch: Aramaic fragments of Qumran Cave 4* (Oxford: Clarendon Press), p. 251.
7　Wintermute, *Jubilees: A New Translation and Introduction* in *The Old Testament Pseudepigrapha Vol. 2*, pp. 35-50.
8　Jubilees 1:15-18; 22-25.
9　These concepts are also found in Deuteronomy 10:16; 30:6; Jeremiah 9:26.
10　Translation by Wintermute, *The Old Testament Pseudepigrapha Vol. 2.*
11　Translation by Wintermute, *The Old Testament Pseudepigrapha Vol. 2.*
12　Jubilees 23:8-15.
13　Isaiah 45:1.
14　Daniel 11:40.
15　Daniel 11:41.
16　Daniel 11:41.
17　Jeremiah 40:11-12.
18　Daniel 11:37.
19　Daniel 11:37.
20　Daniel 11:38-39.

Chapter 15

1　Laurie, *The Rock and the Tower*, pp. 138-46.
2　Jonah 2:1-6.
3　Mark 16:2.

Chapter 16

1 Mark 14:17-26.
2 Mark 14:26-52.
3 Mark 14:53-72.
4 Mark 15:1-20.
5 Mark 13:35.
6 Mark 15:21-22.
7 John 19:41.
8 Mark 15:23-32.
9 Mark 15:33-41.
10 W.D. Davies and Dale C. Allison Jr, *Matthew*, Vol. 3 (Edinburgh: T&T Clark Ltd, 1997), pp. 629-31.
11 Mark 15:42-46.
12 Davies and Allison, *Matthew*, Vol. 3, p. 524.
13 John 19:41-2.

Chapter 17

1 Mark 15:9-14.
2 Matthew 26:15; Zechariah 11:12.
3 Mark 14:49.
4 Strong's Greek 3860.
5 Laurie, *The Rock and the Tower*, pp. 559-60.
6 Romans 6:17; 1 Corinthians 11:2; 15:3.
7 Galatians 3:1.
8 Pliny the Younger, Epistulae 10.96.
9 Matthew 12:27.

Chapter 18

1 2 Kings 18:2 states that Hezekiah was 25 when he became king. The Sennacherib invasion took place in 701 BC when he had been on the throne for 26 years assuming that his reign started in 727 BC.
2 Isaiah 6:1; 7:1.

Chapter 19

1 2 Kings 15:32-38.
2 2 Chronicles 27:1-9.
3 2 Kings 14:21-22; 15:1-7.
4 2 Chronicles 26:1-23.
5 H.G.M Williamson, *The New Century Bible Commentary: 1 and 2 Chronicles* (Grand Rapids: Eerdmans, 1982), p. 133.

6   2 Kings 11:1-16; 2 Chronicles 22:10-12; 23:1-17.
7   2 Kings 14:21-2.
8   2 Kings 14:23; 15:1.
9   Isaiah 7:1.
10 Numbers 21:6-9; Isaiah 30:6.
11 2 Kings 18:4.
12 Laurie, *The Rock and the Tower*, pp. 200-06.
13 Mark 14:3.
14 Luke 7:36-50.

Chapter 20

1   2 Kings 18:2.
2   Isaiah 37:2; 38:1; 39:3.
3   2 Kings 16:2; 18:2.
4   2 Kings 16:2.
5   Laurie, *The Rock and the Tower*, pp. 421-56.
6   1 Samuel 28:7-25.
7   Isaiah 20.
8   2 Kings 10:1-11.
9   Exodus 21:32.

Chapter 21

1   2 Chronicles 28:5-8.
2   2 Chronicles 28:20.
3   2 Kings 16:9.
4   2 Kings 17; 18:9-12.
5   2 Kings 17:24.
6   Hosea 7:1.
7   John 13:27.
8   1 Samuel 16:15-16.
9   1 Samuel 18:10-11; 19:9-10.
10 Isaiah 7:4.

Chapter 22

1   Finkelstein, *The Forgotten Kingdom*, p154-5.
2   Finkelstein, *The Forgotten Kingdom*, Chapter 7.
3   2 Chronicles 30:18.
4   2 Kings 23:13-4.
5   Finkelstein and Silberman, *The Bible Unearthed*, pp. 347-353.
6   Isaiah 37:6.
7   Isaiah 38:1.

8   Jeanna Bryner, *Ancient Egyptian Sundial Discovered at Valley of the Kings in
     Live Science* 20 March 2020, <https://www.livescience.com/28057-ancient-
     egyptian-sundial-discovered.html> [accessed 13 May 2020].

Chapter 23

1   2 Chronicles 29:4-19.
2   Strong's concordance 5180.
3   2 Chronicles 29:16.
4   Acts 28:3-6.
5   Acts 28:8.
6   Laurie, *The Rock and the Tower*, pp. 111-46.
7   1 Corinthians 10:9 in Nestle-Aland 28, *Novum Testamentum Graece*
     (Stuttgart: Deutsche Bibelgesellschaft, 2013).
8   Hyppolitus, Refutation of all Heresies 5:2.
9   There is an ancient Egyptian myth of the god Arum who is sometime
     portrayed as a primaeval snake surrounding the universe. The Naassenes
     have perhaps combined this myth with the early Christian tradition of
     Christ as a snake, and the disciple as temple. For a view of the importance
     of Arum to the gnostics see April D. DeConick, *The Gnostic New Age: How
     a Countercultural Spirituality Revolutionized Religion from Antiquity to Today*
     (New York: Columbia University Press, 2016) pp. 54-57, 216.
10   Epiphanius, Panarion 37:5-8. *Kurt Rudolph, Gnosis: The nature and history of
     Gnosticism* (San Francisco: Harper & Row, 1987), p. 247.
11   Hyppolitus, Refutation of all Heresies 5:11.
12   2 Chronicles 26:6.
13   2 Chronicles 28:18.
14   2 Kings 18:8.
15   Mark 2:5-8.

Chapter 24

1   Mark 14:10-11.
2   Matthew 26:25.
3   John 13:26-30.
4   The best account is Stephen C. Carlson, *The Gospel Hoax: Morton Smith's
     Invention of Secret Mark* (Waco, Texas: Baylor University Press, 2005). See
     also Ehrman, *Lost Christianities*, pp. 67-89.
5   Strong concordance 1068; 1660; 8081). Both "gath" and "yeqeb" (Isaiah 5:2)
     mean winepress.
6   Dever, *Did God Have a Wife?*, p. 146.

Chapter 25

1   Ezekiel 4:5.
2   1 Enoch 86:4.
3   Finkelstein and Silberman, *The Bible Unearthed*, pp. 259-64; *David and Solomon*, pp. 146-49.
4   2 Samuel 21:1-5.
5   Genesis 19:30-38.
6   Ezekiel 23:4.

Chapter 26

1   1 Chronicles 8:35 and 9:41.
2   2 Kings 25:18-21; Jeremiah 52:24-27.
3   Nestle-Aland 18, Mark 14:51.

Chapter 27

1   Mark 3:19.
2   1 Corinthians 15:5.
3   William Klassen, *Judas: Betrayer or Friend of Jesus?* (London: SCM Press, 1996), pp. 32-33. Gunther Schwarz, Jesus und Judas, pp. 6-12.
4   Isaiah 1:1.
5   Acts 5:1-11.
6   Apollinaris, Catena in Evangelium S. Matthaei and Catena in Acts Apostolorum.

Chapter 28

1   2 Chronicles 24:20-21.
2   2 Chronicles 26:5.
3   Zechariah 1:1.
4   Zechariah 14.
5   Exodus 21:32.
6   2 Kings 8:16-17; 8:26; 11:3; 12:1; 14:1-2; 15:1-2.
7   Strong's Concordance 3582.
8   2 Chronicles 24:21-22.
9   2 Kings 11:1-16; 2 Chronicles 22:10-12; 23:1-15; 24:15-22.

Chapter 29

1   Jeremiah 7:31-32; 19:6.

2   1 Chronicles 3:5.

Chapter 30

1   Origen, Commentary on Matthew.
2   Daniel 10:20-21; 3 Enoch 26:12.
3   See Laurie, *The Rock and the Tower*, pp. 200-06.
4   Isaiah 14:12-15.
5   1 Enoch 6-10.

Chapter 31

1   Mark 14:65.
2   Mark 15:15.
3   Mark 15:19.
4   Mark 14:65.
5   Mark 15:42-6.
6   Isaiah 53:10-11.

Chapter 32

1   2 Kings 21:1; 2 Chronicles 33:1.
2   2 Kings 21:2-6.
3   2 Chronicles 33:15-17.
4   Shaye J.D. Cohen, *From the Maccabees to the Mishnah* (Philadelphia: Westminster Press, 1987), p.46.
5   Translation by C.D. Yonge, from *The Works of Philo: New Updated Edition* (Hendrickson Publishers, Eleventh printing 2013), p. 728.
6   Philo, Flaccus 39.
7   2 Kings 21:19-24; 2 Chronicles 33:21-5.

Chapter 33

1   2 Kings 22:1; 2 Chronicles 34:1.
2   Finkelstein and Silberman, *The Bible Unearthed*, pp. 347-53.
3   2 Kings 22:8-23:3.
4   For a good exposition of this theory see Nadav Na'aman, *The "Discovered Book" and the Legitimation of Josiah's Reform* (Journal of Biblical Literature, Vol. 130, No. 1, 2011), pp. 47-62.
5   First put forward by Katherine Stott, *Finding the Lost Book of the Law: Re-reading the Story of "The Book of the Law" (Deuteronomy–2 Kings) in Light of Classical Literature* (Journal for the Study of the Old Testament, No. 30, 2005),

Vol. 30 No. 2), pp. 153-169.

6   2 Chronicles 35:20-24.

7   Nadav Na'aman, *The Kingdom of Judah Under Josiah* (Tel Aviv, 18:1, 1991), pp. 3-71. See also Finkelstein and Silberman, The Bible Unearthed, p. 291.

8   2 Kings 23:31-5; 2 Chronicles 36:1-4.

9   2 Kings 23:36; 2 Chronicles 36:5.

10   2 Kings 24:1.

11   2 Kings 24:6.

12   2 Chronicles 36:6.

13   Jeremiah 22:18-19; 36:30.

14   2 Kings 24:8; 2 Chronicles 36:9. The literal reading of the 2 Chronicles text is that he was just eight years old, but this would seem to be a mistake.

15   Thomas 42; TC 3.2.

16   Matthew 27:32; Luke 23:26.

Chapter 34

1   2 Kings 24:18; 2 Chronicles 36:11; Jeremiah 52:1.

2   2 Kings 25:23; Jeremiah 40:7-8.

3   It is excluded from the text of Nestle-Aland 28.

4   Luke 22:37.

5   Mark 14:48.

6   Mark 11:17.

7   Laurie, *The Rock and the Tower*, pp. 306-7.

8   John 10:1.

9   Felicity Harley-McGowan, *Picturing the Passion* in *The Routledge Handbook of Early Christian Art*, ed. Robin M. Jensen, and Mark D. Ellison (Routledge, 2018), pp. 291-93.

10   Mark 15:32; Matthew 27:44.

11   Luke 23:39-43.

12   See also Jeremiah 1:14-15; 6:1; 6:22; 10:22; 47:2.

13   Wilhelm Schneemelcher *The Gospel of Peter: Introduction* in *New Testament Apocrypha Vol. 1*, Ed. Wilhelm Schneemelcher, translated E. McL. Wilson (London: Westminster John Knox Press, 2003) pp. 217-21. J. K. Elliott, *The Apocryphal New Testament* (Oxford: Oxford University Press, 2005), pp. 150-51.

14   Matthew 27:62; 28:4,11-15.

15   Translation by J.K. Elliott, *The Apocryphal New Testament*, pp. 156-57.

16   Mark 15:46; Matthew 27:59; Luke 23:53; John 19:40.

Chapter 35

1   1 Chronicles 3:17-19; Matthew 1:12; Jeremiah 22:30.

2   2 Kings 25:27-30.

3   Matthew 26:61; 27:40.

4   John 2:19-21.

Chapter 36

1   Laurie, *The Thomas Code*, pp. 110-13.
2   Translation by E. Isaac, *The Old Testament Pseudepigrapha Vol. 1.*
3   Translation by E. Isaac, *The Old Testament Pseudepigrapha Vol. 1.*
4   Isaac, *The Old Testament Pseudepigrapha Vol. 1*, p. 7.
5   E. Isaac, *1 Enoch* in *The Old Testament Pseudepigrapha Vol. 1.*
6   1 Enoch 46:2-5.
7   1 Enoch 48:1.
8   1 Enoch 48:4.
9   1 Enoch 48:10.
10 1 Enoch 71:1.
11 Isaac, *The Old Testament Pseudepigrapha Vol. 1*, p. 50, n. 71 s.
12 Leviticus 12:2-8.
13 Translated by Alexander Roberts and William Rambaut, *Ante-Nicene Fathers, Vol. 1.* Edited by Alexander Roberts, James Donaldson, and A. Cleveland Coxe. (Buffalo, NY: Christian Literature Publishing Co., 1885).
14 John 7:50-51.
15 *On the Origin of the World*, NHC II (5) 104:20-31.
16 Alexander, *3 Enoch* in *The Old Testament Pseudepigrapha Vol. 1*, pp. 225-29.
17 Alexander, *3 Enoch* in *The Old Testament Pseudepigrapha Vol. 1*, p. 259 n. 4l.
18 3 Enoch 4:9.
19 Alexander, *3 Enoch* in *The Old Testament Pseudepigrapha Vol. 1*, p. 259 n. 4t.
20 3 Enoch 16.
21 b. Hagigah 14b-15a. For a discussion of the Aher traditions see: Alexander, *The Old Testament Pseudepigrapha Vol. 1*, pp. 229-239, and Alan F. Segal, *Two Powers in Heaven: Early Rabbinic Reports about Christianity and Gnosticism* (Boston: Brill, 2002), pp. 60-67.

Chapter 37

1   1 Enoch 46:1
2   Jeremiah 41:1-43:18.
3   The Lives of the Prophets 2:1-2.
4   Laurie, *The Rock and the Tower*, pp. 679-729.
5   The Apocryphon of John, NHC II (1) 29:16-30:10.
6   The Apocryphon of John, NHC II (1) 30:16-31:10.

Afterword

1   Finkelstein, *The Forgotten Kingdom*, pp. 155-58.
2   1 Samuel 16–1 Kings 11.
3   2 Samuel 21:19.
4   1 Samuel 25:2-42.
5   1 Samuel 24:1-22; 26:1-25; 28:1-6; 29:1-31:13; 2 Samuel 1:1-2:7.

6   2 Samuel 4.
7   2 Samuel 3:6-39.
8   2 Samuel 16:5-8; 21:1-14.
9   2 Samuel 13:1-14:33.
10   2 Samuel 18:1-19:7.
11   2 Samuel 20:3-13.
12   2 Samuel 11.
13   2 Samuel 6.
14   1 Samuel 7:1.
15   Joshua 15:9, 1 Chronicles 13:6.
16   1 Samuel 21:1-7; 22:6-22.
17   2 Samuel 11:1-12:25.
18   1 Kings 1.
19   1 Kings 11:3.
20   1 Kings 1:41-53; 2:13-25.
21   2 Kings 16:3.
22   2 Kings 23:11.
23   2 Kings 12. See also Finkelstein and Silberman, *David and Solomon*, pp. 171-73.

Appendix A

1   Translation by E. Isaac, *The Old Testament Pseudepigrapha Vol. 1.*
2   Nickelsburg, *1 Enoch 1*, p. 446, section 6.
3   Translation by Nickelsburg, *1 Enoch 1*. The second part of this line is uncertain. E. Isaac has "...and after him one (other) shall emerge as the eternal plant of righteousness." This reading reflects Ethiopian commentators who consider this to be a reference to Isaac (E. Isaac, *The Old Testament Pseudepigrapha Vol. 1.*,p.74 n.93l.). However, it makes more sense for this second "plant of righteousness" to represent the Jewish people.
4   Translation by E. Isaac, *The Old Testament Pseudepigrapha Vol. 1.*
5   Translation by E. Isaac, *The Old Testament Pseudepigrapha Vol. 1.*

Appendix B

1   The account of the murder of Onias is in 2 Maccabees 4:30-38. See also 2 Maccabees 15:12-14. Diodorus implies that Antiochus IV secretly arranged for Antiochus, the young son of Seleucus IV, to be murdered by Andronikos whom he then had executed. This happened in the same year as the supposed death of Onias III. See Jonathan A. Goldstein, *II Maccabees: Anchor Bible* (New York: Doubleday, 1983), p.238 note to 31-38.
2   2 Kings 25:27-30; Jeremiah 52:31-34.
3   Ezekiel 8:14.
4   Jeremiah 50:21,26; 51:3.
5   Jeremiah 50:9,41; 51:2;27-28
6   Jeremiah 50:42; 51:36,42,55.

7   Jeremiah 51:25,53.
8   The prophecy is addressed to "your mother", but it is clear from the context that the subject is Babylon as the motherland of the Babylonians.

Appendix C

1   Luke 3:23-38.
2   Luke 3:23.
3   Luke 3:33. Some manuscripts have Arni between Hezron and Admin, others omit this name. Nestle Aland 18 includes Arni.
4   2 Samuel 7:1-17. Laurie, *The Rock and the Tower*, pp.265-66.
5   Luke 3:29-30.
6   Laurie, *The Rock and the Tower*, pp.266-69.

Appendix D

1   D.R.A. Hare, *The Lives of the Prophets: A new translation and introduction* in *The Old Testament Pseudepigrapha Vol. 2*, ed. James H. Charlesworth (New York: Doubleday, 1985), pp. 380-81.
2   The Lives of the Prophets 2:2-7.
3   Translation by D.R.A. Hare, *The Lives of the Prophets* in *The Old Testament Pseudepigrapha Vol. 2*.
4   1 Corinthians 15:20.

About the author

S.P. Laurie lives in a cottage in rural Shropshire, England (think of the Shire but without the hobbits!). He read mathematics at Balliol College, Oxford—although that was a long time ago. When not researching Christian origins or writing books he attempts to grow things, often without success. He is also a keen astrophotographer. His other books include *The Thomas Code* and *The Rock and the Tower*.

For articles, news and information on his books go to:
JesusOrigins.com

Made in the USA
Coppell, TX
04 July 2023

18747948R00296